S0-AXJ-854

Teaching Mathematics Online:

Emergent Technologies and Methodologies

Angel A. Juan
Open University of Catalonia, Spain

Maria A. Huertas
Open University of Catalonia, Spain

Sven Trenholm
Loughborough University, UK

Cristina Steegmann
Open University of Catalonia, Spain

Senior Editorial Director:	Kristin Klinger
Director of Book Publications:	Julia Mosemann
Editorial Director:	Lindsay Johnston
Acquisitions Editor:	Erika Carter
Development Editor:	Michael Killian
Production Editor:	Sean Woznicki
Typesetters:	Christen Croley, Adrienne Freeland
Print Coordinator:	Jamie Snavely
Cover Design:	Nick Newcomer

Published in the United States of America by
Information Science Reference (an imprint of IGI Global)
701 E. Chocolate Avenue
Hershey PA 17033
Tel: 717-533-8845
Fax: 717-533-8661
E-mail: cust@igi-global.com
Web site: http://www.igi-global.com

Library of Congress Cataloging-in-Publication Data

Teaching mathematics online: emergent technologies and methodologies / Angel A. Juan ... [et al.], editors.
p. cm.
Summary: "This book shares theoretical and applied pedagogical models and systems used in math e-learning including the use of computer supported collaborative learning, which is common to most e-learning practices"-- Provided by publisher.
Includes bibliographical references and index.
ISBN 978-1-60960-875-0 (hardcover) -- ISBN 978-1-60960-876-7 (ebook) -- ISBN 978-1-60960-877-4 (print & perpetual access) 1. Computer-assisted instruction. 2. Web-based instruction. 3. Mathematics--Study and teaching-- Technological innovations. I. Juan, Angel A., 1972-
QA20.C65T434 2011
510.78'54678--dc22
2011013010

British Cataloguing in Publication Data
A Cataloguing in Publication record for this book is available from the British Library.

Editorial Advisory Board

List of Reviewers

Ciarán Mac an Bhaird, *National University of Ireland Maynooth, Ireland*
Maria Meletiou-Mavrotheris, *European University of Cyprus, Cyprus*
Travis Miller, *Millersville University, USA*
Morten Misfeldt, *The Danish School of Education, Denmark*
Diana S. Perdue, *Pride Rock Consulting, USA*
Fernando Pestana da Costa, *Universidade Aberta, Portugal*
Francesca Pozzi, *Istituto Tecnologie Didattiche - CNR, Italy*
Jordi Saludes, *Universitat Politecnica de Catalunya, Spain*
Teresa Sancho, *Open University of Catalonia, Spain*
Fernando San Segundo, *Universidad de Alcala, Spain*
Jason Silverman, *Drexel University School of Education, USA*
Cristina Steegmann, *Open University of Catalonia, Spain*
Dirk Tempelaar, *Maastricht University School of Business and Economics, The Netherlands*
Sven Trenholm, *Loughborough University, UK*
Alexander Vaninsky, *Hostos Community College - CUNY, USA*
Joe Ward, *Loughborough University, UK*

Table of Contents

Section 2
Pure Online Experiences in Mathematics E-Learning

Section 3
Mathematics Software & Web Resources for Mathematics E-Learning

Foreword

There is a global perception that mathematics is surrounded by a special aura that places this discipline in a rather unbalanced position. On the one hand, mathematics is all around us, permeating everything, and has been created to simplify our world by building models to better explain and understand our reality. On the other hand, mathematics appears rather complex due to a broad range of variables; for example, its intricate notation. Nevertheless, and also quite inexplicably, mathematics enjoys a massive consensus around the world: theorems, formulas, principles, methods, and so forth are identical from one continent to the other. As if to further enhance its splendour, mathematics is known as the "queen and servant of the sciences" because it supplies the needs of other sciences (physics, economics, geology, engineering, etc.).

However, teaching mathematics is not mathematics itself, it is a completely different issue. Curricula, teachers, and institutions must deal with the perceptions and emotions provoked by this divine discipline. Hundreds of papers have been written on the subject of the anxiety caused by mathematics learning, not to mention feelings of frustration and a lack of self-confidence experienced along the path towards accomplishment. Linked to this, a common belief can be identified in the educational arena: students have the sense that one is either good or bad at mathematics. Those who are gifted at mathematics are believed to be blessed with divine inspiration thus making their locus of control more external. These feelings are virtually exclusive to learning mathematics. Of course, successfully learning mathematics is also related to enthusiasm and empowering, both of which are required for achieving the prized goal of autonomy. It is not easy to find the middle ground when talking about perceptions and behaviour and that makes the teaching work in a mathematics classroom all the more difficult. It is also a challenge for teachers to gracefully cross the bridge separating mathematics (as a discipline) from teaching mathematics (making it meaningful), tackling Chevallard's evocative "didactical transposition".

In this context, teaching and learning mathematics has an ally in online education. Like all partnerships it can be for better or for worse; in the end, it mostly depends on one's willpower and ability.

In equal shares, online education has the ability to either improve or worsen mathematical teaching. It is taken for granted that when designing an online course the ultimate aim is to improve teaching and learning and not simply to reach the greatest possible number of students with the least amount of effort by breaking through barriers of space and time. However, in both the design and implementation phases there are important decisions to be made that have no routine answers, much less any solutions that can copied directly from face-to-face education. On the contrary, teaching delivered using a technological medium is supposed be extremely considerate due to the fact that technology mediation is able to take us from one extreme to the other without us really being aware of the journey. Teachers are able to bring together a group of elements that enhance significant learning all in the same course. In this modality of learning it is easy to succumb to the temptation of teaching large numbers of students while expending the minimum amount effort. Nonetheless, quality online education without a reasonable and continuous investment is as yet unknown.

In consequence, different online decisions can standardise teaching and make it poorer, but in their favour they are easy to implement in online classes. Some examples of these decisions include: choosing increased automation; making teaching homogeneous; a preference for quantity as opposed to personalisation; opting for formalisation that reduces flexibility; or an inclination towards poor feedback and study based on repetition and low skills levels.

Putting aside this negative aspect, online teaching has been called to do much more and to truly provide an amplifier for teachers that goes beyond borders and offers an authentic study framework to help students better understand and live in today's world.

Among its more positive aspects, the online alternative has the potential to catapult the educational community towards providing more transparent ideas and processes that present facts and events neatly from the inside. Moreover, thanks to its ability to bring the real world into online classrooms by simulating or capturing everyday situations, students are encouraged to develop high-level skills, such as argumentation and reflection relating to the processes they have experienced at first hand.

This approach does not ignore the scalable values technology provides education in terms of measurability, counting, and more, but we all need to go a step further. More than simply building a stereotype of online mathematical education by making the most basic choices, we aspire to use online education as a *mindtool* as a whole (extending on Jonassen's terminology) thus giving teachers and students the right to expand their competences when working with technology to carry out tasks that they would not be able to do alone. Online mathematics education defined as a *mindtool* in this manner helps to better capture, visualise, and manipulate hidden processes, reasoning, and facts that otherwise exist only in teachers' minds and are barely intuited by students. The opportunity we have in online mathematical education nowadays is precious, and our decisions are open to innovation.

Elena Barbera
Universitat Oberta de Catalunya, Spain
December 16, 2010

Elena Barbera *is a Doctor in Psychology from the University of Barcelona (1995). She is currently Director of Research for the eLearn Center at the Universitat Oberta de Catalunya in Barcelona (Spain). She is also an Adjunct Professor for the international doctorate in Nova Southeastern University in Florida (USA). Her research activity is specialised in the area of educational psychology, a field in which she has more than a hundred publications, conferences, and educational courses, relating in particular to knowledge-construction processes and educational interaction in e-learning environments, evaluating educational quality and assessing learning, distance learning using ICT, and teaching and learning strategies. As head of the EDUS (Distance School and University Education) research group, she participates in various national and international projects related to online teaching and learning and student assessment. She is an external and independent evaluator of research projects promoted by local, national, and European Union (e-learning and lifelong programme) bodies, and she collaborates with international organisations in developing knowledge by organising congresses and international awards as a member of their scientific committees.*

Preface

INTRODUCTION

New developments in the educational technology field are changing the way in which higher education is delivered. These innovations include, for example, virtual learning environments for individual and collaborative learning, Internet resources for teaching and learning, academic materials in electronic format, specific subject-related software, groupware, and social network software.

Over the last few decades, technological innovations have become ubiquitous. They have helped realize the birth and growth of new purely-online universities along with the transformation of how instruction is being delivered in most traditional face-to-face universities – affecting the nature of the courses as well as degree programs being offered. These innovations, such as so-called pure (also known as 100%) online instruction, have driven the growth of distance learning opportunities, as students who are time-bound due to job or travel difficulties or place-bound due to geographic location or physical disabilities can now access courses and degree programs at their convenience. E-learning models are currently being developed and utilized worldwide.

The disciplinary area of Mathematics and Statistics has also seen widespread changes. Many instructors have been encouraged to try new teaching strategies based on innovations that enable such provisions as online support, inter-disciplinary collaborative learning, computer-aided assessment, and integration of mathematical and statistical software in their courses. University departments worldwide have been leveraging technological capabilities in an attempt to create new engaging curricula that promote deeper conceptual understanding (versus shallower procedural knowledge). Realizing this potential in mathematics has not been easy, and there are numerous challenges – some, for example, due to the demographic characteristics of the so-called "Internet-generation" students as well as the intrinsic disciplinary nature of Mathematics and Statistics.

In a broad sense Mathematics e-learning refers to the use of computer hardware, software and/or the Internet to deliver and facilitate mathematics instruction. Emergent technologies (e.g. virtual learning environments) enabling emerging instructional strategies (e.g. computer-mediated collaborative learning) are being used in both new and traditional universities to completely teach (e.g. fully asynchronous online), partially replace (e.g. blended or hybrid), or supplement course offerings in mathematics to a new generation of students. Few doubt that this new modality is here to stay.

With e-learning experiencing what has been characterized as "explosive growth," there remains a dearth of research to inform best practices specific to the disciplinary particularities of Mathematics e-learning in higher education. In effect, there are a growing number of available books generically covering e-learning, books covering computer-mediated collaborative learning and, of course a long history of books covering mathematics education but few, if any, cover all of these topics as a whole (i.e., Mathematics e-learning). This book attempts to begin to fill this gap in the literature by fulfilling two main purposes: (1) to provide insight and understanding into practical pedagogical and methodological issues related to Mathematics e-learning, and (2) to provide insight and understanding into current and future trends regarding how mathematics instruction is being facilitated and leveraged with Web-based and other emerging technologies. In particular, the goal of the book is to: (a) identify and publish worldwide best practices regarding Mathematics e-learning in higher education, (b) share theoretical or applied pedagogical models and systems used in Mathematics e-learning, including the use of computer-mediated collaborative learning common to most e-learning practices, (c) forecast emerging technologies and tendencies regarding mathematical software, virtual learning environments and online Mathematics education, (d) provide the academic community with a base text that could serve as a reference in research in Mathematics education, and (e) present up-to-date research work on how mathematics education is changing in a global and Web-based world. The road ahead looks promising. Our hope is that this book will become a roadmap that will begin to help many successfully realize a deeper and more engaging experience of mathematics instruction.

CHAPTER SYNOPSIS

The chapters in this book have been divided into three sections: (i) Blended Experiences in Mathematics e-Learning, (ii) Pure Online Experiences in Mathematics e-Learning, and (iii) Mathematics Software & Web Resources for Mathematics e-Learning. What follows is a chapter-by chapter overview for each of these areas.

Section 1: Blended Experiences in Mathematics E-Learning

Chapter 1: "A Model for Asynchronous Discussions in a Mathematics Content Course," T. Miller presents an asynchronous model for online discussions in a mathematics content course for elementary mathematics teachers. The model facilitates students' motivation and collaborative learning, representing a natural extension of the in-class discussions, lecture, and activities.

Chapter 2: "A Blended Learning Approach in Mathematics," B. Abramovitz et al. describe a blended experience in Calculus courses for undergraduate engineering students. According to the authors, their blended model contributed to making students more active and motivated learners and also served to promote student-instructor interaction.

Chapter 3: "Screencasting for Mathematics Online Learning: A Case Study of a First Year Operations Research Course at a Dual-Mode Australian University," B. Loch introduces a case study regarding the use of screencasting technology in an Operations Research course taken simultaneously by on-campus and distance students. The chapter discusses issues such as online student's isolation, portability of materials and "just-in-time" guidance and support.

Chapter 4: "Mathematics Education: Teaching and Learning Opportunities in Blended Learning," G. Albano discusses some Web-based experiences developed at two different Italian universities to help provide some insight into opportunities offered by e-learning platforms in blended environments. Among other results, the author concludes that her students prefer the blended mathematics course over the traditional one.

Chapter 5: "Best Practices for Hybrid Mathematics Courses," D. Perdue uses an informal style to discuss some "best practices" she uses in her blended mathematics courses. By using these practices, the author analyzes how she spends more class time discussing the relevant material with her students and how they have become increasingly active participants in their own learning process.

Chapter 6: "Implementation of Learning Outcomes in Mathematics for Non-Mathematics Major by Using E-Learning," B. Divjak presents some experiences related to blended mathematics courses carried out at the University of Zagreb. In these experiences, the author examines how blended courses can be efficiently supported by Information Technologies and social software such as wikis, e-portfolios, et cetera.

Section 2: Purely Online Experiences in Mathematics E-Learning

Chapter 7: "Online Communities of Practice as Vehicles for Teacher Professional Development," M. Meletiou-Mavrotheris explores how Web-based technologies can be effectively employed to promote the creation of online communities of practice that share knowledge and experiences regarding math-related contents and courses. In particular, she analyzes an online learning experience regarding a multinational group of elementary and middle school teachers of Statistics.

Chapter 8: "Mathematics Bridging Education Using an Online, Adaptive E-Tutorial: Preparing International Students for Higher Education," D. Tempelaar et al. describe and evaluate a postsecondary online program designed to facilitate the transition from high-school maths to university maths. The program is based on the administration of an entry test and the organization of an online summer course. A quantitative analysis provides some insight on the relevance of several factors affecting students' academic performance.

Chapter 9: "Teaching Mathematics Teachers Online: Strategies for Navigating the Intersection of Andragogy, Technology, and Reform-Based Mathematics Education," D. Jarvis investigates some of the factors and strategies that, according to his ten-year experience as an online instructor, help to successfully combine technology and emergent online teaching models to provide adult mathematics education.

Chapter 10: "Developing Teachers' Mathematical Knowledge for Teaching through Online Collaboration," J. Silverman and E. Clay provide several case studies that highlight the potential that online collaboration hold for supporting mathematics teachers' collaboration. In their own words, "the asynchronous and permanent nature of online environments allow for potentially pivotal utterances [...] to be taken up as a focus of conversation by the remainder of the class and, when they are not taken up, allow instructors to create bridges between teachers' current understandings and the instructional goals."

Chapter 11: "Self-Regulated Learning and Self Assessment in Online Mathematics Bridging Courses," R. Biehler et al. introduce an innovative way of teaching and learning mathematics online and designed to facilitate the transition from secondary to higher-education. They present some multimedia learning materials developed by an inter-university project and discuss the acceptance and success of their courses among students.

Chapter 12: "Long-Term Experiences in Mathematics E-Learning in Europe and the USA," S. Trenholm et al. perform a comparative study regarding some long-term experiences teaching mathematics online at four different universities in Europe and the USA The analysis highlights common patterns and also differences among the diverse models considered. Some key factors for successful mathematics e-learning practices are identified.

Section 3: Mathematics Software & Web Resources for Mathematics E-Learning

Chapter 13: "My Equations are the Same as Yours! Computer Aided Assessment Using a Gröbner Basis Approach," M. Badger and C. J. Sangwin show an example of how computer-aided assessments can automatically evaluate whether or not two systems of equations are equivalent.

Chapter 14: "Interacive Web-Based Tools for Learning Mathematics: Best Practices," B. Cherkas and R. Welder examine and classify a number of popular and relevant websites for collegiate mathematics based on their interactivity, dynamic capabilities, pedagogical strengths and weakness, the practices they employ, and their potential to enhance mathematical learning.

Chapter 15: "NAUK.si: Using Learning Blocks to Prepare E-Content for Teaching Mathematics," M. Lokar et al. exhibit the NAUK group, which is working on the development of mathematics learning blocks and tools for easy creation of mathematics contents. A practical example completes the chapter and illustrates the flexibility and potential of the NAUK system.

Chapter 16: "Software Tools Used in Math Refresher Courses at the University of Alcala, Spain," J. Alcazar et al. present a mathematics teaching experience based on the combination of the Moodle platform and mathematical software such as WIRIS, GeoGebra, SAGE, and Wolfram Alpha.

Chapter 17: "Formula Editors and Handwriting in Mathematical E-Learning," M. Misfeldt and A. Sanne report on an experience in which they compare Moodle's formula editor with the use of direct scanner-based handwriting. According to their results, despite the existence of modern formula editors, handwriting continues to be a relevant way of communicating mathematics in e-learning programs.

Chapter 18: "The Role of Technology in Mathematics Support: A Pilot Study," C. Mac an Bhaird and A. O'Shea discuss the importance of technology to enhance mathematics education and support. They present their experiences on the development of online mathematics courses and online learning materials. They also provide some feedback from their students and discuss the benefits and challenges of techniques such as screencasting.

FINAL WORDS

To the best of our knowledge, this is the first international book focused on Mathematics e-learning in higher education, an emerging area both in research and academic practice. Accordingly, we expect this book to be a valuable tool for researchers in the fields of Mathematics education and e-learning, academics involved in e-learning research, faculty teaching mathematics online, as well as instructional designers and online coordinators implementing courses in Mathematics e-learning. The text will also be potentially useful for senior year undergraduate or graduate studies in computer sciences, management, or mathematics education.

Angel A. Juan
Open University of Catalonia, Spain

Maria A. Huertas
Open University of Catalonia, Spain

Sven Trenholm
Loughborough University, UK

Cristina Steegmann
Open University of Catalonia, Spain

Acknowledgment

We would like to thank the authors, reviewers, and EAB members for their collaboration and prompt responses to our enquiries which enabled completion of this book in a timely manner. We gratefully acknowledge the help and encouragement of the editor at IGI Global, Mike Killian. Also, our thanks go to the staff involved with the production of the book.

Angel A. Juan
Open University of Catalonia, Spain

Maria A. Huertas
Open University of Catalonia, Spain

Sven Trenholm
Loughborough University, UK

Cristina Steegmann
Open University of Catalonia, Spain

Section 1
Blended Experiences in Mathematics E-Learning

Chapter 1
A Model for Asynchronous Discussions in a Mathematics Content Course

Travis K. Miller
Millersville University, USA

ABSTRACT

In this chapter a model is outlined for using asynchronous online discussions in a mathematics content course for preservice elementary teachers. The model integrates conversational discussion threads as a component of a traditional, face-to-face course. This successful approach is based on elements of the variation theory of learning, and derives from a comprehensive dissertation study examining its effectiveness.

INTRODUCTION

Innovations in the mathematical preparation of preservice teachers mirror trends in K-12 mathematics instruction, incorporating learning activities and technological tools that engage learners in mathematical explorations that promote conceptual understanding, knowledge construction and confrontation of mathematical misconceptions (Mathematical Sciences Educational Board & National Research Council, 1989, 1990; NCTM, 1989, 2000). Additionally, collaboration and reflection are recognized as essential toward developing deep and meaningful understandings of mathematics content (Lloyd & Frykholm, 2000; Newell, 1996; Silverman & Clay, 2010; Staples, 2008).

DOI: 10.4018/978-1-60960-875-0.ch001

Inclusion of online discussions has proven effective in a variety of higher education courses, providing opportunities for collaboration and for written expression of ideas. Their asynchronous nature enables individuals to read others' posts and submit their own messages at a time of their convenience, providing the opportunity for students to contemplate ideas and prepare thoughtful responses (Bender, 2003). These discussions can provide a learner-driven environment in which students explore and construct knowledge (Schellens, Van Keer, De Wever & Valcke, 2007; Hong & Lee, 2008). Discussions occur in threads, which are linked messages relating to a common discussion topic. New messages may be linked to the initial post or to subsequent posts in the thread, indicating the message to which the user is responding. The discussion forums are often part of larger course management systems.

DeBourgh (2002), Hofstad (2003), Brett, Woodruff and Nason (1999, 2002), and Silverman and Clay (2010) have argued that participation in online discussions can improve analytical thinking and problem-solving skills, promote development of deeper understandings of course content, and lead to the redevelopment of preservice teachers' conceptions of mathematical learning. Implementations of online discussions in college courses vary significantly, resulting in a broad spectrum of effectiveness and the lack of a clear model for meeting specific mathematics course goals. In contrast to other disciplines, mathematics content courses generally have not benefited from conversational use of online discussions, apparently due to the lack of an effective implementation model and, for face-to-face courses, a lack of understanding regarding the educational opportunities provided by online discussions. Resultantly, mathematics education has yet to fully benefit from learning experiences enhanced with online discussions.

Popular uses of asynchronous discussions in mathematics education include group work on specific problems (Kosiak, 2004) or discussions of teaching and learning strategies within subsequent methods courses or professional development opportunities (Carey, Kleiman, Russell, Venable, & Louie 2008; Slavit, 2002). Required conversations about and with mathematical concepts, however, has not been a common approach. Content courses for preservice teachers that use a conversational approach to asynchronous discussions about and with mathematics can achieve several key objectives. First, preservice teachers can gain experience communicating about and with mathematics in a more relaxed and explanatory fashion that aligns well with their future career needs. These mathematical discussions are not restricted by the limited time within typical classes, and the asynchronous nature allows participants to organize and reflect upon their contributions and explanations. Second, future teachers become more motivated to learn and understand the mathematics content by including discussions that frame this development as necessary for success in their future careers and to fulfill their desires to meet the needs of future students. Finally, preservice teachers' perceptions and misconceptions of the nature, teaching and learning of mathematics have been documented as limiting factors in the development of deep, conceptual understandings of mathematics content (Ball, 1990; Cady & Rearden, 2007; Ma, 1999). Incorporation of tasks or discussions that cause students to confront these notions may lead to open-mindedness regarding the intent behind their mathematics content courses and the rationale behind employed teaching strategies, subsequently leading to deeper and more meaningful understandings of course content.

This chapter presents a model for effective use of asynchronous online discussions as part of a traditional, face-to-face mathematics content course for preservice elementary teachers. The structure and elements of this model are founded upon the tenets of the variation theory of learning (Bowden & Marton, 1998; Marton & Booth, 1997; Runesson, 2005), and the effectiveness of the model is based upon the findings of a phenomenographic dissertation study (Miller, 2007, 2009) from which it derived. The design relies upon a significant role of the instructor as initiator and moderator of conversations, scaffolding students in their learning and sustaining conversations through a deep exploration of content (Fauske & Wade, 2004; Kienle & Ritterskamp, 2007; Mazzolini, 2003; Mazzolini & Maddison, 2007). The model hinges upon several main principles:

- A theoretical underpinning of the variation theory of learning
- Moderation of discussion by the course instructor
- Discussion threads that focus upon true discussion of mathematical concepts as well as upon the nature, teaching and learning of mathematical concepts
- Connection of discussion threads to other class elements
- A grading scheme that emphasizes quality while establishing a minimum requirement for quantity

Each of these points will be discussed as they developed during the related dissertation study. A brief look at the underlying theoretical foundation of variation is described next as part of the model development.

MODEL DEVELOPMENT

Theoretical Foundation

The guiding principles for this model are the tenets of the variation theory of learning. The theory has its origins in the evolution of phenomenography and the findings of phenomenographic research (Bowden & Marton, 1998; Marton & Booth, 1997; Runesson, 2005). Phenomenography aims to identify the finite number of categories of experience among learners in a given learning situation (Marton, 1986). Variation theory views learning as relational, experiential, qualitative, and tied to the specific context in which it occurs – detailing what learning is and how learning occurs (Marton, 1986; Marton & Booth, 1997; Prosser, 1993). According to variation theory, an individual truly learns something means that he or she experiences that thing in a new way (Bowden & Marton, 1998; Marton & Booth. 1997). The mathematical content to be learned in the learning situation can be referred to as the *object of learning* (Runesson, 2005). From this perspective, the object of learning is established as central, not the learning environment or the classroom methods or structure. Thus, selection of teaching and learning methods is not focused upon means that promote metacognitive development, as the cognitive constructivist perspective would dictate, nor is it focused solely upon approaches aiming to situate students in realistic learning phenomena, as a situative perspective would suggest. Instead, variation theory suggests a broader perspective that invokes any appropriate method for leading students to experience and understand course content in a new way.

Runesson (2005) notes that learning includes a change in which the learner sees, experiences, or understands in relation to the object of learning. These changes are influenced by how the learner experiences the learning situation, including his or her perceptions and assumptions of the learning activity and its goals. Variation theory asserts, therefore, that learning activities must reveal to students the different and desired aspects of the mathematics content that they are intended to learn. That is, to understand a concept in a new way, a student's pre-existing understandings must be modified through exposure of the individual to variation of a particular aspect of the object of learning. The variation of this aspect or dimension is what the student learns.

To state this in another way, a learner develops an awareness of the potential variation of particular dimension of the learning object. To become aware of such variation, however, the individual must be able to discern that the dimension exists (Bowden & Marton, 1998; Pang, 2003; Runesson, 2005). This is a key paradoxical element of variation theory. Students must become aware of a dimension of an object of learning that is defined by its variation, but to discern this dimension the variation must be experienced by the student (Bowden & Marton, 1998). If there is no variation, then the dimension is not discernable and the student will not achieve the learning goal.

Variation theory has clear implications for the teaching of mathematics to preservice elementary teachers, hinging upon the idea of variation in learning opportunities. Three of the primary goals of mathematics content courses for prospective elementary teachers are: (1) mastery of mathematical concepts; (2) the ability to think and communicate with mathematical ideas; and (3) to encourage these prospective teachers to readjust their conceptions of mathematics. Variation theory suggests that a lack of proficiency in these categories may result from a lack of sufficient variation along these dimensions in students' previous mathematics courses. Further, variation along these three dimensions is essential for prospective teachers to accomplish course goals. Learning to think and communicate with mathematics requires variation in the educational opportunities provided.

Most importantly and pivotal for the accomplishment of the first two goals, prospective teachers must begin to reconceptualize mathematics as a way of thinking rather than a subject that consists only of memorization, computation, and procedure application. This can be accomplished via learning activities in which variation across conceptualizations of mathematics is made explicit. Preservice teachers must be focused upon appropriate dimensions of the object of learning and the learning situation. Often, this can be difficult to accomplish due to the perspectives and perceptions formed by the variety of individuals' previous experiences, as well as the variety of their existing understandings of the course content.

Implementation of technology in a manner consistent with variation theory can prove effective in meeting course goals (Miller, in press). The inclusion of online discussions in mathematics courses can be particularly valuable. By requiring prospective teachers to participate in carefully designed online discussions in their mathematics courses, variation and subsequent learning can occur within the three goals of these classes, which can be thought of as dimensions of the learning of the course content and the learning context. Questions can be included which promote the sharing and exploration of various solution strategies of mathematical concepts. Topics can be addressed that explore the nature, teaching and learning of mathematics through expression of personal experiences, resulting in reconceptualization of these ideas.

Lastly, these online discussions provide a forum in which prospective teachers are required to communicate using mathematical ideas, strengthening their ability to do so and making them more comfortable in doing so. As Runesson (2005) observes, instruction must bring into focus the essential and relevant dimensions or aspects of the object of learning as well as the learning situation. By the very nature of the online discussion forum, leading students to share their personal beliefs and understandings exposes them to variation. By requiring students to respond to their peers' posts, this variation is brought to the forefront of their considerations. Preservice teachers therefore experience the variation of the topic under discussion, and learn this dimension's demonstrated variation.

Dissertation Study Purpose

The study from which this model evolved examined preservice elementary teachers' perceptions of the discussions, their approaches to participating in the forums, their development of meaningful understandings of mathematics, and the revision of their conceptions of the nature, teaching and learning of mathematics (Miller, 2007, 2009). Discussions regarding the nature of mathematics were viewed as pivotal in leading students to recognize that mathematics is more than memorization and application of algorithms, so that development of new conceptual understandings of mathematics concepts would be more welcomed and more readily achieved. The instructor capitalized upon the preservice teachers' interests and future career concerns by including themes regarding the teaching and learning of mathematics as a motivation for exploring and discussing mathematics content. Through framing many discussions as necessary for meeting the needs of future students, the preservice teachers were provided a rationale for discussing, explaining, and developing connections between different mathematical ideas. Threads concerning the nature of mathematics focused on specific instances concerning larger questions such as "What is mathematics?" and "Is mathematics algorithmic or conceptual?" Threads examining the teaching and learning of mathematics explored students' past and current experiences in learning mathematics, how they might introduce specific course topics to their future students, and the challenges they might encounter when teaching mathematical ideas.

A pilot program for the dissertation study introduced online discussions that were entirely student-driven, with students initiating and moderating threads (Miller, 2005, 2007, 2009). Students were asked to focus on the broader mathematical concepts of the mathematics content as well as the nature, teaching and learning of mathematics. Despite these instructions, the resulting discussion threads focused upon specific homework questions, each with one or two direct responses of how to do the problem. Discussions reached only surface levels of depth, with no development of more meaningful understandings. These results mirror the fact that students are often unfamiliar and uncomfortable with speaking conceptually about mathematics, calling for a more structured approach to facilitate and motivate students' progress using online contributions.

As a result of the pilot program, the dissertation model for online discussions developed a central instructor role guided by course goals and a theoretical framework on mathematical learning. Such a leading role is supported by the literature (Fauske & Wade, 2004; Kienle & Ritterskamp, 2007). Further, the model integrated the online discussions with other course elements by blending in-class and online explorations of mathematical ideas; framing discussions through the lens of the teaching profession; and leading preservice teachers to confront their own math course experiences and beliefs about mathematics and mathematics learning.

Dissertation Study Approach and Findings

The dissertation study tracked students' work in one section of a three-credit university-level mathematics content course at a large, Midwestern university operating on a 16-week semester schedule. The course was part of a required trilogy of mathematics courses designed for the preparation of elementary teachers, with a prerequisite of passing the first course with a C- or above (this and the remaining course could be taken in either order). Topics included geometric, measurement and spatial reasoning in one, two and three dimensions as the basis for elementary school geometry, as well as metric, non-metric and transformational geometry. The course did not include study of teaching methods, which were the focus of an additional course taken after this sequence was completed. The class met three days per week for 50-minute periods. Thirty-nine first- and second-year future elementary and/or special education majors were enrolled in the course, which aimed to develop deeper and more interconnected understandings of mathematics. Students were exposed to alternative models while emphasizing the exploration of multiple solution processes and representations of problems. Communication of mathematical ideas was also emphasized.

Thirty-eight of the preservice teachers agreed to be followed for the study, which used a mixed methods pheonomenographical approach (Marton, 1986) to examine the different experiences of students in learning with the online forum. Online posts, quiz work, and student feedback via surveys and interviews provided the primary sources of data. Quiz questions were directly linked to online discussion threads, and the level of understanding was examined using content analysis (Gunawardena, Lowe & Anderson, 1997; Hara, Bonk & Angeli, 2000) and open, thematic coding (Patton, 2002) of the online discussion, survey, and interview transcripts. Subsequent work on quizzes indicated students' mastery and retention of concepts discussed in the threads. To check the reliability of the coding process, a subset of the data was later recoded by applying the resulting broad categories; agreement of the two rounds of coding was greater than 90%.

Findings suggested that online participation provided students with the opportunity to develop new and deeper understandings of mathematics while drawing connections among multiple representations, contexts and concepts. Students also confronted and modified many existing misconceptions regarding the nature, teaching and learning of mathematics. Students' perceptions of the online discussion model and the academic benefits they provided were largely positive. Thirteen of sixteen survey respondents (81%) believed that participation in the discussions led them to better undersandings of the material by requiring them to think more deeply and critically about the content than would have been possible or necessary in the traditional class setting alone. Fourteen students (87.5%) noted the benefit of increased interaction and communication resulting from online participation, and suggested that this was lacking in typical mathematics courses. Especially noteworthy were comments that exposure to others' views, ways of thinking, or explanations was something new to them as part of a course in mathematics. One student noted that "there were a lot of people who brought up really good points, and it was cool to see other peoples' opinions about math, which you usually don't get" in mathematics courses. Another student expanded on this notion:

"Reading other peoples' posts kind of made me think, 'Oh, well they think about it this way, where as I think about it this way.' And I think that's going to help me when I become a teacher to understand how kids can think of different things differently.... I think that the topics and everything that we talked about, I think that everybody can perceive in different ways and I think that doing the online discussions, it helps people understand other peoples' thought processes about it."

Still another student suggested that by reading peers' posts and participating, "maybe the content of the course becomes more relevant to your way of thinking instead of just getting it from the teacher." It is worthwhile to note that these students had already completed one or two of the other courses in the mathematics sequence that subscribed to a common philosophy (but did not use online discussions), but students did not feel that they had heard alternate solution methods and interpretations of the math concepts in those courses.

Several students explained why they believed that participation in the online discussions led to more meaningful understandings of mathematical concepts. Several reiterated that the additional reading of students' explanations helped to solidify concepts covered in class. One student stated

"I learned that I can figure some things out on my own, without knowing a definition, but just by really sitting down and thinking about it. And that's what the discussions kind of forced me to do."

Another student compared her learning progress to that of students in other sections of the course:

"I always understood things so much better than my peers who were with other sections. That could be difference in teaching styles [of the instructors], but I really think it had a lot to do with the [online] discussions."

Of the 16 students who responded to subsequent questionnaires and interviews, 13 could identify one or more discussions that they believed led

Table 1. Performance on discussion-related quiz questions

Quiz Percentage	N (%)
100-90	5 (14%)
89-80	21 (58%)
79-70	4 (11%)
69-60	5 (14%)
Below 60	1 (3%)

them to develop deeper and new understandings of mathematics content. When prompted, they were each able to describe the content-specific new level of understanding that they had developed in the online discussion.

Quiz assessments supported students' claims, revealing that students who took an active role in the discussions (the majority of students) developed high levels of understanding of the discussed course content and were able to apply this knowledge in extension problems. Six of the ten weekly quizzes included questions that related directly to the online discussions and that were written in a fashion that was prohibitive to successful completion without a familiarity with the actual online discussions. From these scores on individual items, a percentage of correct answers out of those which were attempted was calculated. That is, the percentage is out of those quizzes that were taken by the individual rather than the total possible for the semester, as many students missed at least one quiz over the course of the semester. Two participants were omitted, as they took less than 50% of the quizzes under consideration.

The results are provided in Table 1. As the table indicates, a majority (72%) of the students retained and applied the mathematical concepts developed and explored in the online forum. In fact, only one individual demonstrated that she retained less than 60% of the ideas explored online through the application and synthesis of these ideas. A 60% in the course was required to pass. On quizzes, students were able to apply and synthesize knowledge and understandings from the online discussions on in-class work and assessments. Those who were led to post online contributions of increasing depth by analyzing their peers' comments, negotiating meaning, and testing others' ideas against their personal knowledge performed at higher levels beyond the online discussions.

Three students consistently provided minimal posts with little to no depth or thoughfulness. These students did not exhibit positive perceptions of the online discussions, could not provide examples of beneficial prompts, and did not demonstrate an understanding of topics discussed online in the discussion forum, on surveys, or on in-class assessments. For the remaining students, however, the online discussion model was shown to provide freedom and flexibility for students to participate in personally preferred and equally effective methods of participation leading to achievement of measured academic goals.

IMPLEMENTATION MODEL

The implementation model builds upon variation theory by considering multiple aspects of the students, content, and learning context. A view of the dynamic nature of the online discussions is presented in Figure 1. Discourse cycles through the indicated elements repeatedly between the initial instructor prompt and the eventual evaluation of newly developed understandings of mathematics content. Most of the considerations depicted have been discussed previously in the description of variation theory. The remaining considerations, and how all elements are put into action, are detailed next.

Course Management Software Features

The online discussion forums were part of a larger course management system. To encourage students to visit the online discussion forums frequently, other available features were used to relay course information and sustain regular traffic to the course management system. Document sharing capabilities were utilized to make available the course syllabus, schedule for homework assignments, course handouts, and detailed quiz solutions. The online grade book was also used.

Moderation

To achieve the goals of variation theory and to a to address the pilot study concerns, the instructor initiated most discussions. Multiple discussion threads on different topics were initiated each week to include an appropriate mix of content-specific threads and threads regarding the nature, teaching and learning of mathematics. Generally one thread was available at any given time. When the instructor determined that a conversation had run its course or needed to be refocused, the thread was locked and a new thread was begun. This method was particularly effective for directing students to respond to a peer's post or to begin looking at the thread from a new, specific perspective. This strategy did not preclude students from posting thoughts regarding earlier messages; they could include their ideas in a response to the new, related discussion thread.

The online discussions needed consistent and logical start/end times in order to establish a routine for the students and to minimize confusion that could have led students to "forget" to participate. In this model, a new discussion thread began after class on Friday and ended at the beginning of class on the following Friday when the weekly quiz was given. As students took the quiz, the instructor locked the concluding thread(s) and began a new discussion thread for the following week. This scheduling procedure reminded students to post before coming to class and to review their

Figure 1. The dynamic nature of the online discussions

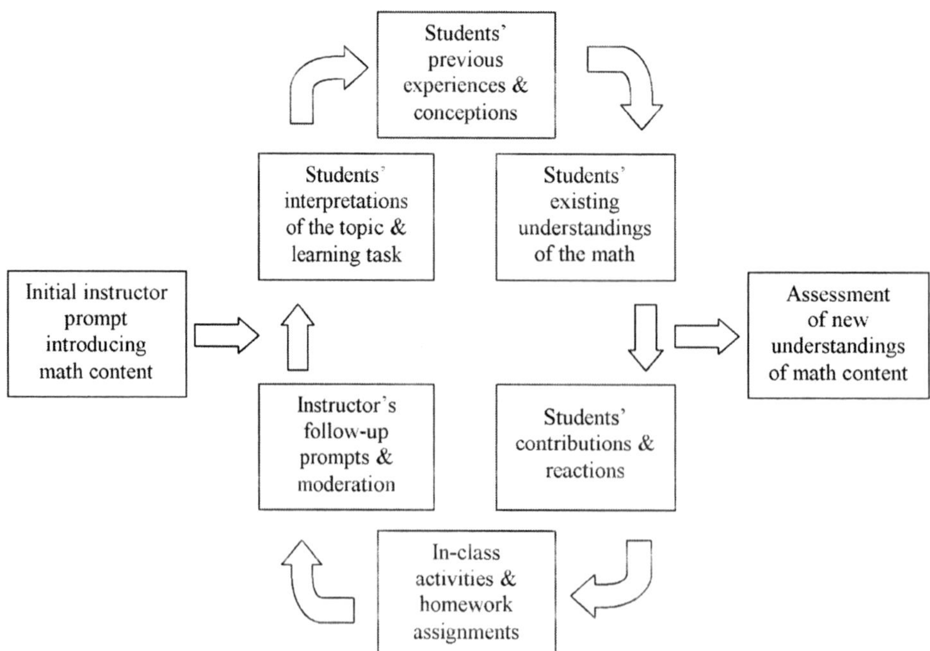

peers' contributions in advance of assessments on discussion-related content. When possible, the instructor did not correct errors in thinking expressed online unless the post had the potential to adversely affect students' performances in current homework assignments, impending quizzes or approaching exams. On some occasions, the instructor began the next class by directly addressing the error, and students responded appropriately in the online forum afterward.

Instructor intervention also proved necessary due to the timeline established for in-class presentation and exploration of material. Many threads were intended as advance organizers (Ausubel, 1960) or opportunities for students to develop personal conceptualizations of content before the material was presented in class. Others were meant to develop deeper or more advanced understandings of concepts that were already presented. Still other threads were designed to progress through both stages. Sometimes, it became necessary to quickly advance, modify or shuffle threads to meet these deadlines established by the course curriculum. On occasion, an intended discussion topic was dropped in favor of pursuing an idea or question raised in previous threads. Careful yet flexible planning of discussion threads alongside the course curriculum was critical as a basis for using the forum effectively.

Promoting Variation and Lively Discussion

Two principles of teaching to experience, as detailed by the variation theory of learning (Marton & Booth, 1997), guided the selection of online discussion threads. The first principle concerned building a relevance structure by creating situations under which students could encounter new abstractions, theories and explanations of mathematical concepts, procedures, and interpretations. Discussions aimed to connect the preservice teachers' previous, current, and future everyday lives and experiences to course content. The value of communication with and about mathematics was also emphasized; mathematical ideas were often developed together before formalizing them. The second principle concerned the "architecture of variation" which emphasized the process of building upon the expected variation in the group of prospective teachers and their varied problem solving approaches, conceptions about mathematics, and motivations behind becoming elementary teachers.

These principles were enacted by leading students to consider and explore variation among differing viewpoints and frames of reference that arose from the conversations. The discussion threads and tasks engaged students in discussing different aspects of mathematics by promoting reflective collaboration. For example, threads for development of exam review problems along with in-depth discussions regarding course content and the nature, teaching and learning of mathematics were included. Scenarios intended to stimulate cognitive conflict were presented, allowing prospective elementary teachers to recognize and confront their assumptions about mathematics content and the nature of mathematics that could impede development of conceptual understanding. Debate of course content issues has been argued as an effective means of engaging students in thoughtful and dynamic online discussions in other disciplines (see, for example, Gunawardena, Lowe & Anderson, 1997; Sloffer, Dueber, & Duffy, 1999). Because students often do not possess or express strong beliefs about models, solution processes, and representations of mathematics content, the type of lively online debate common in other disciplines can be harder to achieve in mathematics courses. To encourage more lively conversations, several threads provided the opportunity to share and debate their experiences in their previous and current mathematics courses. These discussion threads included conversations concerning the appropriateness of specific teaching methods used in the course, the students' academic performance and struggles in math classes, and students' individual learning styles.

Many threads were presented through the lens of the students' future teaching profession, asking how they will explain a concept and what teaching methods they could use. This perspective capitalized on the homogeneity of the group and built upon the interests and desires of these future teachers, motivating them to consider the course content and the nature, teaching and learning of mathematics. This approach aimed to lead the preservice teachers toward recognizing the importance of developing deep and meaningful understandings of mathematics in preparation for a successful teaching career and to best meet the needs of their future students. The threads led them to reflect upon their own experiences, confronting and modifying their perceptions of and attitudes toward mathematics while identifying sources of their developed attitudes. Threads regarding their varied methods and perspectives often led to discussions of the similarities and differences of these contributions, as well as attempts to construct mathematical connections between them.

Connecting Threads to the Course

Thread sources included: in-depth problems from the course textbook and activity book; material presented in previous semesters through in-class lecture and/or the Socratic Method; conversations begun in class; assigned online tasks that explicitly provided assistance in preparing for exams; responses to class readings from the textbook; students' questions and concerns posed in class or during office hours; and expansion of ideas that students posted online. The topics were not simply extensions of additional tasks beyond the presented material. This array of threads engaged students in discussions that varied in focus while establishing the forum as an important and integral part of the course. A partial list of discussion prompts is provided in Table 2.

Online discussion threads often evolved from presentation, exploration, or discussion of mathematics during within the traditional classroom setting. Students' contributions and questions concerned both specific mathematics content as well as the nature, teaching and learning of mathematics. Often the instructor or a student posed a meaningful question without an immediate or clear answer, and the discussion was deferred to the online forum. One particular example concerned the necessary conditions for two polygons to be congruent. Through a series of threads, students provided counterexamples to multiple scenarios, leading to the in-class presentation of the necessary and sufficient conditions for congruence several days later. Excerpts from another example regarding the sums of the vertex angles of a polygon are provided in Figure 2. This asynchronous approach was found to be much more effective than previous in-class attempts to lead students to develop understandings of the relationship between sums of the angles and the number of sides of the polygon. In instances such as these, the asynchronous nature of the discussions enabled students to contemplate the ideas individually before sharing their thoughts. Threads allowed for joint exploration of teaching/learning concerns and development of deeper understandings of course content in ways not possible in the time-constrained class period.

As online discussions unfolded, students' online contributions were often referenced during class to introduce or summarize a thread, draw connections to other concepts, or to incorporate an example, question, or concern posed by a student in the online forum. If a meaningful context, scenario, or diagram was posted online, it was often used in a lecture to stimulate further discussion. In the case of the discussion regarding sums of vertex angles, the images students provided with their posts were subsequently incorporated during an in-class discussion concerning the underlying formula that could be applied to the scenarios. Students expressed pride when one

Table 2. Weekly online discussion prompt topics

Week #	Nature, Teaching and Learning of Mathematics Topic(s)	Mathematics Content Topic(s)
2	Compare/contrast geometry with other types of math	What is an angle?
3	What does it mean to take an intuitive approach to teaching geometry?	Reconciling the different definitions/interpretations of an angle shared last week
4	Examine/critique the different learning methods in the course	Exploring the sums of vertex angles in polygons
5	After the exam concerns	Developing and solving exam review problems
6	The value and concerns of an intuitive approach from the teacher's perspective	What is congruence, and what does it mean for two polygons to be congruent?
7	Evaluating online tools for exploring transformations	What is symmetry, and what does it mean for a polygon to have symmetry?
9	The role of technology in mathematics teaching/learning	Developing and solving exam review problems
10	None	Necessary and sufficient conditions for two polygons to be congruent
11	Similarity or congruence – which should be taught first? When does order matter in teaching and learning math concepts?	Comparing/contrasting the concepts of similarity and congruence
12	None	What is the difference between accuracy and precision? What does it mean to measure?
13	Is our measuring activity an example of the intuitive approach?	How accurate/important were your estimation skills? What were your informal units of measure, and why? Did the conversion to standard units make sense?
14	How prepared do you feel to teach mathematics?	Developing and solving exam review problems

of their online contributions appeared in class, viewing the event as a validation of their post.

Another discussion example concerned the concept of an angle. The full discussion is represented in the posts provided below and in Tables 3, 4 and 5. For this analysis, order of the posts has been adjusted and both spelling and typographical errors have been corrected, but more substantial grammatical errors remain. Note how, for some students, the motivation behind their descriptions and thinking are the needs of their future elementary mathematics students and appropriate methods for explaining and demonstrating the mathematics concepts at hand. By framing the content course as preparation for the students' future teaching careers, in-class activities and online discussions led the students to think about the mathematics and about meaningful explanations that extended beyond traditional textbook definitions prescribed for memorization.

During the first week of discussions and before the class had begun a formal study of geometry, students had been asked to define the concept of an angle. Most responses included reference to rays and angle measures. But one particular student's post, called Emily here, was significantly different and deviated from the textbook definitions that students had been asked to avoid. As a result, her post became a topic of online discussion the following week, which coincided with the start of formal in-class lessons on geometric topics. Below are the initial prompt and the first student response (Emily was notified in advance that her post would be the foundation of one of the week's discussions, and she was therefore anxious to participate in the thread, responding first to the initial instructor prompt).

Instructor: "Last week we wrestled with the idea of what an angle really is, and I would like to continue this conversation. Is an angle a physical

Figure 2. Excerpts from a discussion thread examining the sums of the vertex angles of polygons

Prompt: Consider the three figures in the attached word document [provided below]. How could you go about determining the sum of the vertex angles in each of the figures? Exclude the use of protractors or a simple formula.

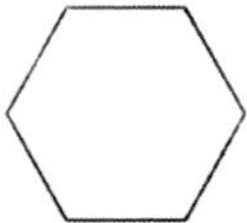

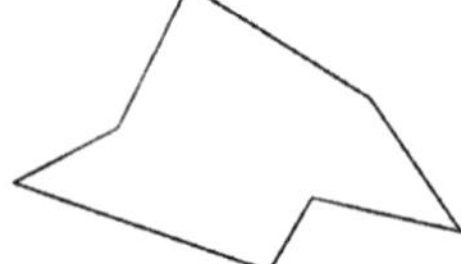

Student A's response: One way you could find the sum of the angles is to start by dividing each polygon into smaller triangles. Make sure that each angle of the newly formed triangle is shared with an interior angle of the polygon. For example, in the hexagon... you could first divide it in half and then make two triangles out of the top half and two out of the bottom half....After you have done that, then you can simply add up the number of triangles that are formed and multiply by 180, since you already know that each triangle equals 180 degrees. You can do the same thing with the other shapes, just make sure that the triangles always share their angles with the interior angles of the polygon (even if it is only part of an angle). This way when you add the triangles together you are only adding segments of the interior angles of the polygon.
Here's a visual explanation of what I'm talking about because it's a lot easier to explain with a picture.

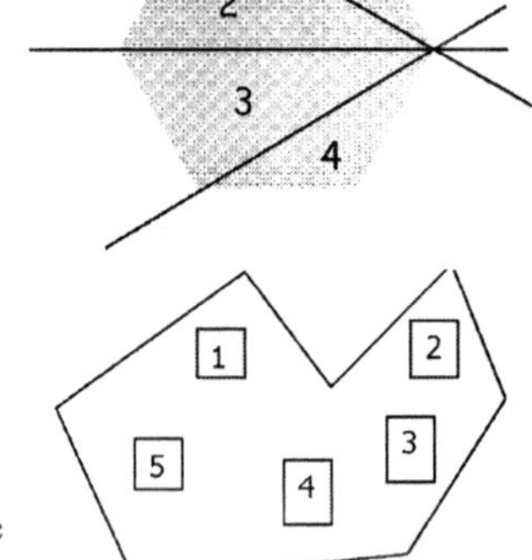

Student B's response: I agree with your answer and how you solved it. I went ahead and did the second shape the same way. I was careful to make sure that my triangles covered every angle inside the shape. I have included a picture to illustrate my answer.

5 triangles = 180 x 5 (900 degrees)

Student C's response: I couldn't help but notice something interesting in both... illustrations. For both shapes, there are two less triangles than there are vertices. For example, the first shape has 6 vertices and it has 4 triangles inside, and the second shape has 7 vertices and 5 triangles. I went ahead and did the last shape and it also has 7 vertices and 5 triangles. I'm sure there is a formula for this, but I just thought it was interesting to see this correlation.

thing, or is it more like an abstract idea? Consider a part of Emily's post from last week: An angle is a type of measurement. When we want to find this measurement we use a tool that is called a protractor, which measures degrees. These are not degrees like temperature. An easy way to think of it is like taking steps. There are 360 'steps' in a circle, or 360 degrees. Measuring an angle is like measuring how many steps it takes to get to a specific spot. What Emily is describing doesn't quite sound like a physical thing that you can see or touch. The most common response last week involved the intersection of two lines or two rays. In the real world, there are few objects that have actual rays or lines drawn on them, but people talk about finding the angle on them. Do these things not have angles? Are these people wrong? And I'm still not convinced either way that a circle has angles or not...."

Emily: "I think that angles are a pretty abstract idea. My example from last week was an attempt at making it a physical concept so that children can better understand what an angle is. If all the

Table 3. Posts Describing an angle as a physical entity

I think that an angle is a physical thing. An angle is formed when 2 rays share an endpoint. In the "real world" everything is formed sharing a common endpoint. Take a building for example...the ground and the wall share an endpoint, making a right angle. Even the rays of light that shine from an object to the ground from the sun cause make an angle. Whenever 2 planes intersect, there is an angle at their intersection. Even the V formation better each letter on a keyboard forms and angle. Not all angles in the world are as easily shown as drawing 2 rays connected at one end, but everything has at least one angle: the angle between that object and the ground (thanks to gravity!).
Just because something does not have a specific line or ray on it, does not mean that is is not there. Let's take for example a table...the table top can be a line and the leg can be a line. Where the two "lines" meet is the point. This is an angle. There are many "real world" examples all around us.
I think that the actual physical angle itself if something that you can physically see, however, the degrees of an angle is something that you can't physically see but you can measure. I agree with Betsy that everything has at least one angle, the angle of where an object meets the ground. There are angles all around us for example where a building and the ground meet, the V where the two sides of the roof meet, the angle when you form an L with your thumb and index finger, they are everywhere. However, what you can't always see is the measure of an angle. You may be able to guess that something is a right angle or you may be able to tell if it is greater than 90 or less than 90 degrees, but unless you actually physically measure it you don't know. So I think that the angle itself is something that you can touch, but the measure of the angle is something that you can't physically touch.
I believe an angle is a physical thing. An angle is not an abstract idea because you can physically measure an angle and you can also see an angle. The way that Emily is describing an angle would qualify it as an abstract idea because you cannot physical see the "steps" she is describing. You also cannot touch these step that she is describing.
I think like everyone else that an angle is an actual thing or object. It is something you see when two objects come into contact with one another. This can be formed by putting two pieces of wood together, or bending your arm. Angles are just not in math but all around us. So why I could of looked up the definition of an angle I did not think that that was needed. An angle occurs when two things touch.
I think that angles are physical things. Just as many people stated, it come when two things meet at the same point. A building on pavement forms an angle. The place between your two fingers forms an angle. When two rays meet at an endpoint, it forms an angle. Also, anything can be considered a line. From one point to another point, it forms a line. Maybe not a line that you can literally SEE like you can draw in math, but it is a line and it meets with some other line, and potentially forms an angle.

Table 4. Posts sharing an abstract interpretation of angles

I personally think that angles aren't physical. I do consider something physical as something you can touch. Yes, they are something you can see...on paper. Can you really see angles in the physical world? Do you really even think about seeing angles in the physical world? Probably not. I've never seen anybody, anywhere "draw" an invisible angle in a place where they think one goes. So they're only physical in one aspect - if they are visible. Otherwise, they are completely abstract. Twolinesortworays,asfarasIknow,haveangles.Ihaven'tseenasituationinwhicheitherdoesn'tformanangle...butmaybeit'sjustsomethingIdon'tknow. As for circles...I was never taught circles had "angles". I always believed that circles had degrees, so unless I'm told by a reliable source otherwise, I'm sticking to what I was taught. 360 degrees forever!
I believe that an angle is both a physical thing and an idea. On paper an angle is two rays or lines that have an intersection. You can measure these angles with a protractor and find how many degrees are actually in the angle. In the real world though many different objects have angles. The difference between paper and the real world is that you can't really take objects in the real world and measure them with a protractor. I'm sure there are so exceptions, but for the most part in the real world you would need a bigger tool to do this measurement or sometimes you can just guess the measure of the angle and you will be close. Physical objects DO have angles though. The people that responded to the question last week and said that an angle was 2 lines or rays with an intersection are not wrong. There are just 2 different ways of saying what an angle is. I'm not sure if an circle has angles either, but if I had to make a guess I would say no. A circle has 360 degrees inside of it which is a measure, but there is not 2 rays or 2 lines with an intersection inside a circle.
I believe that an angle is a physical thing, but can be described, like what Emily did, in other terms or nonphysical events. All items have endpoints even if you don't think they are there. Everything has an edge that can be measured in one way or another. Emily's way of describing an angle is just simply an easier way to teach students or even a great way to introduce the idea to a class. Yet, to contradict what I said, I do not believe that a circle has angles. It is the only thing that can not be measured by simply measuring 2 angles. The way to prove that a circle is 360 degrees is by creating angles inside it to measure. Example as in creating four 90 degree angles inside by making to perpendicular (spelling?) lines in the center of the circle and adding all their degrees together to equal 360.

Table 5. Concluding posts about angles that Build upon in-class activities

Do the ideas discussed in Wednesday's class make anyone think differently about the idea of an angle, or whether it is something physical or abstract? Were any of the ideas we talked about ways that you think about angles?
What we talked about in class doesn't change what I think about angles. I don't believe that circles have angles, but they do both have degrees. I think that since a circle has degrees, the degrees can be shown with angles. I also think that angles are physical. Since they can be drawn out physically and they are everywhere, I think it is concrete.
I found Wednesday's class kind of intriguing. It has been a long time since i have even considered any of this stuff which is unlike most of the class. If you think about the fact that we have said that when you put things together you can figure how big they are or how many degrees the shape is etc. We did all these things with shapes well if you put several triangles together you can make a full circle so in that aspect yes a circle is full of angles depending on how you think about it or look at it. I still think that angles and rays in some aspects are very abstract but you can try to make them more tangible.
The ideas and topics discussed in class actually helped refresh my memory of many of the basic geometry terms that I hadn't seen since my sophomore year of high school. After discussing these things in class the way in which I thought of an angle in comparison to things such as rays, segments and lines became a little different. Things became clearer and then different terms more distinct when we discussed and defined them in the order and the way in which we did. I think angles are more abstract because you have to sort of use your imagination when seeing them on paper, it is hard sometimes to visualize something that would be much easier to visualize as a 3 dimensional figure, yet instead it is just a series of lines and shapes on a piece of paper. To help make angles and different geometric things easier to understand especially with younger students I think you need to make them more visual or hands on Physical so they can better understand the concepts. Once you can visual the physical it is much easier to understand the abstract parts of geometry.

other people go into a fourth grade classroom and talk about rays, etc., the kids are going to look at them like they are crazy. Also, this would be a boring way to teach math. From [the instructor] I learned that hands on teaching is by far the most enjoyable way to learn or even relearn a topic, so my approach still makes sense to me, although I do agree that angles really are a pretty abstract concept overall."

Emily's quick response to the prompt corroborated the instructor's belief that she viewed angles on a more abstract level and through their attributes in contrast to the majority of her peers, who had provided very concrete and textbook definitions during the previous discussion.

The first portion of this subsequent topic is presented in Tables 3 and 4. In general, other students held to the belief that angles are a physical, concrete concept, but wrestled with the more abstract concern of turning through an angle. Broader, more abstract claims became more prevalent as the discussion progressed. This online discussion laid a foundation for future in-class lessons on transformations, when emphasis was placed upon rotations as being the act of turning through an angle. Students also wrestled here with differentiating between 360 degrees in a rotation and whether there are angles in a circle and, more generally, between an angle and its measure; their confusion of these topics was a confounding factor in the discussion. Again, the importance of this distinction was addressed in subsequent lessons on transformations.

The remainder of this discussion thread is presented in Table 5. As the instructor's prompt suggests, the in-class lesson on Wednesday (the online discussion ran from Friday to Friday) focused upon figure and angle comparisons and, as a student notes, included hands-on activities with manipulatives. The instructor specifically leads the students to connect the ongoing discussion to what they have recently learned in class, tying together both elements of the course learning structure and further validating their codependency and academic benefits.

On occasion, online discussion extended tasks that students had begun in class. One such example was the development of review problems in groups or pairs. During the week preceding each in-class examination, students were asked to post review questions to share online with their classmates in preparation for the test. Working as pairs, one student posted the question and another student later posted the solution. These questions were developed in advance during time set aside in class. The review questions often acted as a starting point for more in-depth discussions about course content. Similarly, if a student posed a thoughtful question in class that did not have an immediate answer or was too complex to be analyzed in the available class time, the question likely formed the basis of a subsequent online discussion. This allowed the students to explore the idea individually before sharing their thoughts, resulting in the development of deeper understandings of course content that were otherwise unattainable in the time-constrained class period.

The technological nature of online discussions was also exploited in the online conversations. Several threads linked students to existing websites that allowed them to explore mathematics content through guided or self-paced activities. For example, during the unit on transformations, threads linked students to several transformation applets available online. The purpose of these threads was two-fold: to facilitate the incorporation of meaningful and dynamic virtual technologies as a means to enhance students' understandings of the course material, and to make students aware of the free mathematical learning tools available on the internet. Subsequent discussion threads asked students to discuss the educational benefits and limitations these technologies present, and to develop means of using of them. Students often chose to revisit the still visible links in the locked threads. Subsequently, students shared effective use of internet-available technologies that they discovered on their own by including links in their posts to other relevant online activities, resources and videos.

Grading

To ensure sufficient and effective engagement of all students in the online forums, it proved necessary to provide motivation with an appropriate grading scheme. This decision resulted, in part, from the pilot study (Miller, 2005), in which posts were graded on completion only and did not demonstrate deep levels of thought development. The grading rubric was designed to encourage students to post meaningful and timely messages and to read and respond to peers' contributions. Therefore, students were graded on both the frequency and quality of their posts. The use of such a rubric that assesses the quality, depth, or value of a post has been demonstrated as necessary and effective in the literature (Klisc, McGill & Hobbs, 2009; Sain & Brigham, 2003; Wolff & Dosdall, 2010). Students were expected to read all posts each week and were required to post at least once per week; if multiple threads were discussed, students did not need to post in each thread. Students were not broken into smaller groups, assigned specific roles, or scheduled to participate during specific discussions, thereby promoting continued engagement of all students within the discussions but freedom in their approach to participation. Further, it was determined that forming groups would have added a layer of tracking and scheduling that may have obstructed meaningful participation.

Students were graded on the depth of their post, and their score reflected whether or not their contribution furthered the conversation and built upon the previous contributions of their peers. Acceptable examples of posts were provided to the students, and the expectations were modeled by posts that the instructor made to the forum. The five-point grading rubric shown in Table 6 was applied each week to students' online posts. Students' lowest online participation score for the semester was dropped in recognition that a student may, on occasion, forget to post a message. This also avoided the negative perception some students developed in the pilot study toward the online discussions, claiming that they "lost points" because they did not post a message. Approximately seven percent of a student's course

Table 6. Grading rubric for online posts

Score	Message Characteristics
0	No post
1	A single post providing minimal contribution to the development of the conversation
3	A meaningful contribution, but no response to follow-up requests for clarification or no expansion of already expressed ideas
5	A meaningful contribution that addresses ongoing questions and comments

grade was earned through participation in the online discussions.

This grading scheme focused upon the quality of students' posts, but the quantity of posts was also inherently addressed. A requirement of at least one post per week (with the lowest dropped) established a minimum threshold for quantity of posts for the semester. In the dissertation study, all students who regularly attended class met this minimum requirement. Time committed to grading posts was most significant during the first three weeks of online discussions, in order to establish and enforce clear expectations for online participation. Five-point, in-depth and meaningful posts quickly became the norm, and those that did not meet expectations became readily identifiable among the majority of five-point earning contributions. The use of a 0-1-3-5 scale also facilitated grading, reducing the need to discern between additional rubric levels and eliminating the needs for written grade feedback. Many course management systems allow instructors to evaluate posts as they are read, reducing the need to revisit posts for evaluation. No students indicated displeasure with the rubric, although two asked for a clarification of the system upon receiving a less-than-perfect grade.

Accountability for reading and thinking about all weekly posts was established by linking online discussions to weekly in-class quizzes. At least one quiz question each week pertained specifically to the online discussions, providing further motivation for students to participate thoughtfully online. Some quiz questions asked students to summarize the discussions, others asked them to respond to issues raised during the conversations, and still others asked them to apply or expand the mathematics examined in the discussions. Students were encouraged to revisit the online forum and read more recent posts in preparation for the quiz. The number of messages that each student actually read varied from person-to-person and week-to-week, but the weekly quizzes provided an additional incentive for the students to read and contemplate the contributions of their peers in a timely fashion.

CONCLUSION

This model for online discussions allows students individual freedom in their approaches to online participation. Students are free to log onto the system at times of their choosing, can wait for a different thread before posting, and can choose which ideas from their peers to respond to. Simultaneously, the model also establishes and promotes clear expectations and academic goals. The instructor's leadership in the forums ensures that course learning objectives are met and enable students to begin thinking deeply about mathematics content while drawing connections and honing their mathematical communication skills. The model permits the instructor to encourage (enable) students to confront their beliefs and conceptions of the nature and learning of mathematics, particularly as they related to their understandings of the course content. Students tend to experience little difficulty adjusting to online conversations and appreciated the format.

Without the multiple connections established to the face-to-face facets of the course, online discussions would, from the students' perspectives, operate as a separately functioning entity with little bearing on meeting course objectives. Through this model, students are motivated by the continual impact of their engagement in the online conversations upon their course grade via their discussion scores and quiz grades. They come to view the online discussions as an extension of the in-class discussions, lecture, and activities. Subsequently, a natural back-and-forth between these elements is established. Students develop a better appreciation for their own and for their peers' contributions, and begin to reconcile the multiple solution methods and perspectives that are shared. Finally, the students quickly become accustomed to participating through the logical discussion forum structure and schedule that coincides with other course components.

Since the completion of the dissertation study, this model has continued to be incorporated into similar mathematics content courses for future elementary teachers at another university with a significantly different mission and student population. While several prompts have been modified to align with changing curricula and the dynamic nature of students' contributions, the model itself has continued to prove effective. Students' appreciation for the learning opportunity persists, as do similar levels of achieved educational outcomes.

Adaptations would be necessary for use of this model in mathematics courses with differing content and student populations. As the examined course focused upon content necessary for becoming an elementary school teacher, the population was homogeneous and motivation was framed through the students' common aspirations and career expectations. Additionally, the level of mathematics discussed did not require inclusion of higher-level notation and symbolism necessary in other college mathematics courses. The need for a cohesive group of students in this model should not be overlooked; the framing of online discussions through common interests and career goals among students of a like major are necessary to motivate discussions and drive a variety of responses. In homogenous mathematics courses for majors other than education, topics regarding the nature, teaching and learning of mathematics may be replaced with motivating topics related to the future careers and interests of the group. As technology progresses, the inclusion of mathematics-specific notation and symbolism is increasingly facilitated, allowing for more formal and more advanced levels of mathematics to be discussed without difficulty. With larger classes, students may need to be broken into weekly groups that post to discussions while others observe, reducing the number of posts students must read and limiting the work load for students and the instructor. With classes of 60 or more, it may be necessary to split the class into separate, parallel discussion forums to limit students' workload while ensuring sufficient variation across student contributions.

With asynchronous online discussions, careful planning and structure are paramount, but flexibility is also critical. A well-planned discussion thread may be abandoned in favor of exploring a point made by a student, or to extend a conversation that the instructor feels has not yet reached a conclusion. Through careful alignment with other planned learning opportunities, the full potential and academic benefits provided by online discussions can be realized in a mathematics courses.

REFERENCES

Ausubel, D. P. (1960). The use of advance organizers in the learning and retention of meaningful verbal material. *Journal of Educational Psychology, 51*, 267–272. doi:10.1037/h0046669

Ball, D. (1990). The mathematical understandings that prospective teachers bring to teacher education. *The Elementary School Journal, 90*, 449–466. doi:10.1086/461626

Bender, T. (2003). *Discussion-based online teaching to enhance student learning*. Sterling, VA: Stylus Publishing.

Bowden, J., & Marton, F. (1998). *The university of learning: Beyond quality and competence in higher education*. London, UK: Cogan Page.

Brett, C., Woodruff, E., & Nason, R. (1999). *Online community and preservice teachers' conceptions of learning mathematics*. Paper presented at the Annual Meeting of Computer Supported Cooperative Learning, December. Retrieved September 15, 2006, from http://home.oise.utoronto.ca/ ~cbrett/ FOV10- 00013878/

Brett, C., Woodruff, E., & Nason, R. (2002). *Developing identity as preservice elementary mathematics teachers: The contribution of online community.* Paper presented at the Annual Meeting of the American Educational Association, New Orleans, April, 2002. Retrieved September 15, 2006 from http://home.oise.utoronto.ca/ ~cbrett/ FOV10- 00013878/

Cady, J., & Rearden, K. (2007). Pre-service teachers' beliefs about knowledge, mathematics, and science. *School Science and Mathematics*, *107*, 237–245. doi:10.1111/j.1949-8594.2007.tb18285.x

Carey, R., Kleiman, G., Russell, M., Venable, J. D., & Louie, J. (2008). Online courses for math teachers: Comparing self-paced and facilitated cohort approaches. *Journal of Technology, Learning, and Assessment, 7*(3). Retrieved September 30, 2010, from http://www.jtla.org

DeBourgh, G. A. (2002, May/June). *Simple elegance: Course management systems as pedagogical infrastructure to enhance science learning.* The Technology Source. Retrieved online August 25, 2004, from http://ts.mivu.org

Fauske, J., & Wade, S. E. (2004). Research to practice online: Conditions that foster democracy, community, and critical thinking in computer-mediated discussions. *Journal of Research on Technology in Education*, *36*, 137–153.

Gunawardena, C., Lowe, C., & Anderson, T. (1997). Analysis of a global online debate and the development of an interaction analysis model for examining social construction of knowledge in computer conferencing. *Journal of Educational Computing Research*, *17*, 397–431. doi:10.2190/7MQV-X9UJ-C7Q3-NRAG

Hara, N., Bonk, C., & Angeli, C. (2000). Content analysis of online discussion in an applied educational psychology course. *Instructional Science*, *28*, 115–152. doi:10.1023/A:1003764722829

Hofstad, M. (2003, August). *Enhancing student learning in online courses*. Presented at the 111th Annual Convention of the American Psychological Association: Toronto, Ontario, Canada.

Hong, K., & Lee, A. C. (2008). Postgraduate students' knowledge construction during asynchronous computer conferences in a blended learning environment: A Malaysian experience. *Australasian Journal of Educational Technology*, *24*, 91–107.

Kienle, A., & Ritterskamp, C. (2007). Facilitating asynchronous discussions in learning communities: The impact of moderation strategies. *Behaviour & Information Technology*, *26*, 73–80. doi:10.1080/01449290600811594

Klisc, C., McGill, T., & Hobbs, V. (2009). The effect of assessment on the outcomes of asynchronous online discussion as perceived by instructors. *Australasian Journal of Educational Technology*, *25*, 666–682.

Kosiak, J. J. (2004). Using asynchronous discussions to facilitate collaborative problem solving in college algebra (Doctoral dissertation, Montana State University, 2004). *Dissertations Abstracts International, 65,* 2442.

Lloyd, G. M., & Frykholm, J. A. (2000). On the development of "book smarts" in mathematics: Prospective elementary teachers' experiences with innovative curriculum materials. *Issues in the Undergraduate Mathematics Preparation of School Teachers: The Journal, 2.* Retrieved September 29, 2005 from www.k12prep.math.ttu.edu/ journal/ journal.shtml

Ma, L. (1999). *Knowing and teaching elementary mathematics: Teachers' understanding of fundamental mathematics in China and the United States*. Mahwah, NJ: Lawrence Erlbaum Associates.

Marton, F. (1986). Phenomenography: A research approach to investigating different understandings of reality. *Journal of Thought, 21*, 28–49.

Marton, F., & Booth, S. (1997). *Learning and awareness*. Mahwah, NJ: Lawrence Erlbaum Associates.

Mathematical Sciences Education Board & National Research Council. (1989). *Everyody counts: A report to the nation on the future of mathematic education*. Washington, DC: National Academy Press.

Mathematical Sciences Education Board & National Research Council. (1990). *Reshaping school mathematics: A framework and philosophy for curriculum.* Washington, DC: National Academy Press.

Mazzolini, M. (2003). Sage, guide, or ghost? The effect of instructor intervention on student participation in online discussion forums. *Computers & Education, 40*, 237–253. doi:10.1016/S0360-1315(02)00129-X

Mazzolini, M., & Maddison, S. (2007). The role of the instructor in online discussion forums. *Computers & Education, 49*, 193–213. doi:10.1016/j.compedu.2005.06.011

Miller, T. (2009, March). *Online discussion in a mathematics content course for preservice elementary teachers.* Twenty-first Annual International Conference on Technology in Collegiate Mathematics, New Orleans, LA.

Miller, T. K. (2005, October). *Online discussion in a mathematics content course for preservice elementary teachers.* Poster presented at the 27th Meeting of the North American Chapter of the International Group for the Psychology of Mathematics Education, Roanoke, VA.

Miller, T. K. (2007). *Prospective elementary teachers' experiences in learning mathematics via online discussions: A phenomenographical study.* (Doctoral Dissertation). Purdue University, West Lafayette, IN.

Miller, T. K. (in press). A theoretical framework for implementing technology for mathematics learning . In Ronau, R., Rakes, C., & Niess, M. (Eds.), *Educational technology, teacher knowledge, and classroom impact: A research handbook on frameworks and approaches*.

National Council of Teachers of Mathematics. (1989). *Curriculum and evaluation standards for school mathematics*. Reston, VA: Author.

National Council of Teachers of Mathematics. (2000). *Principles and standards for school mathematics*. Reston, VA: Author.

Newell, S. T. (1996). Practical inquiry: Collaboration and reflection in teacher education reform. *Teaching and Teacher Education, 12*, 567–576. doi:10.1016/S0742-051X(96)00001-7

Pang, M. F. (2003). Two faces of variation: On continuity in the phenomenographic movement. *Scandinavian Journal of Educational Research, 47*, 145–156. doi:10.1080/00313830308612

Patton, M. Q. (2002). *Qualitative research & evaluation method* (3rd ed.). Thousand Oaks, CA: Sage Publications.

Prosser, M. (1993). Phenomenography and the principles and practices of learning. *Higher Education Research & Development, 12*, 21–31. doi:10.1080/0729436930120103

Runesson, U. (2005). Beyond discourse and interaction. Variation: A critical aspect for teaching and learning mathematics. *Cambridge Journal of Education, 35*, 69–87. doi:10.1080/0305764042000332506

Sain, R., & Brigham, T. A. (2003). The effect of a threaded discussion component on student satisfaction and performance. *Journal of Educational Computing Research, 29*, 419-430. Schellens, T., Van Keer, H., De Wever, B., & Valcke, M. (2007). Scripting by assigning roles: Does it improve knowledge construction in asynchronous discussion groups? *International Journal of Computer-Supported Collaborative Learning, 2*, 225–246.

Silverman, J., & Clay, E. (2010). Online asynchronous collaboration in mathematics teacher education and the development of mathematical knowledge for teaching. *Teacher Educator, 45*, 54–73. doi:10.1080/08878730903386831

Slavit, D. (2002). Expanding classroom discussion with an online medium. *Journal of Technology and Teacher Education, 10*, 407–422.

Sloffer, S. J., Dueber, B., & Duffy, T. M. (1999, January). Using asynchronous conferencing to promote critical thinking: Two implementations in higher education. In the *Proceedings of the 32nd Hawaii International Conference on System Sciences*. Maui, Hawaii.

Staples, M. (2008). Promoting student collaboration in a detracked, heterogeneous secondary mathematics classroom. *Journal of Mathematics Teacher Education, 11*, 349–371. doi:10.1007/s10857-008-9078-8

Wolff, B., & Dosdall, M. (2010). Weighing the risks of excessive participation in asynchronous online discussions against the benefits of robust participation. *MERLOT Journal of Online Learning and Teaching, 6*, 55–61.

ADDITIONAL READING

Johansson, B., Marton, F., & Svensson, L. (1985). An approach to describing learning as change between qualitatively different conceptions . In West, L. H. T., & Pines, A. L. (Eds.), *Cognitive structure and conceptual change* (pp. 233–258). New York: Academic Press.

Mishra, P., & Koehler, M. J. (2006). Technological pedagogical content knowledge: A framework for teacher knowledge. *Teachers College Record, 108*, 1017–1054. doi:10.1111/j.1467-9620.2006.00684.x

Prosser, M., & Trigwell, K. (1997). Using phenomenography in the design of programs for teachers in higher education. *Higher Education Research & Development, 16*, 41–54. doi:10.1080/0729436970160104

Putnam, R. T., & Borko, H. (2000). What do new views of knowledge and thinking have to say about research on teacher learning? *Educational Researcher, 29*, 4–15.

Runesson, U., & Marton, F. (2002). The object of learning and the space of variation . In Marton, F., & Morris, P. (Eds.), *What matters? Discovering critical conditions of classroom learning*. Göteborg: Acta Universitatis Gothoburgensis.

Wilcox, S. K., Schram, P., Lappan, G., & Lanier, P. (1991). *The role of a learning community in changing preservice teachers' knowledge and beliefs about mathematics education.* (Research Report 91-1). (ERIC Document ED 330 680).

Zenios, M., Banks, F., & Moon, B. (2004). Stimulating professional development through CMC – A case study of networked learning and initial teacher education . In Goodyear, P., Banks, S., Hodgson, V., & McConnell, D. (Eds.), *Advances in research on networked learning* (pp. 123–151). Boston: Kluwer Academic Publishers. doi:10.1007/1-4020-7909-5_6

KEY TERMS AND DEFINITIONS

Asynchronous: Not occurring in real time; users may log in and participate at different times.

Mathematics Content Course: Focuses upon mathematics, not teaching methods.

Object of Learning: The concept or aspect of a concept focused upon in a learning opportunity.

Online Discussion: A conversation consisting of messages posted by various users and stored collectively online for access by all users.

Phenomenography: Research approach examining the qualitatively different ways in which students experience a learning phenomenon or opportunity.

Preservice Teacher: University student majoring in education who has not yet taught in the classroom.

Variation Theory: Theory of learning positing that what individuals learn is the variation along a particular aspect, or dimension, of the object of learning.

Chapter 2
A Blended Learning Approach in Mathematics

B. Abramovitz
ORT Braude College, Israel

M. Berezina
ORT Braude College, Israel

A. Berman
Technion Israel Institute of Technology, Israel

L. Shvartsman
ORT Braude College, Israel

ABSTRACT

In this chapter we present our work aimed at interweaving e-learning and face-to-face learning in Calculus courses for undergraduate engineering students. This type of blended learning (BL) contains the best properties of e-learning and face-to-face learning and helps overcome many obstacles in traditional teaching. We use our approach in order to improve students' conceptual understanding of theorems. We describe online assignments specifically designed to help students better understand the meaning of a theorem. These assignments are given to students in addition to traditional lectures and tutorials with the objective that they can learn to learn on their own. Students "discover" the theorem and study it independently, by using a "bank" of examples and a lot of theoretical exercises we supply. The assignments are built in such a way that students receive feedback and instructions in response to their Web-based activity.

DOI: 10.4018/978-1-60960-875-0.ch002

INTRODUCTION

Using today's advanced computers and Internet networks, a wide spectrum of different ways of learning and teaching are being developed: from supplying students with learning materials in traditional universities through to studying in new purely online universities. We are Mathematics lecturers in a traditional engineering university where face-to-face teaching is prevalent; however, some elements of online learning are widely used. Almost all courses have websites through which the lecturer stays in touch with students and uploads different materials for them in addition to face-to-face lectures, tutorials and office hours. In attempting to resolve problems related to our face-to-face teaching (for details, see the "Problems and Trends" section), we exploited the opportunities offered by the worldwide web. We knew that our students needed additional special material to supplement our lectures. They were simply not getting enough "face time" with us in class, owing to the shortage of lecture hours. Moreover, we wanted our students to get used to learning theory independently.

In order to overcome these problems we developed a web-based learner-centered approach as a component of BL, which has thus far been implemented in Calculus courses.

We constructed online theoretical assignments to help students better understand the meaning of a theorem. These self learning assignments are of an unusual type and given to the students in a special order to turn them from passive receivers of knowledge into active partners in the learning process. During our face-to-face teaching we used these assignments to complete the learning process.

We called our approach the Self Learning Method (SLM). SLM has three main parts that are presented in detail in the "Description of the Method" section.

In the first part of SLM students learn how to formulate a conjecture. We use the Integral Mean Value Theorem as an illustration. Students "discover" the theorem independently, by using a "bank" of examples we supply.

In the second part students study assumptions and conclusions of theorems. We illustrate this part by means of Lagrange's Mean Value Theorem. Students conduct their own research by using a set of especially composed assignments.

The third part of SLM focuses on proving a theorem. Three Calculus theorems were used to illustrate different types of assignments: "scattered puzzles", "fill in puzzles" and "puzzles". The main aim of these assignments was to teach students that a theorem's proof has a logical order, and each its step is based on information given in a theorem's assumptions.

In the "SLM Implementation and Some Results" section we describe our positive experience in operating SLM as a part of BL.

As an Internet self learning environment, we used the Webassign system (see www.webassign.net). Webassign was developed at North Carolina State University, and it is used by more than 300,000 students at over 1,500 institutions. In our teaching we apply the version that was adapted to Hebrew. Here we present examples translated from Hebrew to English.

PROBLEMS AND TRENDS

We teach different Mathematics courses designed for engineering students. One of these courses is Calculus, which is an important part of the curriculum of most of the students in our university. Usually, this course consists of a four-hour weekly lecture (standard frontal teaching) and a two-hour weekly tutorial, plus homework assignments. Students take midterm and final pencil-and-paper exams.

In our teaching we encounter problems that are difficult to solve in a face-to-face teaching framework. Many of our students are not interested in Mathematics: they are not intending to specialize in it, and they see it as a necessary evil. Some students came from schools that aim to make Mathematics teaching as simple as possible, focusing on standard methods and paying little attention to students' understanding of basic mathematical concepts. This problem is particularly acute when students begin to study Mathematics at university. Similar problems were mentioned in the paper of Naidoo & Naidoo (2007).

Our students generally find it difficult learning theory, and as a result, are frightened of it. Possible reasons are the abstractness of mathematical concepts, the formal way subjects are presented and the special language of a theorem or a definition. In addition, many students do not appreciate the importance of theory. They see the theoretical part of Mathematics as separate from the computing part. This distorted understanding of Mathematics is the result of students being taught Mathematics as a set of algorithms used in problem solving. Obviously, when Mathematics is learned this way, students have difficulties in solving problems that they have not yet seen.

Another important problem we encounter is freshmen's overloaded compulsory syllabi of mathematical courses. Engineering students are required to cover a lot of Mathematics material, which is essential for their professional studies. As a result, there are not enough teaching hours to ensure that students properly understand the material they have to cover.

The modern world needs highly educated, qualified engineers who have a full grasp of mathematical concepts and advanced skills. Ensuring that the students who graduate from our college are indeed fully grounded engineers is our aim, but under the circumstances it is difficult to achieve this goal. Of course, some required material could be given to students to study on their own; however, experience shows that freshmen have a hard time accomplishing this because they do not have the necessary skills for independent study. Moreover, the books we recommend are usually written in a formal Mathematics style, which students also find daunting (see, for instance, Spivak (2006); Kon & Zafrany (2000)).

In an attempt to solve these problems we developed a different approach in our teaching. We understood that students have to study additional advanced Mathematics material on their own in order to supplement face-to-face lectures and tutorials. Looking to the Internet as a medium that could help us achieve our target was only natural. We had already used some elements of e-learning in our teaching, for example, uploading teaching material onto course websites: syllabus, lecturer notes and lists of homework problems. We could have simply put additional material on the site, but that would just be duplicating existing textbooks. We wanted to develop an easy, understandable way for students to independently study theoretical material. We wanted our students to be active in their learning and to "discover" Mathematics, plus be given the feedback they needed as they work on their own. Thus our goal was to make their learning interactive; we did not want our students to perform, as in the words of Tall et al. (2008), "surface learning" (p. 13). Our aim was to reach "deep learning approaches… and conceptual learning" (p. 13).

We understood that we could use Webassign to build a system for students' online self learning that would complement the traditional learning of one of the most important parts of Mathematics, the learning of theorems. Theorems contain all the essential properties of concepts and relations between concepts. They justify the algorithms and formulate the conditions under which these algorithms are applicable.

As we noted above, students, particularly freshmen, have difficulties in studying theorems. Students believe

> *…that the theorem can be memorized as a "slogan", and then it can easily be retrieved from memory under the hypnotic effect of a magic incantation. However, using a theorem as a magic incantation may increase the tendency to use it*

carelessly with no regard to the situation or to the details of its applicability. (Hazzan & Leron, 1996, p. 25)

To this end we developed SLM. We have been using it for about five years as a student online self learning system, in addition to traditional face-to-face teaching experiences. We originally described the method in a 2007 paper, and in two subsequent papers (Abramovitz et al., 2009a, 2009b).

BACKGROUND

A new culture, known variously as the digital, Internet or cyber culture, which transcends ethnic, national and regional boundaries, and allows millions to be part of a global virtual community has arisen (Fang, 2007). It has had an indelible effect on the academic world and initiated a transformation of the learning and teaching processes in universities. Moreover, today's students, have grown up on cyber culture, and accept the Internet as a natural teaching medium. As noted by Cross (2006) "e-learning covers over the multiple possibilities born of the marriage of the learner and the Internet" (p. xxi). There are indisputable merits in e-learning, such as flexibility: learners can be independent of space and time (Garrison & Kanuka, 2004). Students' activities can be carried out when the learners so desire, anytime and anywhere (Alonso et al., 2005). In this paper the authors also pointed out that e-learning is personalized: each student selects the activities most suitable for him/her (most relevant to his/her background). Online study provides more than one opportunity for satisfying each student's learning style (Moore, 2006). Also e-learning helps students develop learning independence and fosters their self-reliance: much more time is spent on the assignment before consulting the teacher; students learn to trust their own judgment (Harding et al., 2005b; Garrison & Kanuka, 2004). E-learning encourages shy learners to be confident (Naidoo & Naidoo, 2007).

On the other hand, Engelbrecht and Harding (2005b) noticed that one e-learning problem is the lack of face-to-face-contact. Students are dissatisfied with the lack of personal attention when they have to confront a problem. They generally want weekly contact sessions so that they can get an opportunity to ask questions face-to-face (Harding et al., 2005b). Even teachers may feel isolated when they undergo the experience of being an online student (Czerniewicz, 2001). Traditional teaching will always be an effective means of learning, because of the face-to-face interaction with both the instructor and classmates (Alonso et al., 2005). Moreover, the teacher is the ultimate key to educational change and a significant part of the successful implementation of online learning, through his or her readiness to exploit the medium (Condie & Livingston, 2007).

The problem is how to ensure that the benefits of e-learning are realized, e.g., keeping the student-teacher interaction. Blended learning (BL) could be a solution to this problem. Usually BL is described as learning with the convenience of online environments, without losing face-to-face contact (Harding et al., 2005b). At its simplest, BL is the integration of classroom face-to-face learning experiences with online learning experiences, against the backdrop of limitless design possibilities. Using BL does not mean that students are deprived of the traditional study format. BL only seeks how best to utilize face-to-face and online learning for purposes of higher education (Garrison & Kanuka, 2004). In the words of Graham (2006): "BL combines the best of both worlds" (p. 8). According to a report by the U.S. Department of Education (2009), BL has a larger advantage relative to purely online learning or purely face-to-face instruction. The report was based on reviewing a great number of research papers.

In recent years the BL approach has been implemented in the teaching of Mathematics at the undergraduate level in many universities in different countries. Getting this to happen was not a simple enterprise; it can perhaps be blamed on the strong role of tradition in Mathematics teaching (Harding et al., 2005a). According to Bookbinder (2000), enhancing the mathematical curriculum with web-based technology takes time and effort, but the effort is well worth it.

A wide overview of works on implementation of BL ideas at different levels in Calculus courses is given in the paper by Tall et al. (2008). They summarized their findings and said: "There is little evidence that the "brand" or type of technology makes any significant difference, beyond the obvious fact that some tasks require more powerful tools than others... The important thing is not *which* tools are used but *how* they are used" (p. 18). The authors argued that many approaches to students' conceptual understanding of the subject can be developed based on the proper use of technology.

Engelbrecht & Harding (2005a, 2005b) published comprehensive papers regarding a study aimed at analyzing Internet teaching of undergraduate Mathematics. In their first paper they described a variety of technologies used to teach undergraduate Mathematics online. They also mentioned some not-so-successful attempts at using online teaching, such as reading texts on screen and visiting a few web sites. Many of the Internet courses they reviewed could be characterized as attempts to digitally replicate traditional teaching. The authors also listed different types of cases that combined Internet teaching with face-to-face teaching and described the experiences of various universities. In their second paper they listed research issues connected to Internet teaching, among them – "Students as independent learners".

Outcomes of BL implementation in teaching of Mathematics at a collegiate level were studied by several researchers. Naidoo & Naidoo (2007) in their work on BL in an elementary Calculus course for engineering students, found that the students in an experimental BL group had deeper conceptual understanding and made fewer essential mistakes than the students in the control group.

Iozzi & Osimo (2004) studied BL implementation in undergraduate Mathematics courses at Università Bocconi in Milan, which started with a notice board and ended with a virtual classroom for advanced studies. They also raised the issue of whether the students' online participation is positively correlated with their overall performance in Mathematics. In their research they did not come to a definitive conclusion regarding gains in final grades, but did find that BL positively influenced the development of some cognitive abilities: cognitive empowerment, capacity for life-long learning, attitudes towards Information Technology and attitudes towards collaborative work.

Groen & Carmody (2005) conducted a research experiment designed to answer the question of "How do learners respond to the blend?" Most of the students who participated in the BL experience learned how to approach the issue of knowledge construction, found that their cognitive skills had increased and developed a positive attitude to learning Mathematics. Ahmad et al. (2008) showed similar results.

As a solution to the problems described in the "Problems and Trends" section, we constructed our approach, SLM, which is a model of BL implementation, and used it in a Calculus course. We related to research questions that are, to some extent, similar to the issues highlighted in the above mentioned papers. Particularly, we studied the issue of "students as independent learners," which is actually a subject for BL research. SLM aims to improve students' conceptual understanding of theorems. Based on our research (see, for instance, the "SLM Implementation and Some Results" section), we can argue that our BL approach results in students developing a positive attitude to the theoretical part of Mathematics.

DESCRIPTION OF THE METHOD

SLM was constructed using the WebAssign system (http://www.webassign.net/how_it_works/), which is a provider of online instructional tools for faculty and students. Instructors create problems and compose assignments online within WebAssign and electronically transmit them to their class. Students enter their answers online, and WebAssign automatically grades the assignment and gives students instant feedback on their performance and hints about how to correct their errors.

Webassign is highly suited to implement SLM. SLM gets students involved in the step by step process of learning the meaning of a theorem, which enables them to better understand the subject. The way in which the material is presented encourages them to take part in formulating, discussing and proving a theorem. Our approach is governed by the fundamental principle of classical teaching – the sequence of in which the material is learned is critical. We agree with Ramasamy's (2009) assertion that in face-to-face learning/teaching the learners/teachers are there to elaborate and explain the steps.

SLM has three main parts:

1. Formulation of a conjecture;
2. Study of the assumptions and conclusions of a theorem; and
3. Proving a theorem.

We constructed different kinds of web-based assignments for each SLM part. The assignments are written in a way that does not appear unusual to students, yet is intended to teach them theoretical knowledge. The assignments are supplemented by a "bank" of specially constructed simple examples. Students are asked to solve given theoretical problems regarding theorems by using these examples. Examples have been a part of Mathematics teaching throughout history. The significance of examples and their use in Mathematics education was reported in several studies (for example, Hazzan & Zazkis (1999); Bills et al. (2006)). Some Mathematics education researchers have proposed asking students to construct the examples (for instance, Watson & Mason (2005)). In our opinion, this is too difficult a task for freshmen. We see our "bank" of examples as the first step in students learning to construct an example. We believe that following our method they will be able to start constructing their own examples, including counterexamples.

We would like to note that as they work on the assignments, students can get help if they want it. Help is built in. In some cases they may be given a simple hint, and in other cases – a full explanation; it depends on the complexity of the question. In an assignment, to access help, students move their cursor to the "click here" hyperlink. Thus, a student not only gets feedback to his or her answer, but also the needed help if the task becomes too difficult. This ensures that the student does not give up, and moves forward.

Formulation of a Conjecture

First, students are asked to review the concepts and theorems that are needed to learn a new theorem. We use the Integral Mean Value Theorem as an example:

If the function $f(x)$ is continuous on $[a,b]$, then there exists a point $c, c \in (a,b)$, such that

$$\int_a^b f(x)dx = f(c)(b-a)$$

This theorem concerns the continuity and integrability of a function. In Assignment 1 students are asked to review these concepts. They are provided with examples, in our case, functions and their graphs. For each given function students have to determine if it is continuous and if it is integrable (see Figure 1). As the reader can see, students can check and correct their answers. In this

Figure 1. Assignment 1 (Formulation of a Conjecture)

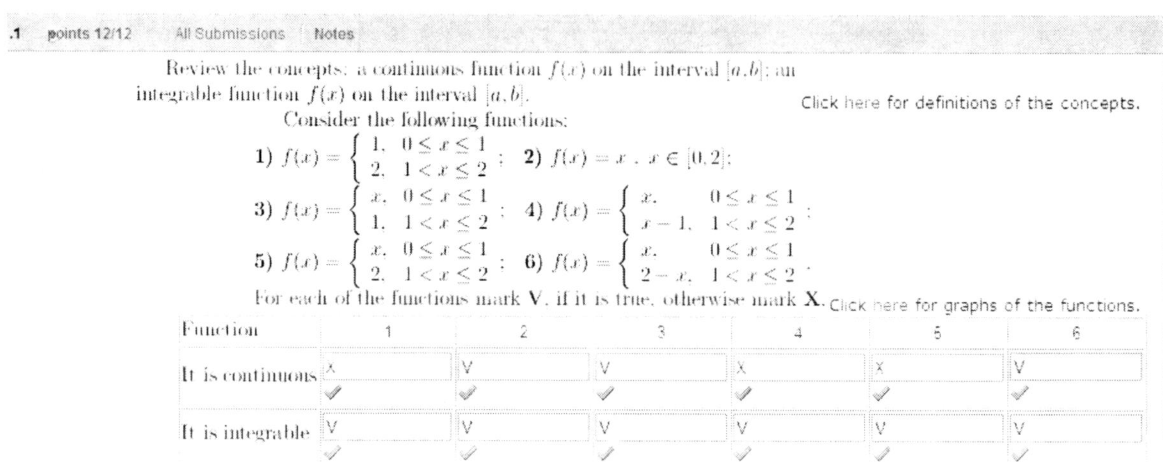

Description

Dear Student, you are going to study the integral Mean Value Theorem - one of the most well-known Calculus theorems. Enjoy your work!

Instructions

We recommend that you print the assignments, solve them and then submit your answers. If you make a mistake, you can correct it and determine its cause.

.1 points 12/12 All Submissions Notes

Review the concepts: a continuous function $f(x)$ on the interval $[a,b]$; an integrable function $f(x)$ on the interval $[a,b]$. Click here for definitions of the concepts.

Consider the following functions:

1) $f(x)=\begin{cases}1, & 0\le x\le 1\\ 2, & 1<x\le 2\end{cases}$; 2) $f(x)=x,\ x\in[0,2]$;

3) $f(x)=\begin{cases}x, & 0\le x\le 1\\ 1, & 1<x\le 2\end{cases}$; 4) $f(x)=\begin{cases}x, & 0\le x\le 1\\ x-1, & 1<x\le 2\end{cases}$;

5) $f(x)=\begin{cases}x, & 0\le x\le 1\\ 2, & 1<x\le 2\end{cases}$; 6) $f(x)=\begin{cases}x, & 0\le x\le 1\\ 2-x, & 1<x\le 2\end{cases}$.

For each of the functions mark **V**, if it is true, otherwise mark **X**. Click here for graphs of the functions.

Function	1	2	3	4	5	6
It is continuous	X ✓	V ✓	V ✓	X ✓	X ✓	V ✓
It is integrable	V ✓	V ✓	V ✓	V ✓	V ✓	V ✓

After checking your answers, reach a conclusion about the relation between continuous functions and integrable functions.

way they both verify their theoretical knowledge of the concepts and improve it. Particularly, the assignment re-emphasizes that every continuous function on an interval is integrable on it and that there exist functions that are integrable, but not continuous. By using these simple examples, students are reviewing the theoretical aspect of the relation between continuous functions and integrable functions once more.

In Assignment 2, still using the same examples, students are asked to make calculations that will help them verify the theorem's conclusion. Students calculate the integral $\int_0^2 f(x)dx$, as the area under the graph of $f(x)$ for every one of the given functions. In the next step they find a rectangle with the base $[0,2]$ and height h, a rectangle whose area is equal to the integral $\int_0^2 f(x)dx$. Toward the end of the assignment students need to determine if a point c, $c\in[0,2]$, exists, such that $\int_0^2 f(x)dx\ /\ 2 = h = f(c)$. For some given functions the conclusion is true, and for others, it is not. In this way students learn the sufficient conditions of the theorem on their own (see Figure 2).

Assignment 3 contains a set of statements (see Figure 3). Students have to mark the statements as true or false. For every false statement a student can find a counterexample by using the "bank" of given functions. Only one given statement is true – the theorem. So, without their noticing, students analyze the obtained results and formulate the theorem. In such an active (creative) way, students, as part of their research, figure the theorem out on their own.

The functions considered in these assignments are very simple, thus even students with a poor

Figure 2. Assignment 2 (Formulation of a Conjecture)

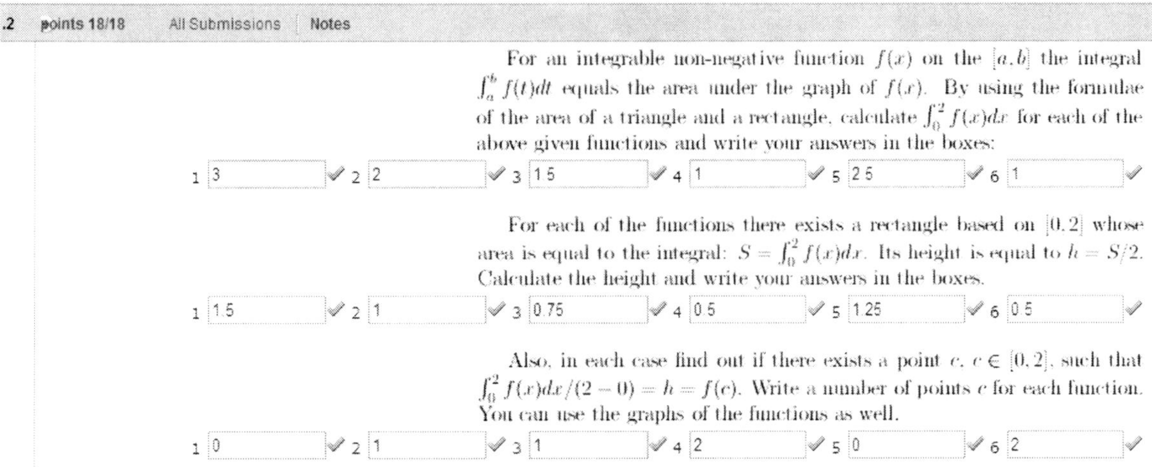

.2 points 18/18 All Submissions Notes

For an integrable non-negative function $f(x)$ on the $[a,b]$ the integral $\int_a^b f(t)dt$ equals the area under the graph of $f(x)$. By using the formulae of the area of a triangle and a rectangle, calculate $\int_0^2 f(x)dx$ for each of the above given functions and write your answers in the boxes:

1 3 ✓ 2 2 ✓ 3 1.5 ✓ 4 1 ✓ 5 2.5 ✓ 6 1 ✓

For each of the functions there exists a rectangle based on $[0,2]$ whose area is equal to the integral: $S = \int_0^2 f(x)dx$. Its height is equal to $h = S/2$. Calculate the height and write your answers in the boxes.

1 1.5 ✓ 2 1 ✓ 3 0.75 ✓ 4 0.5 ✓ 5 1.25 ✓ 6 0.5 ✓

Also, in each case find out if there exists a point c, $c \in [0,2]$, such that $\int_0^2 f(x)dx/(2-0) = h = f(c)$. Write a number of points c for each function. You can use the graphs of the functions as well.

1 0 ✓ 2 1 ✓ 3 1 ✓ 4 2 ✓ 5 0 ✓ 6 2 ✓

Figure 3. Assignment 3 (Formulation of a Conjecture)

.3 points 9/9 All Submissions Notes View Last Response

Using the previous results, mark each of the following statements as true (**V**) or false (**X**). If the statement is false, write the functions' numbers that are counterexamples. If there is no counterexample for the statement than write **0**.

Statements

1. *If there exists a point c, $c \in [0,2]$ such that $\int_a^b f(x)dx = f(c)(b-a)$, then function $f(x)$ is continuous on $[a,b]$.*
2. *If $f(x)$ is continuous on an interval $[a,b]$, then there exists a point c, $c \in [a,b]$, such that $\int_a^b f(x)dx = f(c)(b-a)$.*
3. *If $f(x)$ is integrable on an interval $[a,b]$, then there exists a point c, $c \in [a,b]$, such that $\int_a^b f(x)dx = f(c)(b-a)$.*
4. *If $f(x)$ is continuous on an interval $[a,b]$, then there exists an unique point c, $c \in [a,b]$, such that $\int_a^b f(x)dx = f(c)(b-a)$.*

Statement	1	2	3	4
True or False	X ✓	V ✓	X ✓	X ✓
The counter-example is function number	4 ✓	0 ✓	1 ✓ or 5 ✓	6 ✓

If your answers are correct, you already know what Integral Mean Value Theorem is.

mathematical background will not find it difficult to solve them. Also, the required calculations are simple; they are based on the area of a triangle and a rectangle. Consequently, students are able to use these functions easily and check their answers at every step. Nevertheless, the functions provide students with a variety of possible cases: 1) there exists only one point c, such that $\int_a^b f(x)\,\mathrm{d}x = f(c)(b-a)$; 2) there exists more than one such point; or 3) no such points exist.

The assignments are specially constructed so that students can work without the help of an instructor and "discover" for themselves the theorem.

Assumptions and Conclusions of a Theorem

We start by presenting the theorem in a schematic way, emphasizing what is assumed and what is concluded. Then we provide students with different assignments that focus on the following questions: What are the assumptions of a theorem and what are its conclusions? What is the geometrical meaning of a theorem? What happens when one or more of the theorem's assumptions are not fulfilled? What assumptions are necessary and which are sufficient? Generally speaking, what does the theorem mean?

We use Lagrange's Mean Value Theorem:

If the function $f(x)$ is continuous on $[a,b]$ and differentiable on (a,b), then there exists a point c, $c \in (a,b)$, such that $f'(c) = \dfrac{f(b)-f(a)}{b-a}$,

as one example to show students how to understand a theorem as a set of conditions that are needed so as to reach a conclusion.

In Assignment 1 of this section students are asked to check if the assumptions of the theorem hold true and to determine the number of points c satisfying the conclusion. This assignment is also given by Webassign. Here we present the non-electronic version, as it is a more convenient one for the reader.

In Assignment 2 we focus students' attention on the geometrical meaning of the theorem.

Assignment 3 asks students to review certain geometrical concepts and their relations. Thus we invite our students to explore another aspect of the theorem – its geometrical interpretation, which helps them better understand the meaning of the theorem. Assignment 3 differs from the other ones because there are no examples (given functions). Here students are asked simple theoretical questions that were carefully chosen to ensure that students, even those with a poor mathematical background, succeed.

Assignment 3 aims to teach students to "respect" a theorem's assumptions and to build counterexamples. Students should understand that a function cannot be a counterexample if a conclusion is true. Such functions are $f_1(x)$, $f_2(x)$ and $f_4(x)$. Also a function cannot be a counterexample of a statement if it does not satisfy the assumptions: for the first statement – functions $f_3(x)$, $f_6(x)$; for the second statement – functions $f_3(x)$, $f_5(x)$.

It has been our experience that students often replace the assumptions with the conclusion and make the inverse statement. Some of the given functions allow students to disprove the third statement, so we ask students to find appropriate counterexamples. We believe that over the course of time our students will be able to construct their own counterexamples.

We realize that this assignment is not a simple one for freshmen, so we added a "click here" for help.

Proving a Theorem

We purposely put the assignments of proving a theorem at the end of the process because the proof distracts students from understanding the theorem.

Box 1. Assignment 1 (Assumptions and Conclusions of a Theorm)

Description
Dear Student, you are already aware of Lagrange's Mean Value Theorem. We invite you to study this theorem and to understand it more deeply. Enjoy your work!
Instructions
We recommend you download the assignments, solve them and then submit your answers. Remember that you can correct wrong answers, and try to figure out the reasons for your mistakes.

Consider the following functions

1. $f_1(x) = x^2 - 2x + 1\ ,\ x \in [0,3]$

2. $f_2(x) = x^3 - x\ ,\ x \in [-2,2]$

3. $f_3(x) = x + \sin x\ ,\ x \in [0, 2\pi n]$, where n is a given natural number

4. $f_4(x) = 2x + 5\ ,\ x \in [0,4]$.

For the graphs of the functions, click here.
Mark each function **V** if it satisfies the assumptions of the theorem on the given interval, otherwise mark **X**:

1.	V	**2.**	V	**3.**	V	**4.**	V

If the function satisfies the assumptions, calculate the number of points c, such that $f'(c) = \dfrac{f(b) - f(a)}{b - a}$. Write down the number of points c that exist for each function. If the number is infinite, write **101**. If the function does not satisfy the assumptions, write **0**.

1.	1	**2.**	2	**3.**	$2n$	**4.**	101

Consider the following function:

5. $f_5(x) = x^2 2^x\ ,\ x \in [0,1]$.

Prove that the function satisfies the theorem's assumptions. Check if it is possible to find the exact values of the points c.

○ Yes
● No

For a detailed explanation of the solution, click here.

The assumptions were satisfied by all five examples. The meaning of the concept – there exists a point c – is not always clear to students. So the examples were chosen in order to show that there are several possibilities for the number of points c. Example 5 was chosen to illustrate that the exact value of c cannot always be determined even when its existence is known. This example also demonstrates the rationale of an existence theorem, which states that you do not have to compute a point in order to prove its existence.

Box 2. Assignment 2 (Assumptions and Conclusions of a Theorm)

Description
Dear Student, we invite you to answer the following theoretical questions and deduce the geometrical meaning of the theorem.

1. Consider the straight line defined by the equation: $y = kx + b$, k, b – given real numbers. What is the geometrical meaning of number k? Mark the correct answer.

- If $k = 0$, then the straight line goes through the origin of coordinates $(0,0)$.
- $k = \tan\beta$, where β is the angle between the straight line and the positive direction of the *y* axis.
- k is the slope of the straight line: $k = \tan\alpha$, where α is the angle between the straight line and the positive direction of the *x* axis.
- 'he straight line intersects the *y* axis at the point $(0,k)$.

2. Consider the straight lines defined by the equations: $y = k_1x + b_1$, $y = k_2x + b_2$. The lines are parallel if and only if (complete the sentence):

$k_1k_2 = -1$ $k_1 = k_2$ $b_1 = b_2$ $b_1b_2 = -1$

3. Consider the straight line $y = kx + b$ passing through points $(x_1, y_1), (x_2, y_2)$, $x_1 \neq x_2$. The slope k is (complete the sentence):

$\frac{x_2 - x_1}{y_2 - y_1}$ $\frac{y_2}{y_1}$ $\frac{x_2}{x_1}$ $\frac{y_2 - y_1}{x_2 - x_1}$

4. Consider the function $f(x)$ defined on $[a,b]$ and the secant line $y = kx + b$ connecting the ends of the function graph – points $(a, f(a)), (b, f(b))$. What is k? Mark the correct answer.

$k = \frac{f(b) - f(a)}{b - a}$ $k = \frac{f(b)}{f(a)}$ $k = \frac{b}{a}$ $k = \frac{b - a}{f(b) - f(a)}$

5. Consider the function $f(x)$ defined on $[a,b]$ and differentiable at a point c, $c \in (a,b)$. The straight line $y = kx + b$ is the tangent line of the function graph at point $(c, f(c))$. What is k (the slope of the tangent line)? Mark the correct answer.

$k = \frac{f(c)}{c}$ $k = \frac{f(b) - f(c)}{b - c}$ $k = f'(c)$ $k = \frac{f(c) - f(a)}{c - a}$

6. Consider Lagrange's Mean Value Theorem: *If the function* $f(x)$ is continuous on $[a,b]$ and differentiable on (a,b), then there exists a point c, $c \in (a,b)$ such that $f'(c) = \frac{f(b) - f(a)}{b - a}$.

Which of the following statements is equivalent to the conclusion of the theorem?

- *c is a point where the tangent line is orthogonal to the secant line connecting* $(a, f(a))$ and $(b, f(b))$.
- *c is a point where the tangent line is parallel to the secant line connecting* $(a, f(a))$ and $(b, f(b))$.
- *c is a point where the tangent line is parallel to axis* x.
- *c is a point where the tangent line is parallel to the line connecting* (a,b) and $(f(a), f(b))$.

Click here for another formulation of the theorem and an illustration.

Box 3. Assignment 3 (Assumptions and Conclusions of a Theorm)

Description

Dear Student, we are continuing to study Lagrange's Mean Value Theorem. This theorem has two assumptions. If the assumptions are fulfilled, then the conclusion of the theorem is always true. Under other circumstances we are not able to know beforehand whether there exists a point c, $c \in (a,b)$, such that $f'(c) = \dfrac{f(b)-f(a)}{b-a}$ for a given function. It will be interesting to find out what happens if at least one assumption does not hold. Below you will explore this problem and along the way find out many interesting facts.

Instructions

Below there are two incorrect statements. Why are they false? Because for each statement there exists a function that satisfies the assumption, but the conclusion is not fulfilled. Such a function is called a counterexample for a statement: it disproves the statement. As you work on the assignment, you'll find a counterexample for each statement. Good luck!

Statements

1. *Let* $f(x)$ be a function continuous on $[a,b]$. Then there exists c, $c \in (a,b)$, such that $f'(c) = \dfrac{f(b)-f(a)}{b-a}$.

2. *Let* $f(x)$ be a function defined on $[a,b]$ and differentiable on (a,b). Then there exists c, $c \in (a,b)$, such that $f'(c) = \dfrac{f(b)-f(a)}{b-a}$.

Consider the following functions

1. $f_1(x) = \sqrt[3]{x}\sin x$, $x \in \left[\dfrac{-\pi}{2}, \dfrac{\pi}{2}\right]$

2. $f_2(x) = |\sin x|$, $x \in [0, 2\pi]$

3. $f_3(x) = [x]$, $x \in [0,2]$

4. $f_4(x) = \begin{cases} x^2, & x \le 0 \\ 1 - x^2, & x > 0 \end{cases}$, $x \in [-1,1]$

5. $f_5(x) = \sqrt[3]{x^2}$, $x \in [-1,1]$

6. $f_6(x) = \begin{cases} x^2, & 0 \le x < 1 \\ 4, & x = 1 \end{cases}$, $x \in [0,1]$

For the graphs of the functions, click here.

For each function mark **V**, if it is true, otherwise mark **X**:

Function	1	2	3	4	5	6
The function satisfies the assumption of st. 1	V	V	X	X	V	X
The function satisfies the assumption of st. 2	V	X	X	X	X	V
The conclusion is true for the function	V	V	X	V	X	X

Based on the results, find a counterexample for each statement among the given functions. Write down your answer.

Function number **5** is a counterexample of the first statement.

Function number **6** is a counterexample of the second statement.

Look at the table with your answers and answer the following question: can the conclusion of the theorem be true when all the assumptions of the theorem are not satisfied?

◉ Yes ○ No

Which of the given functions can be a counterexample of the following incorrect statement?

Statement

If there exists c, $c \in (a,b)$, such that $f'(c) = \dfrac{f(b)-f(a)}{b-a}$, then the function $f(x)$ is continuous on $[a,b]$ and differentiable on (a,b).

Write down your answer:

Function number **4** is a counterexample of this statement.

For help, click here.

Box 4. Assignment 1 (Proving a Theorm)

Description
Dear Student, you have already seen Fermat's Theorem:
If the function $f(x)$ is differentiable at x_0 and x_0 is a local extreme point of $f(x)$, then $f'(x_0) = 0$.
You have also seen the theorem's proof, but do you really understand it? Let's check.
Instructions
The steps of the proof are given below, but they are mixed-up and their order is illogical. We ask you to put the steps in the right order and get the correct proof. We consider the case when x_0 is a maximum point.

Steps

Step 1
$\lim_{x \to x_0^-} \frac{f(x) - f(x_0)}{x - x_0} \geq 0$ and $\lim_{x \to x_0^+} \frac{f(x) - f(x_0)}{x - x_0} \leq 0$ by the properties of the limit.

Step 2
It is given that $f(x)$ is differentiable at point x_0, so there exists a finite limit

$$\lim_{x \to x_0} \frac{f(x) - f(x_0)}{x - x_0} = f'(x_0).$$

Thus

$$\lim_{x \to x_0^-} \frac{f(x) - f(x_0)}{x - x_0} = \lim_{x \to x_0^+} \frac{f(x) - f(x_0)}{x - x_0} = f'(x_0).$$

It follows that $f'(x_0) = 0$.

Step 3

$$\frac{f(x) - f(x_0)}{x - x_0} \leq 0 \text{ when } x - x_0 > 0.$$

$$\frac{f(x) - f(x_0)}{x - x_0} \geq 0 \text{ when } x - x_0 < 0.$$

Step 4
It is given that x_0 is a maximum point, then $f(x) - f(x_0) \leq 0$ for every x from a neighborhood of x_0.

Write the proper order of the steps from left to right:

4	3	1	2

Normally, we present a proof during the lecture and ask students to solve the given web-based assignments independently. In this way we can find out whether students really understand the proof or have only learned it off by heart as they would a poem.

In our teaching we use some Calculus theorems. We usually give students a proof of a theorem written as a chain of logical steps. The different assignments are designed to help students better understand and remember the theorem's proof. Once they understand how a theorem is proved we hope that students will be able to prove simple statements independently.

The first type of assignment is a "scattered puzzle" where the steps of the proof are written in the wrong order. Students have to rearrange the steps of the proof so that they are in the correct

Figure 4. Interweaving SLM and Face-to-Face Lectures (FTFL)

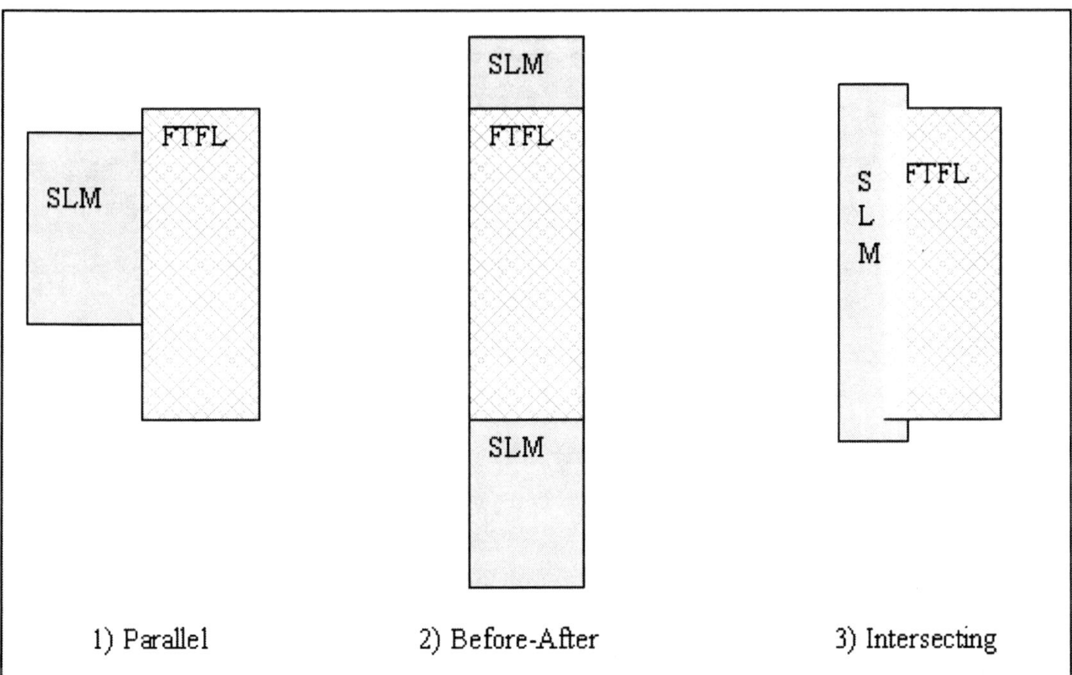

order. We consider here the assignment concerning Fermat's Theorem.

Assignment 1 has only four steps, so it is quite an easy one, even for freshmen. We use such assignments at the beginning of the Calculus course. During the course we give proofs with more steps or whose correct order is not unique. We also use a more advanced type of assignment such as a "fill in puzzle".

In the "fill in puzzle" assignment students have to fill in the missing parts of the proof. In our opinion, this assignment is comparatively more complicated and demands a deeper understanding of a proof than the rearrange the order assignment. Below we present the assignment focusing on the proof of the Main Theorem of Calculus:

If $f(x)$ is a continuous function on $[a,b]$, and $g(x)=\int_a^x f(t)\,dt$, then $g(x)$ is differentiable on $[a,b]$ and $g'(x)=f(x)$ at every point x in $[a,b]$.

In another type of assignment students are asked to explain why every step in the proof is correct. This requires students to figure out on which theorem or definition the step is based. Students receive a list of numbered theorems and definitions and they have to write the appropriate number from the list alongside each step of the proof. Obviously, the theorems and the definitions in the list are not given in the correct order; moreover, there are other, superfluous theorems or definitions in the list. We write the entire statements (not their names) in order to compel students to read these statements once more. This helps to improve students' understanding of the statements.

SLM IMPLEMENTATION AND SOME RESULTS

We have been implementing SLM in Calculus courses since 2006, intertwining its use with face-to-face teaching. We should note that the

Box 5. Assignment 2 (Proving a Theorm)

Description
Dear Student, you have already studied the Main Theorem of Calculus. It's now time to check whether you have completely understood its proof.
Instructions
Below you will find the incomplete proof of the theorem; some parts are missing. The list of the missing parts also appears below, but note that it also contains some additional unnecessary items. Write down the number of the missing part in the right place. You can use a number more than once. By the definition of the 7

$$g'(x) = \lim_{\Delta x \to 0} \frac{g(x+\Delta x) - g(x)}{\Delta x}.$$

$$g(x+\Delta x) - g(x) = \int_a^{4} f(t)dt - \int_a^{x} f(t)dt = \int_x^{4} f(t)dt$$ using the **9**

Suppose $\Delta x > 0$ (in the case of $\Delta x < 0$ the proof is similar). By the **11** there exists a point $c(\Delta x)$ such that

$x < c(\Delta x) < 4$ and $\int_x^{x+\Delta x} f(t)dt = f(c(\Delta x))\Delta x$.

Hence, $g'(x) = \lim_{\Delta x \to 3} \frac{g(x+\Delta x) - g(x)}{\Delta x} = \lim_{\Delta x \to 3} \frac{f(c(\Delta x))\Delta x}{\Delta x} = \lim_{\Delta x \to 3} f(c(\Delta x))$.

When Δx converges to 0, then $c(\Delta x)$ converges to **1** by **12**

$g'(x) = \lim_{\Delta x \to 0} f(c(\Delta x)) = f(x)$ by the definition of a **8**

The list of the missing parts:
1) x ; 2) a ; 3) 0 ; 4) $x + \Delta x$; 5) Δx ; 6) $c(\Delta x)$; 7) derivative; 8) continuous function; 9) properties of a definite integral; 10) Rolle's Theorem; 11) Integral Mean Value Theorem, 12) the Pinching Theorem.

impetus for this activity was students' requests for understandable self learning material about the theoretical part of the subject and theoretical exercises. Our current SLM design evolved through three stages. First stage: SLM and face-to-face lectures took place in parallel; second stage: SLM was available before and after face-to-face lectures; and finally, third stage: SLM and face-to-face lectures were intersecting (see Figure 4).

First Stage

From the start we developed assignments for the Basic Theorems of the differential part of Calculus: Fermat's Theorem, Rolle's Theorem and Lagrange's Mean Value Theorem. The assignments were given to students as optional self learning material. The students were not required to carry out the assignments, but we strongly recommended that they do so. Moreover, students received extra points, which could improve their final grades, for completing SLM tasks. Our experiment lasted for two semesters in academic year 2006/2007. In the winter semester we noticed some improvement in students' understanding of these theorems. In the spring semester we collected data and drew certain conclusions. First, we wanted to know how the students responded to SLM, so we asked about one hundred students to fill in a three-question survey. The three questions in the survey were:

Question 1: Did SLM help you in understanding the theorems and how they are applied?

Box 6. Assignment 3 (Proving a Theorm)

Description

Dear Student, you have already studied Lagrange's Mean Value Theorem, including its proof. We would like to check whether you have understood the proof properly.

Instruction

The step by step proof of the theorem is given below. Point out which theorems or definitions (let's call them statements) are used in each step. The list of the statements is given below. Pay attention: there are some unnecessary statements. Please fill in the table: mark V next to each correct statement.

Proof

Define the function $g(x)$ by

$$g(x) = f(x) - f(a) - \frac{f(b) - f(a)}{b - a}(x - a).$$

Step 1 The function $g(x)$ is continuous in $[a, b]$.

Step 2 The function $g(x)$ is differentiable in (a, b). The value of g at $x = a$ is

$g(a) = f(a) - f(a) - \dfrac{f(b) - f(a)}{b - a}(a - a) = 0$ Similarly, $g(b) = 0$ and thus $g(a) = g(b)$.

Step 3 There exists a point $c \in (a, b)$ such that: $g'(c) = 0$

Step 4 $g'(x) = f'(x) - \dfrac{f(b) - f(a)}{b - a}$

Thus

$$g'(c) = f'(c) - \frac{f(b) - f(a)}{b - a} = 0$$

and

$$f'(c) = \frac{f(b) - f(a)}{b - a}$$

List of Statements

S1 *If the function* $f(x)$ is continuous at x_0, then for every real number k the function $kf(x)$ is continuous at x_0.

S2 *If the function* $f(x)$ is differentiable at x_0, then for every real number k the function $kf(x)$ is differentiable at x_0 and $(kf)'(x_0) = kf'(x_0)$.

S3 *If the function* $f(x)$ is continuous on $[a, b]$ and $f(a)f(b) < 0$, then there exists a point c, $c \in (a, b)$, such that $f(c) = 0$.

S4 *If the functions* $f(x)$ and $g(x)$ are continuous at x_0, then the function $f(x) + g(x)$ is continuous at x_0.

S5 *If the functions* $f(x)$ and $g(x)$ are differentiable at x_0, then the function $f(x) + g(x)$ is differentiable at x_0 and $(f + g)'(x_0) = f'(x_0) + g'(x_0)$.

S6 *If the function* $f(x)$ is differentiable at x_0, then the function $f(x)$ is continuous at x_0.

S7 *If the function* $f(x)$ is differentiable at x_0 and x_0 is a local extreme point of $f(x)$, then $f'(x_0) = 0$.

S8 *If the function* $f(x)$ is continuous on $[a, b]$ and differentiable on (a, b) and if $f(a) = f(b)$, then there exists a point c, $c \in (a, b)$, such that $f'(c) = 0$.

Fill in the Table:

	S1	S2	S3	S4	S5	S6	S7	S8
Step 1	V			V				
Step 2		V			V			
Step 3								V
Step 4		V			V			

Table 1. A summary of the answers

Answers	Absolutely yes	Yes	Yes, but not much	No	Absolutely no
Question 1	14%	54%	31%	1%	0%
Question 2	17%	67%	12%	4%	0%
Question 3	63%	29%	6%	2%	0%

Table 2. Grades

Problems	1	2	3	4
Grades of "differential" problems	74	57	72	47
Grades of "integral" problems"	23	20	27	43

Question 2: Did SLM help you in solving problems?

Question 3: Would you like to get similar SLM for other topics covered in the course?

A summary of the answers is given in Table 1. Each number in Table 1 is the number of the students who chose to answer the particular question (in percent).

Another source of feedback from the students was an Internet forum that we opened on the course web site, where students could express their opinion about the given material. For example, one student wrote that after he had studied the given material, his eyes "opened" and he "saw" these theorems. Another student wrote that he had understood *what a theorem means and how to learn it*.

At the end of the course we decided to compare students' knowledge of the theorems that were used in SLM with their knowledge of another topic – the definite integral and the basic theorems of integration, which was taught without the use of SLM. For every "differential" problem in the exam, we inserted a similar "integral" one. The problems were theoretical, and not procedural. The numbers in Table 2 are the grade averages (a scale 0-100 was used). For example, the average grade in the first differential problem was 74, while the average grade in the first integral problem was only 23.

It should be noticed that problem #4 asked students "to build a counterexample for a given wrong statement". The low grades in both cases (differential and integral) showed that students were still finding this task difficult. Even when they had worked on the SLM assignments, our students had not learned enough to enable them to build counterexamples.

Nonetheless, we were encouraged by these results and decided to develop SLM for most of the basic theorems of One Variable Calculus. This work was completed by the end of the spring semester of academic year 2006/2007, during which time SLM was being used in parallel to face-to-face lectures.

Second Stage

In order to make SLM implementation more effective, the following year we changed the delivery sequence of assignments: we uploaded the first part – "Formulation of conjectures" – before the face-to-face lecture and the other parts – after. We recommended to students that they do the assignments just before the lecture. We tried this assignment sequence for a few semesters, but did not notice great improvement. According to students' feedback, the assignments were helpful in understanding theorems but because of their heavy workload, they could not prepare for each lecture (doing the assignment just prior to class) and preferred to do the assignments when convenient for them.

Third Stage

In the winter semester of academic year 2009/2010 we conducted an experiment: in one group (about 40 students) the lecturer used some SLM assignments only in the lecture (in our university every classroom is provided with a computer, a projector and access to the Internet). The lecturer and the students together solved the tasks, and based on the answers, formulated a conjecture. In these lectures the students were more active than in regular lectures, and they liked this process of learning a theorem.

In the spring semester we repeated the experiment with more theorems, and collected some data by observing lectures, surveying the students and talking to the lecturer. Analyzing the data we came to the conclusion that the experiment's results were positive. For the students, the lectures were more interesting, and as one student put it, "now they aren't scared by theorems. They are fun." The lecturer claimed that the lectures were more fruitful qualitatively, but not quantitatively: the students understood the theorems better, but the lecturer presented less material. Unfortunately, we could not analyze the experiment in term of students' grades, but we intend to continue our research in the near future.

Summing up our experience of SLM implementation and using the data collected by final exams, students' surveys, online forums, students' and lecturers' interviews, we conclude that SLM implementation has:

1. Changed students' attitude towards the theoretical part of Calculus, particularly theorems, so that they now think that the subject is more intelligible and interesting;
2. Increased students' capability for learning Mathematics theory;
3. Improved the results of students' final exams;
4. Provided lecturers with the opportunity to extend students' knowledge of the subject.

FUTURE RESEARCH DIRECTIONS

By using SLM we attempted to improve our face-to-face teaching in order to turn it into interactive one.

Particularly, we want to teach our students to find different approaches to prove some theorems independently. We are also planning to extend SLM to our entire Calculus 1 course, and afterward to Calculus 2 and other subjects.

We are aware there are different aspects of SLM that require further research. For instance, we intend to study the issue of how students' grades are influenced by the interweaving of SLM and face-to-face lectures as a type of BL.

CONCLUSION

SLM was developed to supplement our usual traditional teaching system; yet, by using this method in our Calculus lectures we in fact improved our overall regular way of teaching. This method allows us to overcome the shortcomings of traditional teaching: the overloaded courses, the lack of lecturers' time, and as a result, the lack of adequate time for discussing theoretical problems. We noticed that SLM implementation changes students' self-study for the better: students become more active learners compared to when studying in the traditional way. At the same time SLM permits us to overcome some e-learning challenges, for instance, the lack of student-teacher interaction. Moreover, our approach is also useful for students with a poor mathematical background and lack of motivation. Solving our assignments does not require students to create their own examples; they use the provided bank of examples. The analysis of the data in the section "SLM implementation and some results" suggests that even students who lack mathematical knowledge are able to solve theoretical problems, thereby acquiring abstract thinking skills. Students' learning becomes motivated by their success.

Based on our study we maintain that using SLM helped our students more easily comprehend the concept of a theorem: the meaning of the assumptions and the conclusion, what the necessary conditions are and what the sufficient ones are. We would like to point out that using SLM, our students are not given a theorem as a known fact; on the contrary, they "discover" it as a result of their own research. This learning approach improved students' attitude toward the theoretical part of the subject in general and towards theorems in particular.

We realized that the combination of different learning approaches, such as face-to-face learning and e-learning, provides excellent results, confirming what Juan et al. (2008) wrote: "the convergence between e-learning models and face-to-face educational models is an important fact that will significantly change the way mathematical education is delivered at universities" (p. 467). We came to the conclusion that not a simple combination of face-to-face learning and e-learning, but a delicate interweaving of them, could be applied to teach the theoretical part of Mathematics successfully.

REFERENCES

Abramovitz, B., Berezina, M., Berman, A., & Shvartsman, L. (2009a). How to understand a theorem? *International Journal of Mathematical Education in Science and Technology, 40*(5), 577–586. doi:10.1080/00207390902759618

Abramovitz, B., Berman, A., Berzina, M., & Shvartsman, L. (2007). Lagrange's theorem: What does the theorem mean? In D. Pitta-Pantazi & G. Phillipou (Eds.), *Proceedings of the 5th Congress of the European Society for Research in Mathematics Education (CERME 5)* (pp. 2231-2240). Cyprus: ERME.

Abramovitz, B., Berman, A., Berzina, M., & Shvartsman, L. (2009b). Proofs and puzzles. In L. Paditz & A. Rogerson (Eds.), *Proceedings of the 10th International Conference Models in Developing Mathematics Education* (pp. 5-9). Drezden, Germany: ME21.

Ahmad, F., Shafie, A., & Janier, J. (2008). Students' perceptions towards blended learning in teaching and learning mathematics: Application of integration. *Electronic Proceedings of the Thirteenth Asian Technology Conference in Mathematics*, Bangkok, Thailand. Retrieved from http://atcm.mathandtech.org/EP2008/papers_full/2412008_15274.pdf

Alonso, F., López, G., Manrique, D., & Vines, J. M. (2005). An instructional model for web-based e-learning education with a blended learning process approach. *British Journal of Educational Technology, 36*(2), 217–235. doi:10.1111/j.1467-8535.2005.00454.x

Bills, L., Dreifuss, T., Mason, J., Tsamir, P., Watson, A., & Zaslavsky, O. (2006). Exemplification in mathematics education. *Proceedings of the 30th Conference of the International Group for the Psychology of Mathematics Education* (vol. 1, pp. 122-154). Prague, Czech Republic.

Bookbinder, J. (2000). *Enhancing the mathematics curriculum with Web-based technology*. Hangzhou, China: International Congress on Mathematical Education.

Condie, R., & Livingston, K. (2007). Blended online learning with traditional approach: Changing practices. *British Journal of Educational Technology*, *38*(2), 337–348. doi:10.1111/j.1467-8535.2006.00630.x

Cross, J. (2006). Foreword . In Bonk, C. J., & Graham, C. R. (Eds.), *Handbook of blended learning: Global perspectives, local design* (pp. xvii–xxx). San Francisco, CA: Pfeiffer Publishing.

Czerniewicz, L. (2001). Reflections on learning online – The hype and the reality. *South African Journal of Higher Education*, *15*(3), 17–23.

Engelbrecht, J., & Harding, A. (2005a). Teaching undergraduate mathematics on the Internet. Part 1: Technologies and taxonomy. *Educational Studies in Mathematics*, *58*(2), 235–252. doi:10.1007/s10649-005-6456-3

Engelbrecht, J., & Harding, A. (2005b). Teaching undergraduate mathematics on the Internet. Part 2: Attributes and possibilities. *Educational Studies in Mathematics*, *58*(2), 253–276. doi:10.1007/s10649-005-6457-2

Fang, L. (2007). Perceiving the useful, enjoyable and effective: A case study of the e-learning experience of tertiary students in Singapore. *Educational Media International*, *44*(3), 237–253. doi:10.1080/09523980701491682

Garrison, D. R., & Kanuka, H. (2004). Blended learning: Uncovering its transformative potential in higher education. *The Internet and Higher Education*, *7*(2), 95–105. doi:10.1016/j.iheduc.2004.02.001

Graham, C. R. (2006). Blended learning systems: Definitions, current trends, and future directions . In Bonk, C. J., & Graham, C. R. (Eds.), *Handbook of blended learning: Global perspectives, local design* (pp. 3–21). San Francisco, CA: Pfeiffer Publishing.

Groen, L., & Carmody, G. (2005). Blended learning in a first year mathematics subject. *Proceedings of UniServe Science Blended Learning Symposium*, Sydney, Australia, (pp. 50-55).

Harding, A., Engelbrecht, J., Lazenby, K., & le Roux, I. (2005a). Blended learning in undergraduate mathematics at the University of Pretoria . In Bonk, C. J., & Graham, C. R. (Eds.), *Handbook of blended learning: Global perspectives, local design* (pp. 400–416). San Francisco, CA: Pfeiffer Publishing.

Harding, A., Kaczynski, D., & Wood, L. (2005b). Evaluation of blended learning: Analysis of qualitative data. *Proceedings of UniServe Science Blended Learning Symposium* (pp. 56–61).

Hazzan, O., & Leron, U. (1996). Students use and misuse of mathematical theorems: The case of Lagrange's theorem. *For the Learning of Mathematics*, *16*, 23–26.

Hazzan, O., & Zazkis, R. (1999). A perspective on "give an example" tasks as opportunities to construct links among mathematical concepts. *Focus on Learning Problems in Mathematics*, *21*, 1–13.

Iozzi, F., & Osimo, G. (2004). The virtual classroom in blended learning mathematics undergraduate courses. *ICME10 Topic Study Group 15 Proceedings*, Copenhagen, Denmark. Retrieved from http://www.icme-organisers.dk/tsg15/Iozzi&Osimo.pdf

Juan, A., Huertas, A., Steegmann, C., Corcoles, C., & Serrat, C. (2008). Mathematical e-learning: State of the art and experiences at the Open University of Catalonia. *International Journal of Mathematical Education in Science and Technology*, *39*(4), 455–471. doi:10.1080/00207390701867497

Kon, B.-Z., & Zafrany, S. M. (2000). *Differential and integral calculus* (5th ed.). Haifa, Israel: BAK Press. (in Hebrew)

Moore, M. G. (2006). Foreword . In Bonk, C. J., & Graham, C. R. (Eds.), *Handbook of blended learning: Global perspectives, local design* (pp. xvii–xxx). San Francisco, CA: Pfeiffer Publishing.

Naidoo, K., & Naidoo, R. (2007). First year students understanding of elementary concepts in differential calculus in a computer laboratory teaching environment. *Journal of College Teaching and Learning*, *4*(4), 55–70.

Ramasamy, R. (2009). Mathematics on online-learning: The difference in its approach compared to face to face teaching. *Proceedings of ICI9 – International Conference on Information*, Kuala Lumpur, (pp. 33-39).

Spivak, M. (2006). *Calculus* (3rd ed.). Cambridge University Press.

Tall, D., Smith, D., & Piez, C. (2008). Technology and calculus. In M. K. Heid & G. M. Blume (Eds.), *Research on technology and the teaching and learning of mathematics, vol. 1: Research syntheses* (pp. 207-258). Charlotte, NC: IAP, National Council of Teachers of Mathematics.

U.S. Department of Education, Office of Planning, Evaluation, and Policy Development. (2009). *Evaluation of evidence-based practices in online learning: A meta-analysis and review of online learning studies*. Washington, DC: Center for Technology in Learning.

Watson, A., & Mason, J. (2005). *Mathematics as a constructive activity: Learners generating examples*. Mahwah, NJ: Lawrence Erlbaum Associates.

Chapter 3
Screencasting for Mathematics Online Learning:
A Case Study of a First Year Operations Research Course at a Dual Delivery Mode Australian University

Birgit Loch
Swinburne University of Technology, Australia

ABSTRACT

This chapter presents a case study of technology integration to support student learning in a first year operations research course at a dual delivery mode university. The course is taken by on-campus and distance students at the same time. It is shown how both groups are treated the same in this course in terms of provision of course material, access to the course learning management system, and to screencasts of live classes and additional explanations. The only difference between the two groups is the on-campus students' ability to attend live face-to-face classes and to interact with the lecturer. The chapter demonstrates how screencasting is used effectively in online learning. Its objective is to share good practice of technology enhanced learning.

DOI: 10.4018/978-1-60960-875-0.ch003

INTRODUCTION

Distance learning in mathematics has changed enormously in the last forty years or so, from an entirely paper-based, isolated student experience, to the provision of online multi-media learning objects and the encouragement of collaborative learning of students in different time zones scattered across the globe (Loch, Reushle, Jayne & Rowe, 2010). Technologies have become available now that were not even dreamt of in the past, with opportunities to use them in new and innovative ways to enhance student learning. This has also meant that the difference in study experience between on-campus and distance students is getting blurred, as even traditional universities with only face-to-face enrolments are embracing online education.

This chapter takes a case study approach, describing a first year operations research course at an Australian regional dual delivery mode university ("the university") in which various technological approaches were embedded to enhance the student experience. Some of these technologies are: web conferencing for one-on-one support, where students asking for help were walked through a problem by explaining on a shared whiteboard whilst talking; electronic assignment submission, including trials of digital note pens to enable students to electronically (hand-)write their assignments; and electronic marking of assignments with pen-enabled technology. In this chapter, we will discuss neither of those, but instead focus on screencasting, an asynchronous technology, to effectively support not only distance students but also on-campus students in first year mathematics. A screencast in this context is an audio and video screen capture recording of an instructor's oral and computer-based visual explanation, also capturing electronic writing, for example on a tablet PC. These screencasts are recordings of live lectures, or they are created in response to student enquiries on online discussion groups, or they are short recordings linked to the study material to explain topics students usually find difficult to understand.

The chapter will commence with a discussion of the value of and concerns with lecture recording for on-campus and distance students, summarizing what is now becoming quite an extensive literature base. By placing this in a mathematical context, the use of screencasting in mathematics learning is motivated. This is followed by an overview of where distance education started at the university, to where it is now. It will then describe in more detail the context of the course being investigated, and briefly outline the course material production environment which provides a basis for effective integration of multi-media learning objects. The three ways screencasting is used in the course are then demonstrated and discussed. The chapter will point out implications of technology enhanced teaching, for instance on lecturer workload and training requirements. The objective of this chapter is to share good practice of technology integrated online learning in mathematics, and encourage others who are moving towards online instruction to explore the presented techniques and to go beyond.

BACKGROUND

Traditionally, the lecture model is the most commonly used teaching approach in universities, and this is particularly true in the mathematical sciences. Most current mathematics lecturers would have studied mathematics through face to face lectures and this model is the one they are familiar and comfortable with. However, while lectures accomplish important and valuable purposes (Ayers, 2002), they may not fulfill "learning potential of typical students today", particularly from the Net Generation. These students want interactive approaches, using computers, but also with the lecturer and fellow students (McNeely, 2005). On the other hand, more flexible options should be investigated since many (Australian) university students are of mature age and combine studies with work and family commitments (Phillips, McNeill, Gosper, Woo, Preston & Green, 2007), and students' learning styles and approaches to learning vary (Britain, 2004; Clow, 1998), even between on-campus and distance students (Diaz & Cartnal, 1999).

There is agreement that lectures can be made more effective and accessible for students by recording them (Williams & Fardon, 2007; Laurillard, 1993). While some disciplines lend themselves to the recording of video, for mathematics, in particular, it is vital that the visual component of mathematical explanation is captured together with the lecturer's aural explanations as "writing the symbols down gives the student a chance to read what has been spoken and thus access the content via several senses" (Townsley, 2002). This means that some form of electronic capturing of writing is required, be it via recording of writing on a piece of paper and capturing with a document camera, or directly onto the computer via tablet technology. This type of recording ("screencast"), used in an online mathematics learning context, is the particular focus of this chapter.

The following is a summary of the discussion on lecture recordings, in part from a general Higher Education point of view, but equally applying to mathematics. Lecture recordings allow students to revise the material whenever they want, wherever they are, at their own pace, and to repeat for reinforced learning as often as they like. Students have also been found to ask fewer repetitive questions when provided with recordings (Kates, 2006). While not necessarily meant as a substitute for the face-to-face lecture for on-campus students, students may catch up on missed lectures, and this learner-centred approach puts students in control of their learning experience. Concern has been voiced over the educational value of full recordings of live lectures to *on-campus* students (see, for example, Chang (2007)), and the question has been raised if recorded lectures result in lower class attendance, since students have more freedom to turn on or off, fast forward or backward the recorded lecture whenever they like. McCrohon, Lo, Dang and Johnston (2001) found that the flexibility of different modes of delivery offers more options for stimulating deeper approaches to learning. There seems to be consensus that making lecture recordings available online to students shortly after the lecture does not have a significant impact on lecture attendance (Larkin, 2010; Chang, 2007). An earlier study (Loch, 2010) investigated if mathematics students who were given a choice and purposely enrolled on campus would access live lecture recordings, and if so, for what purpose. Individual students were followed throughout a semester, observing lecture attendance, weekly screencast access, and taking into account survey responses. "While a number of students used the recordings to catch up on missed classes, the majority of enrolled students stated that they attended classes because they had decided to enroll on-campus rather than in distance mode, as they valued interaction with the lecturers and the ability to receive an immediate answer to questions" (Loch, 2010). The ability to ask questions and receive immediate answers from an expert is important to students as learning is facilitated through social interaction, by being in a class with peers (McNeely, 2005). Attending scheduled live lectures also gives students a structure and guidance to their study. Most importantly, students "realized that watching a recorded lecture takes as much time to absorb as a live lecture, without the opportunity to ask questions" (Loch, 2010).

What do students think of the impact recorded lectures have on the practice of learning and teaching in their courses? A comprehensive study (Gosper, Green, McNeill, Phillips, Preston & Woo, 2008) surveying students across four large universities found that 76% of students reported positive experiences. The flexibility of access and support for learning appears to be appreciated by students. Moreover, since according to a national survey of university students conducted by Universities Australia, about 25% of on-campus students regularly miss classes to undertake paid employment (Australian University Student Finances, 2006), the flexibility for an on-campus student to work through recorded material may provide the difference between dropping out and succeeding at university. Particularly in mathematics, where content is built in hierarchical order and missed lectures may hinder a student's understanding of new concepts and halt their progress, providing the opportunity to "catch up" ought to be high on the agenda. This chapter focuses on enhancing the ways a lecturer communicates with students and on introducing more flexibility for students by complementing traditional face to face teaching with online learning in a blended approach, for example by providing a more classroom-style learning experience to students who cannot (or choose not to) attend lectures. One important example of this latter group of students are distance students.

A few questions could be raised here regarding good practice and student benefit: Can a full lecture recording be counted as good practice? Would it be more sensible to edit the lecture recording, and make the lecture available in shorter chunks, maybe focusing on some important topics rather than making available the whole lecture hour? Would it be better if the lecturer recorded the lecture (or components considered as very important and possibly difficult to understand without aural and visual explanation) in an office environment, most likely leading to shorter, more targeted recordings, and excluding student comments and questions? As will be described later in this chapter, such short recordings may prove to be useful when produced for self-paced study material.

In addition to recording lectures for students who don't attend classes, other forms of communication are required to support students who struggle with some concepts. Asynchronous discussion forums, included in all current learning management systems (LMS), provide opportunities to address the traditional independence and isolation of distance learners, for example as described by Juan, Faulin, Fonseca, Steegman, Pla, Rodriguez and Trentholm (2009) in a statistics and operations research teaching context. Moreover, rather than being kept separate, on-campus and distance students may be brought together in the same environment and interact with each other. However, these features tend not to be used extensively in symbol-based disciplines such as mathematics where visual explanations are important for communicating concepts. These explanations require specialised tools for online communication not necessarily available through a standard LMS, for instance the option to write or draw on a (synchronous) shared whiteboard while being able to talk about a topic through a text or voice-based channel (Smith & Ferguson, 2004; Loch & McDonald, 2007). Web conferencing software has been trialled and then rolled out at distance education focused universities (Loch et al., 2010) to bridge this gap in mathematics education. This type of software allows synchronous communication including electronic writing on a whiteboard with students who may be located anywhere in the world, as long as they have at least a dial-up Internet connection. However, as a lecturer participating in a web conferencing trial commented, "flexibility comes from asynchronicity" (Loch & Reushle, 2008), synchronous tutorials may not meet all students' study preferences or time tables. Also, asynchronous technological methods "continue to leave the students in charge of his own work times" (Galusha, 1997). As part of the case study described in this chapter, an approach to combine the benefits of the asynchronicity of a discussion board and whiteboard explanation will be demonstrated: The recording of handwritten explanations in a screencast in response to student questions on the discussion forum.

Heilesen (2010) sums up that the positive effects that have been observed from the use of podcasts (these include video recordings, although screencasts find no specific mentioning) in higher education most likely relate to the "use of the technology rather than the technology itself", as the technology may support "well known techniques for improving academic performance, such as active engagement and revision".

CONTEXT: DISTANCE EDUCATION AT THE UNIVERSITY IN THE PAST

The university described in this study is located in regional Queensland and is a major distance education provider in Australia, with about 75 percent of its students enrolled in distance mode. The university moved into distance education via dual mode teaching in 1977 as a viable alternative to the offerings at traditional universities (Reushle & McDonald, 2000). In these early times, "on-campus" students were instructed in face-to-face mode, while the typical learning package sent to a "distance" student consisted of print-based materials sometimes supported by audio, and later by video and computer-based resources (Loch et al., 2010). The learning package was designed to enable learners to interact independently with the materials. On-campus students would not necessarily be given access to distance study material as they were expected to attend classes, while distance students would not attend classes. These two groups of students were therefore treated quite differently. In addition, the on-campus student would be able to access support from teaching staff or fellow students in person and face-to-face, while the distance student quite often would rely on phone conversations and, before emails, letters exchanged via the postal system. In some cases, distance students were supported by tele-tutorials or face-to-face workshops once or twice a semester, during "residential week", the mid-semester break week (Harman & Dorman, 1998).

CASE STUDY: OPERATIONS RESEARCH

Operations Research (OR) is a first year course offered annually to about thirty to forty students from various programs such as teacher education, IT, science, and double majors in commerce and science. It is taught from a mathematical perspective by mathematics lecturers. About a third of these students are enrolled in traditional on-campus mode and can be expected to attend lectures and tutorials. However the majority study in distance mode: They usually never set foot on campus, and may be located in remote parts of Australia or somewhere else in the world. They are required to have access to a computer and an Internet connection. In the past, these distance students were provided with a printed study book, complemented by online, type-based discussion groups facilitated through an LMS and email and phone contact with the lecturer. Technological advances and reduced cost of equipment in the last few years have allowed a rethinking of course delivery mechanisms for distance students, from which on-campus students may also benefit. The major changes that have been implemented relate to the way study materials are created and presented to students, the way instructors interact with students, the way students interact with each other, and the capturing of the classroom experience for distance students or those students who have not been able to attend class.

Integrated Content Environment

Today, OR study material is produced in multi-modal format using the university's Integrated Content Environment (ICE), which allows course writing in word processors such as Microsoft Word or Open Office (with MathType support for mathematical formulae), and will produce the material in printable format (PDF), and in web delivery as well as CD formats (HTML) (Sefton, 2006). Students receive their study book on a CD and no

Figure 1. OR study material produced in ICE, displayed in HTML version within the LMS. Screencast 7.1 explains how the North-west corner rule was applied in this example, to arrive at the table listed above.

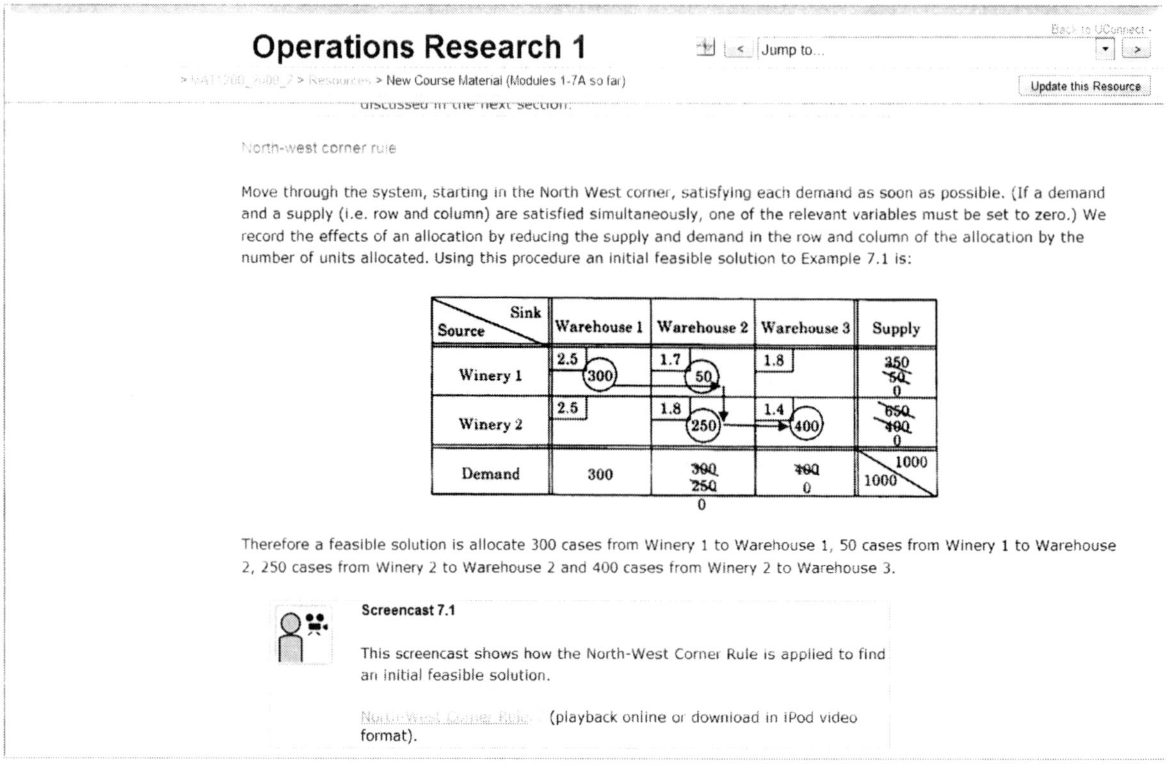

Operations Research 1

Jump to...

Back to UConnect

> New Course Material (Modules 1-7A so far)

Update this Resource

North-west corner rule

Move through the system, starting in the North West corner, satisfying each demand as soon as possible. (If a demand and a supply (i.e. row and column) are satisfied simultaneously, one of the relevant variables must be set to zero.) We record the effects of an allocation by reducing the supply and demand in the row and column of the allocation by the number of units allocated. Using this procedure an initial feasible solution to Example 7.1 is:

Source \ Sink	Warehouse 1	Warehouse 2	Warehouse 3	Supply
Winery 1	2.5 (300)	1.7 (50)	1.8	~~350~~ ~~50~~ 0
Winery 2	2.5	1.8 (250)	1.4 (400)	~~650~~ ~~400~~ 0
Demand	300	~~300~~ ~~250~~ 0	~~400~~ 0	1000 / 1000

Therefore a feasible solution is allocate 300 cases from Winery 1 to Warehouse 1, 50 cases from Winery 1 to Warehouse 2, 250 cases from Winery 2 to Warehouse 2 and 400 cases from Winery 2 to Warehouse 3.

Screencast 7.1

This screencast shows how the North-West Corner Rule is applied to find an initial feasible solution.

North-West Corner Rule (playback online or download in iPod video format).

longer in print, but may print from the PDF document themselves if they prefer reading on paper. This move away from paper towards electronic materials has meant that lead times for material production and for updates to the material have reduced significantly, and that multimedia objects such as screencasts explaining difficult topics can now be embedded in a meaningful way to enhance student learning. Figure 1 shows a screenshot of a section of a study module in web (HTML) format. ICE facilitates breaking up of the material into learning activities such as watching a screencast, searching for information on the Web, or starting a discussion on the discussion forum.

Screencasting

In OR, screencasts were recorded on a tablet PC to enable electronic handwriting of mathematical explanation, with the screen capture packages Camtasia Studio and Camtasia Relay (Techsmith, 2010). This chapter describes three different uses of screencasting:

- Screencasting of live lectures;
- Screencasting in response to student enquiries in the online discussion group; and
- Screencasting of short "snippets", explanations of topics students usually find difficult to understand.

The effective use and integration of all three are explained in detail in the next sections, including a description of the methodology behind the use of these technologies from a lecturer's perspective, and a summary of student feedback on the value of screencasts. Suggestions of best practice for those who may be interested in implementing such an approach are provided.

Figure 2. A frame of a typical lecture screencast. Mathematical explanation is written on PowerPoint slides or in Windows Journal, and recorded in Camtasia Relay or Studio.

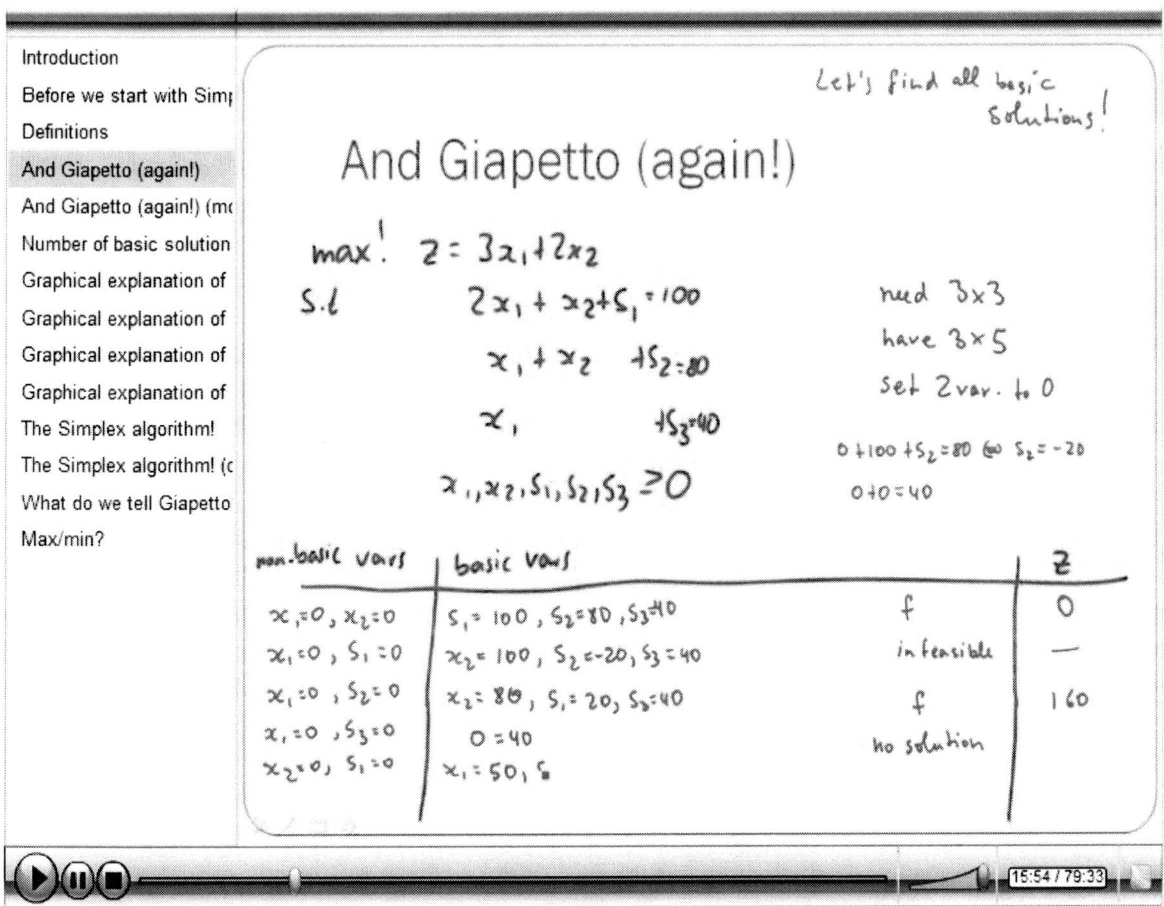

Screencasting of Live Lectures

In OR, three hours of lectures were offered to on-campus students each week, one in the morning and two consecutive hours in the afternoon of the same day, for 11 weeks in a 13 week semester. The remaining weeks were used to refresh material and prepare students for the final exam. All lectures were recorded and recordings made available through the LMS. Printed copies of the lecture PowerPoint or Windows Journal slides with blank spaces for writing were handed out to students attending the classes. These slides, together with the slides annotated in the lecture, were later made available to students via the LMS. Lecture recordings were usually produced in flash format (SWF), to create small files while keeping a reasonable quality. On average, full screen recordings, taken in Camtasia Relay, then edited and produced in Camtasia Studio, were of the size of 1 MB for three minutes, resulting in 20 MB files for one hour of lectures. If requested by students, lecture recordings were made available for download in zip format for offline viewing.

Figure 2 shows a screenshot of a typical lecture screencast, to be played back through the web browser. A table of contents, automatically populated if a PowerPoint presentation was recorded, helped students navigate quickly through the recording.

In 2008/2009, two distance students in OR commented on the availability and effectiveness of lecture recordings in the following way, on end of semester surveys or via unsolicited emails:

Just wanted to let you know that I was struggling week 2, however watching the lectures you posted helped me so much and now I have a deep understanding of those topics. I would really appreciate it if you could keep putting them up, as I think this will be the difference between staying on track, and falling behind - for me anyway.

To be honest, without these online screencasts, I would not have understood concepts or passed this course. I hope that all my future subjects have this online lecture material.

A distance student who had not seen screencasts in other maths courses commented that he felt that "this aspect of delivery was particularly valuable and well worth pursuing", while another said that "simply working through material sometimes takes longer to grasp the point/understand the concept. It was good at times to hear and follow an explanation as provided in the lecture screencasts".

Positive feedback was also given by on-campus students:

The screencasts were extremely helpful. I wasn't able to attend all of the lectures so this allowed me to go at my own pace.

I usually sit with a blank piece of paper and scribble down thoughts as I'm watching the lecture. The student questions provide little intervals of time to write down notes and reflect. (Loch, 2010)

On the other hand, not all feedback from students regarding screencasts was positive. One distance student reported that he found the handwritten annotations difficult to read, and would prefer a PowerPoint animation, revealing content one line at a time. For tricky and complex steps and also as a reminder of rules, he asked for annotations. He also said he didn't like watching the lecture screencasts because he could not fast forward until the whole recording was downloaded. He preferred short, targeted recordings rather than a complete lecture recording. Another on-campus student made it clear that she preferred interactivity in lectures and was concerned that recordings could replace lectures:

I watched the first screencast, but I don't really find this artificial environment useful to my learning. I require a more personal one on one exchange when learning allowing for feedback and gestures to assist in the message. (Loch, 2010)

Attending scheduled live lectures gives students a structure and guidance to their study, for instance an on campus student commented: "I work better in a face-to-face classroom environment where I can't day dream, get bored etc."

To give an indication of student use and acceptance of the lecture screencasts, data from the teaching semester in 2008 is presented here. Out of the 20 distance students enrolled at the end of the semester, ten had engaged with the course and completed all assessment items (three assignments, final exam). One of these failed because of low performance, the other nine passed. Out of the other ten students, four had stopped submitting assignments and failed. Six had not submitted any items; these will be disregarded in the following. The pass rate for students who had engaged at least for some part of the semester was therefore 64% (9/14). This is not atypical for a mathematics distance education cohort. Student use of the lecture screencasts was as follows. On average, each student watched 14 of the 24 screencasts, and each screencast was viewed by six of the 14 students on average. It is difficult to deduce from the data if screencasts increased the retention rate, however the continued use does show that students regarded the screencasts as valuable.

Students were certainly following different strategies – three students watched all recordings (all passed), but of those who watched less than 50% of the screencasts, five also passed.

Interestingly, the situation is quite different for on campus students, where the screencasts were used to catch up on missed classes or for revision, and 13 of the 14 students passed (for more detail, see Loch (2010)).

SCREENCASTING IN RESPONSE TO A STUDENT ENQUIRY ON THE ONLINE FORUM

A discussion forum was maintained in OR, where students enrolled in both modes could ask questions which were answered by the instructor or by other students. Students were encouraged to ask course related questions on this forum rather than via private email, so question and answer could be seen by all students. While most on-campus students used the opportunity of talking to the lecturer during or after a lecture or during consultation hours, distance students quite often utilized the forum. Rather than provide a static response to a mathematical question in the form of a typed explanation, in OR, responses were written on the tablet PC and recorded. The link to these screencasts was then posted on the discussion forum for all students to access.

This usually took less time than typing an answer (keeping in mind that mathematical symbols often require proper typesetting). Recordings were deliberately kept short, as they targeted a specific student question and focused on the explanation of this question. Figure 3 shows a typical online forum thread between student and instructor.

A frame from this recording is shown in Figure 4. The typed text, table and mathematical equations are screenshots from the material, to which was added by handwritten annotations to explain how to calculate the values of certain cells in the Simplex tableau. These values were blanked out for the screencast to create space for writing.

The screencast responses have without exception led to students reporting they understand now. A typical student response is the third post in Figure 3. The use of screencasts to support students on the discussion forum has alleviated the previously experienced repeated exchange of forum posts between students and instructor because the typed explanation wasn't clear or detailed enough.

One of the benefits of responding to students via the discussion group is that the question and answer sequence is available to all students, not just to the student who asked the question. Other students might have had a similar question which is now answered, or weren't thinking of this question but appreciate the discussion. Screencast responses to student questions may also be used in study material for future semesters, as the topics explained in the screencasts are those that students have identified as difficult and requiring further explanation. To create the short screencasts, a section of the screen was recorded in Camtasia Studio, leaving "private space" on the desktop for typed mathematical formulae or screenshots taken from the material to be moved into the recording area when needed. Writing was typically done in Microsoft PowerPoint, and the recordings were produced in SWF format.

There were two types of student responses to the end-of-semester survey question of what they thought about these screencasts in response to forum questions. Students either hadn't looked at the screencasts, or they commented very positively, i.e. that the recordings "really cleared things up", but also that they pointed the student to where they had gone wrong, "The screencasts… in response to my questions were very helpful as I could see at what point I had begun to get off track, or not understand." Another student commented:

Yes, I watched them all. They are fantastic, much better than a typed response.

Figure 3. Forum post. A distance student asks for an explanation of a concept from the study material. The explanation is provided by an instructor in the form of a screencast, which satisfactorily answers the student's question.

No quantitative data is available on student access of these screencasts.

SCREENCASTING TO PROVIDE SHORT SNIPPETS FOR STUDY MATERIAL

The first time that the OR study material was made available in ICE was in 2008, and in the same semester lecture screencasts and screencasts in response to student questions were introduced to the course. Students were asked at the end of semester if they thought there should be short screencasts in the study material to further explain algorithms, or concepts students find difficult to grasp and which may need to be understood before a student can proceed in a course ("threshold concepts"; e.g. Galligan, 2010). On-campus students attending one of the last lectures in the semester, seemed to be divided as to the purpose for short screencasts in the study material. Out of the nine students who answered this question, five said they would like to see these recordings embedded. One said he would appreciate screencasts but not embedded in the material. The remaining three

Figure 4. A short screencast in response to a student enquiry on the discussion forum

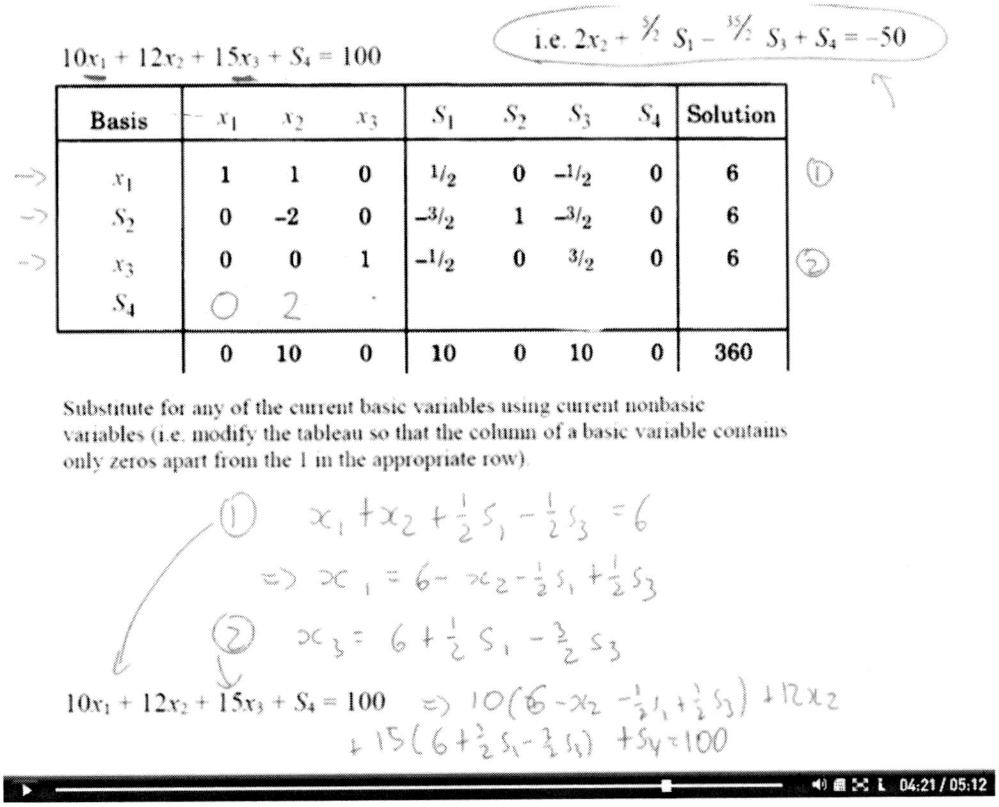

$10x_1 + 12x_2 + 15x_3 + S_4 = 100$

Basis	x_1	x_2	x_3	S_1	S_2	S_3	S_4	Solution
x_1	1	1	0	1/2	0	−1/2	0	6
S_2	0	−2	0	−3/2	1	−3/2	0	6
x_3	0	0	1	−1/2	0	3/2	0	6
S_4								
	0	10	0	10	0	10	0	360

Substitute for any of the current basic variables using current nonbasic variables (i.e. modify the tableau so that the column of a basic variable contains only zeros apart from the 1 in the appropriate row).

$10x_1 + 12x_2 + 15x_3 + S_4 = 100$

04:21 / 05:12

appeared to be concerned that an increase in the number of available screencasts might lead to a reduction of face-to-face classes on offer. Of the distance students who responded, most students said that they thought short, targeted screencasts would be beneficial. One student said that shorter snippets in the material meant no distraction by student questions and answers, as experienced in the lecture recording.

In the teaching semester in 2009, the course material was updated and screencasts were recorded while the course was being taught to explain all algorithms introduced in the study material, and additional concepts that students had struggled with in that year. It was decided to focus on individual topics, and produce very short recordings rather than cover all material with a long recording, which would have copied a lecture style. This type of screencast is an approach to provide only information important to students at this point in learning, and concentrates "on the pedagogical design of podcasts, rather than just repeat lecture content", for which there is a need to focus on (Sutton-Brady, Scott, Taylor, Carabetta & Clark, 2009). These short "just in time" recordings also put students in control of what they watch, as students can directly target concepts they may struggle with while leaving out others.

Figure 5 shows a frame of the screencast corresponding to the example printed in the study material shown in Figure 1. While the study material gives the algorithm in abstract form and expects students to be able to apply it to the given example, leaving out intermediate steps, (in this case, only the final table was shown), the screencast walks students through this example, step by step, and allows them to watch for initial understanding of the algorithm, for reinforcing

Figure 5. Screencast 7.1 explains the application of the North-west corner rule to the example printed in the study material (see Figure 1)

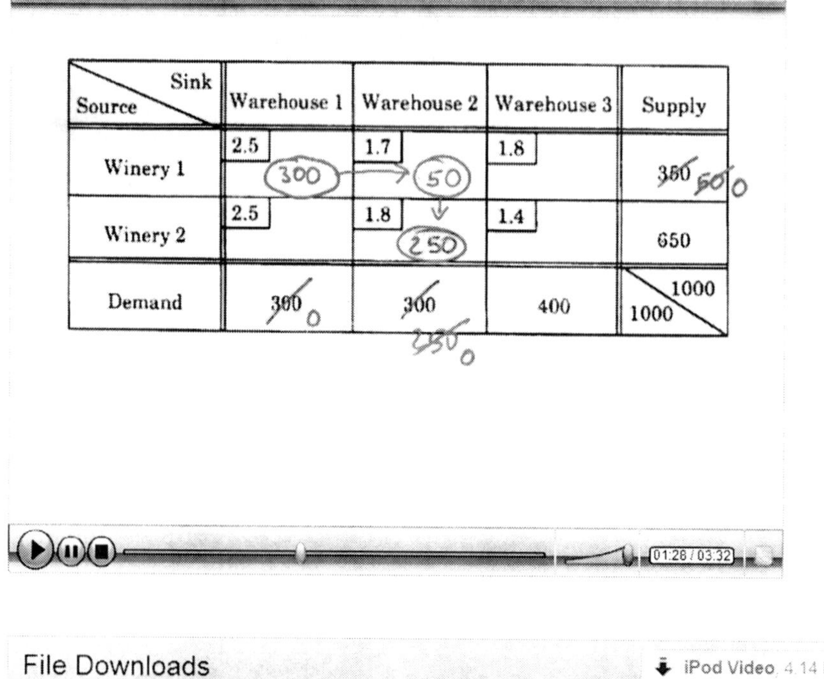

Source \ Sink	Warehouse 1	Warehouse 2	Warehouse 3	Supply
Winery 1	2.5 (300)	1.7 (50)	1.8	350 50 0
Winery 2	2.5	1.8 (250)	1.4	650
Demand	300 0	300 250 0	400	1000 1000

their already gained understanding, or to compare where they might be going wrong in their approach if their solution differs from that given in the material. It is the walking through, with voice and visual explanation, that gives additional information which cannot be captured easily in printed study material. Short snippets are produced in Flash format (SWF), with an additional option to download in iPod video format for playback on a portable multi-media player. "Mobile learning, which utilizes such technologies, offers educators a means to design learning activities and resources that allow students to individualise their learning" (Sutton-Brady et al., 2009; Kukulska-Hulme, Traxler & Pettit, 2007).

In 2009, these snippets were available to students for the first time, and students were asked on the official student evaluation form if they would prefer more short screencasts in the material. The three students leaving comments did not agree – one wanted more, one thought there were sufficiently many recordings, and the third wanted "more screencasts demonstrating methods", and "summaries of material covered". Asked the same question as part of an informal student evaluation, most students commented that the number of recordings available was sufficient, and that they found them very useful for their studies. A distance student remarked:

Early in the semester I watched everything but as I fell behind in my study I only used them if I was having trouble grasping something.

IMPLICATIONS OF INTRODUCING SCREENCASTING

The use of the technologies described in this chapter may have an impact on a lecturer's workload, as flexibility comes at a cost and this is often underestimated. While the recording of live lectures delivered to on-campus students may fit into a lecturer's existing workload (the lecture will be given anyway), the creation of short snippets for study material does take additional time, and if new to these technologies, training and experience. Time and opportunity for professional development need to be made available to lecturers, and this includes training in the effective use of these tools, rather than just focusing on the technical side. Such workload allocation will need to be factored into course delivery time.

It should also be noted that none of the described technology implementations were designed to replace or reduce face-to-face contact with students. It was clear from student comments that they feel quite strongly about the service that is provided to them when they are enrolled on-campus. The reason for introducing technologies was to provide more flexible learning options to on-campus students, and to attempt to bridge the gap between what is available to distance students and on-campus students. The technologies were not meant to make teaching more efficient or to reduce the cost of course delivery. An encouraging outcome following local success stories of tablet and recording technology use such as described in this case study (and also, for example, by Galligan, Loch, McDonald and Taylor (2010)), is that most mathematics lecturers at the university have now commenced recording of screencasts of their lectures, with electronic writing on a tablet PC. It is clearly worth noting that screencasting for mathematics teaching "has opened up for new ways of integrating classroom teaching and net-based learning on the basis of pedagogical concerns rather than mere administrative convenience" (Heilesen, 2010).

When moving towards multi-media recording of narration and/or image, an important consideration is how provision of offline and online screencasts differs. A screencast that is played back through a web browser online, and requires authentication to access via the LMS, can be accessed only by authorized viewers such as students enrolled in a course. It cannot easily be downloaded by a student, handed to a friend, uploaded in modified form to YouTube or copyright-violated in other ways. On the other hand, a screencast that is available for download and playback off-line, either via a computer or portable multi-media player, provides students with the flexibility to play back wherever they are, but the further use of the recording is out of the hands of the lecturer. Copyright expectations, i.e. what students are allowed to do with a recording, need to be made clear to students before screencasts are made available.

Finally, from a lecturer's point of view, copyright of the presented material may need to be observed. For example, video playback of protected content in the class may need to be removed from the lecture recording. Alternatively, recording could be paused while this material is shown. While this issue has not yet found widespread discussion in Australia, UK academics have been deliberating actively how student contributions to a lecture, recorded as part of the screencast, should be dealt with, and what needs to happen when a student withdraws consent to have their contribution recorded (ALT, 2010).

CONCLUSION

This chapter has provided a demonstration and discussion of the use of screencasting in a first year Operations Research course taught to on-campus and distance students at a dual delivery mode university. It has shown how all students are treated the same in OR in terms of provision of course material, access to the course learning management system, and to screencasts of live classes and additional explanations. The only difference between on-campus and distance students is the ability to attend live face-to-face classes and to interact with the lecturer and students.

What are the implications of using screencasting for mathematics online learning? Some of the implications drawn out of the work discussed above are

- Online students may remain engaged and overcome a feeling of isolation when the instructor is given a voice and becomes a "real person", rather than an impersonal technology-facilitated entity.
- Screencasts may be downloaded to portable devices, enabling students to study wherever they are, whenever they like, e.g. while travelling on a train or while other family members are playing games on the computer next door. This increased flexibility would appeal to part time students juggling study and personal/work life.
- Particularly in mathematical sciences, guided "walks" through solving of difficult problems by an expert are a common face to face approach, and screencasting allows an extension of this to online education. Whilst this idea has been in use for decades in the form of recorded videos of a presenter writing on a whiteboard, the ease of creating these recordings from a desk without the help of technical staff makes it more accessible and appealing, and allows "just-in-time" creation of material.

A thorough analysis of how (when, how often, for what purpose) distance students used the lecture recordings, and comparison of these results with those reported in Loch (2010) for on-campus students is currently being undertaken. This may take a similar shape to the investigation of the impact of the use of lecture recording and engaging students with tablet technology in a first year finance course at the same university (Phillips & Loch, forthcoming). Other studies to gauge if a student understands better by watching a screencast rather than just reading through material have commenced in mathematics Master training level and in tertiary mathematics support. Future research may explore the benefit of student generated screencasts to explain topics to each other, to include in study material or as assignment tasks. However, particularly when communicating mathematics, these students may need to be given access to appropriate hardware for electronic handwriting. A trial of student mini tablet PCs is currently being evaluated at the university to identify the feasibility and pedagogical value of electronic handwriting by students, both in face to face classrooms and in online education (see Loch, Galligan, Hobohm and McDonald (2010) for preliminary results).

ACKNOWLEDGEMENT

This study was undertaken while the author was employed at the university, teaching and redeveloping OR, and coordinating and evaluating a number of educational technology trials.

REFERENCES

ALT (Association for Learning Technologies). (2010). *Discussion via members email list on the topic: Guidelines for copyright etc for lecture capture*. April-August, 2010.

Australian University Student Finances. (2006). *Final report of a national survey of students in public universities*. Universities Australia. Retrieved from http:// www.universitiesaustralia.edu.au/ documents/ publications/ policy/ survey/ AUSF-Final-Report-2006.pdf

Ayers, E. (2002). Technological revolutions I have known . In Burton, O. V. (Ed.), *Computing in the social sciences and humanities*. Champaign, IL: University of Illinois Press.

Britain, S. (2004). *Review of learning design: Concept, specifications and tools*. London, UK: The Joint Information Systems Committee.

Chang, S. (2007). Academic perceptions of the use of Lectopia: A University of Melbourne example. In *Proceedings ascilite Singapore 2007 ICT: Providing choices for learners and learning*. Retrieved from http:// www.ascilite.org.au/ conferences/ singapore07/ procs/ chang.pdf

Clow, D. J. M. (1998). Teaching, learning, and computing. *University Chemistry Education*, *2*(1), 21–28.

Diaz, D. P., & Cartnal, R. B. (1999). Students' learning styles in two classes: Online distance learning and equivalent on-campus. *College Teaching*, *47*(4), 130–135. doi:10.1080/87567559909595802

Galligan, L. (2010). *Examining personal and contextual threshold concepts in academic numeracy*. Paper presented at the Third Biennial Threshold Concepts Symposium. University of NSW, Sydney. From http:// www.thresholdconcepts2010. unsw.edu.au/ Abstracts/ GalliganL.pdf

Galligan, L., Loch, B., McDonald, C., & Taylor, J. (2010). The use of Tablet and related technologies in mathematics teaching. *Australian Senior Mathematics Journal*, *24*(1), 38–51.

Galusha, J. M. (1997). *Barriers to learning in distance education*. The Infrastruction Network. http:// www.infrastruction.com/ barriers.htm

Gosper, M., Green, D., McNeill, M., Phillips, R., Preston, G., & Woo, K. (2008). *The impact of Web-based lecture technologies on current and future practices in learning and teaching*. ALTC report. Retrieved from http:// www.cpd.mq.edu. au/ teaching/ wblt/ docs/ report/ ce6-22_final2.pdf

Harman, C., & Dorman, M. (1998). Enriching distance teaching and learning of undergraduate mathematics using videoconferencing and audiographics. *Distance Education*, *19*(2), 299–318. doi:10.1080/0158791980190208

Heilesen, S. (2010). What is the academic efficacy of podcasting? *Computers & Education*, *55*, 1063–1068. doi:10.1016/j.compedu.2010.05.002

Juan, A., Faulin, J., Fonseca, P., Steegman, C., Pla, L., Rodriguez, S., & Trentholm, S. (2009). Teaching statistics and operations research online: Experiences at the Open University of Catalonia . In Olaniran, B. (Ed.), *Cases on successful e-learning practices in the developed and developing world: Methods for the global information economy* (pp. 298–311). Hershey, PA: IGI Global. doi:10.4018/978-1-60566-942-7.ch020

Kates, P. (2006). *Lecture podcasting*. Retrieved from http:// www.math.uwaterloo.ca/ ~pkates/ LT3/ podcasting.html

Kukulska-Hulme, A., Traxler, J., & Pettit, J. (2007). Designed and user-generated activity in the mobile age. *Journal of Learning Design*, *2*(1), 52–65. Retrieved from http:// www.jld.qut.edu.au/.

Larkin, H. (2010). "But they won't come to lectures …" The impact of audio recorded lectures on student experience and attendance. *Australasian Journal of Educational Technology*, *26*(2), 238–249.

Laurillard, D. (1993). *Rethinking university teaching: A framework for the effective use of educational technology*. London, UK: Routledge.

Loch, B. (2010). What do on-campus students do with mathematics lecture screencasts at a dual-mode Australian university? *Proceedings of 'Opening Windows on Mathematics and Statistics', the Continuing Excellence in the Teaching and Learning of Maths, Stats and Operational Research Conference* (CETL-MSOR 2009), Milton Keynes, United Kingdom, 07-08 September 2009.

Loch, B., Galligan, L., Hobohm, C., & McDonald, C. (2010). *Students using mini tablets: Preliminary results of three case studies*. Presented at ATiEC2010, Australasian Tablets in Education Conference, Monash University, December 8-10, 2010. Retrieved from http:// www.monash.edu/ eeducation/ events/ atiec2010/ index.html

Loch, B., & McDonald, C. (2007). Synchronous chat and electronic ink for distance support in mathematics. *Innovate, 3*(3).

Loch, B., & Reushle, S. (2008). The practice of Web conferencing: Where are we now? In *Proceedings of ascilite: Hello! Where are we now in the landscape of educational technology?* (pp. 562-571). Melbourne 2008, Nov 30-Dec 3.

Loch, B., Reushle, S., Jayne, N., & Rowe, S. (2010). Adopting synchronous audiographic Web conferencing - A tale from two regional universities in Australia . In Mukerji, S., & Tripathi, P. (Eds.), *Cases on technology enhanced learning through collaborative opportunities*. Hershey, PA: IGI Global.

McCrohon, M., Lo, V., Dang, J., & Johnston, C. (2001).Video streaming of lectures via the internet: An experience. *Meeting at the Crossroads: Proceedings of the 18th Annual Conference of the Australian Society for Computers in Learning in Tertiary Education,* Melbourne 2001. Retrieved from http:// www.ascilite.org.au/ conferences/ melbourne01/ pdf/ papers/ mccrohonm.pdf

McNeely, B. (2005). Using technology as a learning tool, not just the cool new thing. In D. Oblinger & J. Oblinger (Eds.), Educating the Net generation. Retrieved from http:// www.educause.edu/ educatingthenetgen

Phillips, P., & Loch, B. (forthcoming). Building lectures and building bridges with socio-economically disadvantaged students. [forthcoming]. *Journal of Educational Technology & Society.*

Phillips, R., McNeill, M., Gosper, M., Woo, K., Preston, G., & Green, D. (2007). Staff and student perspectives on Web-based technologies: Insights into the great divide. In R. J. Atkinson & C. McBeath (Eds.), *ICT: Providing choices for learners and learning. Proceedings of ascilite*, Singapore. Retrieved from http:// www.ascilite.org.au/ conferences/ singapore07/ procs/ phillips.pdf

Reushle, S., & McDonald, J. (2000). *Moving an Australian dual mode university to the online environment: A case study*. In: ED-MEDIA 2000: World Conference on Educational Multimedia, Hypermedia and Telecommunications, 26 June - 01 July 2000, Montreal Canada.

Sefton, P. (2006). *The integrated content environment*. In: 12th Australasian World Wide Web Conference (AusWeb06): Making a Difference with Web Technologies, 1-5 July 2006, Noosa, Australia. Retrieved from http:// prints.usq.edu.au/ 697/

Smith, G., & Ferguson, D. (2004). Diagrams and math notation in e-learning: Growing pains of a new generation. *International Journal of Mathematical Education in Science and Technology*, *35*(5), 681–695. doi:10.1080/0020739042000232583

Sutton-Brady, C., Scott, K., Taylor, L., Carabetta, G., & Clark, S. (2009). The value of using short-format podcasts to enhance learning and teaching. *ALT-J*, *17*(3), 219–232. doi:10.1080/09687760903247609

Techsmith. (2010). *Website*. Retrieved from http:// www.techsmith.com

Townsley, L. (2002). Multimedia classes: Can there ever be too much technology? *Proceedings of the Vienna International Symposium on Integrating Technology into Mathematics Education*, Vienna, Austria.

Williams, J., & Fardon, M. (2007). Perpetual connectivity: Lecture recordings and portable media players. In R. J. Atkinson & C. McBeath (Eds.), ICT: *Providing choices for learners and learning, Proceedings ascilite Singapore*. Retrieved from http:// www.ascilite.org.au/ conferences/ singapore07/ procs/ williams-jo.pdf

KEY TERMS AND DEFINITIONS

Lecture Recording: Any form of recording to capture a live lecture. This can be an audio-only recording; a video recording of the lecturer plus whiteboard, document camera or electronic writing; or a screencast of the lecture.

Screencast: A screencast is a video file. It contains a recording of audio and video screen capture of an instructor's oral and computer-based visual explanation, also capturing electronic writing, for example on a tablet PC.

Snippet: In this context, a short screencast of the path to the solution of a mathematical problem, written on a tablet PC.

Chapter 4
Mathematics Education:
Teaching and Learning Opportunities in Blended Learning

Giovannina Albano
Università di Salerno, Italy

ABSTRACT

This chapter is concerned with the integration of research in mathematics education and e-learning. Its main aim is to provide a perspective on the teaching/learning opportunities offered by e-learning platforms in a blended learning setting, as experienced at the Universities of Salerno and of Piemonte Orientale. Two types of teaching actions have been set above all: a) tailored units of learning, which have required the design/implementation of a huge pool of learning objects, according to domain-specific guidelines from mathematics education research and to various educational parameters from e-learning research; b) cooperative or individual teacher-driven learning activities together with various practice for self or peer assessment, which have been designed according both to e-learning and mathematics pedagogies based on the active role of the learner, the interaction with tutors and peers, and the importance of critical thinking and communication skills. Finally some feedback from students is reported, and some opportunities for future research are outlined.

DOI: 10.4018/978-1-60960-875-0.ch004

INTRODUCTION

This chapter is framed in the areas of e-learning and mathematics education. We assume that integrating research outcomes in both areas is of paramount importance. Lately web-based educational environments specific for mathematics have been developed (e.g. MUMIE, WebALT, MEI online resources for mathematics, MathWiki). Even if we acknowledge the need for specific domain tools, we aim at understanding the potentials of standard e-learning applications and methods for undergraduate education in mathematics. The effort of the author has been devoted to exploit the generic outcomes about e-learning (tools, theories, practices) according to the domain-specific results from research in mathematics education. With this concern, we provide a comprehensive description of e-learning practices related to the state of the art in both e-learning and mathematics education as well as an overview of research in both areas as wide as possible.

Through the chapter we focus on some e-learning experiences in mathematics education, carried out over the last few years at the Universities of Salerno and of Piemonte Orientale (Italy). Some mathematics courses have been supported with e-learning platforms, in a blended way, that mixes face-to-face lectures and distance mathematical instruction. The e-learning platforms used are IWT (Intelligent Web Teacher) in Salerno and Moodle (Modular Object Oriented Dynamic Learning Environment) in Piemonte. The first one is equipped with features of LCMS (Learning Content Management System), adaptive learning system and allows the definition of personalized and collaborative teaching/learning experiences by means of the explicit representation of the knowledge and the use of techniques and tools of Web 2.0. The second one is an open source CMS (Content Management System), an adjustable environment for learning communities, designed to support a social constructionist framework of education.

The main features of the e-learning practices described in the chapter are:

1. generation of personalized units of learning;
2. cooperative or individual, teacher-driven learning activities, along with various practices for self or peer assessment.

As regards item a), platform IWT (compared to Moodle and similar ones) adds the opportunity to effectively represent knowledge domains and manage the related contents. This allows the platform to automatically run a learning process, in terms of contents assessment and remedial materials to be delivered. Moreover IWT can also store and manage learning-related information on the student (e.g. preferred learning style or previous knowledge), which allows it to tailor the learning process, delivering just the contents needed according to the student's preferred style. In order to exploit such feature of IWT, various learning objects (LOs) have been created related to the domain of Linear Algebra and Analytic Geometry. Further, we note that personalization can be student-driven, as he/she can access alternative resources available in the platform and then choose the most fitting to his/her needs or preferences.

Regarding item b), the personalised course has been supported by some teacher-driven learning activities on the platform. Some facilities for cooperative and individual work, such as wiki, forum and task, available both in IWT and Moodle have been exploited for designing mathematical activities in order to encourage students to deepen their knowledge on the subjects at stake. All of these activities are open-ended and thus the problem of their assessment has been posed, and some self- or peer-evaluation procedures have consequently been designed and implemented. The first ones are based on the availability in the platform of solution-patterns students can compare to their products (after they have completed the task). The second ones consist in a peer-evaluation process among students.

At beginning in the section "Background" we give an overview of the theoretical framework, taking into consideration e-learning theories, mathematics education research, integration of ICT and e-learning in mathematics education. Next the section "The platform IWT" describes the main features of the e-learning platform which have been exploited for this work. Later the section "Didactic transposition the learning objects" describes the different kinds of LOs and the rationale underlying their creation. Next in the sections "Learning activities" and "Self and peer assessment" we show examples of didactical material and teaching and assessment activities which exploit some opportunities provided by IWT and fulfil some of the research outcomes sketched in the background. Finally, the section "Some experimental outcomes" includes some discussion of the implementation related to the previous sections from a qualitative point of view and the section "Future research directions" explores some opportunities for future research.

BACKGROUND

The theoretical framework draws from at least two research areas: e-learning and mathematics education. In the following sub-sections we provide an overview of the state of the art in e-learning, mathematics education, ICT and e-learning in mathematics education.

E-Learning Theories, Methods and Technologies

Many definitions of e-learning can be found in literature, all related to an educational experience, whose differences depend on the electronic means (CD-ROM, LMS, Virtual Worlds, etc.) or on the method used (distance, blended, mobile). A more general and inclusive definition can be found in Kahligi *et al.* (2008): "*a learning method that uses ICTs to transform and support teaching and learning process ubiquitously*".

At beginning e-learning has been guided by traditional learning theories, such as behaviourism, cognitivism and constructivism.

Then some models of learning pedagogy specific for e-learning have been developed. Among them we cite Mayes' Conceptualisation Cycle (1995), Laurillard's Conversational Mode (1993), Salmon's E-tivities (2002). The first one is based on three steps: (1) conceptualisation, where students acquire information, (2) construction, where learners are involved in processing the information acquired by performing meaningful tasks, (3) dialogue, where the new knowledge is assessed through conversation with tutors and peers and feedbacks are provided in order to resolve erroneous concepts. Laurillard's model is based on Vygotsky's theories in which learning occurs by means of the dialogue between tutor and students. Laurillard underlines that such dialogue should involve both the theoretical and the practical level. The interactions needed are: (1) narrative, that is imparting knowledge to the learner, (2) communicative/discursive, where the tutor supports students' discussion and reflection on their learning, (3) interactive, giving feedback to the students after tasks performance in order to overcome misconceptions or validate the knowledge acquired, and to guide further learning. Finally, e-tivities refer to educational online activities. Salmon defines the key features of e-tivities as: "…1) A small piece of information, stimulus or challenge (the 'spark'), 2) online activity which includes individual participants posting a contribution, 3) an interactive or participative element- such as responding to the postings of other, 4) summary, feedback or critique from an e-moderator (the 'plenary')… ".

The e-learning pedagogy has been the source of various changes in the state of the art: the creation of more effective learning resources; the empowering of the communication tools; the shift from educational models just based on the delivery of learning material to others based on more complete processes involving participation in learning activities.

Mathematics Education Framework

In mathematics education the main task for the teacher is the so-called didactic transposition (Chevallard, 1985), that is the action of moving from *knowledge* (originating from research) to *knowledge to be taught* (decided by institutions) to *taught knowledge* (chosen by the teachers as specific object of their action). The second passage is filtered by teachers' epistemological choices and by information derived from the classroom's context (student's background, goals, etc.). The *didactic transposition* comes along with the problem of the *didactic engineering* (Artigue, 1992), which concerns the elaboration of teaching sequences, the setting up of teaching tools and materials organised and structured according to the given goals. The tools offered by e-learning platforms allow to strengthen both didactic transposition and didactic engineering, making it possible the construction of various teaching sequences according to different parameters.

Both didactic transposition and didactic engineering have to take into account some key issues and skills in mathematics education, such as reasoning, critical thinking, problem solving, process mastering.

According to Schoenfeld (1992), this requires some effort to focus on seeking solutions, not just memorizing procedures; exploring patterns, not just memorizing formulas; formulating conjectures, not just doing exercises. This requires the students to be engaged in suitable learning activities involving communication and various semiotic systems in appropriate settings. Schafersman (1991) underlines the key role of writing: "*The best way to teach critical thinking is to require that students write. Writing forces students to organize their thoughts, contemplate their topic, evaluate their data in a logical fashion, and present their conclusions in a persuasive manner. Good writing is the epitome of good critical thinking*". This is in line with more recent studies. Sfard (2001) interprets thinking as communication and languages are regarded as builders of meanings, not just as carriers of pre-existing ones. Thus learning is the outcome of a mathematical discourse, with others or with oneself, verbal or with the help of any other representation system. Ferrari (2004) shows that some students' troubles in mathematics can be ascribed to their poor linguistic resources and in particular to the divergent use of everyday-life and mathematical language. According to him, linguistic competence is a powerful factor in mathematics learning (even though a disregarded one). Finally, also Duval (1995) states that knowledge is not separable from representations: in other words, conceptualisation (*noesis*) is strictly linked to representation processes (*semiosis*). In Duval's framework an important step in learning is the *coordination of the semiotic systems*, which is the ability at using multiple representations of the same concept and moving quickly from one to another and is the key of the construction of new knowledge.

ICT in Mathematics Education

In the last decades, Information and Communication Technologies have entered in our daily life and involved all activities we are engaged in. As far as education is concerned, according to NCTM (2000), "*Technology is essential in teaching and learning; it influences the mathematics that is taught and enhances students' learning*". Much research is still devoted to the examination and application of new technological approaches to mathematics teaching and learning (Glendon W. Blume & M. Kathleen Heid (eds.), 2008; Guin, D., Ruthven, K., & Trouche, L. (eds.), 2005). First of all, technologies seem to match a constructivist approach. Mariotti (2002) discusses in depth potential and limits of the use of a computer taking into account different theoretical stances. As far as the constructivist approach is concerned, new learning environments have been designed, the so-called 'microworlds', which explicit the two main innovative aspects: they make accessible (i.e. 'concrete') originally 'abstract' concepts through visualization and manipulation, and they promote the construction of meanings through a problem-solving activity and interaction with the environment. To overcome some limits of microworlds, more complex computer-based environments such as Computer Algebra Systems (CAS) have been developed. Despite of their user-friendly interface and their high computational power, even symbolic, CAS pose a semiotic issue: the interpretation of the phenomena on the computer screen might require the mathematical knowledge which is the aim of the computer activity itself. Following Mariotti's discussion, some weakness of mathematical activities in microworlds and CAS can be interpreted within the instrumental approach, which distinguishes between artifact and instrument. The first one is a particular object with its intrinsic characteristics, designed for performing a specific task; the second one is an artifact together with the modalities of its use by a particular user. The instrument is then an evolving object and the process of such evolution is called 'instrumental genesis'. The complexity of such process can explain some failures. Moreover, it is not obvious that the mathematical meaning incorporated in the artifact is easily accessible through instrumental genesis. The key theoretical hypothesis stated and showed by Mariotti is that "*their [of the meanings] evolution is achieved by means of social construction in the classroom, under the guidance of the teacher*", that is the process of semiotic mediation.

For completeness we want to cite some internet-based use of CAS (Sangwin, 2004; Albano *et al.*, 2003) for mathematics learning and assessment. Maple and Mathematica have been used in order to create quizzes, exercises or problems with the following characteristics: a) they contain some parameters whose value is randomly generated in order to have multiple instantiations of the same object; b) CAS is able to symbolically compare students' and teacher's answer so that equivalent expressions are marked in a consistent way; c) appropriate, immediate and tailored feedback is returned to the students; d) students can have exercise sessions as many as they want. Furthermore it is possible to create other kinds of tasks, which consist in requiring the students to generate an example of an object satisfying given constraints. Internet gives the students freedom of times and spaces and does not ask them to have CAS in local settings, by means of plug-in components.

E-Learning and Mathematics

In the case of mathematics, e-learning offers new, almost unexplored opportunities. Clearly enough, learners' needs are different according to the kind and the level of instruction considered, and all-embracing answers are not available. Anyway, some efforts (Descamps *et al.*, 2006, Albano & Ferrari, 2008, Juan *et al.*, 2008, Faulin *et al.*, 2009, Engelbrecht & Harding, 2005, Bringslid, 2002, Huertas *et al.*, 2006, Lee, 2005, Miner & Topping, 2001, Rodrıguez & Villa, 2005) can be found to understand how to direct the technological potential in order to improve quality and quantity of mathematics learning.

Bass (in Descamps *et al.*, 2006) recognizes five topics in mathematics education which can be helped by technology:

1. Drawing mathematically accurate and pedagogically valid graphs, to be used for exploring, investigating what happens if some elements vary, prove/show ideas, explanations, solutions.
2. Keeping trace of the classroom work and errors. This helps teachers to re-direct work, and allows them to keep trace of students' mathematical progress.

3. Coordinating lectures and textbooks.
4. Easy access for the teacher. Technology gives the opportunity to adopt a flexible timetable for meeting students.
5. The repetitive nature of individual, out-of-schedule sessions. Most often some understanding problems cyclically recur and the teacher is compelled to replicate his/her explanations each time. FAQ's and fora allow teachers to make accessible to all students topical discussions potentially useful.

Further opportunities and improvements can be recognised (Albano & Ferrari, 2008):

1. Personalisation: the belief that there exist 'best' teaching methods has been long discarded, and now it is largely agreed that methods are more or less effective for particular individuals depending upon their specific skill and aptitude. In this respect e-learning platforms allow teachers to create learning situations *appropriate* for *each* student, as far as a choice of teaching materials (such as written texts, multimedia file, interactive exercises and so on) and a wide range of stimuli through different sensorial channels (auditory, visual, manipulative, …) for each teaching unit is made available. The tracing of the individual work and errors, offered by e-learning platforms, can be used to dynamically adjust the learning path of each student.
2. Cooperative and constructive learning: an e-learning platform allows the learners to actively construct new knowledge as they interact with their environment and generally provide a number of activities involving peer interactions or interactions between learners and tutors. Modules such as Moodle's 'workshop', 'wiki', 'task', 'quiz' or 'lesson' are generally suitable for designing activities of this kind.
3. Language and representations: the potential of information and communication technology as regards semiotic or linguistic issues is largely underestimated. According to Sfard (2001) and Ferrari (2004), an e-learning platform provides plenty of opportunities for planning activities aimed at improving linguistic competence, including competence in verbal language, through the availability of a wide range of communication situations and the opportunity to design tasks forcing students to use more refined linguistic resources as well as to attain the coordination of semiotic systems.

THE PLATFORM IWT

In this section we describe the main features of the platform IWT (Intelligent Web Teacher), used in our practices. It is a distance learning platform, realized at the Italian Pole of Excellence on Learning & Knowledge, equipped with features of LCMS, adaptive learning system and allowing the definition of personalized and collaborative teaching/learning experiences by means of the explicit representation of knowledge and the use of techniques and tools of Web 2.0. Due to the presence of three models (Didactic, Student, Knowledge), IWT allows the student to reach the learning objectives defined by delivering a personalised course which takes into account his/her specific needs, previous knowledge, preferred learning styles, didactical model more suitable to the knowledge at stake and to the mental model (then engagement) of the learner.

Let us briefly describe the three models.

The Knowledge Model

The Knowledge Model (KM) is able to represent in an intelligible manner for the computer the information associated to the available didactic material. It distinguishes three levels:

Figure 1. A zoom on the Geometry ontology

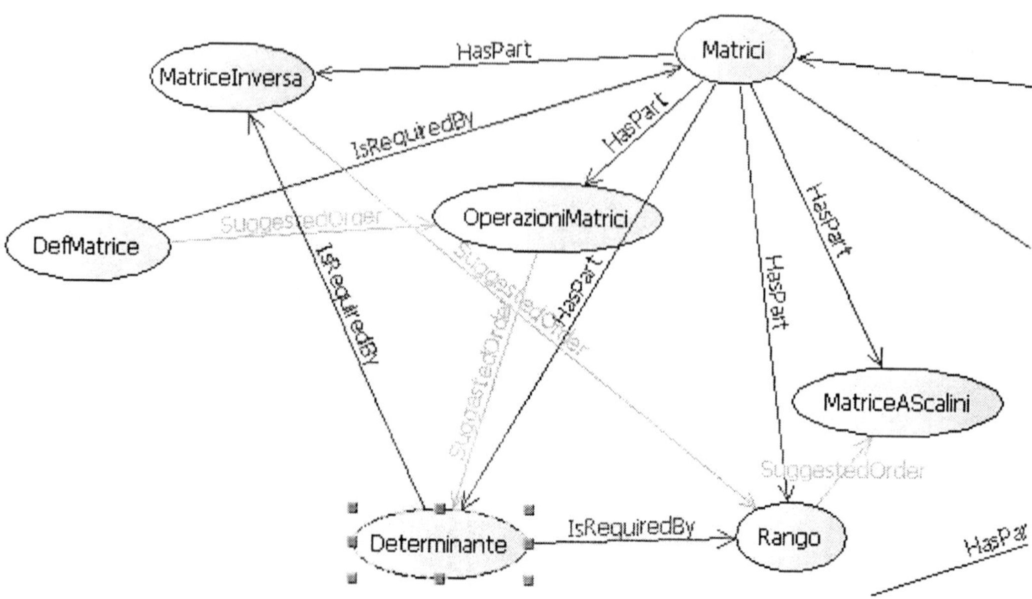

1. the ontologies, that allow to formalise cognitive domains through the definition of concepts and relations between the concepts;
2. the learning objects (LOs), that are defined as "any digital resource that can be reused to support learning" (Wiley, 2000);
3. the metadata, that are descriptive information and allow to tag each LO in order to associate it to one or more concepts defined in an ontology.

Let us describe in more details the first and the third levels, while the second level will be considered in next sections.

The ontologies have been implemented in IWT using the graph paradigm. The first step is the choice a suitable level of granularity in splitting the various types of knowledge into atomic parts. So a suitable decomposition of the Geometry domain has been done. A glossary consisting of about 150 terms, i.e. elementary concepts, has been created. A graph, whose nodes are the elements of the glossary, has been designed. The arcs connecting the nodes are mainly related to two order relations called "Is Required By" (pre-requisite) and "Suggested Order", and a decomposition relation called "Has Part". The Figure 1 zooms in, to highlight such relations:

As you can see, the concept "Matrici" (i.e. Matrices) has been split into five sub-concepts, which are connected by the relation "Has Part" with "Matrici". Among these nodes, some order relation is mandatory, e.g. you need to know what is a determinant (node "Determinante") in order to learn what is the rank of a matrix. So the relation "Is Required By" connects the node "Determinante" to the node "Rango" (i.e. rank). On the other hand, there is no pre-requisite relation between the concepts of rank and echelon matrix (node "MatriceAScalini"). Anyway the author of the ontology (an expert of the knowledge domain) may suggest a preference. This is why in the Figure 1 you can see that the node "Rango" is linked to the node "MatriceAScalini" by the relation "Suggested Order". If this latter relation

Figure 2. Metadata: association of the LO to a specific concept of a given ontology

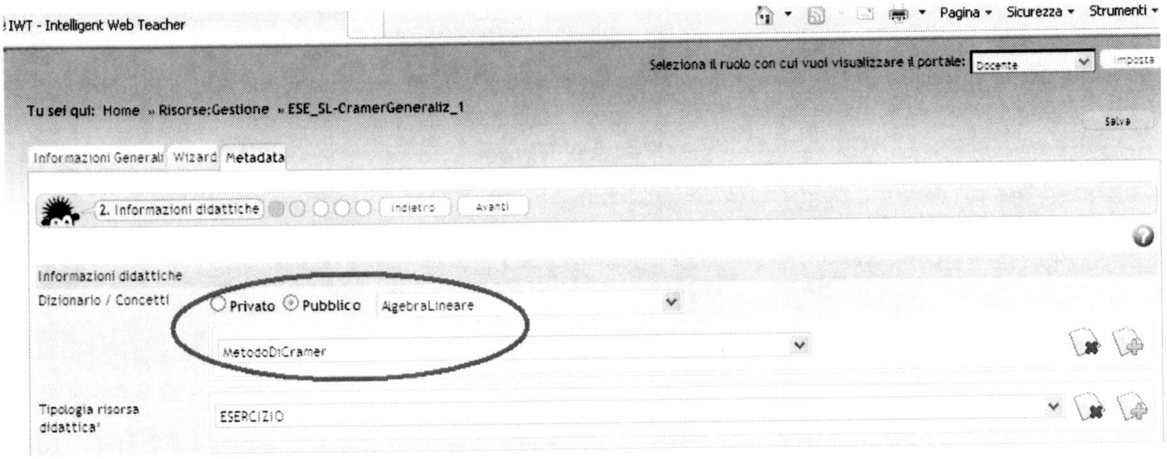

occurs, the platform will take into account, otherwise a random choice is done.

Once an ontology is made, we need to associate the teaching material available in the platform to the nodes of the graph. This means that IWT has to be able to recognize that a specific material explains a certain concept. The material is organized in LOs. Each of them is annotated with a metadata, that allows to specify a concept (or more than one) inside a domain which the content of the LO itself is referring to. For instance, the Figure 2 shows the metadata of a LO associated to the concept "Metodo di Cramer" (i.e. Cramer method) in the ontology "Algebra Lineare" (i.e. Linear Algebra, see within circle).

In this way, it is possible to link the LOs to the concepts of the ontologies: indeed, by associating a LO with one or more concepts, we can assume that the content of such LO "explains" the correlated concepts.

The Didactic Model

The Didactic Model (DM) defines the optimal modalities for the knowledge transfer to the students on the basis of the domain (formalised in the KM) and to the characteristics of the involved student (formalised in the Learner Model – see below).

IWT uses a simplified representation of the DM that are associated to specific typologies of LOs. For instance, a LO, whose content is a simulation, is associated with an inductive didactic model, while a LO of textual type is typically associated with a deductive didactic model. The information on the DM (as we meant it) are stored using once again the metadata associated with the LOs. Such information consists in the following parameters: typology of didactic resource, typology and level of interaction, difficulty, semantic density, didactic context, age range, as shown in the Figure 3.

The Learner Model

The Learner Model (LM) is able to catch (automatically) information about the student, which are:

1. Cognitive State, which is the knowledge the student have acquired through the learning process. It is modelled as a matrix with three columns, corresponding to glossary (related to a specific ontology), concept and grade. For instance the row framed in the rectangle in Figure 4 indicates that the student has learnt the concept "MatriceAScalini", within the ontology "AlgebraLineare", with grade 8. Cognitive state is automatically update

Figure 3. Metadata: setting of the parameters associated to the DM

Figure 4. Cognitive state in the Learner Model

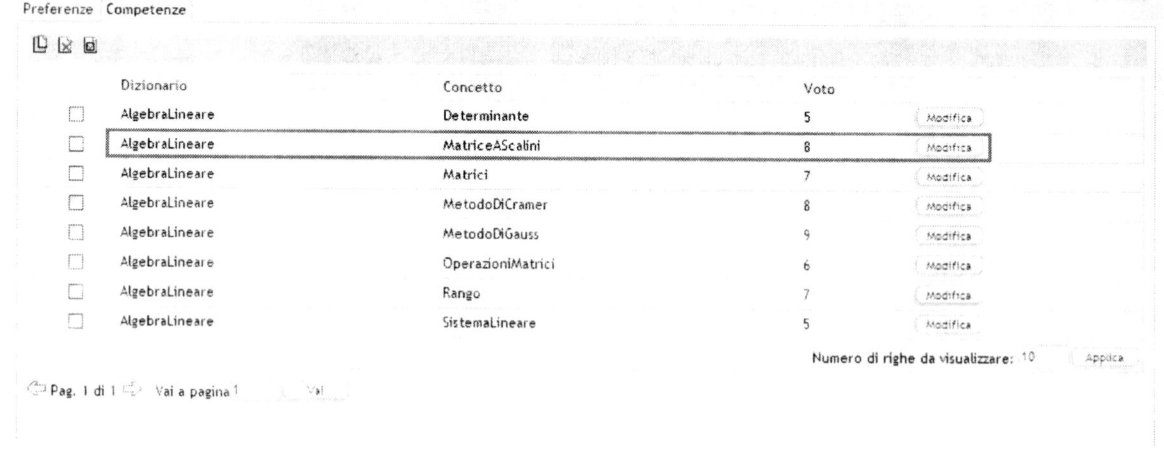

after each evaluation phase, such as pre- and intermediate quiz. Anyway, the teacher can be update it by hand (see button at the end of the row in Figure 4), after activities with no automatic assessment.

2. Learning Preferences, that are pedagogical parameters associated to a DM (see previous section and Figure 3). They are first set by submitting the student various student profiles (Figure 5, within circles, e.g. *active*, *pragmatic*, *holistic*, *analytic*, etc.), described in a narrative way (Figure 5, the paragraph after the circle), and the student has to choose one of them. The choice made by the student corresponds to set a specific preferred DM, in terms of fixed values for the associated pedagogical parameters. Subsequently, after failed evaluation phases, as IWT proposes recovery material according a different DM, if the student is successful with the new DM, IWT automatically updates the Learning Preferences according the experienced successful DM.

Figure 5. Learner profile: questionnaire presenting various profiles to be chosen

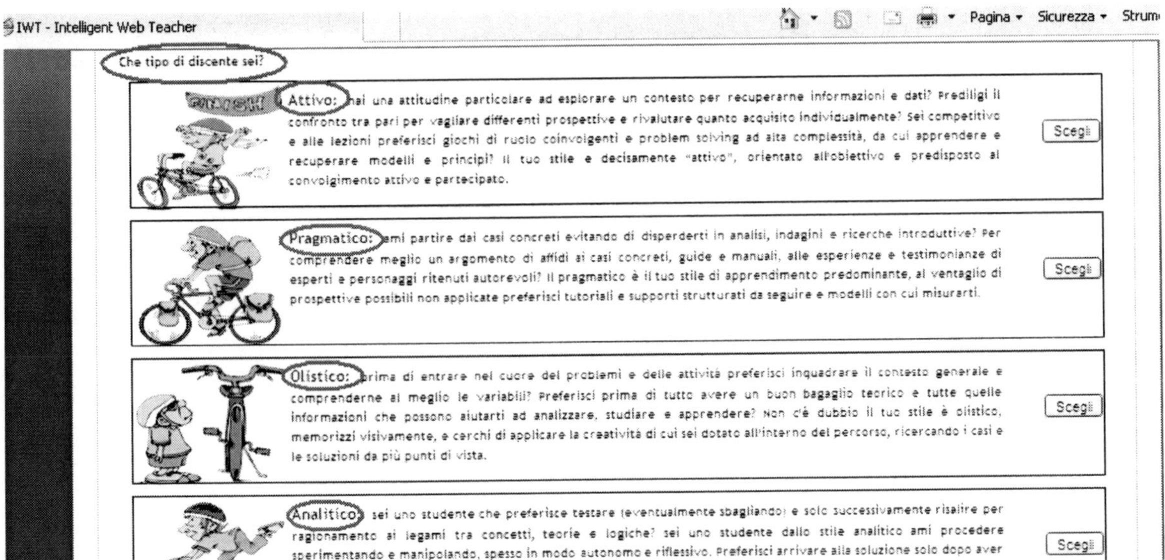

The Generation of Personalized Units of Learning

The models previously described allow IWT to take care of the didactic engineering, elaborating learner-tailored courses, setting up tools, times, feedbacks and updating according to individual needs and outcomes in order to promote individual learning success. There are many paths to personalised learning. Martinez (2000) describes the personalisation types, which vary from name-recognised personalisation to the whole-person one. Among these, in IWT we refer to the cognitive-based personalisation, which uses information about cognitive process, strategies and ability to delivery suitable tailored LOs for the specific learner. In our case, this approach to personalisation, which is more 'teacher-centered' rather than 'learner-centered' as the flow of the LOs is predefined and determined by the platform (that is the teacher/instructor), is combined with a non-linear approach, which allows the learners to navigate among the various alternative resources available and to select and also to create their own preferred ones.

Let us sketch how IWT is able to create a personalised Geometry course. First of all, we as expert of the knowledge domain, have designed an ontology for Geometry, making use of an easy graphical tool in IWT (Figure 6).

Then, we have set a personalised course, that from our side consists in defining the course specifications: ontology (among those stored in IWT), target concepts (i.e. learning objectives, among the concepts of the selected ontology), some milestones (e.g. intermediate tests, if desiderable).

On the other hand, when a student gets into the course the first time, IWT automatically generates the best possible units of learning according to the information available in the student profile (by means of the LM), to the course specifications and to the LOs available in the repository. This is done through various phases (Albano et al., 2007; Gaeta et al., 2009):

1. IWT, due the specified ontology, creates the list of the concepts needed to reach the target concepts of the course;

Figure 6. Tool for editing an ontology

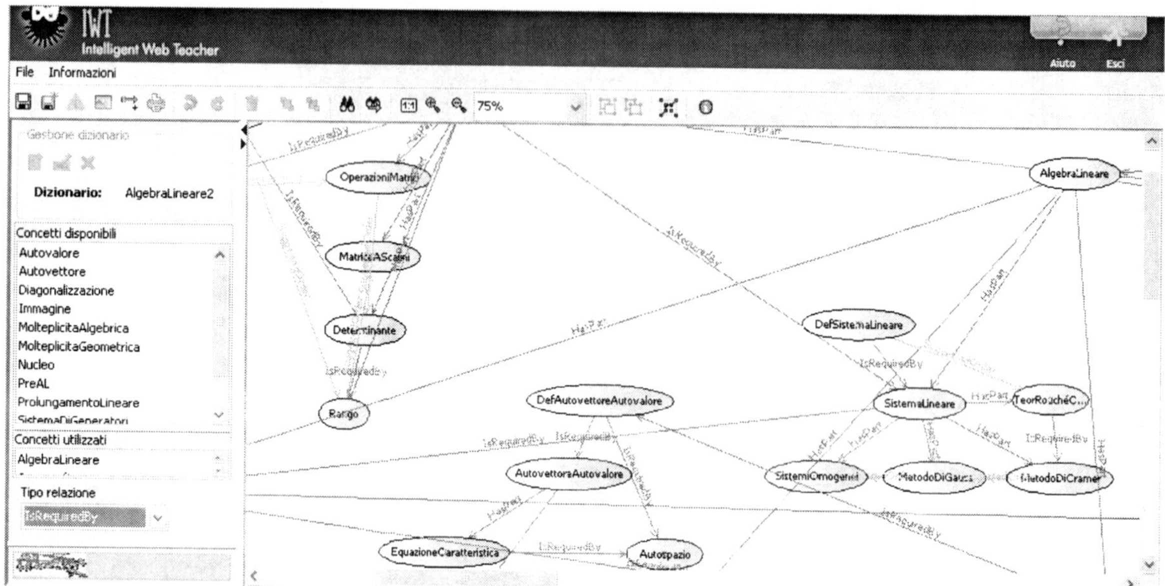

2. IWT, by means of the information of the student profile, updates this list according to the cognitive state;
3. IWT chooses the more suitable LOs according to the learner preferences. The choice is made possible taking the LOs whose metadata best match with the learner preferences data.

For instance, if we have fixed "Rango" ("Rank") as target concept, the Figure 7 illustrates the three phases of the IWT work in order to create a personalised course: at first IWT creates the learning path, constituted by the ordered list *DefMatrice*, *OperazioniMatrici*, *Determinante*, *Rango*, then looking at the cognitive state of the specific student it eliminates the nodes already acquired (i.e. *OperazioniMatrici*), finally looking at the learner preferences it chooses the more suitable LOs for that student.

The student has also a chance to personalize the course on her/his own with a non-linear approach. In fact, for each didactical resource of the course he/she has the possibility to access alternative resources related to the same concept, in order to explore and choose what he/she considers as the most suitable. Moreover, he/she can create his/her own resources, adding annotations (textual or multimedia), and also decide to let them public or not.

Finally, the personalization process is dynamic along the student's attendance of the course. In fact, IWT, after each evaluation phase (intermediate tests), dynamically re-directs the subsequent work and updates the units of learning, according to the trace of the students' errors (Bass in Descamps *et al.*, 2006). So remedial work is proposed to the student, consisting in further LOs related to the knowledge concepts not already grasped. In order to make effective such updating, the evaluation phase assumes a key role. In our case, it consists in questions (closed answer) with automatic assessment. These objective tests, which refer to previously specified criteria, are useful for a "summative" assessment, aimed at verifying the level of the acquired knowledge with respect to fixed learning objectives (Rodriguez Conde, 2008).

Figure 7. Phases of the IWT creation of a personalized course

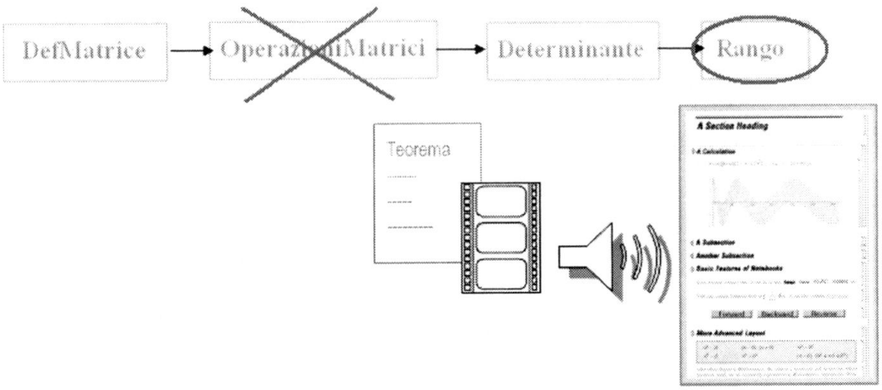

DIDACTIC TRANSPOSITION: THE LEARNING OBJECTS

The exploitation of the potential of personalisation in IWT needs the availability of various LOs. This has a key role as it allows to support diversity in student's methods, which in the constructivist perspective is viewed being the driver of mathematical learning (Balacheff & Sutherland, 1999). Moreover interaction with LOs (that is information) is the first step in all of Mayes', Salmon's and Laurillard's models. Thus attention has been paid to the didactic transposition in the platform, which consists in designing various LOs, taking into account both e-learning and mathematics education pedagogies. Let us see them in more details in the following sections.

Hypermedia

Related to the need for underlining connections stressed by NCTM (2000), some generalized hypermedia LOs have been designed. They are composed of a main HTML text with keywords, which bring to other LOs, allowing the students to make connections among different topics of the mathematical knowledge; to see the same concept from different viewpoint (e.g. geometrical meaning of an algebraic concept such as the determinant of a matrix); to expand historical or motivational references; to make explicit technical details; to use and coordinate various semiotic representations; to recall definitions or theorems which are needed for the topic at stake.

Structured Video

According to Rav (1999), the whole mathematical know-how is plunged in mathematical proofs, which contain all the mathematical methodologies, concepts, strategies for problem solving, connections among theories and so on. A proof is not a whole inseparable text, but it is possible to single out a structure composed by several autonomous blocks, which have a proper meaning and a specific role within the proving path (e.g. sub-goals). Each block can be considered as a module which it is possible to refer to in a more or less concise way. The composition of more modules leads to the construction of new knowledge. Note that various theorems share some modules within their proofs and the overall structure of proofs is not univocally determined. Thus it becomes crucial that students are able to identify such modules and to understand their role within the frame, because this allows them to look at the text at different levels (a whole text, a list of modules, list of expanded modules), and it highlights proving strategies

Figure 8. Structured video

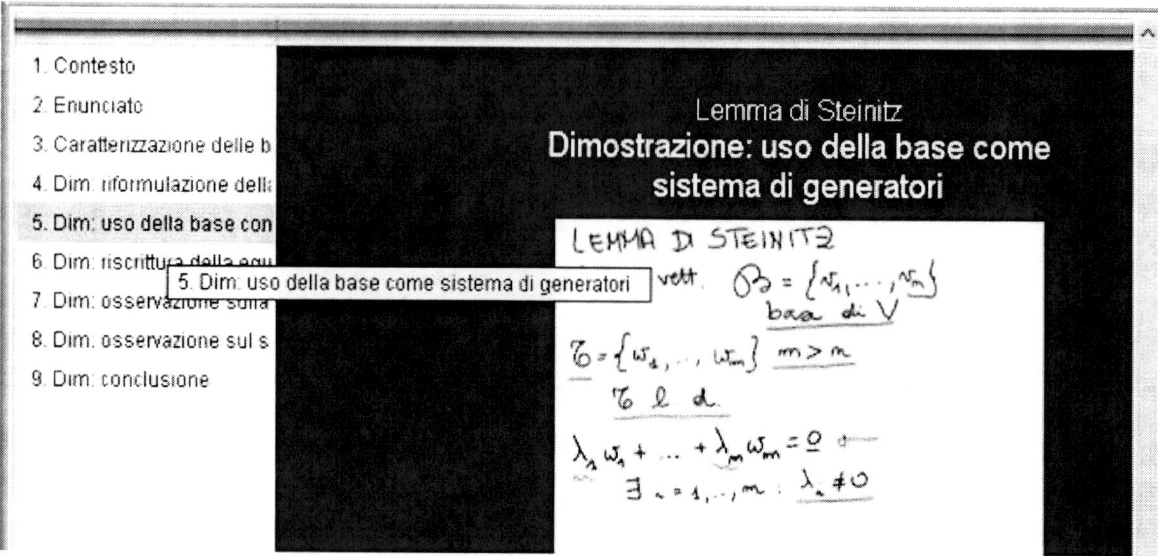

and solving techniques. On this basis, suitable structured videos have been created, by means of a multimedia blackboard. Various colours have been used to address attention balancing. Pieces of previous knowledge (even in a different digital format) have been stored in other pages of the blackboard and then suitably recalled. Moreover, the videos have been split into modules, directly accessible by a side menu (Figure 8).

Static and Dynamic Problems

In order to cover the knowledge domain with problem solving activities, we have tried to offer LOs on basic solving techniques. Thus static and dynamic exercises/problems have been implemented. The first one consists in a solving patterns in plain text, equipped with many comments and theoretical remarks. Dynamic problems have also been designed and implemented (Figure 9). Mathematica and WebMathematica have been used to create suitable algorithms generating an infinity of problems, based on the divide and conquer strategy, splitting each one into one or more elementary steps (Albano et al., 2003). We define an "elementary" step as a sub-problem which is seen the first time (very fine granularity) or a sub-problem corresponding to a task already developed step by step. At each step an interaction is required and an automatic evaluation of the correctness of the answer is done, through Mathematica. The algorithms have been designed in order to recognize errors and distinguish 'theoretical' ones (e.g. logical inconsistencies) from computational ones, giving the students different feedback and requiring further interaction.

Some semi-dynamic problems have been created using structured video to show some algorithmic procedures to solve certain exercise typologies (Figure 10).

Animated Slides

Animated slides are particularly meaningful when some drawings are shown. The construction of a drawing is often the first and the key task to properly solve a problem. To this purpose, the conversion between verbal description and figural representation is crucial (Ferrari, 2004). The animation and the synchronisation between the textual description and the corresponding graphical representation might guide the student in the

Figure 9. Dynamic Problems using Mathematica

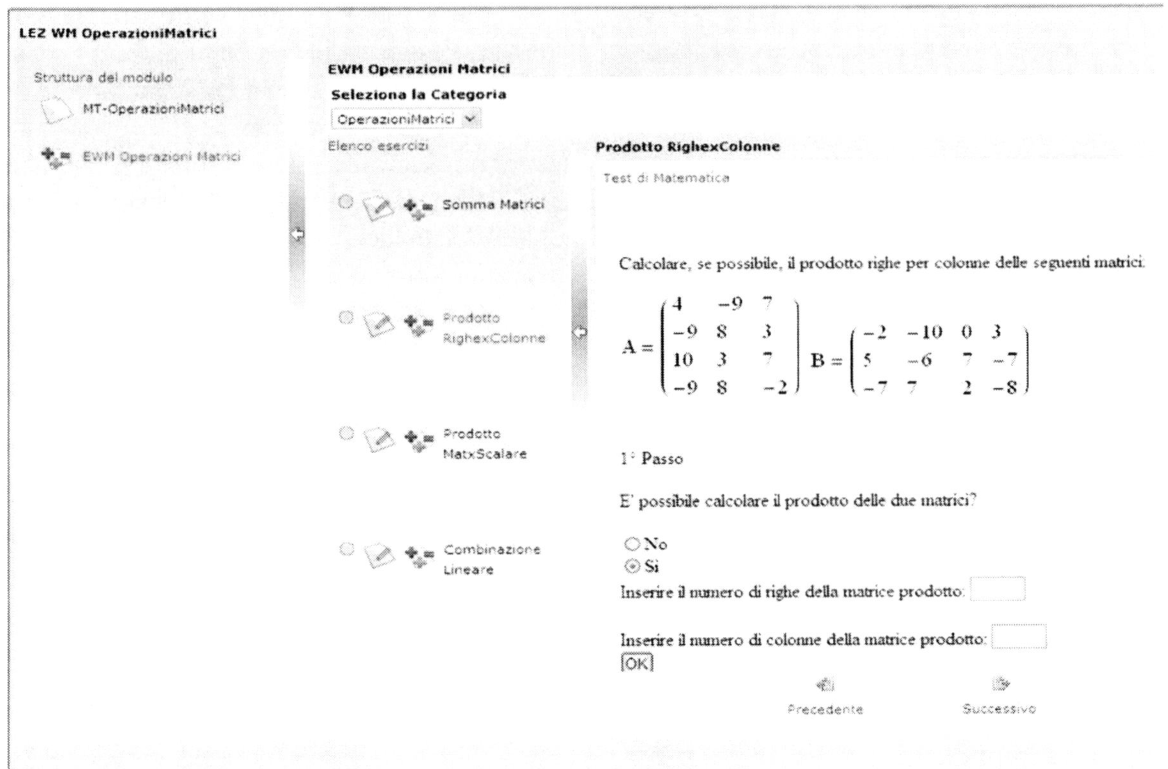

Figure 10. Semi-dynamic problems using videos

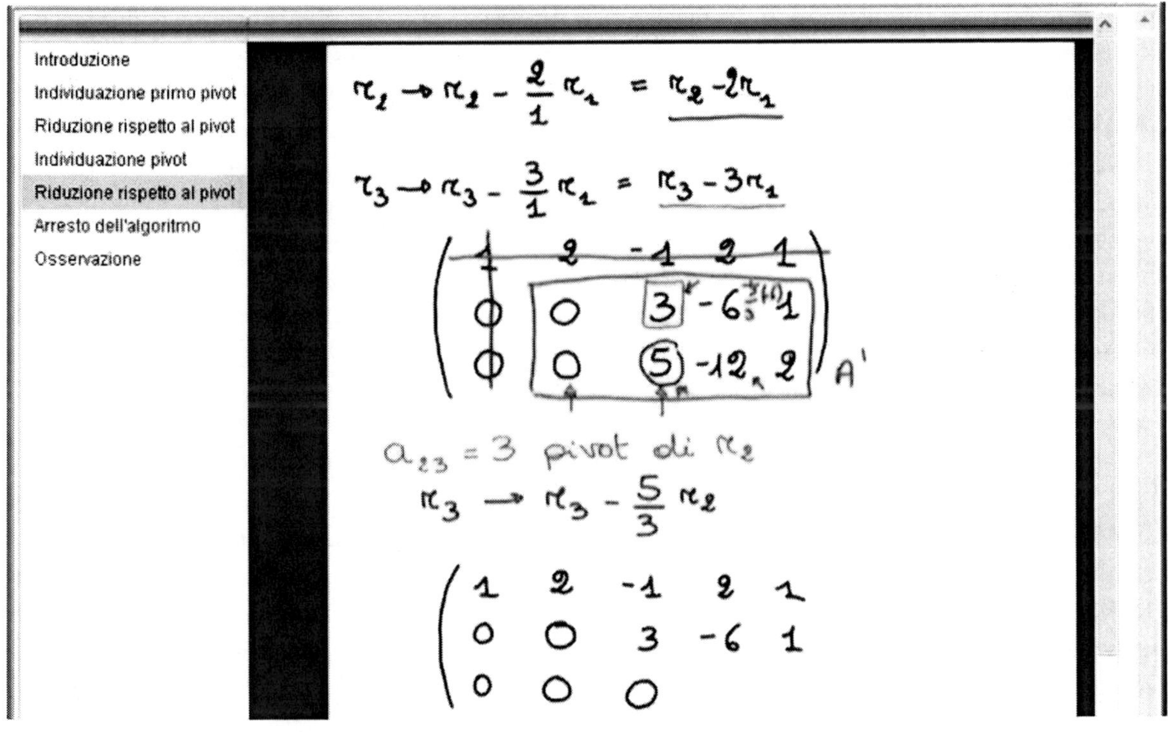

conversion from the graphical situation to the verbal description and to the algebraic formula. So the learner gains experience in the coordination of different semiotic systems.

Lessons

According to the purpose of disposing of various LOs with different granularity, we have created some modules, called Lesson, which consists of a collection of elementary LOs among the types seen above. These can be grouped according to various parameters: didactical (e.g. an Exercise Lesson, including only various problems), difficulty (e.g. a Lesson including LOs with fixed difficulty level), typology (e.g. a Lesson including only hypermedia), and so on.

Junction Elements

A further element to enrich the connection structure consists in the so called "Junction Elements". They allow to add a new LO acting as connectors between adjoining LOs which are apparently disjoint, giving the learning path a non homogeneous look. For instance, this is the case of a plain text based on an historical approach to a given concept followed by a dynamic exercise. Then a junction element allows to bridge the gap between them. IWT offers three types of junction elements according the following goals: to state the objective, in order to bridge the gap between theoretical notions and their applications; to settle the learning process, fostering curiosity, pointing at connections and so on; to stimulate the fruition of further learning objects which make evident interesting aspects related to the concept at stake.

LEARNING ACTIVITIES

Besides the personalised units of learning previously described, e-learning platforms can support learning process by allowing to design additional learning activities, as suggested by Bass (in Descamps *et al.*, 2006). In this section we focus on the exploration of the potential of tools such as *wiki* and *task*, available in IWT and Moodle, in e-learning and in mathematics.

It is worthwhile to underline the key role of an e-learning platform in the implementation of such kind of activities, as it allows both the design of situations of interaction among peers where the teacher can get involved without assuming the institutional role unavoidably played in a lecture, and the use of various semiotics systems and various registers of verbal language.

In the following sub-sections we give some examples of implementation. We note that these activities include "open" answers, thus the evaluation cannot be automatic. The problem of their assessment will be faced in the section "Self and peer assessment".

Cooperative Activities

Classroom practice points out students' inclination to mechanically learn resolution procedures of problems. This leads to various learning troubles: inability at controlling their own products, at individuating the simplest or briefest resolution procedures in specific cases, at facing problems slightly different from the ones already met, bad management of the time available in written examinations, improper application of procedures etc. Such learning problems are raised because some students seem to assume that solving procedures are disconnected by theoretical results. This is why we have promoted the activity described below aimed at fostering student's change of attitude towards problems.

These activities have been consisted in requiring the students to write a common document, which answers to given requirements. The authoring of the document has been realised by using the *wiki* tool, which allows a group of people to write on the same document. In a dedicated area of the platform, the teacher has started a wiki, with a specific request. The e-learning pedagogy underpinning can be assimilates to Mayes' conceptualisation cycle and to Salmon's e-tivities, since they start from interaction with LOs available in the platform, then they foresee to process retrieved information through active participation to dialogue and own products' construction with peers and teacher.

The flow of the activities is:

1. The students start form an acquisition of information, which consists in some worked-out problems suggested by the teacher and made available in the platform (static problems);
2. Then they are required to individuate and write down (in the wiki environment) all the definitions, properties and theorems which get involved in the procedures, indicating where they are applied too. We underline that the assignments will start with the words "*Read and solve the problems ...*" (Figure 11, see within rectangle for teacher's request and the following for students' answers). This explicit requirement would stress two different activities needed to learn;
3. For problems allowing more than one solving procedure, students are required to apply at least one alternative procedure. Note that different solving methods are available in the platform. So the task aims at promoting students' awareness of the availability of a range of opportunities to solve the same problems and that the choice of one or another can depend on a range of parameters;
4. For those problems which differ just in the way data are represented, which means that the resolution procedures have to differ as well, the students are required to individuate and write the various types of problems and for each of them to sketch the solution as sequence of actions to perform;
5. The teacher reads the product when completed and points out the unsatisfactory parts, distinguishing among wrong concepts or unclear and incomplete answers.
6. The students are required to explain why the sentences are unsatisfactory, providing counter-examples if possible, then to write down the corresponding appropriate answers.

Individual Activities

These activities consisted in assigning the students some homeworks, to be completed and returned to the teacher by a fixed deadline. This has been realised using the *task* tool, which allows the teacher to open a one-to-one private communication with each student, giving all of them the same homework. After the deadline, the tool does not allow the student to deliver the homework. The e-learning pedagogy underpinning agrees with Laurillard's conversational model, since the task feature enhances the communication process between tutor and learner. In fact, once the student has delivered the homework, the teacher can give his feedback on the students performance, both in terms of grade (see Figure 12, within the circle low on the left) and guide to overcome misconceptions or to validate the acquired knowledge. If the teacher feedback allows for further submission by the student, this latter can give back a new version of the homework, and the cycle can continue until the teacher considers it appropriate.

The platform IWT takes trace of all the messages exchanged between the teacher and the student related to a fixed homework (see Figure 12, within circle up to right the list of the exchanges), that is both the student's deliverables student and the corresponding teacher's feedbacks. This allows to access anytime each student performed homework's history and to see his/her advancements (Bass in Descamps *et al*., 2006).

Here we describe two examples of homeworks, implemented by *task* tool. From mathematics education viewpoint, they both regard the proof,

Figure 11. Screen-shot from wiki tool

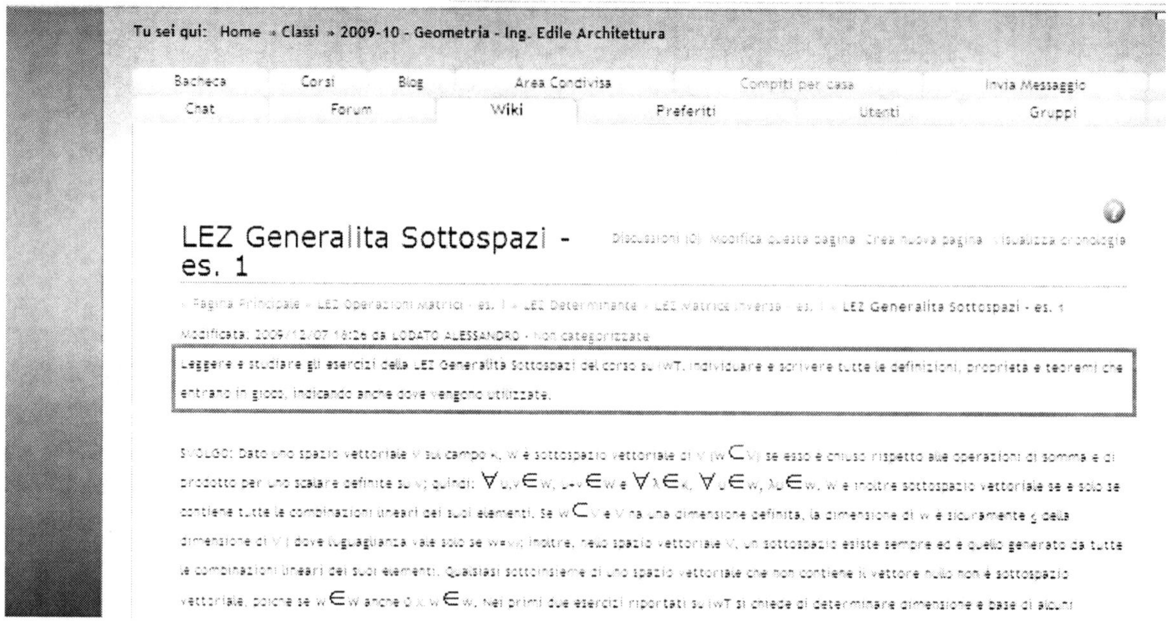

Figure 12. Screen-shot from task tool

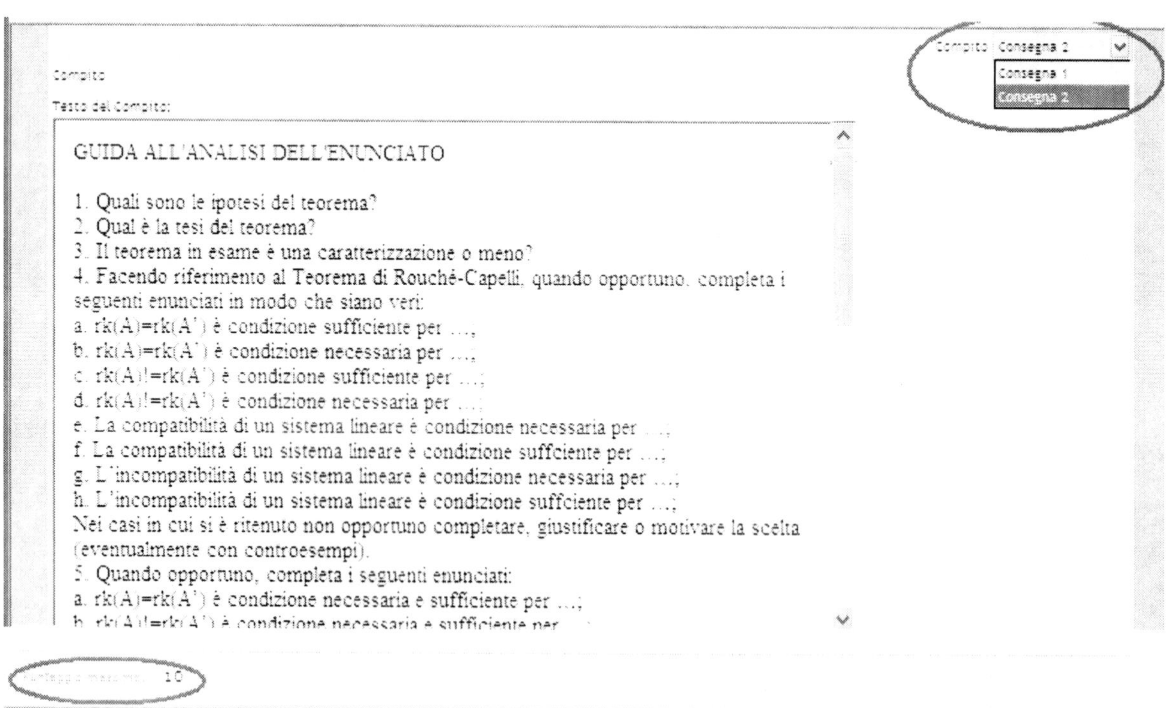

as it is intended in school practice. Their design's guidelines can be found in the discursive approach to mathematics (Sfard, 2001) and in the usefulness of various semiotic systems (Duval, 1995) and various linguistic registers, from colloquial to advanced ones (Ferrari, 2004).

Let us see them the details.

Homework 1

The teacher has individuated four models of problems, for each model three problems have been submitted to the students as *task*. The models are:

(C1) the teacher provides a true statement and a list of reasoning pieces to be used in order to construct the related proof; the student is required to order the list so to have the proof and to individuate the goal of each piece and its role in the context of the global proof;
(C2) the teacher provides a true statement and a scheme of its proof, as list of sub-goals; the student has to add some reasoning pieces in order to prove the sub-goals;
(C3) the teacher provides a statement and its synthetic proof and some questions which require the students to explicit the meaning or the goal of some sentences, to convert them in formulas or to explain them by words.
(C4) the teacher provides a statement and a related proof (not necessarily correct); the student has to establish if the statement is true and if the proof is correct. If the student considers the statement false, then he/she is required to give a counter-example and to indicate which steps of the given proof fail.

The three problems of each model were ordered in an increasing degree of difficulty and the third one involved visual proofs.

Homework 2

The teacher has individuated a model for guiding the student towards the comprehension of a given proof, so the instantiation of the model to some theorems proved during face-to-face lectures has been submitted to the students as *task*. The model consists in a form, containing questions or statements with gaps to be filled by the student, divided into three sections, as described below:

1. *guide to the analysis of the statement*: the focus markers are posed on the identification of hypothesis and thesis within the statement;
2. *guide to the proof*: the focus markers regard the proof process and on the explanation and justification of each step of such process;
3. *guide to a global view*: the focus markers are moved to the macroscopic viewpoint defined by the "logical thread" of the proof.

With the aim of encourage student to autonomously use the focus markers, the activity has been performed along three levels: a) I level: the questions on each theorem are specific, and then different from a theorem to another one; b) II level: standard questions have been proposed, that are not dependent on the specific content of the theorem at stake, in order to make evident what is invariant in the study of a theorem; c) III level: in this case, the students are required to formulate the questions by themselves as they are teachers who want to assess the learning of the theorem at stake, exploiting what they have done in the previous two levels.

SELF AND PEER ASSESSMENT

Actually, the description of the learning activities in the previous section is not complete if we do not consider the related assessment phase, which constitutes itself a further learning activity as we have conceived it. As the described learning activities have been carried out along all the teaching process with the aim of improving the learning process, the evaluation has to be of "formative" type (Rodriguez Conde, 2008). Nowadays, assessment research goes in this direction, as confirmed from the importance given to meta-cognition (that is learners' control of their own learning processes) which can be fostered by a continuous reflexive phase after the feedback received along the teaching process. This is particularly true for activities which include "open answers", like the previous ones. So some patterns of evaluation have been experimented in both cases of cooperative and individual activities, exploiting various tools of an e-learning platform, such as forum, shared repository of didactical material, task, wiki. For each pattern of evaluation pros and cons will be considered.

In any case, after the deadline, the teacher examines the answers submitted and classifies the errors if any. Then assessment continues along various patterns.

Correspondence One-To-One between Student and Teacher

The teacher comments the product, so to trigger student's thinking and to promote self-correction of mistakes, if any. Then he/she sends it back to the student requiring a new submission. The correspondence between student and teacher can continue according to the teacher's judgement. It is implemented through the task tool.

This evaluation pattern is viable with small groups of students, whereas it becomes unprofitable with larger classes.

We have applied it to the homework 2 (level III). This is because this activity is strictly individual as the answers greatly differ from a student to another one. Then individual feedback is needed. Anyway, it is needed to well distribute tasks and deadlines, as the correspondence on each task can be long. This is why this activity fits the evaluation of transversal skills (e.g. abilities of understanding a mathematical text, of conversion among different semiotic representations, of constructing a proof, etc.) better than specific knowledge. In fact, the student is discouraged to continue discussions on topics too long disconnected from the ones treated in the face-to-face lectures. This is not the case of the transversal skills.

Correspondence One-To-One Student-Teacher and Online Availability of Homework Solution

The teacher points out the wrong parts, without commenting nor correcting them, and gives them back to the students by the task tool. Moreover he/she makes available a solution sketch (more or less detailed) in a shared area on the platform. Students are required to think over their products (including their errors, if any) comparing it to the given proper solution model.

This evaluation pattern is suitable in case of large numbers of students. We have applied this to homework 1 and 2 (levels I – II). Differing from the previous cases, students have the whole responsibility to understand and correct their errors. At the same time they also have the responsibility of performing such assessment activity, as there is no manifest control by the teacher. This can be considered a limit. So we plan the use of the *blog* tool requiring the students to have something like a learning diary where they have to annotate their remarks deriving from the comparing activity. This also interesting in order to trace the history of the student's learning process.

Online Availability of Homework Solution

The teacher makes available a solution sketch (more or less detailed) and students are invited to compare it with their own product. This requires them to think over their products, their correctness, the probable equivalence between their own and the teacher's solving strategies, etc.

Figure 13. Screen-shot from forum tool

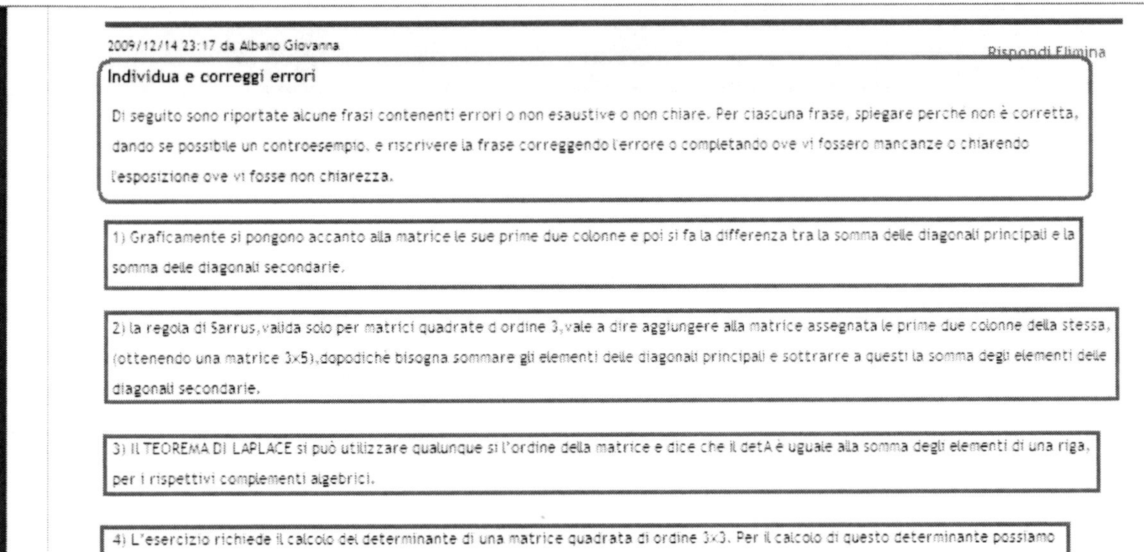

Besides the remarks made in the previous case, we note that here students are also required to individuating his/her errors.

This evaluation pattern is suitable in case of quite large numbers of students and of procedural problems. We experimented it in the latter case, for problems assigning during the face-to-face lectures.

Forum on Common Mistakes

The teacher just individuates and posts in a forum the mistakes (Figure 13, within the rectangles from the second one on), so the learning community is required to understand and correct them (Figure 13, within the first rectangle). Here everyone works on the mistakes of everyone and the comprehension of one enriches all the others.

We applied this assessment to the homework 2, I level, and to the cooperative activities previously described. In fact, it is well experienced by teachers that students make repetitive errors both in the comprehension of a proof and of problem solving strategies. Then such forum allows the teacher to drive the attention of the students on some critical issues at stake and to foster collaboration to overcome the difficulties commonly encountered.

We note that tools such as forum and wiki usually do not support mathematical editing. This is why activities using these tools should be more focused on the use of verbal language instead of symbolic one, otherwise students are discouraged to take part in the activity due to technical problems.

SOME EXPERIMENTAL OUTCOMES

In this section we try to discuss some outcomes of the experimental implementation of the above ideas as on-line support of a standard 12-weeks, first term Geometry course for Engineering freshman students. The discussion will be supported by reports obtained automatically by IWT and by questionnaire submitted to the students after examination sessions.

The students attending the course were 100. The on-line sessions have been considered as part of the lectures, so students were required to

Figure 14. Mathematical editing in some areas of IWT

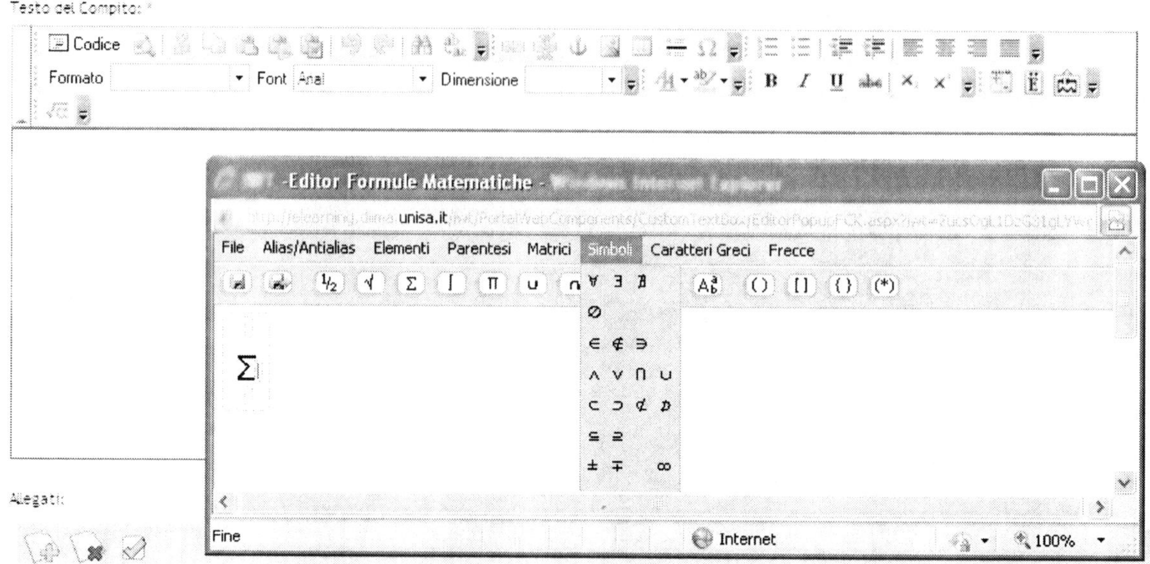

register in an on-line classroom of "Geometry" in IWT, even if they were free to attend or not both the face-to-face and on-line lectures.

At the beginning students took time to get familiar with the new artifact even related to basic operations such as registering, looking for materials, homeworks, etc. Note that Geometry was for them the only course with on-line support. The first two weeks were dedicated to exploration of the possible utilization schemes. Some problems soon arose regarding mathematical editing. Some working areas of IWT, such as homework, makes available a user-friendly interface similar to Equation Editor, allowing to insert mathematical basic input (Figure 14).

Some other areas, such as wiki and forum do not. In this latter case, the difficult has been overcome by giving the students the chance to upload files in these areas (Figure 15, within the big rectangle). We notice that students have adopted such practice also in the first case, making evident their preference for working off-line using already known editors and reducing the connection time (probably because of connection slowness).

Editing constraints affect the cooperative philosophy of wiki as some students have been discouraged from participating whereas some others have uploaded individual products (Figure 15, small rectangles). This remark specially holds for the case of forum, whose participation has been very low. Perhaps students are less interested to others' errors and do not consider the activity fruitful for themselves.

The Figures 16 and 17 show some data reported in IWT.

We can see that participation in the personalized course is larger than the one in learning activities. This can be explained taking into account two factors: the LOs have much more direct reference to the program of the course which is listed in terms of concepts to know instead of skills to be acquired. This leads students to give more importance to content rather than skills, let alone competence. Furthermore, interaction with LOs is not under explicit control of the teacher and thus students can feel themselves more free and less under judgment. Finally there are no deadlines so students can access wherever they want, even after the end of the 12 weeks. As

Figure 15. Screen-shot from activities

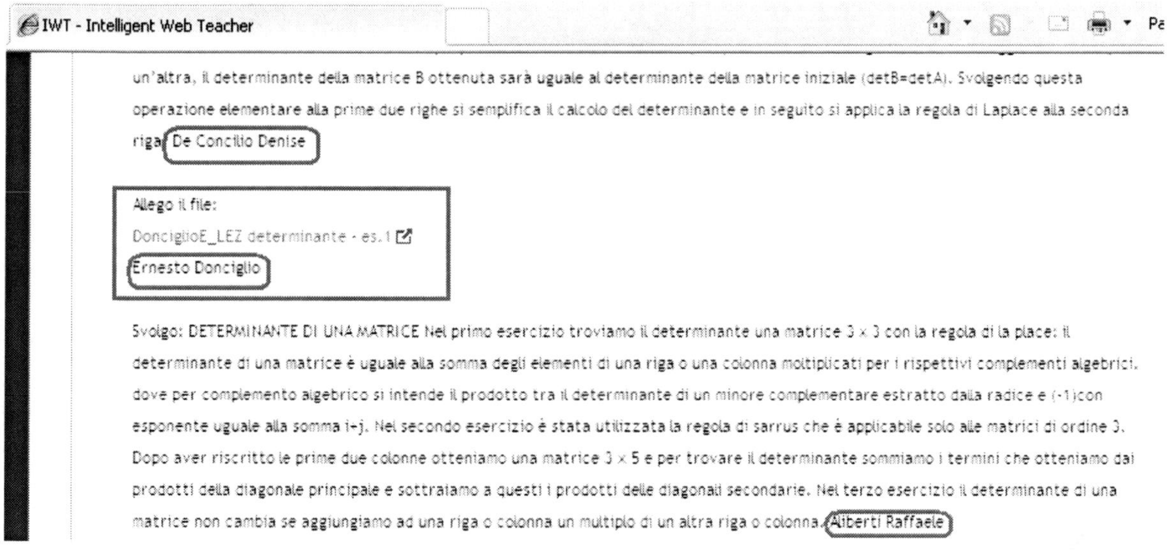

Figure 16. Data about students engaged in IWT

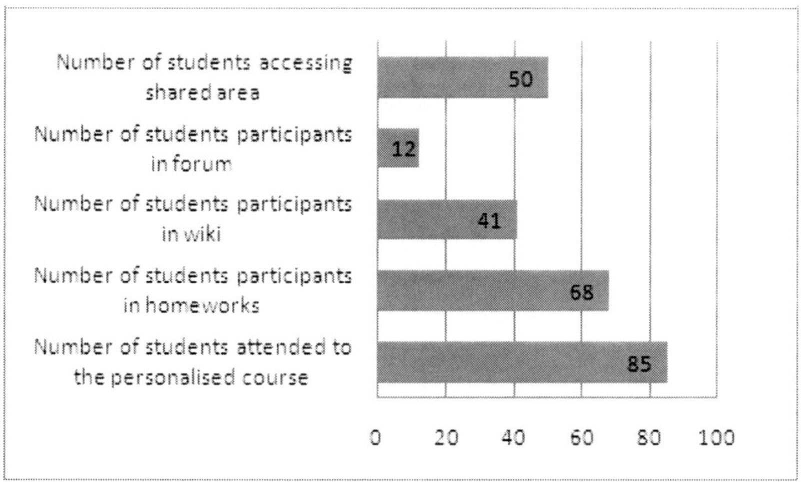

Figure 17. Data about engagement in on-line activities

Number of accesses to personalised course	Number of files downloaded from shared area	Number of posts in wikis	Number of posts in forum	Number of homeworks (1st submission)	Number of homeworks (2nd submission)
2481	547	270	29	194	180

Figure 18. Satisfaction rating about on-line engagment

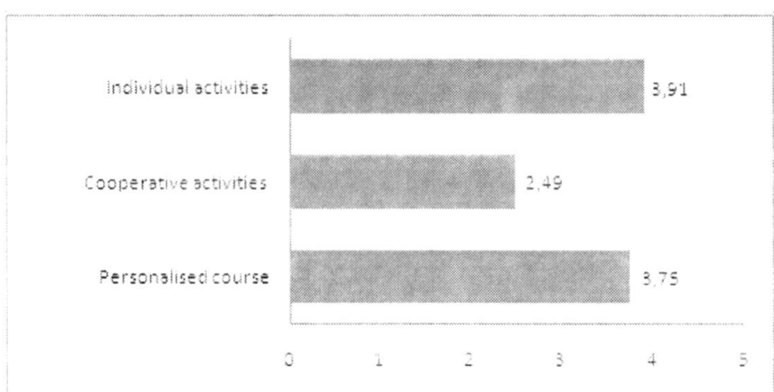

Figure 19. Satisfaction rating about LOs

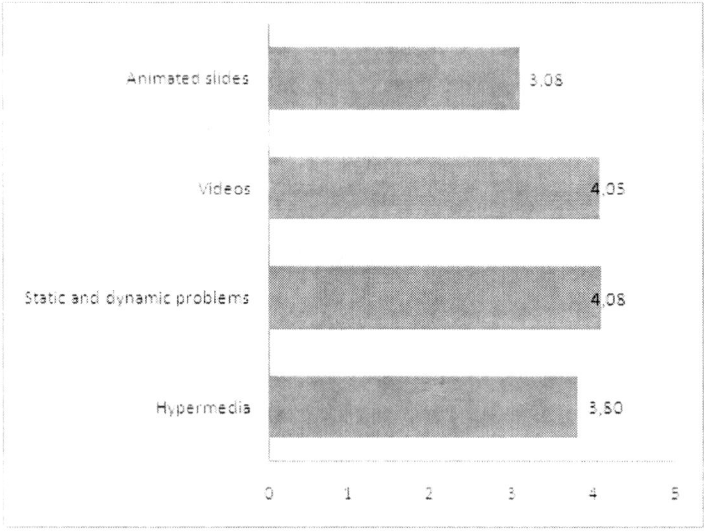

concerns the learning activities, we noted a decreasing participation from homeworks to forum.

The above data are generally coherent with satisfaction rating obtained by questionnaire. Among the others, we asked students to say which LOs and activities they regard as more useful for their training. The students have been required to give a grade between 0 and 5, according to the following legenda: 0 means that the LO or the activity has been of no help and pleasure; 3 means that it has been useful; 5 means that it has been much useful and much interesting. The Figures 18, 19, 20 indicate the arithmetic mean of the answers collected.

From students' comments came out their preference for the videos and the static and dynamic problems: most likely the first ones offer them the opportunity of attending a lesson on demand; the second ones are regarded as interesting in order to be successful in the written examination, as the static problems offer models of solutions and the dynamic problems allow to exercise more and more.

The preference for self-assessment most likely is caused by the practical difficulties in the authoring of mathematical formulas.

Figure 20. Satisfaction rating about individual and cooperative activities

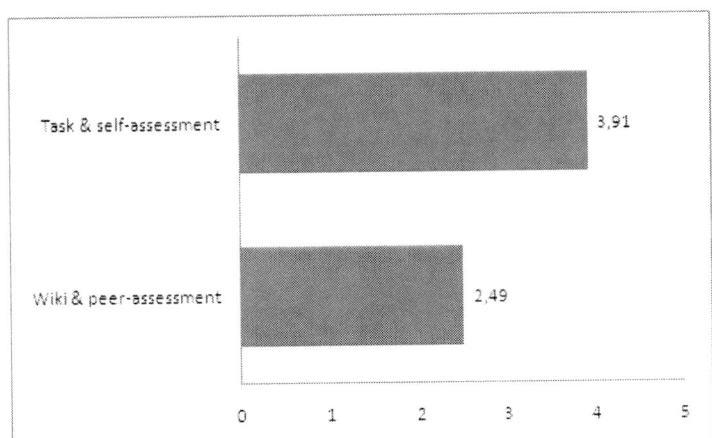

Figure 21. Trend of successful in examinations

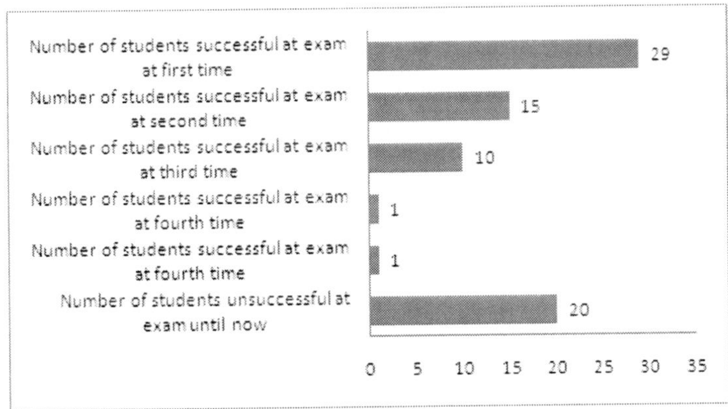

The graph in Figure 21 shows the successful trend at the exams. The total number of students giving the exam was 76.

Looking at the names of the successful students, we note that most of them have been more contact with the on-line course with respect to the others. We know that this does not necessarily means that the on-line course was effective. Further we note that results on meta-cognitive level need long time practices, thus almost 10 weeks cannot be considered sufficient time.

A further question has been posed in order to investigate what kind of impact the activities performed in the platform have had on the exam training. The graph in the Figure 22 shows the related distribution of the answers:

FUTURE RESEARCH DIRECTIONS

In the above sections, we have investigated the potentialities of e-learning in undergraduate mathematics education. The main issues include: (1) the design of effective e-learning activities; (2) the (external or self) assessment of e-learning activities; (3) the personalization of the teaching/learning process. We plan to go on with research in these areas. In the following paragraphs we

Figure 22. Distribution of the kind of impact of the distance practices

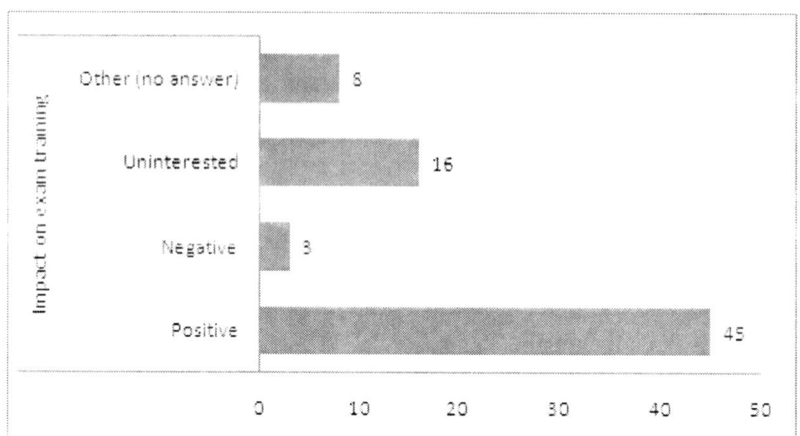

give some research guidelines we consider of particular interest:

1. Here we have presented some patterns of e-learning activities in mathematics. Further research is needed to enlarge the proposal. In particular, for mathematics learning, the design of open-answer activities based on CAS should be investigated. In fact, one of the main features of CAS is the availability of various semiotics representations (formulas, graphs, tables of values, verbal language). As Duval (1995) pointed out, the coordination of semiotics systems is far from being a natural activity, thus CAS would be exploited in order to plan activities involving the use of multiple representations, the conversion between representations, the choice of one rather than another one due to efficient treatments available according to the problem to be solved, etc.
2. As already said, some important mathematical skills cannot be assessed by means of automatic tools (closed-answer). On the other hand, for large groups of students, it is not practicable one-to-one assessment on open-answer tasks. Here we have investigated some patterns of self-assessment, which include peer-to-peer assessment and situations of communication. The self-assessment has been conceived as an e-tivity itself, becoming a learning chance. It is worthwhile to invest research efforts in this topic, as on one hand it allows to overcome some technological constraints and on the other hand it opens to the possibility of creating effective occasions of learning.
3. Here we have focused on cognitive-based personalization, but it is well known that a whole-person perspective is needed. Recent studies (Damasio, 1994) have asserted the key role of emotions and intentions in determining learning success. This has been investigated and confirmed in mathematics learning too (Di Martino & Zan, 2007; Brown et al., 2006). The whole-person personalization uses learning orientations (Martinez, 2000), which differ from learning styles, as the latter recognize the dominant influence of cognitive factors, whilst the first ones recognize the dominant influence of emotions and intentions. In mathematics, learning orientations can be matched to the attitudes towards mathematics, whose definition (Di Martino & Zan, 2007) is based on three correlated dimensions: (a) the learner

emotional disposal; (b) the learner's view of the mathematics; (c) the view which the learner has of his/her relationship with the mathematics. Attitude-personalisation has been validated in face-to face learning environment, whilst the exploiting of this construct in e-learning studies is at beginning. In Albano & Ascione (2008) a model and a tool to assigning an affective profile to a learner have been proposed. Further investigations and implementations are needed to go on with research.

CONCLUSION

In this chapter we have reported some web-based practices in mathematical education, supporting traditional courses with e-learning platforms, at the University of Salerno and at the University of Piemonte Orientale. Such practices have consisted in two main strands:

- on one hand, various kind of learning objects have been created, according to the outcomes of the research in mathematical education; such richness of the LOs repository allow to have personalised units of learning, by IWT automatic generation or by self-selection of the students;
- on the other hand, various cooperative and individual learning activities with self or peer assessment have been set.

Data reports in IWT have shown more students' engagement in personalized course than in learning activities. This can be ascribed both to technical difficulties and major interest in content rather than skills. Anyway, satisfaction rating obtained by questionnaire states students' preference for the attended blended course with respect to a traditional one, due to the chance of various learning styles, of lessons on demand, of direct and continuous contact with the teacher.

ACKNOWLEDGMENT

This work has been partially financed by the Italian Ministry of University and Research under grant 2007H752XT, PRIN project "Insegnamento-apprendimento della matematica ed e-learning: utilizzo di piattaforme per personalizzare l'insegnamento nella scuola secondaria superiore, nel raccordo secondaria-università, e all'Università".

REFERENCES

Albano, G., & Ascione, R. (2008). E-learning and affective student's profile in mathematics. *International Journal of Emerging Technologies in Learning, 3*, 6-13. ISSN: 1863-0383

Albano, G., D'Auria, B., & Salerno, S. (2003). A webMathematica application for mathematics learning . In Sloot, P. M. A. (Eds.), *ICCS 2003, LNCS 2657* (pp. 754–763). doi:10.1007/3-540-44860-8_78

Albano, G., & Ferrari, P. L. (2008). Integrating technology and research in mathematics education: The case of e-learning . In Peñalvo, G. (Ed.), *Advances in e-learning: Experiences and methodologies* (pp. 132–148). Hershey, NY: Information Science Reference. doi:10.4018/978-1-59904-756-0.ch008

Albano, G., Gaeta, M., & Ritrovato, P. (2007). IWT: An innovative solution for AGS e-learning model. *International Journal of Knowledge and Learning, 3*(2/3), 209–224. doi:10.1504/IJKL.2007.015552

Artigue, M. (1992). Didactic engineering. In R. Douady & A. Mercier (Eds.), Research in didactique of mathematics: Selected papers (Special issue). *Recherches en didactique des mathématiques, 12*, 41-65.

Balacheff, N., & Sutherland, R. (1999). Didactical complexity of computational environments for the learning of mathematics. *International Journal of Computers for Mathematical Learning*, *4*, 1–26. doi:10.1023/A:1009882419704

Blume, G. W., & Heid, M. K. (Eds.). (2008). *Research on technology and the teaching and learning of mathematics, vol. 1 & 2. Cases and perspective*. NCTM, Information Age Publishing.

Bringslid, O. (2002). Mathematical e-learning using interactive mathematics on the Web. *European Journal of Engineering Education*, *27*, 249–255. doi:10.1080/03043790210141564

Brown, L., Evans, J., Hannula, M., & Zan, R. (Eds.). (2006). Affect in mathematics education. *Educational Studies in Mathematics*, *63*(2).

Chevallard, Y. (1985). *La transposition didactique. Du savoir savant au savoir enseigné*. Grenoble, France: La Pensée Sauvage.

Damasio, A. R. (1994). *Descartes' error: Emotion, reason, and the human brain*. Avon Books.

Descamps, S. X., Bass, H., Bolanos Evia, G., Seiler, R., & Seppala, M. (2006). E-learning mathematics. Panel promoted by the Spanish Conference of Mathematics' Deans. In *Proceedings of International Conference of Mathematicians*, Madrid, Spain, 2006. Retrieved February 18, 2010, from http://webalt.math.helsinki.fi/ content/ e16/ e301/ e787/ eLearningMathematics _eng.pdf

Di Martino, P., & Zan, R. (2007). Attitude toward mathematics: Overcoming the positive/negative dichotomy. *The Montana Math Enthusiast*, *3*, 157–168.

Duval, R. (1995). *Sémiosis et pensée humaine*. Peter Lang.

Engelbrecht, J., & Harding, A. (2005). Teaching undergraduate mathematics on the Internet. Part 2: attributes and possibilities. *Educational Studies in Mathematics*, *58*, 253–276. doi:10.1007/s10649-005-6457-2

Faulin, J., Juan, A., Fonseca, P., Pla, L., & Rodriguez, S. (2009). Learning operations research online: Benefits, challenges and experiences. *International Journal of Simulation and Process Modelling*, *5*(1), 42–53. doi:10.1504/IJSPM.2009.025826

Ferrari, P. L. (2004). Mathematical language and advanced mathematics;earning. In M. Johnsen Høines & F. A. Berit (Eds.), *Proc. of the 28th Conf. of the International Group for the Psychology of Mathematics Education* (vol. 2, pp. 383-390). Bergen, Norway.

Gaeta, M., Orciuoli, F., & Ritrovato, P. (2009). Advanced ontology management system for personalised e-learning. *Knowledge-Based Systems– Special Issue on AI and Blended Learning, 22*, 292–301.

Guin, D., Ruthven, K., & Trouche, L. (Eds.). (2005). *The didactical challenge of symbolic calculators: Turning a computational device into a mathematical instrument. Mathematics education library* (*Vol. 36*). New York, NY: Springer.

Huertas, M., Juan, A., Serrat, C., Corcoles, C., & Steegmann, C. (2006). Math online education: State of the art, experiences and challenges. In *Proceedings of the International Congress of Mathematicians*, Madrid, Spain, August 22–30, 2006, (pp. 578–579).

In *Proceedings of the Eighth International Conference on Reform, Revolution and Paradigm Shifts in Mathematics Education*, Johor Bahru, Malaysia, Nov 25–Dec 1, 2005, (pp. 238–243).

Juan, A., Huertas, M., Steegmann, C., Corcoles, C., & Serrat, C. (2008). Mathematical e-learning: State of the art and experiences at the Open University of Catalonia. *International Journal of Mathematical Education in Science and Technology*, *39*(4), 455–471. doi:10.1080/00207390701867497

Kahiigi, E. K., Ekenberg, L. Hansson, H., Tusubira, F. F., & Danielson, M. (2008). Exploring the e-learning state of art. *The Electronic Journal of e-Learning, 6*(2), 77–88.

Laurillard, D. (1993). *Rethinking university teaching: A framework for the effective use of educational technology*. London, UK: Routledge.

Lee, Y. (2005). Integrating constructivism approaches in e-learning to enhance mathematical self-study.

Mariotti, A. (2002). The influence of technological advances on students' mathematics learning . In English, L. D. (Ed.), *Handbook of international research in mathematics education* (pp. 695–723). Mahwah, NJ & London, UK: Lawrence Erlbaum.

Martinez, M. (2000). Designing learning objects to mass customize and personalize learning. In D. A. Wiley (Ed.), *The instructional use of learning objects: Online version*. Retrieved February 18, 2010, from http://reusability.org/ read/ chapters/ martinez.doc

Mayes, T. (1995). Learning technology and Groundhog Day . In Strang, W., Simpson, V. B., & Slater, D. (Eds.), *Hypermedia at work: Practice and theory in higher education*. Canterbury, UK: University of Kent Press.

Miner, R., & Topping, P. (2001). Math on the Web: A status report - Focus: Distance learning.

NCTM The National Council of Teachers in Mathematics. (2000). *Principles and standards of school mathematics*. Reston, VA: Author.

Rav, Y. (1999). Why do we prove theorems? *Philosophia Mathematica, 7*(3), 5–41.

Retrieved November 15, 2010, from http://www. dessci.com/ en/ reference/ webmath/ status

Rodrıguez, G., & Villa, A. (2005). *Can computers change the trends in mathematics learning? A Spanish overview*. Plenary lecture at the 4th International Conference APLIMAT. Retrieved November 15, 2010, from the dmath.hibu.no/ Rodrigez-De_la_Villa Aplimath.pdf

Rodriguez Conde, M. J. (2008). Designing an online assessment in e-learning . In Peñalvo, G. (Ed.), *Advances in e-learning: Experiences and methodologies* (pp. 301–317). Hershey, PA: Information Science Reference.

Salmon, G. (2002). *E-tivities: The key to active only learning*. Sterling, VA: Stylus Publishing Inc.

Sangwin, C. (2004). Assessing mathematics automatically using computer algebra and the Internet. *Teaching Mathematics and Its Applications: An International Journal of the IMA, 23*(1), 1–14. doi:10.1093/teamat/23.1.1

Schafersman, S. D. (1991). *An introduction to critical thinking*. Retrieved February 18, 2010, from http://www.freeinquiry.com/ critical-thinking.html

Schoenfeld, A. H. (1992). Learning to think mathematically: Problem solving, metacognition, and sense-making in mathematics . In Grouws, D. (Ed.), *Handbook for research on mathematics teaching and learning* (pp. 334–370). New York, NY: MacMillan.

Sfard, A. (2001). There is more to discourse than meets the ears: looking at thinking as communicating to learn more about mathematical learning. *Educational Studies in Mathematics, 46*, 13–57. doi:10.1023/A:1014097416157

Wiley, D. A. (2000). Connecting learning objects to instructional design theory: A definition, a metaphor, and a taxonomy. In D. A. Wiley (Ed.), *The instructional use of learning objects: Online version*. Retrieved February 18, 2010, from http:// reusability.org/ read/ chapters/ wiley

ADDITIONAL READING

Downes, S. (2005). E-Learning 2.0. Retrieved February 18, 2010, from http://www.elearnmag.org/ subpage.cfm? article=29- 1§ion=articles

Hall, R. (2009). Towards a Fusion of Formal and Informal Learning Environments: the Impact of the Read/Write Web. *Electronic Journal of e-Learning,* Volume 7 Issue 1 2009, 29 – 40.

Jeschke, S., Richter, T., & Seiler, R. (2005). Mathematics in Virtual Knowledge Spaces: User Adaptation by Intelligent Assistants. Retrieved February 18, 2010, from http://www.mumie.net/ publications/ intell-assis_tu-berlin_ full-article.pdf

Leventhall, L. (2004). Bridging the Gap between Face to Face and Online Maths Tutoring. Presented at ICME 10 (International Congress on Mathematical Education). Retrieved February 18, 2010, from http://dircweb.king.ac.uk/ papers/ Leventhall_L.H.2004_242915/ leventhall_ ICME10.pdf

Mc Leod, A. (Ed.). (1989). *Affect and Mathematical Problem Solving.* Springer Verlag.

Melis, E., Andrès, E., Büdenbender, J., Frishauf, A., Goguadse, G., & Libbrecht, P. (2001). ActiveMath: A web-based learning environment. *International Journal of Artificial Intelligence in Education, 12*(4), 385–407.

Noss, R., & Hoyles, C. (1996). *Windows on Mathematical Meanings. Learning Cultures and Computers.* Kluwer Academic Publishers.

Peñalvo, G. (Ed.). (2008). *Advances in E-Learning: Experiences and Methodologies.* Hershey, NY: Information Science Reference. doi:10.4018/978-1-59904-756-0

Pugalee, D. K. (2004). A comparison of verbal and written descriptions of students' problem solving processes. *Educational Studies in Mathematics, 55,* 27–47. doi:10.1023/B:EDUC.0000017666.11367.c7

Sfard, A. (2008). *Thinking as communicating: Human development, the growth of discourses, and mathematizing.* Cambridge, UK: Cambridge University Press. doi:10.1017/CBO9780511499944

Skemp, R. (1976). Relational understanding and instrumental understanding. *Mathematics Teacher, 77,* 20–26.

Strijbos, J. W., Martens, R. L., & Jochems, W. M. G. (2004). Designing for interaction: Six steps to designing computer-supported group-based learning. *Computers & Education, 42,* 403–424. doi:10.1016/j.compedu.2003.10.004

Tall, D. (2000). Cognitive Development In Advanced Mathematics Using Technology. *Mathematics Education Research Journal, 12*(3), 210–230. doi:10.1007/BF03217085

VV.AA. (2008). ICME 11. TSG22, Theme 3: Design of technology for the learning and teaching of mathematics. Retrieved February 18, 2010, from http://tsg.icme11.org/ tsg/ show/23

Watson, J (2010). A Case Study: Developing Learning Objects with an Explicit Learning Design. *Electronic Journal of e-Learning,* Volume 8 Issue 1 2009, 41 – 50.

Way, J. (2004). Multimedia learning objects in mathematics education. Presented at ICME 10 (International Congress on Mathematical Education). Retrieved February 18, 2010, from http://www.icme-organisers.dk/ tsg15/ Way.pdf

KEY TERMS AND DEFINITIONS

Blended Learning: A mix between face-to-face and distance instruction/learning.

E-Learning: Any distance technology based teaching/learning practice.

Learning Activities: Any educational setting aimed to the acquisition of specific skill.

Learning Objects: Any self-contained digital resource aimed to explain a certain concept from a knowledge domain.

Mathematics Education: Learning methods/strategies specific for mathematics teaching/learning.

Online Assessment: Any web-based evaluation practice.

Personalization: Tailored learning practice according to pedagogical/technical parameters and to the needs of the learner.

Chapter 5
Best Practices for Hybrid Mathematics Courses

Diana S. Perdue
Intare Educational Resources, USA

ABSTRACT

This chapter is designed for the mathematics teacher, experienced or not, who is interested in incorporating Web-based content and activities into her face-to-face (F2F) classroom (i.e. creating "blended" or "hybrid" classes). It is not a "technical manual" nor is it meant to be exhaustive; rather, the intent is that of describing, colleague to colleague, things that work in an online environment. I will discuss, as if we are sitting in the teacher's lounge with a laptop in front of us, how I use Web-based content in my mathematics instruction and how my students benefit from it in their mathematics learning. I will attempt to present some specific examples for clarity; be aware that these are just guides for you and not strict demarcations. For ease of discussion I will choose common tools / programs (e.g. Microsoft Word, GoogleDocs, Adobe Acrobat, etc.) and for cost effectiveness I will choose Open Source items whenever possible.

DOI: 10.4018/978-1-60960-875-0.ch005

INTRODUCTION

The chapter will have a workbook-like structure in that, for each tool or best practice, there will be a description (including advantages / disadvantages), action example(s) related to mathematics teaching and learning, and a practice assignment (e.g. "now you try it"). There will be screenshots and links to give the teacher a picture of what it would look like in his or her own hybrid course, plus, websites and other resources will be included for "where to go to learn more". Specific topics will include: Content Presentation, Interactive Elements, Communication, Demonstration, and Assessment.

For each topic, I will discuss one or more web-based tools that I use in my mathematics classes; also, I will explain how I use that tool to accomplish a specific goal. Please note that the topic categories: content presentation, interactive elements, etc. are just used to describe the tools that I generally use for that purpose, not to rigidly define them. In other words, a tool like YouTube, which I include in the "interactive elements" category (as I most often use it for that purpose: to increase student interaction and engagement with the content) could also be including in a category like "communication" or "assessment" if the teacher wanted to use it in that way. For example, if I give my students a cooperative learning project in which they are to create some type of presentation to make to the class as a whole and, instead of having them do in during regular F2F class time, I ask them to create a video and upload it to YouTube, then I have used that tool for multiple purposes: to increase interaction, to communicate information, and to assess performance.

A word of caution is also in order before we begin: please do not make the mistake of thinking just because you provide a list of websites to your students that you have "incorporated technology". That applies for every "new thing" in education and educational practices: manipulatives, problem solving, reading, modeling, student-centered learning, etc. None of those items can simply be put "on top of" an existing, otherwise-unchanged, traditional course – no, they must be truly incorporated, and this requires much thought and effort. You must thoughtfully integrate the tools and techniques with a clear and defined purpose in order for them to have the chance to transform both your course and your teaching practice.

Lastly, I offer a bit of context and some caveats: this chapter reflects my personal experiences in teaching mathematics and mathematics education courses at several different universities for over twenty years; it is not meant to be an extensive and exhaustive "proof" for hybrid instruction. Instead, it is meant to be personalized evidence of one teacher's journey and what she has learned in the process. My experience has included: two-year colleges, four-year colleges, universities, K-12, fully online courses, hybrid courses, fully face-to-face courses, private institutions, public institutions, HBCUs, nationally located institutions (United States: mostly South, Midwest, and East coast), and internationally located institutions (Rwanda). My students met with me in F2F time approximately 3 – 4 hours per week and spent, on average (taken from both the LMS records and their self-reports) 4 – 5 hours per week online (as well as an additional 2 – 4 hours on outside-of-class but not online work). The specific examples and screenshots used in this chapter were drawn from the following courses: History of Mathematics (offered to mathematics majors as well as secondary mathematics education majors), Algebra & Functions (offered to middle school and elementary school education majors), and Geometry & Measurement (offered to secondary mathematics education majors as well as middle school and elementary school education majors) taught from 2008-2010. Although these particular courses were not heavily symbolic mathematically, I have taught courses that were (both hybrid and fully online) and had similar successful results as those I present here. However, the scope and intent of this chapter is not to convince anyone that abstract mathematics concepts and notation can be taught virtually; instead, the intent is, for those who are interested in hearing from someone who's "been there" and "done that", the absolutely best practices, ideas, strategies, and techniques that I have developed over the years and that my students have told me are the most helpful in their learning of mathematics and mathematics education topics.

Background

As mentioned in the previous section, this chapter is not intended to be a comprehensive description and defense of hybrid instruction; however, in order to understand some of the tools I discuss here, a little background information is appropriate. The "multimedia era" (late 1980's – early 1990's) was the precursor to the e-learning movement begun in the late 90's when the World Wide Web and Internet technologies began influencing teaching and learning (Bersin, 2004). As early as 1997, educators have sought to bridge the gap between traditional classroom instruction and the use of a wide-range of technologies. Initially, email, online discussion groups, intranet websites, in-house CD-ROMs, and so-forth were the media used in order to facilitate this fusion of classroom and electronic or distance learning. As instructional technologies advanced, more educators began to see the practicality of their use overall. Increased student enrollment in universities as well as elementary/middle-schools led them to consider other options that provide the same, if not better, instructional benefits to their students. Thus, hybrid courses came into being. Hybrid courses gained popularity due to their inherent flexibility as they utilize both web-based learning and traditional classroom learning formats in varying combinations (Pape, 2006). Educators were successful in using them to elicit the maturity, responsibility, and judgment skills required to complete projects and focus on long-term solutions that could extend into real-world applications. They found that, when the instructor's physical presence was minimized, the opportunities for students to collaborate with each other on projects, class work, etc., allowed them to develop complex thinking and decision-making skills that would not have happened under the traditional classroom format (Spilka, 2002).

Hybrid courses are sometimes referred to as "blended learning" or "mixed mode instruction" and the combination of modalities used, in addition to the reduced classroom time, provided much-needed pedagogical improvements:

"... blended learning should be viewed as a pedagogical approach that combines the effectiveness and socialization opportunities of the classroom with the technologically enhanced active learning possibilities of the online environment, rather than a ratio of delivery modalities.... Our research has shown that, while student success and high levels of student and instructor satisfaction can be produced consistently in the fully online environment, many faculty and students lament the loss of face-to-face contact. Blended learning retains the face-to-face element, making it—in the words of many faculty—the 'best of both worlds'." (Dzuiban, Hatman, Moskal, 2004, pg. 3)

Traditional F2F is the original model of instruction and, initially, online instruction was viewed as the model of the future; however now "... a large part of the future of education will involve providing content, resources, and instruction both digitally and face-to-face in the same classroom.... This blended approach combines the best elements of online and face-to-face learning. It is likely to emerge as the predominant model of the future — and to become far more common than either one alone." (Watson, 2008, pg. 3) My personal experience echoes these findings: combining both models allows my students and me to have more of the advantages and less of the drawbacks than one model alone. These "blended models (part online and part traditional face-to-face)" of instruction, though focused on here in the university setting, also hold a great deal of potential in K-12 teaching and learning (Picciano & Seaman, 2009). As my students are often K-12 teachers in training, this is of particular importance to me as well. I feel they are receiving the additional benefit of additional teaching methodology and modeling as well as the student-centered benefits. "One clear measure of the benefits *(of hybrid and online instructional models)* — and perhaps the most important — is increased student learning." (SREB, 2009, pg. 2, additions mine). There are also benefits to the institution itself.

In using a hybrid class format, a school's physical resources can be maximized (i.e. they can increase enrollment, reduce budget strain, and balance equipment needs more effectively) while enhancing the student-learning environment. Another reason that the hybrid course format is useful is that it has demonstrated success in compelling less-experienced teachers to improve the quality of their instruction methods in order to boost student performance – something I have witnessed both in my students during their student teaching experiences and in my colleagues during the semester as we discuss coordinated courses. For example, by supplementing his or her content presentation with videos of more experienced teachers, the less-experienced teacher can gain both the benefit of seeing and hearing how a master teacher presents the material and the added bonus that his or her own students are being exposed to excellent instruction as the same time. As occurs in many other professions, the use of a master to demonstrate for the apprentice, often results in benefits and marked improvement of the entire profession, not just the individuals involved: again, the best of both worlds can result.

Although the focus of this chapter is on teaching mathematics and mathematics education via hybrid courses, the research shows that the benefits are not limited to only one subject matter:

"Online classes, whether completely online or hybrid, on average produce stronger student learning outcomes than those conducted solely in a traditional classroom environment.

Online learning is more conducive to an expansion of learning time; therefore, students in virtual (online) classes benefited from more time-on-task.

Hybrid learning plus the expansion of time-on-task for online learners produced observed learning advantages." (SREB, 2009, pg. 3)

In closing, I will mention that I am not stating that every teacher must teach every class with both online and F2F components; however, I will state that, in my personal experience, when I do combine both models, I get better results. Apparently, I am not alone in this discovery:

*In addition to the directed questions about online learning, all faculty members were asked a number of open ended questions in which they could provide as much information as they desired. One such question asked of those with any experience teaching online was "What do you like most about online instruction?" A total of 2,536 free-text responses were received from faculty members with online teaching experience. ... The 2,500+ responses were overwhelmingly student-centered responses (the word "student" was used over 1,500 times) –**what faculty like most about online instruction is how it is better for students.** (NASULGC-Sloan, 2010, pg. 6, emphasis mine)*

SECTION 1: CONTENT PRESENTATION

Description

One of the main reasons I use web-based materials is that they give me the ability to provide specific content information to my students without taking away from class time. Effective and efficient use of instruction time is one of the hallmarks of master teachers, and one way to accomplish this is to ensure that students arrive to class with all necessary preparation to allow the teacher to begin the lesson at the appropriate starting point. Web-based materials afford the teacher a way to achieve this goal. In addition, after the lesson, web-based materials allow the teacher the ability to require students to synthesize information and reflect upon their own learning process, to make connections to previous lessons and topics, and to practice in order to ensure understanding and mastery of the subject.

Depending upon the LMS (Learning Management System) that is used (Blackboard, Moodle, etc.), there are a variety of ways to include content presentation into your hybrid course. I will discuss three ways here: course announcements, course documents, and course discussion boards. The focus here is on the pre- and post-class learning, so that is how these three components will be discussed. It should also be mentioned that an LMS is not required to use these components or ideas; that is just the context of how I have used them in my courses in a university setting. You could, of course, have all three components located on your personal (or school-housed) web site, as there are easy (and open-source) ways to post files and have discussions online.

Course announcements (which can also include additional web-based items discussed in the next sections like screencasts or videos) can be used to let the students know what is happening for the week and, consequently, for each class session. I make students aware of my expectations and the class topics / goals in three different ways through my course announcements. For my weekly announcement, I include:

1. A "to-do" list of what they must do before and after each class session
2. Reminders of upcoming assignments and due dates
3. Requests for information or feedback

In general, I think of my course announcements as a way to communicate both before and after the lesson so I can "set the stage" and "sum it up" without taking any time from the actual "doing" of the lesson (see Figure 1).

Course documents can be used as a repository for information. The information can take any form that you wish, but I mostly opt for a list of files. I usually save these files in Adobe PDF format (as AdobeReader is a free download and important aspects like font choices and formatting are preserved). Course documents can include the "basics" like the syllabus, assignments list, course calendar, and lecture notes as well as other, perhaps more creative, items like in-class activity sheets, group recording forms, lab instruction sheets, and assessment items (like reviews or take home exams). Basically, I think of the course documents section of my LMS as a place to store any information that I want my students to know or know about (see Figure 2). Note: Course documents do not have to be restricted to text-based files - If there is a "cool" article on Yahoo! or a related video on YouTube (or any other, more advanced, web-based tool like VoiceThread or Wave or Wiki) that you want to have your students read, view, think about, participate in, or look at, then you can include those in the course documents as well; see more about some of those types of tools in the other sections of this chapter.

Course discussion boards can be used to extend class time by adding virtual discussions. In a course discussion board, students can be asked to continue any F2F discussion, to have a new discussion (for which there is no time during the F2F class), or to create a type of online journal for the entire class to share thoughts or questions and further communicate with each other. What is beautiful about online discussion boards is that the entire conversation is recorded and therefore accessible for review, contemplation, or further extension at any time throughout the whole course. As a teacher, I have seen students that would never open their mouths during F2F class time become the leader and most articulate champion for an idea or

Figure 1. Course announcement

Fri, Aug 21, 2009 -- ***Information for the 2nd Week of Class*** Posted by: Dr. Di

First, a little bit of "housekeeping": (1) Please bring your first, second, and third choices for the month you'd like to do for your calendar assignment. Please have these choices written or typed on a piece of paper with your name on it and be ready to turn it in at the beginning of class. I will look them over during class and create a "master list" so you can begin work on your calendars now. (2) Please download and print a NEW copy of the course calendar. I have made revisions since our first class discussion and important changes have been made. Make sure you have the correct copy! (3) Please begin reading! Ideally, you should have Chapters 1-2 read before class; however, at minimum, have the first chapter "actively and thoughtfully" read. I encourage you to take notes as you go on things you learn, find interesting, are confused about, or want to ask questions about and bring those with you to class to use in our class discussions. (4) Please download and print the "guidelines & grading rubrics" for all our upcoming assignments. Again, revisions have been made since our first class so make sure you have the correct / current version!

This week's class will be all about the Egyptians. Please read Chapter 1 before class and be ready to discuss, do ancient mathematics, and have fun! I will be using a PowerPoint presentation to guide our discussion on Tuesday. Please download, print, and bring to class the lecture notes found in the **Lecture Notes** folder from the COURSE DOCUMENTS link.

Reminder: Your calendar assignment and first article assignment are due soon (see Calendar)! You may begin work now. The articles are all found in the **Readings** folder from the COURSE DOCUMENTS link. **Note:** there are more articles than we need; I wanted to give you choices! Please download and read all of the articles before making your choices! Most of the articles are from *Mathematics Teaching in the Middle School* (NCTM's journal for middle school teachers) but there are also some from the *Mathematics Teacher* (NCTM's journal for high school teachers) and *Teaching Children Mathematics* (NCTM's journal for elementary school teachers). All of the articles I selected are related to history of mathematics so please remember to incorporate that key element into your abstract. In addition, the guidelines and grading rubrics for all of the assignments can be found in the **Assignments** folder from the COURSE DOCUMENTS link. Don't forget to "scroll down" and be sure you've read all previous announcements since you were last on BB.

stance via the online discussion. Including online discussion boards, a.k.a mandatory reading and writing components, to your F2F class allows for students who are better able to represent themselves in writing to demonstrate their knowledge and take leadership positions in the class discussions. In addition, it sometimes exposes areas of weakness in those masterfully verbal students we notice in the F2F class by revealing an otherwise overlooked skill that needs honing.

Before I show you the action examples for each of these three ideas, let me make one more observation: these three aspects of content presentation do not have to function as independent entities. Let me describe how I use all three together as a single way to accomplish my goals for a particular class. Let's say that, for a specific lesson, I want the following things to happen:

1. The students to prepare for the lesson by reading an article and answering a series of questions that we will use in the beginning of class to jumpstart our discussion.
2. To determine what prior knowledge (or misconceptions) the students have about the topic by having them answer a short series of questions that I will review before class begins.
3. The students to have specific information and activity sheets for use and completion during the class.
4. The students to continue the discussion after class by both making additional comments & posing questions and also responding to others' ideas.

My responsibility, as the teacher, would involve preparing the following at least three days before the day of the lesson:

- The article saved as a PDF file or similar format
- The discussion questions typed and saved in a file so they can be easily copied and pasted
- The prior knowledge questions typed and saved in a file so they can be easily copied and pasted
- The information and activity sheets (for use during class) saved as PDF files or similar format
- The prompt questions and description statement for how I want the after-class discussion to continue typed and saved in a file so they can be easily copied and pasted

Figure 2. Course documents

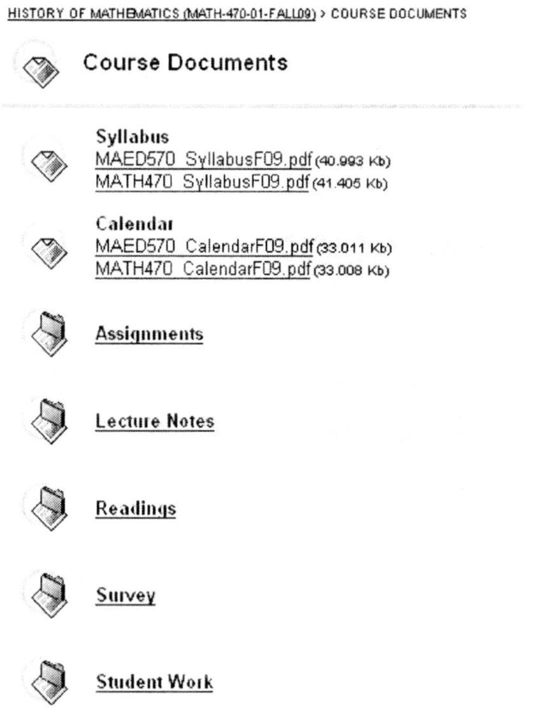

HISTORY OF MATHEMATICS (MATH-470-01-FALL09) > COURSE DOCUMENTS

Course Documents

Syllabus
MAED570_SyllabusF09.pdf (40.993 Kb)
MATH470_SyllabusF09.pdf (41.405 Kb)

Calendar
MAED570_CalendarF09.pdf (33.011 Kb)
MATH470_CalendarF09.pdf (33.008 Kb)

Assignments

Lecture Notes

Readings

Survey

Student Work

Then, I would use the three components simultaneously to extend my students' learning time on task by creating a course announcement in which I:

- Describe for them the topic for that day's lesson (the "introduction")
- Instruct them to go to the discussion board and post their response to the questions I've asked in order to determine their current level of knowledge for the topic to be discussed (due date would be on or before the day before the class day)
- Instruct them to go to the course documents and download the article, then write their responses to the questions (including as part of the course announcement), and bring those with them to class for use during our discussion (and that likely they will be submitted to me as part of their work for the day)
- Instruct them to go to the course documents and download the activity / information sheets, print, and bring those to class with them for use during our class time
- Inform them that, after class, they need to visit the discussion board and post at least one comment or question that they have AND post at least two responses to other students' comments or questions

I would also mention that any portion of the work mentioned in this announcement (the preparation work, the in-class work, or the post-class work) might be collected by me and assessed, depending upon my goals for that lesson. So, whether you use them separately or as a collective whole, these three web-based components of content presentation offer a wonderful way in which you can ensure that your students are prepared for class, participate fully in class, and continue thinking about the lesson after class.

Advantages and Disadvantages

The biggest advantage for using web-based materials is the ability to provide specific content information to my students without taking away from face-to-face class time. To me, supplementing class time with web time is a good way to extend my reach; this results in students spending more time with the material and that is always a good thing. When surveying current in-service teachers, the number one comment is about time and needing more of it to accomplish the stated educational goals. Using web-based materials to enhance and increase presentation of content is a viable way to add instruction time. I have discovered, again from specific student comments, that by incorporating web-based materials, my students spend, on average 3 hours more per week on the course material than they did before I started adding these tools to my educational toolbox.

The only disadvantages to using web-based materials in content presentation are the same as any method of content presentation, including F2F: the potential for students to misunderstand. All teachers have had the experience where, after a completed lesson, the students demonstrate that they did not hear what you said or learn what you intended to teach. Teachers must constantly keep this danger in mind, particularly in written course announcements or instructions. I have found, for example, that something that I think is written clearly will result in students doing or thinking things that were entirely unintended. For example, I used to write in the "reminder" section of the weekly course announcement things like, "Remember that Quiz 1 is due by Monday, August 25, 2010 at noon" but quickly realized that, by offering such a detailed reminder, I was actually causing my students to never consult the course calendar which had due dates plus other important information. I should mention that I made that realization because students would repeatedly make comments like, "No, I haven't looked at the calendar, I just read your reminder." After that, I started making my reminder section a bit less specific: "Remember that Quiz 1 is due by noon on the due date listed in your Course Calendar." This small change had a big impact in that I now see the benefits of training my students to keep up with their own responsibilities with the use of the tool, the course calendar, that I provide them. Another way I combat this potential disadvantage is identical to how I do it F2F as well: use multiple means of communication. Instead of merely written instructions, I may include a link to a video, an additional audio recording, or even a screencast to ensure that they "get" what I am saying in the way that I intend it. Again, these tools will be discussed in more detail in later sections of this chapter.

Action Examples

In the next three action examples, you will see screenshots of my initial Welcome to Class announcement that includes an audio Voki greeting (in my voice) (see Figure 3), a partial course documents listing (showing the course readings) (see Figure 4), as well as a one of my discussion boards (used as an online journal) (see Figure 5).

Action Example 1.1: Welcome to Class Course Announcement

Welcome to Math 230, Geometry & Measurement! First, let me say how glad I am you are in this class and how much I am looking forward to our time together. This class will be fun, exciting, and most of all, educational. There are a few things you need to do ASAP: download several things from COURSE DOCUMENTS including the syllabus, course calendar, and lecture & activities sheet. The course calendar will be vital to your success in this class -- it tells you exactly what we will be doing, when it's due, and what it's worth (point-wise). Read it carefully, print out a copy, refer to it daily, and bring it with you to each class. You will need to purchase the textbook for this course and you will need a calculator (NOT a cell phone). You need to get in the habit of checking BB daily for announcements and to download the needed materials for class (whether activities or lecture notes). Most activities will require you doing some amount of work before class begins so don't wait until the last minute. The lectures require readings from the text before that class as well. I will be sharing with you some words of advice from previous students on our first class day as well as going over our first lecture. To be prepared, you need to download the lecture notes (found in COURSE DOCUMENTS in the Lecture Handouts folder) and print them out and bring them with you to class. Again, welcome & I'm looking forward to a wonderful and productive semester with you!:-)

Figure 3. Fri, Aug 14, 2009. Welcome to Class!

Things to notice / think about:

- What advantages might there be for including an audio component to the written announcement? If you had one minute to speak, what would you say to your class in the first announcement?
- When I wrote this, I thought of five specific things I wanted to convey – help me test how well I did: write down the five things you think I wanted to communicate and check your answers (found at the end of the action examples section)
- Are there sections or sentences you would rewrite for clarity? How important do you think it would be to proofread your course announcements before posting?

Figure 4. Course readings

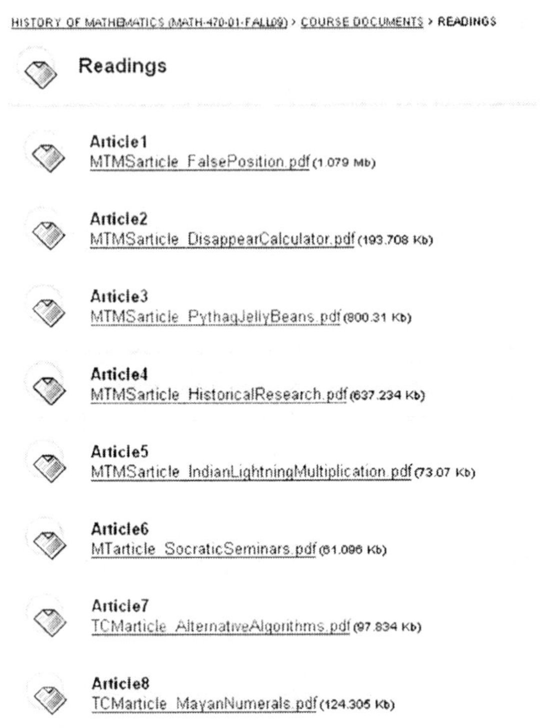

Action Example 1.2: Readings from Course Documents

This section of my course documents listing consists of various readings that I use as both pre- and post-class tools for extending the learning. In addition to the readings, I will often have lecture notes, lab notes, activity sheets, test reviews & study guides, university documents (like tutoring schedules or exam schedules), and additional computer-related files (like Excel files, PowerPoint presentations, Sketchpad files, or graphing calculator files) included in the course documents section of my course's web presence.

Action Example 1.3: Online Journal Discussion Board

In the discussion board shown here, I have my students discuss items that we normally don't have

Figure 5. Discussion board

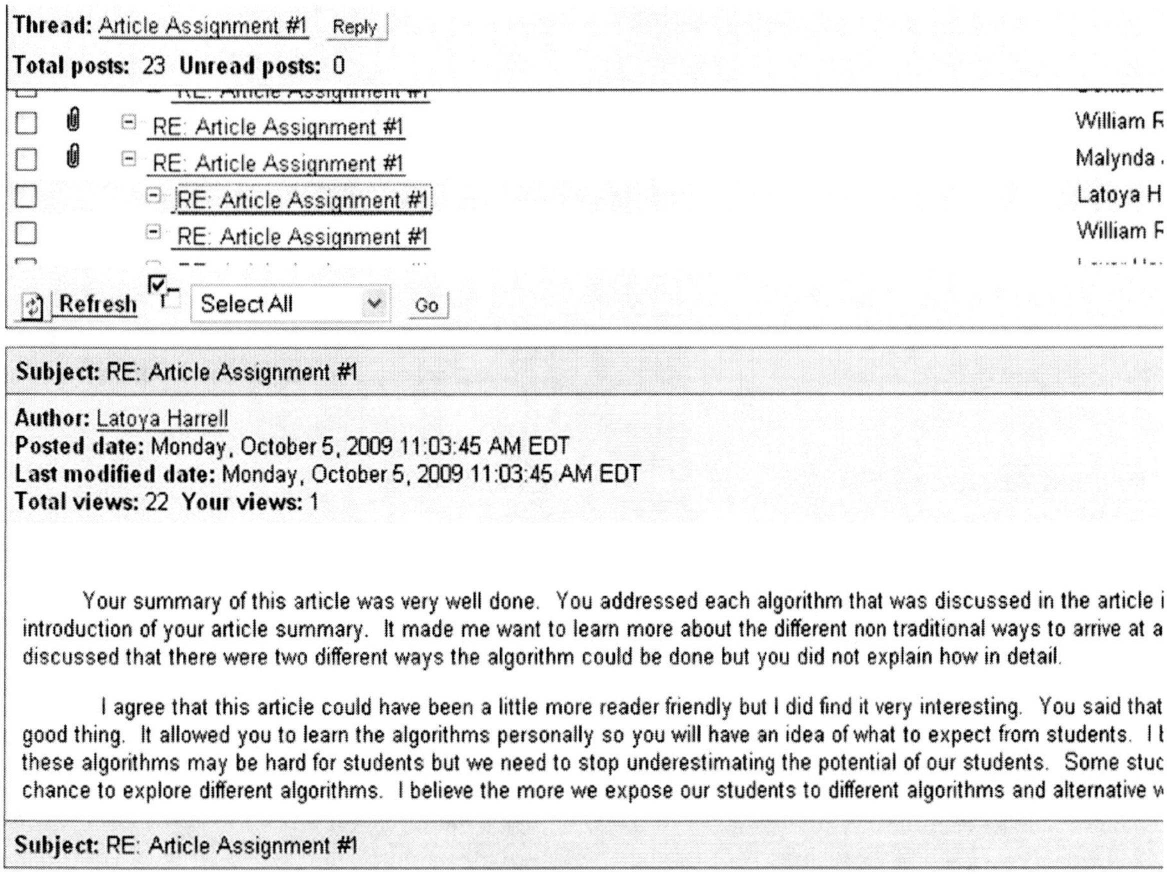

Thread: Article Assignment #1 Reply
Total posts: 23 **Unread posts:** 0

RE: Article Assignment #1 William F
RE: Article Assignment #1 Malynda
RE: Article Assignment #1 Latoya H
RE: Article Assignment #1 William F

Refresh Select All Go

Subject: RE: Article Assignment #1

Author: Latoya Harrell
Posted date: Monday, October 5, 2009 11:03:45 AM EDT
Last modified date: Monday, October 5, 2009 11:03:45 AM EDT
Total views: 22 **Your views:** 1

Your summary of this article was very well done. You addressed each algorithm that was discussed in the article i introduction of your article summary. It made me want to learn more about the different non traditional ways to arrive at a discussed that there were two different ways the algorithm could be done but you did not explain how in detail.

I agree that this article could have been a little more reader friendly but I did find it very interesting. You said that good thing. It allowed you to learn the algorithms personally so you will have an idea of what to expect from students. I t these algorithms may be hard for students but we need to stop underestimating the potential of our students. Some stuc chance to explore different algorithms. I believe the more we expose our students to different algorithms and alternative v

Subject: RE: Article Assignment #1

time for in our F2F class time. By coordinating the topics of each discussion with those from the course calendar, I can assure that my students are both thinking about and writing about the topic during class time as well as outside of class time when working on their journal entries. I write the initial "thread" or topic for discussion (which typically includes two to three open-ended questions) and each student is responsible for writing a response, posting that response properly and on-time, and reading / responding to other students' posts. This online activity is part of their overall course grade and they are aware of both its' value (point-wise) and the grading rubric on the first day of class (as it is included in their course calendar). More detailed discussion of web-based tools and other assessment-related issues are discussed in later sections of this chapter.

Answers

The five specific items I wanted to convey in my announcement were: (1) my excitement for class and hope that the students would share in it (2) instructions for them to download needed files from the course documents along with brief information on what use those files will be to them during the class (3) information that they needed a textbook & calculator for class (4) general information that they needed to form some new habits (checking BB regularly, printing documents for class, and doing preparation work before class) and (5) specific information for what they needed

Figure 6. Interaction between students, teachers, and content

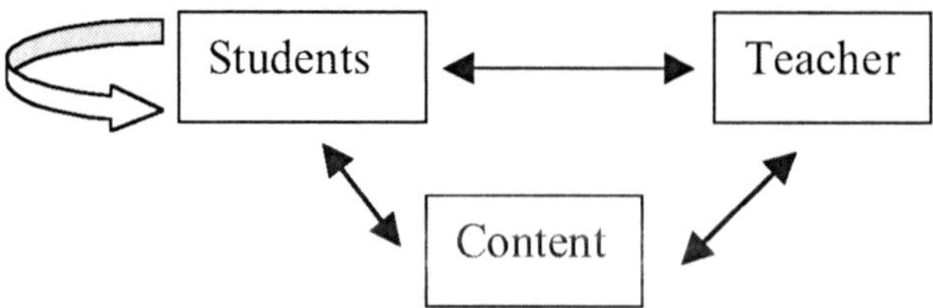

to do for the first day of class (downloading the lecture notes, printing them, and bringing them to class to use in note taking).

How'd I do?

Practice Assignment: "Now You Try It"

Think of a specific lesson that you have taught before in which you felt your students needed more "time on task" in order to fully understand the topic and pull out that particular lesson plan (or recreate it in outline form if you don't have it in written form already). Now break the content into three pieces: preparation, in-class, and follow-up. Think about each of these three parts of your lesson and make specific notes about what your students needed to spend more time on and what activity or action you could use to achieve that goal. For example, you may have realized, before your lesson on graphing linear equations, you're your students needed a review of slope in the form of seeing pictures of various graphs of lines and answering simple questions like, "Which of the following lines have positive slopes?" Using your previous lesson plan and your notes as guides, create a web-based item to help you add "virtual time" to both your instruction and your students' learning. You may choose to:

- Create files for a course documents listing
- Create a discussion board item to "continue the conversation"
- Or, if you are really brave, create a course announcement that incorporates all three aspects into one cohesive whole

SECTION 2: INTERACTIVE ELEMENTS

Description

Often, when teachers are first introduced to web-based learning they incorrectly assume that the only option for delivery is text-based. However, with the Web 2.0 tools available today (and more being dreamed of and developed every day), that is simply not the case. Instead, teachers can provide as much interaction in the hybrid parts of their courses as they do in the F2F portions. The diagram shown in Figure 6 illustrates this interaction best.

In other words, interactive elements can facilitate interaction between students, between student(s) and teacher, and between student(s) and the content. Interactive web-based elements engage the students by acting on their senses of sight, hearing, and touch and often illustrate the content in a fresh, unanticipated, and exciting way that causes the student to become more interested, pay more attention, and to become more motivated to continue their learning. I have found in my own classes, for example, that students will watch a video (like the YouTube one shown in Figure 7) three or four times (thus increasing the time they are spending on the material) whereas they will not review their written notes at all (or

Figure 7. Parametric equations video

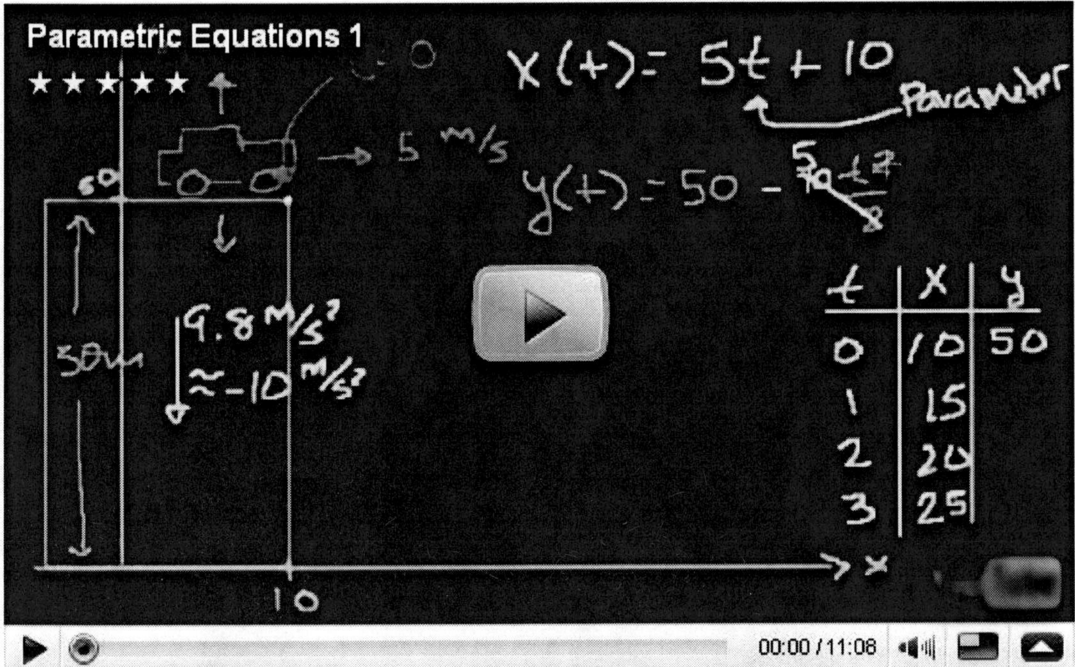

very little). Note: the preceding is not simply an opinion-statement: I have documented proof in the form of the records of my LMS (which records the number of "clicks" and time spent on a particular link in the course) and the words of my students (again, from the benefits of asking survey questions in my LMS which I can then refer to as future guides to instructional practices, a.k.a. "to inform future instruction").

We know that students who use multiple senses when learning a new skill are more likely to enjoy, remember, and master the skill than when a single sense is used. We also know the same is true for learning styles and types of intelligences. For example, the artistic student will respond much more positively and enthusiastically to a presentation that incorporates color, sound, and shapes in a creative way rather than static black and white text. Incorporating web-based interactive elements into a hybrid course allow the teacher to engage the student more fully and in more ways and allow the students to engage both with each other and with the content in different and varied ways.

I will discuss three types of interactive elements: audio / video, collaborative authorship, and creative. Here are some of the tools for each element: (Note: this list is by no means exhaustive!)

- Audio / Video: Voki, Viddler, YouTube
- Collaborative authorship: Wiki's, GoogleDocs, VoiceThread
- Creative: Prezi, Wordle

Audio / Video tools are helpful web-based additions to a hybrid mathematics course because they most resemble the face-to-face interaction in the classroom. The students can both hear and see the presenter and the material being discussed (in video tools) or hear the instructor's voice describing additional information (in audio tools). I often use these tools to supplement my interaction with the students. For example, in class, I may have only ten minutes allotted for

Figure 8. Viddler video

discussing a particular topic, say the connection between our base-ten numeration system and other ancient systems of numeration like the Romans or Egyptians. However, this might be a topic that captures my students' interest due to connections to things that may be relevant to their "real lives" like: in football, why is each year's Superbowl given a Roman numeral? So, in order to utilize that potential for additional motivation and subsequent learning, I may create a Viddler video (see Figure 8) in which I discuss in more detail, for an extra ten minutes, those specific things that are relevant and "cool" but not necessarily required for the lesson itself or appropriate / beneficial to spend class time on.

Then, during the F2F time, I can simply give my students the link to these "extras" and they can, on their own time, go check them out. Now, before you even bring it up, let me state that I know what you're thinking: "I can't even get my students to do the 'required' things for class; there's no way they'd do something 'extra'!" Well, you may be correct; however, look at it this way: for the ones who do, you have "added instructional time" without very much additional effort on your part. Also, there are ways by which you can encourage your students to check out these extras: one method I've used to great success is the "hidden bonus". Here's how it works, somewhere (say six minutes in to the 10 minute video), I will say, "I am so impressed by your motivation and that you took the time to watch this extra video that I want to give you a token of appreciation. If you will write me an email titled 'extra' in which you describe two additional things you learned by watching this extra video, then I will give you a 'bonus' two points on our next in-class quiz." You will be AMAZED by (a) how quickly this "word gets out" in your classroom after you do it the first time (b) how many students will take you up on this offer for "appreciation" and (c) how thoughtful and well-written their emails are (because, I think, they are viewing it as a "favor" and therefore the pressure is off). Try it! You really have nothing to lose and your students have a lot to gain.

Although increasing my instructional interaction time with my students is the major way I utilize the audio / video tools, it is not the only way. Increasing students' interaction with me and students' interaction with each other are also ways in which these tools can be used. For example, I can ask for one-minute class summaries from each student where, using Voki, they choose an avatar then create a one-minute (as that is the limit for this particular tool) recording where they summarize (a) what class was all about (b) the major thing they learned and (c) any questions or parts they remain unsure about or have questions on. Then, the class posts their links to a common location (usually within the LMS). We can all then watch and hear about how class went for that day. It is not just a valuable tool for the students to hear from each other but also for the teacher to "check in" with the students and see if what they are learning matches with what the teacher thinks is being taught. The one-minute time limit has two big advantages for this: it is not very stressful because they students think, "it's only a minute, that's easy" and it forces them to be concise and make every sentence count. I will often, the first time I make this assignment, encourage my students to write out their "script", practice reading it aloud, and time themselves so they can be sure they can say everything that they want to in the allotted time.

Collaborative authorship tools can be a wonderful way to increase student ↔ student interaction and student ↔ teacher interaction. They can also be used to involve more people in the learning process, including other classes, other learners, other teachers, and other people who are interested in the topic. To me, these tools are simply a jazzed-up way of allowing individuals to work together on a single item. The three tools I listed earlier (Wiki's, GoogleDocs, VoiceThread) all share the common ability to have people contribute individually in a way that produces a finished group product. In my classes, I have chosen which tool on the basis of how many people I want to work together. Let me explain by describing a series of examples.

First, I think of GoogleDocs as the best tool when I want a small group of students to truly collaborate and co-write something as part of a cooperative learning group project. So let's say, as an example, I have groups of students whose task it is to solve a particular problem, then create a report that describes the process (description of the problem, their plan for solving the problem, how they carried out that plan and the results that occurred, their statement of the solution or solutions to the problem, their reflection on both the solution and the process, and their contributions and evaluations as both individuals and a group). I may require them to produce this final group document using GoogleDocs because the features of this particular web-based tool coincide with my goals for the project as a whole: it shows who contributed to the document, when they did so, and what they added / changed; it keeps the "current" copy so, at any time in the collaborative writing process, one can see the entire document; it "stores" this document online so everyone has access to it all times during the process.

Next, I think of Wikis as the tool of choice when my goal is to create a class-wide product. As an example, consider a class of pre-service teachers and the educational goal of teaching them how to create an effective and complete lesson plan on a particular mathematics topic, say graphing linear functions. I will often begin the page on the Wiki by creating the layout for the lesson plan and including the topic and grade level. Then, I will ask my students to join with me in writing various parts to the lesson plan, editing each other's work, and, finally, creating a truly collaborative final product that we can all use. Wikis have the added bonus that, if you share the link and include keywords and other items to make it "searchable", then other people can also benefit from your effort (and give you feedback as well). Of course the most famous example of this is Wikipedia, the collaborative online encyclopedia that the entire online community is writing continuously.

Finally, I consider VoiceThread the ideal tool to use when I want my students to participate in a conversation with each other AND the outside community (defined however you'd like: other classes, other schools, "regular people", etc.). Their site describes the tool better than I can:

"With VoiceThread, group conversations are collected and shared in one place from anywhere in the world. All with no software to install. A VoiceThread is a collaborative, multimedia slide show that holds images, documents, and videos and allows people to navigate pages and leave comments in 5 ways - using voice (with a mic or telephone), text, audio file, or video (via a webcam)." (www.voicethread.com)

Creative tools are often overlooked because they do not fall into a critical category (like content presentation or assessment) and, as a result, teachers may not (a) be familiar with them or (b) understand how they could be incorporated into a classroom setting. Wordle is my favorite "creative" web-based tool. Again, I will let the creators tell you about their product in their own words:

"Wordle is a toy for generating "word clouds" from text that you provide. The clouds give greater prominence to words that appear more frequently in the source text. You can tweak your clouds with different fonts, layouts, and color schemes. The images you create with Wordle are yours to use however you like." (www.wordle.com)

I have used Wordle in a lot of ways in my class:

- As a diagnostic tool to see what my students know or think of when given a particular topic, like "probability"
- As a brainstorming tool to have my students think of examples they can use with future students to describe where a particular mathematics concept comes up in real life, like "geometry all around us"
- As a summarizing tool to ask my students to synthesize an entire section, chapter, or class, like "all about functions"

Advantages and Disadvantages

Incorporating web-based interactive elements into your mathematics course share the same main advantage that incorporating interactive elements into your F2F course has: increasing student participation, including interest-level, motivation, and involvement. Increasing your students' level of participation increases their chances of both understanding and retaining the content you are conveying to them. We all know that when we are interested and engaged, then we pay better attention, focus more, and, as a result, learn more easily (and certainly more enjoyably).

In addition, there are specific advantages for each of the particular interactive tools related to the way in which they are incorporated to meet the educational goals of the lesson or course. For example, if your major goal is to have your students truly "work together" in a learning group, edit and interact with each others' work and thoughts, and then produce a finished product in which they can all see themselves in it, then a tool like GoogleDocs has the tremendous advantage of providing you with an interactive, dynamic, always-available platform from which your students (and you) can accomplish this goal.

The disadvantages for the interactive elements are better discussed for each category. In the case of the audio / video tools, the major disadvantage depends upon which tool you select. For example, the major disadvantage to the Voki tool is the one-minute restriction on recording time. The major disadvantage for using a Wiki is that your students must learn some basic formatting items prior to creating or contributing to the forum. The major disadvantage to VoiceThread is that it does make some, albeit small, demands upon the computer used in terms of Flash, Java, and required plugins. In addition, the specific tools I've discuss here also share two common disadvantages: (1) they require the students (and the teacher) to create online accounts (though these are free) and (2) to fully participate, they require some additional hardware (for example, speakers to hear the audio and a webcam to create video).

Action Examples

In the following three action examples, you will see examples of an audio component (Voki), a collaborative authorship tool (Wiki), and a creative element (Wordle) that I have used in my class to add an interactive element and increase student interest and engagement with the material (and me).

Action Example 2.1: Audio / Video

Sample Voki

I used Voki as a component of my weekly course announcement to provide a more personal touch to the information I was trying to relay (refer to Figure 3). What I discovered, again through student comments and survey results, was that my students paid more attention to details when they heard my voice saying the information rather than when they read it for themselves from a printed form. In addition, they were "into" seeing what form my Voki took from week to week as the avatar would change depending upon my mood, the season of the year, or the content of the mes-

Figure 9. History of math Wiki

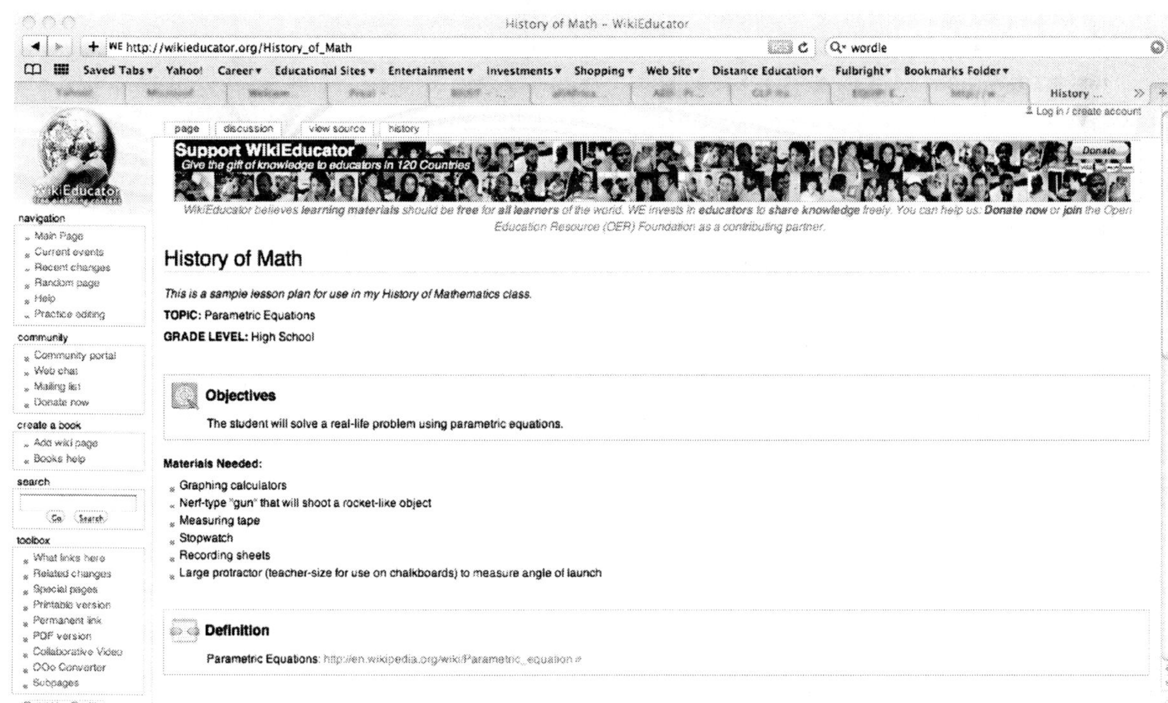

Figure 10. Wiki lesson

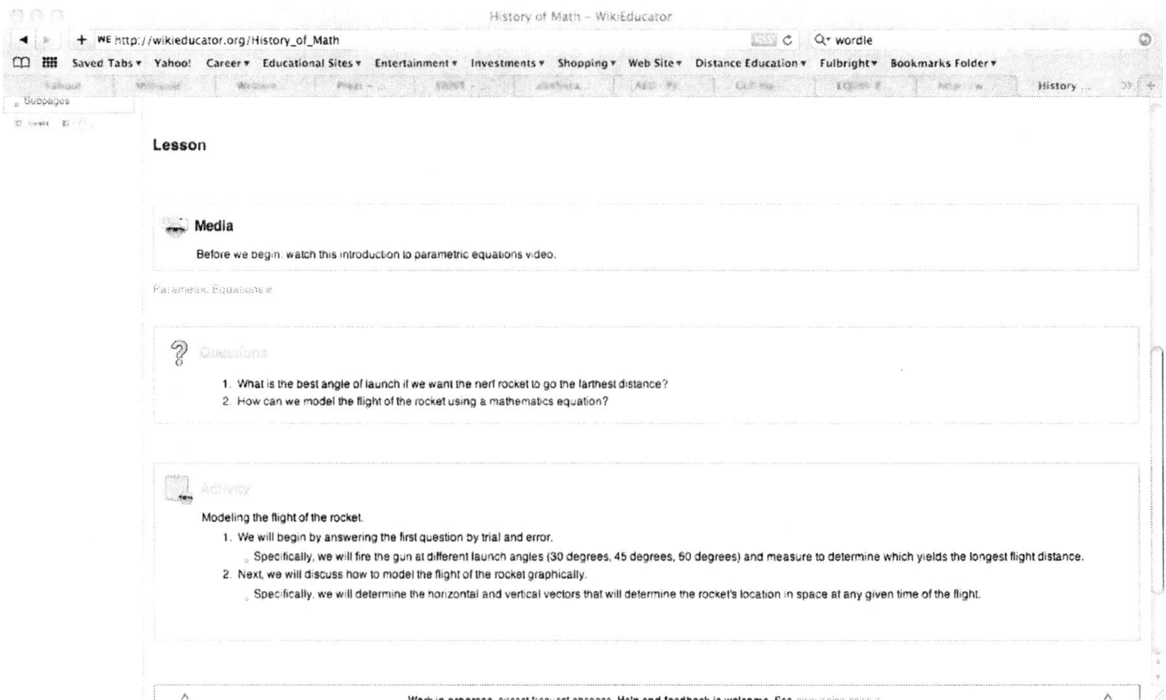

sage. For example, my students would know, before even clicking on the link and hearing my message that if the course announcement title was "test results" and the Voki avatar was a "cool dude" on the beach, that I was happy.

Action Example 2.2: Collaborative Authorship

Sample Wiki

The sample Wikis highlighted in Figure 9 and Figure 10 show an interactive lesson plan that I created with my History of Mathematics class in which I started with the basic outline, then asked my students to contribute additional pieces to complete the lesson.

Action Example 2.3: Creative

Sample Wordle

The Wordle shown in Figure 11 was created by one of my History of Mathematics students as part of her take-home final exam. The question required her to "Create a history of mathematics "wordle" consisting of at least 25 words at http://www.wordle.net/. Then, save your wordle to the gallery (title it "History of Mathematics" and use your name as the author) AND print a copy to turn in with your exam."

Practice Assignment: "Now You Try It"

First, choose a tool from one of the interactive categories (audio / video, collaborative authorship, creative) and then create a "plan" that describes, in some detail, how you will incorporate that tool into a particular lesson, unit, activity, assessment, or project.

Figure 11. History of math Wordle

SECTION 3: COMMUNICATION

Description

Hybrid courses provide an ideal platform from which a teacher can get to know her class and communicate with them, both individually and collectively. The communication tools available may vary with the LMS used, but the basics remain the same. Web-based tools allow teachers to communicate with their students in four specific ways: (1) assessments and grades given in real time with dynamic, current calculations (2) immediate responses to questions or problems via virtual office time (3) long-term dialogs (e.g. over the entire semester or school year) via email and (4) virtual classroom discussions via course discussion boards or online meeting tools.

Most of the communication tools that I use in my classes are part of my university's LMS; however, if your school does not have a license to a commercial LMS like Blackboard and you do not want to create your own online presence with an open-source LMS like Moodle, you can still incorporate these items. There are sites like RCampus which offer, free of charge, all the tools for a complete LMS including the dynamic grade reporting, email, and messaging capabilities. Gmail is one of many sites where you can create an email account, again free of charge, and with Google's new Wave feature, the future of email organization and collaboration is brighter than ever. Virtual meetings can be arranged by using an open-source tool called DimDim, while course discussion boards and virtual chat rooms can be created using the tool Chatzy. Again, for almost every area discussed in this chapter, there are myriad tools available for use; the ones I'm suggesting here are simply my favorites and the ones I have used successfully in my courses.

Advantages and Disadvantages

Making use of the tools for increased communication in your classes is one area where I am hard-pressed to think of any disadvantages. In my experience, having multiple ways for students to communicate with me (and with each other) has always been advantageous and often indispensable as both insurance that the message sent is the one received and as a record of agreements or arrangements. There is no better way to keep everyone involved "honest" than to realize there is a written record of what was said and agreed upon beforehand. I have simply pulled up an email correspondence and shown it to the student to stop the argument of "you told us that..." before it even gets started and, I think, it has the additional bonus of teaching my students to read carefully and pay attention to details (like requirements for an assignment, due dates, procedures for submitting it, etc.).

Action Examples

Action Example 3.1: Immediate and Dynamic Grade Reporting

Sample Grade Report

The screenshots highlighted in Figure 12 and Figure 13 show a sample grade report for an individual student in one of my classes. This screen is indicative of what she would see when she logs into our course using the LMS. As you can see, the report includes a lot of information including her grade for each assessment item, a description of the item (if the teacher wrote one), and statistics (mean and median) for each item.

Practice Assignment: "Now You Try It"

If your school has an LMS like Blackboard or Moodle, create an online presence for your class to use as its "base of operations" – for this assignment, pay particular attention to the communication aspects. Ensure that you have a clear

Figure 12. Sample grades report

Sample Grade for Jade

Grade Information

Item	Grade	Description	Average	Median
Total	166.50 (84.47%)	The unweighted sum of all grades for a user.	73.14	78.89
Survey1	✓		0.00	0.00
Survey2	✓		0.00	0.00
SurveyPts	6.00		4.96	6.00
Act1	2.00		1.50	2.00
Act2	1.50		1.89	2.00
Quiz1	2.00		1.48	2.00
Act3	1.00		1.67	2.00
Lab1	9.50 (A)		8.83	8.00
J1	2.00		1.20	1.00
Test1	14.00 (C-)		13.41	14.00
Quiz2	2.00		1.74	2.00
Act4	1.00	Compass & Straightedge construction	1.65	2.00
Act5	0.00	Patty paper construction	2.13	3.00
J2	2.00		1.13	1.50
Act6	2.50		1.80	2.00
Act7	3.50		2.35	2.50
Midterm	15.00 (50.00%)		15.20	15.00

Figure 13. Sample grades report, continued

Quiz3	3.00		2.22	3.00
J3	1.50		1.28	2.00
Act9	3.00	Lateral logic	2.70	3.00
Congruence	2.00	Worth up to 5 bonus points from problems in sect 4.4 and 4.5	0.76	0.00
Act10	5.00	Hypatia Airlines	4.87	5.00
Lab2	17.00		14.74	15.00
Test2	15.00 (C)		13.33	14.50
Act12	6.00	Proof activity + chance for bonus points from book problems.	3.54	4.00
Quiz4	2.00		2.34	2.00
J4	0.50		0.96	1.00
Act11	1.50		2.07	2.00
Act13	6.00		4.04	3.00
Final Survey	✓		0.00	0.00
Survey_Pts	5.00		3.91	5.00
Final	35.00 (87.50%)		26.13	27.25

way to send and receive emails (both to individual students and to the whole class or selected students, if necessary). Create at least one discussion board or virtual chat room to be used for communication purposes when your class is not meeting F2F.

If your school does not have an LMS already set up for use, create your own educational management system by using some of the tools listed in the resources section. Ensure that you can communicate with your students in the four specific ways mentioned in this section.

SECTION 4: DEMONSTRATION

Description

Often in mathematics courses, especially those designed for pre-service teachers, one of the primary goals is familiarizing the teacher-in-training with the "tools of the trade", whether these are manipulatives, a new graphing calculator, or a useful computer program or web-based applet. Learning a new tool requires a lot of time to become confident and proficient. However, as already mentioned, time is in short supply in our classes and therefore learning these new tools is sometimes overlooked or purposefully avoided. One way to introduce students to new tools without sacrificing F2F class time is to use demonstration tools and put the material online for students to access on their own time. This use of web-based tools to add demonstration time offers the added benefit that the learner can view and review the information as many times as necessary.

Screencasting tools (like Screencast-o-matic and Jing) as well as audio / video tools (like YouTube, Voki, or Viddler) can be put to amazing use in demonstrating how to use software, graphing technology, manipulatives, or other web-based components like applets or virtual models. By creating a screencast, you can record everything you are doing on your computer screen (each item you click on, each menu choice you make, etc.) along with your own voice describing the goals and procedures for whatever it is you are demonstrating. The student then watches it back (like a movie), seeing everything on the screen and hearing you describe it all. Plus, with certain tools like Screencast-o-matic, you can also add notes (specific to a particular timestamp in the screencast), and the student can pause and play any section (for as many times as needed). In creating a video, using a tool like YouTube or Viddler, you can demonstrate anything (not just technology-dependent items like how to use software) just as you would in front of your class. With simple equipment like a microphone and web-camera, you can record yourself discussing, demonstrating, and using a new tool or technique for your students. I will often Viddler myself performing some of the basic, but repetitive, tasks that I know my students must learn how to perform in my class. Some examples include: (listed in parentheses next to each item is the course for which I use these videos)

- Identifying the various types of manipulatives that are in their classroom kit so that they know the name, the primary use, and the major advantages / disadvantages of each manipulative before we actually begin to use them in instruction (Mathematics for Teachers)
- Creating basic graph types (line graph, bar chart, box-and-whiskers graph, and histogram) by hand with small data sets so that they will understand the "basics" before we begin utilizing the graphing technology in the classroom (Probability & Statistics)
- Performing the standard compass-and-straightedge and patty-paper-and-straightedge constructions so my students can review the details of each, both before and after the in-class demonstration (Geometry & Measurement)

I will mention that you don't have to be the one *creating* the demonstration in order to *use* it with your students. I have often supplemented my own instruction and demonstration with those created by others that I found with a simple search on YouTube. I also have offered the links (both my own creations and those I've found created by others) to my colleagues for them to use with their students. Obviously, you want to view the demonstrations yourself before you recommend or require your students to watch them to ensure that (a) the information is accurate (b) the content is an appropriate level for your students (c) the intent of the demonstration is the same as your own.

Advantages and Disadvantages

As with many of the web-based tools discussed so far, the primary advantage of using demonstration tools in your hybrid mathematics class is that of saving F2F instruction time and adding virtual instruction time. With the tools discussed in this section, you can effectively demonstrate something exactly twice (once in front of your students during the F2F meeting and once in front of your computer or webcam) and thus ensure that, at any time for the rest of the course (and even longer if you save the movie files to your own computer hard drive). To me, this is SO much better than, week after week, demonstrating the same tasks to your students during regular class time. In that scenario, part of the class is watching and paying attention (because they needed the review) and part of it is completely bored and ignoring you (because they got it the first time you demonstrated it). So much better then to simply provide the link and let those students who need the extra viewings recognize their own responsibility in their education and watch the demonstrations on their own time.

The main disadvantages I've found to using web-based demonstration tools are (a) I must take the time and make the effort to create the web-version of the demonstration – sometimes I am tempted to try to skip this if I think I can get away with it; however, I always find, after the third or tenth time a student asks me, "Now how did you do….?" that the time is well-spent if I can simply respond, "Here's the link so you can watch it again." (b) I must be careful *when* I let my students know of this additional demonstration material. I find that, if I tell them *before* I have demonstrated it in class, then they will often not be as interested or pay as much attention (as their thinking is, "Well, I can always watch it later."). So, if I plan to both demonstrate in class and provide an online version, then I always tell them about the online version *after* I finish the F2F version. On the other hand, if I only plan to offer them the online version, then I can tell them about all

Figure 14. Screencast article assignment

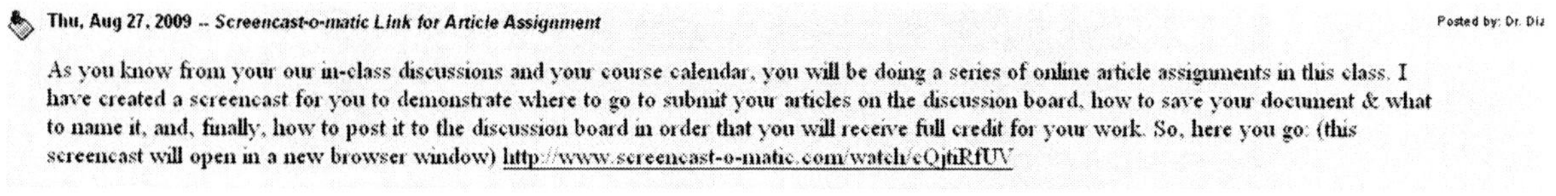

Thu, Aug 27, 2009 -- *Screencast-o-matic Link for Article Assignment* Posted by: Dr. Diz

As you know from your our in-class discussions and your course calendar, you will be doing a series of online article assignments in this class. I have created a screencast for you to demonstrate where to go to submit your articles on the discussion board, how to save your document & what to name it, and, finally, how to post it to the discussion board in order that you will receive full credit for your work. So, here you go: (this screencast will open in a new browser window) http://www.screencast-o-matic.com/watch/cQjtiRfUV

of those links at the beginning of the class, unit, or lesson (as appropriate for their preparation).

Action Examples

Action Example 4.1: Screencast Instructions on How to Post Online Journal

The screenshots shown in Figure 14 and Figure 15 include the course announcement where I inform my students that the procedure for posting their online journals is now available for viewing as a screencast. I also include what the screencast screen looks like. You will notice that it looks just like the LMS (in this case, Blackboard). For this particular demonstration, I show them once (in class) by "walking through the process" that they will perform each week in submitting their online journal assignments. Before the demonstration, I encourage them to take detailed notes and to pay attention even if "it seems easy". After the demonstration in class, I do NOT mention the screencast that I've made. Instead, in the next weekly announcement, I post that there is a screencast that will show them the process again (if, after they have attempted their first journal posting, they realize that their notes and memory are not as good as they thought).

Action Example 4.2: YouTube Demonstration on Solving Parametric Equations

The screenshot seen earlier in the text in Figure 7 is the opening scene of a YouTube video in which the presenter, using a type of interactive whiteboard, is introducing the concept of parametric equations. I chose this video because (a) the presenter has a very non-technical approach and I thought this would be good for my students as they would not, at this stage in the lesson, be familiar with too much vocabulary around this topic (b) the approach of the demonstration is very common-sense and the presenter uses an example (a car driving along a road) that I felt my students would easily understand. Finally, this video was a good choice because this particular presenter has continuation movies (part 2, 3, etc.) on this topic that my students could view for additional information and insight. Also, by choosing a video created by someone else, I saved some of the time it would have taken for me to create it myself. I used this demonstration by asking my students, as part of their preparation work before class, to view the video then answer a series of questions about what they saw, which they then brought to class with them for use in discussion.

Practice Assignment: "Now You Try It"

Decide upon a particular demonstration that you normally give to your students in the F2F meeting. Now, choose the best web-based tool and make a "copy" of that demonstration so your students can view it anytime (and as many times) as they wish. Repeat this assignment so that, when you are done, you have both a screencast-type demonstration and a video-based demonstration to use with your students.

Figure 15. Blackboard course announcement

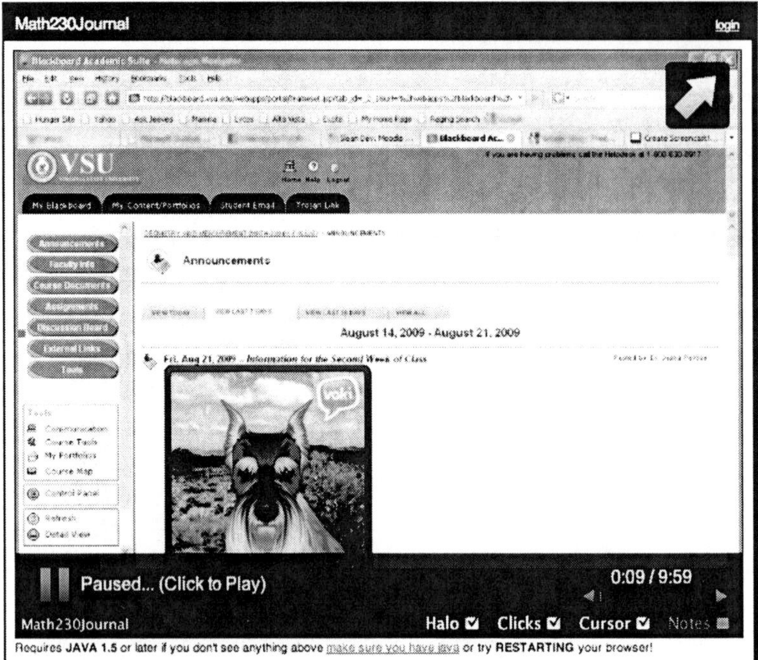

SECTION 5: ASSESSMENT

Description

Assessment is an area often overlooked by teachers in terms of web-based tools. Perhaps this is because of fears of academic dishonesty or privacy issues. However, these concerns, though valid, can be easily resolved with the proper tool and the appropriate use of that tool. I tend to use the assessment tools in primarily three ways: (1) for periodic, low-stakes (a.k.a low percentage) individual evaluation of content (e.g. short weekly quizzes that include more procedural questions) (2) to create and store grading rubrics and student results (e.g. for projects or assignments that often occur over a longer time frame) (3) for occasional individual or group assessment of content that is more open-ended (e.g. take-home exams).

One of my favorite web-based assessment tools is iRubric: a site that can be used to both create online grading rubrics as well as store class grades and individual student results / comments. In the first action example, I show one of the online rubrics I have created and used in iRubric to grade an article abstract assignment. Obviously, you can create a grading rubric using any word processing or spreadsheet program (or even, for that matter, using regular old pen and paper); however, the benefits from using an online service like iRubric include: (1) long term storage, revision, and organization of your rubrics (2) dynamic, "fill-able" forms that you can then save & send to your students (3) access to additional rubrics created by others that you can use and revise (4) a virtual "space" in which to save the grades and results of all your students (which I often use as a backup to my LMS).

Advantages and Disadvantages

To me, the primary advantage to using web-based tools for assessment purposes is that it cuts down on the amount of paper I must carry around with me (and keep up with until I give it back to the students). I used to, for example, ask students to write journal-type entries during the last ten minutes of class or as homework assignments. Then, I would collect them, take them home, grade them (marking grades / comments as I went), and, finally, pass them back to the students. When you multiply the number of students I had in each class by the number of classes I had by the number of times per week I had them doing this type of assignment, the amount of paper I was hauling around easily became equivalent to a few more textbooks. In addition, the process was not always flawless; occasionally, I would lose a particular students journal entry (especially if it was written on a different-sized paper than the others in the class or if was turned in at a different time than the rest) or, when students were absent, end up carrying around "old" papers for days or even weeks before I was able to return them. By moving this particular assessment item to the online realm, I alleviated all of these issues. Now, the students submit their online journal entries electronically. I "collect" them all and save them to my computer or portable storage device. Then, using my online assessment tool (like a fill-able grading rubric), I evaluate each journal (still making comments and assigning a grade as I go), and simply post the results to the online gradebook or email the link to my student so they can retrieve the marked document whenever they wish.

There are two primary disadvantages to using web-based assessment tools: (1) the "up front" time it takes to design the assessment / grading rubric and (2) the "learning curve" (again, in terms of time, but also sometimes patience) it takes to learn how to use the tool in the most efficient and effective manner. Both of these disadvantages turn into advantages, however, if you tend to teach the same types of classes as the revision / re-use of these items is MUCH easier to do in an online format than a hardcopy one.

Action Examples

Action Example 5.1: iRubric Tool

The grading rubric shown in Figure 16 was created using iRubric and I used it to assess the individual assignment where I ask students to read an article then write an abstract about it. Although it is not obvious in this screenshot, there is an additional column for each assessment item that allows the teacher to enter comments for the student (e.g. explanations describing what was good or lacking in their work). In addition, each cell of the form is selectable and, once you have completed the entire thing, iRubric will display the student's score in a form like: "11 out of 14 points (79%)". Lastly, the site will both store the grades for the entire class and give you the option to save each student's completed rubric as separate files.

Action Example 5.2: Take-Home Midterm Exam

This course announcement informs my students that their take-home midterm exam is available for download (see Figure 17). Note that I include details like telling the students that the file itself is password-protected and giving them detailed instructions on how to save and submit their finished work. I should also mention that, unlike traditional exam questions, take-home exam questions tend to be questions that are unique to an individual student (thus, taking away the ability to "copy" from someone else's work). Here are some examples of the types of questions on this particular exam:

1. Write the day and year of your birth in each of the following numeration systems:
    a. Hindu-Arabic numerals
    b. Egyptian hieroglyphics
    c. Babylonian cuneiform
    d. Ionic (Roman) Greek numerals
    e. Traditional Chinese

Figure 16. Grading rubric

Article Abstract			
	Poor or Missing 1 pts	Satisfactory 1 pts	Superior 2 pts
Format?	Poor or Missing More than 1 item INCORRECT from guidelines: margins, font size, spacing, etc.	Satisfactory 1 item INCORRECT from guidelines: margins, font size, spacing, etc.	Superior All items CORRECT from guidelines: margins, font size, spacing, etc.
Length?	Poor or Missing Less than half a single-spaced page long.	Satisfactory At least 1 full single-spaced page long.	Superior More than 1 full single-spaced page long.
Information?	Poor or Missing More than 1 item MISSING from guidelines: author, journal, title, date, etc.	Satisfactory Only 1 item MISSING from guidelines: author, journal, title, date, etc.	Superior All items INCLUDED from guidelines: author, journal, title, date, etc.
Submission?	Poor or Missing File name and/or posting are INCORRECT.	Satisfactory Posting is CORRECT but file name has minor error (e.g. .rtf format instead of .doc).	Superior BOTH file name AND posting are CORRECT.
Spelling & Grammar?	Poor or Missing Major spelling and/or grammar errors are present.	Satisfactory Less than 2 minor spelling and/or grammar errors are present. Example of good quality graduate writing.	Superior No spelling or grammar errors are present. Example of high quality graduate writing.
Quality of Summary?	Poor or Missing The summary section of the abstract does NOT clearly, accurately, and/or succinctly convey the basic ideas presented in the article in the student's own words. Three or more quotations are given and may not be cited properly.	Satisfactory The summary section of the abstract clearly, accurately, and succinctly conveys the basic ideas presented in the article in the student's own words. Less than three quotations are given and are cited properly.	Superior The summary section of the abstract clearly, accurately, and succinctly conveys the detailed ideas presented in the article in the student's own words and shows deep understanding and connection of the material discussed. Less than three quotations are given and are cited properly.
Quality of Reaction?	Poor or Missing The reaction section of the abstract includes mostly vague sentiments that do not demonstrate understanding of how the material presented	Satisfactory The reaction section of the abstract includes specific, detailed information that demonstrates adequate understanding of how the	Superior The reaction section of the abstract includes specific, detailed information that demonstrates excellent understanding of how the

2. Go to our course page on Blackboard and read everyone's article submissions for the first online article assignment. Then, choose TWO people. For each, reply to their post and address the following prompts and then take a "screen shot" (by using the "Print Screen" key on your keyboard) of each reply that you post and include it in your exam (both file and hardcopy):
    - Give a thoughtful and thorough evaluation of their summary of the article; include comments discussing what you found particularly well-written or insightful as well as comments on what you believe might have been overlooked or misunderstood
    - Give a thoughtful and thorough evaluation of their reaction to the article; include comments discussing your personal experience and whether or not it agreed with what they wrote

Did you notice how, by asking for personal information (like the day and year of the student's birth), it creates a unique question for each person and thus makes it harder for students to cheat? In the second question, including "comments discussing your personal experience" achieves the same result: as everyone's personal experience is different, the way they answer the question is unique for each student. Also did you notice how, as I've mentioned before, the web-based tools themselves may be used in different categories? In

Figure 17. Midterm exam announcement

Wed, Sep 30, 2009 -- ***Information about Midterm Exam*** Posted by: Dr. Dian.

Look, it's not even 11:59 pm when I'm posting this! :-)

As per your decision in our last class, I have created a take home midterm exam for you. You may download the take-home exam from the **Assignments** folder from the COURSE DOCUMENTS link. **Important Note: you will need a password to open this file! The password is my last name (proper spelling and capitalization).** Please carefully read and follow the directions given in the exam itself and here in this announcement. The electronic copy of your midterm should be saved in a file named "*yourlastname*_midterm.doc" and submitted via the "safe assign" link titled "Submit_Midterm" (also from the **Assignments** folder from the COURSE DOCUMENTS link). Additional Note: I'm "testing" this new feature in BB so there may be "issues". If you have technical issues, then you must call the 800 help desk number for BB; if you have other issues, then you may contact me via email (or come to my office). Please remember that we ARE meeting on Tuesday of midterms for (a) you to turn in your hardcopy of your exam and (b) us to discuss lesson plans (that means you need to bring your lesson plan draft with you to class along with your notebook and any additional items you have for your lesson plan). Email me if you have questions, concerns, etc. Good luck & make me proud!! :-)

this case, I am using the course discussion board as part of assessment.

Practice Assignment: "Now You Try It"

Think of a particular assignment that you typically give to your students and assess as part of their overall course grade. Now add a web-based element to it. You may, for example:

- Create a short (e.g. three question) online quiz that does a "quick check for understanding"
- Create an online grading rubric for use with a more in-depth assessment item like a project or paper
- Create a longer, more substantial, evaluation of content that includes more personalized questions in the form of a take-home exam

CONCLUSION

Before the decision to incorporate web-based tools and appropriate technology into my mathematics courses, I found myself spending more time re-teaching and noticed a distinct lack of both involvement and responsibility in my students. After transforming my classes into a hybrid format, I see distinct, measurable, positive improvements in both areas. First, I am able to spend more class time discussing the material that my students needed to learn (rather than reviewing material they should have already learned or preparing them for some future material that we can't get to since they are not ready yet). Second, my students are now active participants in their own learning process – there are now specific tasks assigned to each role of teacher and learner; and, because of this, the onus of responsibility has moved to a more correct location rather than being centralized solely around the teacher. These web-based tools allow both of us (me and my students) to get the most out of our time together.

In this chapter on best practices for teaching a hybrid mathematics course, I discussed five types of web-based tools: Content Presentation, Interactive Elements, Communication, Demonstration, and Assessment. I have listed what I believe to be the major advantages and disadvantages for each tool. To explain further, I presented specific examples to illustrate how I have successfully incorporated these times into my classes and the benefits and rewards that both my students and I reaped from them. Practice assignments are offered as an opportunity to put to use what you have learned. Resources are listed for each set of tools in an effort to provide further information and the chance to learn more. Finally, I hope that, collectively, this chapter describes a useful set of best practices that you can incorporate into your hybrid mathematics course.

Resources: Where to Go for More

Learning Management Systems

- http://demo.moodle.net/ (Moodle Demonstration Site)
- http://www.rcampus.com/help/about/course_and_learning_management_system.cfm? (Open source LMS)
- http://www.rcampus.com/ (RCampus website)

Moodle Video Tutorial Sites

- http://www.moodletutorials.org/
- http://moodle-tutorials.blogspot.com/
- http://www.lynda.com/home/DisplayCourse.aspx?lpk2=47547

Blackboard Video Tutorial Sites

- http://ondemand.blackboard.com/
- http://www.lynda.com/home/websearch.aspx?q=Blackboard

Audio / Video Tools

- www.voki.com (Voki website)
- www.viddler.com (Viddler website)
- www.youtube.com (YouTube website)

Collaborative Authorship Tools

- http://wikieducator.org/Wikieducator_tutorial (Wiki Tutorials)
- www.wikipedia.org (Wikipedia)
- http://www.youtube.com/docs (GoogleDocs learning videos)
- http://www.slideshare.net/Andreatej/voicethread-tutorial (VoiceThread tutorial)
- http://voicethread.ning.com/ (VoiceThread for Educators)

Creative Tools

- www.wordle.com (Wordle website)
- http://www.ideastoinspire.co.uk/wordle.htm (47 interesting ways to use Wordle in your classroom)

Online Meeting Tools

- http://www.dimdim.com/ (DimDim website)
- http://www.chatzy.com/ (Virtual Chat Rooms)

Email Tools

- http://gmail.com (Gmail)
- http://wave.google.com (Google Wave)

Screencasting Tools

- http://www.techsmith.com/jing/ (Jing website)
- www.screencastomatic.com (Screencast-o-matic website)

Assessment Tools

- http://www.respondus.com (Respondus website)
- http://www.irubric.com (iRubric website)

REFERENCES

Bersin, J. (2004). *The blended learning book: Best practices, proven methodologies, and lessons learned*. San Francisco, CA: Jossey-Bass.

Dzuiban, C., Hartman, J., & Moskal, P. (2004). Blended Learning. *EDUCAUSE Center for Applied Research. Research Bulletin (Sun Chiwawitthaya Thang Thale Phuket), 2004*(7). http://www.educause.edu/ ECAR/ BlendedLearning/ 157515.

NASULGC. (2010). *Sloan National Commission on Online Learning benchmarking study: Preliminary findings*. Needham, MA: The Sloan Consortium. Retrieved on October 26, 2010, from http://sloanconsortium.org/ sites/ default/ files/ NASULGC.pdf

Pape, L. (2006, August 1). *From bricks to clicks: Blurring classroom/cyber lines: Blended learning combines the elements of online and face-to-face teaching approaches*. The Free Library. Retrieved October 26, 2010, from http://www.thefreelibrary.com/From bricks to clicks: blurring classroom/ cyber lines: blended...-a0149514814

Picciano, A., & Seaman, J. (2009). *K–12 online learning - A 2008 follow-up of the survey of U.S. school district administrators*. Needham, MA: The Sloan Consortium. Retrieved October 26, 2010, from http://sloanconsortium.org/ sites/ default/ files/ k-12_online_learning_ 2008.pdf

Southern Regional Education Board. (2009). *Overcoming doubts about online learning*. Atlanta, GA: Educational Technology Cooperative.

Spilka, R. (2002). Approximately "real world" learning with the hybrid model. *Teaching with Technology Today, 8*(6). Retrieved from http:// www.uwsa.edu/ ttt/ articles/ spilka.htm

Watson, J. (2008). *Blended learning: The convergence of online and face-to-face education*. Vienna, VA: The North American Council for Online Learning.

KEY TERMS AND DEFINITIONS

Applet: Any small application that performs one specific task and sometimes runs within the context of a larger program (i.e. browser plugin). It usually refers to programs written in the Java programming language that can be included in an HTML web page.

Avatar: A computer user's representation of himself/herself or alter ego whether in the form of a three-dimensional model used in computer games, a two-dimensional icon (picture) or a one-dimensional username used on Internet forums and other communities, or a text construct found on early systems such as MUDs (multi-user dungeon). It is an object representing the user.

BB: BlackBoard Learning Management System; incorporates course management, content management and community/portal systems to facilitate e-learning.

Collaborative Authorship: The act of co-creating and consulting within a group of people to create a project, in which the author of the project is the group itself rather than a single person.

Distance Education: A field of education that focuses on the pedagogy, technology, and instructional system with the goal of delivering education to students who are not physically "on site" in a traditional classroom or campus.

Hybrid Course: A course with mixed medium instruction featuring a combination of the traditional classroom format and a distance-learning format (i.e. web-based learning, videoconferencing, etc). It is also referred to as "blended learning" or "mixed mode instruction".

F2F: Face-to-Face interaction with students

Learning Management System: A software application for the administration, documentation, tracking, and reporting of training programs, classroom and online events, e-learning programs, and training content.

Open-Source Software: Computer software that is available in source code form for which the source code and certain other rights normally reserved for copyright holders are provided under a software license that permits users to study, change, and improve the software.

PDF: Portable Document Format, an open standard document exchange file format that was created by Adobe Systems in 1993. It is a *de facto* document format standard that allows users to share files with others who don't have the same software, computer platform (i.e. Mac, Windows, Linux, etc) as well as use many other web-centric document features.

Screenshot (Screen Capture or Screen Dump): An image taken by the computer to record the visible items displayed on the monitor, television, or another visual output device. A *screenshot* is when one saves the output of an entire screen into a common image format such as a bitmap, PNG file or JPEG file. A *screen dump* literally "dumps" the contents of whatever application it is using into an internal data file. A *screen capture* captures the contents of your screen over an extended period of time to create a video file (also known as a *screencast*).

Screencasting: A digital recording of a computer screen that is shared with other users in video format. In online education, this technology allows the student and teacher to interact easily over any distance.

Voice-Thread: A collaborative, multimedia slide show that holds images, documents, and videos and allows people to navigate pages and leave comments in 5 ways - using voice (with a microphone or telephone), text, audio file, or video (via a webcam).

Web 2.0: The second generation of the World Wide Web, especially the movement away from static webpages to dynamic and shareable content and social networking. Examples of Web 2.0 include social networking sites, blogs, wikis, video-sharing sites, hosted services and web applications.

Webcam: An abbreviation for "web camera".

Wiki: A website that allows the easy creation and editing of any number of interlinked web pages via a web browser using a simplified markup language or a WYSIWYG text editor.

Chapter 6
Implementation of Learning Outcomes in Mathematics for Non-Mathematics Major by Using E-Learning

B. Divjak
University of Zagreb, Croatia

ABSTRACT

Learning outcomes are considered to be a key tool for student-centered teaching and learning. They can be successfully implemented in teaching and learning mathematics on higher educational level and together with appropriate level of technology enhanced learning can provide the framework for successful learning process even for students that have not been primarily interested in mathematics. The aim is to present the case study of implementation of learning outcomes and e-learning in several mathematical courses at the Faculty of Organization and Informatics of the University of Zagreb. First of all, there are examples of mathematical courses in the first year since the first study year is crucial for retaining students. Further, there are mathematical courses taught at higher years of undergraduate study and the first year of graduate study. Again, educational process is appropriately supported by ICT and executed through blended e-learning, as well as the use of social software.

DOI: 10.4018/978-1-60960-875-0.ch006

INTRODUCTION

In this chapter the aim is to present the case study of implementation of learning outcomes in several mathematical subjects within study programs of informatics that is supported by e-learning. There are several reasons for implementation of e-learning and learning outcomes and they will be explained later in this chapter. Besides, the theoretical background of learning outcomes, blended learning and teaching mathematics to non-mathematics major will be discussed. There are four courses that serve as case studies and they will be described and analysed in this chapter: Mathematics 1 (1st semester undergraduate study), Mathematics 2 (2nd semester undergraduate), Selected chapters in mathematics (4th semester undergraduate) and Discrete mathematics with graph theory (5th semester undergraduate and 1st semester graduate). These courses are a part of the Information and Business Systems (IBS) study program at the Faculty of Organization and Informatics of the University of Zagreb.

University of Zagreb is the oldest and biggest Croatian and Southeast European University. It was founded in 1669 and today it has around 60 000 students and it consists of 29 faculties, three art academies and two centers. One of the faculties is the Faculty of Organization and Informatics (FOI) founded in 1962, which is today a teaching and research institution providing research in information technology, business system, information sciences in general, as well as in mathematics. There are 2700 students enrolled in the academic year 2009/10 and they are mainly taught in accordance with the blended learning approach. FOI itself has study programs at all levels: undergraduate, graduate and postgraduate, following the Bologna Declaration requirements enforced by law in 2003 and incorporated into the organization of studies.

The main objectives for implementation of e-learning and learning outcomes are to increase retention of students, improve unfavourable position of some underrepresented groups in ICT study, meet the demands of employability, as well as of teaching large heterogeneous student groups. Here, we will briefly introduce two important problems we have been facing: a high drop-out rate and the under-representation of female students in ICT. A high drop-out rate and the fairly long study duration are problems plaguing many Central and East European countries including Croatia. The approach in higher education teaching, which can be summed up as an ex cathedra, teacher-centered approach, used to be a typical pattern of teaching in Croatia before the Bologna reform. This approach was especially common in teaching mathematics. It was one of the factors which caused the high drop-out rate in Croatian universities, especially in those study programs that had mathematics in its first study year. According to two different sources, only 1/3 or 1/2 of enrolled students completed their course of study. The percentage of those who got their diploma in the time set for the course is even lower. The average duration of the study of Informatics (ICT) was between 6 and 7 years instead of 4.5 or 5 years specified by official regulations. The system was inefficient and highly traditional. In such circumstances, even though it has not been widely accepted by all academics, the significance of the Bologna reform is in its contribution to creating solutions and introducing necessary changes. In this context it is particularly necessary to reflect on teaching and learning mathematics.

Furthermore, women seem to be strongly underrepresented in ICT. This is partly the result of many myths about underperformance of women in typically male areas such as ICT and mathematics. Between 250 and 300 students enrol in the undergraduate study programs of Informatics at FOI each year and among them only about 20% are female students. Therefore the specific objective of the research reported here is to improve student retention in mathematics by means of enhancing teaching methods, with the awareness of gender issues. Further, because the University of Zagreb and especially FOI has introduced an E-learning strategy, one can investigate the capacity of ICT in order to fulfill the abovementioned objective.

Let us emphasize at the beginning that our approach to teaching and learning is based on the paradigm that pedagogy precedes technology and that setting educational goals comes before looking for appropriate ICT tools or other media. The dilemma about the appropriate usage and influence of media on learning is not something new. There was the great "media debate" started in the 1990s by Richard Clark and Robert Kozma, when Clark (Clark, 1983) presented the analogy of technology's role in learning as having no more effect than a grocery truck contributes to the quality of the produce it carries and Kozma (Kozma, 1994) stressed that the usage of computer technology is the most effective when it supports active engagement within the curriculum. That is the reason why we start this chapter with the section on learning outcomes. In this section on learning outcomes the theoretical background of teaching and learning in higher education (HE) is provided as an introduction to the approaches to and key principals of teaching in HE. Further, case studies of implementation of learning outcomes on the program and the course level are given, as well as the example of fulfilling the learning outcome concerning mathematical modeling in different mathematical courses. The section is concluded with recommendations about the evaluation of learning outcomes.

The next section concerns blended learning approach where the case studies are mainly taken from courses Mathematics 1 and Mathematics 2 that are taught in the first year of undergraduate IBS study program. At the beginning of the section the fundamental guidelines of the E-learning strategy are presented. After that, two examples are described where the blended learning approach contributes to the solution of the problem: enhancing students' pre-knowledge and retention. At the end of the section there are results of several student evaluations of the blended learning approach. The third section is dedicated to the use of social software in mathematics and two case studies are described and analysed. First, there is a subsection on the use of wiki in the course Discrete mathematics with graph theory, with the aim of supporting collaborative learning and problem solving and then a subsection on the implementation of an e-portfolio in the course Selected chapters in mathematics where the intention is to stimulate students' reflection on their learning and progress. Again, student evaluation of the implementation is provided.

A LEARNING OUTCOMES APPROACH TO TEACHING AND LEARNING MATHEMATICS

Approaches to Teaching in Higher Education

In theory, as well as in practice, we distinguish between three basic approaches to teaching (Ramsden, 2003; Entwistle, 2000). The first one, often called traditional, is the one in which the teacher is in the centre of the teaching process. In the second one, the teacher can also appear as the one who organizes activities directed to learning. The third approach puts the student in the centre of the teaching and learning process. It is important to implement the third approach in teaching mathematics in order to awake interest and enhance retention of students (Din & Wheatley, 2007). Especially, (Haruta & Stevenson, 1999) reported on student-centred approach integrated into an institution-wide first year college curriculum. Findings of the project indicated increased freshmen enrolment and retention rates in science, mathematics, engineering and technology disciplines.

In professional public the topic of recognizing the key principles of teaching in higher education is widely discussed. Being inspired primarily by (Ramsden, 2003), but also taking into consider-

Table 1. Teaching principles in higher education

Principles	Instruments
Clear goals and intellectual challenge	Learning outcomes and goals setting in line with the demands of modern life and the appropriate use of *technology* that also communicate high expectations
Interest, understanding and deep learning	Good teaching and appropriate literature as well as quality *online material* and various ways of student-student and student-teacher communication including *online communication* that encourages deep learning
Concern and respect for students and student learning	Appropriate student's workload (expressed for example in European Credit Transfer System – ECTS), taking into account student's effort invested in working in *Learning management system* (LMS) that has to help diverse student population, and emphasizing time on task
Appropriate assessment and prompt feedback	Implementation of taxonomy, rubrics, creative ways of problem solving and the *use of technology* for regular and motivating assessment that respects diverse talents and ways of learning and after each assessment activity prompt feedback on task performed
Development of subject specific as well as generic skills	Learning outcomes that besides subject specific skills also include generic skills development and assessment methods that stress their importance, as well as the use of *social software* in order to enhance the development of generic skills
Learning from students	Quality assurance system and enhancement of teaching and teacher's personal development that takes into account students evaluation of teaching and learning (*online evaluation and reflection*) as well as analysis of results of students learning in order to introduce effective changes

ation (Chickering & Gamson, 1987), (Smittle, 2003) and our own teaching and research experience, we give the most important principles and corresponding instruments in Table 1. According to (Chickering & Gamson, 1987), which are perhaps the most widely used general principles for good practice in undergraduate education, this good practice includes: encourage student-faculty contact, promote cooperation among students, encourage active learning, give prompt feedback, emphasize time on task, communicate high expectations, and respect diverse talents. Additionally, (Smittle, 2003) put more emphasis on the commitment to teaching under-prepared students and diverse student population, providing an open and responsive learning environment, as well as on engaging in an ongoing evaluation and professional development. Finally, it is an assumption that quality assessment can be used to improve the quality of student learning and to promote deep learning style (Entwistle, 1995; Entwistle, 2000). Principles that are listed in Table 1 are mainly taken from (Ramsden, 2003) and then slightly modified. Instruments that are given in the second column are closely related to the practice we introduce in teaching mathematics at FOI and emphasize the use of technology enhanced teaching-learning environment. These instruments will be thoroughly described later.

Learning Outcomes Approach

One of the most important instruments that supports student-centred approach and key principles of teaching in higher education is learning outcomes. Let us emphasize that learning outcomes are statements about what is expected of the student to know, to understand, to be able to do and to evaluate as a result of the learning process. They are connected with measurable level descriptors in national and European qualifications framework. In the implementation of learning outcomes both the top-down approach and the bottom-up approach need to be combined. Whereas the former takes into account the overall study program and the level of study, the latter departs from the level of a particular unit and course. In devising the instructions in mathematics for non-mathematics majors it is essential to recognize the role which mathematical tools and models play in such a study program. In doing so, students' pre-knowledge of

Table 2. Cox taxonomy – MATH-KIT

Level	Description	Verbs
Knowledge – K	defining and understanding of terms; routine skills and techniques; simple application of formulas and theorems	remember, recognize, define, identify
Interpretation – I	interpretation of theorems and problems, awareness of consequences and limitations of theorems, proof of theorems;	understand, analysis, distinguish, investigate, prove
Transfer – T	transfer to new context; application theorems and theory in new areas; creating of new application; formulation of hypothesis; construction of new up-graded methods and models	application, evaluation, synthesis/create, design, formulate

mathematics should by no means be disregarded and we will refer to it in the next section.

In the process of construction of learning outcomes, taxonomy should be used. The most widely used taxonomy for the construction of learning outcomes is Bloom's taxonomy (Bloom et al., 1956). He identified three domains of educational activities: cognitive or mental skills (knowledge), affective or growth in feelings or emotional areas (attitude) and psychomotor or physical skills (skills). According to Bloom, a learner who is able to perform at higher levels of the taxonomy also demonstrates a more complex level of cognitive thinking. Bloom's classification of cognitive skills has six hierarchical stages: knowledge, comprehension, application, analysis, synthesis and evaluation. All these stages can be defined by verbs that describe related behaviours. Anderson, a former student of Bloom, revisited the cognitive domain in the learning taxonomy and changed the names of the six categories from noun to verb forms and slightly rearranged them (Anderson et al., 2001). According to Anderson, the revised Bloom taxonomy has the following categories: remembering, understanding, applying, analysing, evaluating and creating. The Bloom taxonomy is a very useful tool in the process of construction of a study program learning outcomes.

However, according to our teaching experience and reference literature (Cox, 2003; Biggs, 2005) Bloom's taxonomy is not very suitable for the construction of learning outcomes in mathematics as it is too complicated for everyday use, especially if the teacher wants to use it to systemize the assessment process. Therefore we have to look for taxonomies which have been designed primarily for mathematics. Several taxonomies have been taken into consideration for the purpose of this research: Galbraith & Haines (Galbraith & Haines, 1998 and 2001), Smith et al. (Smith et al., 1996) – MATH taxonomy, TIMSS (TIMSS, 2003), SOLO (Biggs, 1995) and Cox (Cox, 2003) – MATH-KIT taxonomy. We have decided to use MATH-KIT since it is a practitioner friendly taxonomy of learning objectives for mathematics and enables the design of teaching, learning and assessment strategy according to the learning outcomes of a study program. As it is shown in Table 2, MATH-KIT, similarly to MATH taxonomy, divides mathematical skills into three levels: knowledge, interpretation and transfer.

Case Study of Implementing Learning Outcome on the Program and Course Level

It will be explained in the following sections how the MATH-KIT taxonomy is used in order to build the data base of exercises and how we can combine the usage of the Bloom taxonomy on the study program level and the MATH-KIT taxonomy on the course level. Further, the choice of teaching methods must be done according to the defined level of the learning outcome. Finally, this should help us to design a valid and reliable assessment strategy. We will illustrate it by using

Table 3. Learning outcomes at the study program level and course level

Learning outcome at the IBS study program	Learning outcomes at Mathematics 1 course associate with given learning outcome on the IBS study program level
(LO1) The ability to understand and apply mathematical methods, models and techniques appropriate for solving problems in the field of information and business systems	*students have to be able to … differ between methods for solving systems of linear equations and apply appropriate method in a given system;… … understand and reproduce correctly formal mathematical proof of selected number of statements by applying mathematical logic.*
(LO2) The ability to understand and apply study skills needed for life-long learning and continuation of education at the graduate study level	*students have to be able to … use mathematical literature from different sources (including online), at least one tool for mathematical text editing and the system for e-learning taking into consideration characteristic of mathematics*
(LO3) The ability to model business processes and data in organizations and implement these models in the development of information and business systems	*students have to be able to … describe mathematical concepts that are needed as prerequisites for IT courses*

Table 4. Mathematical modeling tasks in different courses

Courses	Mathematics 1 (Math 1)	Mathematics 2 (Math 2)	Selected chapters of mathematics (SCM)	Discrete mathematics with graph theory (DMGT)
Semester	**1st semester undergraduate**	**2nd semester undergraduate**	**4th semester undergraduate**	**5th semester undergraduate and 1st semes. graduate**
Size of teaching groups	Big	Big	Big/Medium	Small
Main requirement	*Literature search* about given problem and correct compilation into 3 pages text	*Simple real problem given* to be solved using math techniques that are explained in advance	*Complex real problem given* that needs to be researched on; theoretical and practical solution (for ex. software) must be provided	Problems and solution provided by students; transfer of mathematical knowledge in *new context* (explained further in separate section)
LO taxonomy MATH-KIT Bloom (verb)	**Knowledge** Describe	**Knowledge /Interpretation** Solve	**Interpretation /Transfer** Analyze/Combine	**Transfer** Evaluation
Project type	Essay	Problem exercise	Problem solving two-disciplinary (math/IT)	Interdisciplinary problem solving and setting
Team work /Individual	Individual	Individual	Team	Team
ICT support On-line work	Upload essay Assessment in Moodle	Upload exercise Feedback in Moodle	Upload theoretical and practical work Analyzes in e-portfolio	Development, solving in wiki Communication in Moodle

More about introduction of learning outcomes in mathematics can be found in (Divjak & Ostroški, 2009) and for those who are specially interested in the outcome-based education (Biggs & Tang, 2007) can be recommended.

an example of problem solving and essay writing exercises in mathematics (Table 4).

After determining the levels of the study programme and agreeing about professional competencies required by students, the learning outcomes of the study programme are developed. To illustrate this some of the learning outcomes at the level of undergraduate study program of Information and Business System (IBS) that are recognized to be fulfilled on mathematical courses are listed in Table 3 in the first column and in the second column there are a few learning outcomes of the course Mathematics 1 associated with the given learning outcomes on the IBS study program level.

Consequently it is clear that mathematics courses are not in the program as independent subjects but have to serve the given purpose – contribute to the fulfilment of learning outcomes of the study program. In this respect teaching and learning mathematics in study programs that don't have mathematics per se as ultimate goal has to be researched separately from the case of study programs of mathematics as a major.

Learning outcomes of the study program have to be refined at the course level e.g. learning outcomes on a course level have to be much more operational and have to describe teaching and learning process but they need to enable student assessment and course evaluation. For example, some of learning outcomes in Mathematics 1 are given in Table 3.

Case Study of the Learning Outcome Concerning Mathematical Modeling

Further, the "responsibility" for fulfilment of the learning outcome (LO1) of study program concerning mathematical modelling has been divided among four mathematical courses: three on the undergraduate level and one that can be taken on both the undergraduate and graduate level. Further, these tasks also contribute to (LO2) because problem setting and assessment have been supported by ICT, since students use LMS and social software to work on problem-solving exercises. Learning outcome, similar but stronger in the sense of requirement, exists also on the graduate level. Afterwards, learning outcomes at the level of teaching units are detailed and appropriate methods of teaching and assessment are chosen. The aim is, at least for the courses in a higher semester, to promote deep strategic approach to studying, which is only possible if assessment procedures emphasise and reward personal understanding (Entwistle, 2000).

In Table 4, main characteristics of our approach are presented. Some of the examples are described in more details further in the text. There are four different courses that we analyse and they differ considerably regarding listed characteristics. Mathematics 1 and Mathematics 2 have big teaching groups that consist of 130-150 students to be lectured and 30-40 in seminar groups and in Discrete mathematics with graph theory there are usually 15-30 students all together. Main requirements regarding mathematical modelling tasks vary from very simple in Mathematics 1 and Mathematics 2 to rather complex in Selected chapters in mathematics (SCM) and those that require transfer of knowledge into a new context (DMGT). All of them can be described by Bloom as well as MATH-KIT taxonomy and the associated verbs are given in Table 4, but distinctions between various tasks are more obvious when we apply Cox taxonomy. Further, students start with an essay type task (Math 1), then they have to produce a problem solving exercise (Math 2) and broaden the scope by combining mathematics and informatics disciplines in problem solving. Finally they have to participate not just in problem solving but also in problem setting. This step by step approach helps them to build up problem solving and research skills. At the same time they gradually need to develop their team working abilities (generic skills!) because they start with individual work and progress towards rather complex team collaborative learning. Finally, all these exercises are supported by ICT and on-line work and that will be described in more details in the following sections.

BLENDED LEARNNING APPROACH: CASE STUDIES OF MATHEMATICS 1 AND MATHEMATICS 2

Strategy for E-Learning Implementation

Although it is very important, pedagogy is not the only factor in determining the course design and especially not the whole study program. Other factors will include available finances, time and resources, as well as intended audience (Weller, 2007) and therefore the organization should have the strategy for e-learning implementation where all above mentioned factors can be considered.

For some years we at FOI have been considering e-learning as an unavoidable and a very important element of the teaching process at our institution, which essentially contributes to the quality of the teaching process and especially to the accessibility of the teaching materials. The result of such an approach is the acquired E-learning strategy of the Faculty of Organization and Informatics (E-learning Strategy of the FOI, 2007), which relies on the E-learning Strategy of the University of Zagreb (E-learning Strategy of the UniZg, 2007).

By introducing and actively using e-learning, FOI intends to improve the quality of the teaching process and the learning outcomes, to render students (future citizens of the society of knowledge) capable for lifelong learning, enable widening participation in higher education and ensure the conspicuous position of the faculty on the international education market. In the framework of the strategy, the blended learning has been chosen as the most appropriate one for the needs of teaching at our faculty, and conforming to this, three levels of blended learning have been determined. Today at the Faculty level there are 260 online blended learning courses at all three study levels. It means that all courses have been "covered" by their counterparts in LMS and that every student and teacher has experience with e-learning.

In the next two subsections two examples will be described where the blended learning approach contributes to the solution of problems. These problems are the enhancement of students' pre-knowledge in order to be able to progress in first year mathematics and the improvement of the retention rate of students, which is very often heavily influenced by the retention rate of the students in first year mathematical courses.

Enhancing Students' Pre-Competencies

After the learning outcomes have been recognized, they are harmonized with students' pre-competencies, teaching methods, student workload (ECTS), continuous monitoring of students' achievements and their assessment, while taking into account different learning and motivation styles as well as their attitudes towards mathematics. Students' performance in a particular study program depends on many factors but is initially heavily influenced by the background pre-knowledge and especially, the motivation for entering the study program (Bruinsma, 2004). Our recent research on this topic has been described in (Divjak et al., 2010) and (Vidacek Hains et al., 2009) and the results of the survey of motivation factors for entering a study program show equal influence of intrinsic and extrinsic motivation. As it was pointed out earlier, in that research special emphasis was put on gender differences in learning mathematics because female students are strongly underrepresented in ICT.

It is important to evaluate initial students' competencies (pre-knowledge) in every course and to compare them with output competencies, in order to evaluate the students' progress in a specific subject. It is clear that this assessment is not an easy or unambiguous procedure. Initial competencies are described through a prerequisite in the form of the whole course, but also as a set of necessary pre-knowledge that should be acquired through the previous formal, non-formal and informal learning. For this purpose, in the subjects Mathematics 1 and 2 we do the pre-knowledge assessment and we use taxonomy for classifying tasks and students' success.

For the first time we analysed male and female students' pre-knowledge (background) in mathematics in the academic year 2006/2007, to detect any potentially significant gender differences in that respect (Divjak et al., 2010). Firstly, there was no significant gender difference regarding the number of mathematics classes they attended in the secondary school. Naturally, there is a correlation between the number of classes and the grades they obtained in the secondary school and their respective success in the first-year mathematics tests. Secondly, there was no significant difference, either in the range or depth of their knowledge of mathematics as measured by the entrance test at the beginning of the course. To sum up, we cannot be satisfied with students' pre-knowledge of mathematics gained in the secondary school. According to our expectations, students are better at numeric and verbal questions and unfortunately they underperform in geometry and graphics, especially in problem solving. Thus it was necessary to introduce a significant level of support for students to help them gain the necessary pre-knowledge in mathematics. In order to lessen these lacks in their pre-knowledge, tutorial classes have been organized where older students help those attending specific subject classes, then frequent teacher consultations and extra material for revision in the e-learning system. To stimulate students to do graphic tasks and to achieve better results we have created a great number of self-testing tasks in Mathematics 1 and 2, with graphical tasks and problems, for example the self-tests implemented in LMS Moodle for Mathematics 2. The tasks are classified according to Cox (MATH-KIT) taxonomy in three levels and put into the data base. For each student, exercises are generated randomly from the data base according to the predefined criteria (content, level and number of exercises of each type) and time constrains are placed for solving them.

Concerning under-representation of female students, the data from (Divjak et al., 2010) show that mathematics is not an obstacle for their retention. Obviously, the problem of increasing number of female students in ICT has to be considered in much more broader frame than just taking into consideration the pre-knowledge and retention on mathematics in ICT programs.

Finally in the last decade there has been an additional trend that causes a varied range of abilities within class. It is the proportion of secondary school population entering higher education, which increased rapidly in the last decades. This proportion is now higher than 40% in many countries (Biggs & Tang, 2007) and for Croatia it is 47% and as a consequence many teaching-related problems have emerged ranging from rather poor pre-knowledge in fundamental disciplines like mathematics to the demand of working with big groups of students, especially in the first year of undergraduate programs. They all have negative influence on the retention of students.

Enhancing Retention of Students

In the implementation phase the blended learning approach is used in order to contribute to the retention of students. In general, retention can be defined as student's continued participation in the learning event until its completion, which in HE could be a course, a programme, an institution, or a system (Berge, 2003). At FOI the drop-out rate among first-year students was around 60% before the Bologna reform. The situation at this Faculty is changing for the better after the reform, with the drop-out amounting to less than 40%, which is at "Tinto's average" (Tinto, 1982). For this reason, efforts are being made toward improving this situation, as was reported in (Divjak & Erjavec, 2007). Enhancing retention in mathematics can be achieved by using different teaching methods (Juan et al., 2008) which cater for different learning styles and for gender differences as it was described before. In general, the students' pass rate has been considerably higher after the mathematics course had been redesigned and the learning environment improved.

Two Phases of Transformation of Math 1 and Math 2

There were two phases in which transformations were implemented. The first change to be made in the year 2003 was the classification of the first year mathematics curriculum under two headings: Mathematics 1 and Mathematics 2, each lasting for one semester. Subsequent changes included adjustments in the content (more discrete mathematics and an emphasized use of mathematical models in practice), teaching methodology (student-centred teaching, more interaction with students, team work, use of ICT in problem solving and essay writing), learning methodology (more work in seminars, researches on given themes, essay writing, weekly homework, short tests, monthly tests, tests analysis), in examination methods (continuous assessment) and in student support (new textbook and exercise book, individual tutorials, well prepared web page with additional e-learning facilities). These changes resulted in a much higher pass rate. Details and results of that first phase are given in (Divjak & Erjavec, 2007).

In the second phase, the learning outcomes of the course were formulated. Therefore we tried to find a suitable mathematical taxonomy to help us in that respect. As it was mentioned earlier, we decided to use MATH-KIT (Cox taxonomy). Since 2007 the Mathematics 1 and Mathematics 2 courses in the first year have been taught as a blended course, which means that we combine face to face teaching with an on-line virtual learning environment. In this respect we use an open source LMS Moodle.

It can be concluded that the introduction of certain methods and the concept of a blended learning environment into teaching and learning mathematics depends upon the role played by mathematics in the study program, wherein the fact that mathematics is a part of the study program in engineering or social sciences (rather than the study of mathematics itself) makes a significant difference in the approach to developing a course.

Challenges of the Second Phase of Blended Learning Implementation

Several challenges were identified that influenced a still relatively high drop-out rate within the first year Mathematics courses and tremendous workload of professors and teaching assistance, before the implementation of e-learning and after the first phase of restructuring. These challenges are named in Table 5. Interestingly, female students have a significantly lower drop-out rate that their peers (Divjak et al., 2010). It means that less female students enter mathematics courses but when they are there, they do better than male students. In Table 5 strategies are specified that have been used in blended teaching and learning process in order to help overcome the issues that teachers and students faced in traditional, face to face, classes of Mathematics.

There is diversification of students' work and assessment in class and online that includes weekly homework assignments, written essays on given mathematical themes and problems, short tests performed through a virtual learning environment model, activity in the classroom and in Moodle as well as three mid-term tests that provide for 60% of the final grade. All these assessments are summative i.e. they contribute to the summative function, but homework, short tests in LMS and the activity in the classroom have the additional capability of serving formative functions. Each of these assessment methods is correlated with some of the defined learning outcomes (Divjak & Ostroški, 2009). Furthermore, in LMS Moodle there is a lot of teaching mate-

Table 5. Mathematical modeling tasks in different courses

Challenge	Strategy in blended e-learning to deal with it	How the strategies helped
Large heterogeneous student groups; high workload of teachers	• Continuous monitoring, recording and all guidelines available in LMS Moodle • (Self)evaluation database with exercises • Forum with information and for communication • Survey on satisfaction with on-line work	• Every data on monitoring students' progress is at one virtual place • Reduced teacher workload because data from on-line tests and survey results are notified automatically • Information is available on forum for all students
Low level of pre-knowledge	• Evaluation of pre-knowledge, feed-back to students with recommendation how to overcome identified gap • Student tutors (on-line peer tutoring and face to face tutoring), • Additional material available in Moodle for individual learning	• Students have opportunity to identify gaps and fill them by using different tools according to their learning styles and time available
Low motivation of students for learning mathematics	• Students of ICT like technology and therefore in the most cases like LMS and mathematical software we introduced • Different learning styles – presentations, animations are done having in mind learning styles of students and teachers • Different motivations taken into account (goal-oriented students appreciate guidelines how to pass the course fast; learning-oriented students welcome references for further learning; relationship-oriented ones enjoy working in groups etc.)	• Students learn mathematics through diverse activities • Different assessment methods motivate students • Motivation is higher – can be seen from students surveys
Low achievement level of learning outcomes within prescribed semester	• Enhancement of the methodology of teaching and learning by clear implementation of taxonomies of learning outcomes • Exercises and additional activities available in Moodle – examples and homework • Diversification of assessment methods and their mapping to levels in learning outcome taxonomy	• Students know what is expected from them • Examples, exercises and self-evaluation in LMS help them to test their readiness • Students use different abilities to raise their achievement level • Retention level is higher
High drop-out rates of some underrepresented groups of students (part-time students, adult learners, students with disabilities)	• Teaching material available on line • Communication enhanced by forums and e-mails • Digitalized material for visually impaired students • Assistants for students with disabilities available	• Students with disabilities and part-time students can access material on-line • Visually impaired students can use digital library and transform written material to audio

rial. For example every week students can read prepared interactive teaching material and download smart board in form of images of notes and exercises from face to face classes.

Special emphasis has been put on the data base of questions and exercises prepared according to the Cox taxonomy, which only for Mathematics 2 contains 532 items and enables generation of individualized tests (example in *Figure 1*).

Students' Evaluation of Math 1 and Math 2

Evaluations of mathematical courses done by students have confirmed the statement that it is rational and relevant to invest in blended teaching and learning mathematics. For example in the year 2009, 244 freshmen students were asked to evaluate different aspects of teaching mathematics, their attitudes towards mathematics and especially teaching mathematics with technology. Among other questions, we also asked if *Mathematics*

Figure 1. Example of exercise taken from the database for Mathematics 2 (translated into English)

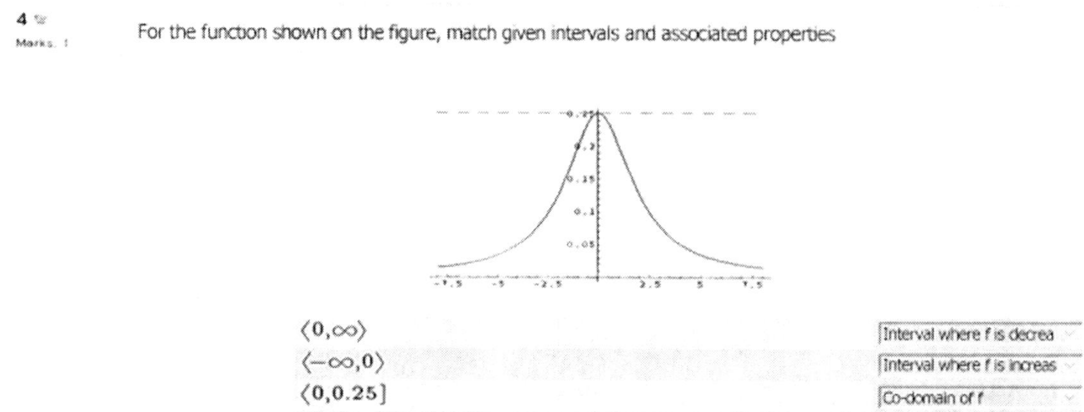

is more interesting when it uses ICT for making models, presentations and solving problems and if *Moodle helps them to learn mathematics better*. In that research students were divided into two almost equal groups: those who passed Mathematics 2 due to their work during the semester (continuous monitoring of students achievements through tests, quizzes, homework etc.) and those who didn't. Those who fail to pass the course due to their work during the semester, have three additional examination opportunities to pass the exam in the same academic year. Since the survey was performed in June, 117 out of 244 students passed the exam through the activities in the course of the semester and 127 didn't pass at that time. In the scope of the academic year approximately 75% of students passed Mathematics 1 and more than 50% passed Mathematics 2. In the scope of two academic years around 85% passed both courses. Extracts from students' survey results are given on the Figure 2 and they show that both groups of students (those who passed and those who didn't) have been satisfied with using ICT and problem solving in Mathematics. Similarly, both groups thought in general that Moodle helped them in learning Mathematics, but as we had expected, the perspective of those students who passed Mathematics in the first examination period was more affirmative.

Student Evaluation of Blended Learning Approach

Students have also recognized the possibilities and advantages of blended learning in relation to classical learning. In the survey, which was conducted in the academic year 2007/2008 and in which 240 students of the first year participated, we asked: „Do you prefer when teaching is done: a) mostly with the support of a computer b) in a classical way with oral teacher's lecture c) with a combination of the first two ways." 69% of the questioned students prefer blended learning, 24% classical way, and 7% computer-supported teaching.

Further, at the end of the academic year 2009/2010, a questionnaire of students' satisfaction on Selected chapters in mathematics was conducted and 120 students answered. More than 83% of students expressed their satisfaction with the usage of e-learning.

Figure 2. Mathematics is more interesting when it uses ICT for making models (presentations and solving problems)

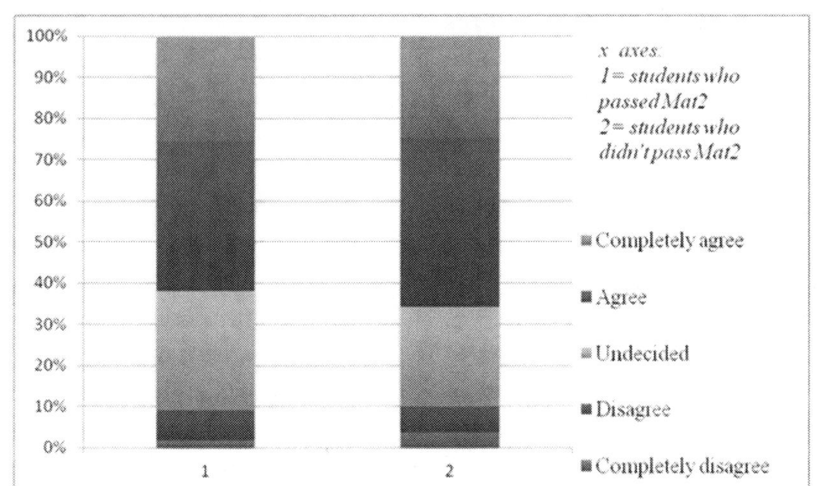

USE OF SOCIAL SOFTWARE IN MATHEMATICS: CASE STUDY OF DISCRETE MATHEMATICS WITH GRAPH THEORY AND SELECTED CHAPTERS IN MATHEMATICS

There are mathematical courses we teach in the second year of undergraduate IBS study and the first year of graduate study of Information Systems. Again, the entire process of teaching and learning mathematics is heavily supported by ICT and executed through blended e-learning but also by the use of social software such as wiki and e-portfolio. In this part of the proposed chapter we will elaborate these two case studies.

Wiki in the Course: Discrete Mathematics with Graph Theory

The course *Discrete mathematics with graph theory (DMGT)* is taught in the last year of undergraduate level of IBS and in the first year of graduate level of study programs Information Systems and Software Engineering. In comparison with mathematical courses on the undergraduate level, the number of students in DMGT is usually between 15 and 30. The syllabus consists of two parts: in the first part different topics in discrete mathematics are covered and the second half is dedicated to the graph theory and its applications. The topics have sound mathematical theoretical foundations but there are also a lot of applications of mathematical theory in informatics and business, e.g. problem solving exercises that are performed individually or in teams. For example, when integer numbers, their properties and corresponding theorems have been introduced, different applications like RSA cryptosystem, the usage of congruencies in ISBN (International Standard Book Number) and UPC (Universal Product Code) is discussed and investigated. An interesting exercise that we use is to provide communication between students and teachers by using the RSA cryptosystem and public and private keys for encryption and decryption. A teacher sends encrypted exercise to a student and the student has to decrypt it, solve it, and then again send encrypted solution back to the teacher. The whole process was implemented in Moodle by use of open source mathematics software Sage (a year ago we used Mathematica software). Further, especially fruitful opportunities for students' investigations can be found in the graph theory when particular emphasis is put on applications and problem solving in the area of ICT. In this process, we keep in mind that "The innovations which have used problems from outsides schools as a part of their material have improved students' motivation and succeeded in other ways, and have demonstrated that problem-cantered approaches can indeed have an important part to play in mathematics education." (Black & Atkin, 2005, p. 89).

Let us describe the way which we used in this course in order to assure the fulfillment of the learning outcome (LO1) concerning mathematical modelling and problem solving. Usually, problem solving is regarded as the thinking and behaviour we engage in to obtain the desired outcome we seek (Treffinger et al., 2008). The outcome could be attaining a certain goal or finding a satisfactory answer to our question. Besides classical problem solving, when the description of a problem is given to students by teachers, we try to develop additional student's competence connected with recognizing real life problems that can be formulated and afterwards solved by the usage of non-trivial mathematical theories and techniques which students have learned in the course. In such a case students become problem owners (replacing the industrial representatives) and they are interested to formulate it carefully and also to monitor the solution finding process, as well as to evaluate the final solution. This teaching method engages students actively in a deep conceptual mathematical activity, to develop their ability in mathematical reasoning and collaborative learning. Collaborative learning is all about sharing knowledge but there must be common ground, language, joint focus and compatible perspective (Stahl & Hesse, 2009). Therefore it is very important at the beginning of collaborative work to explain the educational goals of the activity and to provide students with the joint problem space. The central issue in the theory of collaborative learning is how students can solve problems, build knowledge, accomplish educational tasks, and achieve other cognitive accomplishments together. The wiki and the virtual reality were designed to create shared perceptual space, where salient objects could be seen by all (Cakir et al., 2009).

However, this process can be extremely demanding for the teacher to follow and assess. Luckily there are ICT tools and social software available that can enhance and enable implementation of such a challenging, problem solving exercise. Therefore students need virtual learning environment that allows them to discuss potential real world problems suitable to be solved by some mathematical theory or approach, construct mathematical solutions collaboratively and exchange references in situations where they are not co-located.

Hence, in the course *Discrete mathematics with graph theory,* wiki has been introduced in order to support student team work, problem setting and problem solving exercises and to enable monitoring of students' work and progress. In this particular situation students are divided into teams of three and in the first part of their team work each group has to identify and describe one real world problem that can be, in their opinion, solved by methods of discrete mathematics or graph theory. The proposed problem has to be described correctly and references have to be given by the use of *delicious* social bookmarking. After this first phase teams exchanged their problem assignments and the second stage of the problem solving phase starts. In this phase each team has to investigate and work on finding the solution to the assignment, prepared by some other team. The whole collaboration has to be recorded in the wiki system implemented in the LMS Moodle.

Students' Opinion about DSTG

Since there is a rather small number of students enrolled in the course, it is not appropriate to analyse students' answers from students' evaluation survey statistically, but we can say that they are very positive and pass rate is near 100%. Instead of that, let us cite some qualitative evaluation that students wrote:

"...In my opinion it is by far the most interesting and useful mathematics... I recommend every student to enroll", "It has to be even more practically oriented exercise than those about RSA and Python.", "All in all it is a very interesting and well designed course.", "It was one of the most useful courses I enrolled during my study and I know that algorithms we learnt are very applicable in my professional work.", "It is a very broad and interesting course and it might be better if it is defined more precisely what is important and what is not so important."

E-Portfolio in the Course: Selected Chapters in Mathematics

According to (Knoerr & McDonald, 1999), in a reflective portfolio, students are asked to explicitly consider their progress over the length of the course and a reflective portfolio helps students assess their own growth. At the same time, the collection of portfolios can help a teacher reflect on the strengths and weaknesses of the course. In *Selected chapters in mathematics* (SCM), reflective portfolio type is used, but it is web-based and therefore more accessible and manageable for students and teachers.

We introduced the e-portfolio in the course *SCM* (4th semester of the undergraduate study) in the academic year 2008/2009 in order to monitor student progress and evaluate the achievement of prescribed learning outcomes. The portfolio represents systematic, multidimensional and organized collection of evidence about students' knowledge, skills and attitudes. With e-portfolio this collection is available in electronic way or on-line. „In a nutshell, the portfolio assessment is considered an effective means of measuring the change in students' cognition and learning process, involvement and interaction, and assessing higher-order cognition abilities and attributes." (Frankland, 2007). The role of an e-portfolio in the course is dual: reflection on the subject, the students' activities in the subject and their execution and evaluation of the learning outcomes of the subject. (Blackburn & Hakel, 2006) recommend that electronic portfolios provide the means for students to set learning goals, to monitor and regulate their progress towards these goals, as well as develop their self-assessment skills. Further, they suggest that these goals be focused on learning objectives rather than performance objectives. Such a delivery mode does not only enhance student motivation for learning mathematics and the availability of teaching and learning materials but also improves communication between the student and the teacher, as well as that among the students themselves. In addition, it enables the teacher to store a lot of students' artefacts, which opens many possibilities for the evaluation of learning outcomes. This is in line with (Stefani et al., 2007) that points out that e-portfolio must encourage personal reflection and involve the exchange of ideas and feedback.

The course SCM was considered a "hard one" and not easy to pass because it covers variety of mathematical topics and requires a certain level of student mathematical pre-knowledge. Therefore one of the goals of e-portfolio implementation was to investigate problems students have in the course and find possible teaching strategies to overcome them. In order to do so, we ask students to write reflections about the course itself (lecture matters, the role of the course in the curriculum, the possibility of usage and implementation of mathematical knowledge and tools in informatics, etc.), course activities and accomplishment of the same. Furthermore, there is also a discussion about the difficulties and success in the course, about clarifying the concepts of the course and its integration with the study program as well as reflections about mathematical modelling and in general the role of mathematics in the ICT profession. The course is structured into six chapters and students write their reflections on the topics they have learned, referring to the learning outcomes, for each chapter continuously. Student's reflections in the e-portfolio need to be written in the period of two weeks after lectures in particular chapter are finished. In doing so, the open source e-portfolio system Mahara is used. This system enables students to write their reflections in the form of a blog with six posts corresponding to each of the before mentioned chapters. This blog system is very functional because one can see the date of the last post editing and the attachments can be commented separately (you can leave a feedback to students for each attachment). Together with their reflection, students also need to attach a single artefact (homework, solved test, solved midterm exam, solved exercise from lecture presentation, model, description of the possible application, organized lecture notes, computer experiment – for instance, in Wolfram Mathematica and so on…) with explanation why they decided to attach a certain artefact. The example is given on the Figure 3. The work on the e-portfolio was not an obligatory condition for fulfilling their course requirements, but in this way students could collect 6% from the total amount of points during the coursework on SCM (that is 6 points – one for each chapter). In (Knoerr & McDonald, 1999) that also considers e-portfolios in mathematics, it is proposed that the portfolio is 5% of student's final grade. In assigning these points, teachers use the following criteria: student's understanding of the basic course concepts presented in the reflection, student's achievement through the attached artefacts and creativity of their choice. The motivation on the side of teachers for introducing this kind of new assessment is the systematical gathering of reflections and the evaluation of learning outcomes in working with large group of students (approximately 250 students on SCM and only 3 teachers – 1 professor and 2 teaching assistants). In such teaching environment there is a significant number of students who do not have an opportunity to express their opinion and also the teacher does not get to monitor special achievements of each one of them. The intention was to obtain a certain insight into the progress and work of each student by using the e- portfolio. It is important to mention that activity related to the e-portfolio represents contribution to the usage of technology in education and on the other hand, it serves to raise the student's awareness about their own work and the progress on the course. This progress is followed by the interference of pointing out the personal choice of the best course achievement (exercise, assignment, etc.) and writing reflections about the course matter and progress, written in unconstrained form.

Students' Evaluation of E-Portfolio Implementation

After the lectures are over, a questionnaire on students' satisfaction implemented in the learning management system Moodle is conducted. Usually the questions are about learning and teaching environment on SCM and in 2009 two new questions were added to this questionnaire concerning the e-portfolio activity: Was the e-portfolio useful for them and how much time on average they spent working on their reflections. In the sample of 34% of the total number of students examined, around 55% of them answered that the e-portfolio was useful or even very useful to them, which is a rather good result considering the fact that the e-portfolio was a novelty to them. Others were indifferent or slightly negative. We have to point out that among those examinees there were also students who had not participated in the e-portfolio exercise. Besides, we asked for the qualitative analysis of the usefulness of the e-portfolio and we prepared some improvements for the next academic year based on it we prepared some improvements for the next academic year. In students' answers, most criticism was pointed towards the fact that the portfolio exercise is very time consuming and that six reflections in one semester were too much. In the academic year

Figure 3. Extract from e-portfolio (translated into English)

OPM poglavlja

Blog o poglavljima iz OPMa, svrha su bodovi bodovi bodovi!

Functions with several variables

Functions with several variables is one of the most interesting and graphically the most attractive chapters in the course. Quadrics are excellent, most of them I used in 3D modelling as starting objects and then I modified them to look like something from real world. In this chapter there are limits that I don't like because each exercise is solving by its own trick, as far as I remember form Math 2. Partial derivatives don't look difficult, if you learn derivatives of functions with one variable in Math 2. I remember we solve problems with finding extremes and it means that more or less Im familiar with topics but it has to be risen on higher level.

Attached files:

derivacije.jpg (231.2K) - Download

zadatak sa demonstratura, parcijalne derivacije

Posted by on 02 June 2009, 10:47 PM

Polynomials

Polynomials! Finally something I know well from secondary school and from some other courses. Nothing difficult. Horner algorithm is super useful, it was explained in tutoring before second monthly test and I used it for finding characteristic polynomial of a matrix. Cardan formula is practical, but boring... Ferrari method is somewhere between Horner and Cardan, not so interesting as F4 30 ili Enzo, but what it is – it is. In almost every chapter I try to see how to implement problems in Maya, here I can't, at least not from a user perspective. I believe that from developer perspective is different, but I'm not familiar with it.
On the third test I need 10 points and therefore I will exercise more...
I attached here the solution of one interesting problem from tutorial.

Attached files:

zadatak.doc (17K) - Download

Posted by on 02 June 2009, 9:42 PM

Linear operators

When I'm writing this reflection I already know results from the previous test and for me it was much better than the first. Now only one test left. This chapter was not so unfamiliar to me since I prepared the project that referred to it at the beginning of the semester. Things like rotations, reflections, central symmetry etc. Rank and nullity is not very difficult to calculate but I did something wrong. ..

2009/2010 the results were better because 80% of those who used e-portfolio responded that e-portfolio was useful or even very useful to them. It can be considered that better results are due to some organizational changes we introduced in that academic year. First of all, that students have to write their reflections only three times in one semester.

Further, we can notice that a great majority of students who passed the course in the first exam period were in the group that had been writing the e-portfolio regularly. Whereas the e-portfolio is associated with the learning outcomes, it's reasonable to analyse the artefacts students attach (notes, short tests, midterm tests, homework…) and perhaps the nature of their reflections, in order to assess if they reason with understanding or they just do the copy-paste of the definitions and homework assignment. This is a possible course for the further investigation and thorough analysis. Finally, we would like to emphasize that the e-portfolio contributes to the process of raising students' awareness and critical thinking about their own achievements and motivation, as well as self-monitoring of their learning progress, which has a vast influence on their study success. More about the implementation of e-portfolio at FOI can be found in (Balaban et al., 2010a) and (Balaban et al., 2010b).

CONCLUSION

From the cases described in this chapter it can be concluded that it is very important to use technology enhanced learning, especially in teaching ICT students, who are in general inclined to technology and are non-mathematics majors. It is considered that the delivery of teaching by using only the model of teacher-cantered learning will have little effect on equipping students with the competencies, knowledge and skills required for their successful future participation in the knowledge based economy and society (OLCOS Roadmap 2012, p. 12). It means that a shift has to be made towards competency based, student-cantered education. Therefore, other than learning the indispensable mathematics, "students should strive to acquire self-direction and creativity, critical thinking and problem-solving skills, collaborative team work and communication skills". (OLCOS Roadmap 2012, p. 16).

On the other hand it is essential that pedagogy precedes technology in planning the teaching and learning process. Therefore, first educational goals and learning outcomes on the level of a study program, the course level and the level of teaching units have to be set and analysed. At the same time, the student population needs to be taken into consideration: their pre-knowledge and motivation, the existence of part-time students, underrepresented groups etc. Teaching methods and assessment, as well as e-assessment methods, have to be mapped to the learning outcomes, the study level and to the specifics of mathematics as a science, but also to the characteristics of students' pre-knowledge, motivation and learning styles. The wise usage of LMS and blended learning approach can contribute to better retention of students and the decrease in dropping out. After that, appropriate additional ICT tools can be found and applied. As very useful, social software can be considered, such as wiki, the e-portfolio and social bookmarking we presented here.

Therefore, our aim is to use technology in order to enhance the quality of teaching and learning process and especially to meet the requirements of prescribed learning outcomes, having in mind the fulfillment of pedagogical and mathematical goals and not only the imperative of application of modern technology. It will be challenging to research further on the dark side of using technology for teaching and learning mathematics. For example, are there any educational goals connected especially with mathematics that are harder to achieve by using technology supported learning, as well as what misconception might developed in the case when face to face teaching is missing. It can be the extension and focusing on mathematics of the review (Schmid et al., 2009) where the authors examine different uses of technology in higher education classrooms and their impact on learning achievement.

On the other hand, the use of ICT in teaching and learning motivates students for learning and problem solving tasks, especially those who are by orientation of their study inclined to technology. Yet in order to achieve that, the process must be carefully planned, prepared, implemented and monitored. Besides, if we want to stimulate problem solving and collaborative learning, rich learning environment must be provided to enable collaborative work when team members are physically distant. Consequently, creativity in problem solving can be enhanced by using an appropriate pedagogical approach and engaging tasks, which can also be supported by ICT, but it is also useful that students reflect on their work and progress. In this respect, e-portfolio tools can be helpful. The collection of reflective portfolios besides as a tool for collecting feedback of students' mathematical understanding and progress through the course can serve also to realign teaching methods and material and to recommend for spending greater time on particularly difficult concepts. Additionally, portfolio usage is writing-intensive form of assessment which is unusual in mathematic courses. Concerning implementation of wiki in online collaborative problem-based learning there is a need for thorough research comparing students' achievements in online and face-to-face problem-solving, since it has been hard any work in this direction done so far.

Thereafter students' workload has to be considered very carefully, because using an e-portfolio system and reflecting on one's own achievement progress can be very time consuming. It would be interesting to research further if there is any significant change of attitude towards learning and usefulness of mathematics as a result of the use of e-portfolios as we proposed (as a place to reflect and store the best artefacts).

At the same time when student-cantered approach tries to be implemented, it is important to consider costs in terms of teachers' workload that has to be invested, especially when a problem-solving oriented course is considered. There are good examples how ICT and e-learning can help on the long run, but we have to be aware that in the first phase of the implementation of e-learning there is a need for extra workload and training for teachers involved. Therefore, it can be advised to implement blended learning gradually i.e. to improve system step-by-step in accordance with accepted strategy Additional training for students in the usage of e-learning tools has to be provided, too.

Finally, nowadays it is the ultimate goal to raise interest for mathematics, especially in those students who do not study mathematics. Mathematics is supposed to be a strong engine for their professional development and the development of the discipline in general. On the other hand we are witnessing the descending interest and motivation for learning and studying mathematics. It is therefore noteworthy to research further why students' motivation for learning mathematics today is not particularly high, what possible paths there are in designing teaching and enhance learning that have to be explored and how we can wisely use ICT to support and improve the journey along these paths.

REFERENCES

Anderson, L. W., Krathwohl, D. R., Airasian, P. W., Cruikshank, K. A., Mayer, R. E., & Pintrich, P. R. … Wittrock, M. C. (Eds.) (2001). *A taxonomy for learning, teaching and assessing: A revision of Bloom's taxonomy of educational objectives*: Abridged edition. New York, NY: Longman.

Balaban, I., Divjak, B., Grabar, D., & Žugec, B. (2010). Towards successful implementation of ePortfolio in blended learning. In S. Ravet (Ed.), *Learning Forum London 2010 proceedings* (pp. 146-153). London, UK: EIfEL.

Balaban, I., Divjak, B., & Kopić, M. (2010). Emerging issues in using e-portfolio. In S. Ravet (Ed.), *Learning forum London 2010 proceedings* (pp. 212-218). London, UK: EIfEL.

Berge, Z. L., & Huang, Y. P. (2004). A model for sustainable student retention: A holistic perspective on the student dropout problem with special attention to e-learning. *Distance Education Online Symposium, 13*(5).

Biggs, J. (1995). Assessing for learning: Some dimensions underlying new approaches to educational assessment. *The Alberta Journal of Educational Research, 41*(1), 1–17.

Biggs, J., & Tang, C. (2007). *Teaching for quality learning at university. What the student does* (3rd ed.). Mc Graw Hill – Society for Research into Higher Education & Open University Press.

Black, P., & Atkin, J. M. (2005). *Changing the subject. Innovations in science, mathematics and technology education.* Paris, France: Ruthledge, OECD.

Blackburn, J. L., & Hakel, M. D. (2006). Enhancing self-regulation and goal orientation with e-portfolios . In Jafari, A., & Kaufman, C. (Eds.), *Handbook of research on e-portfolios* (pp. 83–89). Hershey, PA: IGI Global. doi:10.4018/978-1-59140-890-1.ch009

Bloom, B. S., Engelhart, M. D., Furst, E. J., Hill, W. H., & Krathwohl, D. R. (1956). *Taxonomy of educational objectives: The classification of educational objectives. Handbook 1: Cognitive domain*. New York, NY: David McKay.

Bruinsma, M. (2004). Motivation, cognitive processing and achievement in higher education. *Learning and Instruction*, *14*(6), 549–568. doi:10.1016/j.learninstruc.2004.09.001

Çakır, M. P., Zemel, A., & Stahl, G. (2009). The joint organization of interaction within a multimodal CSCL medium. *International Journal of Computer-Supported Collaborative Learning*, *4*(2), 115–149. doi:10.1007/s11412-009-9061-0

Chickering, A. W., & Gamson, Z. F. (1987). Seven principles for good practice in undergraduate education. *American Association for Higher Education Bulletin*, *39*(7), 3–7.

Clark, R. E. (1983). Reconsidering research on learning from media. *Review of Educational Research*, *53*(4), 445–459.

Cox, W. (2003). A math-KIT for engineers. *Teaching Mathematics and Its Applications*, *22*(4), 193–198. doi:10.1093/teamat/22.4.193

Din, F. S., & Wheatley, F. W. (2007). A literature review of the student-centered teaching approach: National implications. *National Forum of Teachers Education Journal*, *17*(3), 1–17.

Divjak, B., & Erjavec, Z. (2008). Enhancing mathematics for informatics and its correlation with student pass rates. *International Journal of Mathematical Education in Science and Technology*, *39*(1), 23–33. doi:10.1080/00207390601002732

Divjak, B., & Ostroški, M. (2009). Learning outcomes in mathematics: Case study of their implementation and evaluation by using e-learning. In M. Pavleković (Ed.), *The Second International Scientific Colloquium Mathematics and Children (Learning outcomes)*(pp. 65-77*)*. Monography. April 24, 2009, Osijek. Zagreb, Croatia: Element.

Divjak, B., Ostroški, M., & Vidaček Hainš, V. (2010). Sustainable student retention and gender issues in Mathematics for ICT study. *International Journal of Mathematical Education in Science and Technology*, *41*(3), 293–310. doi:10.1080/00207390903398416

Entwistle, N. (1995). The use of research in student learning in quality assessment. In Gibbs, G. (Ed.), *Improving student learning through assessment and evaluation* (pp. 24–43). The Oxford Centre for Staff Development.

Entwistle, N. (2000). *Promoting deep learning through teaching and assessment: conceptual frameworks and educational contexts.* TLRP Annual Conference, 2000. Retrieved October 18, 2010, from http://www.tlrp.org/acadpub/Entwistle2000.pdf

Frankland, S. (Ed.). (2007). *Enhancing teaching and learning through assessment: Deriving an appropriate model*. The Netherlands: Springer. doi:10.1007/978-1-4020-6226-1

Galbraith, P., & Haines, C. (1998). Disentangling the nexus: Attitudes to mathematics and technology in a computer learning environment. *Educational Studies in Mathematics*, *36*, 275–290. doi:10.1023/A:1003198120666

Galbraith, P., & Haines, C. (2001). Conceptual and procedural demands embedded in modelling tasks. In Matos, J. F., Blum, W., Houston, K. S., & Carreira, S. P. (Eds.), *Modelling and mathematics education: ICTMA 9 - Applications in science and technology* (pp. 342–353). Chichester, England: Horwood Publishing.

Geser, G. (Ed.). (2007). *OLCOS roadmap 2012 – Open educational practices and resources.* Retrieved October 18, 2010, from www.olcos.org

Haruta, M. E., & Stevenson, C. B. (1999). *Integrating student-centered teaching methods into the first year SMET curriculum: The University of Hartford model for institution-wide reform* (ERIC Document Reproduction Service No. ED440977).

Juan, A., Huertas, M., Steegmann, C., Corcoles, C., & Serrat, C. (2008). Mathematical e-learning: State of the art and experiences at the Open University of Catalonia. *International Journal of Mathematical Education in Science and Technology*, *39*(4), 455–471. doi:10.1080/00207390701867497

Knoerr, A. P., & McDonald, M. A. (1999). Student assessment through portfolios. In Gold, B., Keith, S. Z., & Marion, W. A. (Eds.), *Assessment practices in undergraduate mathematics*. Washington, DC: The Mathematical Association of America.

Kozma, R. (1994). Will media influence learning? Reframing the debate. *Educational Technology Research and Development*, *42*(2), 7–19. doi:10.1007/BF02299087

Ramsden, P. (2003). *Learning to teach in higher education*. London, UK: Routledge Farmer.

Schmid, R. F., Bernard, R. M., Borokhovski, E., Tamim, R., Abrami, P. C., Wade, C. A., & Lowerison, G. (2009). Technology's effect on achievement in higher education: A Stage I meta-analysis of classroom applications. *Journal of Computing in Higher Education*, *21*(2), 95–109. doi:10.1007/s12528-009-9021-8

Smith, G. H., Wood, L. N., Coupland, M., Stephenson, B., Crawford, K., & Ball, G. (1996). Constructing mathematical examinations to assess a range of knowledge and skills. *International Journal of Mathematical Education in Science and Technology*, *27*(1), 65–77. doi:10.1080/0020739960270109

Smittle, P. (2003). Principle for effective teaching. *Journal of Developmental Education*, *26*(3), 10–12, 14, 16.

Stahl, G., & Hesse, F. (2009). Paradigms of shared knowledge. *International Journal of Computer-Supported Collaborative Learning*, *4*(4), 365–369. doi:10.1007/s11412-009-9075-7

Stefani, L., Mason, R., & Pegler, C. (2007). *The educational potential of e-portfolios: Supporting personal development and reflective learning*. New York City, NY: Routledge.

Strategy of e-learning FOI, (2007). *Strategija E-učenja Fakulteta organizacije i informatike*, Varaždin. Retrieved October 18, 2010, from http://www.foi.hr/sluzbe/tajnistvo/dokumenti.html

TIMSS. (2003). *International report on achievement in the mathematics cognitive domains: Findings from a developmental project*. IEA. Retrieved October 18, 2010, from http://timss.bc.edu/timss2003.html

Tinto, V. (1982). Limits of theory and practice in student attrition. *The Journal of Higher Education*, *53*(6), 687–700. doi:10.2307/1981525

Treffinger, D. J., Selby, E. C., & Isaksen, S. G. (2008). Understanding individual problem-solving style: A key to learning and applying creative problem solving. *Learning and Individual Differences*, *18*, 390–401. doi:10.1016/j.lindif.2007.11.007

UniZg. (2007). *Strategija E-učenja Sveučilišta u Zagrebu*. Retrieved October 18, 2010, from http://www.unizg.hr/nastava_studenti/strategija_eucenja.html (In Croatian)

Vidaček-Hainš, V., Divjak, B., & Ostroški, M. (2009). Motivation for study and gender issue. *DAAAM International Scientific Book*, Paper Number 564.

Weller, M. (2007). *Virtual learning enviroment. Using, choosing and developing your VLE*. Routledge Taylor & Frances Group.

KEY TERMS AND DEFINITIONS

Blended Learning: Learning that combines face-to-face instruction with computer-mediated approach.

E-Learning: Comprised of all forms of electronically supported learning and teaching.

Higher Education: Refers to a level of education that is provided at academies, universities, colleges, vocational universities etc.

Learning Management System (LMS): Software application for the administration, documentation, tracking, and reporting of training programs, classroom and online events, e-learning programs and content.

Learning Outcomes: Statements about what is expected of the student to know, to understand, to be able to do and to evaluate as a result of the learning process.

Mathematical Software: Software used to model, analyze, or calculate numeric, symbolic, or geometric data.

Problem Solving: The thinking and behaviour we engage in to obtain the desired outcome we seek.

Section 2

Pure Online Experiences in Mathematics E-Learning

Chapter 7
Online Communities of Practice as Vehicles for Teacher Professional Development

Maria Meletiou-Mavrotheris
European University, Cyprus

ABSTRACT

The affordances offered by modern Internet technologies provide new opportunities for the pre-service and in-service training of teachers, making it possible to overcome the restrictions of shrinking resources and geographical locations and to offer high quality learning experiences to geographically dispersed teachers. The focus of this chapter is the question of how information and communication tools made available online could be effectively exploited to build and study network-based services with the aim of fostering online communities that promote teacher learning and development. The chapter presents an overview of the main experiences gained from a study which investigated the forms of collaboration and shared knowledge building undertaken by a multinational group of teachers participating in EarlyStatistics, an online professional development in statistics education targeting European elementary and middle school mathematics teachers. Findings from the study provide insights into the factors that may facilitate or hinder the successful implementation of an online community of teaching practitioners.

DOI: 10.4018/978-1-60960-875-0.ch007

INTRODUCTION

In a world where the ability to analyze, interpret and communicate information from data are skills needed for daily life and effective citizenship, statistical concepts are occupying an increasingly important role in mathematics curricula worldwide. Statistics has already been established as a vital part of school mathematics in many countries. The subject, however, has been introduced into mainstream math curricula without adequate attention paid to teachers' professional development. There is some evidence of poor understanding and insufficient preparation to teach statistical concepts among both pre-service and practicing teachers (e.g. Watson, 2001; Chick & Pierce, 2008). Many of the senior teachers have never formally studied the subject. Younger teachers may have taken an introductory statistics course at college, such a course however does not typically adequately prepare future teachers to teach statistics in ways that develop students' intuition about data and uncertainty (Rossman, Medina, & Chance, 2006). College-level statistics courses are often lecture-based, not allowing future teachers to experience the model of data-driven, activity-based, and discovery-oriented statistics they will eventually be expected to adopt in their teaching practices. As a result, some teachers tend to have weak knowledge of the statistical concepts and to focus their instruction on the procedural aspects of statistics, and not on conceptual understanding (Watson, 2001).

The direct relationship between improving the quality of teaching and improving students' learning in mathematics is a common thread emerging from educational research (Stigler & Hiebert 1999). Thus, it is critical for mathematics teachers to have rich teaching and learning experiences in statistics and its pedagogy. Technology advances, and especially web-based training, provide new opportunities for teacher initial and in-service training in statistics education. Internet technologies make it possible to overcome restrictions of shrinking resources and geographical locations and to offer, in a cost-effective and non-disruptive way, high quality learning experiences to teachers.

Numerous initiatives in online teacher training serving large numbers of educators are underway. Several of these programs exploit the richness of interactions fostered by the Web to build and study network-based services with the aim of fostering online communities of teaching practitioners. Communities of practice is a construct grounded in an anthropological perspective that examines how adults learn through social practices (Gray, 2004). A community of practice consists of a group of individuals with a shared domain of expertise, who engage in a process of collective learning about practices that matter to them (Wenger, 1998). A promise of new web-based technologies is that they can enable geographically dispersed teachers to engage in online communities, in which they can exchange ideas with other teachers and garner support as they try new strategies in their classrooms (Cochran-Smith & Lytle, 1999).

This chapter focuses on the question how the information and communication tools made available by modern internet technologies could be effectively utilized in order to build and study network-based services with the aim of fostering online communities that promote mathematics teachers' learning and development. It first provides an overview of the existing literature on online communities of practice. It then reports on some of the experiences from an exploratory study designed to investigate the forms of collaboration and shared knowledge building undertaken by a multinational group of mathematics teachers participating in online professional development in statistics education. The main insights gained from the study regarding enabling and constraining factors to the successful implementation of an online community of practice are discussed. Based on the analysis of these data, some recommendations for mathematics educators involved in pre-service and/or in-service teacher training who wish to incorporate online communities of practice in their work are provided. The chapter concludes with some implications for at-distance training of mathematics teachers and for future research.

BACKGROUND

Educational leaders and professional organizations in mathematics education have, for several years, been stressing the need for providing active learning environments that encourage students through authentic inquiry and discussion to establish the relevance and meaning of mathematical concepts. Despite, however, the significant reform efforts taking place worldwide, changing teaching practices is proving to be quite difficult. Empirical classroom research indicates a disconnection between the calls for reform and actual classroom practice and suggests the persistence of traditional, teacher-centered approaches.

In recent years, it has been recognized that for mathematics teacher training to become more effective in producing real changes in classroom practices, it ought to promote continuous, professional development opportunities that are cumulative and sustained over the career of a teacher (Joubert & Surtherland, 2009). The financial and logistic difficulties of engaging teachers in face-to-face training, as well as the need for professional development which can fit with teachers' busy schedules and can draw on powerful resources often not available locally, have encouraged the creation of online teacher professional development programs (Dede, Ketelhut, Whitehouse, Breit, & McCloskey, 2006).

Distance education is a useful framework for teacher training, but it can represent a large variety of pedagogical perspectives. The traditional approach is to provide teacher training and support mainly through a well-designed and predefined course package. The consequence of such an approach is that distance education could potentially be very authoritarian, with pre-packaged course material that could present only a particular perspective (Simpson, 2002). The expansion, however, in the modes of communication enabled by recent advances in communications and information technologies is revolutionizing distance education, opening up new possibilities for communication and collaboration among teachers (Baran & Cagiltay, 2006). The appearance of a variety of new tools and technologies fostering computer-supported collaborative learning (CSCL) is helping to remove the idea of distance from online education, leading to the development of new forms of online professional development settings, in accord with socio-constructivist views of learning (Vygotsky, 1978). There is increased interest in online communities of practice as vehicles which can promote teacher learning and development (Renninger & Shumar, 2002).

Several online communities of practice have been created in recent years to mitigate mathematics teachers' usual isolation and to support productive collaboration. One of the largest online communities in mathematics education is the Math Forum (Renninger & Shumar, 2004), a highly successful and active community which promotes online communication among mathematics teachers by allowing them to discuss issues, share ideas, and exchange resources and professional expertise. Teacher educators, administrators, and students interested in mathematics teaching and learning can also join the Math Forum. The Inquiry Learning Forum (ILF) is another online community of practice that has been used to support both pre-service and in-service mathematics and science teachers in sharing, improving, and creating inquiry-based, pedagogical practices (Barab, Makinster, & Scheckler, 2004). Another example is Connect-Me (Dalgarno & Colgan, 2007), a virtual mathematics community for novice elementary mathematics teachers.

Online communities of practice are constantly evolving into many forms and styles as they embrace new and evolving technologies. While, however, they proliferate in cyberspace, little is still known about best practices for their effective design and implementation, as empirical research on this topic is still at an initial stage. Conducted research studies in this area indicate that online communities of practice are, indeed, a promising model for both pre-service and in-service mathematics teacher training (Cady & Rearden, 2009; Koc, Peker, & Osmanoglu, 2009; Sinclair & Owston, 2006). They have a great potential to support teacher professional development through placing educators at the center of their learning (Kayler & Weller, 2007), thus promoting their independence and self-directed learning. Online communities of practice facilitate not only communication, but also the collaborative finding, shaping, and sharing of knowledge (Faulin et al., 2009).

Despite the potential of online communities of practice, several studies have found their introduction in educational contexts to be less successful than anticipated (e.g.Wagner, 2005; Kennard, 2007). These studies highlight several difficulties in building and maintaining online communities involving shared professional learning. Despite the early enthusiasm and encouragement of participants, many online communities of practice fail to thrive (Maloney-Krichmar, Abras, & Preece, 2002; Riverin & Stacey 2007). For example, after examining twenty eight studies, Zhao and Rop (2001) reported that there was little conclusive evidence to demonstrate the effective use of reflective online communities of practice. Other studies (e.g. McGraw, Lynch, & Koc, 2007; Sinclair & Owston, 2006; Stephens & Hartman, 2004) raise several issues that consistently create challenges for community building among participating teachers and for sustainability, including barriers around access, usability, sociability, lack of time to spend in online discussions, and language. Language barriers are a particularly serious challenge for international communities of practice, where members come from different countries and time zones, and communicate with other teachers in a foreign language (Trayner, Smith, & Bettoni, 2007).

Timely postings by all group members are considered to be a necessary component in building a functional community of practice (Kayler & Weller, 2007). However, collaborative learning does not suit all learners, and online collaboration may, in itself, cause stress for some of the learners (Allan & Lawless, 2003). There is strong research evidence indicating that many distance learners join discussion forums, read messages, but do not contribute to discussions (Simpson, 2002). Studies of participation demographics in online communities and social networks have found that between 46 percent and 82 percent of users are invisible observers who rarely or never participate (Preece, 2000; Nielsen 2006). As a result, while online education holds the potential for vibrant interaction and rich dialog, "online instructional experiences can become quite wooden and lifeless at times" (Muirhead, 2007, p. 8).

As Kling and Courtright (2003) note "transforming a group into a community is a major accomplishment that requires special processes and practices" (p. 221). The design of cognitive tools to promote learner participation in online communities of practice involves many interrelated considerations (e.g. moderator involvement, reliability and stability of the technology, etc.), most of which are not yet well understood (Stahl, 2006). More research is still needed to shed light into how to best support the development of healthy and sustaining online communities of teaching practitioners. Below some experiences related to educating statistics teachers at a distance are analyzed.

EXPERIENCES OF TRAINING STATISTICS TEACHERS AT-A-DISTANCE

This section provides a brief description of the main experiences gained from implementing

EarlyStatistics, an intercultural online professional development course in statistics education. The course aims at helping teachers improve their pedagogical and content knowledge of statistics through exposure to innovative web-based educational tools and resources, and cross-cultural exchange of experiences and ideas.

The *EarlyStatistics* course is the main outcome of a 3-year project (2005-2008) funded by the European Union under the Socrates-Comenius Action, which exploited the affordances offered by open and distance learning technologies to help improve the quality of statistics instruction offered in European schools. Recognizing teachers' ongoing professional development and learning as a linchpin of instructional innovation and success for their students, the project harnessed the power of the Internet to provide European teachers with access to a wide array of colleagues, discussions, and resources eluding them in their workplace.

The *EarlyStatistics* project consortium, comprised of five universities in four countries (Cyprus, Spain, Greece, Norway), spent the first two years of the project designing and developing, using contemporary web-based tools and resources, a line of research-based curricular and instructional materials to be used during the professional development course. In parallel to the development of the instructional material, the team worked on the technical design and implementation of the infrastructure and services for a dedicated online information base to support the project activities and outputs. A pilot delivery of *EarlyStatistics* took place during the final year of the project. To evaluate the applicability and success of the course, there was also follow-up classroom experimentation. Participating teachers developed and delivered teaching episodes integrating the use of the course tools and resources provided to them.

After final revisions of *EarlyStatistics* based on feedback from the pilot delivery and the follow-up classroom experimentation, and updating of the project information base with the latest version of all content, the course entered the European Union Lifelong Learning-Comenius database for European wide recruitment. It will be offered to the European educational community as a Comenius in-service course targeting elementary and middle school mathematics teachers. The course has been scheduled for offering three times during 2011. The consortium intends to continue offering the course in subsequent years, thus increasing access to large numbers of teachers involved in statistics education.

The study presented in this chapter, which took place during the *EarlyStatistics* pilot delivery, aimed at investigating the forms of collaboration and shared knowledge building undertaken by the multinational group of teachers participating in the pilot delivery. Specifically, the study had the following objectives:

- Study the online interactions in which the teachers engage during the course;
- Gather evidence in the teachers' online interactions of the formation of an online community of practice that facilitates intercultural communication and knowledge sharing;
- Gain understanding of the ways in which conditions in the pedagogical setting, the tools, and the context of teachers' collaborative work, facilitate or hinder the formation of a functional online community of practice;
- Provide expert and practitioner recommendations for improving the implementation of online communities of practice in teacher professional development;
- Provide groundwork for further research in the area of CSCL.

Methodology

Context and Participants

A case study design with mixed methods was employed in the current study. This approach is suitable given that the key purpose of the study was to allow us to gain comprehensive understanding of the online interactions and knowledge sharing among teachers engaged in online professional development, rather than to prove/disprove underlying hypotheses. The case studied consisted of the group of fourteen in-service teachers that participated in the pilot delivery of the professional development course, which took place during the spring of 2008 in three of the partner countries – Cyprus, Spain and Greece. Participants voluntarily enrolled in the course. They did not gain any extrinsic rewards such as compensation, or academic credit incentives. A prerequisite for participation in the course was proficiency in English, since English was the language of instruction.

Nine of the course participants were female and five male. Half were aged between 31-40, while three were younger (21-30 years old) and four older (41-50 years old). The majority had been teaching for more than ten years. Since they originated from three different European countries, they were geographically, culturally, and linguistically heterogeneous. They came from different educational systems, and had varied educational backgrounds. They were either elementary or secondary school teachers (9 elementary school teachers, 5 secondary school teachers), and differed considerably in their mathematical and statistical knowledge, and in their confidence and experience in teaching statistics. There was also variety in teachers' experience and comfort with internet technologies, and in their previous experience in taking online courses. Although all of the teachers were familiar with computers and the majority rated their computer skills as fairly or highly competent, only five teachers had ever taken a distance learning courses in the past. No participant had ever used any videoconferencing facilities prior to this course.

Pedagogical and Didactic Approach

Recognizing that teachers bring a diverse variety of strategies into the course as a result of their own professional experiences, and that professional development is often most effective when deeply contextualized in teachers' professional activity, *EarlyStatistics* adopted an approach that respects and utilizes teachers' professional knowledge. The distance education environment was designed as a framework for flexible learning, regarding teachers as the main agents of their professional development, supported by an environment rich in challenges and interactions.

A central conviction underlying *EarlyStatistics* is that learning as part of a community of practice can provide a useful model for teacher professional development in statistics education. The *EarlyStatistics* course provided a virtual space where European teachers of statistics with a broad range of experiences and expertise came together to reflect upon pedagogical theory and practice, to exchange ideas and resources, and to build collaborations. Teachers were encouraged and expected to engage in joint discussions and to work collaboratively in completing projects and other assignments. The aim was to build an open knowledge-building and sharing environment that would foster sustained participation, and would allow teachers opportunities for increased social presence. Social presence creates a greater sense of belonging in the community, providing a context that facilitates critical discourse and reflection (Vaughan & Garrison, 2005).

Central to the course design was the functional integration of technology with existing core curricular ideas, and specifically, the integration of statistics educational software (the dynamic software Tinkerplots© and Fathom©), as well as a variety of activities and resources available online (e.g. simulations, animations, video clips, etc.), which stimulate and engage teachers and provide them with the opportunity to model and investigate real world problems of statistics.

EarlyStatistics Course Content and Structure

Table 1 shows the EarlyStatistics course agenda. The course lasted 13 weeks, and was made up of six Modules (Meletiou-Mavrotheris et al., 2008). In Modules 1-3 (Weeks 1-6), the focus was on enriching the participants' statistical content and pedagogical knowledge by exposing them to similar kinds of learning situations, technologies, and curricula to those they should employ in their own classrooms. The conceptual "Framework for Teaching Statistics within the K-12 Mathematics Curriculum" (Franklin et al., 2005), developed by a group of leading statistics and mathematics educators, had been used to structure the presentation of content. Statistics was presented as an investigative process that involves four components: (i) clarifying the problem at hand and formulating questions that can be answered with data; (ii) designing and employing a plan to collect appropriate data; (iii) selecting appropriate graphical or numerical methods to analyze the data, and (iv) interpreting the results. To help teachers go beyond procedural memorization and acquire a well-organized body of knowledge, the course emphasized and revisited a set of central statistical ideas. Through participation in authentic educational activities such as projects, experiments, computer explorations with data, group work and discussions, participating teachers learned where the "big ideas" of statistics apply and how, and developed a variety of methodologies and resources for their effective instruction.

In Modules 4-6, the focus shifted to classroom implementation issues. Teachers customized and expanded upon provided materials (Module 4; Weeks 7-9), and applied them in their own classrooms with the support of the design team (Module 5; Weeks 10-11). They wrote up their experiences, including a critical analysis of their work and that resulting from their pupils. Once the teaching experiment was completed, they reported on their experiences to the other teachers, and also provided video-taped teaching episodes and samples of their students' work, for group reflection and evaluation (Module 6; Weeks 12-13).

Each module involved a range of activities, readings and contributions to discussion, as well as completion of group and/or individual assignments. Both the dialogue and the assignments were structured so as to explicitly make ties among theory and practice. Reflective questions created situations for the participating teachers to critically examine the subject matter through additional personal research or reading of the course material, thus giving them the opportunity to make new connections between theory and their personal and professional experiences. Table 2, which presents the activities included in Module 1, is indicative of the activities in which teachers engaged during the course.

A number of strategies were employed by the project consortium to promote online dialogue and transnational collaboration among participating teachers, and to ensure that all teachers would actively contribute to course activities and discussions, including the following:

- Monitored discussion forums allowed teachers to discuss content and help each other;
- Discussion questions were assigned bi-weekly. These were conceptual questions keyed to a major theme, and addressing content as well as pedagogical concerns;
- Participation in discussion forums and other collaborative activities was a compulsory element of the course;
- Participants were assigned to small groups, and each group was facilitated by a tutor. Groups received periodic assignments

Table 1. The EarlyStatistics course agenda

Week	Topic	Activities
1st f2f meeting	*Introduction to Course*	• Video-conferencing session: "Meet" teachers from other participating countries • Pre-assessment of teacher pedagogical and content knowledge of statistics • Discussion on importance of statistics • Familiarization with course objectives • Familiarization with online course website
Week 1 Week 2	**Module 1: Statistical Problem Solving/ Statistical Problem Posing**	• Statistics as a Problem Solving Process • Big Ideas of Statistics • Formulate questions that can be answered with data
Week 3 Week 4	**Module 2: Data Collection**	• Design a plan to collect appropriate data • Employ the plan to collect the data
2nd f2f meeting	*Familiarization with statistics educational software*	• Familiarization with educational software Tinkerplots • Computer-based practice and experimentation • Use of simulation and visualization • Computer supported teaching
Week 5 Week 6	**Module 3: Data Analysis and Interpretation**	• Select appropriate graphical or numerical methods • Use these methods to analyze the data • Interpret the analysis • Relate the interpretation to the original question
Week 7 Week 8 Week 8	**Module 4: Preparation for teaching intervention**	• Customize and expand materials
3rd f2f meeting	*Logistics of Teaching Intervention*	• Help teachers get prepared for the teaching intervention • Give teachers guidelines about how to build their portfolio (e.g. video-taping, samples of student work)
Week 10 Week 11	**Module 5:Teaching intervention**	• Apply customized materials • Write up experiences • Provide samples of student work
Week 12 Week 13	**Module 6: Reflection and Evaluation**	• Preparation of portfolio
4th f2f meeting	*Reflections on the Course*	• PowerPoint presentations • Viewing of videotaped classroom episodes

which they jointly completed using social software such as wikis.

Members of the *EarlyStatistics* consortium with expertise in statistics education facilitated the course. Their role was to moderate discussions, encourage full, thoughtful involvement of all participants, and provide feedback. Facilitators helped to deepen the learning experience for course participants by encouraging productive interaction and critical reflection on workplace practices.

Mode of Delivery

The course was delivered through a blended learning approach. There were a few face-to-face meetings with local teachers, but the biggest part of the course was delivered online, by utilizing the project information base for teaching, support and coordination purposes. In addition to the course content, the e-learning environment offered access to a variety of other links and resources, as well as to tools for professional dialogue and support.

Table 2. Module 1 Activities

Activity 1 – Discussion Forum *Researching and Enhancing Children's Reasoning about Statistical Problem Solving (Whole class forum; Weeks 1-2)* In this activity, you will participate in a whole class forum to discuss based on some suggested readings and your own ideas, the statistical problem-solving process, and ways in which the mathematics curriculum can help promote statistical problem solving. 1) First we suggest that you read carefully the following research article, in order to reflect on some underlying questions: Nitko, A.J. and Lane, S. (1990). Solving Problems is Not Enough: Assessing and Diagnosing the Ways in Which Students Organize Statistical Concepts. In *Proceeding of the 3rd International Conference on Teaching Statistics* (pp. 467-474). New Zealand: Dunedin. [REMOVED HYPERLINK FIELD] 2) Participate in the discussion forum by posting a response addressing the following: - What type of student activities encompasses statistical problem solving? - Nitko's article suggests that solving problems is not adequate to construct statistical knowledge. Do you agree with this view? Why or why not? - To which extent do you agree with the view that problems must be based on real scenarios in order for learning to be adequately contextualized? Revisit the discussion forum multiple times throughout the two weeks. Be sure to respond to your classmates' postings and to questions posed by the course facilitators. Contribute at least one additional substantive posting. ***Activity 2 – Individual Assignment*** The aim of this individual assignment, which is due at the end of Week 2 of the course, is to help you reflect on how you could integrate Statistical Problem Solving into your instructional practices. Read the introductory chapter of the Guidelines for Assessment and Instruction in Statistics Education (GAISE) Report (Franklin et al., 2005) which provides a curriculum framework for Pre-K-12 (Pre-kindergarten to high school) statistics instruction. Also review your national mathematics curricula. In no more than 1000 words, respond to the following questions: - Which is the proposal regarding the promotion of statistical problem solving within the mathematics curriculum put forth by the GAISE report? - How much emphasis is placed on problem solving in the statistics strand of your national mathematics curriculum? How is this related with the GAISE report? - Which are the potential benefits of using statistical problem solving at school? - Which problem settings are relevant to your real classroom situation and could provide an appropriate context for your students to learn statistics? - Which difficulties do you anticipate to encounter if you introduce statistical problem solving in your classroom? When you finish answering the questions, you must remember to upload the file (.doc, .pdf) in your e-portfolio. ***Activity 3 – Phase I of "Conducting a Statistical Study" project*** This is Phase I of the "Conducting a Statistical Study" project, which will span the first six weeks of the course. In the project, you will work in small groups of 4-5 teachers of similar grade levels to carry out a real statistical study to investigate one or more questions of your choice. Completing the project will help you see the "big picture" of statistics by taking you through all four stages of the statistical problem solving process: posing the question, collecting the data, analyzing the data (using appropriate technological tools), and interpreting the results. This will deepen your content knowledge of statistics and will serve as a model as to the type of learning situations, technologies and curricula you should employ in your own statistics classroom. *Phase I (Weeks 1-2): Formulate Questions* In order to begin the preparation for the teaching experiment that you will design and implement in your classroom, choose a set of problems related with statistical knowledge that would be interesting for your students. Working jointly with your group, do the following: 1) Decide on a topic that you think would be of interest to students of your grade level. 2) Formulate one or more questions that would be appropriate for your grade level, and that could be addressed by collecting and analyzing data. 3) Post a message in the discussion forum for Activity 3, describing to the rest of the course participants the question(s) formulated by your group. Revisit the discussion forum multiple times throughout the two weeks. Be sure to respond to your classmates' postings and to questions posed by the course facilitators. Contribute at least one additional substantive posting.

To offer teachers flexibility and to accommodate different time zones, the largest portion of the course was conducted asynchronously through discussion and mail groups. There was also some synchronous communication through use of technologies such as audio/video streaming, and videoconferencing. One-way informational postings such as articles and videos also served as objects for supporting interaction.

The course was developed by using Moodle, an easy to use, open source course management system designed to help educators in creating

Figure 1. Screenshots from a discussion forum in the EarlyStatistics portal

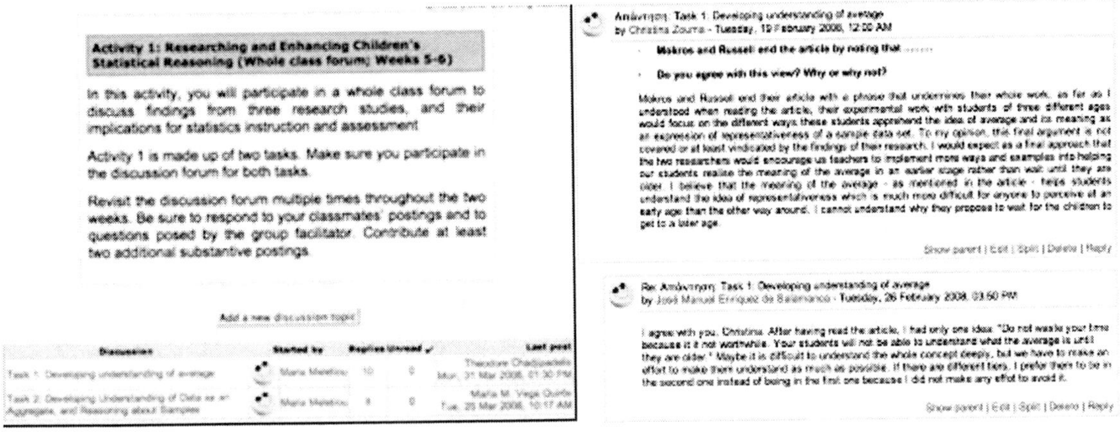

quality online courses. While Moodle is freeware, it has a user-friendly and reliable interface, with good pedagogical design, and offers many excellent applications that can be used to support the learning process. For example, the system offers a variety of distance collaboration tools (e.g. discussion forums, wikis, chat rooms, etc.) which were utilized in *EarlyStatistics* to allow interaction among peers and course facilitators (see Figure 1). Moreover, to support learners not fluent in English, the course used multilingual interfaces (Greek, Spanish, English).

Instruments, Data Collection and Analysis Procedures

Documenting online interactions and collaborative knowledge construction is a multifaceted phenomenon that requires complementary methods of data collection and analysis in order to understand how learning is accomplished through interaction, how learners engage in knowledge building, and how designed media support this accomplishment (Hmelo-Silver, 2003). Consequently, to increase understanding of the research setting, the current study employed a variety of both qualitative and quantitative data collection techniques, including:

- The contents of the online discussion boards, chats, and wikis in which teachers participated during the course;
- Group assignments completed by teachers throughout the course;
- Quantitative statistics automatically collected by the system (e.g. number of teachers participating in a discussion forum or successfully completing group assignments, number of postings by each participant, etc.);
- An open-ended web-based survey administered at the course completion, aimed at determining teachers' perceptions, opinions, feelings and motives regarding their participation in collaborative course activities and the impact these might have had on their professional development;
- Semi-structured interviews of a selected group of teachers that surveyed their views on the effectiveness of the online communication during the course.

Quantitative data were used to account for the occurrence of actions or events and to capture general tendencies regarding community dynamics, and to relate them with the qualitative categories derived though qualitative data analysis. Qualitative data were analyzed using the constant comparison analysis method. Constant comparison analysis, which involves unitizing, categorizing, chunking, and coding by choosing words, phrases, or sentences that specifically address the research aims, assisted in the search for patterns and themes that were used to develop the study's interpretation.

Lessons Learned from *EarlyStatistics* Course Pilot Delivery

The overall feedback from the target user groups from all partner countries participating in the *EarlyStatistics* course pilot delivery, as well as from external experts in statistics education regarding the course content, services, and didactical approaches was generally very positive. Key conclusions from the analysis of the user feedback were that *EarlyStatistics* was quite successful in helping teachers to improve their pedagogical and content knowledge of statistics by offering interactive, technology-rich instructional materials and services that enhance the teaching and learning process, and by providing course participants the opportunity to collaborate with other teachers and begin the construction of a community of practice. Moreover, data obtained from the teaching experimentations in the course participants' classrooms suggest positive gains in student learning outcomes and attitudes towards statistics (for more details see Chadjipadelis & Andreadis, 2008).

In the survey administered at the completion of the pilot course delivery and the follow-up interviews, teachers were asked to indicate *"what they liked the most about the EarlyStatistics course"*. The following aspects of the course were the ones which were most appreciated by the course participants:

- Flexibility and convenience associated with distance education;
- Opportunity for communication and collaboration with others teachers;
- Exchange of experiences and ideas with teachers from other European countries;
- Close ties between the course material and teachers' personal and professional experiences.

All of the course participants considered the fact that *EarlyStatistics* was offered at-distance to be an advantage of the course, since it made it possible for teachers to determine their own place, pace, and time of study: *"It is a form of training that does not place stifling limits and restrictions of freedom on the teacher"; "You decide your own workload"; "You can follow your own pace of work"*. Further, a few teachers noted that the distance option gave them the opportunity to attend a course in statistics education offered by experts in the field originating from different European countries.

The promotion of communication and collaboration among teachers was an aspect of the *EarlyStatistics* course that was considered by all of the course participants to be an important strength of the program:

I liked the interaction with the other teachers. It is useful to share your ideas and problems with other teachers from different educational levels.

I liked the regular communication for exchange of opinions with other teachers and reflection, with the help of technology, and the sense of permanent support.

It was very useful to be able to communicate with teachers of different levels and perspectives. This direct communication with everyone has helped to continue the hard work of self-learning.

In particular, teachers praised the fact that *EarlyStatistics* had allowed them, through computer-mediated communication, to share content, ideas, and instructional strategies with teachers from different countries and educational systems:

What I liked the most was the direct communication with the help of the internet with colleagues from other countries.

Distance training has helped me to understand that the problems that I have when teaching statistics are also common in other European Countries.

It helps to enrich our experiences, when contrasting information with other teachers around Europe.

It is good to 'hear' colleagues from other countries that face similar problems like you and sometimes, because of a different view on a point, suggest ideas that you didn't think of.

An important motivational factor influencing the success of an online community of practice is the nature of the group tasks in which learners are engaged. Merely forming a discussion forum and providing the technology will not automatically lead to the development of a community of practice that supports well-managed, conducive to learning conversations (Doolan, Hilliard, & Thorton, 2006). Similarly, mere provision of social software such as a wiki will not be adequate to generate collaborative co-creation and shared learning (e.g. Kennard, 2007). In *EarlyStatistics*, both the dialogue and the assignments were carefully designed to be learner-centered, and to make explicit ties between theory and practice by utilizing participating teachers' own experiences as learning resources. This aspect of the course was very much appreciated by the course participants. Several of them pointed out that *EarlyStatistics* offered them professional development which addressed their workplace educational needs, because it was deeply contextualized in their professional activity:

From the cognitive point of view this type of training obviously helps construction of knowledge, though the exploitation of experiences of teachers and the interaction with other teachers.

The organization of the program with the aim that teachers self-learn, analyze what they know, and reflect about their practices, is a different way of permanent in-service learning.

It is a form of training that respects teachers' professional experience and contributes to the improvement of their educational work through the enrichment of experiences and the exchange of opinions with other teachers that work in different cultural and educational environments.

The *EarlyStatistics* project won, ex-aequo with *Maths4Stats* (a joint project coordinated by Statistics South Africa), the 2009 Best Cooperative Project Award in Statistical Literacy. This award is given every two years by the International Association of Statistics Education (IASE) "*in recognition of outstanding, innovative, and influential statistical literacy projects that affect a broad segment of the general public*".

Issues, Controversies, Problems

Despite the overall success of the *EarlyStatistics* project and the very positive feedback from the groups of teachers participating in the pilot delivery and from external experts in statistics education, a number of shortcomings have also been identified. The biggest difficulty experienced by the consortium was its limited success in establishing a functional online community of practice, which was a main objective of the project.

From the outset of the project, the course team was well aware of the challenges in developing such a community, of the fact that providing the technology does not automatically lead to the establishment of relations and group cohesion (Gordon, Petocz, & Reid, 2007). The experience from the pilot testing of *EarlyStatistics* further alerted them to the fact that community building is

Figure 2. Distribution of messages in the EarlyStatistics Discussion Forums per Module

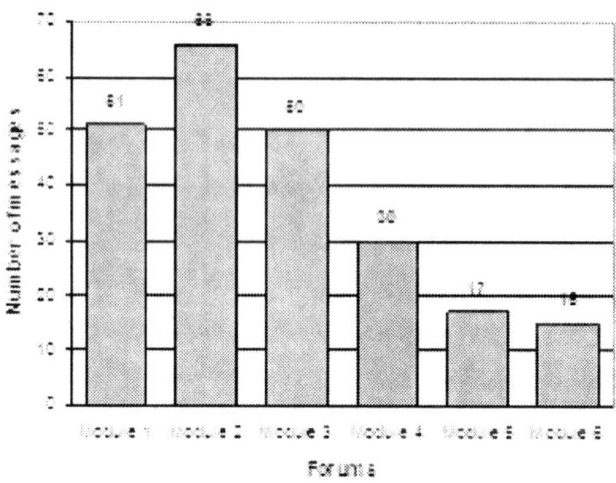

very challenging. Despite the fact that the course team employed several strategies to promote teacher dialogue and collaboration, and that the course facilitators tried their best to ensure that all teachers actively contributed to discussion forums, there was often a lower than anticipated learner-to-learner interaction.

Figure 2 shows the distribution of messages in *EarlyStatistics* per forum:

We can see that while at the beginning of the course there was big enthusiasm and very high participation in the discussion forums, interaction dropped off over time. A total of 229 messages had been sent to *EarlyStatistics* during the 13 weeks that the course lasted (76 messages/month on average). However, the vast majority of the messages (167 messages, 73% of all messages) were sent during the first six weeks of the course. The forums in which there was high participation were the ones in Modules 1-3. The last two forums of the course had a very limited number of messages. In contrast to the vibrant interaction and rich dialog characterizing the earlier part of the course, often what happened towards the end of the course was that only 3-4 teachers would actively participate in the discussion forums, while the rest would make minimal or no contributions.

Figure 3 shows the distribution of messages written in the forums per community member (P1-P14 stand for the 14 teachers participating in the course, and CF1-CF3 for the course facilitators):

As we can see, there was a huge variation in the degree of participation among community members. There were a few teachers whose level of engagement was very high. One of the teachers (P1, 31 messages) was so active in the discussion forums that she ended up sending more messages than any of the three course facilitators moderating the forums. At the same time, several of the teachers participated only sporadically. These teachers exhibited a silent manner of participation. Checking their records of participation, we discovered that despite them not being active in the discussion forums, they continued to join the discussion forums and to read the messages posted by the other community members.

Figure 4 provides information about the initiation of discussion threads by community members, considering only those threads which resulted in subsequent discussion.

Naturally, the three course facilitators initiated half of the threads. However, it is very interesting to see that P1 – the teacher with the highest number of messages among course participants – had also been very active in provoking discussions among community members (7 thread initiations). In total, 5 out of the 14 teachers participating in the course (36%) initiated at least one discussion thread.

Based on the analysis of the data collected during the study, we have identified a number of factors that adversely affected online participation of course participants. These factors, which have also been pointed out by previously conducted research studies, are discussed below.

Course Workload

A reason that might have contributed to the pilot *EarlyStatistics* course limited success in building an online community of practice is the pilot course workload, which proved to be overwhelming. When asked, in the end-of course survey and in

Figure 3. Distribution of messages written by community members in the EarlyStatistics Discussion Forums

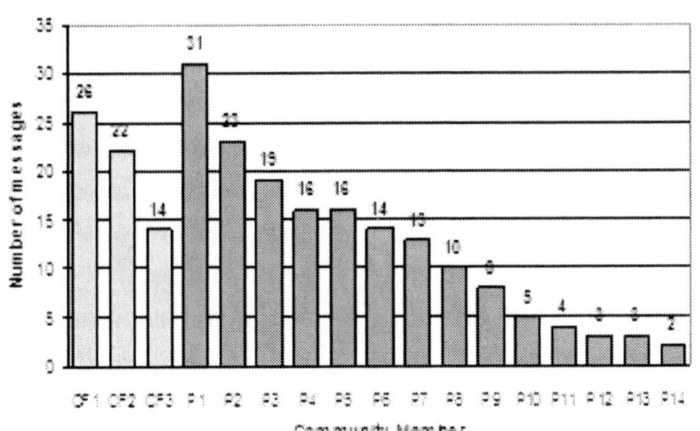

Figure 4. Initiation of discussion threads by community members in the EarlyStatistics Discussion Forums

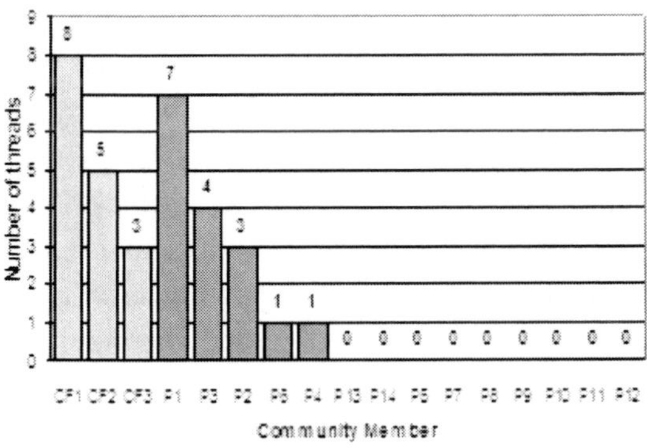

the follow-up interviews, to indicate *"what they liked the least about the EarlyStatistics course"*, most participants mentioned the course workload which made it very difficult for them to keep up with the course requirements due to their overburdened schedules. Responses such as the following were typical:

The papers we had to read in the first modules were too many and our time to work on them limited, because of our jobs.

There was too much studying involved.

Teachers' difficulties in finding time to engage in online activities is the most frequently faced challenge uncovered by research studies investigating teacher participation online communities of practice (Davis & Resta, 2002; Forrester et al, 2006; Hartnell-Young, 2006). It takes a lot of time and commitment for teachers to engage online, and the implications of an over length course can be extremely serious (Juan et al., 2008).

Duration of Discussion Forums

The short duration of the discussion periods was another aspect of the course criticized by participants. Several participants noted that the study pace had been too high for them, and that the time allocated to each discussion forum was not adequate:

The course had too many assignments on the theoretical part, and there was not enough time for working on them and posting on the forums.

The tight time schedule - I believe that more time is required for every part or module since every one of us works or is involved in so many other things at the same time.

Other studies have also found that many learners have difficulties in formulating and articulating contributions to an online discussion when under time pressure (Hardless et al., 2001; Jakobsson, 2006).

Technical Issues

Some technical difficulties experienced during the *EarlyStatistics* pilot course testing, might have also discouraged the course participants from fully contributing to the discussion forums: *Because of the bad state of my e-connection, sometimes it was difficult to get or send prompt replies.*

The server was down sometimes and made it impossible to access the course website.

Impact of technology can be an issue that directly affects online participation (Bradshaw et al., 2005). Access also continues to be one of the most important factors affecting online participation (Geibert, 2000; ten Cate, 2007). Even when all participants have access to a computer with internet connection, like in our case, online access might be difficult and time consuming for some of the participants due to issues such as low speed connectivity, outdated browsers, forgetting of passwords, etc. (Klecka et al, 2005; Forrester et al, 2006).

Lack of Physical Proximity

The fact that there was *"no personal contact with teachers from other countries"* was also a shortcoming of the pilot course that might have negatively affected the building of a successful online community of practice. During the pilot delivery there were a few face-to-face meetings with local teachers, but not with the group as a whole. Course participants got the chance to virtually meet teachers from the other countries through video-conferencing, this however cannot be as effective as face-to-face interaction. Moreover, planning of videoconferencing and other activities that required synchronous communication (e.g. chat sessions) proved very difficult to schedule, as it was almost impossible for all of the teachers to be available at the same time. Similarly to previous research (Stodel, Thompson, & MacDonald, 2006; Thomas, 2002; ten Cate, 2007; Juan et al., 2008), this lack of physical proximity and social cues characterizing ICT-mediated interaction impacted negatively the sense of togetherness within the online community, increasing teachers' feelings of isolation and decreasing social presence online. Teachers built strong local groups but had more limited than desired interaction with teachers from other countries.

Language Barriers

Researchers that have studied the dynamics of international online communities of practice (e.g Trayner, Smith, & Bettoni, 2007) have found communication among people who speak different first languages to be a very serious challenge for such communities. In this study, language of communication also proved to be an obstacle to participation for some of the course participants. While most of the teachers did not seem to have any problems with reading and writing in English, for a few of them language was a barrier that prevented them from fully participating in online discussions:

The bibliography presented in the course was rich and modern but hard to read for those of us not used to reading in English.

It was a bit difficult and time consuming for us to read bibliography in English and to post our thoughts in the forum.

Teachers with language difficulties did not post as often as their peers who had better English writing skills, and their contributions tended to be shorter.

Limited Experience of Course Facilitators in Online Instruction

The important role of facilitators and moderators is a main theme emerging from research studies examining online communities of practice. Most of these studies find that prompt and effective moderation of online interactions is important to motivation and feedback (Henderson, 2007; Forrester et. al, 2006) and that course facilitators should be skilled with good online moderating practices (Hewitt, 2005; Stodel et al., 2006). In *EarlyStatistics*, the limited experience of the course facilitators in distance learning was a drawback of the pilot course. The team members that facilitated *EarlyStatistics* are very experienced statistics educators who have been involved for several years in teacher training. Nonetheless, this was the first time they were offering professional development online. Consortium partners with extensive previous expertise in distance education acted as mentors and provided hands-on training on a number of topics relating to distance learning. This certainly helped course facilitators to improve their instructional skills in distance education. However, they still faced difficulties in leading the discussion forums, and particularly in achieving full, thoughtful involvement of all participants. As Gould and Peck (2005) point out, leading a discussion of substance on a "discussion board" than in a real classroom is quite challenging.

Solutions and Recommendations

Ensuring the successful building of an online community of practice is a particularly important issue for online teacher professional development. As the first experiences with the *EarlyStatistics* teacher professional program indicate, building online communities of practice is difficult. Based on the findings from the pilot delivery, we have identified several reasons that might have contributed to our limited success in online community building. These have informed the revision of the course to better support community building among participating teachers.

The heavy course workload was corrected in the revised version of the course, and the length of time allocated to each discussion forum was increased from two to three weeks, to allow teachers more time for reflection and for online communication. Similarly, the technical difficulties experienced in the pilot delivery have been resolved. Additionally, the lack of a face-to-face meeting with participants from other countries will not be an issue in future offerings of the *EarlyStatistics* course, which will have a blended-learning format. At the beginning of the course, teachers around Europe will gather together to attend a one-week intensive seminar (they can finance their expenses by applying for a grant under the Lifelong Learning/Comenius In-Service Training Program). During this meeting, they will get familiarized with the course and its objectives, and with the facilities offered by the course e-Learning system. More importantly, they will get the chance to meet and interact with each other. We believe that this initial in-person meeting will reinforce teacher online engagement by helping mitigate the problem of trust and social presence online (Ardichvili, Page, & Wentling, 2003). Finally, the limited experience of the *EarlyStatistics* course facilitators in online instruction will not be such a big issue in future offerings of the course. Undoubtedly, the valuable experiences gained from this pilot delivery will allow the employement of more effective moderating strategies in future offerings of the course.

Online communities of practice is a promising model for ongoing teacher professional development. Institutions involved in in-service teacher professional development could utilize online communities of practice as a means for ongoing teacher professional growth and support. Higher education teacher training institutions could also exploit online communities of practice in order to introduce their pre-service teachers into the teaching profession. Participation in online communities of practice can allow novice teachers to obtain different perspectives, teaching strategies, and ideas from more experienced teachers, and to see how different aspects of learning theories are applied in real classroom environments (Sutherland, Scanlon & Sperring, 2004; Garcia, Sanchez, Escudero & Llinares, 2006).

Despite their potential, experiences gained from the *EarlyStatistics* course suggest that online communities of practice also present some unique challenges. Teachers participating in such a course are likely to be characterized by diversity in a number of parameters (pedagogical and content knowledge of statistics and mathematics, educational level and grade they teach, cultural and/or professional backgrounds, level of comfort with technology and with distance learning, etc.). Given their overburdened schedules, they will be willing to invest time on the course only if it stimulates and engages them, and addresses their specific educational needs and preferences. Several pedagogical and technical issues should be taken into account in the design of an online professional development course, in order to provide an effective environment that motivates teachers and supports the development of a functional online community of practice:

- Choice of accessible media;
- User-friendly interface and navigation services;
- Multimedia presentation of content to ensure effective knowledge transfer;
- Activities and resources (simulations, animations, video clips, etc.) that stimulate and engage teachers participating in professional development, and address a variety of teaching and learning styles;
- Access to multiple distance collaboration tools that promote interaction with peers and with course facilitators;
- Course content addressing teachers' workplace educational needs;
- Respect and utilization of teachers' professional knowledge;
- Careful scheduling of course activities to offer teachers flexibility, and to accommodate different time zones;
- Adoption, whenever possible, of a blended learning approach, to allow teachers to personally meet and interact with each other.
- Setting of realistic work expectations so as not to overburden teachers;
- Provision of adequate time for teachers to formulate and articulate contributions to online discussions;
- Prompt and effective moderation of online interactions by course facilitators;
- Support, in the case of international online communities, of members experiencing difficulties in oral and/or written communication in English.

Expecting all members of a community of practice to have the same level of participation is unrealistic. It is very natural to have different levels of participation due to differences in members' learning styles, experiences, and personal circumstances. It is a very common phenomenon to have some of the participants acting as invisible observers, spending many hours lurking, and knowing the topics of conversation and key players very well, but never crossing the threshold of observation. This silent participation in online communities, which has been described as legitimate peripheral participation (Lave and Wenger 1991), is characteristic of online communities of practice and should not be discouraged, because it plays an important role in professional and personal development (Sutherland, Scanlon & Sperring, 2004). A viable online community of practice needs a steady flow of members with a range of commitment levels—peripheral, moderately engaged, as well as highly active. However, online community members who do not contribute because they feel insecure (e.g. people with language difficulties) should be supported by other members of the community, and especially by the moderator(s).

CONCLUSION

A common thread emerging from educational research is the direct relationship between improving the quality of teaching and improving students' learning. Thus, the provision of high-quality, ongoing professional development for teachers has become a paramount issue in school reform efforts. The need for the training of large numbers of teachers makes distance learning an attractive option. The traditional approach is to provide teacher training through a well-designed course package. The *EarlyStatistics* project has adopted a different approach, guided by contemporary visions of web-based instruction which support "learning" and "community" rather than "instructional" models of professional development. A central conviction underlying the program is that learning as part of a community of practice can provide an effective model for professional development. Unlike traditional, individualistic approaches to teacher professional development, properly designed online communities of practice can foster a culture of sharing and sustained support for teachers. By allowing geographically dispersed teachers to exchange experiences and ideas, communities of practice can enable them to connect and learn from each other in ways not possible in more traditional, face-to-face professional development programs.

Despite the potential of online communities of practice, the existing research literature indicates that their introduction in educational contexts is often less successful than anticipated. Findings from the current study concur with the existing research literature, indicating that successful building of an online community of practice, particularly in a cross-national context, is very challenging. An online community of practice will not automatically take shape through the availability of online space but requires carefully crafted designs – both technical and social (Rourke & Kanuka, 2007).

Teaching online courses is a new, unexplored territory for most statistics instructors. Online instruction is similar yet different from face-to-face learning, and requires new teaching skills and strategies (Juan et al., 2008). Online instructors' new role as course facilitators turns them into both guides and learners (Heuer & King, 2004). Teachers must be trained in this new mode of instruction, to facilitate learner success and online participation, as they develop in the art of becoming online guides. Garfield and Everson (2009), who developed an at-distance statistics teacher training course that has been quite successful in achieving learner participation and collaboration, explain that their online courses go through a continuous cycle of evaluation and improvement. Each time the online course is taught, changes are made in the way in which discussion assignments are structured and used, based on feedback received from learners and on careful study of the patterns of interaction occurring within different discussion groups.

Research in the area of online communities of practice is still at a developmental stage. More research is needed to advance our understanding of how to best take advantage of computer-mediated communication tools to support the development of effective virtual communities of practice that can act as vehicles for promoting teacher learning and growth. By exploring the forms of collaboration and shared knowledge building undertaken by the multinational group of teachers participating in the online in-service training course *EarlyStatistics*, the current case study has contributed to the growth of scientific knowledge in the field. Despite the tentative and non-generalizable nature of the study findings, we were still able to contribute some useful insights into the factors that may facilitate or impede the successful implementation of an online community of practice, suggesting possible methods for improving their implementation in distance education. These insights have helped to further improve the quality and effectiveness of the *EarlyStatistics* course, which is the first of its kind in Europe, and sketch a road map for our future research work, and for other similar online community building endeavors.

REFERENCES

Allan, J., & Lawless, N. (2003). Stress caused by online collaboration in e-learning. *Education + Training*, *45*(8/9), 564–572. doi:10.1108/00400910310508955

Ardichvili, A., Page, V., & Wentling, T. (2003). Motivation and barriers to participation in virtual knowledge-sharing communities of practice. *Journal of Knowledge Management*, *7*(1), 64–77. doi:10.1108/13673270310463626

Barab, S. MaKinster, J., & Scheckler, R. (2004). Designing system dualities: Characterizing and online professional development community. In S. Barab, R. Kling & J. Gray (Eds.), *Designing for virtual communities in the service of learning* (pp. 53-90). Cambridge, UK: Cambridge University Press.

Barab, S. A., & Duffy, T. (2000). From practice fields to communities of practice . In Jonassen, D., & Land, S. M. (Eds.), *Theoretical foundations of learning environments* (pp. 25–55). Mahwah, NJ: Lawrence Erlbaum Associates.

Baran, B., & Cagiltay, K. (2006). Teachers' experiences in online professional development environment. *Turkish Online Journal of Distance Education*, *7*(4), 110–122.

Bradshaw, P., Powell, S., & Terrell, I. (2005). Developing engagement in Ultralab's online communities of enquiry. *Innovations in Education and Teaching International*, *42*(3), 205–215. doi:10.1080/01587910500167886

Cady, J., & Rearden, K. (2009). Delivering online professional development in mathematics to rural educators. *Journal of Technology and Teacher Education*, *17*, 281–298.

Chadjipadelis, T., & Andreadis, I. (2008). *Early statistics evaluation report* (Internal document. Project: 226573-CP-1-2005).

Chick, H. L., & Pierce, R. U. (2008). Teaching statistics at the primary school level: Beliefs, affordances, and pedagogical content knowledge. In C. Batanero, G. Burrill, C. Reading, & A. Rossman (Eds), *Joint ICMI/IASE study: Teaching statistics in school mathematics. Challenges for teaching and teacher education. Proceedings of the ICMI Study 18 and 2008 IASE Round Table Conference.* Monterrey, Mexico: ICMI and IASE. Retrieved October 15, 2010, from www.stat.auckland.ac.nz/~iase/ publications.

Cochran-Smith, M., & Lytle, S. L. (1999). Relationships of knowledge and practice: Teacher learning in communities . In Iran-Nejad, A., & Pearson, P. D. (Eds.), *Review of research in education* (pp. 249–305). Washington, DC: American Educational Research Association.

Dalgarno, N., & Colgan, L. (2007). Supporting novice elementary mathematics teachers' induction in professional communities and providing innovative forms of pedagogical content knowledge development through information and communication technology. *Teaching and Teacher Education: An International Journal of Research and Studies*, *23*, 1051–1065. doi:10.1016/j.tate.2006.04.037

Davis, B., & Resta, V. (2002). Online collaboration: Supporting novice teachers as researchers. *Journal of Technology and Teacher Education*, *10*(1), 101–117.

Dede, C., Ketelhut, D., Whitehouse, P., Breit, L., & McCloskey, E. (2006). *Research agenda for online teacher professional development*. Cambridge, MA: Harvard Graduate School of Education.

Doolan, M., Hilliard, A., & Thorton, H. (2006). Collaborative learning: Using technology for fostering those valued practices inherent in constructive environments in traditional education. *Journal for the Enhancement of Learning and Teaching*, *3*(2), 7–17.

Faulin, J., Juan, A., Fonseca, P., Pla, L., & Rodriguez, S. (2009). Learning operations research online: Benefits, challenges and experiences. *International Journal of Simulation and Process Modelling*, *5*(1), 42–53. doi:10.1504/IJSPM.2009.025826

Forrester, G., Motteram, G., & Bangxiang, L. (2006). Transforming Chinese teachers' thinking, learning and understanding via e-learning. *Journal of Education for Teaching International research and pedagogy*, *32*(2), 197–212.

Franklin, C. A., Kader, G., Mewborn, D., Moreno, J., Peck, R., Perry, M., & Scheaffer, R. (2005). *Guidelines for assessment and instruction in statistics education* (GAISE) *report: A pre-K–12 curriculum framework*. Alexandria, VA: American Statistical Association. Retrieved October 15, 2010, from www.amstat.org/ Education/gaise/

Garcıa, M., Sanchez, V., Escudero, I., & Llinares, S. (2006). The dialectic relationship between research and practice in mathematics teacher education. *Journal of Mathematics Teacher Education*, *9*, 109–128. doi:10.1007/s10857-006-0003-8

Garfield, J., & Everson, M. (2009). Preparing teachers of statistics: A graduate course for future teachers. *Journal of Statistics Education, 17*(2). Retrieved October 15, 2010, from http:// www.amstat.org/ publications/ jse/ v17n2/ garfield.html

Geibert, R. (2000). Integrating web-based instruction into a graduate nursing program taught via videoconferencing: Challenges and solutions. *Computers in Nursing*, *18*(1), 26–34.

Gordon, S., Petocz, P., & Reid, A. (2007). Tools, artefacts, resources and pedagogy-Stories of international statistics educators. In P. L Jeffery (Ed.), *Australian Association for Research in Education 2006 Conference Papers*, AARE, Adelaide. Retrieved October 15, 2010, from http:// www.aare.edu.au/ 06pap/ gor06358.pdf

Gould, R., & Peck, R. (2005). Inspiring secondary statistics. *MSOR Connections*, *5*(3). Retrieved October 15, 2010, from http:// mathstore.ac.uk/ headocs/ 53inspiringstats.pdf

Gray, B. (2004). Informal learning in an online community of practice. [from http://www.cnd-webzine.hcp.ma/IMG/pdf/GRAY_article.pdf]. *Journal of Distance Education*, *19*(1), 20–35. Retrieved October 15, 2010.

Hardless, C., Lundin, J., & Nulden, U. (2001). Mandatory participation in asynchronous learning networks. In *Proceedings of HICSS-34*, Maui, USA. Retrieved October 15, 2010, from http:// www.viktoria.se/ nulden/ Publ/ PDF/ UNALN.pdf

Hartnell-Young, E., & Morriss, M. (2007). *Digital portfolios: Powerful tools for promoting professional growth and reflection* (2nd ed.). Thousand Oaks, CA: Corwin Press.

Henderson, M. (2007). Sustaining online teacher professional development through community design. *Campus-Wide Information Systems*, *24*(3), 162–173. doi:10.1108/10650740710762202

Heuer, B. P., & King, K. P. (2004). Leading the band: The role of the instructor in online learning for educators. *The Journal of Interactive Online Learning, 3*(1). Retrieved October 15, 2010, from http:// www.ncolr.org/ jiol/ issues/ PDF/ 3.1.5.pdf

Hewitt, J. (2005). Toward an understanding of how threads die in asynchronous computer conferences. *Journal of the Learning Sciences*, *14*(4), 567–589. doi:10.1207/s15327809jls1404_4

Hmelo-Silver, C. E. (2003). Analyzing collaborative knowledge construction: Multiple methods for integrated understanding. *Computers & Education*, *41*, 397–420. doi:10.1016/j.compedu.2003.07.001

Jakobsson, A. (2006). Students' self-confidence and learning through dialogues in a Net-based environment. *Journal of Technology and Teacher Education*, *14*(2), 387–405.

Joubert, M., & Surtherland, R. (2009). *A perspective on the literature: CPD for teachers of mathematics*. Bristol, UK: National Centre of Excellence in the Teaching of Mathematics.

Juan, A., Huertas, M., Steegmann, C., Corcoles, C., & Serrat, C. (2008). Mathematical e-learning: State of the art and experiences at the Open University of Catalonia. *International Journal of Mathematical Education in Science and Technology*, *39*(4), 455–471. doi:10.1080/00207390701867497

Kayler, M., & Weller, K. (2007). Pedagogy, self-assessment, and online discussion groups. *Journal of Educational Technology & Society*, *10*(1), 136–147.

Kennard, C. (2007). Wiki productivity and discussion forum activity in a postgraduate online distance learning course. In C. Montgomery C., & J. Seale (Eds.), *Proceedings of World Conference on Educational Multimedia, Hypermedia and Telecommunications 2007* (pp. 3564-3569). Chesapeake, VA: AACE.

Klecka, C. L., Clift, R. T., & Cheng, Y.-M. (2005). Are electronic conferences a solution in search of an urban problem? *Urban Education*, *40*(4), 412–429. doi:10.1177/0042085905276434

Kling, R., & Courtright, C. (2003). Group behavior and learning in electronic forums: A sociotechnical approach. *The Information Society*, *19*, 221–235. doi:10.1080/01972240309465

Koc, Y., Peker, D., & Osmanoglu, A. (2009). Supporting teacher professional development through online video case study discussions: An assemblage of preservice and inservice teachers and the case teacher. *Teaching and Teacher Education: An International Journal of Research and Studies*, *25*, 1158–1168. doi:10.1016/j.tate.2009.02.020

Lave, J., & Wenger, E. (1991). *Situated learning. Legitimate peripheral participation*. Cambridge, UK: Cambridge University Press.

Maloney-Krichmar, D., Abras, C., & Preece, J. (2002). Revitalizing an online community: Beyond user-centered design. *Proceedings of the 2002 International Symposium on Technology and Society* (pp. 13-19). Raleigh, NC.

McGraw, R., Lynch, K., & Koc, Y. (2007). The multimedia case as a tool for professional development: An analysis of online and face-to-face interaction among mathematics pre-service teachers, in-service teachers, mathematicians, and mathematics teacher educators. *Journal of Mathematics Teacher Education*, *10*(2), 95–121. doi:10.1007/s10857-007-9030-3

Meletiou-Mavrotheris, M., Paparistodemou, E., & Mavrotheris, E. Azcárate, P., Serradó, A., & Cardeñoso, J. M. (2008). Teachers' professional development in statistics: The Earlystatistics European Project. In C. Batanero, G. Burrill, C. Reading, & A. Rossman (Eds), *Joint ICMI/IASE study: Teaching statistics in school mathematics. Challenges for teaching and teacher education. Proceedings of the ICMI Study 18 and 2008 IASE Round Table Conference.* Monterrey, Mexico: ICMI and IASE. Retrieved October 15, 2010, from http:// www.ugr.es/~icmi/ iase_study/ Files/ Topic6/ T6P6_Meletiou.pdf

Muirhead, B. (2007). Integrating creativity into online university classes. *Journal of Educational Technology & Society*, *10*(1), 1–13.

Nielsen, J. (2006). *Participation inequality: Encouraging more users to contribute*. Nielsen's Alertbox Column on Web Usability. Retrieved October 15, 2010, from http:// www.useit.com/ alertbox/ participation_inequality.html

Nitko, A. J., & Lane, S. (1990). Solving problems is not enough: Assessing and diagnosing the ways in which students organise statistical concepts. *Proceedings of the 3rd International Conference on Teaching Statistics* (pp. 467-474). New Zealand: Dunedin.

Preece, J. (2000). *Online communities: Designing usability, supporting sociability*. Chichester, United Kingdom: John Wiley & Sons.

Renninger, K. A., & Shumar, W. (Eds.). (2002). *Building virtual communities: Learning and change in cyberspace*. New York, NY: Cambridge University Press. doi:10.1017/CBO9780511606373

Renninger, K. A., & Shumar, W. (2004). The centrality of culture and community to participant learning at and with the math forum . In Barab, S., Kling, R., & Gray, J. (Eds.), *Designing for virtual communities in the service of learning* (pp. 181–209). Cambridge, MA: Cambridge University Press.

Riverin, S., & Stacey, E. (2007). The evolution of an online community – A case study. *Research and Practice in Technology Enhanced Learning, 2*(3), 267–297. doi:10.1142/S1793206807000361

Rossman, A., Medina, E., & Chance, B. (2006). A post-calculus introduction to statistics for future secondary teachers. In A. Rossman & B. Chance (Eds.), *Proceedings of the Seventh International Conference on Teaching Statistics*, Salvador, Brazil. Voorburg, The Netherlands: International Statistical Institute.

Rourke, L., & Kanuka, H. (2007). Barriers to online critical discourse. *International Journal of Computer-Supported Collaborative Learning, 2*(1), 105–126. doi:10.1007/s11412-007-9007-3

Simpson, O. (2002). *Supporting students in online, open and distance learning*. London, UK & New York, NY: Taylor and Francis Group.

Sinclair, M., & Owston, R. (2006). Teacher professional development in mathematics and science: A blended learning approach. *Canadian Journal of University Continuing Education, 32*(2), 43–66.

Stahl, G. (2006). *Group cognition: Computer support for collaborative knowledge building*. Cambridge, MA: MIT Press.

Stephens, A. C., & Hartmann, C. E. (2002). *Using an online discussion forum to engage secondary mathematics teachers in teaching with technology*. Paper presented at Annual Meeting of the American Educational Research Association, New Orleans (ERIC Document Reproduction Service No. ED468891).

Stigler, M., & Hiebert, J. (1999). *The teaching gap*. Free Press.

Stodel, E. J., Thompson, T. L., & MacDonald, C. J. (2006). Learners' perspectives on what is missing from online learning: Interpretations through the community of inquiry framework. *The International Review of Research in Open and Distance Learning, 7*(3). Retrieved October 15, 2010, from http:// www.irrodl.org/ index.php/ irrodl/ article /viewArticle/ 325/743

Sutherland, L. M., Scanlon, L. A., & Sperring, A. (2005). New directions in preparing professionals: examining issues in engaging students in communities of practice through a school-university partnership. *Teaching and Teacher Education, 21*(1), 79–92. doi:10.1016/j.tate.2004.11.007

ten Cate, G. (2007).*Supporting a community of trainers: Can a community of practice help address trainers' need for continuous, easily accessible, and context-appropriate support?* International Institute for Communication and Development, The Hague. Retrieved October 15, 2010, from www.ciera.org/ library/ reports/ inquiry-3/ 3-014/ 3-014.pdf

Thomas, M. J. W. (2002). Learning within incoherent structures: The space of online discussion forums. *Journal of Computer Assisted Learning, 18*(3), 351–366. doi:10.1046/j.0266-4909.2002.03800.x

Trayner, B., Smith, J. D., & Bettoni, M. (2007). Participation in international virtual learning communities: A social learning perspective. *Lecture Notes in Business Information Processing, 1*(Part IV), 402–413. doi:10.1007/978-3-540-74063-6_32

Vaughan, N., & Garrison, D. (2005). Creating cognitive presence in a blended faculty development community. *The Internet and Higher Education, 8*(1), 1–12. doi:10.1016/j.iheduc.2004.11.001

Vygotsky, L. S. (1978). *Mind in society: The development of higher psychological processes*. Cambridge, MA: Harvard University.

Wagner, C. (2005). Supporting knowledge management in organizations with conversational technologies: Discussion forums, weblogs, and wikis. *Journal of Database Management, 16*(2), i–viii.

Watson, J. M. (2001). Profiling teachers' competence and confidence to teach particular mathematics topics: The case of chance and data. *Journal of Mathematics Teacher Education, 4*(4), 305–337. doi:10.1023/A:1013383110860

Wenger, E. (1998). *Communities of practice: Leaning, meaning, and identity*. Cambridge, UK: Cambridge University Press.

Zhao, Y., & Rop, S. (2001). *A critical review of the literature on electronic networks as reflective discourse communities for inservice teachers*. Retrieved October 15, 2010, from www.ciera.org/ library/ reports/ nquiry-3 /3-014/ 3-014.pdf

ADDITIONAL READING

Beuchot, A., & Bullen, M. (2005). Interaction and Interpersonality in Online Discussion Forums. *Distance Education, 26*(1), 67–87. doi:10.1080/01587910500081285

Birney, R., Barry, M., & Eigeartaigh, M. (2006). The Use of Weblogs as a Tool to Support Collaborative Learning and Reflective Practice in Third-Level Institutions. In E. Pearson E. & P. Bohman, (Eds.), *Proceedings of World Conference on Educational Multimedia, Hypermedia and Telecommunications 2006* (pp. 1047-1052). Chesapeake, VA: AACE.

Browne, E. (2003). Conversations in Cyberspace: A Study of Online Learning. *Open Learning, 18*(3), 245–259. doi:10.1080/0268051032000131017

Chua, A., & Lam, W. (2007). Quality Assurance in Online Education: The Universitas 21 Global approach. *British Journal of Educational Technology, 38*(1), 133–152. doi:10.1111/j.1467-8535.2006.00652.x

Collazos, C. Guerrero, L., Pino, J., Ochoa, S., & Stahl G. (2006). A Model and a Game for Investigating and Designing Collaborative Learning Environments. *Proceedings of 8th International Symposium on Computers in Education*, SIIE'06, León, Spain. Retrieved October 15, 2010, from http:// gerrystahl.net/ pub/ siie06.pdf.

Ebersbach, A., Glaser, M., & Heigl, R. (2006). *Wiki: Web Collaboration*. Berlin: Springer-Verlag.

Evans, S. R., Wang, R., Haija, R., Zhang, J., Rajicic, N., Xanthakis, V., et al. (2007). Evaluation of Distance Learning in an Introduction to Biostatistics Course. *Statistical Education Research Journal, 6*(2), 59-77. Retrieved October 15, 2010, from http:// www.stat.auckland.ac.nz/ ~iase/ serj/ SERJ6(2)_Evans.pdf.

Hiltz, S. R., Coppola, N., Rotter, N., & Turoff, M. (2001). Measuring the Importance of Collaborative Learning for the Effectiveness of ALN: A Multi-Measure, Multi-Method Approach. *Journal of Asynchronous Learning Networks, 4*(2). Retrieved October 15, 2010, from http:// citeseerx.ist.psu.edu/ viewdoc/ summary?doi=10.1.1.105.4825.

Kavanaugh, A., Carroll, J. M., Rosson, M. B., Zin, T. T., & Reese, D. D. (2005). Community Networks: Where Offline Communities Meet Online. *Journal of Computer-Mediated Communication, 10*. Retrieved October 15, 2010, from http:// jcmc.indiana.edu vol10/ issue4/ kavanaugh.html.

Kearsley, G. (1995). *The Nature and Value of Interaction in Distance Education.* Distance Education Symposium 3: Instruction. University Park, PA: American Center for the Study of Distance Education.

Lamb, B. (2004). Wide Open Spaces: Wikis, Ready or Not. *EDUCAUSE Review, 39*(5), 36–48.

McConnell, D. (2000). *Implementing Computer Supported Cooperative Learning*. London: Kogan Page.

Nicaise, M., & Barnes, D. (1996). The Union of Technology, Constructivism, and Teacher Education. *Journal of Teacher Education, 47*, 205–212. doi:10.1177/0022487196047003007

Philips, B. (2003). Overview of Online Teaching and Internet Resources for Statistics Education. In *Proceedings of the IASE Satellite Conference on Statistics Education and the Internet*, Berlin:Voorburg, The Netherlands: International Statistical Institute and International Association for Statistical Education. Retrieved October 15, 2010, from http:// www.stat.auckland.ac.nz/ ~iase/ publications/ 6/ Phillips.pdf.

Picciano, A. G. (2002). Beyond Student Perceptions: Issues of Interaction, Presence, and Performance in an Online Course. *Journal of Asynchronous Learning Networks, 6*(1), 21–40.

Plaisted, T., & Irvine, S. (2006). Learning from Web 2.0 Practices: A Tool to Support Realtime Student Collaboration. *Proceedings of the 23rd annual ascilite conference: Who's learning? Whose technology?* Retrieved October 15, 2010, from http:// www.ascilite.org.au/ conferences/ sydney06/ proceeding/ pdf_papers/ p112.pdf.

Roschelle, J. (1992). Learning by Collaborating: Convergent Conceptual Change. *Journal of the Learning Sciences, 2*(3), 235–276. doi:10.1207/ s15327809jls0203_1

Scardamalia, M., & Bereiter, C. (1994). Computer Support for Knowledge-Building Communities. *Journal of the Learning Sciences, 3*(3), 265–283. doi:10.1207/s15327809jls0303_3

Schwartz, L., Clark, S., Cossarin, M., & Rudolph, J. (2004). Educational Wikis: Features and Selection Criteria. *International Review of Research in Open and Distance Learning.* Retrieved October 15, 2010, from http:// www.irrodl.org/ index.php/ irrodl/ article/ view/ 163/ 244.

Selwyn, N. (2000). Creating a 'Connected' Community? Teachers' Use of an Electronic Discussion Group. *Teachers College Record, 102*(4), 750–778. doi:10.1111/0161-4681.00076

Speed, F. M., & Hardin, H. (2001). Teaching Statistics via Distance: Duplicating the Classroom Experience. *Communications in Statistics Simulation and Computation*, *30*(2), 391–402. doi:10.1081/SAC-100002374

Stephenson, R. W. (2001). Statistics at a Distance. *Journal of Statistics Education, 9*(3). Retrieved October 15, 2010, from http:// www.amstat.org/ publications/ jse/ v9n3/ stephenson.html.

Tallent-Runnels, M. K., Thomas, J. A., Lan, W. Y., Cooper, S., Ahern, T. C., Shaw, S. M., & Liu, X. (2006). Teaching Courses Online: A Review of the Research. *Review of Educational Research*, *76*(1), 93–135. doi:10.3102/00346543076001093

Thorpe, M. (2002). Rethinking Learner Support: The Challenge of Collaborative Online Learning. *Open Learning*, *17*(2), 105–119. doi:10.1080/02680510220146887a

Tudor, G. (2006). Teaching Introductory Statistics online – Satisfying the Students. *Journal of Statistics Education, 14*(3). Retrieved October 15, 2010, from www.amstat.org/ publications/ jse/.

Utts, J., Sommer, B., Acredolo, C., Maher, M. W., & Matthews, H. R. (2003). A Study Comparing Traditional and Hybrid Internet-Based Instruction in Introductory Statistics Classes. *Journal of Statistics Education, 11*(3). Retrieved October 15, 2010, from http:// www.amstat.org/ publications/ jse/ v11n3/ utts.html.

Van Petegem, P., De Loght, T., & Shortridge, A. M. (2004). Powerful Learning is Interactive: A Cross-Cultural Perspective. *E-Journal of Instructional Science and Technology, 7*(1). Retrieved October 15, 2010, from http:// www.ascilite.org.au/ ajet/ e-jist/ docs/ Vol7_No1/ content2.htm.

Ward, B. (2004). The Best of Both Worlds: A Hybrid Statistics Course. *Journal of Statistics Education, 12*(3). Retrieved October 15, 2010, from http:// americanprinter.com/ press/ digital/ printing_hybrid_printing_best_2/.

Wenger, E., McDermott, R., & Snyder, W. M. (2002). *Cultivating Communities of Practice: A Guide to Managing Knowledge*. Boston: Harvard Business School Press.

Whitetaker, S., Kinzie, M., Kraft-Sayre, M. E., Mashburn, A., & Pianta, R. C. (2007). Use and Evaluation of Web-based Professional Development Services across Participant Levels of Support. *Early Childhood Education Journal*, *34*(6), 379–386. doi:10.1007/s10643-006-0142-7

Chapter 8
Mathematics Bridging Education Using an Online, Adaptive E-Tutorial:
Preparing International Students for Higher Education

Dirk T. Tempelaar
Maastricht University School of Business & Economics, the Netherlands

Bart Rienties
University of Surrey, UK

Wolter Kaper
Universiteit van Amsterdam, the Netherlands

Bas Giesbers
Maastricht University School of Business & Economics, the Netherlands

Sybrand Schim van der Loeff
Maastricht University School of Business & Economics, the Netherlands

Leendert van Gastel
Universiteit van Amsterdam, the Netherlands

Evert van de Vrie
Open Universiteit Nederland, the Netherlands

Henk van der Kooij
Universiteit Utrecht, the Netherlands

Hans Cuypers
Technische Universiteit Eindhoven, the Netherlands

ABSTRACT

This contribution describes and evaluates a postsecondary remediation program in mathematics, aiming to ease the transition from high school to university and to improve the success rates in the first year of bachelor studies. The remediation program consists of the administration of an entry test and the organisation of voluntary bridging education in the format of an online summer course, using the adaptive e-tutorial ALEKS. Participants are prospective students of the university programs business and economics of Maastricht University, and are mostly students with an international background. Effect

DOI: 10.4018/978-1-60960-875-0.ch008

analysis suggests a strong treatment effect of successful participation in the summer course. However, given the quasi-experimental setup of this study, with non-equivalent groups, selection effects may be responsible for part of that effect. Correction of the treatment effect by applying the propensity score method indicates that indeed a selection effect is present, but that a substantial treatment effect remains, of about 50% the size of the effect of being educated in advanced math versus basic math, in high school.

INTRODUCTION

This contribution focuses on a type of education that is referred to in different ways: bridging education, developmental education, or remedial education. Whatever the label, the type of education subject of this contribution is education directed to ease the transition from high school to college and to improve the success rates in the first year of bachelor studies. In the Netherlands, the main advising council for educational affairs, the Educational Council of the Netherlands, has stressed the importance of bridging education in a range of studies and recommendations (Onderwijsraad 2006, 2007, 2008). The dating of these advices makes evident that Dutch interest in bridging education beyond the institute of open education is recent. Nation wide projects, supported by SURF, the Dutch collaborative organisation for higher education institutions and research institutes aimed at innovations in ICT, run from 2004 onwards. Some of these Dutch initiatives have acted as pioneer for European projects, indicating that interest in (continental) Europe is also of very recent date. EU projects M.A.S.T.E.R., S.T.E.P. and MathBridge collect experiences with bridging education with a specific European focus: that of internationalisation of European higher education. This internationalization development is going very fast; for example, some Dutch universities located at short distance of country borders, like the case elaborated in this article, the share of international students in the inflow of new bachelor students has risen to 75% (mostly from continental Europe). Although most of these students are not very international in terms of the geographical distance they have to bridge, there is certainly a huge diversity with respect to high school education they have received. Secondary school systems, even in neighbouring countries as Netherlands, Germany and Belgium, are very different, producing strong heterogeneity in knowledge and skills of prospective students. That heterogeneity brings about a strong need for bridging education in the transfer from secondary to university education, which adds to the more national focused needs for bridging education that have existed for some time: to bridge knowledge and skills deficiencies in areas that are part of the national secondary school program, but are not sufficiently mastered by students transferring to university.

US Context

The longest tradition of bridging education is without doubt to be found in the Anglo-Saxon education system, and specifically, in the US. Developmental education for underprepared students, as it is generally labelled, is in the US quite often organized state-wise, and has achieved an enormous reach: estimates of participation of undergraduate students in developmental education in any format offered by community colleges and universities ranges between 40% and 58% of first year students (Attewell et al., 2006; Bailey, 2009; Kozeracki, 2005). Most recent discussions in the US on the topic of developmental education is focusing on the question if there is any way back: the opinion that too large a share of public funding of education is finding its way into developmental education is shared by many, opening the debate how to improve regular education to diminish the need of developmental education (see e.g. the special edition of New Directions for Community

Colleges, 2008). No surprise therefore that by far the most empirical studies into the effect of bridging education refer to the US context: Bahr (2008), Bettinger and Long (2008), Calcagno and Long (2008), Jamelske (2009). The specific US context of these studies steers to a large extent the way the research question of the impact of bridging education is approached: the US higher education system is strongly based on selection, and part of most selection procedures is that prospective students participate in a placement or entry test and, in the case that they score less than a certain cut-off point, are required to take developmental education. In such a typical US context, impact studies compare the academic success of students scoring just below the cut-off score (who are obliged to participate in the bridging education) with that of students who score just above the cut-off score (and who are excluded from bridging education), using so-called regression-discontinuity models.

European Context

In the (continental) European context, such an approach cannot be followed: in most cases, no selection takes place upon entering university education, so the option is missing to obligate some, and to exclude other, students from bridging education (Brants & Struyven, 2009; Rienties et al., in press; Tempelaar & Rienties, 2008). In countries where no selection takes place, as e.g. the Netherlands, the legal basis is lacking to require prospective students to participate in an entry exam, and/or remedial program. Another difference between the US and European case is that where in the US placement tests are used to place students in different levels of their first math course, with the lowest level being a remedial course that usually does not earn credits toward a degree, in the typical European case all students are placed in one math course, with remedial educational playing the role of bridging toward that single course, again without earning credits. But although contexts are rather different, from a methodological point of view both European and US contexts share important characteristics: in the investigation of the impact of bridging education, one cannot use the experimental design, since participation in bridging education does not take place on the basis of randomized assignment, but on the basis of the outcome of a placement test (US), or self-selection (Europe). A direct comparison of academic success of participants and non-participants of bridging education is therefore not a proper way to find a treatment effect, since the composition of the two groups of prospective students will, in general, be different. The relevant research design is that of the quasi-experiment with non-equivalent groups, that requires a correction of the differences observed between experimental and control group on the basis of differences in background statistics of students in both groups (the covariates). In the US-based empirical studies, it is one single background factor, the score on the placement test that distinguishes the students in the treatment group from students in the control group, and so allows the use of regression discontinuity methods. The typical European case lacks such a discontinuity, and directs the investigator to methods recently developed for the quasi-experimental setup without pre-test and with non-equivalent groups: propensity score-based methods (Fraas, 2007; Shadish, Cook, & Campbell, 2002; Yanovitzky, Zanutto, Hornik, 2005).

The effect analysis presented in this contribution makes use of experiences achieved in the bridging courses mathematics for prospective bachelor students of the Maastricht University School of Business and Economics. Those courses are designed as optional summer courses that take place in the summer before the start of the regular bachelor program. In the European context, it is one of the longest lasting cycles of bridging education: from summer 2003 on, these summer courses have been offered without major changes, and in seven consecutive runs, 750 prospective students have participated. The bridging courses focus on the international students, entering the bachelor study with a non-Dutch prior education, and indeed 90% of the participants are of international background. Is an optional summer course an effective instrument to help international students bridge math deficiencies caused by differences in national secondary school systems? This is the central question of this contribution, against the background of cumulating evidence in the US context that developmental education certainly is expensive, but doubtful in its effects.

THE UM SUMMER COURSE MATHEMATICS

The characteristics of students flowing in into the programs in Business and Economics, combined with the outcomes of the entry assessments to be discussed in more detail in the next section, have been conclusive with regard to major design choices of the bridging education, including the preference for a summer school format. Some of the major considerations at play were:

- The large differences in prior math mastery require a bridging course of considerable size: up to a workload of approximately 100 hours for students with the most basic forms of prior math schooling. This size is incomparable with that of most of the existing national bridging courses, which are quite often scheduled in a couple of days of intensive teaching.
- For a bridging course of this size and the strong heterogeneity of students, it is crucial that the course is tailor-made: adapting to the students' mastery. Each student should be able to enter the course at the appropriate level.
- To achieve this adaptive feature, (repeated) diagnostic testing is crucial, as well as the ability to adapt learning materials to the outcomes of individual, diagnostic tests.
- The size of the bridging course, and the large variation in work load for students depending on their prior mastery, prevents offering such a bridging course 'in the gate' (that is: intra-curricular, during the first few weeks of the regular program), but forces it to be offered 'before the gate' (that is: extra-curricular, during the summer that precedes the start of the regular program).
- Since participants of the bridging courses are -predominantly- international students, the bridging course cannot be offered on site, but should be offered according the model of distance e-learning.
- Since the period in which the summer course is offered is also occupied by holidays, jobs, and practical work, the format of the summer course should be very flexible: the summer course should be available over a relative long period (June, July, August), with a maximum of freedom for students to schedule their individual learning around other activities in that summer.

Based on all these grounds, it was concluded that face-to face education could not meet several of the above requirements, making the decision to organize the bridging course around an existing adaptive, electronic tutorial inevitable: ALEKS (Assessment and LEarning in Knowledge Spaces) College Algebra module. The tool makes use of server based computing, and can be characterised as supporting individual, distance learning. The ALEKS system (see also Doignon & Falmagne, 1999; Falmange et al., 2004; Tempelaar et al., 2006) combines adaptive, diagnostic testing with an electronic learning and practice tutorial in several domains relevant for higher education. In addition, it provides lecturers an instructor module where students' progress can be monitored, both in the learning and assessment modes.

The ALEKS assessment module starts with an entry assessment in order to evaluate a student's

Figure 1. Sample of an ALEKS assessment item

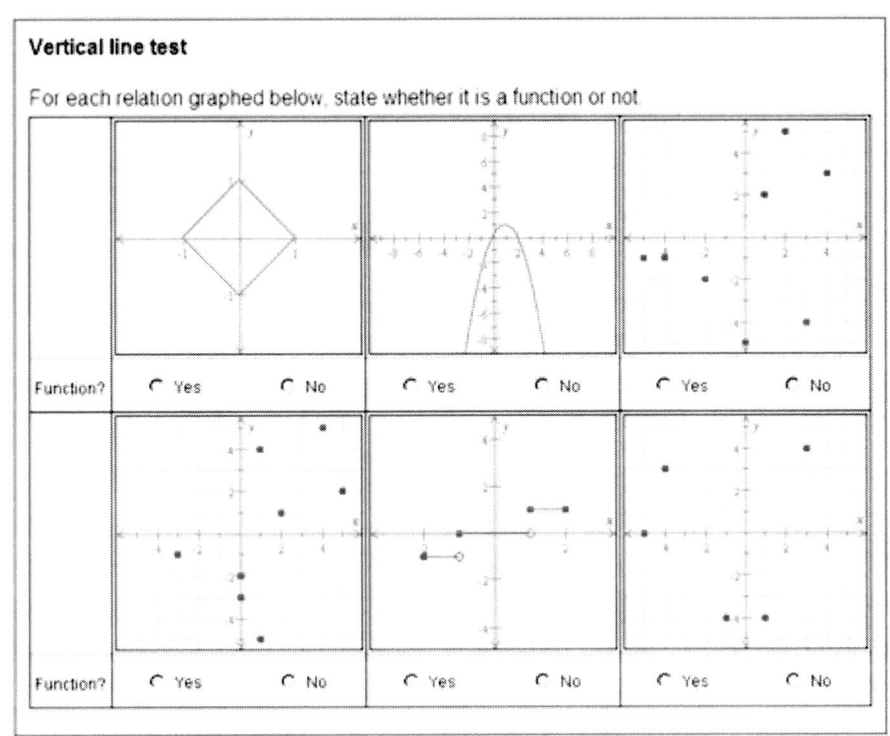

knowledge state for the domain. Following this assessment, ALEKS delivers a graphic report analyzing the student's knowledge within all curricular areas for the course. The report also recommends concepts on which the student can begin working; by clicking on any of these concepts or items the student gains immediate access to the learning module.

Some key features of the assessment module are (see Figure 1 for a sample):

- All problems require that the student produce authentic input.
- All problems are algorithmically generated.
- Assessment questions are generated from a carefully-designed repertoire of items ensuring comprehensive coverage of the domain.

The assessment is adaptive: the choice of each new question is based on the aggregate of responses to all previous questions. As a result, the student's knowledge state can be found by asking only a small subset of the possible questions (typically 15-25).

The learning report, of which Figure 2 shows part of, provides a detailed, graphic representation of the student's knowledge state by means of a pie-chart divided into slices, each of which corresponds to an area of the syllabus. In the ALEKS system, the student's progress is shown by the proportion of the slice that is filled in by solid colour: if the slice is entirely filled in, the student has mastered that area. Also, as the mouse is held over a given slice, a list is displayed of items within that area that the student is currently "ready to learn," as determined by the assessment. Clicking on any of these items gives access to the learning mode (beginning with the item chosen).

Figure 2. Partial sample of an ALEKS learning report

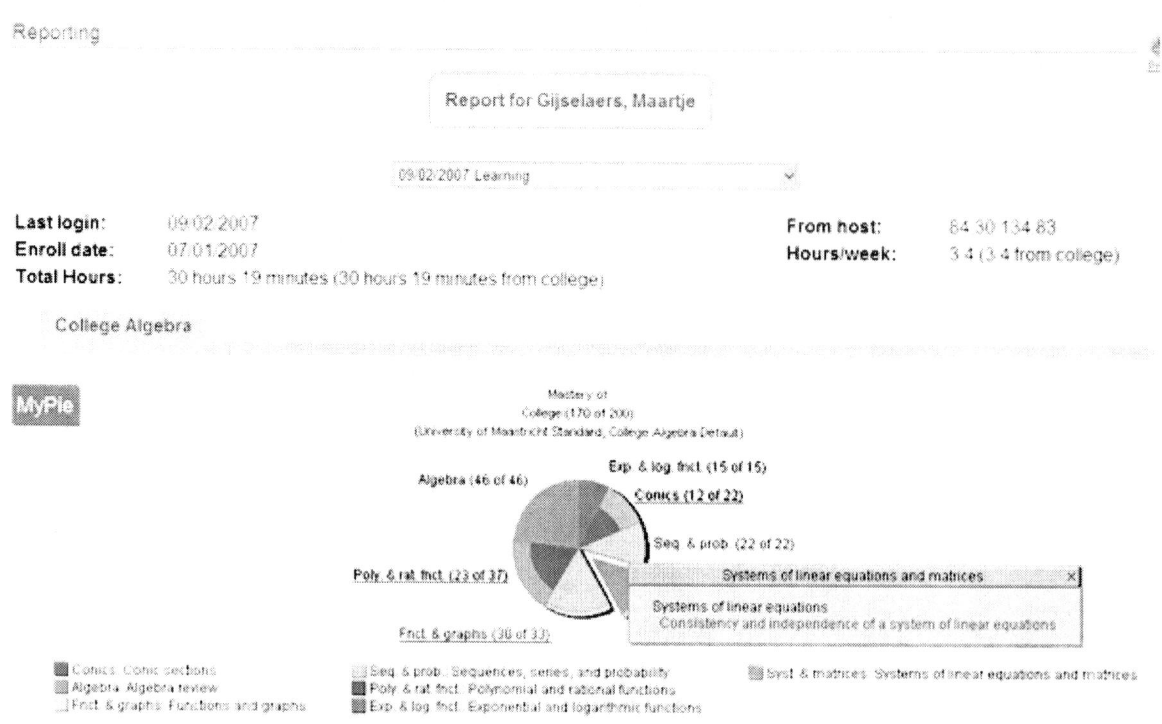

At the conclusion of the assessment ALEKS determines the concepts that the student is currently ready to learn, based on that student's current knowledge state. These new concepts are listed in the report, and the learning mode is initiated by clicking on any highlighted phrase representing a concept in the list. The focus of the learning mode is a sequence of problems to be solved by the student, representing a series of concepts to be mastered. The facilities offered by the learning mode are as follows:

- Practice (that is, the problems themselves);
- Explanations of concepts and procedures;
- Dictionary of technical terms;
- Calculator (adapted to the topic studied, e.g. in statistical items, a special "statistics calculator" is provided).

For example, a student working on a particular problem may "ask for" an explanation of that problem (by clicking on the button marked "Explain"). The explanation typically provides a short solution of the problem, with commentary. After reading the explanation(s), the student may return to "Practice", where she or he will be presented with another problem exemplifying the item or concept just illustrated. If the student is successful in solving the problem, the system will offer (usually) two or three more instances of the same item to make sure the student has mastered it. In the text of problems and explanations, certain technical terms such as "addition", "factor" and "square root" are highlighted. Clicking on any highlighted word or phrase will open the dictionary to a definition of the corresponding concept. The dictionary can also be used independently of the current problem to look up any term the student may be curious about. A graphing calculator is available for computing and displaying geometrical figures in analytical geometry and calculus. Other, related features of the learning mode are Feedback, Progress Monitoring, and Practice. Whenever the student attempts to solve a problem in the learning mode, the system responds to the input by saying whether or not the answer is correct and, if it is incorrect, what the student's error might have been. More generally, ALEKS follows the student's progress during each learning sequence, and will at times offer advice. For example, if a student has read the explanation of a problem a couple of times and yet continues to provide incorrect responses, ALEKS may suggest -- depending on the circumstances -- that the student looks up the definition of a certain word in the dictionary. ALEKS may also propose that the student temporarily abandon the problem at hand and work instead on a related, but easier, problem. When a student has demonstrated mastery of a particular item by repeatedly solving problems, ALEKS will encourage the student to proceed to a new item.

The instructor module enables lecturers to monitor individual student progress and achievement, both in learning and assessment mode, and to monitor class progress, again in both modes.

Participants and Non-Participants

This study is based on the investigation of five cohorts of first year students in the programs business and economics; these are all cohorts for whom full data is available on both the summer course, and relevant students' background characteristics needed for the statistical investigation. In total, these five cohorts contain about 4500 first year students, amongst them 68% are international students. Of these students, 578, or 13%, decide to participate in the voluntary math summer course. That decision to participate follows a chain of information and recruitment activities:

- In the period March to May, prospective students are informed on the option of participating in a free math summer course. Part of the information is a short, digital introductory test that provides the students a global picture of expected math mastery, and their position in this.
- Yearly, about 300-500 people take part in these introductory tests. Serious test takes are selected, receive feedback on their test attempt, and are asked for their interest in participation in the math summer course. Students reacting positively are required to express their willingness to invest at least 80 hours of study efforts in the summer course offered by the university. Yearly, between 150 and 250 prospective students qualify and receive an invitation.
- About half of these invitations, so yearly somewhat more than 100 students, are accepted; these students receive a certificate for the use of ALEKS College Algebra in the summer period.

However, expressing willingness to invest an appropriate amount of time is by far identical to really spending sufficient time: only 52% of all participants manage to achieve a pass for the summer course. To achieve such a pass, students were required to study and master at least 55% of the topics covered in the electronic learning tool. Since this required coverage also includes topics already mastered at the start of the summer course, these passing requirements are rather mild. That is also clear from a comparison of real time investment: total connect time in the e-tutorial of students passing the summer course is on average 52.1 hours, whereas average connect time of students failing the summer course, that is, not achieving the 55% coverage requirement for passing, is only 15.1 hours. Tool connect time is a conservative estimate of total study efforts: it measures how much students study within the tool, but misses study time outside the tool.

After finishing the summer course, end of August, the regular program of the bachelor studies International Business and International Economics starts early September. Both programs begin with two eight-week (half semester) integrated, problem-based learning designed courses, each having a 50% study load. The first course is an introduction into organizational theory and marketing, the other course, called Quantitative Methods I or QM1, an introduction into mathematics and statistics. That second course is of special interest for this study, since the ultimate aim of the summer course is to optimally prepare students for this QM1 course. The very first activity in the QM1 course is to administer an entry test, for several reasons: for longitudinally monitoring the math mastery of prospective students, to provide individual students with diagnostic feedback, and to collect data relevant for the design of both the summer course, and the QM1 course. The coverage of the QM1 course mirrors the circumstance that strong heterogeneity in math mastery, due to students educated in different national systems and at different math levels, necessitates a fair amount of repetition. Most topics covered repeat topics educated in the grades 11 and 12 of Dutch secondary schooling, basic math level (the last two years of high school), with some time devoted to new topics. There is no overlap between QM1 and the content of the summer course, since that content is covering topics of grades 7-10 of secondary schooling (middle school and first year of high school). Effect analysis in this study will focus on student achievements of both participants, and non-participants in the summer course, in this QM1 course. However, outcomes of our study are rather robust with regard to the specific choice of effect variable, due to institutional regulations in Dutch higher education. E.g., both programs are characterized by the presence of a so-called system of binding study advice: students with insufficient academic achievements cannot enrol the program for a second year. Achieving a pass for QM1 is practically a requirement, and in fact the most binding requirement, for achieving a positive binding study advice, implying that academic success in the first year, and that in the QM1 course, do not deviate very much.

The most powerful predictor of academic achievements in QM education is the level of math schooling in high school. In this study, we will distinguish two different levels: basic and advanced. Students who take high school according to the Dutch national system, called VWO (pre-university education), are either taught math at one of two different basic levels (A1 or A1,2), or one of two advanced levels (B1 or B1,2). The lowest level, A1, does not qualify for studies in business or economics, so what remains is one basic, and two different advanced levels. Only a minority of prospective students (32%) is educated within the Dutch national system. Many more, somewhat more than 50%, of the prospective students are educated in a German speaking high school system. That system has again two different levels of math prior education, the advanced level or 'Leistungskurs', and the basic level or 'Grundkurs'. The remaining students either have an International Baccalaureate (IB) diploma, or are educated within a national system outside the Dutch or German speaking part of Europe. IB again allows distinguishing advanced level (HL) from basic level (SL), whereas for the last category, students were asked to classify their own math prior education either as math major, or as math minor. The binary variable achieved this way is an important predictor of academic achievement. However, it should be realized that it is no more than a very crude classification, given the strong differences between national educational systems. Figure 3 contains the decomposition of both participants and non-participants in the math summer course with regard to different types of prior education, and the level of math prior education, of students of which data on prior education are available. With regard to nationality, two different groups are distinguished: Dutch versus International. Students with an IB diploma are regarded as being part of the last group, but can be of any nationality; this implies that International refers to the type of prior education, rather than nationality.

Figure 3. Composition of five cohorts of first year students with regard to prior education

Summer course participation	Dutch-prior education		International prior education		Total
	math basic	math advanced	math basic	math advanced	
Participant	44 (4.3%)	10 (2.7%)	394 (18.2%)	104 (12.8%)	552
Non-participant	971 (95.7%)	403 (97.3%)	1769 (81.8%)	708 (87.2%)	3851
Total	1015	413	2163	812	4403

In agreement with the main goal of the bridging course, participation is much stronger amongst international students, than amongst Dutch students, and much stronger amongst students educated at basic level, than amongst students educated at the advanced level. Still, there are relatively many summer course participants amongst the international students with advanced math prior education. Main explanation is the tradition in German speaking countries to halt study in between high school and university for one or several years, either forced by military service, or voluntary, a tradition that is not present in other continental European countries. Most international participants with advanced math prior education have interrupted their study, and regard the summer course as a crucial opportunity to refresh.

STATISTICAL ANALYSES

An important focus of this contribution is the methodology of the effect analysis. Since participation in the summer course is on a voluntary basis, a quasi-experimental setup for the effect analysis is required. Besides, the design contains a post-test, but no pre-test, so that it is best characterized as a quasi-experimental design with non-equivalent groups and post-test only (Shadish e.a., 2002). Such a design embodies the risk of self-selection. In line with recent advices with regard to finding causal effects in observational studies[1], quasi-experimental elements are added to the research design, the most important one being the inclusion of a broad range of students' background factors that may be related to potential self-selection effects. These students' background characteristics are measured both for students participating the voluntary summer course, and for students who have opted not to participate the summer course, and originate from long-term longitudinal research into student related factors explaining academic success. These background characteristics refer to: type of secondary education (Dutch or international), level of math prior education (basic or advanced), learning approaches, goal orientations, metacognition, academic motivations, and subject specific achievement motivations.

Traditional approaches for effect analysis in observational studies determine the treatment effect with a multiple (logistic) regression model or ANCOVA containing as predictor variables, beyond the treatment, also covariates that correct the effect for variation in the effect variable that is not caused by the treatment variable (but is e.g. the outcome of a selection effect). In specific applications, especially when experimental and control group strongly deviate with regard to these background characteristics, this approach has its limitations (Fraas, 2007; Yanovitzky et al., 2005). Therefore, the preferred methodological approach is based on the method of propensity scores, where the treatment effect is corrected

(Fraas, 2007; Shadish et al., 2002; Yanovitzky et al., 2005). Basis of that correction are the propensity scores: the conditional probabilities that an individual belongs to the experimental group, or to the control group, given the set of covariates. Propensity scores are generally estimated with logistic regression analysis. The correction of the treatment effect can take place in different ways: using the propensity scores as matching variables, as stratification variables, or as covariates. In this study both of these last approaches will be used.

One background characteristic will not be used in determining the propensity scores, but will be included into the model as a separate factor, together with the propensity score: the level of prior math education. This will allow us to make an explicit comparison of the treatment effect of successfully participating in the summer course, with the effect of being educated at advanced math level in high school.

The Covariates: Students' Background Characteristics

In finding relevant covariates, we profited from long term research into study achievements in the first year of study undertaken in our school. The first set of background factors refer to students' approaches to learning, and are investigated in the context of the learning patterns model of Vermunt (Entwistle & Peterson, 2004; Vermunt, 1996) and the instrument based on that model: ILS or Inventory of Learning Styles. Vermunt distinguishes in his model four domains or components of learning: cognitive processing strategies, metacognitive regulation strategies, learning conceptions or mental models of learning, and learning orientations. Next, students' goal orientations are measured with an instrument designed by Grant and Dweck (2003), that classifies goal orientations into six types: intrapersonal outcome goals, intrapersonal ability goals, normative outcome goals, normative ability goals, and two different types of learning goals, that differ in the extent the student is longing for challenge: the learning goal (in the strict sense) and the challenge-mastery focused goal orientation. Metacognitive abilities are measured by the AILI instrument (Elshout-Mohr, Daalen-Kapteijns, & Meijer, 2001; Tempelaar, 2006), that is based on Flavells' three component model of metacognition, which decomposes metacognition into the components knowledge, skills, and attitudes. The Academic Motivation Scale (AMS; Guya, Mageau, & Vallerand, 2003); Ratelle et al., 2007; Vallerand et al., 1992), based upon Ryan and Deci's (2000) model of intrinsic and extrinsic motivation, is applied to achieve motivational profiles of students containing different types of intrinsic, extrinsic, and a-motivation. Lastly, subject achievement motivations based on Eccles' expectancy-value theory (Eccles & Wigfield, 2002) are measured with an instrument derived from the Survey of Attitudes Toward Statistics (SATS) developed by Schau and co-authors (Tempelaar et al., 2007). The SATS instrument measures six aspects of post-secondary students' subject attitudes, amongst which two expectancy factors that deal with students' beliefs about their own ability and perceived task difficulty: Cognitive Competence and Difficulty, and three subjective task-value constructs that encompass students' feelings toward and attitudes about the value of the subject: Affect, Interest and Value. The sixth aspect, Effort, is assumed to be the outcome of the process of weighting expectancy against value.

RESULTS

The National Entry Test

In the framework of several, consecutive national projects in the Netherlands to improve transition from high school to college, and study success in college, national entry tests for mathematics have been constructed. In three out of the five cohorts in this study, the same version of the national entry test is administered, implying more than 2600 test

Figure 4. Proportion correct scores entry test and its topics, broken down into prior education

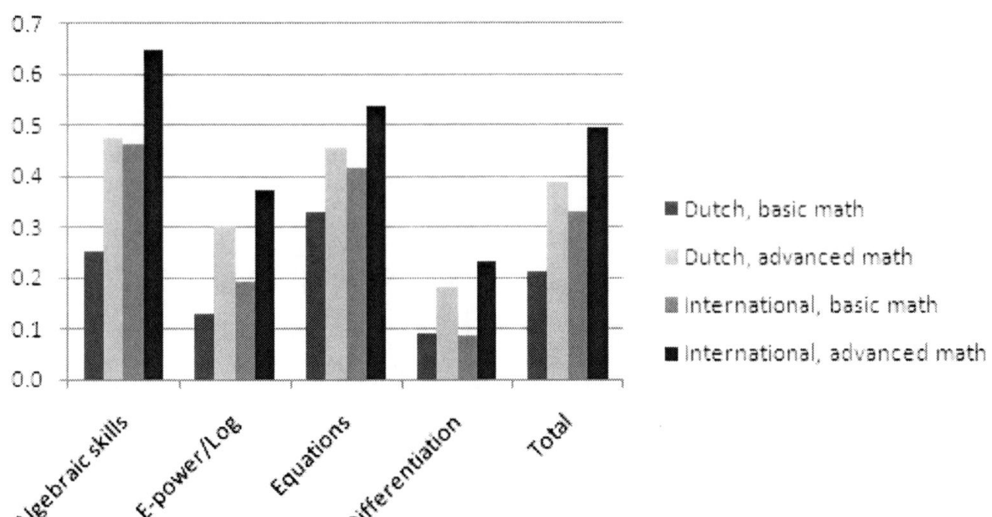

takes of that test. The short test consists of four categories of math competency, all being part of middle school coverage, or early high school math programs at basic level. Two topics, algebraic skills and e-powers & logarithms, are the most elementary of the topics, the other two, equations and differentiation, slightly more advanced. Figure 4 contains the scores for each of those four topics, and the total score, for four different categories of students: students educated in the Dutch secondary school system or not, crossed with students educated at advanced level, versus basic level, with regard to their math prior education. Scores in the figure are p-values or proportion of correct answers, after correction for guessing (since the entry test contains multiple choice items).

Scores in the entry test are (disappointing) low. Some low scores have been expected: it was known that more advanced topics as solving equations and differentiation, although being taught in programs for basic math all over Europe, are not fully mastered by prospective students, and are in need of a repetition within the regular program of first year university education. Important outcome of the entry test is however that crucial math deficiencies exist beyond these advanced topics: also topics like algebraic skills and e-powers and logarithms, although firmly rooted in any middle school program, produced no better than very incomplete mastery. Traditionally, these basic topics are no part of regular university teaching, implying that any deficiency would stay if not addressed in a bridging course.

Another crucial observation from the entry test scores is that whereas the bridging courses have been primarily designed for international students being educated in programs deviating from the typical Dutch program, deficiencies of Dutch prospective students seem to be larger than those of the international students. One should be cautious in generalising the interpretation of such differences in group means, since selection effects are highly probable, but relative to the total score, it is surprising to see how meagre students with a Dutch prior education score in especially the algebraic skills topic. In fact, with regard to this topic students educated at the advanced level do not perform better than international students educated at the basic level. A finding that justifies the large scale national projects in math bridging

Figure 5. Non-corrected treatment effect of successful participation in summer course on QM1 total score

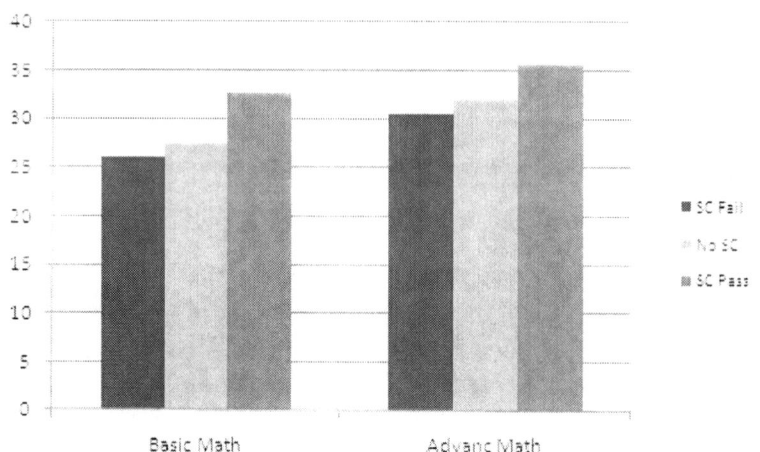

education within the Netherlands: beyond reasons of internationalization, there are urgent reasons related to the national state of affairs of math education for providing remedial education.

Descriptive Analyses

Figures 5 and 6 exhibit the non-corrected treatment effects of successful participation in the summer course of students being educated at basic math level versus advanced math level in high school, respectively for the total score in the course, QM1 total score in Figure 5, and for the QM1 passing rate, in Figure 6. The effect of prior education at advanced level, compared to basic level, is 4.6 points in the QM1 total score (or expressed as effect size, 0.64 standard deviations), against 23% in the passing rate (0.53 standard deviations). The effect of successful participation in the summer course, with no participation as reference, equals 5.3 points in total score (0.76 standard deviations), respectively 28% in passing rate (0.56 standard deviations) for students educated at basic level, and 3.8 points (0.54 standard deviations), respectively 13% (0.31 standard deviations) for students educated at advanced level. As to be expected, the treatment effect is much larger for students educated at basic math level, than for students educated at advanced math level. For the principal target group of students in the summer course, those with a basic math prior education, the non-corrected effect of successful participation in the summer course is even that large, that they outperform students with an advanced prior education who do not participate the summer course, both with regard to QM1 total score, and with regard to QM1 passing rate.

Propensity Scores

The selected instruments of self-perception surveys relevant for learning processes appear to be appropriate resources for potential selection effects. Out of the 42 learning related scales, 30 demonstrate statistically significant differences in means when contrasting summer course participants with non-participants, always in the direction that participants in the summer course achieve on average more favourable scores than non-participants. Only 12 scales do not demonstrate significant differences. Propensity scores or conditional probabilities to participate in the math summer course have been estimated for all 3240 students for which a full data record of background

Figure 6. Non-corrected treatment effect of successful participation in summer course on QM1 passing rate

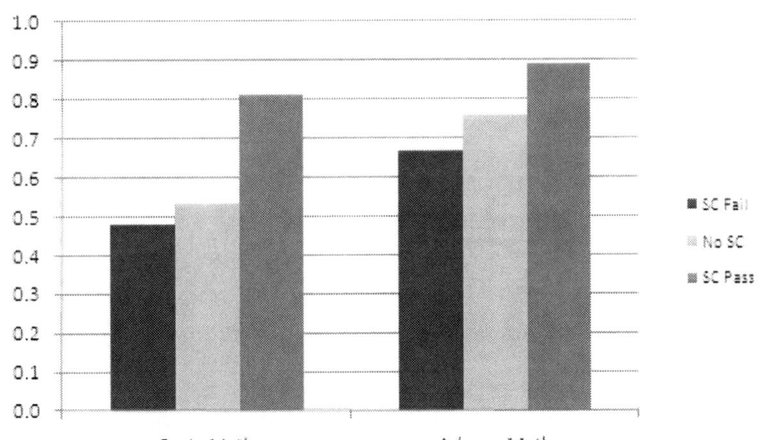

characteristics is available, using binary logistic regression. Since most of these learning characteristics are associated, in the logistic regression determining the propensity scores, only six of the 42 students' background characteristics appear to be a statistically significant predictor of summer course participation (beyond prior math education). By far the strongest predictor is, in agreement with the design aims of the summer course, the indicator variable distinguishing international students from students with a Dutch prior education. Next, in the order of decreasing impact, the vocational learning orientation, self-perception of cognitive competence (negative), metacognitive knowledge, the constructivist learning conception, and amotivation (negative). The outcomes of the logistic regression, both in terms of statistical significance of predictors and the sign of the regression coefficients, are intuitive: international background, the conception that learning takes place through self-construction of knowledge, and good metacognitive skills strengthen the probability to participate the summer course, whereas lack of learning motivation, and one's perception to be already rather competent in the area of quantitative methods, weaken that probability.

In agreement to procedures advised in the literature (Fraas, 2007; Shadish e.a., 2002; Yanovitzky e.a, 2005), propensity scores are estimated on the basis of the full model, that is all covariates included, both those being statistically significant and those being non-significant.

Propensity Score as Covariate

After the estimation of propensity scores, the effect analysis is repeated, with the propensity score added as extra predictor, next to the indicator variable of math prior education, and the treatment variable of summer course participation. Depending upon the choice of the effect variable, QM1 total score versus QM1 passing rate, the proper method for doing effect analysis is that of multiple regression in case of the score variable, respectively logistic regression in case of passing rate. Figure 7 contains the outcomes of multiple regression of QM1 total score on de predictor variables propensity score and three indicator variables (dummies): math prior education at advanced level, successful participation in the summer course, and non-successful participation in the summer course (this choice of indicator variables implies that math prior education at

Figure 7. Outcomes of effect analysis of summer course participation on QM1 total score with propensity score as covariate

	beta	*t*-value	significance
Propensity score	0.072	4.116	0.000
Advanced math dummy	0.271	15.978	0.000
Successful participation summer course dummy	0.154	8.899	0.000
Non-successful participation summer course dummy	-0.086	-5.002	0.000

Figure 8. Outcomes of effect analysis of summer course participation on QM1 passing rate with propensity score as covariate

	B (S.E.)	significance	Exp(B)
Propensity score	1.298 (0.456)	0.004	3.663
Advanced math dummy	0.967 (0.091)	0.000	2.629
Successful participation summer course dummy	1.097 (0.181)	0.000	2.996
Non-successful participation summer course dummy	-0.494 (0.149)	0.001	0.610

basic level, and no participation in the summer course, serve as reference groups). Propensity scores and the three indicator variables together explain 11.2% of the variation in total score.

Figure 7 confirms the picture sketched in the last results section: participants of the summer course stand out from non-participants in terms of background characteristics that have a positive impact on learning. The consequence of this is that in the corrected calculation of the effect of summer course participation, part of explanation of academic success by successful summer course participation is absorbed by the propensity score, as compared to the non-corrected model. The obvious implication of this is that the contribution to explained variation by summer course participation becomes smaller, and the variable is no more the strongest predictor: the indicator variable distinguishing math prior education at advanced level takes over that position. However, a substantial effect of successful participation in the summer course remains: the beta (standardized regression coefficient) exceeds 50% of the value of the beta of the predictor math at advanced level.

Shifting the focus to passing or failing the QM1 course as outcome variable, a similar picture emerges. The proper method is now that of logistic regression; Figure 8 contains the outcomes of such a regression. The explained variation, expressed as the Nagelkerke R^2, equals 8.1%.

For the interpretation of the outcomes of the logistic regression, it is especially the last column of Figure 8, which provides the changes in the odds of passing the QM1 course as the result of a unit change in the predictor variable, that deserves attention. Students' background characteristics that influence the participation in the summer course are the strongest determinant of the odds to pass QM1: see the coefficient of the propensity score. Next come the two indicator variables for math at advanced level in prior education and successful participation in the summer course, with the notable detail that predictive power of the summer course participation dummy exceeds that of the advanced math dummy.

Propensity Score as Stratification Variable

The best protection against the impact of potential selection effects in a quasi-experimental research design with non-equivalent groups is offered by the matching approach, in our case through quintile stratification of all subjects on the basis of the propensity scores as stratification variable (Fraas et al., 2007; Guo & Fraser, 2010; Shadish et al., 2002; Yanovitzky et al., 2005). This literature suggests the creation of five strata, based on the quintiles of the distribution of the propensity scores. Each of these five strata this way contains subjects with propensity scores of the same magnitude, so that effect analysis within each stratum is minimally influenced by differences between subjects in their value on the propensity score, providing a correction for the selection effects that depend on background characteristics used in the estimation of the propensity scores. We applied this approach, and repeated the multiple regression analysis described in the last section for each of the five strata created by distinguishing the five quintiles of the propensity score. The outcomes of these regression analyses are collected in Figure 9.

Stratification appears to achieve exactly what it is intended for: the influence of students' background characteristics, expressed as propensity score, is statistically insignificant in all five strata, where it had been the strongest predictor before stratification taking place. Since treatment and control group overlap in all five strata, we can do an even more thorough check of the adequacy of the propensity score based stratification by performing difference in means tests for all 42 predictors in all five strata (Guo & Fraser, 2010). Doing these test at a 5% significance level, we find 3, 2, 1, 0, 1 significant differences in strata 1-5 respectively, so 1.4 on average in each stratum. This compares quite well to the expected 2.1 significant difference one expects when testing at 5% level. As a reminder, in the complete data set we found 30 out of 42 differences to be significant, indicating that stratification indeed succeeds in taking away any selection effect induced by these 42 predictors.

Other regression outcomes are quite similar to the outcomes achieved on the complete data set, with the first stratum producing slightly deviant outcomes. In that first stratum, the quintile of students with the lowest score for students' background characteristics that contribute to participation in the summer course, the positive effect of successful participation in the summer course is outshined by the negative effect of failing the summer course. This different position of the first stratum is an artefact of the way the strata are created: due to the very low propensity scores of students in this first stratum, that stratum counts by far the fewest number of participants of the summer course, and amongst those participants, the large majority drops out of the summer course (amongst the 660 students in this stratum, there are only 23 participants in the summer course, of which 17 drop out). The other four strata, each containing many more summer course participants and especially many more successful participants, all demonstrate the same patterns as found in the full data set: the largest effect is that of the indicator variable of prior math education at advanced level, with the treatment effect of successful participation in the summer course in the second position, having an effect size of at least 50% of the effect size of advanced math. Average treatment effect (ATE; Guo & Fraser, 2010), calculated by averaging the stratum-specific differences of the mean QM1 scores, equals $t = 4.75$, which is clearly significant at 5% or 1% level. Focusing on the four strata with a substantial amount of summer course participants, so excluding the first stratum form the calculation of the ATE due to the very small number of participants, the statistical significance even achieves a value of $t = 11.27$.

Redoing the logistic regression analysis to determine the treatment effect of participation in the summer course on the passing rate of the QM1 course after stratifying the data set into five

Figure 9. Outcomes of effect analysis of summer course participation on QM1 total score with propensity score as stratification variable

Stratum 1: propensity score < 0.055	beta	*t*-value	significance
Propensity score	0.062	1.715	0.087
Advanced math dummy	0.365	10.065	0.000
Successful participation summer course dummy	0.061	1.674	0.095
Non-successful participation summer course dummy	-0.118	-3.251	0.001
Stratum 2: 0.055 < propensity score < 0.117			
Propensity score	0.022	0.563	0.573
Advanced math dummy	0.310	8.124	0.000
Successful participation summer course dummy	0.173	4.511	0.000
Non-successful participation summer course dummy	-0.050	-1.308	0.191
Stratum 3: 0.117 < propensity score < 0.166			
Propensity score	0.008	0.201	0.841
Advanced math dummy	0.222	5.697	0.000
Successful participation summer course dummy	0.127	3.257	0.001
Non-successful participation summer course dummy	-0.090	-2.315	0.021
Stratum 4: 0.166 < propensity score < 0.217			
Propensity score	0.041	1.063	0.288
Advanced math dummy	0.195	4.990	0.000
Successful participation summer course dummy	0.146	3.735	0.000
Non-successful participation summer course dummy	-0.117	-2.996	0.003
Stratum 5: 0.217 < propensity score			
Propensity score	0.007	0.191	0.849
Advanced math dummy	0.268	7.071	0.000
Successful participation summer course dummy	0.210	5.485	0.000
Non-successful participation summer course dummy	-0.068	-1.769	0.077

strata based on the quintiles of the distribution of the propensity scores, we achieve equivalent outcomes. Within each of the strata, the propensity score has no statistically significant effect anymore on passing rate. And except for the first quintile, where success in the summer course appears to be insignificant for the QM1 passing rate, the other four strata demonstrate significant effects of both math prior education at advanced level and successful participation in the summer course, with the odds-ratio of the last everywhere exceeding the one of the first. The average treatment effect, ATE, for the success rate equals $t = 2.59$ when calculated over all five strata, and up to $t = 9.18$ when calculated over the four non-sparse populated strata, so statistically significant at 5% level.

Summarizing the outcomes of the statistical analyses: a direct comparison of academic success of students successfully participating the summer course, and that of non-participants, demonstrates a large treatment effect. The treatment effect exceeds the effect of math schooling at advanced level, with math schooling at basic level as reference. However, part of this effect may be caused by selection bias due to the voluntary participation in the summer course. In order to decompose the total treatment effect into such a selection effect, and a corrected treatment effect, propensity scores of summer course participation were estimated based on a very wide range of learning related students' background data. After stratification based on these propensity scores the presumption of the existence of selection bias was confirmed, and correction for this selection effect did indeed diminish the treatment effect, but still a very substantial treatment effect remained, of the size of about half of the effect size of being schooled at advanced level.

CONCLUSION

Many first year university programs contain elements of remedial education: only after revisiting topics that have been taught in the last grades of high school, the program continues with the coverage of completely new topics. Our study suggests that such an approach to bridging is insufficient: important deficiencies exist in the mastery of more basic mathematical competencies, and these stay outside the scope of such a refreshment approach. Based on our experiences with entry tests over a sequence of years, the UM has opted for a very broad and basic coverage of topics in our math summer course, and individual learning routes controlled by repeated administrations of adaptive, diagnostic tests.

Effect analysis suggests that this kind of bridging education is very effective: the non-corrected effect of successful participation in the summer course exceeds the effect of math prior schooling at advanced level, with basic schooling as reference. The relevant research design of this study is however that of a quasi-experimental setup with non-equivalent groups, requiring a correction of the calculated treatment effect for potential selection effects. Correction on the basis of the propensity score method indicates that indeed part of the non-corrected treatment effect should be attributed to the circumstance that participants in the summer course possess more favourable background characteristics for achieving academic success in their study, than students who choose not to participate in the summer course. At the same time, after correction for the non-equivalent composition of both groups, a substantial treatment effect remains, in the order of size of about half the effect size of being educated at advanced math level in high school.

The outcomes of the effect analysis suggest that the chosen format for bridging education, to know that of an online summer course with a very broad coverage of basic math topics, and learning controlled by individual, adaptive testing, is a very efficient one to bridge math skills deficiencies. The average study load of being successful in the summer course is much less than the difference in study load between high school math education at advanced, versus basic level. Notwithstanding, the treatment effect of successful summer course participation is about 50% of the effect size of advanced prior math education. The question if such an outcome is unique for the chosen format of bridging education, or that other formats, like offering additional bridging classes parallel to regular education as part of the first year university program –a format used by many Dutch and European bridging initiatives–, is as effective, suggests to be an important question for future research.

ACKNOWLEDGEMENT

The authors would like to thank the EU Lifelong Learning programme funding the S.T.E.P. project and the Dutch SURF funding the NKBW project being part of the Nationaal ActiePlan e-Learning, which enabled this research project. This publication reflects the views only of the authors, and the Commission cannot be held responsible for any use which may be made of the information contained therein.

REFERENCES

Attewell, P., Lavin, D., Domina, T., & Levey, T. (2006). New evidence on college remediation. *The Journal of Higher Education*, *77*(5), 886–924. doi:10.1353/jhe.2006.0037

Bahr, P. R. (2008). Does mathematics remediation work? A comparative analysis of academic attainment among community college students. *Research in Higher Education*, *49*(5), 420–450. doi:10.1007/s11162-008-9089-4

Bailey, T. (2009). Challenge and opportunity: Rethinking the role and function of developmental education in community college. *New Directions for Community Colleges*, *145*, 11–30. doi:10.1002/cc.352

Bettinger, E. P., & Long, B. T. (2009). Addressing the needs of underprepared students in higher education: Does college remediation work? *The Journal of Human Resources*, *44*(3), 736–771.

Brants, L., & Struyven, K. (2009). Literature review on online remedial education: A European perspective. *Industry and Higher Education*, *23*(4), 269–276. doi:10.5367/000000009789346112

Calcagno, J. C., & Long, B. T. (2008). *The impact of postsecondary remediation using a regression discontinuity approach: Addressing endogenous sorting and noncompliance*. NBER working paper series, 14194.

Doignon, J. P., & Falmagne, J. C. (1999). *Knowledge spaces*. Berlin, Germany: Springer. doi:10.1007/978-3-642-58625-5

Dweck, C. S. (1999). *Self-theories: Their role in motivation, personality, and development*. Philadelphia, PA: Psychology Press.

Eccles, J. S., & Wigfield, A. (2002). Motivational beliefs, values, and goals. *Annual Review of Psychology*, *53*, 109–132. doi:10.1146/annurev.psych.53.100901.135153

Elshout-Mohr, M., van Daalen-Kapteijns, M. M., & Meijer, J. (2001). *Constructie van het instrument "Rapportage Autonoom Studeren."* Amsterdam, The Netherlands: SCO-Kohnstamm Instituut en Instituut voor de Leraren Opleiding (ILO).

Entwistle, N. J., & Peterson, E. R. (2004). Conceptions of learning and knowledge in higher education: Relationships with study behavior and influences of learning environments. *International Journal of Educational Research*, *41*(6), 407–428. doi:10.1016/j.ijer.2005.08.009

Falmange, J., Cosyn, E., Doignon, J., & Thiéry, N. (2004). *The assessment of knowledge, in theory and in practice*. Retrieved December 1, 2010, from http:// www.aleks.com/ about_aleks/ Science_Behind_ALEKS.pdf

Fraas, J. W. (2007). *A comparison of propensity score analysis to analysis of covariance: A case illustration*. Invited paper American Educational Research Association annual conference Chicago.

Grant, H., & Dweck, C. S. (2003). Clarifying achievement goals and their impact. *Journal of Personality and Social Psychology*, *85*(3), 541–553. doi:10.1037/0022-3514.85.3.541

Guya, F., Mageau, G. A., & Vallerand, R. J. (2003). On the hierarchical structure of self-determined motivation: A test of top-down, bottom-up, reciprocal, and horizontal effects. *Personality and Social Psychology Bulletin*, *29*(8), 992–1004. doi:10.1177/0146167203253297

Jamelske, E. (2009). Measuring the impact of a university first-year experience program on student GPA and retention. *Higher Education*, *57*(3), 373–391. doi:10.1007/s10734-008-9161-1

Kozeracki, C. A. (2005). Editor's notes. *New Directions for Community Colleges*, *129*, 1–4. doi:10.1002/cc.180

Onderwijsraad. (2006). *Reinforcing knowledge in education: Study*. Den Haag, The Netherlands: Onderwijsraad. English summary. Retrieved December 1, 2010, from http:// www.onderwijsraad.nl/ upload/ english/ publications/ reinforcing_knowledge_in_education.pdf

Onderwijsraad. (2007). *Reinforcing knowledge II: Advice*. Den Haag, The Netherlands: Onderwijsraad. English summary. Retrieved December 1, 2010, from www.onderwijsraad.nl/ upload/ english/ publications samenvatting_versteviging_van_kennis_ii_engels.pdf

Onderwijsraad. (2008). *A successful start in higher education: Advice*. Den Haag, The Netherlands: Onderwijsraad. English summary. Retrieved December 1, 2010, from http:// www.onderwijsraad.nl/ upload/ english/ publications/ a_succesfull_start_in_higher_education.pdf

Ratelle, C. F., Guay, F., Vallerand, R. J., Larose, S., & Senécal, C. (2007). Autonomous, controlled, and amotivated types of academic motivation: A person-oriented analysis. *Journal of Educational Psychology*, *99*(4), 734–746. doi:10.1037/0022-0663.99.4.734

Rienties, B., Kaper, W., Struyven, K., Tempelaar, D. T., van Gastel, L., & Vrancken, S. (in press). Virgailaitė-Mečkauskaitėe [Describing the current transitional educational practices in Europe. *Interactive Learning Environments*.]. *E (Norwalk, Conn.)*.

Ryan, R. M., & Deci, E. L. (2000). Self-determination theory and the facilitation of intrinsic motivation, social development, and well being. *The American Psychologist*, *55*(1), 68–78. doi:10.1037/0003-066X.55.1.68

Schneider, M., Carnoy, B., Kilpatrick, J., Schmidt, W. H., & Shavelson, R. J. (2007). *Estimating causal effects: Using experimental and observational designs*. Washington, DC: AERA.

Schuetz, P., & Barr, J. (2008). Are community colleges underprepared for underprepared students? *New Directions for Community Colleges*, ▪▪▪, 144.

Shadish, W. R., Cook, T. D., & Campbell, D. T. (2002). *Experimental and quasi-experimental designs for generalized causal inference*. Boston, MA: Houghton Mifflin Company.

Tempelaar, D. (2006). The role of metacognition in business education. *Industry and Higher Education*, *20*(5), 291–298. doi:10.5367/000000006778702292

Tempelaar, D. T., Gijselaers, W. H., Schim van der Loeff, S., & Nijhuis, J. F. H. (2007). A structural equation model analyzing the relationship of student personality factors and achievement motivations, in a range of academic subjects. *Contemporary Educational Psychology*, *32*(1), 105–131. doi:10.1016/j.cedpsych.2006.10.004

Tempelaar, D. T., & Rienties, B. (2008). Remediating summer classes and diagnostic entry assessment in mathematics to ease the transition from high school to iniversity . In *Proceedings Student Mobility and ICT: Can E-LEARNING overcome barriers of Life-Long learning* (pp. 9–17). Maastricht, The Netherlands: FEBA ERD Press.

Vallerand, R. J., Pelletier, L. G., Blais, M. R., Brière, N. M., Sénécal, C., & Vallières, E. F. (1993). On the assessment of intrinsic, extrinsic, and amotivation in education: Evidence on the concurrent and construct validity of the academic motivation scale. *Educational and Psychological Measurement*, *53*(1), 159–172. doi:10.1177/0013164493053001018

Vermunt, J. D. (1996). *Leerstijlen en sturen van leerprocessen in het Hoger Onderwijs*. Amsterdam/Lisse, The Netherlands: Swets & Zeitlinger.

Yanovitzky, I., Zanutto, E., & Hornik, R. (2005). Estimating causal effects of public health education campaigns using propensity score methodology. *Evaluation and Program Planning, 28*(2), 209–220. doi:10.1016/j.evalprogplan.2005.01.004

KEY TERMS AND DEFINITIONS

Adaptive E-Tutorial: Web-based tutorial that intelligently adapts to student interaction and knowledge level.

ALEKS: Assessment and LEarning in Knowledge Spaces, adaptive e-tutorial for mathematics and other subjects that allow for hierarchical classification in knowledge spaces.

Bridging Education: Remedial education with the aim to ease the transition between subsequent educational systems.

Effectiveness: Systematic investigation of the impact of educational innovations.

Postsecondary Remediation: Bridging education in the transition from high school to college or university.

Propensity Score: Probability that a student opts for participating in voluntary remedial education, or to opt out, given this students' background characteristics: the covariates.

Quasi-Experimental Design: Research design in an educational effectiveness study in which effectiveness is based on the comparison of achievements of two groups of students, the experimental group and the control group, but where groups are not created through random assignment.

Selection Effect or selection bias: Distortion of statistical analysis resulting from experimental and control groups being non-equivalent. In educational research, selection effects result quite often from self-selection: instead of comparing groups designed by random assignment, group composition is the result of students opting to participate, or not, different types of education.

ENDNOTE

1 See the AERA 'think tank white paper': Schneider, Carnoy, Kilpatrick, Schmidt & Shavelson (2007).

Chapter 9
Teaching Mathematics Teachers Online:
Strategies for Navigating the Intersection of Andragogy, Technology, and Reform-Based Mathematics Education

D. H. Jarvis
Nipissing University, Canada

ABSTRACT

Online course offerings in continuing teacher education are rapidly becoming standard features for faculties of education involved with the professional development of in-service teachers. However, instructors of mathematics education courses which are offered online must navigate certain formidable obstacles in the planning and delivery of their online learning experiences. In an era of reform-oriented mathematics education (National Council of Teachers of Mathematics, 2000; Ontario Ministry of Education, 2005), which emphasizes the increased use of manipulatives, technology, groupwork, problem-based learning, and varied assessment, the "virtual" instructor must develop creative methods for modeling these important aspects of teaching and learning. Drawing upon the relevant research literature, and based on nearly a decade of online instructor/course evaluation feedback and on the author's own observations, the following paper presents five key strategies for bridging this technological gap, and for navigating the intersection of andragogy (i.e., adult education), technology, and reform-based mathematics education within emergent online teaching models.

DOI: 10.4018/978-1-60960-875-0.ch009

INTRODUCTION

Online learning, or distance education, is quickly becoming a commonplace feature of the post-secondary education landscape (Guruz, 2008; Howell, Williams, & Lindsay, 2003; Varnhagen, Wilson, Krupa, Kasprzak, & Hunting, 2005). This reality is clearly, and in an ever-expanding manner, evidenced within pre-service and in-service teacher development programs across North America, and internationally. Online professional learning in higher education presents certain affordances and challenges for participants, and for the online instructor (Juan, Huertas, Steegmann, Corcoles, & Serrat, 2008). A list of the former would include such benefits as greater flexibility and choice regarding course selection and the actual times at which learning takes place; increased access to different courses, particularly for those in remote areas; the ability to take part in "threaded" discussion forums, allowing time for reflection and an historical record of conversations; and, an overall broader and deeper fostering of shared knowledge throughout educational jurisdictions.

The challenges of online learning often hinge on technological limitations (e.g., lack of highspeed Internet connection, difficulty with typing and/or related computer skills, Content Management System (CMS) software malfunction—particularly in terms of different Internet browsers being used), a preference for face-to-face interaction among participants, and the amount of required reading/posting, often done at length in front of a computer monitor. Further, as noted by Russell et al. (2009), some have questioned the effectiveness of online delivery in terms of the achievement of actual learning outcomes.

[S]ince its introduction more than a decade ago, educational leaders have questioned whether professional development delivered in an online environment is as effective as traditional face-to-face sessions in increasing teachers' content and pedagogical knowledge and in improving their instructional practices. . . . While researchers have reached a broad consensus on the general components of high-quality K–12 teacher professional development in face-to-face contexts, many questions remain about the design and delivery of effective online professional development. (pp. 71-73)

Mathematics education, by the very nature of its thick content and varied representations (e.g., symbolic, numeric, textual, graphical), brings with it a unique set of challenges and opportunities when taught online, particularly from a reform-oriented perspective such as that encouraged by the National Council of Teachers of Mathematics (National Council of Teachers of Mathematics, 2000). Beyond the lack of face-to-face social connectedness that often is perceived as characterizing online learning environments (Slagter & Bishop, 2009), the added challenges of mathematics education courses offered in such a format are significant, particularly in light of reform-oriented pedagogy and practice. What are these particular obstacles? Some of the main components of reform-oriented mathematics are the use of manipulatives (hands-on learning tools, either physical or virtual), groupwork, increased communication, incorporation of technology, problem-based learning, and varied assessment. How can instructors facilitate meaningful interaction and select appropriate activities that will serve to enhance the learning and professional growth experience within an online environment?

Several research studies have recently examined the effectiveness of online professional development models for mathematics educators (Carey, Kleiman, Russell, Douglas-Venable, & Louie, 2008; Russell, Carey, et al., 2009; Russell, Kleiman, Carey, & Douglas, 2009; Silverman & Clay, 2010). Russell et al. (2009) compared the effects of a professional development course delivered in an online and a face-to-face format, examining changes in teachers' pedagogical beliefs, instructional practices, and understanding of

Figure 1. Three components of instructional intelligence for mathematics teaching

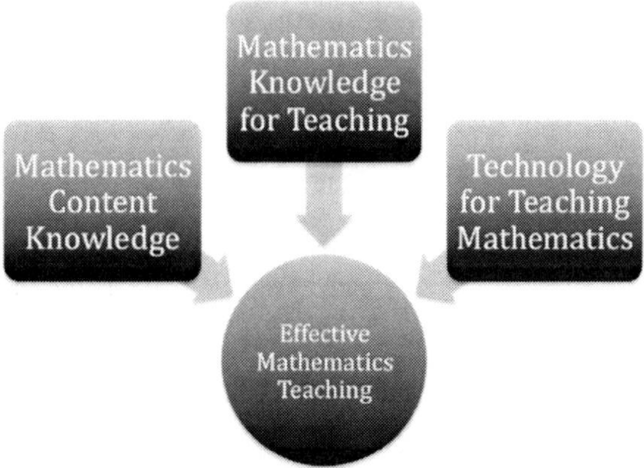

teaching certain mathematical concepts. Using a combination of surveys (by teachers, and by their students), a math content assessment, teacher logs, and course evaluations with both groups, the researchers found that while both formats of the course showed significant impact on teachers' mathematical understanding, pedagogical beliefs, and instructional practices, there was no significant differences in these gains between the two delivery methods. Further, those participants experiencing the online version indicated that they were more likely to take an online course in the future. According to Russell et al., this finding is consistent with prior research regarding online versus face-to-face instruction, indicating that while little may be lost in the online experience in terms of learning outcomes, all of the above-mentioned advantages of online learning may still be enjoyed.

Teaching mathematics to children involves at least three major components of instructional intelligence (see Figure 1). First, there is the *mathematical content knowledge*, something with which many elementary school generalist instructors struggle, especially in the light of newer strands of mathematics curriculum being introduced in North America over the past two decades (e.g., statistics, data management, probability). Second, there is what Shulman (1987) referred to as *pedagogical content knowledge*, or what has further been developed, based on his work, by Ball and her colleagues (D. Ball, Lubienski, & Mewborn, 2001; D. L. Ball, 2000; Deborah L. Ball & Bass, 2000) as *Mathematical Knowledge for Teaching* (MKT). The premise of MKT is that the ability to teach mathematics with effectiveness involves not only a deep understanding of the mathematical content itself, but also a related understanding of connections between mathematical ideas, an awareness of common misconceptions of students, and, the ability to analyze, interpret and discuss novel student solutions to mathematics problems shared in class. More specifically, it "consists of (i) pedagogically productive images and conceptually unpacked understandings, images, and representations of the content for students to learn, and, (ii) awareness of the connections to related mathematical ideas, concepts, and applications" (as cited in Silverman & Clay, 2010, p. 55). Third, teachers must be able to use, and to implement in their instruction, various forms of technology for teaching mathematics (Galbraith, 2006; Roulet, 2006). Depending on school level, this might include familiarization with the following types of tools/programs: graphing calculators (e.g., TI-83), computer software titles (e.g., dynamic geometry, Computer Algebra Systems), online interactive websites, motion detectors (e.g., TI Calculator-

Table 1. Class Profile chart of professional and personal information

AQ Candidate	Location	School	Courses Taught	Years Teaching	Interests/Other Information
Imran	Toronto, Ontario	AASS	Mathematics/Business	2a	Worked in Business; MBA; likes new technologies
Jean-Jacques	Montreal, Quebec	BBSS	Mathematics/Computers	18a	Physics/Science background; enjoys cycling and climbing
Elizabeth	Ottawa, Canada	CCSS	Mathematics/Visual Arts	7a	Black belt in karate; loves to sketch, paint, and integrate

Based Ranger), handheld/mobile technologies (e.g., iPod, laptop, cell phone), and, increasingly popular at the elementary level, interactive whiteboards (e.g., SmartNotebook).

INSTRUCTIONAL STRATEGIES FOR EFFECTIVE ONLINE MATH LEARNING

Having taught many online mathematics courses within three different online Content Management Systems (WebCT, Blackboard, ICZ) at two Canadian universities during the past decade, I have attempted to develop several strategies that I believe, based on candidate feedback and my own repeated observations and reflections as facilitator, enhance the overall professional learning experience for mathematics educators enrolled in such teacher development courses. In this chapter, I will highlight five such strategies which have been implemented with hundreds of online participants and which may offer some insight into effective instructional practice.

Building Community with Class Profiles

Like in any regular classroom, the first few instructions given and interactions experienced within the online forum are of extreme importance in terms of setting the tone or "creating the ambience" for learning (Kimball, 1995, p. 55). Adult learners enrolled in my Honours Specialist Mathematics courses are first asked to "sign in" online within the "Aftermath Café" folder, sharing various details about their professional experiences and personal interests. After several days, I have found it very useful, for both myself and the candidates, for me to take the time to collate this data in two forms: a simple table or chart (see Table 1) with columns highlighting their location, school, courses taught, years teaching, and other miscellaneous information; and a geographical map upon which each individual is situated according to location and name. These files are shared with candidates online, and I ask them to provide me with feedback regarding any possible errors or omissions. As the second and often third drafts are posted, I am already *modeling* positive collaboration, personal interest, and direct involvement within the course (Childers & Berner, 2000; Slagter & Bishop, 2009).

The Class Profile chart provides the instructor with instant access to important facts which often become helpful throughout the course in terms of mentally "locating" an individual, asking good questions, and mindfully drawing upon candidate expertise as one extends or redirects online interaction. The map (see Figure 2) serves to actually situate learners within a visual context, allowing them to obtain a general "feel" for what the course looks like in terms of geographical representation, and rendering a sense of "place" in an otherwise distant or disconnected context. One obvious benefit of online learning is that it allows the

Figure 2. Class Profile map of candidate names and locations

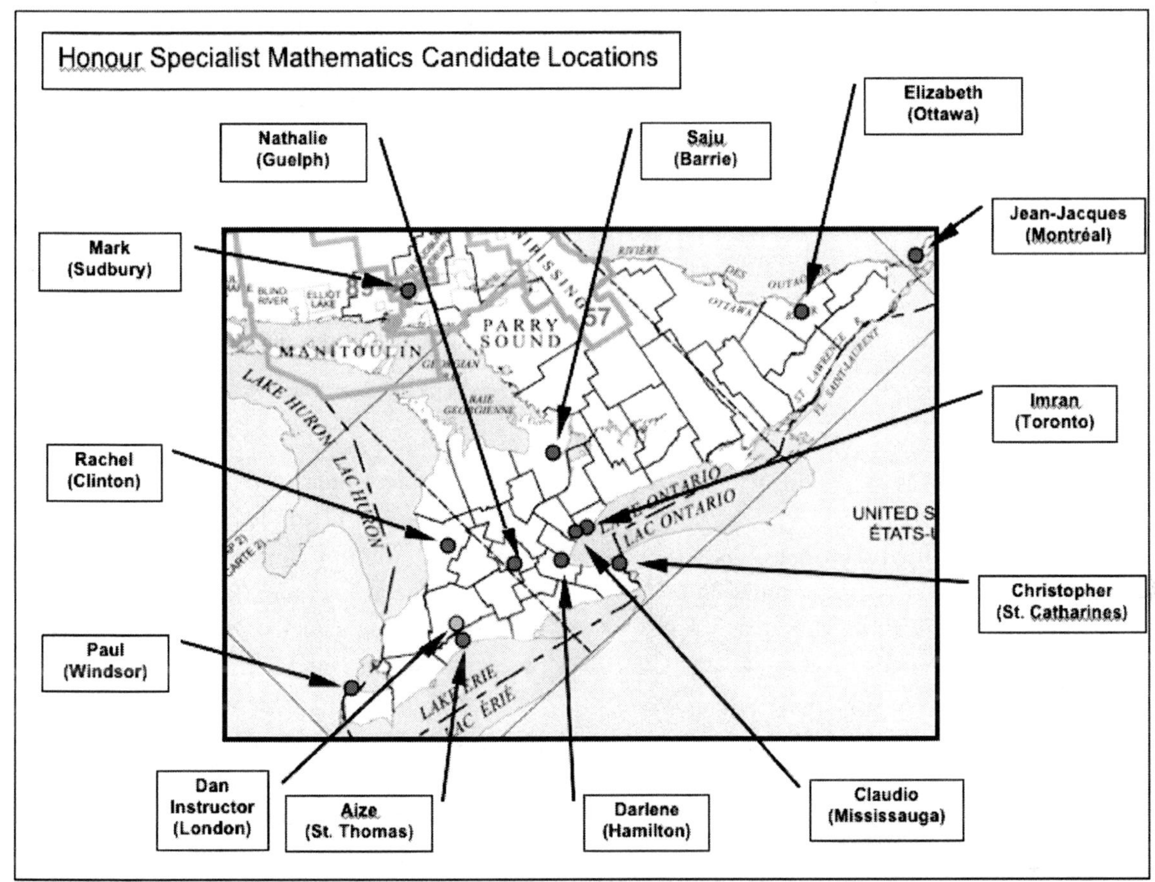

learner to not only participate at her/his leisure, but also permits she/he from studying at great distances or while on the move. I've had candidates take my mathematics education courses while teaching in China, working in western Canada, and touring Europe with a backpack and laptop.

Because the instructor and course participants are often denied the visual element (i.e., as in onsite settings or video-conferencing situations) in much of distance education, this chart/map Class Profile is very much a part of building community and constructing individual "portraits" of each learner. Mounted near my monitor for the duration of the course, the Class Profile provides for quick identification regarding *who is who*, and *who is where*.

Engaging Minds with Rich Mathematical Problems or Tasks

The importance of both teachers' mathematics content knowledge (i.e., the curriculum expectations) *and* Mathematics Knowledge for Teaching (Ball, 2000)(D. L. Ball, 2000) (i.e., deeper understanding of mathematical connections, and, how children learn, err, and represent/communicate their mathematical thinking) cannot be understated. Within the online learning environment, it is often difficult to engage in the types of rich tasks/problems and rich assessment activities that speak to these required skills and competencies, insofar as face-to-face engagement is arguably

Table 2. Sample engaging problem, question, and response posting instructions

Problem: Strider and Boromir are sitting at a back table in a dark, smoky tavern of Middle Earth known as the Prancing Pony. Strider has three loaves of bread; Boromir has two. Just before they eat, however, in walks Bilbo Baggins, obviously famished, and asks if he may share their meal. They agree, and each of the three characters eat equal amounts of bread. Before departing, Bilbo pulls out five identical gold coins and says, "Please accept these few coins as thanks." Strider and Boromir watch the hobbit depart but then become puzzled as to how they should distribute the gift. Unable to solve the riddle, they take it to Gandalf the Grey and ask him for advice. As this represented a difficult "two-pipe" problem, they had to wait some time outside the wizard's dwelling. Finally, he emerged from the interior, and delivered his recommendation.
Question: What was Gandalf's conclusion, and why was it the only fair and just way to divide up the golden coins? Further, think of as many different ways (at least three) to tackle this mathematical problem as possible. What role would the teacher play in these? At what grade levels might this problem be appropriate, and where might it be used in terms of curriculum?
Note: Again, please wait until Monday July 18th before posting solutions/ideas/comments, so that all of the class participants will have a chance to think through the problem.

more conducive—at least *prima facie*—to this type of learning.

In an attempt to interpret MKT in light of online learning environments, and building on the social-constructivist learning theory of Vygotsky (1986/1934), researchers Silverman and Clay (2010) developed what they refer to as *Online Asynchronous Collaboration* (OAC). Through several iterations of online learning experiences for mathematics teachers, and subsequent modifications based on feedback and observations, the researchers present a revised model that includes (a) posting initial thoughts, comments, questions, and solutions in a private online space (i.e., weblog), (b) small-group discussion focusing on comments and questions to the now public initial posts, (c) revision of initial posts, and (d) a synthetic discussion (p. 71).

Having adopted a somewhat similar approach in my own teaching (i.e., using threaded discussion folders rather than weblogs), I have found that one way to involve online participants in rich tasks, or problem-based activities, is to post engaging mathematics problems at regular intervals throughout the online course, allow participants time to work on these independently over a pre-determined time allocation, and then have participants post/discuss solution strategies in designated discussion folders. This allows all participants more time to grapple with a given problem (see Table 2 for sample problem and related instructions; this is a classic ratio problem rewritten using Tolkien's *Lord of the Rings* characters in order to provide a more interesting context). These mathematics problems can be selected to reflect the types of problems implemented at the educational level for which the course/qualification is being taught (e.g., elementary, secondary, or post-secondary), and may be more word-based or numeric in content.

Four or five such problems are selected for the course, one being featured for each of the online modules, which may last one or several weeks, depending on the course structure. Not only does this process model the use of rich problems in mathematics classrooms, but the multiple solutions that are often presented by candidates lead to important pedagogical discussions surrounding issues of mathematical communication, teacher questioning, consolidation of learning, and the encouragement of invented algorithms and novel approaches to problem solving among students (Jarvis, 2008). Technology now permits these solutions to also be posted in video format, allowing candidates to visually share how they used pencil/paper, or manipulatives, or software to model a problem and to create/present a viable solution in written/visual form. YouTube, for example, now offers a feature that allows one to upload *video comments* to previously-posted videos, providing a means to further breech the

Table 3. Sample web-based and web-access resources for online technology explorations

eWorkshop (ON, Canada): http://www.eworkshop.on.ca/edu/core.cfm
GeoGebra: Dynamic Mathematics for Everyone: http://www.geogebra.org/
Leading Math Success (ON, Canada): http://www.edu.gov.on.ca/eng/studentsuccess/lms/library.html#TIPS4RM
LearnAlberta (AB, Canada): http://www.learnalberta.ca/
NCTM Illuminations (VA, USA): http://illuminations.nctm.org/
National Library of Virtual Manipulatives (UT, USA): http://matti.usu.edu/nlvm/nav/vlibrary.html
Statistics Canada E-Stat Educational Resource: http://www.statcan.ca/english/Estat/licence.htm

face-to-face and online experiential divide. Where such video capability exists, children and/or teachers can be shown posing/modeling/solving problems, leading to further discussions and analysis within the online forum.

CREATING ANTICIPATION WITH LIVE TECHNOLOGY TUTORIALS

A third online teaching strategy is the use of scheduled chat-line technology tutorials in which candidates meet virtually, at scheduled dates/times to share comments/questions/insights regarding the many software/website resources and related explorations that I, as instructor, have posted earlier in the course. Like with the math problems, I have found it beneficial to maintain a separate folder specifically focused on mathematics technology, in which I can post these various resources and links. Candidates are asked to have relevant software "up and running" and/or available during the virtual class sessions wherever possible, and to have specific questions/comments prepared in advance. During the scheduled tutorials, the instructor acts as facilitator, sometimes answering specific questions but more often than not simply guiding the conversation and offering insights where possible, yet always present and available for support.

As technology is now such a vital part of reform-oriented mathematics education (Gadanidis, Gadanidis, & Schindler, 2003; National Council of Teachers of Mathematics, 2000, pp. pp. 24-27; Ontario Ministry of Education, 2005, pp. pp. 27-28; Richards, 2002; Sinclair, 2005), and since online learning prohibits the use of technology software/hardware in an actual classroom, this teaching strategy serves to address this important area of pedagogy within the distance education forum. I currently have candidates examine several types of mathematics software (see Table 3) with related introductory activities [geometric/algebraic modeling; spreadsheets; data manipulation]; online virtual manipulatives and interactive activities (note: these are also excellent for reviewing mathematics content knowledge); and, Statistics Canada's *E-Stat* learning resources). Note that all of these products are freely-available, either as "open-source" titles, or as virtual/interactive manipulatives, allowing teachers to experiment at no extra cost during the online course, even without access to an actual classroom.

At the post-secondary level, open-source alternatives are becoming more popular and widely-available as well, such as "R" for statistics, "SAGE" for computer algebra system (CAS) symbolic manipulation, and, "GeoGebra" for combined geometric, algebraic, and numeric representations of mathematical phenomena. Relating to the latter, Todd, Lyublinskaya, and Ryzhik (2010) have described such software as "next level" programs that allow for interactive modeling and a powerful moving back-and-forth between various representations:

Dynamic Geometry… has facilitated an inductive approach to geometry. These technologies have been widely adopted in the last 20 years and a vast amount of creativity has been brought to bear on applying it to the educational process.... However, this technology is not without its shortcomings. First it is construction-based; geometric configurations which are easy to state declaratively must be expressed in terms of sequential constructions... . Secondly, the existing software is numeric only, and does not have a convenient way of interacting with Computer Algebra Systems (CAS). . . . Recently developed symbolic geometry software . . . allows geometric and algebraic representations to coexist in the same model. Such software takes a geometric configuration and outputs algebraic expressions for quantities measured from the model. A combination allowing geometry to be modeled and expressed algebraically and then solved automatically in an algebra system provides a powerful toolkit for taking the inductive exploration-based approach facilitated by the original dynamic geometry systems to the next level, integrating geometric and algebraic exploration for developing proofs. (pp. 151-152)

The fact that the above-mentioned software titles are freely available and open-source in nature cannot be overstated in terms of access issues within all forms of online/onsite learning. This has changed the "rules of the game" the world over, allowing dozens of developing nations first-time access to, and input into, powerful mathematical tools that were heretofore beyond the reach of jurisdictional education budgets, and permitting the use of such software in all distance learning.

I have treated these chat-line tutorials as both optional/voluntary and as a required component of various courses, in terms of candidate participation. Both approaches have their advantages/disadvantages. As a voluntary activity, those more inclined to use software are able to explore this in-depth, while others who may not like the technology aspect as much, or have issues regarding accessibility, are not required to take part. By making the chat-line experience a required component, one ensures that all participants have at least tried to access, experiment with, and prepared questions based on the software(s) being examined. If it is mandated, it is best to provide multiple dates/times so that participants can be sure to find a time that works for them. For those not able to join the group online during selected dates/times, transcripts of the sessions are converted to PDF and posted for everyone following the chat-line sessions. As one teacher shared following the tutorial: "I found the online chat the most fun part of the course. It was quite engaging and I would encourage you to include more live chat sessions."

SHARING WEB-BASED DISCOVERIES USING SOCIAL BOOKMARKING TECHNOLOGY

In studying the effects of integrating technology, observation, and writing into a teacher education method course, Jang (2008) describes how that the nature of online learning provides for certain affordances that instructors and adult students often find highly beneficial:

The technology is used in four ways as: a knowledge source, a data organizer, an information presenter, and a facilitator. . . . Therefore, most teachers, especially those who endeavor to provide students with a stimulating teaching and learning environment, have been attracted by the powerful capacity of Internet technology in collecting information that is scattered over different information sectors around the world. The main idea behind their desire to use this technology is not only to teach their students how to access their teaching materials on the Internet and the World Wide Web, but also to train their students how to effectively explore the Internet to search for needed information. (pp. 854)

The most recent addition to my online courses has been the implementation of a web-based social bookmarking tool known as "Delicious" (http://

Figure 3. Screen capture of the Delicious social bookmarking "Network Bundle"

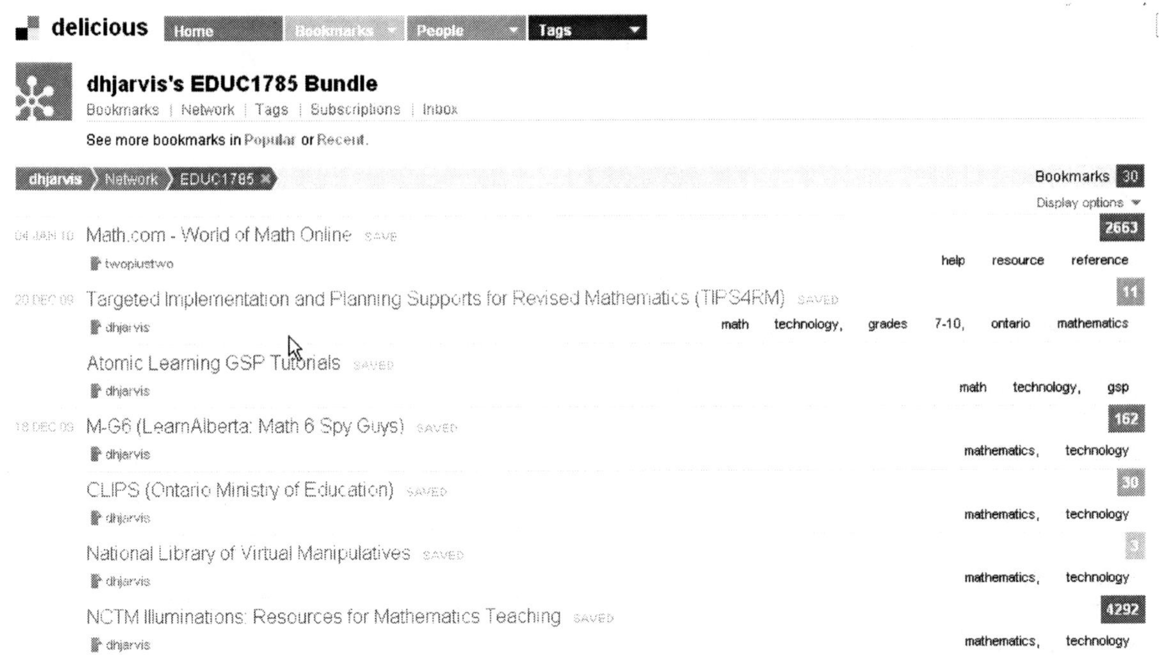

delicious.com/). Participants are asked to sign up for this free online tool, email me their individual usernames, and then I have created what is known as a "network bundle" (see Figure 3) of contacts specifically named/dedicated to the course. In this way, when students find websites that are related to mathematics teaching or learning, or to specific educational issues that arise in the discussion forums, they can easily "bookmark" these sites using a "Delicious" icon, add keywords making it searchable for course participants, and then benefit from everyone's discoveries as the course progresses. All marked sites are therefore housed in one convenient location, including those added regularly by me, the instructor, and this compendium can be referenced, searched by keyword, and added to throughout the online course session. This process not only emphasizes a knowledge sharing, or sense of community endeavour, but also underscores the tremendous potential for information gathering that is now possible through Internet access.

PROVIDING SPECIFIC AND ONGOING FEEDBACK WITH *CANDIDATE ASSESSMENT FILES*

Like all students, adult learners desire meaningful and ongoing feedback throughout the online learning experience. I have found that the best way to respond to this need in a consistent and appropriate manner is to construct what I've simply labeled as "Candidate Assessment Files (CAFs)." Sent privately to each participant via the online MailBox, all four installments of this CAF provide candidates with both general and individual comments regarding course progress and assignment achievement, respectively. These CAFs are Microsoft Word files with each candidate's name typed on a title page with course information and colourful graphics. Inside, each course module is briefly synopsized and then individual comments are made regarding the modular assignments. Particularly effective, in terms of feedback, is the copying and pasting of specific quotations made by each candidate within their various assignments, accompanied by related instructor comments, questions, and/or suggested readings.

Even in the very first installment of the CAF, all modules and assignments are represented in blank outline form. Also included are rubrics for major assignments (i.e., the cells of which are simply shaded to indicate achievement upon assessment), a "Course in Review" page with all assignments listed and their respective value (i.e., these left blank for the moment), and a copy of the university grading scales (e.g., what characteristics constitute a mark of "A" or "B+"). This complete CAF, although primarily blank at the point of first installment, provides each candidate with a clear framework for assessment in the online course. They can be confident that there will not be any surprises in terms of how or when they will be evaluated. By providing both general (i.e., course reading and online discussion highlights) and individual (i.e., referencing specific assignment quotations and online participation tracking) comments, not only is the instructor more likely to be in tune with all participants and the course in general, but candidates are reassured that their instructor is carefully monitoring all that transpires.

CONCLUSION

When I first began teaching online courses I assumed that they would be very limiting in terms of possible interaction with candidates, student assessment, and my ability to deal, in any meaningful way, with the immensely important area of technology within mathematics education. In looking back now, however, and comparing my university courses taught online with those taught onsite in faculty of education classrooms, I must say that not only have I enjoyed the online immensely, but that in developing and implementing the above-detailed strategies, I have been much more "connected" to candidates and able to closely monitor what and how they were thinking as a given course progressed. The archives of threaded discussion forums—with no real equivalent mechanism in face-to-face courses—not only provide for rich discussion experiences, but also facilitate more valid assessment, since the instructor's recollection of participant comments (sketchy at the best of times) is replaced by a documented record. Although I could not "see" them, in the end I felt that I actually "knew them" better.

Some participants will always prefer taking part in a face-to-face forum where they can see and hear the instructor and the other students, and can share their thoughts in public, as they occur to them within the discussions. Others prefer time to think about their responses and to craft online discussion forum postings at their leisure and often following some research into literature, or on the web, or from the course textbook. The ongoing discussion of, and access to, relevant mathematics software titles, mathematical problems, and other web-based resources (mutually shared using Delicious) during the online course delivery, was consistently met with positive comments from adult learners. Although not reflective of all course participants, as one would expect in any teaching context, the following course evaluation responses do provide a sense of overall teacher feedback based on learning experiences that featured these online strategies:

This course was thorough and exceeded my expectations in terms of interactivity, enriching tasks and 'sense of community.'

The course met my expectations. I am at a point in my teaching career where I am ready to experiment. This course helped to bring me up to date on current research and theory in all aspects of teaching and learning.

This is an excellent course that meets the needs of the experienced mathematics teacher. It builds on our teaching experience and is an essential step in our professional development.

The instructor participated in the on-line discussions, provided us with new and relevant articles and research, offered on-line tutorials . . . was excellent!!!!

With an increasing number of digital conferencing programs now becoming available (some free, like Moodle and GoToMeeting; others commercial such as Adobe Connect, Elluminate, and Blackboard), many with video capacity, teachers taking online courses will be able to benefit from both the asynchronous and visual/personal nature of new "hybrid," online formats.

By creating detailed Class Profiles, posting/discussing rich and engaging mathematics problems, hosting virtual technology tutorials, facilitating centralized social bookmarking of discovered websites, and providing ongoing and meaningful assessment files, I have been able to provide mathematics educators with meaningful online professional development. Future, more formal research that would be of interest to me would include comparing the online learning experiences of Bachelor of Education (preservice), Additional Qualification (inservice), and graduate students (MEd/PhD) within our program. Does the online learning format adequately meet the needs of instructors and adult learners within these three programs? Online learning does have its inherent limitations, to be sure; yet the opportunities it affords the "virtual" instructor of mathematics education, and the participating course candidates, are indeed worth investigating.

REFERENCES

Ball, D., Lubienski, S., & Mewborn, D. (2001). Research on teaching mathematics: The unsolved problem of teachers' mathematical knowledge . In Richardson, V. (Ed.), *Handbook of research on teaching* (4th ed., pp. 433–456). New York, NY: Macmillan.

Ball, D. L. (2000). Bridging practices: Intertwining content and pedagogy in teaching and learning to teach. *Journal of Teacher Education, 51*(3), 241–247. doi:10.1177/0022487100051003013

Ball, D. L., & Bass, H. (2000). Interweaving content and pedagogy in teaching and learning to teach: Knowing and using mathematics . In Boaler, J. (Ed.), *Multiple perspectives on mathematics teaching and learning* (pp. 83–104). Westport, CT: Ablex.

Carey, R., Kleiman, G., Russell, M., Douglas-Venable, J., & Louie, J. (2008). Online courses for math teachers: Comparing self-paced and facilitated cohort approaches. *The Journal of Technology, Learning, and Assessment, 7*(3), 3–35.

Childers, J. L., & Berner, R. T. (2000). General education issues, distance education practices: Building community and classroom interaction through the integration of curriculum, instructional design, and technology. *The Journal of General Education, 49*(1), 53–65. doi:10.1353/jge.2000.0001

Gadanidis, G., Gadanidis, J., & Schindler, K. (2003). Factors mediating the use of online applets in the lesson planning of preservice mathematics teachers. *Journal of Computers in Mathematics and Science Teaching, 22*(4), 323–344.

Galbraith, P. (2006). Students, mathematics, and technology: Assessing the present-Challenging the future. *International Journal of Mathematical Education in Science and Technology, 37*(3), 277–290. doi:10.1080/00207390500321936

Guruz, K. (2008). *Higher education and international student mobility in the global knowledge economy*. New York, NY: SUNY Press.

Howell, S. L., Williams, P. B., & Lindsay, N. K. (2003). Thirty-two trends affecting distance education: An informed foundation for strategic planning. *Online Journal of Distance Learning Administration, 6*(3), 1–18.

Jang, S.-J. (2008). The effects of integrating technology, observation and writing into a teacher education method course. *Computers & Education*, *50*(3), 853–865. doi:10.1016/j.compedu.2006.09.002

Jarvis, D. H. (2008). Thinking outside the rectangular prism: Fostering problem-based mathematics learning. *Ontario Mathematics Gazette*, *47*(2), 23–28.

Juan, A., Huertas, M., Steegmann, C., Corcoles, C., & Serrat, C. (2008). Mathematical e-learning: State of the art and experiences at the Open University of Catalonia. *International Journal of Mathematical Education in Science and Technology*, *39*(4), 455–471. doi:10.1080/00207390701867497

Kimball, L. (1995). Ten ways to make online learning groups work. *Educational Leadership*, *53*(2), 54–56.

National Council of Teachers of Mathematics. (2000). *Principles and standards for school mathematics*. Reston, VA: Author.

Ontario Ministry of Education. (2005). *The Ontario curriculum, grades 9 and 10: Mathematics, Revised*. Toronto, ON: Queen's Printer for Ontario.

Richards, G. (2002). The challenges of the learning object paradigm. *Canadian Journal of Learning and Technology*, *28*(3).

Roulet, G. (2006). The practice of information technology in mathematics education: A critical look. *The Mathematics Educator*, *9*(2), 16–32.

Russell, M., Carey, R., Kleiman, G., & Douglas-Venable, J. (2009). Face-to-face and online professional development for mathematics teachers: A comparative study. *Journal of Asynchronous Learning Networks*, *13*(2), 71–87.

Russell, M., Kleiman, G., Carey, R., & Douglas, J. (2009). Comparing self-paced and cohort-based online courses for teachers. *Journal of Research on Technology in Education*, *41*(4), 443–466.

Shulman, L. S. (1987). Knowledge and teaching: Foundations of the new reform. *Harvard Educational Review*, *57*(1), 1–22.

Silverman, J., & Clay, E. L. (2010). Online asynchronous collaboration in mathematics teacher education and the development of mathematical knowledge for teaching. *Teacher Educator*, *45*(1), 54–73. doi:10.1080/08878730903386831

Sinclair, M. (2005). Using technology in the junior grades. *Ontario Mathematics Gazette*, *43*(4), 30–34.

Slagter, P. J., & Bishop, M. J. (2009). Theoretical foundations for enhancing social connectedness in online learning environments. *Distance Education*, *30*(3), 291–315. doi:10.1080/01587910903236312

Todd, P., Lyublinskaya, I., & Ryzhik, V. (2010). Symbolic geometry software and proofs. *International Journal of Computers for Mathematical Learning*, *15*(2), 151–159. doi:10.1007/s10758-010-9164-8

Varnhagen, S., Wilson, D., Krupa, E., Kasprzak, S., & Hunting, V. (2005). Comparison of student experiences with different online graduate courses in health promotion. *Canadian Journal of Learning and Technology*, *31*(1).

Vygotsky, L. S. (1986). *Thought and language*. Cambridge, MA: MIT Press.

ADDITIONAL READING

Borba, M. C., Malheiros, A. P., & Zulatto, R. B. (2010). *Online distance education*. Rotterdam, Netherlands: Sense.

Veletsianos, G. (2010). *Emerging technologies in distance education*. Edmonton, AB: AU Press.

KEY TERMS AND DEFINITIONS

Assessment: Often defined in education as the collection of various forms of student data with a view to facilitating evaluation, which is the judging of the data in terms of levels of student achievement.

Mathematics Education: Learning in mathematics including strands such as numeration, patterning, geometry, spatial sense, algebra, data management, and probability.

Online Learning: A form of learning that is experienced at a distance, using the Internet and often some form of online learning software/platform such as Blackboard, Adobe Connect, Elluminate for interaction.

Problem-Based Learning: Learning that focuses on the understanding and solving of a rich problem that is explored through the use of numbers, pictures, words, and various types of mathematical models.

Professional Development: In-service teacher learning which can be experienced externally from the classroom in the form of workshops/conferences, or that is more ongoing in nature and embedded within actual classroom practice (e.g., lesson study, Action Research).

Reform-Oriented Mathematics: Mathematics education characterized by the frequent use of cooperative groupwork, manipulatives, problem-based learning, technology, and varied assessment.

Social Bookmarking: An Internet-based software that allows for the tagging and sharing of annotated, bookmarked Internet favourite websites among a defined group of users.

Chapter 10
Developing Teachers' Mathematical Knowledge for Teaching through Online Collaboration

Jason Silverman
Drexel University, USA

Ellen L. Clay
Drexel University, USA

ABSTRACT

In this chapter, we discuss our perspective on mathematical knowledge for teaching and present an emerging instructional model for supporting the development of that knowledge through an instructor facilitated online environment. We focus on the ways in which online collaboration can support teachers as they wrestle with, and ultimately make sense of, the mathematical structures that underlie a variety of the school mathematics curriculum. Three cases are provided to highlight the potential that online collaboration hold for supporting teachers' as they collaborate about specific mathematical ideas and reflect on those collaborations. We believe that these cases can also serve as a starting point for further conversations about supporting online mathematical collaboration and online mathematics teacher development.

DOI: 10.4018/978-1-60960-875-0.ch010

INTRODUCTION

The importance of teachers' mathematical knowledge has been well documented in the literature (Ball, 1993; Bransford, Brown, & Cocking, 2000; Ma, 1999; Shulman, 1986) and increasing teachers' mathematical knowledge continues to be a major focus in both education research and policy (Greenberg & Walsh, 2008; National Mathematics Advisory Panel, 2008). In this chapter, we discuss our perspective on mathematical knowledge for teaching and present an emerging instructional model for supporting the development of that knowledge through an instructor facilitated online environment. Because of the scarcity of models for supporting the development mathematical knowledge for teaching for secondary mathematics (face-to-face *or* online), the primary focus of this chapter will be on detailing three "case studies" of teachers engagement and collaboration about one big mathematical idea that underlies a large portion of the school mathematics curriculum: similarity, equality, and congruence. These cases will highlight the potential online collaboration holds for supporting teachers as they collaboratively engage with these big mathematical ideas and reflect on those collaborations. We believe that these cases can also serve as a starting point for further conversations about supporting online mathematical collaboration.

THEORETICAL BACKGROUND

Mathematical Knowledge for Teaching

Ball and her colleagues (Ball, 1993, 2007; Ball, Hill, & Bass, 2005; Ball & McDiarmid, 1990) have focused on understanding the special ways one must know mathematical procedures and representations to interact productively with students in the context of teaching. Their pioneering work has succeeded in identifying a statistical relationship between this *mathematical knowledge for teaching* (MKT) and student achievement (Ball, et al., 2005; Hill, Rowan, & Ball, 2005). We extend this work by focusing not only on particular mathematical understandings but also the conceptual structures within which those particular understandings lie. Our reason for this focus is pragmatic:

If a teacher's conceptual structures comprise disconnected facts and procedures, their instruction is likely to focus on disconnected facts and procedures. In contrast, if a teacher's conceptual structures comprise a web of mathematical ideas and compatible ways of thinking, it will at least be possible that she attempts to develop these same conceptual structures in her students (Thompson, Carlson, & Silverman, 2007)

Rather than focusing on identifying the mathematical reasoning, insight, understanding and skill needed in teaching mathematics, we focus on the mathematical understandings "that carry through an instructional sequence, that are foundational for learning other ideas, and that play into a network of ideas that does significant work in students' reasoning" (Thompson, 2008). We refer to these understandings as *coherent* understandings: powerful, generative "big ideas" from which an understanding of a body of mathematical ideas and its relation to other bodies can emerge.

It is important to note that coherence is not a characteristic of one's understanding of a particular mathematical idea, for coherence in curricula or students' understandings depends on the way in which they fit together (Thompson, 2008). This notion of coherence is a challenge to traditional mathematics teacher education efforts that seek to support teachers in "gain[ing] the ability to do the mathematics … and understand[ing] the underlying concepts so they will be able to assist their students, in turn, to gain a deep understanding of mathematics" (Musser, Burger, & Peterson, 2008). When a focus is on coherence, the emphasis is not just on doing and learning "the mathematics," but rather on developing a scheme of understanding within which a variety of mathematical ideas are connected and that can serve as a conceptual anchor for mathematics curricula and instruction. The research described in this chapter is grounded in the development of coherent mathematical knowledge for teaching.

RESEARCH IN ONLINE COLLABORATION

While there are numerous internet sites devoted to information sharing and collaboration (most notably social networking sites like *Facebook* and *LinkedIn* and Web 2.0 environments such as blogs and wikis), a review of mathematics internet sites reveals that most exist for the purpose of disseminating information and are therefore not ideal for studying mathematical collaboration. One mathematics site that is focused on using the power of the Internet to support mathematical communication and collaboration is the Math Forum @ Drexel. Since the mid-1990s, the Math Forum has focused on the development of interactive services that bridge higher education, K-12, and workplace communities. As of 2008, the Math Forum and its members have collaboratively developed over one million pages of content and have generated over three million visits a month. In addition, the Math Forum has supported more than 100,000 K-12 students through its interactive Problem of the Week services. Through the development of these services, the Math Forum has developed into a community of practice that is defined by the shared purpose of supporting people learning math together and the professional practices of making one's own mathematical thinking public, analyzing student thinking and using the results of that analysis as a starting point for further mathematical interactions (Renninger & Shumar, 2002; Shumar, 2003; Shumar, 2009; Shumar & Sarmiento, 2008).

Outside of a mathematics disciplinary focus, there is growing interest in online collaboration in distance learning settings. Instructors and instructional designers believe that in order for a participant to be successful in online learning, they must actively *participate* in the class, which may take on the form of discussion boards, blogs, or other computer-supported interactional environments. The importance of interaction and collaboration in online learning is also well accepted by researchers (Paloff & Pratt, 1999; Ravenscroft, 2001; Shale & Garrison, 1990; Su, Bonk, Magjuka, Liu, & Lee, 2005; Wegerif, 2006). Much of the research on this collaborative learning seeks to identify quantitative relationships between variables (such as measures of participation, prominence, etc.) and stands in contrast to the significant push towards the importance of communication and discourse in knowing and learning (Perressini & Knuth, 1998; Sfard, 2008; Wertsch & Toma, 1995). In contrast, a relatively new field of Computer-Supported Collaborative Learning uses ethnomethodology (Garfinkel, 1967) and other derivative methodologies (conversation analysis, video analysis) to develop detailed case studies describing the methods through which groups accomplish of collaborative meaning making (Stahl, Koschmann, & Suthers, 2006).

Our primary goal of our work over the past three years has been to develop a model for online mathematical collaboration that builds on the work of our colleagues at the Math Forum and to document the ways in which particular systems – specific combinations of participants, facilitation, and technology – support and constrain participation and collaboration in mathematics. Through a design research methodology, we have developed and explicated a model that holds promise for supporting teachers' development of deep, connected understandings of school mathematics and that allows them to experience and explore the pedagogical implications of those understandings through authentic online collaboration (Clay & Silverman, 2008a, 2008b; Silverman & Clay, 2010). Our environment, which we call Online Asynchronous Collaboration in Mathematics Teacher Education (OAC), has its roots in the belief that replicating traditional (face-to-face) instructional practices is insufficient for the creation of online learning environments (Reeves, Herrington, & Oliver, 2004) and required that we fundamentally rethink what legitimate and productive mathematical collaboration for teachers might look like in the online environment. We discuss the specifics of OAC in the following section.

ONLINE ASYNCHRONOUS COLLABORATION IN MATHEMATICS TEACHER DEVELOPMENT

Our current model for OAC involves cycles of individual "private" problem solving followed by analysis, discussion, and reflection on the individual solutions in small groups. We provide three to four days for work on each phase and at any given time in our course, teachers are concurrently working on different phases for different problems. Each online "unit" begins with teachers working in a private workspace where they draft solutions, describe their initial approaches, or pose questions they have on a set of purposefully selected, mathematics tasks. We use a Blog to provide a space for teachers to record their initial thoughts, questions, and solutions. Throughout the three to four-day "private" phase, teachers have the ability to edit and revise their posts (during the "private" period, these posts are only viewable by the author of the post and the course instructor). We accomplish this through the use of an online Blog developed by Learning Objects, Inc. and integrated within Blackboard[1]. The blog module has built in features that allow the moderator to determine both when others are allowed to view posts and when they are allowed to comment or discuss the individual postings. Rather than traditional Blogs that have one blog per person, we create one blog per problem, to which everyone produces their own entry.

We feel this private phase is invaluable for a variety of reasons. First, it is important to create an open and safe environment for teachers to engage in mathematical activity (National Council of Teachers of Mathematics, 1991). The private Blog becomes a space where teachers can "think out loud," mull over ideas, and ultimately create mathematics. Second, the teachers' individual work in the Blog results in a permanent record of each student's initial thinking. One challenge for mathematics education is not only to have productive mathematical conversations among small numbers of teachers (those who understand the content or are able to synthesize the focus of each utterance with their own understandings), but to ensure that the conversation intersects with the current understandings of as many teachers as possible. Using this permanent record as a catalyst for instructional conversations increases the likelihood of such intersection. In addition, we see the permanent record transcending individual and group mathematical development and serving as a "representative sample" of teachers' thinking about a particular mathematics task. In this way, the permanent record can also serve as the bridge between developing mathematical understandings and a focus on the pedagogical implications of those understandings. We are currently involved in other projects that study the ways in which these samples of teachers' work, often containing interpretations, solutions, and comments similar to typical school students, can catalyze shifts in teachers' pedagogical beliefs and practices.

In the individual problem solving phase, we provide teachers with mathematics tasks that have multiple entry points, that can be solved with a variety of methods and that involve important mathematical ideas that cut across a variety of mathematics content and courses. We begin by asking the teachers to share all the things that they notice about the given scenario, to ask clarifying questions, and to attempt to solve the problem and describe the solution method employed. In our previous work, we have found these prompts to be open enough that teachers who are comfortable with a particular solution method and those who may need support interpreting the problem – and all teachers in between – can, at a minimum, begin to engage with the problem. In the private phase, we do not expect that everyone in the class will be able to complete each of these activities, but we do expect each student to attempt the assigned task and either pose a solution method and solution or ask relevant questions that would assist in the completion of the activity. The instructor's role at this phase is simply to encourage legitimate mathematical engagement, and not to judge the correctness or appropriateness of each posting.

The second stage in OAC involves catalyzing public discourse about the mathematical thinking and reasoning that has been generated in the individual thinking phase. After the teachers have had three to four days to post their initial thoughts, questions, and solutions to the private Blog, we open up the individual postings for public discussion. In our Blog system, we accomplish this by switching the Blog type from "Private Journal" to "Group Blog," which activates the feature that allows all Blog participants to post and view comments to each posting. During this public stage, everyone has an opportunity to read, comment on and ask questions about each other's solutions. As teachers work through this phase, they are provided with opportunities to comment on and discuss the various interpretations of the problems, strategies, and representations. In addition, these dyadic and small group interactions are public and are thus able to be viewed by others in the class. As stated previously, our explicit goal is to support teachers' mathematical development and the development of MKT, but as a result of the public and permanent nature of OAC, opportunities for examination and discussion of mathematics pedagogy in the context of mathematical activity are almost impossible to avoid. Blanton (2002) and Zeichner (1996) note that such sites hold much potential for the development of mathematics teachers.

The third stage of OAC involves the synthesis and supporting reflective discourse and collective reflection, which Cobb, Boufi, McClain, and Whitenack (1997) describe as "repeated shifts such that what the students and teacher do in action subsequently becomes an explicit object of discussion [and] the joint or communal activity of making what was previously done in action an object of reflection" (p. 258). The goal of these discussions is to facilitate the transition from doing math and supporting each others' mathematical development (individual and collective) to synthesis and reflection on the big mathematical ideas and pedagogical practices that each set of problems was selected to be a case of. It is in this phase that the teacher educator is invaluable: in order to orchestrate these discussions, the instructor must devise follow-up prompts and pose additional mathematical tasks and scenarios that are designed to support further discussion and that exist at the confluence of the participants' understandings and the relevant key mathematical and pedagogical ideas to be learned (Clay & Silverman, 2009).

SETTING AND PARTICIPANTS

In this article, we will discuss the first two weeks of a 10-week course titled *Geometry and Geometric Reasoning*. This online graduate course is a content-based course required for a master's degree in mathematics education at a university in the Northeastern United States. The particular goals of the course were to support teachers in developing mathematical knowledge for teaching geometry, including polygons and polyhedra, transformation, similarity and congruence, and proof through authentic engagement in collaborative online problem solving. The course was developed and taught by the authors. Tasks and activities were taken from the *Re-Conceptualizing Mathematics* program (Sowder, Sowder, & Nickerson, 2008, 2010) and the authors' personal repertoire developed over a combined 25 years of work in mathematics teaching and teacher development.

The class consisted of 17 (13 women, 4 men), 16 of which who were geographically distributed throughout the United States and one who resided overseas. The 10-week course was hosted in the Blackboard Learning Management System and was offered during the 2009-2010 academic year. Within Blackboard, participants accessed course materials (readings and activities) from their homes or workplaces and participated in both threaded discussion boards and blogs. The data for this paper comes from one iteration of OAC. Stage 1 and 2 (individual problem solving and small group discussions) was hosted in a Blog course add-in, developed by Learning Objects, Inc., and integrated within Blackboard. Stage 3 of OAC (synthetic discussions) took place in a Blackboard discussion forum.

METHOD

As was described previously, the goal of this chapter is to highlight the potential online collaboration holds for supporting collaboration and reflective conversations about sophisticated mathematical and pedagogical understandings. As such, a variant of the traditional case-study methodology was used in the preparation of this chapter. The goal of the research is to explore a particular phenomenon (online collaboration in mathematics) and ultimately to provide an "existence proof" of the potential affordances of the online environment in mathematics learning and teaching. The process began by reviewing the entire data set chronologically and identifying instances of mathematical activity. 43 instances were identified. Of these instances, three were selected to be analyzed and presented in this chapter. Selection was based on alignment with course goals and potential significance of the collaboration as well as to provide an example of a unit of instruction, where future activities build on previous collaboration. Because the focus of this chapter is on supporting mathematical collaboration, we do not address student learning and individual development explicitly. The next phase of our work involves conducting more detailed analysis of the remainder of the instances of mathematical activity and developing a framework for documenting learning and development in that context.

ANALYSIS AND RESULTS

The first two weeks of the geometric reasoning course focused on polygons and transformations. We began with the assumption that the teachers were familiar with, and teach or have taught, the ideas of congruence and transformation of polygons. We also assumed that teachers' understandings of congruence would be grounded in the idea that congruent polygons have "the same size and the same shape," which is consistent with typical texts and state standards. In addition, based on prior experiences of the research team, it was assumed that almost all teachers were familiar with the rigid transformations of reflection, translation, and rotation.

In the sections that follow, we provide three "cases" from the transformation and congruence unit. The first case explores one group's work on the initial "standard" problem *given a polygon and a transformation find the resulting polygon*. In the second case, we explore teachers' work on follow-up tasks and discussion prompts that were designed to push teachers beyond their mathematical comfort zone and to provide a setting where significant mathematical discussions could take place (for example, describing and identifying transformations and composition of transformations). Finally, in the third case, we analyze a group discussion designed to (1) focus the teachers' attention on their use of composition as an operation on the set of transformations, (2) look

Figure 1. Diagram from Quinn's post

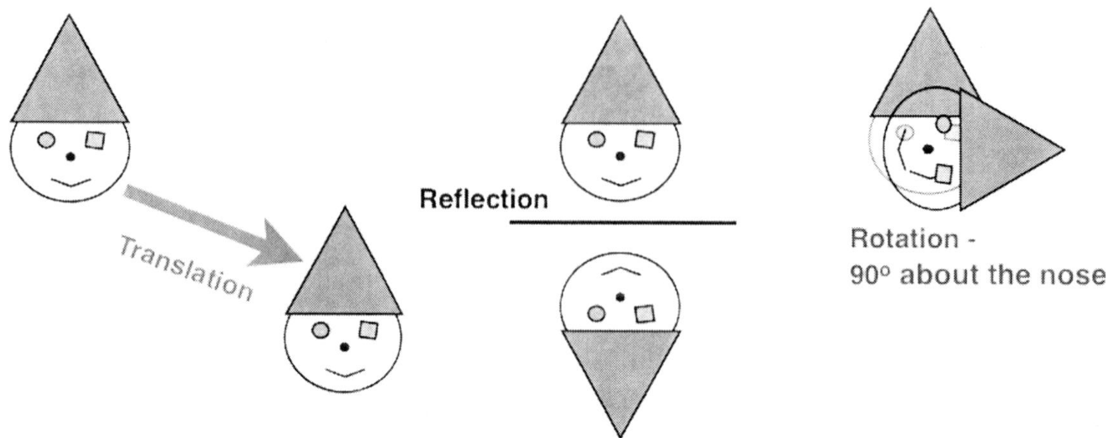

at properties of the set with this new operation, (3) re-examine their understanding of congruence by redefining it from "same size, same shape" to "there exists a rigid transformation" from one polygon to another and (4) explore the implications of this new understanding.

CASE #1: ENGAGING WITH FAMILIAR MATHEMATICS

Teachers were familiar with the notion of transformation and each was able to translate, reflect, and rotate figures in the plane. On a task that asked the participants to translate, rotate, and reflect a given figure, most provided diagrams consisting of the original image and the transformed image and few provided descriptions or explanations of what they did. An paradigmatic example of such a solution is provided below (all names are psuedonuyms).

Quinn: *Working with Mr. Conehead here, I've performed the three transformations:*
He was translated along the green vector.
He was reflected about the black center line.
And then he was rotated about his nose. (see Figure 1)

When engaging with the mathematics they teach, participants' posts were matter-of-fact descriptions of what they did. When the class discussed the posts, there was little conversation about the mathematics – conversations were either affective ("I really liked your diagrams") or focused on the technology used to generate the transformations (grid paper, Geometer's Sketchpad, Adobe Photoshop). Examples included:

Carla: *I love that you named him! Anywhoo... I was wondering what you used to make your pictures. They are very nice.*

Adam: *Yours look like perfect replicas....where you able to copy them or did you draw them? If you were able to copy them, how did you do so? The only thing missing for your rotation is the point that its rotated about*

Una: *I enjoy looking at your work because it is easy to understand. I never thought of using Adobe Photoshop.*

Opall: *Did Photoshop do everything? If so, would you allow your students to use it or make them follow the directions in the book and produce accurate hand drawn transformations?*

It has proven tremendously difficult to orchestrate generative mathematical conversations around mathematical content that teachers believe they know well. This result is consistent with Blanton (2002), who noted the importance of "legitimate mathematical situations" in supporting teachers' mathematical and pedagogical development. While initial engagement with mathematical tasks that teachers are comfortable with has proven not to be particularly useful in supporting teachers' mathematical development, it has proven to be a good jumping-off point for discussions that focus explicitly on coherence in mathematical understandings.

CASE #2: THE SET OF TRANSFORMATIONS AND OPERATIONS ON THAT SET

As a follow-up to transforming figures in the plane, teachers were then asked to define a transformation that would produce the same result as applying two specified transformations in sequence (this new transformation is a *composition* of the two constituent transformations). It was quite apparent that the idea of transformations as a set that we could define an operation on was unfamiliar territory for the majority of the teachers. The following excerpt is taken from the public discussion following individual problem solving focusing on the composition of transformations task.

Carla: *I never heard the terminology "composition" of two motions. I remember in high school doing multiple transformations to an object, but the word "composition" never came up. To me in school it would be doing multiple translations, not doing a single translation with multiple steps as this suggests.*

Therin: *Carla, I also don't remember learning about composition of rigid motions before. I am more familiar with composition of functions from teaching Algebra 2. I have a hard time thinking about the composition of rigid motions as a single rigid motions ...*

Wendy: *I have taught reflections, rotations, and translations, but I had never heard of compositions either. I had always treated them as separate motions. But when I think about it, asking the student to use compositions forces them to see the big picture as the sum of the parts. I think both viewpoints are important to get a true understanding of what is happening. The student needs to see the whole as well as its parts.*

Krystal: *I also never heard the terminology "composition" of two motions. I found that interesting, and created a shift in thought for me – from the individual pieces to the "Big Picture" and the result of the sequence of individual pieces.*

Rachel: *You said in school it would be multiple translations not just one, but the book noted "Any composition of rigid motions can be described by a single reflection, rotation, translation, or glide-reflection," I feel pretty certain that if I had seen it in the past, I would have remembered it - it's beautiful! Now the next thing I want to do is prove it...*

The conversation begins with Carla and her colleagues noting that they are not familiar with the idea of "composition" of two motions, although they are all familiar with the idea of performing multiple translations in succession and are comfortable teaching this idea. Wendy initiates a shift in the conversation, building on her previous experience and the previous posts to describe a composition as a single entity the "sum of the parts." By "sum," it appears that she is not referring to the arithmetic operation of "summing" but rather building up a new entity from its component parts. Krystal, building on Wendy's post, contrasts her previous "school" understanding with "the result" and even explicitly mentions a shift in her thinking, or at least the awareness of a new possibility. Finally, Rachel builds on the previous posts by connecting Krystal's utterance with the definition from the text and introduces the need for a proof as a means to connect the common notion of performing translations in sequence with a theorem from the text.

In the above excerpts, we see teachers engaging in mathematical discourse and thinking about mathematical abstractions in the context of transformations that they ostensibly already know. We believe that it is significant that these conversations do not take place in the context of school mathematics, but require moving beyond school mathematics and problematizing teachers' mathematical understandings (Cobb & Bauersfeld, 1995). The initial posts (Carla, Wendy, and Therin) demonstrate initial engagement and the beginning of a shift in thinking and awareness of potential implications for teaching, while the subsequent posts build on them, delving deeper and reflecting on relevant mathematical ideas and extensions.

CASE #3: EQUIVALENCE RELATIONS

Mathematics teachers are almost universally familiar with the informal notion of congruence of polygons as polygons that have "same size, same shape" or whose "sides and angles match up." While this notion works for most of school geometry, it is not generative and does not easily generalize beyond the particular case of school geometry. It is possible to define congruence more formally using transformations: two polygons are congruent if there exists a rigid transformation that maps one onto the other. Intuitively this definition of congruence makes sense and is internally consistent with teachers' current conceptions of congruence. Additionally, it allows for learners to begin to explore and discuss connections between different notions of "sameness" from various branches of mathematics, ultimately leading to the mathematical idea of equivalence, which, informally speaking, is the way mathematicians define "sameness" on any given set. A canonical example of equivalence involves the set of rational numbers: all fractions that reduce to 2/3 are said to be equivalent and are members of the same *equivalence class*. In this activity, teachers were presented with the following task designed to reconcile their prior understandings with this new notion of congruence[2].

Below are four posts where teachers are discussing their work on the Congruence Task above:

Adam: *The definition of congruent: Two shapes are said to be congruent if one can be transformed into the other through isometry. Since, the definition clearly states two shapes, a single shape cannot be congruent to itself. ... Yes, a = a, and 7 =7 and pi=pi, but those are values...not shapes. To say that a shape is equal to itself, seems silly to me. A shape is inherently discrete...from my perspective. So, to say it is equal to itself just seems improper.*

Carla: *Congruence, by definition, is similar but not the same. When explaining to my students the difference between "equal" and "congruent" I tell them that two congruent objects are so because their properties are the same, same lengths, angles, measurements, etc, but they are not equal because the two objects are still two different objects. They go by different names and in the real world two objects are different because they both occupy their own space. Comparing an object to itself is, what I would think, crossing over from congruence to equivalence.*

Pearl: *Carla - [C]ongruence and equality ... are not the same, but they are related. I know when I have done them with my classes, we use the two kind of interchangeably. Shapes or parts of shapes would be congruent, and the measures are equal. So for example, two angles are congruent if they have the same measure and conversely, if* *two angles have the same measure, then they are congruent. For my geometry classes, that has been an important part of proving different statements.*

Carla: *I agree with you completely. I am just not convinced that a shape is congruent to itself. ... [The] history that I found also said that the words "equals" and "congruent" through out the last 4 centuries has been interchangable in translations of Elements. This has basically reinforced that they really are the same. In all this searching I didn't find anything that conclusively stated why we have the separate terms, but I would like to believe that there was at one time a reason. Why, if we specify different terms for equivalence in Geometry verses Algebra, don't we have different terms for addition? Or other operations?*

In these posts we see evidence of the teachers' collaborative efforts to make sense of the mathematics at hand and reconcile it with their current understandings. We see Adam relying on the definition of congruence "from a transformation point of view" and concluding that this definition implies that a shape cannot be congruent to itself, apparently neglecting the identity transformation (a transformation that translates a figure by a length of zero or rotates it by an angle of zero). It is interesting to note that Adam is no doubt familiar with the idea of an *identity* in other contexts such as the real numbers under addition (add zero) or multiplication (multiply by 1), but that his makes it clear that he is struggling with the same idea in a geometric context: "a = a, and 7 =7 and pi=pi, but those are values...not shapes. To say that a shape is equal to itself, seems silly to me."

Looking beyond Carla's informal (and mathematically incorrect use of the term *similar*), she expresses a similar sentiment as Adam, likely questioning or extending his definition, and introducing the notion that congruence has to do with the space the objects occupy. She is falling back on her intuitive knowledge rather than the more general mathematical definition of equivalence. As is often the case, her intuition comes from her early experience with equivalence: equality (and particularly, equality of numbers). Pearl shifts the conversation to how equality and congruence are really saying similar things, but apply in different contexts: "Shapes or parts of shapes would be congruent, and the measures are equal." We believe that Pearl is using the term "measure" to indicate the magnitude of a quantity (area, angle measure, etc.) and distinguishes this from "equality" of non-numeric entities. Further, her comment that "we use the two interchangeably" indicates that while she is aware there is a difference between equality and congruence her understanding of the specifics of that difference and why such a difference exists is lacking. We then see Carla, who is still struggling with the different "kinds of equivalence" discussed by the others, posing a potentially significant question: "Why, if we specify different terms for equivalence in Geometry verses Algebra, don't we have different terms for addition? Or other operations?" We do not have data to claim that Carla understands the significance of the question she is asking, she is asking about what else she might know that is only an example of something bigger and seeking coherence through that bigger idea.

In these excerpts, we a group of teachers expressing their thinking, building and extending each others' work, and asking significant mathematical and pedagogical questions. It is also clear that as the teachers began to engage with transformations and equivalence at a higher and abstract level, they began to become less sure of their understandings and the function of their posts shifted from telling what they did or can do (univocal) to generating new meanings and understandings (more dialogic). This shift from "telling" to collaboration where discourse functions dialogically is typical for a unit of using OAC.

While we there were clearly shifts in the nature of the teachers' discourse between their initial engagement with the school mathematics content and the increasingly sophisticated follow-up tasks and prompts, we are not able to clearly identify shifts in individual mathematical content knowledge through their participation in the discourse. The shifts are most accurately described as collective development as a result of collaboration and group cognition (Stahl, 2006). While we are currently exploring ways to document these shifts in collective mathematical ability through the emergence of social or sociomathematical norms or mathematical practices (Cobb & Bauersfeld, 1995; McClain & Cobb, 2001), different forms of analysis are needed to study the development of individuals' mathematical knowledge for teaching through authentic mathematical collaboration through OAC.

CONCLUSION

Above, we argued the importance of teachers' coherent mathematical understandings. We have seen teachers willing and able to engage with the broad topics (transformations and congruence) at a limited level: given a particular transformation, they were able to perform that transformation. This activity was not problematic and they were willing and able to relate it to mathematics they already 'know' and teach. It is also clear that as the participants began to engage with transformations and equivalence at a higher, more connected level, they began to become less sure of their understandings. It is important to note that their confusion did not lie in the particular school mathematics ideas; rather it was in the mathematical connections between the school mathematics topics, as evidenced by the conversational themes of *What do you mean you can compose transformations?* and *How can equality and congruence are the same thing?*

At its most basic level, transformations and congruence are mathematical ideas to be taught, but we argue that the significance of these topics for teachers does not lie simply in teaching transformations or congruence. Both are examples of larger mathematical ideas – an abstraction – that it is evident the teachers were not consciously aware of. Transformations *are* functions. Congruence *is* an equivalence relation. While teachers are likely to have experience with transformations and congruence and *may* have some level of familiarity and experience with functions and equivalence relations, they are less likely to be aware of the various different ideas and contexts from which they are abstracted, how they are related, or the value of seeing the relatedness. It is this aspect of understanding – understandings of the ways in which a variety of ideas and contexts fit together – that makes one's understandings coherent (Thompson, 2008).

In this paper, we pose a way of thinking about a mathematics educators' task of supporting teachers as they develop more coherent, connected mathematical understandings. We begin our teacher development activities by meeting teachers where they are and allowing them to engage with familiar content and take up each others' work as an initial focus for conversation. We then focus teachers' attention on additional tasks and activities of mathematical "big ideas" (in this case, functions and equivalence) and scaffold conversations about particular aspects of these tasks that are designed to highlight "big ideas" and invariants across particular solutions or special cases. The activities, including the tasks, the interactional space, and the instructors' scaffolding, create an online system within which mathematical abstractions of school mathematics ideas problematize teachers' mathematical understandings and support legitimate mathematical engagement. We have argued previously that the online environment enables such mathematical engagement: conversations that take place in a face-to-face class are ephemeral and as a result "[p]otentially important or insightful aspects of… mathematical activity are often lost as a result of the chaotic nature of the mathematics classroom, the split-second decisions that teachers in face-to-face classrooms must make …, and the lack of adequate documentation of the conversations" (Clay & Silverman, 2009). The asynchronous and permanent nature of online environments allow for potentially pivotal utterances (like Therin's and Carla's) to be taken up as a focus of conversation by the remainder of the class and, when they are not taken up, allow instructors to create bridges between teachers' current understandings and the instructional goals.

We feel it is important to note, in closing, that such advanced mathematical understandings or schema (Dubinsky & McDonald, 2001) lie at the core of our instructional model, but we do not believe that the significance of the model is limited to mathematics. In order to identify mathematical "big ideas" that cut across various mathematical topics, we turn to the field of professional mathematics, whose primary function is to systematize and advance the field. A significant question is how applicable would the model would be for teacher educators in other disciplines. In social studies education, for example, *are* there similar "big ideas?" The authors acknowledge that they are not aware of any in particular, but argue that a historian or anthropologist would have important thoughts on the issue. While it is still not the norm for academic faculty to engage in sustained collaboration with their teacher education colleagues around teacher preparation, we put forth the notion that this collaboration it is essential – it is only through careful examination of the school mathematics curriculum from mathematical, pedagogical, and curricular perspectives, that the big ideas, tasks, and appropriate online scaffolding can be conceptualized and developed.

FUTURE WORK

We are aware that there is still more needed to understand about supporting online mathematical collaboration. We have begun to explore sequential analysis (Bakeman & Gottman, 1997; England, 1985; Jeong, 2003) to study group interactions. Sequential analysis involves using probability to study relationships between individual posts and predict the characteristics of interactions that support individual contributions with particular characteristics and the conditions under which those posts are more likely. In addition, there is a need to understand the relationship between online mathematical collaboration and the development of collective and individual mathematical understandings. In our current work, we are analyzing teachers' participation from an ethnomethodological perspective and seek to describe and understand the specific ways teachers participate in the mathematical collaboration. This will allow us to develop conjectures about how this participation content and structure supports the particular shifts in discourse practices and to correlate this with individual mathematical development.

ACKNOWLEDGMENT

Research reported in this chapter was supported by National Science Foundation Grant No. DUE-0737178. Any opinions, findings, and conclusions or recommendations expressed in this material are those of the authors and do not necessarily reflect the views of the National Science Foundation.

REFERENCES

Bakeman, R., & Gottman, J. M. (1997). *Observing interaction: An introduction to sequential analysis* (2nd ed.). New York, NY: Cambridge University Press. doi:10.1017/CBO9780511527685

Ball, D. L. (1993). Halves, pieces, and twoths: Constructing and using representational contexts in teaching fractions . In Carpenter, T., Fennema, E., & Romberg, T. (Eds.), *Rational numbers: An integration of research* (pp. 157–195). Hillsdale, NJ: Lawrence Erlbaum Associates.

Ball, D. L. (2007, January 26, 2007). *What kind of mathematical work is teaching and how does it shape a core challenge for teacher education.* Paper presented at the Judith E. Jacobs lecture given at the annual meeting of the Association of Mathematics Teacher Educators, Irvine, CA.

Ball, D. L., Hill, H. C., & Bass, H. (2005). Knowing mathematics for teaching: Who knows mathematics well enough to teach third grade, and how can we decide? *American Educator, 29*(3), 14–22, 43–46.

Ball, D. L., & McDiarmid, G. W. (1990). The subject matter preparation of teachers . In Houston, W. R. (Ed.), *Handbook of research on teacher education* (pp. 437–449). New York, NY: Macmillan.

Blanton, M. L. (2002). Using an undergraduate geometry course to challenge pre-service teachers' notions of discourse. *Journal of Mathematics Teacher Education, 5*, 117–152. doi:10.1023/A:1015813514009

Bransford, J., Brown, A., & Cocking, R. (2000). *How people learn.* Washington, DC: National Research Council.

Clay, E. L., & Silverman, J. (2008a). Online asynchronous collaboration in mathematics teacher education. *Proceedings of the 20th Annual Meeting of the International Society for Information Technology and Teacher Education.* Las Vegas, NV: SITE.

Clay, E. L., & Silverman, J. (2008b). Online collaboration in mathematics teacher education. In J. Cortina (Ed.), *Proceedings of the Joint Meeting of the International Group for the Psychology of Mathematics Education and the North American Chapter of the International Group for the Psychology of Mathematics Education.* Moreila, Michoacán, Mexico: PME.

Clay, E. L., & Silverman, J. (2009). Reclaiming lost opportunities: The role of the teacher in online asynchronous collaboration in mathematics teacher education . In Maddox, C. (Ed.), *Research Highlights in Technology and Teacher Education 2009.* Chesapeake, VA: SITE.

Cobb, P., & Bauersfeld, H. (1995). *The emergence of mathematical meaning: Interacting in classroom cultures.* Hillsdale, NJ: L. Erlbaum Associates.

Cobb, P., Boufi, A., McClain, K., & Whitenack, J. (1997). Reflexive discourse and collective reflection. *Journal for Research in Mathematics Education, 28*(3), 258–277. doi:10.2307/749781

Dubinsky, E., & McDonald, M. (2001). APOS: A constructivist theory of learning in undergrad mathematics education research. In D. Holton (Ed.), *Teaching and learning of mathematics at university level: An ICMI study* (pp. 273-280). Kluwer Academic Publishers. England, E. (1985). Interactional analysis: The missing factor in computer-aided learning design and evaluation. *Educational Technology, 25*(9), 24-28.

Garfinkel, H. (1967). *Studies in ethnomethodology.* Englewood Cliffs, NJ: Prentice Hall.

Greenberg, J., & Walsh, K. (2008). *No common denominator: The preparation of elementary teachers in mathematics.* Washington, DC: National Council on Teacher Quality.

Hill, H. C., Rowan, B., & Ball, D. L. (2005). Effects of teachers' mathematical knowledge for teaching on student achievement. *American Educational Research Journal, 42*(5), 371–406. doi:10.3102/00028312042002371

Jeong, A. C. (2003). The sequential analysis of group interaction and critical thinking in online threaded discussions. *American Journal of Distance Education, 17*(1), 25. doi:10.1207/S15389286AJDE1701_3

Ma, L. (1999). *Knowing and teaching elementary mathematics: Teachers' understanding of fundamental mathematics in China and the United States*. Mahwah, NJ: Lawrence Erlbaum Associates.

McClain, K., & Cobb, P. (2001). The development of sociomathematical norms in one first-grade classroom. *Journal for Research in Mathematics Education, 32*(3), 236–266. doi:10.2307/749827

Musser, G. L., Burger, W. F., & Peterson, B. E. (2008). *Mathematics for elementary teachers: A contemporary approach* (8th ed.). Hoboken, NJ: John Wiley & Sons, Inc.

National Council of Teachers of Mathematics. (1991). *Professional standards for teaching mathematics*. Reston, VA: Author.

National Mathematics Advisory Panel. (2008). *Foundations for success: The final report of the National Mathematics Advisory Panel*. Washington, DC: U.S. Department of Education.

Paloff, R., & Pratt, K. (1999). *Building learning communities in cyberspace*. San Fransisco, CA: Jossey-Bass.

Perressini, D. D., & Knuth, E. J. (1998). Why are you talking when you could be listening? The role of discourse and reflection in the professional development of a secondary mathematics teacher. *Teaching and Teacher Education, 14*(1), 107–125. doi:10.1016/S0742-051X(97)00064-4

Ravenscroft, A. (2001). Designing e-learning interactions in the 21st century: Revisiting and rethinking the role of theory. *European Journal of Education, 36*(2), 133–156. doi:10.1111/1467-3435.00056

Reeves, T., Herrington, J., & Oliver, R. (2004). A development research agenda for online collaborative learning. *Educational Technology Research and Development, 52*(4), 53–65. doi:10.1007/BF02504718

Renninger, K., & Shumar, W. (2002). Community building with and for teachers: The Math Forum as a resource for teacher professional development . In Renninger, A., & Shumar, W. (Eds.), *Building virtual communities: Learning and change in cyberspace* (pp. 60–95). New York, NY: Cambridge University Press. doi:10.1017/CBO9780511606373.008

Sfard, A. (2008). *Thinking as communicating: human development, the growth of discourses, and mathematizing*. New York, NY: Cambridge University Press. doi:10.1017/CBO9780511499944

Shale, D., & Garrison, D. (1990). Introduction . In Garrison, D., & Shale, D. (Eds.), *Education at a distance: From issues to practice*. Melbourne, FL: Krieger.

Shulman, L. S. (1986). Those who understand: Knowledge growth in teaching. *Educational Researcher, 15*(2), 4–14.

Shumar, W. (2003). The role of community and belonging in online learning . In Mardis, M. (Ed.), *Developing digital libraries for K-12 education* (pp. 174–187).

Shumar, W. (2009). Communities, texts, consciousness: The practice of participation at the Math Forum . In Falk, J., & Drayton, B. (Eds.), *Creating and sustaining online professional learning communities*. New York, NY: Teachers College Press.

Shumar, W., & Sarmiento, J. (2008). Communities of practice at the Math Forum: Supporting teachers as professionals . In Hildreth, P., & Kimble, C. (Eds.), *Communities of practice: Creating learning environments for educators* (pp. 223–239). Hershey, PA: Idea Group Publishing.

Silverman, J., & Clay, E. L. (2010). Online asynchronous collaboration in mathematics teacher education and the development of mathematical knowledge for teaching. *Teacher Educator, 45*(1).

Sowder, J., Sowder, L., & Nickerson, S. (2008). *Reconceptualizing mathematics*. New York, NY: W.H. Freeman.

Sowder, J., Sowder, L., & Nickerson, S. (2010). *Reconceptualizing mathematics for elementary teachers*. New York, NY: W.H. Freeman.

Stahl, G. (2006). *Group cognition: Computer support for building collaborative knowledge*. Cambridge, MA: MIT Press.

Stahl, G., Koschmann, T., & Suthers, D. (2006). Computer-supported collaborative learning: An historical perspective . In Sawyer, R. K. (Ed.), *The Cambridge handbook of the learning sciences* (p. xix). Cambridge, UK & New York, NY: Cambridge University Press.

Su, B., Bonk, C. J., & Magjuka, R., J., Liu, X., & Lee, S.-H. (2005). The importance of interaction in Web-based education: A program-level case study of online MBA courses. *Journal of Interactive Online Learning*, *4*(1), 1–19.

Thompson, P. W. (2008). *Conceptual analysis of mathematical ideas: Some spadework at the foundation of mathematics education*. Plenary paper delivered at the 32nd Annual Meeting of the International Group for the Psychology of Mathematics Education, (vol. 1, pp. 1-18). Morelia, Mexico.

Thompson, P. W., Carlson, M., & Silverman, J. (2007). The design of tasks in support of teachers' development of coherent mathematical meanings. *Journal of Mathematics Teacher Education*, *10*(4-6), 415–432. doi:10.1007/s10857-007-9054-8

Wegerif, R. (2006). A dialogic understanding of the relationship between CSCL and teaching thinking skills. *International Journal of Computer-Supported Collaborative Learning*, *1*(1), 143–157. doi:10.1007/s11412-006-6840-8

Wertsch, J., & Toma, C. (1995). Discourse and learning in the classroom: A sociocultural approach . In Steffe, L. P., & Gale, J. (Eds.), *Constructivism in education* (pp. 159–174). Hillsdale, NJ: Lawrence Erlbaum.

Zeichner, K. (1996). Designing educative practicum experiences for prospective teachers . In Zeichner, K., Melnick, S., & Gomez, M. (Eds.), *Currents of reform in preservice teacher education* (pp. 215–233). New York, NY: Teachers College Press.

ENDNOTES

1. For more information, please visit http://www.learningobjects.com/
2. Mathematically, the three parts of this task are significant. Stated more generally, if given a set and an relation on that set (denoted ~), then that relation is an *equivalence relation* if and only if whenever a,b, and c are elements of that set, then the following must hold: (a) if $a \sim b$, then $b \sim a$ (the relation is symmetric), (b) $a \sim a$ (the relation is reflexive), and (c) if $a \sim b$ and $b \sim c$, then $a \sim c$ (the relation is transitive). Relations such as similarity and congruence (for triangles), equality (for numbers), and "is the same age as" (for people) are all examples of equivalence relations.

1 For more information, please visit http://www.learningobjects.com/
2 Mathematically, the three parts of this task are significant. Stated more generally, if given a set and an relation on that set (denoted ~), then that relation is an *equivalence relation* if and only if whenever a,b, and c are elements of that set, then the following

must hold: (a) if $a \sim b$, then $b \sim a$ (the relation is symmetric), (b) $a \sim a$ (the relation is reflexive), and (c) if $a \sim b$ and $b \sim c$, then $a \sim c$ (the relation is transitive). Relations such as similarity and congruence (for triangles), equality (for numbers), and "is the same age as" (for people) are all examples of equivalence relations.

Chapter 11
Self-Regulated Learning and Self Assessment in Online Mathematics Bridging Courses

R. Biehler
University of Paderborn, Germany

P. R. Fischer
University of Kassel, Germany

R. Hochmuth
University of Kassel, Germany

Th. Wassong
University of Paderborn, Germany

ABSTRACT

Varying mathematical skills, rising dropout rates, and growing numbers of first year students confront the universities with major organizational and pedagogical problems. In this chapter, the authors describe an innovative way of teaching and learning designed to improve this situation by bridging courses particularly including self-diagnostic e-assessment and supporting self-regulated learning. The development of highly structured e-learning material has been and still is the most important objective. The material has been implemented, extended, evaluated, and improved since 2003. Our chapter refers to multimedia learning material for bridging courses which was developed by the project "Multimediavorkurs Mathematik" in collaboration of research groups from the German Universities of Kassel and Paderborn and the Technical University Darmstadt.

For providing an overview of our whole bridging-course programme, at first we will discuss our material concerning content-related, didactical, and authoring aspects. Then we will discuss our course scenarios with regard to pedagogical and organisational aspects. Focusing on selected results of an accompanying evaluation study we will finally discuss the acceptance and success of our courses and highlight some interesting findings concerning our learners.

DOI: 10.4018/978-1-60960-875-0.ch011

INTRODUCTION

The transition from school to university studies is a difficult one. The gap between school and university mathematics seems to be larger than in other subjects (cf. Gueudet, 2008; Bescherer, 2003; de Guzman, Hodgson, Robert, & Villani 1998; Holton, 2001; Tall, 1991). Moreover, mathematical requirements vary widely from mathematics majors via mathematics in engineering through to mathematics for future elementary teachers. Universities could in principle change their entrance courses but are mostly not willing to do so. Instead they offer pre-term bridging courses and/or bridging courses which are provided parallel to the first year courses as a kind of additional, remedial courses. Having a look at beginning students of study programmes with mathematical content and discussing with experts of bridging courses from other German universities (cf. Biehler, Hochmuth, & Koepf, 2010), one can identify various problems:

- The students have very heterogeneous mathematical competencies: In Germany, for instance, different government regulations have led to differing intended school curricula. The variability is even larger at the level of the "attained curricula", i.e. students' knowledge.
- The traditional German university entry qualification (the Abitur), has become only one qualification to enrol at a university among some emerging others. Now, also an entitlement to study at a Fachhochschule or an education as a master craftsman qualifies as a prerequisite at some German universities. These different qualifications increase the heterogeneity especially with regard to mathematical competencies.
- Different fields of study need different kinds of mathematics. The lectures on mathematics for electrical engineering have different requirements than lectures for pre-service teachers or mathematicians.
- Universities expect more self-regulated learning than at school level. In general, the contact to teachers and tutors is not as close as in school. There are more opportunities for learners to stay anonymous; no person asks them to learn and do their homework, and, thus, more self-dependent preparation is required. Most first-year students are unfamiliar with this kind of responsibility for their own learning and have difficulties in organizing their learning processes. Following Roll et al. (2006, p. 360) further metacognitive competencies need to be developed at university level. Minguillon, Huertas, Juan, Sancho, & Cavaller (2008) point amongst others to methodological skills, technological skills or the ability of critical appraisal.
- As a general rule, mathematics at university level is more abstract than at school. Most first-year students have problems with this abstractness. Moreover, although they may have passed the final mathematics exam at school level, the mathematical competencies required, for instance fluency in symbolic calculations and deeper understanding of concepts are not available (cf. Juan, Huertas, Steegmann, Corcoles, & Serrat, 2008, p. 5).

The project VEMA – "**V**irtuelles **E**ingangstutorium **Ma**thematik (Virtual Entrance Tutorial for Mathematics) (http://www.mathematik.uni-kassel.de/vorkurs) started in 2003 with the objective to develop multimedia resources primarily for supporting the pre-term bridging courses. The project was initiated at the University of Kassel and was extended to the Universities of Darmstadt and Paderborn later on. The material was also designed to be supportive for students' self-regulated, remedial learning in the first year of study or in bridging courses that run in parallel to the standard courses. In a second step, the project extended its concern and redesigned all pre-term courses by new *course scenarios* that better incorporate the multimedia learning material into the course. In recent years, advantage was taken from integrating the material into a learning management system, mainly moodle (http://www.moodle.org), and enhancing the material by diagnostic tests for improved support of students' self-regulated learning. Moodle was also used as a communication platform with the students. The material as well as course scenarios have been continuously improved taking into account yearly evaluations within the pre-term bridging courses that take place every September and October before the winter term starts.

Our chapter will describe the development and the components of the project including the technical aspects of producing multimedia material for mathematics. We add some details from an accompanying evaluation study, where we analyzed the acceptance and success of our courses as well as the learning behaviour of our students in the various variants of the course scenarios we designed.

A SHORT HISTORY OF VEMA: DEVELOPING LEARNING MATERIAL AND COURSE SCENARIOS

When VEMA started in 2003 the pre-term bridging courses lasted 2 weeks and consisted of lectures in the morning (with up to 200 students) and small-group sessions (30 students) in the afternoon, where the students were supposed to work on mathematical problems related to the morning lecture.

Our first development step was to design multimedia enhanced "lecture notes" according to the "book metaphor": a so-called "interactive book" was delivered to the students on CD-ROM including a printable version of the book's text.

The starting points were personal lecture notes from bridging courses mainly held for future engineering students. The first step goals included:

- Developing a book-type material from the lecture notes
- Conscious didactical restructuring of the content taking into account the differences between school mathematics and university mathematics and deliberately bridging the approaches
- Extending the number of exercises and explicitly redesigning the exercises according to competencies to be developed; adding model solutions to all exercises
- Enhancing the material by numerous visualizations, experimental environments, movies, and applets taking into account recent developments in computer supported mathematics education (see e.g. Rodríguez & Villa, 2005 or Krivsky, 2003).
- Enhancing the material by interactive exercises with immediate feedback
- Using electronic hypertext elements such as linking and search facilities for supporting students' working with the book
- Adding supplementary chapters or parts of chapters for those who want to learn more than the basics, taking into account the variability of students' previous mathematical knowledge and study aspirations
- Extending the content in order to make the resources useful not only for future engineering students but for all students with mathematical courses in the first year.

The development team consists of experienced lecturers of the bridging courses, mathematicians who hold introductory lectures in the first year of study, and mathematics educators who bring in knowledge of how and with which success mathematics is or should be taught at school. Thus, all relevant perspectives were brought together.

The lecturers of our bridging courses were advised to use the CD-ROM as content basis for their courses, use elements of the interactive material within their lectures, take exercises from the interactive book etc. Although the CD-ROM was well accepted as our evaluations showed, we experienced the need to better advice our course lecturers how to integrate the material in their lectures and the small-group afternoon tutorials. Therefore the project decided to redesign the interactive book with two major changes:

- The content was organised in self-contained smaller content packages (modules). This enabled learners as well as teachers to specifically choose those modules that were suitable in view of the deficits of the learner as well as most required from the field of study of the student.
- Each content module got the same "knowledge type" structure (see next section). This did not only assist learners in keeping the orientation but also supported different learning approaches better respecting individual learning preferences and learning goals.

The project group kept on extending the content over the years to cover the whole range of school mathematical topics. This was a result of extending the audience to mathematics majors and mathematics teacher-education courses and due to the demands of the engineering departments to extend the topics of the pre-term bridging courses and to prolong the bridging courses to 4 weeks.

But still, the courses were mainly orientated at the requirements of the field of study and a general assumption on where the collective deficits of the students are situated. The individual deficits of the learners could only be addressed by the little time that could be spent with individual students in the afternoon tutorials. Another problem we faced was that many first-year students were not able to join the whole course starting four weeks before the winter term due to problems with their move to the city of the university or since they had to earn money during the days before the term starts. Consequently, since 2007 a new course scenario (the so-called E-course) with extended phases of self-determined e-learning, integrated use of the learning management system moodle through the internet and much reduced time for lectures and small group face-to-face meetings was developed. In 2007, this new scenario was offered as an alternative to the traditional lecture type of bridging course. As a result, this also led to a reconsideration and adjustment of the traditional course.

Since 2008 the pre-term bridging courses were offered in the following two blended learning variants: a **P-course** with relatively more lectures and small-group meetings and an **E-course** with relatively more self-regulated e-learning. Both new course scenarios combine traditional settings with new forms of learning such as collaborative learning or self-directed distance learning via learning platforms with online-support. This approach combines benefits of both learning scenarios (cf. Mandl & Kopp, 2006, p. 6 or Kerres, 2002). Changing the scenarios also resulted in a fundamental reconsideration and redefinition of the teachers' and learners' roles in both variants. This experience corresponds to findings from other projects, see for instance Vovides, Sanchez-Alonso, Mitropoulou, & Nickmanns (2007, p. 72), Juan et al. (2008, p. 1) or Unwin (2005, p. 46). Consequently, not only the material and the course design were adjusted. The changes led to a complete "*redefinition of the teaching-learning process*" (Juan et al., 2008, p. 1). Such fundamental changes being a result of a technological advance are also described by Raschke (2003), who defines this as a new epistemology of learning or, more drastically spoken, as a "*new paradigm of learner-driven or client-centred education*" (Raschke, 2003, p. 31).

For the E-course, we decided for a student-centred design, which is increasingly used at many universities (cf. Lai, Pratt, & Grant, 2003). Ibabe & Jauregizar underline that "*feedback students receive from the teacher is a key supportive factor in the process of continuous improvement*" (Ibabe & Jauregizar, 2010, p. 244). Whereas in traditional small size classroom courses teachers can give such feedback to the learners, this is often lacking in self-regulated e-learning as well as in lectures. But especially for self-regulated learning, the students need to know about their content-specific and competence-specific performance in order to identify knowledge and competence gaps and to efficiently design their individual learning paths (cf. Niegemann et al., 2008, pp. 295). Since feedback in the interactive book of VEMA is only given in terms of model solutions for self-evaluation, we had to think about an improvement of the individual feedback to our students.

Therefore we developed self-diagnostic pre- and post-tests for each module of our interactive book. We used the learning management system moodle for implementing these tests, which are automatically corrected by the system and give individual feedback to the learner concerning his/her content- and competence-specific performance and, moreover, provide suggestions for next learning steps. Using these diagnostic tests in addition to the interactive book, the learner was now enabled for a self-regulated design of his/her learning-path. Additionally, we worked out recommendations for each study programme that indicate for each module whether it is *unrestrictedly important, partially important* or *not important at all*. We experienced that support in the selection of topics as well as in the structuring of learning is necessary for most students and for first-year students in particular, similar to what Minguillon et al. (2008, p. 8) are suggesting.

The use of moodle has a further advantage with regard to the social facet of learning. It does not only provide features that can partially replace the "classroom" as a central place to meet and learn, but its specific communication tools also allow efficient forms of communication with teachers and fellows. Problems can be discussed in the forum with the whole group and do not need to be asked several times or individual problems can be discussed in confidence via messaging.

THE INTERACTIVE MATERIAL FROM THE LEARNERS' POINT OF VIEW

Overview

In this section we describe our material as it presents itself to the learner in more detail. Our material contains different components: First, we have the interactive book that is the main part of our material. The interactive book has a specific structure which will be described in the *structure of the interactive book* and the *structure of a module*. Every year we publish the actual version of the interactive book on a CD-ROM. All components of the CD-ROM are described in *Components of the CD-ROM*. For the E-course, we integrated our material and diagnostic tests in a learning management system (LMS). Its realization is described in the section *integration of the interactive book into a LMS*. In the end, the developed components support various ways to learn with our material. The most important ones are described in the last section *different learning approaches*.

The authoring process started with identifying the most relevant subject domains for the bridging courses. While at the beginning of our project we originally concentrated on topics from precalculus, we later also introduced topics from calculus and analytical geometry.

First, our authors had to make a choice of the most relevant concepts with regard to the estimated students' knowledge and the content-related goals of the courses. This is followed by a detailed analysis of each subject domain fixing the basic definitions, theorems and algorithms. We took into account text-books both for school and university. In the next step, we enriched the chosen learning objects with examples, applications, and exercises and added a "genetic" introduction to the domain. The third step was to design media and interactive exercises that help the student to understand the domain and its concepts. Currently, we use interactive JavaScript exercises and GeoGebra-applets (http://www.geogebra.org), GeoNEXT-applets (http://geonext.uni-bayreuth.de/), and own Java-applets. The last step was the development of diagnostic tests.

Structure and Content of the Interactive Book

During the years the number of subject domains has been continuously extended. In order to enable students to individually recapitulate certain topics, we decided to structure the content into smaller packages called "modules". Each module essentially concentrates on one mathematical topic and is structured in *knowledge units* as described in the next section. The learning material contains six chapters: arithmetic, powers, functions, higher functions, analysis and vectors in its latest version. Each chapter has about 10 modules. The chapter on higher functions, for instance, consists of three sections with the following modules:

- polynomials: polynomial functions; Horner-scheme; division of polynomials; zeros of functions
- exponential and logarithmic function: rules for powers and logarithms; the general exponential function; functions with the basis e; natural logarithms
- trigonometric functions: intercept theorems; Pi and radians; sine, cosine, and tangent in rectangular triangles; sine, cosine, and tangent as functions; periodic functions

Structure of a Module

Each module consists of *knowledge units* that are identical in type. A well-defined and consistent structure for all modules supports learners in their navigation. This is further supported by the layout of the interactive book. On the left side of each page there is a chapter navigation frame, where the learner can chose the chapters to which s/he likes to switch. We have a module navigation frame where the learner can select the different units of the current module on the top of our pages.

The structure of a module consists mainly of the units *overview*, *introduction to the domain*, *info*, *info/ interpretation/ explanation* (IIE), *application*, *typical mistakes* and *exercises*:

1. We start with the *overview* unit which essentially consists of one html page that lists the major topics and learning goals of a module.
2. The second unit is called *introduction to the domain*. The introduction unit uses guided discovery, inductive and exemplary approaches to familiarize the learner with the new content. We also support the knowledge construction process by interactive exercises. The content is presented on a concrete level for the learners, with visualizations and references to their assumed previous knowledge. The introduction starts from knowledge that is prerequisite and develops the new domain from this basis.
3. The third *info* unit lists the definitions, theorems and algorithms of the module. These are the central concepts of the module. The *info unit* presents the content on an abstract mathematical level so that merely definitions, theorems and algorithms are presented without examples or exercises. This unit can be used as kind of "reference sheet" for the topic.
4. The fourth *IIE* unit (*info / interpretation / explanation)* not only repeats the central definitions, theorems and algorithms of the

info unit but also networks them among each other and illustrates them with examples. With regard to theorems we can find plausible arguments and/or proofs for their correctness. The learner finds interactive exercises as well as flash-films and animations s/he can interact with. These elements help her/him to develop a deeper understanding of the concepts.

5. The fifth unit is called the *application unit,* where some applications from inside and outside mathematics are shown and discussed.
6. The sixth unit is called the *typical-mistakes* unit: The learners are invited to find mistakes in a given solution or argumentation, to correct them and to explain possible reasons for them. These exercises are provided to train the diagnostic competencies of the learners and to depict misconceptions in order to avoid them in the future. The learners can check their answer by reading the corrected model solution and comparing them with their own solutions afterwards.
   For future mathematics teachers this unit is of particular importance for training their diagnostic competence. They have to be enabled to find mistakes in wrong argumentations, to recognize, why a mistake was done, and to know, how the mistake can be corrected (cf. Wittmann, 2007).
   To make errors or mistakes is also important in the knowledge construction process. Following Oser, Hascher, & Spychiger (1999) mistakes belong to the "negative knowledge", which has protection functions against the positive knowledge.
7. The last unit is the *exercises* unit: This unit is important for the learners to check their understanding of the topic and to give opportunities for practicing the concepts. A model solution is available for every exercise, which the learners can use to compare with their own solutions. Clearly this approach is similar to the way traditional books present exercises. This had the advantage that all kinds of complex exercises could be included in our content without taking into account narrow restrictions from software tools that are available for realising interactive exercises. Since recently developed advanced software tools like STACK (http://stack.bham.ac.uk/) nowadays give more freedom in designing didactically sensitive interactive exercises, we plan to include such in the near future.

In addition to this structure we provide two more units: the *visualization* unit and the *supplements* unit. The first one just collects all visualizations of the current module in one list. This supports lectures in their use of the material during the courses so that they do not need to search for the interaction themselves. For the supplements unit, we have another, more learner oriented reason: Some students learn faster than others and some students are more interested in particular content than others. Therefore, we added the supplements unit that contains examples, definitions, interactivities or exercises.

The following screenshot in Figure 1 illustrates the layout of our modules and the representation of the structure with the module navigation frame at the top of the site.

Components of the CD-ROM

The CD-ROM that we give to the students contains the interactive book as an **interactive XHTML script**. We also integrated a search function for the interactive XHTML pages. When starting the CD-ROM the learner first has to configure his/her browser so that all elements of the material can be used. Related to this we developed an interactive html-based installation routine that checks necessary settings for different browser plug-ins. In case of missing software or wrong settings, the installation routine supports the user to install the missing software or adjust the right settings.

Figure 1. Structure of a module within VEMA

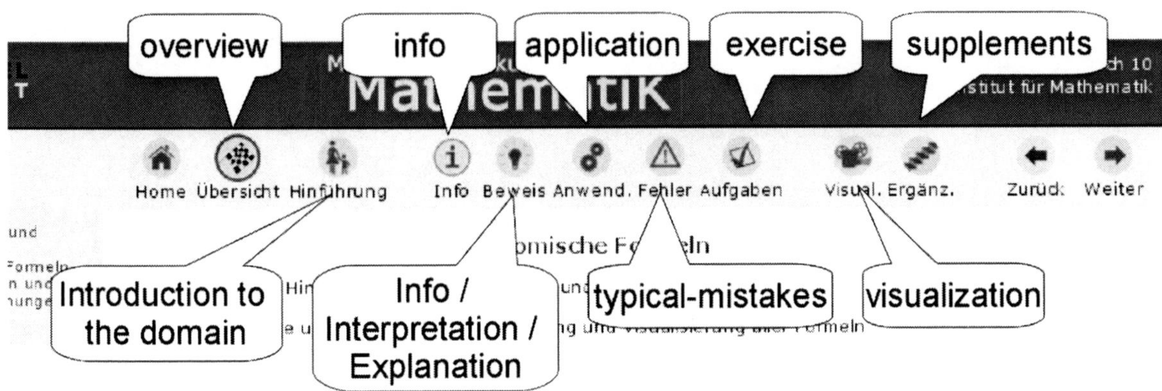

For supporting different online and offline modes of learning with our material, the CD-ROM contains pdf-documents with a printable version of the interactive book. The **short pdf script** consists only of the *info* units. The short script is primarily used for lectures in all course scenarios. With this script the students have a printed document and can take additional notes related to the main concepts, which need not be copied from the blackboard. In the **long pdf script** the material is presented as a book. Due to the limits of the pdf-format only the pictures and graphs are available, other media-LOs than images are only mentioned in form of a comment that this element is missing in this output-format. The model-solutions of the exercises are not shown either. The long pdf script is used for having a printed version of the material that the students can use to read without a computer. Therefore, we only included the IEE unit and the application unit in order to have a condensed but still comprehensive version of our material.

Diagnostic Tests

The interactive book as described above provides feedback to the learner by the interactive exercises in the introduction and in the IEE unit. These exercises are intended to be used in formative self-assessment. As a further elaboration of the material, we decided to develop a *diagnostic module pre-test* for each module to support students' decision whether to work on the topic of a module and on which aspects they should focus. A *diagnostic module post-test* of a module provides summative feedback on how well a learner has acquired the intended knowledge of this module.

Our authoring system (see next section) did not support the editing of interactive exercises. Therefore, we decided to use the exercise editing capabilities of moodle, instead, and use its capabilities of automatic evaluation. We were aware that mathematical-symbolic input's evaluation was not supported by the current version although it is very desirable from the point of view of mathematics. We regard our moodle-constrained diagnostic tests as first steps and intend to add further components to moodle in future work such as the STACK system.

Since an individual diagnosis of deficits (and strengths) is an important requirement for designing a curriculum related to individual needs, self-diagnostic tests are of central importance.

In the meanwhile, a total of 50 tests were developed with about 250 tasks that serve as pre- and post-tests for the VEMA modules. The main goal of the diagnostic tests is providing a basis for a competence orientated feedback to individual students. Therefore we carried out a competence-orientated analysis of our content and identified

Figure 2. Diagnostic test with automatic feedback and learning advice

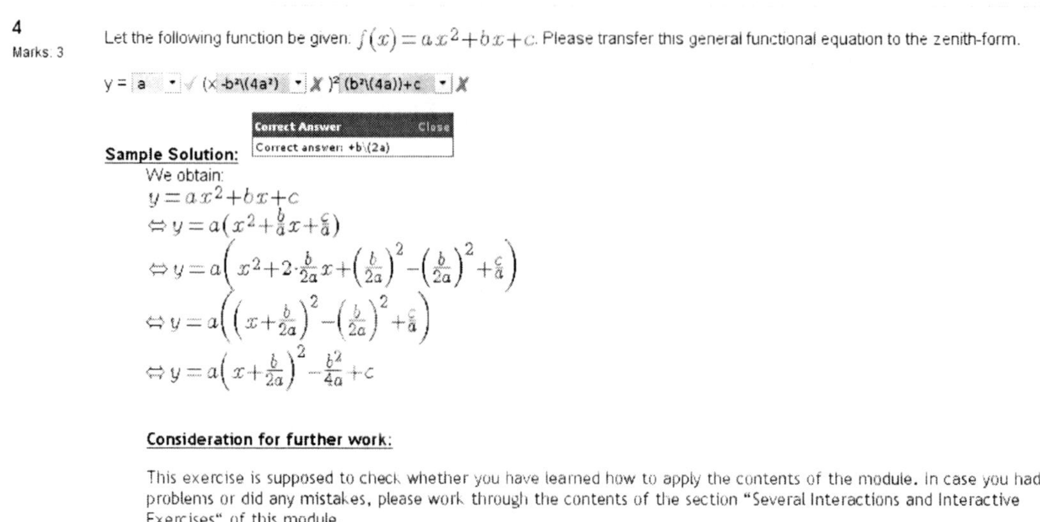

the following competence-categories: *technical aspects*, *understanding*, *application*, and *diagnosis of mistakes*. Each diagnostic test was developed for the content of one module and includes at least one task for each identified competence category. Corresponding to the individual results of a test, the learner gets some advice for his/her learning of the content of the respective module.

We developed as much exercises as possible in form of numeric answers or multiple-choice formats to enable an automatic correction and feedback by the system. Figure 2 shows a screenshot of such a test item including the automatic feedback and the learning advice. As you can see model solutions are always given in addition to the automatic correction, so that the student also gets a correct solution to which s/he can compare the own solution:

We use an open-answer format for modelling and proof tasks in these tests. We decided that for these tests the evaluation of the student's solution by an online tutor is more adequate. This allows a more precise and didactically sensitive feedback to the student. As an alternative, some tests have been designed in a way that the students have to evaluate their solutions themselves with the help of an evaluation scheme. The comparison to the model solution can be seen as a learning step itself. After the evaluation, students will enter their scores into the system and then get automatically feedback and learning advice for the whole test.

In the course scenarios we also implemented other forms of individually tailored human feedback: An individual tutor can be contacted using the forums, mail and chat. Moreover, the drop-in workshops that are offered in the E-course give the students the opportunity of face-to-face communication and feedback.

By offering these different types of diagnostic feedbacks, we also hope to develop the students' abilities in self-regulation and to enhance the accuracy of their self-evaluation. Pointing to the findings of Nota, Sorei, & Zimmermann (2005), Williams & Hellman (2004) and Pintrich (2002), Ibabe & Jauregizar (2010) describe these two elements (self-regulation and self-knowledge) as one of the major factors for the success of individual learning.

Figure 3. Integration of the interactive book into moodle

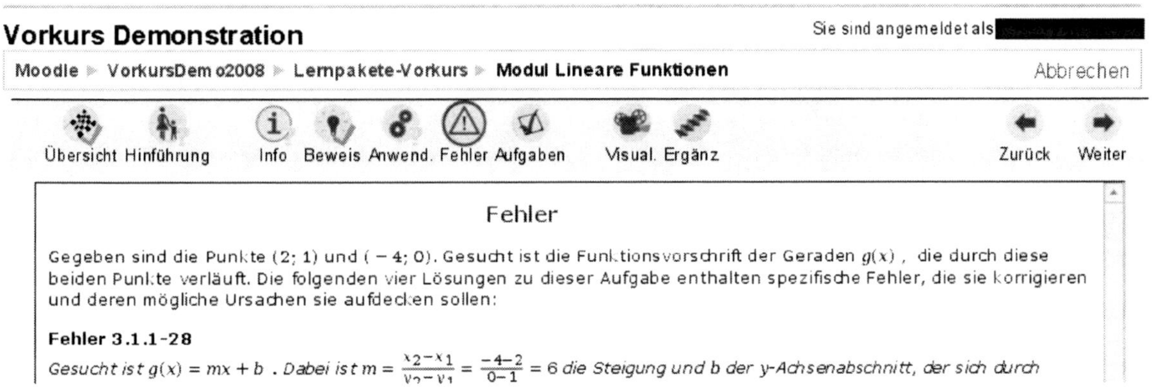

Vorkurs Demonstration Sie sind angemeldet als

Moodle ▸ VorkursDemo2008 ▸ Lernpakete-Vorkurs ▸ **Modul Lineare Funktionen** Abbrechen

Übersicht Hinführung Info Beweis Anwend. Fehler Aufgaben Visual. Ergänz Zurück Weiter

Fehler

Gegeben sind die Punkte (2; 1) und (−4; 0). Gesucht ist die Funktionsvorschrift der Geraden $g(x)$, die durch diese beiden Punkte verläuft. Die folgenden vier Lösungen zu dieser Aufgabe enthalten spezifische Fehler, die sie korrigieren und deren mögliche Ursachen sie aufdecken sollen:

Fehler 3.1.1-28

Gesucht ist $g(x) = mx + b$ *. Dabei ist* $m = \frac{x_2-x_1}{y_2-y_1} = \frac{-4-2}{0-1} = 6$ *die Steigung und b der y-Achsenabschnitt, der sich durch*

Integration of the Interactive Book into a Learning Management System

In a first step of integration, we structured the course according to moodle's learning unit and just added links to our material, which we presented to the students online as a second complete resource on a separate server. We added forums and additional material to the learning units to strengthen the communicative aspects of learning.

For improving the integration of the interactive book into our LMS, we also started to use the SCORM-environment, which provides much more flexibility and supports the arrangement of courses using the interactive book selectively as a resource. The SCORM-environment is also used to increase the support of the learning process by applying the possibilities of communication between the content and the LMS to notify if the learner has already completed or if s/he just browsed through it or not. A yellow question mark stands for a non-finished but viewed page and a green check mark stands for a finished page as you can see in Figure 3.

The other components of the CD-ROM like the pdf scripts or the html-based installation routine are still linked with the LMS, so the learner does not need the CD-ROM anymore.

Different Learning-Approaches

Depending on the individual students' interests and competencies the taken learning approach can and will differ from module to module. The structuring of each module into the same type of units supports different "macro learning strategies", namely working with the complete set of units or a selection of units or changing the sequence of units. A diagnostic pre-test is supposed to help the students with their decision which units of a module to concentrate on.

- The **basic approach with introduction** contains all described module units in the predefined order. The learners start with the *overview* and the *introduction to the domain*, where the new content is introduced - based on the assumed learners previous knowledge. That's why we call this the "genetic approach". Afterwards the learners continue with the *info*, the *IEE* and the *application* units and end with the *typical-mistakes* and the *exercise* units. Working on a module is finished up by doing the diagnostic post-test, and depending on its results requires working again on some units. This approach is recommended when the learners think that a module's content is practically a new domain for them.

- The **basic approach without introduction** differs from this in one aspect only: In this approach, the learners continue after the *overview* with the *info* unit and not with the *introduction*. Sometimes learners just need an overview over the central definitions and theorems of the module for their further learning. This approach is mostly used for rehearse-scenarios.
- **Selective approaches**. We distinguish several typical selective approaches:
  - Use as a **book with short reference sheets**: only the info units,
  - Use as a **workbook to practice**: only the exercise unit,
  - **Prepare for assessments**: info and exercise unit, diagnostic post-test
  - **Develop diagnostic competences**: typical mistakes unit
  - **Deepen domain knowledge**: info, application and supplements unit.

In the European project Math-Bridge, we expanded these approaches and designed several remedial scenarios that can be used by the intelligent tutor system of ActiveMath to generate own books realising those scenarios within specific content contexts. (cf. Biehler, Hochmuth, Fischer, & Wassong, 2010).

THE INTERACTIVE MATERIAL FROM THE AUTHORS' PERSPECTIVE

A big challenge for authoring content in such a great dimension, like in our project, is to establish a user-friendly authoring environment. Especially the different formats in which we intend to use our content makes it more difficult. This section describes our solutions for authoring mathematical content for different output formats.

The Output Formats

We decided to use LaTeX for authoring the content for two reasons: First, it is the easiest way to write mathematical formulae and is hence used by most mathematicians. Second LaTeX provides different output formats, so it is flexible enough for our purposes.

The target of our authoring process is to transform the LaTeX-content into the following output formats:

- a short pdf script which contains only the module units *info* with some space for students' notes,
- a long pdf script which contains only the module units *IEE* and *application*,
- the interactive XHTML script including all units with all applets and visualizations and
- a SCORM version of the XHTML script (also including all units, applets and visualizations)

The first two output formats are just pdf scripts which can be easily transformed from LaTeX with pdflatex, but the selection of certain types of learning objects and units needs to be prepared. For the short pdf script, a small script extracts the info-environments from the LaTeX-sources into separate files and transforms them with pdflatex to a pdf-file. For the long pdf script we use the full LaTeX-sources but exclude the unused units by using the LaTeX-package *comment* and its *excludecomment*-command.

Our most important output format is the interactive XHTML script. By using a XHTML-based platform for our material, we can use the advantages of a hypertext-infrastructure. Moreover, it supports our two-dimensional navigation: the tree structure of the topic-navigation on the one hand and our module-internal navigation on the other hand. Therefore it provides more navigation options than a usual book. Finally, we integrate applets produced with GeoGebra or GeoNext as well as our own Java-applets. We add JavaScript-based exercises on one hand for providing enactive learning possibilities and on other hand to use the possibilities of automatic evaluation. With the use of XHTML for the interactive material, we can combine these components and the text of the script into one comprehensive interactive book.

In our material the mathematical formulae are rendered with Math-ML which has two main aspects: Most of the users can use this rendering without extra software, only users of the Internet-Explorer need to install a plug-in. The more important aspect is that Math-ML is scalable. So with this rendering, we can use the material not only in situations where only one or two persons look at one screen, we can also use the material in a lecture room with 100 and more students looking at this material. For better reading, we can scale the page as well as the formulae.

For the transformation process, we developed and use the following converter:

1. Enriching the LaTeX code with adequate LaTeX environments so that various output formats (long and short pdf, XHTML, SCORM) can be automatically produced
2. Using ttm (http://hutchinson.belmont.ma.us/tth/mml/) for converting the whole LaTeX-sources into one single and big XHTML document
3. After the transformation of the LaTeX-sources to the XHTML document, another script slices this document into several pages, one page for each unit of a module, the navigation frame is added, the interactive exercises are integrated and the applets and the model solutions are linked.

The complex procedure is necessary as ttm does not convert all our used LaTeX-commands; so in some cases, we were forced to define our own LaTeX-environments which convert these LaTeX-commands into the correct Math-ML-commands.

For producing the SCORM-packaged version of our material, we developed a second converter that deletes the navigation frame (SCORM doesn't provide this), creates the needed SCORM-environment and produces the SCORM-package. For the communication of the SCORM-modules with the LMS, we use the SCORM Runtime Environment.

As described above, we use SCORM to communicate the status of a module unit: not viewed, viewed but unfinished and finished. We decided to implement the following rule for the status "finished": if there are interactive exercises in a unit, the learner has to solve all of them correctly. If there are no such exercises, the learner has to spend at least ten seconds on this unit.

Beside the necessary elimination of both navigation frames, the standard SCORM-player does not allow a clear visualization of the status of a unit. To resolve both limitations, we adapted the standard SCORM-player in moodle. This new player provides moodle with our typical navigation frame and adds a yellow question mark to those module units a learner has begun but not finished and a green check mark, if the unit is finished.

The Authoring Environment

Further reasons for using LaTeX include:

- Text with mathematical formulae has to be written.
- Media and interactive learning objects have to be produced.
- These Media has to be embedded into the written text.
- The whole content, the text including formulae, media, and interactive learning objects, has to be automatically converted into the interactive XHTML-Script like described above.
- Authoring should be independent of the output formats' designs.

For these requirements, we extended the standard LaTeX environments by special VEMA environments: First, we defined unit-LaTeX-environments for our different module units, like an *introduction* or an *application* LaTeX-environment. These unit-environments are used to identify the module units to which the text belongs. Second, we defined learning-object-LaTeX-environments for single learning objects (LOs), like an example or a typical-mistakes exercise. Just for the *exercise LaTeX-environments,* we separate the task from the model solution and, for the *typical-mistakes LaTeX-environment,* we separate the wrong solution from the diagnosis and the correction. With this separation, it is possible to generate own pages for model solutions in the XHTML script. Third, we defined *media LaTeX-environments* for the different media we integrate into our material, for instance Flash-films, images, interactive JavaScript-exercises, Java-Applets, GeoGebra-Applets and GeoNEXT-Applets. In these media-LaTeX-environments, all necessary data are defined: the captions of the media and the local references to the media-files. These *media LaTeX-environments* are necessary for a differentiated representation of the different output formats. For instance, there are just hints for the Flash films but not the Flash films themselves in the pdf-output-format. They are only available in the XHTML-output-format.

We implemented several supporting strategies for the authoring process. First, we have written a user-guide where the authoring process and all environments are described. Second, with the use of SVN we implemented an infrastructure for multi-user access.

THE COURSE SCENARIOS

This section describes the different course scenarios we have been experimenting with over the last few years. Following Niegemann et al. (2008), one can distinguish between self-directed-learning and external-regulated-learning. Both represent opposite poles of a continuum of possible learning scenarios and typically do not appear in a pure form. Learning scenarios show aspects of elements from both sides (cf. Niegemann et al., 2008, p. 66). So-called "blended learning scenarios" combine phases of attendance with phases of self-directed-learning with the computer. The attendance phases enable the students to get to know one another, to exchange experiences, to ask specific questions to the teacher/ tutor and to discuss topics face-to-face. The e-learning phases focus on the individual or collaborative construction of knowledge (cf. Mandl & Kopp, 2006, p. 6). Hence, the social components of learning are combined with the advantages of individual self-regulated learning, which exploits the benefits of both methods.

A specification of the most common formats can be found in Niegemann et al. (2008, pp 121). So far, no empirical or theoretical findings have shown that one format is more efficient than the other in general. The correct decision on the instructional format should always be based on an analysis of the specific learning context.

We also combined both types of instructional formats for our bridging courses. Both have their justification in the specific situation of a bridging course: On the one hand, learners are new at the university so they have to acclimatise themselves with the new learning place. Here, attendance phases can help them before they really start with their studies. On the other hand, the university requires a different learning behaviour. In contrast to school, the learners have to be more self-directed in their learning. At this point, the e-learning phases can help to adapt their learning behaviour. As described in the short history of the project, we have developed two different blended-learning course scenarios for our bridging courses: a course scenario with an extensive attendance part (P-course) and a course scenario with an extensive e-learning part (E-course).

Since we offer the bridging courses for a couple of study programmes like electrical engineering, computer science, teacher pre-services, mechanical engineering and mathematics, we grouped these study programmes with regard to their related content needs and provide a separate P-course and a separate E-course for every group.

The Course Scenario with an Extensive Attendance Part (The P-Course)

This course scenario is mainly structured and led by the teacher. The course includes 4 weeks with each week consisting of three days with attendance at the university with three hours of lectures and two hours for a practice-session. The remaining two days are free for individual learning and homework. The homework consists of two parts: one part includes exercises on the topics that were taught in the lectures and another part includes specific tasks for individually working with the modules in order to revise or to prepare for the next attendance day. Thus, this course variant is extensively managed by the teacher, while the learner has fewer opportunities for individual learning. The diagnostic tests can generally be used, but which specific tests are available to the students is administered by the teacher.

The Course Scenario with an Extensive E-Learning Part (The E-Course)

This course includes 4 weeks in September with totally 6 attendance days at the university. The remaining time is kept free for online learning. The first week starts with one or two orientation days during which the learners get acquainted with the learning management system, get some hints of how to learn with the material and the first modules are discussed in the shape of lectures. These first two days introduce the learners to the course, its learning opportunities and to the university in general.

From then on, there is only one attendance day at the end of every week. Here, the learners have the opportunity to ask questions about the learned content in the first part of the morning and to select the content which is to be discussed in the second part of the morning. In the afternoon, there is a small group working opportunity with exercises related to the content that has been discussed in the morning. The small group work is guided by a tutor, who supports the learners in solving the exercises and in revising the content if necessary. The rest of the time is free for learning with the online resources. Beside the orientation days, moodle supports the learners in their learning paths. There are the diagnostic tests with the individual feedback for further learning and there is a list of recommended modules for every study programme. Besides, we provide a text that explains the use of the material, the diagnostic tests and the role of the days at the university. The learning system provides the following communication opportunities: There are synchronous (chat) and asynchronous possibilities (forum and mail). The students can either communicate among each other or ask questions to an online tutor who is reachable via moodle. The tutor helps the learners in case of questions concerning the content or technical problems and corrects open-answer exercises. S/he is the contact person with regard to all questions. The lecturer supports and tries to motivate the students in their individual learning, since the lack of students' motivation is a major problem in online learning environments (cf. Meyer, 2002). On the one hand, s/he designs the lectures for the attendance time according to the learners needs. In the first part of a lecture, s/he concentrates on the learners' questions concerning the content studied by them. In the second part of the lecture, s/he presents new content that is chosen on the basis of a previous discussion with the learners in a forum. On the other hand the lecturer reminds the learners of their learning agenda in the forum.

Table 1. Results for questions concerning the acceptance of the courses

Question	P-course			E-course		
	M	SD	N	M	SD	N
1: *"In general..."*	3.57	0.62	254	3.64	0.53	96
2: *"The participation in..."*	3.69	0.62	254	3.69	0.56	96
3: *"I would decide for ..."*	3.67	0.68	254	3.48	0.79	96

THE EVALUATION-STUDY

In 2008, the bridging courses in Kassel were extensively evaluated in the context of the PhD-project of the second author of this chapter. This PhD project aimed at the design, the evaluation, and the refinement of the bridging course scenarios that have been described above. The evaluation study was piloted in the bridging courses in 2007. Among the major questions of the study were identifying reasons for the students' choice of the course variants, describing the participants concerning personal aspects, identifying course effects on the learners' performance and attitudes, analyzing the acceptance and appreciation of the courses and the learning material, and finally analyzing the students' use of the learning material.

The data were collected within the P- and the E-courses in 2008 using two assessment tests and three questionnaires, one at the beginning of the course, one in the middle of the course and one at the end. These questionnaires were realized as anonymous online-forms with an anonymous personal key in order to trace the student's answers. The questions were taken from different studies (Prenzel et al., 2002, Baumert et al., 2008, Bescherer, 2003 and items from the general course evaluation of the University of Kassel) and were enriched by self-developed items in order to develop a new instrument for a differentiated analysis of blended learning scenarios of mathematical bridging courses. The students' mathematical proficiency level was quantified using an electronic pre- and a post-test which was written under testing conditions in a computer room at the beginning and at the end of the courses. This course pre-test consisted of exercises from school mathematics, while the course post-test was specifically designed with regard to the content of the bridging courses.

In the 2008's bridging courses, 280 students took the E-courses and about 520 the P-courses. The evaluation of the assessments' considers 372 students' pre-test results and 203 students' post-test results. Although the questionnaires used in the study were very substantial with various objectives of investigation, we will only take a closer look at selected results of this study concerning the *acceptance of the courses*, the *results of the assessments*, the *reasons for the student's choice of the course variant* and finally the *usage of the learning materialwithin the E-course* in view of the length of this chapter.

Acceptance of the Courses

For evaluating the acceptance of our bridging courses in general and the two course scenarios in specific, we asked the students for a rating of the following three questions 1. *"In general I was satisfied with the bridging course"*, 2. *"The participation in the bridging courses is absolutely recommendable"* and 3. *"I would decide for the E-/P-course of the bridging course again"*.

The students had to answer these questions using a Likert type scale with four answering categories: (1) "is not true", (2) "is rather not true", (3) "is rather true" and (4) "is true".

Table 2. Assessment results

Test	Results for P-course			Results for E-course		
	M	**SD**	**N**	**M**	**SD**	**N**
Pre-test 2008 Maximum: **19 points**	8.52	3.14	226	8.52	3.64	146
Post-test 2008 Maximum: **20 points**	9.21	3.13	131	10.93	4.02	72

Table 1 shows that all courses got very high scores for these questions in general and the comparison of the two course variants reveals fairly comparable results.

Obviously, the learners were very satisfied with the bridging courses in general and their chosen scenario in specific. Our results approve the success of our course design decisions concerning the participants' validation and are similar to the findings of Sikora & Caroll (2002) who also detected equal satisfaction of students with campus and distance learning courses. But what's about the effect of the courses concerning the students' mathematical proficiency?

Results of the Assessments

Our pre-test in 2008 showed very similar results for the participants of both course types. For the post-test, the results for the E-course are even better than the results of the P-course as you can see in Table 2.

For students that participated in both tests we additionally made an analysis of variance for the results of the post-test considering the course variant as dependent variable and the results of the pre-test as covariant. This proved that the difference in the results of the course variants is highly significant.

This was surprising to us, since we only intended to achieve at least similar results for both course types in order to disprove the critical argument that the E-course is indeed a popular alternative to some students but does not improve the students' performance as much as traditional scenarios.

Besides, one further detail is interesting: From the descriptive perspective, the statistical spread of the E-course's test results is slightly higher than the spread within the P-course. This is the same for both, pre- and post-test. Moreover, the spread within the E-course's results did not decrease from pre- to post-test.

Students' Reasons for Their Choice of the Course Variant

Based on the results of the pilot study in 2007, we identified several possible reasons for the students' choice between E- and P-course. In 2008 the students had to indicate for each of these reasons if they were relevant for their decision or not. Again we used a Likert type scale with four answering categories from (1) "is not true" up to (4) "is true". We calculated for each of these questions a mean score and could hence identify factors with a high impact and factors with a low impact.

For the **E-course,** we found out that the mean scores for *extrinsic* factors such as being on vacation, job-related restrictions, the living situation or other external reasons had low values between 1.24 and 2.4. In contrast to this, the questions concerning *intrinsic* reasons had high mean scores between 2.73 and 3.52 and can therefore be interpreted as main factors for the decision: These include reasons concerning the possibility of individual timing in learning, the possibility of a more self-regulated learning within the E-course

Table 3. Results for questions on learning with computer. Answering categories for the third question: (1) almost every day, (2) 2-5 times a week, (3) about once a week, (4) 1-2 times per month, (5) less often, (6) never.

Question	Results for P-course			Results for E-course		
	M	SD	N	M	SD	N
"I have experiences in e-learning already"	1.97	0.4	376	1.95	0.33	209
"I like to learn with the PC"	3.23	0.74	376	3.4	0.7	209
"In the last year in school, I have learnt with a PC already"	3.32	1.58	376	3.39	1.55	209

as well as an interest in e-learning as teaching method. Besides – which is not very surprising – the reduced numbers of days with compulsory attendance was rated with a mean score of 2.7 and can certainly be interpreted as a further important factor for the choice.

For the **P-course,** the results show that again extrinsic reasons concerning the availability of a computer, internet-access or an internet-flatrate had very low mean scores between 1.06 and 1.32. Bad experiences in e-learning (M = 1.33) or the aversion to learning with the computer (M = 2.13) were also factors with low impact. In contrast to this, reasons concerning the possibility of personal contact to students (M = 3.4) and to the teacher (M = 3.64) as well as the possibility of experiencing typical lectures got high mean scores between 3.4 and 3.64 and can, hence, be interpreted as main factors. The questions concerning doubts in one's ability of self-regulated learning (M = 2.6) and doubts concerning the method e-learning itself (M = 2.61) are neither strong factors for or against the choice of the course variant.

Since we originally assumed that especially those students decide for the E-course that either have an affinity to working with the computer or that already have made (positive) experiences in learning with the PC, we asked respective questions in both course-scenarios. Surprisingly the results in Table 3 do not show any substantial differences in this respect between the answers of P- and E-course participants.

Usage of the Diagnostic Tests within the E-Course

The participants of the E-course were asked to describe their use of the diagnostic tests and of the modules. Amongst others, they had to indicate how often they had used the diagnostic tests (1) "practically all", (2) "most of them", (3) "some of them" (4) "barely none". The results can be found in Figure 4:

This reveals a slightly higher average usage of the diagnostic pre-tests which is also proved by the user numbers: The number of pre-test-users is always higher than the respective number for the post-tests. A major finding is the diversity in using our tests.

Moreover, it is interesting to have a closer look at the results concerning the acceptance of the diagnostic tests: The students had to rate how helpful the diagnostic tests were on a scale from (1) "helpful" up to (6) "not helpful at all". Students who didn't use the tests could indicate it in the answer and were filtered out in Figure 5.

Thus, the evaluation of the tests was very positive for both test types from those who used them at all.

FURTHER PERSPECTIVES

Our project material is transformed and extended in the following two projects. Minguillón et al. (2008) demand the development of efficient web

Figure 4. Use of the diagnostic tests

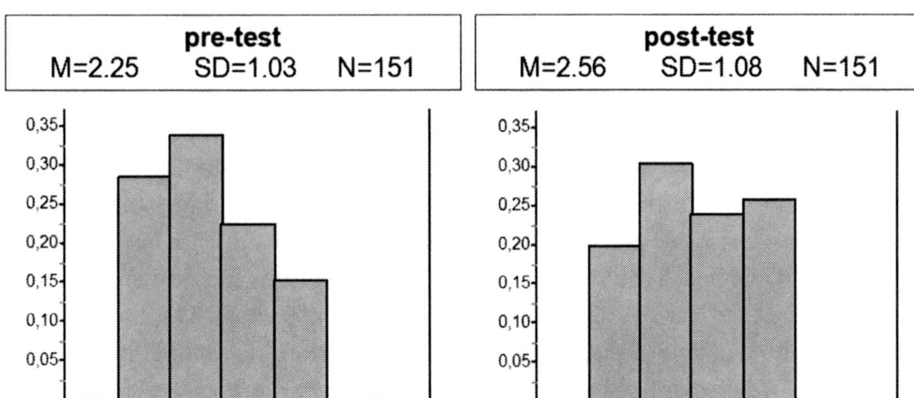

Figure 5. Acceptance of the diagnostic tests

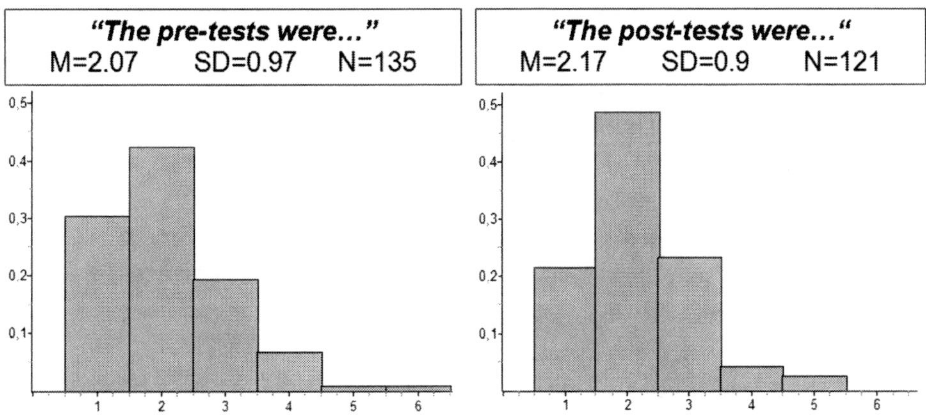

repositories that make materials on mathematics easily available and searchable while Rodriguez & Villa saw the "*need to unify contents with a view to homogenisation in Europe*" (Rodriguez & Villa, 2005, p. 200), which should also lead to the development of effective distance learning. The EU-project "Math-Bridge" is actually establishing such an international repository for material for distance and blended learning bridging courses in mathematics (http://www.math-bridge.org) and aims at the design of an adaptive learning system for mathematical bridging courses in different languages using the learning system ActiveMath that is usable in different learning scenarios. The authors of this chapter are members of the consortium as pedagogical experts and content providers. In particular, the VEMA material will be transformed in the ActiveMath format and will be available for the European community in five languages (English, German, French, Finnish, Hungarian, Dutch). Moreover, we will continue and extend our work on mathematical e-learning in the context of the recently established Centre for Higher Mathematics Education Research of the Universities of Kassel and Paderborn (http://www.khdm.de), which will be directed by the first and third author of this chapter.

CONCLUSION

In this chapter we have reported about the project VEMA, which aims at resolving some of the typical problems that occur within mathematical bridging courses. The project's approach is the design of bridging courses that consider all aspects of learning and that are student-orientated. This includes (1) the design of interactive learning material that enables self-regulated learning and (2) the design of blended learning course scenarios that enables varying levels of self-regulated learning.

With the didactically founded development of interactive learning material we support various uses and reuses, different learning approaches and the opportunity of helping students with their individual deficits. We saw the necessity of implementing diagnostic tests with individual feedback in order to replace the teachers' advices that are missing in self-regulated learning environments and large scale lectures. In accordance with our experience as well as with our evaluation results, we emphasized that it is still necessary to embed our learning material into blended learning scenarios that give students the opportunity of learning in a social framework with physically attendant teachers and learners. For meeting students learning customs we developed two different blended learning course variants – a P- and an E-course – for giving the students the opportunity to decide on the intensity of instructional lead by the teacher respectively the intension of self-regulated learning.

Discussing the technical aspects of the design of our material and of our courses, we argued that these aspects always need to be embedded into didactical and pedagogical design decisions. Hence we developed an authoring environment that separates the design from the content and that enables the reuse of our content for various designs and output formats. For the authoring process of interactive learning material we experienced this procedure as the most efficient and sustainable one.

Giving an insight in our evaluation concept and in some selected results, we showed that many aspects need to be considered when designing blended learning scenarios. A closer look at some of the students' learning strategies revealed interrelations we would not have expected but which are relevant for the design and the organization of bridging courses. The integrative development of both, learning material and course scenarios, calls for an appropriate concept of evaluation to ensure a continuous progress in view of the learners' needs.

We are currently working on a detailed analysis of the user data and intend to develop a more generally applicable instrument for the evaluation of blended learning mathematical bridging courses.

REFERENCES

Baumert, J. (2008). *Professionswissen von Lehrkräften, kognitiv aktivierender Mathematikunterricht und die Entwicklung von mathematischer Kompetenz (COACTIV): Dokumentation der Erhebungsinstrumente (Materialien aus der Bildungsforschung, Nr. 83)*. Berlin, Germany: MPI.

Bescherer, C. (2003). *Selbsteinschätzung der mathematischen Studierfähigkeit von Studienanfängerinnen und –anfängern*. online published doctoral dissertation. Retrieved September 15th, 2010, from http://opus.bsz-bw.de/ phlb/ volltexte/ 2004/ 1626/

Biehler, R., Hochmuth, R., Fischer, P. R., & Wassong, T. (2010). *EU-Project Math-Bridge - D1.3: Pedagogical remedial scenarios*. Retrieved September 15th, 2010, from http://subversion.math-bridge.org/ math-bridge/ public/ WP01_Pedagogical_Preparation/ Deliverables/ D1.3-pedagogical_remedial_scenarios/ D13_remedial_Scenarios.pdf

Biehler, R., Hochmuth, R., & Koepf, W. (2010). Schnittstellenaktivität "Mathematische Brückenkurse". In *Beiträge zum Mathematikunterricht 2010*. Münster, Germany: WTM-Verlag.

De Guzman, M., Hodgson, B. R., Robert, A., & Villani, V. (1998). Difficulties in the passage from secondary to tertiary education. In . *Proceedings of the International Congress of Mathematicians*, *III*, 747–762.

Gueudet, G. (2008). Investigating secondary-tertiary transition. *Educational Studies in Mathematics*, *67*(3), 237–254. doi:10.1007/s10649-007-9100-6

Holton, D. (Ed.). (2001). *The teaching and learning of mathematics at university level. An ICMI Study*. Dordrecht, The Netherlands: Kluwer.

Ibabe, I., & Jauregizar, J. (2010). Online self-assessment with feedback and metacognitive knowledge. *Higher Education*, *59*(2), 243–258. doi:10.1007/s10734-009-9245-6

Juan, A., Huertas, A., Steegmann, C., Corcoles, C., & Serrat, C. (2008). Mathematical e-learning: State of the art and experiences at the Open University of Catalonia. *International Journal of Mathematical Education in Science and Technology*, *39*(4), 455–471. doi:10.1080/00207390701867497

Kerres, M. (2002). Online- und Präsenzelemente in hybriden Lernarrangements kombinieren . In Hohenstein, A., & Wilbers, K. (Eds.), *Handbuch E-Learning*. Köln, Germany: Fachverlag Deutscher Wirtschaftsdienst.

Krivsky, S. (2003). *Multimediale Lernumgebungen in der Mathematik*. Hildesheim, Germany: Franzbecker.

Lai, K. W., Pratt, K. & Grant, A. (2003). *State of the art and trends in distance, flexible, and open learning: A review of the literature*. Report submitted to the Distance Learning Reference Group, University of Otago (commissioned discussion paper).

Mandl, H., & Kopp, B. (2006). *Blended learning: Forschungsfragen und Perspektiven. (Forschungsbericht Nr. 182)*. München, Germany: Ludwig-Maximilians-Universität.

Meyer, K. A. (2002). Quality in distance education: Focus on on-line learning. *ASHE-ERIC Higher Education Report Series, 29*(4).

Minguillón, J., Huertas, A. M., Juan, A. A., Sancho, T., & Cavaller, V. (2008). Using learning object repositories for teaching statistics. In *Proceedings of the First Workshop on the Methods and Cases in Computing Education*, (pp. 53-61).

Niegemann, H. M., Domagk, S., Hessel, S., Hein, A., Hupfer, M., & Zobel, A. (2008). *Kompendium multimediales Lernen*. Heidelberg, Germany: Springer.

Nota, L., Sorei, S., & Zimmerman, B. J. (2005). Self-regulation and academia and resilience: A longitudinal study. *International Journal of Educational Research*, *41*, 198–251. doi:10.1016/j.ijer.2005.07.001

Oser, F., Hascher, T., & Spychiger, M. (1999). Lernen aus Fehlern. Zur Psychologie des negativen Wissens. In W. Althof (Ed.), *Fehlerwelten. Vom Fehlermachen und Lernen aus Fehlern* (pp. 11-42). Opladen, Germany: Leske + Budrich.

Pintrich, P. R. (2002). The role of metacognitive knowledge in learning, teaching, and assessing. *Theory into Practice*, *41*(4), 220. doi:10.1207/s15430421tip4104_3

Prenzel, M., Senkbeil, M., Ehmke, T., & Bleschke, M. (Eds.). (2002). *Konzeption, Evaluationsinstrumente und Unterrichtsmaterialien des SEMIK-Projekts "Didaktisch optimierter Einsatz Neuer Medien im naturwissenschaftlichen Unterricht". (IPN-Materialien)*. Kiel, Germany: IPN.

Raschke, C. A. (2003). *The digital revolution and the coming of the postmodern university*. New York, NY: RoutledgeFalmer. doi:10.4324/9780203451243

Rodríguez, G., & Villa, A. (2005). *Can computers change the trends in mathematics Learning? A Spanish overview*. Plenary lecture at the 4th International Conference APLIMAT. Retrieved November 22th, 2010, from http://dmath.hibu.no/ Rodrigez-De _la_ VillaAplimath.pdf

Roll, I., Aleven, V., McLaren, B. M., Ryu, E., Baker, R. S., & Koedinger, K. R. (2006). The help tutor: Does metacognitive feedback improve students' help-seeking actions, skills and learning? In M. Ikeda, K. D. Ashley, & T. W. Chan (Eds.), *Proceedings of the 8th International Conference on Intelligent Tutoring Systems* (pp. 360-369). Berlin, Germany: Springer.

Sikora, A., & Carroll, C. (2002). *A profile of participation in distance education: 1999-2000*. Washington, DC: National Center for Education Statistics, U.S. Department of Education.

Tall, D. (1991). *Advanced mathematical thinking*. Dordrecht, The Netherlands: Kluwer.

Unwin, T. (2005). Capacity building and management in ICT for education. In D. Wagner, R. Day, T. James, R. Kozma, J. Miller, & T. Unwin (Eds.), *Monitoring and evaluation of ICT in education projects*. Retrieved November 22nd, 2010, from http://www.literacyonline.org/ PDFs/ ICThandbook.pdf #page=83

Vovides, Y., Sanchez-Alonso, S., Mitropoulou, V., & Nickmans, G. (2007). The use of e-learning course management systems to support learning strategies and to improve self-regulated learning. *Educational Research Review*, *2*(1), 64–74. doi:10.1016/j.edurev.2007.02.004

Williams, P. E., & Hellman, C. M. (2004). Differences in self-regulation for online learning between first and second-generation college students. *Research in Higher Education*, *45*(1), 71–82. doi:10.1023/B:RIHE.0000010047.46814.78

Wittmann, G. (2007). Von Fehleranalysen zur Fehlerkorrektur . In *Beiträge zum Mathematikunterricht 2007*. Münster, Germany: WTM-Verlag.

KEY TERMS AND DEFINITIONS

Blended Learning: Blended Learning is a combination of components with self-regulated e-learning and components of teaching and learning in a classroom. There are different types of blended learning which vary in the combination of these components.

E-Learning: Learning with computer resources such as programs, interactive learning material, hypertext or other electronic resources. Usually learning management systems (LMS) are used to organize e-learning, to provide the content and to enable a communication between students and teachers.

Heterogeneous Learning Group: This is a group of learners who strongly differ in their individual knowledge and abilities. Heterogeneous learning groups may result from varying educational backgrounds due to different graduation, mixed educational systems or individual variation for instance due to the personal learning history.

Mathematical Bridging Courses: Courses in mathematics before or at the beginning of the first-year terms. These courses aim at refreshing and deepening the mathematical knowledge of the students in order to prepare them for their studies.

Research in Higher Mathematics Education: Research in Higher Mathematics Education deals with the teaching and learning of mathematics at university level. It is a part of research in mathematical educational and is concerned with the knowledge, misconceptions and dispositions of first-year-students, with the knowledge to be taught in view of the requirements of the different field of studies, and with adequate methods and course scenarios including the use of technology for supporting learning.

Secondary-Tertiary Transition: The Secondary-tertiary transition marks the change from school, job or other activities to studying at University level. This transition mostly goes along with heterogeneous learning groups in first-year university courses which result from the varying previous knowledge and learning strategies.

Self-Assessment: Ability to assess one's own knowledge and competences in view of a certain topic. This ability is particularly needed for self-regulated learning. The term "self-assessment" is also used to describe the process of assessing oneself.

Self-Diagnostic Tests: A test that can be autonomously used by a learner to diagnose her/his knowledge and competences without the help of a teacher or an external person. A self-diagnostic test can be used to support self-assessment and self-regulated learning.

Self-Regulated Learning: Self-regulated learning means that a student designs her/his individual learning herself/himself. Thus s/he is the main actor while a teacher is either absent or only a supporter of the student. The learner autonomously sets his personal learning goals and correspondingly plans the learning process. For this s/he needs to select adequate learning resources and is responsible for the structuring and timing of the learning process. Within self-regulated learning, the student also has to monitor his learning progress to ensure that s/he achieves her/his learning goals. Therefore adequate abilities in self-assessment are needed.

Chapter 12
Long-Term Experiences in Mathematics E-Learning in Europe and the USA

Sven Trenholm
Loughborough University, UK

Angel A. Juan
Open University of Catalonia, Spain

Jorge Simosa
Massachusetts Institute of Technology, USA

Amilcar Oliveira
Universidade Aberta, Portugal

Teresa Oliveira
Universidade Aberta, Portugal

ABSTRACT

This chapter presents a comparative study regarding four long-term experiences teaching mathematics online at four different universities in Europe and the USA. The chapter first begins by discussing general differences in e-learning adoption between the USA and Europe (with specific focus on asynchronous e-learning). Second, some of the major benefits and challenges of mathematics e-learning are discussed. Third, the chapter describes some specific experiences with mathematics e-learning at the four universities (two European and two American) - these descriptions focus on methodological and practical aspects of the e-learning process in mathematics courses. Finally, a comparative analysis highlights common patterns and differences among the different models and some key factors for successful mathematics e-learning practice are identified along with a set of recommendations.

DOI: 10.4018/978-1-60960-875-0.ch012

INTRODUCTION

Information technologies, broadly, have undergone significant evolution over the past two decades. This in turn has led to changes in higher education practice. In particular, in an effort to explore ways to harness technological innovations and thus improve their educational programs, more and more universities are providing online courses and degree programs, as well as so-called hybrid or blended courses, These innovations, such as virtual learning environments (VLE's), have, for example, driven the growth of online and distance learning opportunities by providing students who are time-bound due to job or travel difficulties, or place-bound due to geographic location or physical disabilities, with access to courses and degree programs at their convenience (Simonson et al., 2003). The resultant growth has been rapid, as evidenced by the proliferation of e-learning models worldwide (Allen & Seaman, 2008; Nagy, 2005).

As in most or all of higher education, mathematics also follows a clear trend towards the increasing use of web resources – e.g. VLE's such as Moodle (http://moodle.org/), Sakai (http://sakaiproject.org/portal) or Blackboard/WebCT (www.blackboard.com/) – and mathematics software – e.g. Mathematica, Maple, Minitab, Statistica, SPSS or R. These technologies both promote and enable the research and development of new instructional approaches. This, in turn, is leading to the development of new roles, strategies and methodologies for mathematics instruction in higher education. The current situation is largely one where the requisite research base (and thus understanding of best-practices) is not keeping up with the fluid changes that continue to occur. This chapter seeks to contribute to filling this gap by providing the first comparative analysis (to our knowledge) of long-term experiences with mathematics e-learning between European and American universities. By doing so, the hope is to begin to identify some of the benefits and challenges encountered by online mathematics instructors as well as students.

The structure of the chapter is as follows: First, growth of e-learning in Europe and the US is discussed and some characteristics and trends are suggested (with a particular emphasis on asynchronous e-learning). Second, the chapter analyzes some of the main benefits and challenges related to offering mathematics courses online. Third, mathematics e-learning experiences at the four universities are presented. These universities are: Open University of Catalonia (Spain), Universidade Aberta (Portugal), State University of New York (USA) and Massachusetts Institute of Technology (USA). Fourth, these experiences provide the means for providing a comparative analysis in which key similarities and differences among the models are highlighted. From this analysis, some best practices and fundamental factors for successful mathematics online courses are deduced. Finally, a conclusion section summarizes the main findings and contributions of the chapter.

While the chapter places particular emphasis on the fully online asynchronous modality (i.e. e-learning as a complete replacement for traditional face-to-face instruction) much of the experiences and lessons shared will also have natural applicability to blended (or hybrid) instruction (i.e. e-learning as a partial replacement for traditional face-to-face instruction).

GROWTH IN E-LEARNING: EUROPE VS. USA

Acting as a complete replacement or as a complement to traditional face-to-face (F2F) instruction, asynchronous e-learning is perhaps the fastest growing segment in the US higher education sector. Asynchronous e-learning, commonly facilitated by media such as email and discussion boards, supports interactions among learners and with instructors, even when participants cannot be online at the same time (Hrastinski, 2008). Recent estimates for the US indicate that e-learning, acting as a complete replacement, has seen average annual enrollment increases of just below 20% between 2002 and 2008, with an estimated 300,000 faculty engaged in fully online instruction (including an estimated 20 to 25% of 2008 U.S. college students enrolling in at least one online class; Mayadas et al., 2009).

Similar European statistics are harder to come by. In contrast to the US statistics just cited, Schneckenberg (2009) looks at web-based learning technologies in general and summarizes that "the eLearning (sic) adoption rate of European academic staff appears disappointing" (p. 411). This statement concurs somewhat with a report from the Dutch Center for Higher Education Policy Studies, sub-titled An International Comparative Survey on the Current and Future use of ICT in Higher Education. The report, comparing 5 European countries, the US and Australia, found that while a great deal of similarity was reported among countries, where differences existed, only Finland and US institutions consistently had the highest scores related to "certain aspects of their ICT policy and… their orientations on the ICT agenda" (Collis & Van der Wende, 2002, p. 42). Expanding to 13 countries, the 2005 Organization for Economic Cooperation and Development (OECD; with a largely European membership) Policy brief on E-learning in Tertiary Education concludes, that "fully online provision at campus-based institutions will remain very much a minority in the short to medium term" (Vincent-Lancrin, 2005).

Thus it appears that the development of asynchronous e-learning in Europe has not been the same as that experienced in the US (Schneckenberg, 2006). Some explanations have been offered: First, there have been some "high-profile failures of online universities and a larger number of initiatives that never reached their full potential" (reported failures in the US are much fewer compared to reported successes; Mayadas et al, 2009, p.88). Second, whereas growth in asynchronous e-learning in the US has been robust in traditional institutions this has not been the case in Europe where, currently, Open Universities appear to dominate the market for fully asynchronous courses (Note: Open Universities in Europe may offer optional live classes with their asynchronous courses whereas, in the US, it is common that asynchronous courses are completely online). Several other reasons have been offered for the differences in US vs. European asynchronous e-learning adoption. They include:

- "The greater 'travel to study' distances" in the US (vs. Europe), providing a greater inducement to the development distance e-learning possibilities (Mayadas et al, 2009, p. 88).
- "More 'can do' culture" in the US including strong free market forces that encourage innovation and development (Mayadas et al, 2009, p. 88).
- A greater prevalence and "acceptance of private universities, both nonprofit and for-profit" in the US (Mayadas et al, 2009, p. 88).
- A majority of European universities "stalled in the traditional pedagogical model" (Schneckenberg, 2009, p. 411).
- A "lack of faculty interest and engagement with eLearning (sic)" (Schneckenberg, 2009, p. 411).
- "Skepticism about the pedagogic value of e-learning" associated with the lack of solid empirical evidence demonstrating its value (Vincent-Lancrin, 2005).

To these potential factors, one can add the gap between European and North American Internet usage (as a percent of population) which is currently about 20% or more (http://www.internetworldstats.com/stats.htm).

Despite these mixed reports there are clear global expectations that the demand for this kind of education will continue to grow (Beldarrain, 2006; Glenn, 2008; Mayadas et al, 2009). With the increasing importance of higher education in driving a knowledge-based economy, technological advancements coupled with market force demands for convenience and flexibility, are helping propel the rapid growth of asynchronous e-learning in tertiary education. Of those who project growth, first, the global 2008 survey by the Economist Intelligence Unit, The Future of Higher Education: How Technology Will Shape Learning, concludes that "online learning is gaining a firm foothold in universities around the world" (Glenn, M., 2008, p. 4). Programs such as the University of London International program are one such recent example (http://www.londoninternational.ac.uk/). Second, as reported in a recent BBC article, with governmental pressure, "universities (are seeking to)... find more flexible and cheaper ways to teach... (as well as) expanding chances for students to study long distance" (Bell, 2010, p. 1). Fully asynchronous e-learning is presented as one solution. Third, both of these examples are in agreement with the World Bank statement that, "the emergence of new types of tertiary institutions and new forms of competition (is) inducing traditional institutions to change their modes of operation and delivery and to take advantage of the opportunities offered by the new information and communication technologies" (Bradwell, 2009, p. 47).

Within academia, Bernard et al. (2004) suggests the asynchronous "reality of 'learn anywhere, anytime,'...has set traditional educational institutions into intense competition for the worldwide market of online learners". This view is perhaps more prophetic than a present reality since it appears this is yet to be witnessed with any great participation from the European higher education sector.

However, it is possible that European development may be advanced through changes that encourage use of the Internet among all of its citizens. Finland, for example, the previously mentioned notable exception to European ICT adoption trends, recently enshrined broadband access as a 'legal right' for every Finn (BBC News, July 1, 2010, http://www.bbc.co.uk/news/10461048). Also recently, the European Commission's Viviane Reding, commissioner for information society and media, suggested Internet access should be a 'fundamental human right' (CNET news, May 6, 2009, http://news.cnet.com/8301-13505_3-10234555-16.html). What role that any of these changes may play in the growth of e-learning in general, and asynchronous e-learning in particular, is yet to be understood.

The best picture for current European e-learning development may be provided by the recent London UK-based Demos think tank document, The Edgeless University. This report indicates that it is still unclear to what extent e-learning will replace F2F instruction (Bradwell, 2009, p. 56). While acknowledging the existence of fully asynchronous online e-learning, the report limits a call for e-learning to only "support or supplement offline provision, not simply replace it" (Bradwell, 2009, p. 56). Despite any predictions otherwise, while e-learning in general and full replacement (i.e. fully online) e-learning, in particular, continue to grow rapidly in the US, the emphasis on "supporting or supplementing" may, perhaps, more accurately reflect the current status view of e-learning in much of European higher education.

TEACHING MATHEMATICS ONLINE: BENEFITS AND CHALLENGES

As some authors have pointed out, mathematics e-learning is an emerging area of research and practice which combines e-learning (e.g. technology) issues with mathematics education (Engelbrecht & Harding, 2005; Juan et al., 2008). For example, most universities worldwide are currently integrating VLE's in their higher education programs. These web-based tools can be used to develop both alternative and complementary strategies to traditional F2F learning and permit the delivery of instructions to students who are time or place-constrained (Seufert et al., 2002). This, in turn, has been seen as a potential and efficient means of mitigating the problem, in some developed countries, where the current higher education infrastructure cannot easily accommodate the growing demand due to significant enrollment increases (Howell et al., 2003). Such e-learning platforms currently provide, for example, opportunities for students to conveniently access all or part of their course material, take tests, complete homework assignments, participate in various individual and/or collaborative learning activities, post questions for instructors or for collaborative group student problem solving, etc.

In the area of mathematics e-learning some of the emerging benefits are:

- Flexibility and convenience (Robinson, 2005)
- Improved instruction through adaptive systems that individualize the instructional approach (Clark & Feldon, 2005; Means, Toyama, Murphy, Bakia, & Jones, 2009).
- A reduction in the gap between theory and practice through the use of mathematics software that allows for the modeling and solving of real-world problems or case studies (Faulin et al., 2009).
- Provision of continuous evaluation processes: Students receive timely feedback about their academic progress during the course and, as some authors suggest, interactive self-assessment might improve students' academic results as well as their perception of learning (Peat, 2002).

In contrast, some important challenges have been identified:

- Significant variation in student demographic characteristics regarding incoming mathematics and computer skill sets (Simonson et al., 2003).
- High dropout rates and isolation risk: As Sweet (1986) and Truluck (2007) point out; distance-education programs tend to produce higher dropout rates than F2F education programs. The lack of a personal contact between the agents involved in the learning process increases the risk of a sense of isolation among students. Students may feel disconnected from the instructors as well as from other students.
- The challenge in providing pedagogically sound assessment and continuous feedback. Computer-assisted assessment can be leveraged for these purposes but there remains questions regarding the nature of questions used and problems regarding automated grading systems (e.g. granting students partial credit).
- When assessing at a distance, authorship of problem solutions may be particularly hard to determine in mathematics and mathematics-related subjects where answers tend to be more objective (versus the more varied and subjective nature of student responses typically found in writing-based disciplines; Trenholm, 2007; Juan et al., 2008).

MATHEMATICS E-LEARNING EXPERIENCES AT THE OPEN UNIVERSITY OF CATALONIA

In this section, we will discuss the insight gathered from our experiences in teaching mathematics online at the Open University of Catalonia (UOC) through the UOC Virtual Campus, a proprietary e-learning platform which has been developed and improved over the last decade to fulfill online students' and instructors' needs (Figure 1). The UOC is a purely-online university located in Barcelona, Spain, that has offered undergradu-

Figure 1. A typical session inside the UOC Virtual Campus

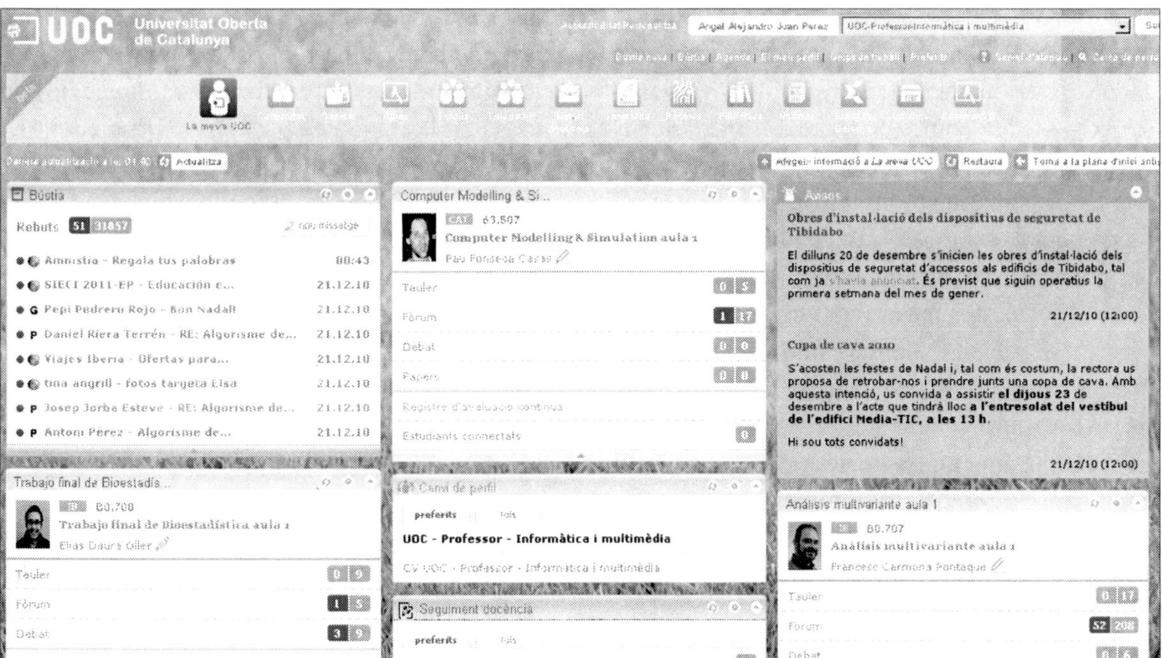

ate and graduate degrees since 1995. Currently, the Open University of Catalonia has more than 40,000 enrolled online students – most of them from Spain, but also includes a growing number of students from other Latin-American countries – and more than 500 online instructors. The UOC uses an asynchronous learning model, which follows a student-centered educational paradigm: at the beginning of the semester, students access the course's online classroom and, following the recommendations provided by their instructors, download a complete syllabus of the course along with all associated learning materials and resources. Throughout the course, students are encouraged to participate actively in discussion forums, to develop collaborative learning projects and, especially, to follow a scheduled continuous assessment process, which typically consists of four or five homework activities. By the end of the semester, students are required to take a short final exam, which in most courses is a F2F test that also helps validate authorship of homework activities. Of course, it is possible to state that learning mathematics-related contents at a distance using technology without F2F instructional support is not easy at all. Most UOC students are working adults, between 25 and 35 years old, and thus, in many cases, have left mathematics-related education several years ago. Therefore, they tend to suffer from a lack of basic statistical background which, additionally, causes them some anxiety. These problems should be addressed before starting the regular courses. For example, introductory courses on using web technology can help prepare students for the actual technological and pedagogical characteristics of the e-learning environment that they will use when completing a degree.

From our experience at the UOC, there are several key ideas to keep in mind when designing an efficient online environment and curricula. During the course development, instructors should make use of different available e-learning methods and strategies–such as dynamic presentations, laboratory tutorials, simulations, concept discussions, interaction and collaboration with other students– to support activity, exploration and creation, which could assist students in constructing their own mathematics knowledge. Students should learn mathematics by actively building new knowledge from experience and prior knowledge. Additionally, feedback from instructors and regular consultation by e-mail or posted notes are fundamental components of an efficient e-learning process. Another important issue to address is the efficiency of the evaluation process. In this sense, it is critical to define evaluation strategies that allow ensuring authorship of all online tests carried out during the semester. At the same time, final F2F exams might be necessary to complement those administered online. These exams should always be consistent –in contents and difficulty levels– with already performed tests. Throughout the course, mathematics and statistical software such as Wiris, Matlab, Minitab, SPSS or R is used by students to solve real-life problems since we follow a professionally-oriented approach. Finally, it should be noted that a mathematics e-learning curriculum is more than a collection of activities: it must be coherent, focused on important content, and it must efficiently integrate the use of mathematics software and Internet resources.

With respect to the challenges associated with learning mathematics online, it is important to highlight that focusing the course on problem-solving by using software contributes to overcoming possible deficiencies in students' mathematics background. Finally, the development of collaborative projects and discussion of common problems in forums help to increase interaction among students and also with the instructor.

MATHEMATICS E-LEARNING EXPERIENCES AT THE UNIVERSIDADE ABERTA

The Universidade Aberta (UAb) was founded in 1988 in Lisbon, Portugal as a pioneer in long-distance higher education with the mission to train large and geographically-disperse audiences. It has provided new opportunities for higher education training in around 24 countries worldwide (in Portugal, in Portuguese-speaking African countries and in several other parts of the world). The UAb currently has about 10,000 students and more than 8,000 student graduates (including about 1,100 masters level and about 100 PhD level students in various subject areas). The staff consists of about 200 instructors and 300 administrative staff employees. UAb is headquartered in Lisbon, with centers in Coimbra and Porto, as well as local learning centers in all district capital cities.

UAb's pedagogical model is based on modern e-learning pedagogies and the intensive use of new tools for on-line communication. This model, which promotes the interaction between students and teachers, is centered on the student as an active and individual builder of his own knowledge. It also allows for more flexibility in learning, where communication and interaction can take place anywhere and accords to the student possibilities for sharing resources, knowledge and collaborative activities. The evaluation of knowledge and skills is oriented as a continuous evaluation process. In undergraduate programs, students have a learning card where they invest throughout the course, preparing e-folios, crediting e-values and completing F2F tests. Students have as an option only one final exam. In graduate programs, the evaluation process is structured in very differently using tools such as: portfolios, blogs, projects, essays, problem solving, group discussions, reports and tests.

Currently the UAb uses Moodle for its virtual learning environment (Figure 2). Some advantages of Moodle are: (i) It facilitates communication by using chats, discussion rooms, e-mails, discussion forums; (ii) It includes tools which allow the creation of evaluation processes; (iii) It is simple to use and user-friendly; (iv) It allows the creation of groups of students to solve different exercises;

Figure 2. Screenshot of UAb online platform

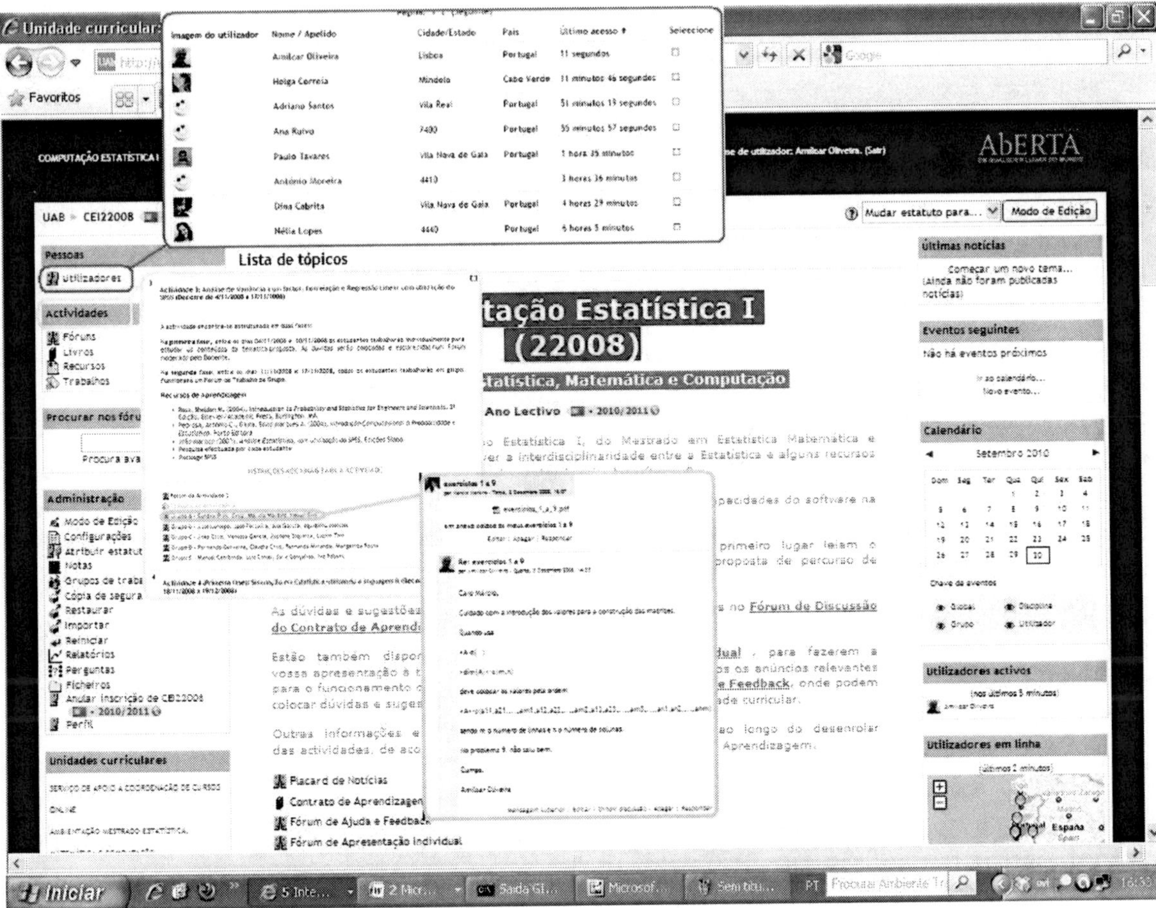

(v) It allows the possibility of writing in the LaTex editor (http://www.latex-project.org/).

Since on-line teaching requires technological skills from the students, all its certified programs include a free preparatory course. Therefore, students are able to acquire the necessary skills before entering the program in which they have enrolled. Moreover, in the case of students enrolled in mathematics courses, there is also a free course on LaTex which is offered every year. LaTex is designed to provide students with the ability to communicate with mathematical symbols such as in discussion forums. Using such introductory classes, to help students get accustomed to the online environment, is strongly recommended for any online education program but particularly in mathematics, given the challenges with two-way symbolic mathematics communication.

The use of computational resources and support in the field of teaching mathematics is becoming increasingly important. Resources, such as spreadsheets, programming languages, web applets, and educational software, can provide strong support for both online instructors and students. At the UAb, SPSS (Statistical Package for Social Sciences) was adopted as a tool in some of the Statistics courses, particularly in graduate courses. SPSS is particularly useful in performing applications of advanced statistics; Linear models such as GLM, mixed models, survival analysis, models for estimating variance, regression models, Anova and Manova. Some activities include exercises resolution using this tool. Another resource, CPLEX, is a software package that was adopted in UAb for use in courses in Operations Research area. However, both programs require commercial licenses for all students and professors. This is a major disadvantage since they are quite expensive.

One possible alternative is the recently developed R-project (http://www.r-project.org/). This is a free open source software program that is part of the larger GNU Project (http://www.gnu.org/), originally developed by Ross Ihaka and Robert Gentleman in the 90's using the language S. This open source resource includes, among other features, a language and an environment for computing and also has a large amount of functionality for Experimental Design or Design of Experiments (DOE). It appears to be an excellent tool for teaching and learning in particularly in online graduate courses, in statistical and mathematics-related areas.

MATHEMATICS E-LEARNING AT THE STATE UNIVERSITY OF NEW YORK

The State University of New York (SUNY) Learning Network (SLN) is a multiple award winning web-based learning network. It provides an estimated 4,000 fully online courses and 107 online degree programs to over 100,000 online students. While individual campuses are responsible for developing and running their own courses, SLN acts to facilitate this work by providing services (e.g. faculty training) and support. While some institutions have chosen to develop and maintain their own web-based learning network (institutions may opt to build and maintain their own network using software such as Blackboard), at present, of the total of 64 SUNY higher education institutions, SLN currently services over 30 (http://sln.suny.edu/as/as_history.shtml). While SLN has been primarily known for fully asynchronous e-learning, the system also supports hybrid (or blended) courses as well as the establishment of virtual presences for F2F course.

For many years the VLE for SLN was IBM's Lotus Notes. "Notes" provided a robust platform that enabled the network to become established. When IBM announced it would no longer support Lotus Notes, and after comparing several products, the commercial product Angel (http://www.angellearning.com) was chosen as the new VLE. The interface (Figure 3) resembles that of other well-known systems such as Blackboard and WebCT. As with any technology-based system, Angel continues to be tweaked and upgraded as new pedagogical tools are created and faculty become more proficient with the system functions.

The development of fully asynchronous e-learning within SLN has tended to focus on writing-based disciplines (tending towards the soft pure and applied in Biglan's taxonomy). Despite this, mathematics course offerings continue to grow. In the fall of 2010, approximately 200 fully asynchronous e-learning courses in mathematics were being offered state-wide. These courses range from basic numeracy to differential equations and linear algebra. Some of the major issues facing SLN mathematics faculty are universal. They are:

- Problems with efficient and naturalistic two-way symbolic communication: It remains a challenge to emulate or find an adequate replacement for mathematics communication traditionally conducted via the still ubiquitous "chalk and blackboard" or "pencil and scrap paper". The 'qwerty' represents an effectual communication bottleneck. This has presented a serious challenge for all learner-learner, learner-instructor and learner-interface interactions.
- Problems with aligning traditional mathematics pedagogy with the dominant e-learning learning theory: social constructivism.

Figure 3. SUNY Angel VLE Course Portal

- Problems with assessment, particularly summative, that attempts to live up to the "anytime, anywhere" creed typical with this form of instruction: While many writing-based courses traditionally will not require an invigilated exam component (utilizing term papers for example), math-based disciplines traditionally have used invigilated summative instruments as a major assessment component.

In comparison to the European system, it appears that much of US higher education practice places a heavier reliance on a partnership with the commercial textbook publishing sector. That is, where American students are likely to be required to purchase a textbook, European students are much less likely to be required to do so. It should then come as no surprise that US publishers have developed VLE's to supplement their textbooks (often sold to students in the form of "bundling" or stand-alone e-texts with VLE access). In mathematics, one of the most significant commercial contenders is Pearson's MyMathLab (MML; see Figure 4). VLE's are being developed with increasing sophistication that provide faculty with, among other provisions, preset question banks, automatic grading (with partial grading), individualized prescriptive study plans, a range of multimedia resources including animations and "canned" web-streamed lecture videos – all with increasing functionality. Currently, when SUNY e-learning faculty decide to use MML (or any other publisher-developed VLE), the student may be forced to contend with the use of two separate VLE's. This may entail Angel being used simply as a point of communication (email, announcements, etc.) whereas the publisher's VLE is used as the primary point of instruction. In these early days of development, it is still unclear how this situation will develop.

Figure 4. Sample Textbook Website VLE

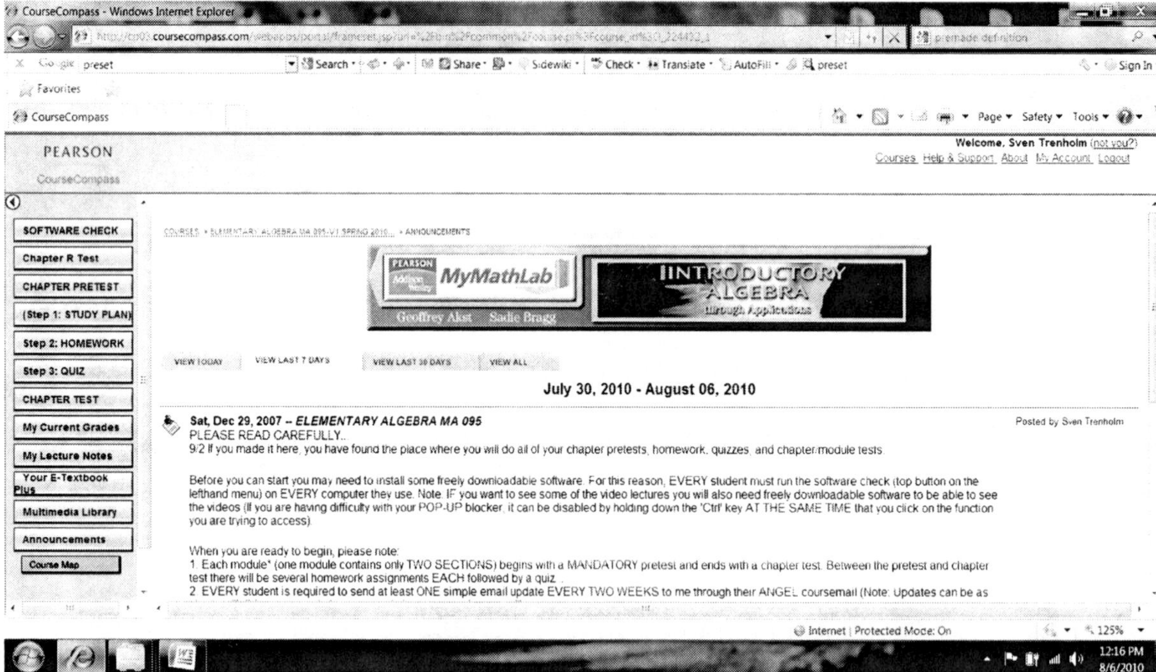

MATHEMATICS E-LEARNING EXPERIENCES AT THE MASSACHUSETTS INSTITUTE OF TECHNOLOGY

Massachusetts Institute of Technology (MIT) is one of the best-known private universities in the United States and has a reputation of being one of the best engineering schools in the world. While MIT does not offer fully online courses, in what they do offer, there is a clear acknowledgement of the importance of online technologies and their role within the educational arena. For example, MIT has advanced their reputation within the online education community with the development of several pioneering instructional tools such as Stellar (MIT's Course Management System) and MIT's OpenCourseWare website. The latter provides online resources for millions of users worldwide. The former, Stellar Course Management System (Figure 5), developed and maintained by the university's IT team, was designed to facilitate efficient communication between students and professors by taking advantage of emerging online technologies. This online platform provides students with a plethora of information on the courses they are taking, including course announcements, syllabi, course calendars, faculty contact information, etc. Meanwhile, it also helps facilitate the administrative role of professors and teaching assistants by providing a single tool from which they can communicate course information and provide course materials. Due to the success of Stellar, the school is using the platform in an effort to structure and standardize all of its course and curricula.

The OpenCourseWare (OCW) website (Figure 6) features a plethora of archival course materials from previously taught semesters. MIT's OCW was proposed in 2000 in order to provide a means of providing MIT course content for the purpose of global knowledge advancement. Currently, it hosts over 1,500 course material items and has achieved over 50 million visits as of 2009 (41%

Figure 5. Screenshot of MIT's Stellar Online Platform

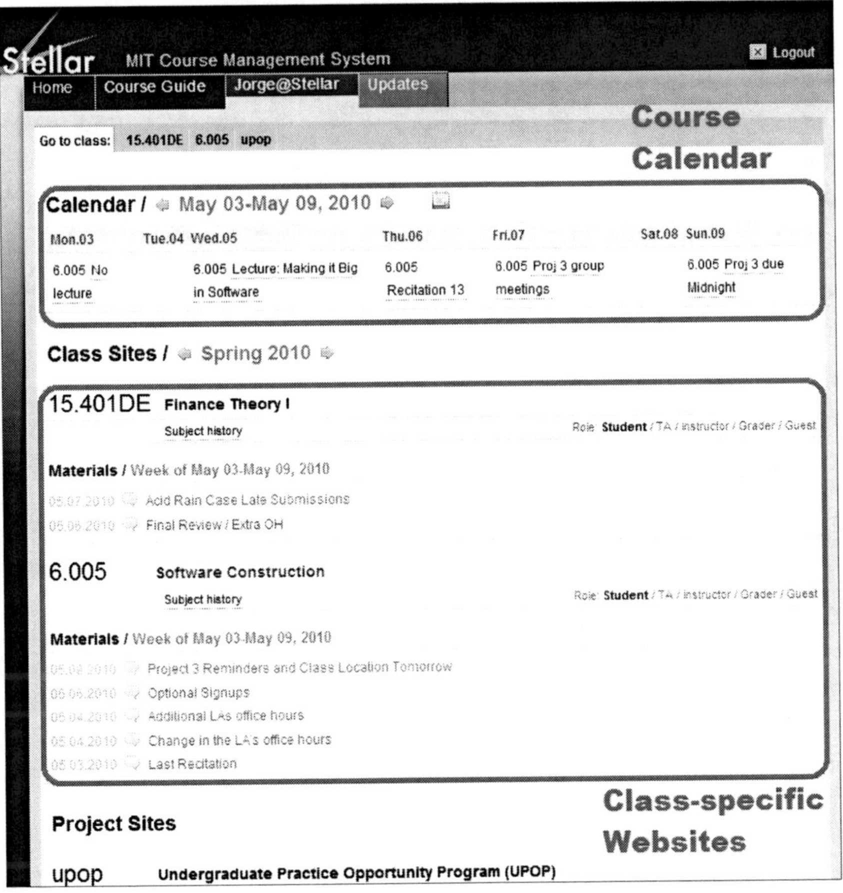

from North-America). The site contains previously used course materials, such as past exams that may help MIT students to prepare for their current courses and multimedia content such as video lectures and course notes for those individuals with a personal desire to advance their knowledge. Going forward, the OCW team is updating existing courses and adding new content and services to the site.

Table 1 shows the wide variety of reasons that users have found the OpenCourseWare website to be valuable; the users mostly include self-learners, students, and educators.

In addition to the OpenCourseWare website and Stellar, mathematics professors make use of a vast number of software programs, including web-based applications, to reinforce critical concepts that are presented in the classroom. Typically, a mathematics course is composed of 2-3 lectures taught by the professor and 2 recitations taught by a teaching assistant per week. In the lecture, new mathematics concepts are introduced and developed; while in recitation, the concepts are illustrated using examples. In case students have trouble mastering any concept, the professors and teaching assistants can be reached at any time of the day using the Stellar website or another course-specific website.

For most mathematics courses at MIT, the overall course grade is mainly composed of 2-3 mid-term exams, one final exam, and weekly assignments. When studying for the exams, students are encouraged to use the online resources to find sample problems to work on; review material such

Figure 6. Screenshot of MIT's OpenCourseWare website

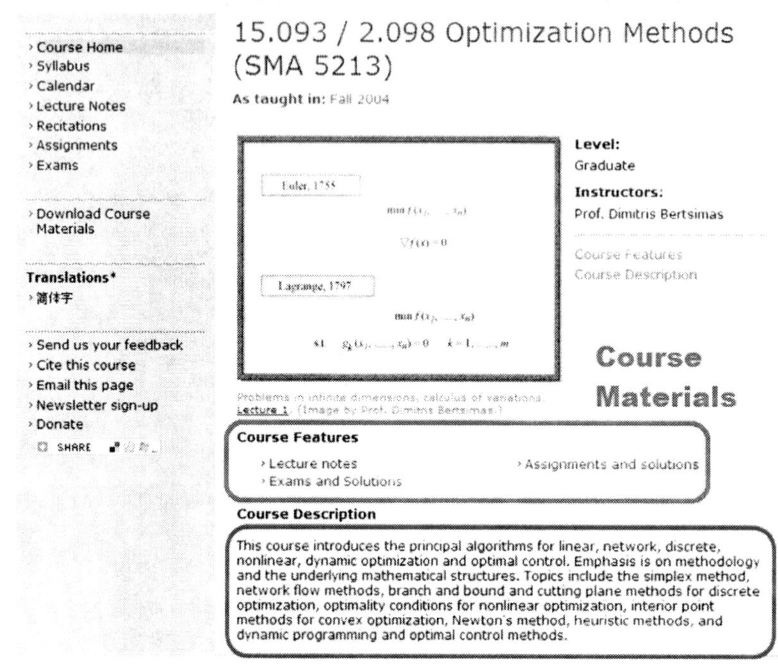

Table 1. Usage statistics of OpenCourseWare users (http://ocw.mit.edu/about/site-statistics/)

Use Scenario		% of Use
Educators	Improve personal knowledge	31%
	Learn new teaching methods	23%
	Incorporate OCW materials into a course	20%
	Find reference material for my students	15%
	Develop curriculum for my department or school	8%
Students	Enhance personal knowledge	46%
	Complement a current course	34%
	Plan a course of study	16%
Self Learners	Explore areas outside my professional field	40%
	Review basic concepts in my professional field	18%
	Prepare for future course of study	18%
	Keep current with developments in my field	17%
	Complete a work-related project or task	4%

as exams from previous terms or other online sample problems. The weekly assignments, however, rely much more heavily on online software programs and mathematics tools. They are posted online, either on Stellar or on the course-specific website, so that the students can browse and access them at their convenience. While a majority of the problems may involve traditional computation (i.e. completed without using any software tools) there is an increasing trend for professors to design their own problems using available software programs. As a whole, available software programs provide an alternate approach for students to be able to grasp and understand concepts in mathematics (e.g. graph or a time/phase-dependent illustration). Both professors and students seem to agree that using such programs, as well as online tools, enrich their mathematics intuition as well as their understanding of the material needed to serve as a foundation for their careers.

COMPARISON OF THE DIFFERENT MODELS

Tables 2 through 6 present some of the main characteristics for each of the mathematics e-learning networks discussed in the previous sections. Following these, some best practices and fundamental factors for successful mathematics-related online courses will be deduced.

COMMON PRACTICES AND USEFUL RECOMMENDATIONS

Reflecting on these four different long-term experiences offering mathematics instruction and full courses online, there are perhaps five fundamental factors that need to be addressed for successful design and developement. In particular:

- ***Core course learning materials:*** They constitute the main source of information for students during the learning process. They must be designed for independent learning. They must also provide students with an insight into all relevant aspects of the course. Ideally, these resources should be designed and written by the same individual who (or design group that) develops all of the assessments. Due to the intrinsic nature of the mathematics knowledge area, where students need to do a lot of thinking and annotations during the learning process, it is strongly recommended that core materials should also be available in PDF format for easy printing. These core learning materials can (and should) be complemented with additional learning materials and resources, such as applets, related articles, simulations, etc.
- ***The role of online instructors:*** Critical to the success of online instruction. There is a pedagogical imperative for the "human" provision of orientation, ongoing guidance and support as well as continuous and timely feedback throughout the learning process. This guidance should be developed through posted messages (e.g. at the beginning of each week) with clear instructions about which contents and activities must be completed in the short-term. While students progress through the course, support should be provided with quick responses to student posts in shared forums and e-mail. This feedback should be timely; provided no later than 48 hours from the posting of the question. Finally, if applicable, coordination among different instructors of the same course is important in order to guarantee homogeneity.
- ***For professionally-oriented courses in particular, effective use of mathematics software:*** Theoretically-oriented mathematics instruction might make sense for students in a pure mathematics degree program, but usually it is not the

Table 2. Summary of general information on each university

	Open University of Catalonia (UOC)	Universidade Aberta (UAb)	State University of New York (SUNY)	Massachusetts Institute of Technology (MIT)
Country	Spain	Portugal	USA	USA
Website	www.uoc.edu	www.uab.pt	www.suny.edu	www.mit.edu
Model	Purely online	Purely online	Purely online (Also supporting F2F blended and traditional)	Blended (face-to-face with web support)
Offering Online/ Blended Courses Since	1995	2007	1995	2000
Language	Catalan & Spanish	Portuguese	English	English
Number of Online Students	40,000	10,000	100,000	10,000*
Number of Online Instructors	500+	200+	approx. 3000	N/A
Number of Online Courses	1,500	830	4,000	2,000**
Relationship with Other Universities	High: most online instructors are professors at other universities.	High: maintains many contacts, programs and projects jointly with researchers around the world.	University level: Maintains quantity and quality of relationships consistent with a large state public university system. Community College level: No research requirements. Maintains limited collaborative research activities.	High: maintains strong research collaboration ties around the world.
Online Library	The UOC online library facilitates learning resources to students.	The UAb online library facilitates learning resources to students.	Links directly to individual campus library	The OpenCourseWare site provides free MIT course content.
Face to Face Activities	Inaugural session and proctored final exams.	Recitations and exams	Varies; More than half of the mathematics courses have no F2F requirements.	Lectures, recitations, and exams.
Students Profile	Most students between 25 and 40 years old. Most of them work while studying at UOC. In most cases, lack of mathematics background.	Most students between 25 and 45 years old. Most of them work while studying at UAb. Students come from various backgrounds and several countries.	Most students are female. More than half between 20 and 29 years. Vast majority work at least part-time while studying. Most require mathematics remediation	The undergraduates are between 18-24 years old, mostly studying as full-time students. Graduate students come from various backgrounds.

*Number of enrolled students in the traditional (non-online) education program at MIT
**Course materials available on OpenCourseWare website and Stellar system

best way to motivate students completing other degrees such as Computer Science or Telecommunications. Therefore, it is important that students understand what mathematics courses provide in terms of practical concepts and skills (i.e. authentic or real world learning). Such an approach is likely to be more appreciated by students and will likely contribute to higher levels of motivation. The available mathematics-related software is of such high quality (Swain, 2009) that the issue is not as much which specific software to use but how

Table 3. Math-related education and research

	Open University of Catalonia (UOC)	Universidade Aberta (UAb)	State University of New York (SUNY)	Massachusetts Institute of Technology (MIT)
Math-related Undergraduate Courses	Computer Science, Electrical Engineering, Business Management.	Computer Science, Management, Sciences, Mathematics.	Applied Mathematics, Business Management, Economics, Finance	Engineering, Sciences, Economics, Management, Mathematics.
Math-related Graduate Courses	Computer Science, Electrical Engineering, Business Management, Bioinformatics & Biostatistics, Financial Mathematics.	Computer Science, Management, Sciences, Mathematics.	Accountancy, Business	Engineering, Sciences, Economics, Management, Mathematics.
Number of Mathematics Courses Online	50+	70	180+	N/A (only blended)
Mathematics Innovation Projects	Video tutorials, online labs, online editor for equations, online repositories with solved exercises, labs and exams, digitalization of hand-writing formulas.	Video tutorials, software exercices.	Video tutorials, interactive online instruction, online editor for equations,	Video lectures, online labs and problem sets, online problem solving, exams and assignments, software exercises.
Math-related Research Areas	Operations Research, Computer Science, Artificial Intelligence, Mathematics E-Learning, Educational Data Analysis.	Operations Research, Mathematics, Computer Science.	Varies among 25+ University Colleges and Centers	Mathematics, Computer Science, Engineering, Economics, Sciences.
Academic Staff per Course	For each course, there is a coordinator (full-time) and several online instructors (part-time).	For each course, there is a coordinator (full-time) and several online tutors (part-time).	Each course is administered by an average of one professor supported by SUNY SLN tech support.	Each course is administered by an average of one course administrator, two professors, and three teaching assistants.

Table 4. VLE and software descriptions

	Open University of Catalonia (UOC)	Universidade Aberta (UAb)	State University of New York (SUNY)	Massachusetts Institute of Technology (MIT)
Virtual Learning Environment (VLE)	UOC Virtual Campus	Moodle	Angel	Stellar
VLE Ownership	Proprietary	Open Source	Commercial	Proprietary
VLE Special Features	Integrates mathematics software (Wiris) and online editor for mathematics formulas.	Wikis to share documents	Mathematics equation editor	Provides links to previous repositories. Simple communications tools.
Other Platforms and Groupware	BSCW, Skype, DropBox.	Skype	Textbook websites	Course-specific websites, Athena.
Mathematics Commercial Software	Wiris, Matlab, Minitab, SPSS.	SPSS	e.g. MyMathLab, Maple. SPSS, Minitab	Matlab, Mathematica, Maple. Simulink, Stata.
Mathematics Open Source Software	Octave, R.	Latex, R	-	LaTex, R, GNUPlot, Maxima, SPlus.

Table 5. Teaching/Learning methodology

Information technologies & mathematics software	**Open University of Catalonia (UOC)**	**Universidade Aberta (UAb)**	**State University of New York (SUNY)**	**Massachusetts Institute of Technology (MIT)**
Size of Online Classes	Between 20 and 75 students per class.	Máx 50	Varies; average of 20-30	Between 10 and 700 students per class.*
Class Dynamics	Regular use of posted notes, forums, assisted debates and e-mail.	Posted notes, group discussion and e-mail.	e.g. Regular use of posted announcements, emphasis on threaded discussions.	Lectures, posted course notes, group discussions and email.
Learning Resources	PDF or Web materials developed by the instructors and published by the UOC Editorial.	Materials written and developed by professors.	Materials written and developed by professors AND/OR textbook website resources	Materials written and developed by professors and teaching assistants.
Web Resources	Online repository with solved exercises, labs and exams from previous semesters	Exams from previous semesters, Applets	Varies	MIT OpenCourseWare and Stellar website contain both previous and current course materials.
Learning Approach	Professionally oriented, applied & problem-solving approach, intensive use of mathematics software.	Emphasis on conceptual knowledge, problem-solving approach, intensive use of mathematics and programming software.	Varies but general emphasis on constructivist approaches (e.g. collaborative learning via the use of threaded discussions)	Heavy emphasis on conceptual knowledge, problem-solving & project-based approach, intensive use of mathematics and programming software.
Evaluation System	Continuous Assessment + Proctored Final Exam.	Continuous Assessment + Proctored Final Exam.	Varies. There is a general emphasis, which tends to be associated with un-proctored courses, of continuous assessment that emphasizes "assessment for learning". The majority of mathematics courses are un-proctored.	Problem Sets, Projects (both individual- and group-based), Exams, Final Exmas.

*Traditional face-to-face classes, since online classes are not offered at MIT.

to effectively integrate it into the course curriculum.

- ***Continuous evaluation process:*** To keep students engaged a continuous evaluation system is imperative (some would argue even more imperative for mathematics instruction) given how strongly related it is to the issue of motivation which thus can significantly contribute to reducing drop-out rates during the semester. Depending on the student demographic, online courses that only require one single final exam and perhaps two to four class tests may not be successful.
- ***VLE usability:*** The most important aspect of any VLE is its usability, i.e., students and instructors should feel comfortable using the VLE and all main options should be intuitive and easy to find. For mathematics courses, as with any other discipline, the system should be able to facilitate an online space for posting instructor's notes – official messages from instructors to students – and another space for students to post notes and hold debates and discussions regarding the course contents. Other desirable VLE options would be the inclusion of a native equation editor and a monitoring feature

Table 6. Factors of success and main challenges

	Open University of Catalonia (UOC)	Universidade Aberta (UAb)	State University of New York (SUNY)	Massachusetts Institute of Technology (MIT)
Key Factors of the Model	(1) Online instructors provide continuous guidance and quick feedback; (2) Continuous assessment system; (3) Up-to-date learning materials developed by instructors; (4) Professionally oriented approach & use of mathematics software; (5) VLE usability.	(1) Online instructors provide continuous guidance and quick feedback; (2) Continous evaluation process through assignments and multiple exams throughout the term; (3) Consistent use of mathematics software; (4) Up-to-date course materials designed by current professors.	Varies; Generally, individual instructors from individual institutions have control over the pedagogy. Typically: (1) SLN, at its core, uses threaded discussions for continuous student-centered, instructor-guided instruction and feedback. (2) Many follow traditional F2F pedagogical approach online.	(1) Continous evaluation process through assignments and multiple exams throughout the term. (2) Focus on conceptual knowledge through problem solving and short-term projects. (3) Consistent use of mathematics software. (4) Up-to-date course materials designed by current professors
Relevant Challenges	(1) Most students have to face professional and personal duties; (2) Students might have a lack of recent mathematics background; (3) Online mathematics students might need extra motivation; drop-out rates; (4) Digital writing of mathematics equations is time-consuming; (5) Monitoring students' evolution is a hard task.	(1) Most students have to face professional and personal duties; (2) Differences in individual learning processes and backgrounds; (3) Differences in origin; students coming from different countries have different skills and needs; (4) Digital writing of mathematics equations by latex preliminary course.	(1) Most students have to face professional and personal duties; (2) Students might have a lack of recent or poor mathematics background; (3) Online mathematics students might need extra motivation; drop-out rates; (4) Digital writing of mathematics equations is time-consuming;	(1) Heavy workload from other classes may decrease the student's time commitment, (2) Differences in individual learning processes and backgrounds. (3) Large class sizes decrease the possibility of one-to-one interaction. (4) Maintaining a comfortable level of difficulty throughout the course.

that could provide regular feedback on students' activity and performance (Juan et al., 2009). While some progress has been made towards the provision of naturalistic two-way communication in virtual learning environments (i.e. given the heavily symbolic nature of mathematics), progress has yet to be made whereby the efficiency of hand-written communication has been replicated. In this respect, software and hardware developments are ongoing.

CONCLUSION

In the absence of consensus literature on best practices, and with the steady growth in both pure and blended online mathematics course offerings, the comparative experiences described in this chapter are offered to help instructors and course developers in their own development and teaching of mathematics online.

With the current growth in the use of e-learning technologies such as VLE's, traditional pedagogic approaches are being challenged including the nature of the roles played by both instructors and students. This new context, with less F2F interaction, requires a particularly unique teaching and learning approach. In this chapter, by drawing on our long-term experiences at four different universities, we have described some of the benefits and challenges associated with teaching mathematics online. We also highlight what we believe to be the main factors that need to be carefully considered when offering online courses in mathematics or related subjects. As a whole, these case studies speak to the viability of teaching mathematics online and also present principles that provide some direction for those considering and actively involved in online mathematics instruction.

ACKNOWLEDGMENT

This work has been partially supported by the IN3-HAROSA KC (http://dpcs.uoc.edu).

REFERENCES

Allen, I., & Seaman, J. (2008). *Staying the course: Online education in the United States*. Needham, MA: The Sloan Consortium. Retrieved August 10, 2010 from http://www.sloan-c.org/ publications/ survey/ index.asp

Beldarrain, Y. (2006). Distance education trends: Integrating new technologies to foster student interaction and collaboration. *Distance Education*, *27*(2), 139–153. doi:10.1080/01587910600789498

Bell, S. (2010). External students at the people's university. Retrieved August 10, 2010, from http:// www.bbc.co.uk/ news/ 10285568

Bernard, R. M., Abrami, P. C., Lou, Y., Borokhovski, E., Wade, A., & Wozney, L. (2004). How does distance education compare with classroom instruction? A meta-analysis of the empirical literature. *Review of Educational Research*, *74*(3), 379. doi:10.3102/00346543074003379

Bradwell, P. (2009). *The edgeless university: Why higher education must embrace technology*. London, UK: DEMOS think tank.

Clark, R. E., & Feldon, D. F. (2005). Five common but questionable principles of multimedia learning . In Mayer, R. (Ed.), *Cambridge handbook of multimedia learning*. Cambridge, UK: Cambridge University Press.

Collis, B., & Wende, M. (2002). *Models of technology and change in higher education: An international comparative survey on the current and future use of ICT in higher education*. Retrieved August 10, 2010, from http://doc.utwente.nl/ 44610/

Engelbrecht, J., & Harding, A. (2005). Teaching undergraduate mathematics on the Internet. Part 1: Technologies and taxonomy. *Educational Studies in Mathematics*, *58*, 235–252. doi:10.1007/s10649-005-6456-3

Faulin, J., Juan, A., Fonseca, P., Pla, L. M., & Rodriguez, S. V. (2009). Learning operations research online: Benefits, challenges, and experiences. *International Journal of Simulation and Process Modelling*, *5*(1), 42–53. doi:10.1504/IJSPM.2009.025826

Glenn, M. (2008). *The future of higher education: How technology will shape learning*. Austin, TX: New Media Consortium.

Howell, S. L., Williams, P. B., & Lindsay, N. K. (2003). Thirty-two trends affecting distance education: An informed foundation for strategic planning. *Online Journal of Distance Learning Administration*, *6*(3), 1–18.

Hrastinski, S. (2008). Asynchronous & Synchronous E-Learning. *Educase Quarterly*, *4*, 51–55.

Juan, A., Daradoumis, T., Faulin, J., & Xhafa, F. (2009). SAMOS: A model for monitoring students' and groups' activity in collaborative e-learning. *International Journal of Learning Technology*, *4*(1/2), 53–72. doi:10.1504/IJLT.2009.024716

Juan, A., Huertas, M., Steegmann, C., Corcoles, C., & Serrat, C. (2008). Mathematical e-learning: State of the art and experiences at the Open University of Catalonia. *International Journal of Mathematical Education in Science and Technology*, *39*, 455–471. doi:10.1080/00207390701867497

Lera, F., Juan, A., Faulin, J., & Cavaller, V. (2009). Monitoring students' activity and performance in online higher education: A European perspective . In Juan, A. A., Daradoumis, T., Xhafa, F., Caballé, S., & Faulin, J. (Eds.), *Monitoring and assessment in online collaborative environments: Emergent computational technologies for e-learning support* (pp. 132–148). Hershey, PA: IGI Global. doi:10.4018/978-1-60566-786-7.ch008

Mayadas, A. F., Bourne, J., & Bacsich, P. (2009). Online education today. *Science*, *323*(5910), 85. doi:10.1126/science.1168874

Means, B., Toyama, Y., Murphy, R., Bakia, M., & Jones, K. (2009). *Evaluation of evidence-based practices in online learning: A meta-analysis and review of online learning studies*. Washington, D.C.: U.S. Department of Education Center for Technology in Learning.

Nagy, A. (2005). The impact of e-learning . In Bruck, P., Buchholz, A., Karssen, Z., & Zerfass, A. (Eds.), *E-content: Technologies and perspectives for the European market* (pp. 79–96). Berlin, Germany: Springer-Verlag.

Peat, M., & Franklin, S. (2002). Supporting student learning. The use of computer-based formative assessment modules. *British Journal of Educational Technology*, *33*(5), 45–55. doi:10.1111/1467-8535.00288

Robinson, L. A. (2005). Consumers of online instruction. *Issues in Information Systems*, *6*, 170–175.

Schneckenberg, D. (2006). *E-competence in European higher education-ICT policy goals, change processes and research perspectives. The challenge for e-competence in academic staff development*. Centre for Excellence in Teaching and Learning NUIG & European eCompetence Initiative.

Schneckenberg, D. (2009). Understanding the real barriers to technology-enhanced innovation in higher education. *Educational Research*, *51*(4), 411–424. doi:10.1080/00131880903354741

Schwartzman, R. (2007). Refining the question: How can online instruction maximize opportunities for all students? *Communication Education*, *56*(1), 113–117. doi:10.1080/03634520601009728

Seufert, S., Lechner, U., & Stanoevska, K. (2002). A reference model for online learning communities. *International Journal on E-Learning*, *1*(1), 43–54.

Simonson, M., Smaldino, S., Albright, M., & Zvacek, S. (2003). *Teaching and learning at a distance: Foundations of distance education*. Upper Saddle River, NJ: Merrill, Prentice Hall.

Swain, J. (2009). A long way from flip charts. *ORMS Today*, *36*(1), 44–47.

Sweet, R. (1986). Student drop-out in distance education: An application of Tinto's model. *Distance Education*, *7*(2), 201–213. doi:10.1080/0158791860070204

Trenholm, S. (2007). An investigation of assessment in fully asynchronous online math courses. *International Journal for Educational Integrity*, *3*(2), 41–55.

Truluck, J. (2007). Establishing a mentoring plan for improving retention in online graduate degree programs. *Online Journal of Distance Learning Administration*, *10*(1), 1–6.

Vincent-Lancrin, S. (2005). *E-learning in tertiary education*. OECD Policy Briefs. Retrieved August 10, 2010, from http://www.cumex.org.mx/ archivos/ ACERVO/ ElearningPolicy briefenglish.pdf

Section 3
Mathematics Software & Web Resources for Mathematics E-Learning

Chapter 13
My Equations are the Same as Yours!
Computer Aided Assessment Using a Gröbner Basis Approach

M. Badger
University of Birmingham, UK

C. J. Sangwin
University of Birmingham, UK

ABSTRACT

In this chapter we explain how computer aided assessment (CAA) can automatically assess an answer that consists of a system of equations. In particular, we will use a computer algebra system (CAS) and Buchberger's Algorithm to establish when two systems of equations are the "same."

INTRODUCTION

Our primary concern in this chapter is the assessment of mathematics with computers, and in particular the ability of CAA software to provide automatic feedback in a formative setting to support students. We focus on mathematical methods that allow for the assesment and provision of feedback on questions involving systems of equations. In Section 1 we consider word exercises. These, we argue, are an important component in mathematics education. In Section 2 we discuss computer aided assessment of mathematics and the role of feedback in CAA. Section 3 covers the mathematics underpinning systems of equations. We discuss what it means to solve equations, and when two systems are the same. We examine Euclid's algorithm and Gaussian elimination and then move onto Gröbner basis techniques for manipulating systems of polynomial equations. Section 4 combines the previous topics by explaining how we can automatically assess the modelling

DOI: 10.4018/978-1-60960-875-0.ch013

component of answers to word exercises using the STACK computer aided assessment system.

Word Exercises and Modelling

The motivation for the work discussed in this chapter is the desire to improve the ability of computer aided assessment to deal with questions that involve modelling. There is a general consensus among researchers of mathematics education that problem solving and modelling are important skills for students of the mathematical sciences. Blum and Niss [1991] offered an overview of arguments for and against such training, their view being summed up in the following quote:

Mastering mathematics can no longer be considered equivalent to knowing a set of mathematical facts. It requires also the mastering of mathematical processes, of which problem solving - in the broadest sense - occupies a predominant position.

In *Mathematical Discovery* [Pólya, 1981, pg. 59], Polya asserts that word problems in particular deserve a special place on the mathematical curriculum:

I hope that I shall shock a few people in asserting that the most important single task of mathematical instruction in the secondary schools is to teach the setting up of equations to solve word problems. Yet there is a strong argument in favor of this opinion. In solving a word problem by setting up equations, the student translates a real situation into mathematical terms; he has an opportunity to experience that mathematical concepts may be related to realities, but such relations must be carefully worked out.

In their report *Mathematics for the European Engineer - A Curriculum for the Twenty-First Century* [Mustoe & Lawson, 2002], SEFI, the Société Européenne pour la Formation des Ingénieurs, wrote

The ability to formulate a mathematical model of a given physical situation, to solve the model, interpret the solution and refine the model is a key aspect of the mathematical development of an engineer.

Word exercises serve as an introduction to modelling and problem solving in general as they require a student to transcribe a situation described in words to a system of equations [Sangwin, 2010]. Such transcription is not as straightforward as one may assume; in [1981] Clement et al. gave the example of the Students-and-Professors Problem:

Example 1

Write an equation for the following statement: "There are six times as many students as professors at this university." Use S for the number of students and P for the number of professors.

When this was given to 150 calculus level students, 37% answered incorrectly with $6S=P$ accounting for two thirds of all errors, [Clement et al, 1981].

Given that students can experience such difficulties with problems that contain very little in the way of technical mathematics, a CAA system that has the ability to pose and mark word exercises could be a very useful tool to a teacher. Asking students to transcribe a given situation into a system of equations creates a number of challenges when it comes to the system marking responses. Choices of variables, co-ordinate systems or origin may lead to situations where correct answers differ greatly in appearance. It is important that a CAA system can handle deftly such differences; marking a correct answer as incorrect could have serious repercussions for a student.

While the student and professors problem contains an element of *modelling*, there are other types of word problems. A comprehensive classification of 1097 high-school algebra story problems was developed by [Mayer, 1981]. The following is a typical example.

Example 2

Chris takes 10 hours to walk up a mountain and back down by the same route. He averages 2km per hour on the way up and 3km per hour on the way down. How far was it from the base to the top of the mountain?

For the purposes of Mayer's analysis, a "story problem" is more complex than an arithmetic question, but requires a numerical answer (not an equation as with the Students-and-Professors problem) and is stated in words with a story line. Hence "A rectangle has an area $80m^2$ and its length is 2m more than its width: find the perimeter" is not a 'story'. Such problems are first placed into major *families* based on their *source formulae*. In our example the source formula involves distance, rate and time: $d = r \times t$, or $d = v \times t$ since our rate is velocity. Interestingly, the language used to write story problems contains only three kinds of proposition.

- Values are assigned to variables, e.g. time taken to walk up =10.
- Relationships between variables, e.g. distance up = distance back.
- Identification of the unknown or goal, e.g. GOAL = distance up.

Within families are *categories*, which are further refined into *templates*.

Problems belong to the same template if they share the same story line and same list of propositions, regardless of the actual values assigned to each variable, the actual relation assigned to a pair of variables, or which variable is assigned to the unknown. (Mayer 1981, pg. 145)

Our example problem is an instance of the *round-trip* template, which is a sub-category of the *distance- time* category of the *rate* family. The underlying system of equations can be written as

Table 1. Round-trip template variables and meanings

Variable	Interpretation	Value
d_1	distance 1 (up)	GOAL
d_2	distance 2 (down)	
d_t	total distance	
t_1	time 1 (up)	
t_2	time 2 (down)	
t_t	total time	10h
v_1	rate 1 (up)	2km/h
v_2	rate 2 (down)	3km/h

$$d_t = d_1 + d_2 \quad (1)$$

$$t_t = t_1 + t_2 \quad (2)$$

$$d_1 = v_1 \times t_1 \quad (3)$$

$$d_2 = v_2 \times t_2 \quad (4)$$

$$d_1 = d_2 \quad (5)$$

where the meaning of each variable, and the values from our example, are given in Table 1.

Substituting in these values results in the following system of equations

$$\{d_t = d_1 + d_2, 10 = t_1 + t_2, d_1 = 2t_1, d_2 = 3t_2, d_1 = d_2\}$$

Since d_t is unspecified, un-required and unused elsewhere, the first equation contributes nothing. The last can be used to eliminate d_2 resulting in an equivalent system

$$\{d_t = 2d_1, d_2 = d_1, 10 = t_1 + t_2, d_1 = 2t_1, d_2 = 3t_2\}$$

This has solution set $\{d_t = 24, d_1 = 12, d_2 = 12, t_1 = 4, t_2 = 6\}$.

In order to assess students' answers to questions such as Example 2, and give them worthwhile feedback in the process, we need to have a robust system for comparing the systems of equations that result.

Computer Aided Assessment

Assessment is a key component in all learning. Early CAA systems implemented only multiple choice questions (MCQs), selections, matchings and true/false interactions. No matter how carefully written, the teacher is often forced to give the game away by presenting choices up front. In choosing a response the student only has to verify which potential response satisfies the given conditions, reducing the process of creating a solution to that of verifying an answer. This is particularly problematic when asking students to "solve" equations, or find equations which model particular situations, the format invalidates the question.

Since 2000, a number of specialist computer aided assessment systems have used an existing CAS to provide tools to assess mathematical expressions as answers. Perhaps the first system to make a mainstream CAS a central feature was the AiM System [Klai et al, 2000], which operates using Maple, as does the Wallis system and the proprietary system MapleTA. Other systems have acces to a different CAS, such as CABLE which uses AXIOM. Such CAA systems use a computer algebra system to randomly generate instances of a problem, allowing students to enter a response which is a *mathematical statement or expression,* and then assess these answers. Deciding whether a student's answer is "correct" frequently means establishing some well-defined properties. The teacher has to articulate these properties and they may also wish, particularly in a formative setting, to generate feedback to help students learn.

STACK [Sangwin and Grove 2006], a *system for teaching and assessment with a computer algebra kernel,* is an open-source CAA system with an emphasis on formative assessment. Developed since 2005, STACK uses the CAS Maxima, also released under the GPL. As with other CAS-based CAAs, STACK works by determining properties of a student's answer. This allows the system to can pose randomised questions, and those such as "Give an example of a function $f(x)$ with a minimum at $x=0$ and a maximum at $x=2$." Multi-part questions are supported, and answers are fed into a *potential response tree*, which allows a teacher to tailor feedback and assign partial marks in instances where students have made common mistakes or deserve some credit for their work.

It is widely asserted that "feedback promotes learning", however the research evidence is less clear. For example, Kluger & DeNisi [1996] examined about 1300 studies and found that, of the 131 feedback interventions which met basic validity and reliability criteria, over one third *decreased performance*: a counterintuitive and largely ignored outcome. It is not feedback itself but the nature of the feedback which determines whether it is effective. Specific *task related* feedback, e.g. how to improve performance, is found to be effective whereas feedback which focuses on the *self* is detrimental. A summary mark may be interpreted as a personal comment, e.g. *"only 45% – you aren't very good at maths are you?"* This may be more harmful than no feedback at all, see for example [Shute, 2007]. 'Task-aware' CAA systems therefore have more to offer the student than do simple correct/incorrect MCQs. Furthermore, it is claimed by [Hassmén & Hunt, 1994], and others, that the MCQ format itself has inherent gender bias.

While syntax is a significant barrier for students, e.g. [Sangwin and Ramsden, 2007], our focus here will be on establishing certain mathematical properties of systems of equations which are answers to mathematical problems. Therefore, we assume the student has entered their intended system of equations.

Once the student has entered their answer into a CAA system such as STACK, the system then compares this answer to the teacher's. In

STACK, the teacher may (i) use CAS commands to manipulate the student's answer and (ii) use pre-defined *answer tests* to establish mathematical properties, such as equivalence with the teacher's answer. Given a student's and a teacher's answers, the output of an answer test is a triple consisting of a numerical *mark*, text-based *feedback* for the student and a *note* for statistical analysis. In broad terms, the *mark* is summative, the *feedback* is formative and the *note* is evaluative. The *mark* and *feedback* are displayed to the student on the screen, though the teacher may choose to hide these on a question by question basis. The *note* is stored in the database for later statistical analysis by the teacher. These answer tests are linked together into a tree structure, enabling the teacher to establish a variety of properties, as the precise situation demands. Each test may provide or modify feedback based on whether a particular test passes or fails.

By using a CAS to determine the various properties of an answer, the feedback which STACK can give to students can be specific and effective. For example, if a student is asked to find the integral of an expression, and is correct but for a constant of integration, the system gives the feedback "You need to add a constant of integration, otherwise this appears to be correct. Well done."

The aim of the work discussed here was the creation of an answer test for STACK that compares systems of equations and provides useful and robust feedback to the student. In the next section we discuss equations and their comparison using modern mathematical techniques.

Systems of Equations

The equals sign, =, was invented by the Welshman Robert Recorde for use in his book *The Whetstone of Witte*, the first book on Algebra written in Britain [Stedall, 2002, pg. 41], published in 1557. Recorde explained his reasoning thus:

...to avoid the tedious repetition of these words: "is equal to", I will set (as I do often in work use) a pair of parallels of one length (thus =), because no two things can be more equal.

Since its invention, nearly 1900 years after the publication of Euclid's Elements, the equals sign has become arguably the most important symbol in mathematics, allowing us to assert the equality of two expressions with unparalleled brevity. An equation is a triple consisting of two well-formed mathematical expressions and an equals sign; a statement, saying *these two things are equal to one another*. Some equations, such as $3 + 4 = 7$ and $11 + 12 = 25$, can be said to be true or false. However, we cannot say whether or not the equation $x + 4 = 11$ is true, because we do not know the value of x. We can *solve* it, i.e. we assume it to be true, and determine the set of values, possibly empty, of variables which maintain its veracity. Using the equality symbol to denote an equation yet to be solved ($x^2 + 1 = 0$) and as a binary infix operator, returning Boolean values *true* or *false* were just two of the six possible uses identified by [Bradford et al, 2009]. Two further uses we have cause to consider here are the assignment of a value to a variable ($x = 1$) and to define a function ($f(x) = x^2$).

To solve equations we apply injective functions to both sides; an extension of the first three *common notions* of Euclid's Elements [Euclid, 1965]:

- Things equal to the same thing are also equal to one another.
- If equals be added to equals the results are equal.
- If equals be subtracted from equals, the remainders are equal.

With our equation $x + 4 = 11$, we may apply the function $f: y \rightarrow -4$ to both sides, giving:

$x + 4 = 11$

$f(x + 4) = f(11)$

$x + 4 - 4 = 11 - 4$

$x = 7$

There are two things to note here. Firstly, it is highly unlikely that someone trying to solve such an equation as $x+4=11$ will go through the rigmarole of explicitly defining the function f, and will instead subtract the appropriate number from either side. It is important to recognise that this is what is happening, however. Secondly, we previously mentioned the restriction that f be an injective function. This is because we must ensure that $x = y \Leftrightarrow f(x) = f(y)$, the definition of an injective function. Thus the function $g: y \rightarrow \sin(y)$ will not suffice because $\sin(x) = \sin(y)$ does not guarantee that $x = y$.

Given a number of equations, we may form a *system of equations* from them. A system of equations is a set of equations, each of which is asserted to be true. For example,

$$\left.\begin{matrix} x + 4 = 11 \\ x = 7 \end{matrix}\right\}$$

is a system of equations. The conventional form for such systems is to write them as a list of equations whose right hand sides are all zero. Thus our example reduces to the somewhat straightforward

$$\left.\begin{matrix} x - 7 = 0 \\ x - 7 = 0 \end{matrix}\right\}$$

If we wrote our system as a *set* we would have the reduction

$$\{x + 4 = 11, x = 7\} \rightarrow \{x - 7 = 0\}.$$

Notice here we have *removed duplicate* elements of the set, using a syntactic definition of equality to recognise sameness of equations written in canonical form. Canonical form is an important concept in computer aided assessment; if we place no restrictions (such as a fraction in lowest terms) on how a student enters their answer, we must reduce both theirs and the teacher's answer to canonical form to compare them.

We introduce a notational convention in which we think of a system of equations all equal to zero as being equivalent to a set of expressions $\{e_1, \ldots, e_n\}$. The set of solutions of such a system is a set of assignments of the variables in the equations such that each equation holds. This set of solutions is called the *variety* of the system. Where there is only one variable, we usually write the variety simply as a set of numbers without reference to the variable. For example, the equations $x^2 - 5x + 6 = 0$ and $x^2 - 3x + 2 = 0$ have solutions $\{2, 3\}$ and $\{1, 2\}$ respectively, so the solution to the system of equations

$$\{x^2 - 5x + 6 = 0, x^2 - 3x + 2 = 0\} \tag{6}$$

is $\{2,3\} \cap \{1,2\} = \{2\}$. This leads us to a fact about solving systems of polynomial equations: given a set of univariate polynomials $\{e_1, \ldots, e_n\}$, the solution of the system of equations $e_1 = 0, \ldots, e_n = 0$ is the solution of the highest common factor of the set of expressions, $HCF(e_1, \ldots, e_n) = 0$. With (6) above:

$$x^2 - 3x + 2 = (x - 2)(x - 1) = 0 \tag{7}$$

and indeed we see that the highest common factor of our two expressions is $(x - 2)$.

The Sameness of Systems of Equations

Systems of equations arise as the result of mathematical modelling. However, there are many choices to be made when modelling a situation, many of which are often taken for granted. For example, in dealing with a clock-face or other circular object, we may choose to use polar co-ordinates rather than cartesian; in cases where position is important we may choose different points of origin. No process yet exists that can encompass the vast range of possibilities when modelling any situation; the best we can hope for is to develop tools that cope with as wide a range of situations as effectively as possible.

Two systems of equations are "the same" when they describe the same situation; that is to say, they have the same solutions. Thus two systems are defined to be equal if and only if their varieties coincide. Take for example the following two systems

$$\{x^3 - 2x^2 - x - 2 = 0, \quad x^3 + x^2 - 4x - 4 = 0\}, \tag{8}$$

$$\{x^2 - x - 2 = 0\} \tag{9}$$

As with our previous example, we can apply Euclid's algorithm to both (8) and (9) to find that they have the same variety, $\{-1,2\}$. It is important to note that two systems need not have the same number of equations, nor polynomials of the same degree, for their varieties to coincide, as it is how the equations in a system interact that is key.

We now hit upon the crux of the matter: if we ask a student to model some particular situation by writing down a system of equations that describes it, they may not choose the same equations as we do. No one person is more correct than another if the varieties of such systems are equal, however. In questions whose answers are systems of univariate polynomials, we may simply apply Euclid's Algorithm to determine the highest common factor of the systems, and compare these. An important goal for students could well be to manipulate their system of equations to identify the highest common factor. For assessment purposes, we may need to identify whether any error is in their original system of equations, or their subsequent manipulation of them. When the highest common factors are not the same, there may still be things that we can learn about the student's incorrect answer. If the highest common factor of a student's system of equations, H_s, divides but is not equal to the teacher's, H_t, we know that the student's system is underdetermined, as H_s is missing some factor present in H_t. Conversely, if $H_s \neq H_t$ and $H_t \mid H_s$, the student's system is overdetermined. Finally, if $H_s = 1$, we know that the student's answer is inconsistent (unless we present them with a system with no solution).

By the deft application of Euclid's algorithm we can efficiently assess a student's response to a question whose answer is a system of univariate polynomials. Whilst this is useful in certain situations, it is very limited in scope. We could not, for example, use Euclid's algorithm to compare answers with more than one variable; for that we require a greater range of mathematical tools. These are needed even in simple questions involving the Pythagorean Theorem, for example.

Beyond Euclid's Algorithm

Next we consider systems of linear equations, such as

$$2x_1 + 4x_2 - 2x_3 = 2 \tag{10}$$

$$3x_1 + 4x_2 + x_3 = -3 \tag{11}$$

$$x_1 + 3x_2 - 3x_3 = 4 \tag{12}$$

These *simultaneous equations* can be solved with *Gaussian elimination*, which works in the following way: given variables $x_1, \ldots, x_n$, eliminate x_1 from all but the first equation by subtracting a suitable multiple of the first equation from each equation in turn. Ignoring the first equation, we now have a system of equations with one fewer variable made up from one equation fewer than before. This process is called the *reduction* of one equation by another. Iterating the process we ultimately have one equation with one unknown, or one equation with a number of *free variables*. The variety is a point, representing the unique solution, or an implicit function of free variables representing a line, plane, hyper-plane etc. For our system (10) - (12), the process works as follows.

Example 1

We want to solve the system (10), (11) and (12). Dividing (10) by 2 gives $x_1 + 2x_2 - x_3 = 1$. Subtracting this from (12) and 3 times this equation from (11) gives

$$x_1 + 2x_2 - x_3 = 1$$

$$-2x_2 + 4x_3 = -6$$

$$x_2 - 2x_3 = 3$$

Repeating this process with the last two equations we notice that the second is a multiple of the third. I.e. when written in canonical form these equations are the same. Hence, our original system is equivalent to

$$\{x_1 + 2x_2 - x_3 = 1, x_2 - 2x_3 = 3\}.$$

An alternative way to represent our variety is in parametric form, such as

$$\{x_1 = -3t - 5, x_2 = 2t + 3, x_3 = t\}.$$

For systems of linear equations we may use Gaussian elimination to determine the variety, a similar result as when using Euclid's algorithm with univariate polynomials. We next discuss Gröbner bases, which allow us to spread our wings a little wider than do Euclid's or Gauss' famous algorithms. The theory of Gröbner bases, [Adams & Loustaunau, 1994, Buchberger, 1997], was developed by Bruno Buchberger in the 1960s for his PhD Thesis [1965, 2006]. Within computational algebraic geometry, this combines the Euclidean algorithm and Gaussian elimination to deal with systems of multivariate polynomials; of which systems of linear and univariate polynomials are special cases. The central element of the theory is Buchberger's Algorithm, which enables us to find the varieties of systems of multivariate polynomials. By implementing the theory, we can solve systems such as:

$$\{x^2 + y^2 - 1 = 0, x - 2y = 0\},$$

which describes a straight line intersecting with a circle, something not possible with either previous method.

Gröbner Bases

Before we can explain the general ideas behind Gröbner bases we must introduce a little notation. We shall not give an exhaustive discussion of Gröbner bases; to find out more we recommend Adams & Loustaunau[1994], though this does rely on a certain amount of abstract algebra. Given a field $\mathbb{F}$ (which can be assumed to be $\mathbb{Q}$), the *affine n*-space is

$$\mathbb{F}^n = \{(x_1, \ldots, x_n) | x_i \in \mathbb{F}\}.$$

A polynomial $f \in \mathbb{F}[x_1, \ldots, x_n]$ is a function from $\mathbb{F}^n$ to $\mathbb{F}$; when values are assigned to the variables of the polynomial it is called an *evaluation*. For example, if $f(x, y) = x + 2y$, the evaluation of f with $(2, 1) \in \mathbb{Q}^2$ is $2 + 2(1) = 4$.

When we want to solve an equation, we want to find the elements of $\mathbb{F}^n$ for which the equation evaluates to zero. As previously mentioned, the *variety*, $V(f)$ is the set of solutions of the equation $f = 0$, i.e.

$$V(f) = \{(a_1,\ldots,a_n) \in \mathbb{F}^n | f(a_1,\ldots,a_n) = 0\}.$$

This definition is generalised to a set of polynomials $F = \{f_1,\ldots,f_t\}$ by

$$V(F) = \{(a_1,\ldots,a_n) \in \mathbb{F}^n | f(a_1,\ldots,a_n) = 0 \, \forall f \in F\}.$$

The *ideal*, *I*, generated by polynomials $f_1,\ldots,f_t$ is written $(f_1,\ldots,f_t)$ and given by

$$I = (f_1,\ldots,f_t) = \left\{ \sum_{i=1}^{t} u_i f_i | u_i \in \mathbb{F}[x_1,\ldots,x_n] \right\}$$

The ideal, as we have defined it, is an ideal in the ring theoretic sense and the set $F = \{f_1,\ldots,f_n\}$ is a generating set of the ideal *I*. Given a set of polynomials *F*, it is easily proven [Adams & Loustaunau, 1994, pg. 3] that the variety of the ideal generated by F is equal to the variety of F itself, i.e. $V(\langle F \rangle) = V(F)$.

To tell if two systems of equations have the same varieties, we can therefore compare their respective ideals. Unfortunately, by generating the same ideal with two different sets of polynomials, it may not be clear that our ideals are indeed the same. This is where Gröbner bases take centre stage; two ideals are the same if and only if their *reduced Gröbner bases* are the same, and any given ideal has a reduced Gröbner basis which is not only unique, but appears unique when written in canonical form. Further, given an ideal we can compute its reduced Gröbner basis with relative ease by using Buchberger's Algorithm.

To calculate the Gröbner basis of a particular ideal, we must first decide how we order the terms in individual polynomials. In the univariate case this was not difficult, we just ordered terms in descending powers of the variable; however in the multivariate case, it is not clear whether x^2y or y^2x should appear first in the sum. We solve this problem by fixing a *term order*, a total order $<$ on the set of all possible power products, i.e. products of variables raised to powers. This is a technicality in the process but one which cannot be ignored.

The definition of a term order guarantees that, given a particular power product, any other power product which divides it appears before it in the term order. This in turn guarantees that division algorithms terminate with polynomials as reduced as possible.

Given a polynomial f its leading power product, *lp*(*f*), is the leading term without its coefficient (for example $lp(2x^2 + x + 1) = x^2$). Division algorithms always deal with the leading power product, whether they be for multivariate or univariate polynomials. With this, we can define what a Gröbner basis is:

Definition 3.2. *A set of non-zero polynomials* $G = \{g_1,\ldots,g_s\}$ *in an ideal* I *is called a Gröbner basis for* I *if and only if for all* $f \in I \setminus \{0\}$ *there exists* $1 \le i \le s$ *such that* $lp(g_i)$ *divides* *lp*(*f*).

A Gröbner basis is said to be *reduced* if the leading coefficient of every g_i is 1 and $lp(g_i) \nmid lp(g_j) \forall i \neq j$. Bruno Buchberger wrote *Buchberger's Algorithm* for computing a Gröbner basis for the ideal of a given set of polynomials F. He also showed that, for a given term order, an ideal I has a unique reduced Gröbner basis. Further, the map $\varphi : I \to G$ which takes an ideal to its reduced Gröbner basis is injective; two ideals are equal exactly when their reduced Gröbner bases are equal. Thus, for a given term order, a reduced Gröbner basis is a canonical form for the generator of an ideal.

Using Gröbner Bases to Assess $d = v \times t$ Word Exercises in CAA

With the theory of Gröbner bases in place, we use the following example, adapted from Ex 61.19 of [Tuckey, 1904], to demonstrate how the system added to STACK works.

Example 1

In a railway journey of 90 kilometres an increase of 5 kilometres per hour in the speed decreases the time taken by 15 minutes. What is the speed?

This example belongs to the distance, rate (v) and time family. Notice the mix of units of time between hours and minutes in the statement of the question calls for careful attention. Taking v and t to be the original speed and time (in hours) we have the equations

$$\left\{90 = vt, 90 = (v+5)\left(t - \frac{1}{4}\right)\right\} \tag{13}$$

Since the goal is to find v, we choose to eliminate t from the second equation, ultimately reducing the second equation a quadratic $v^2 + 5v - 1800 = 0$ which can readily be solved. Only one solution is positive, so a further critical judgement is needed to eliminate the algebraic solution which is unrealistic in the context of this problem.

The first task when dealing with this system of equations automatically is to convert them into the correct form to which we may apply Buchberger's Algorithm. In particular, we must write this system of equations as *expressions* in *rational form*. This leads us to

$$\left\{tv - 90, tv + 5t - \frac{v}{4} - \frac{365}{4}\right\}$$

From this we must clear any denominators to restore a set of polynomials

$$\left\{tv - 90, 4tv + 20t - v - 365\right\}.$$

A polynomial Gröbner basis of this system with respect to the lexicographical term order $\left[t, v\right]$ is

$$\{tv - 90, 4tv + 20t - v - 365,$$
$$-20t + v + 5, -v^2 - 5v + 1800\}$$

and the *reduced* Gröbner basis is

$$\left\{-20t + v + 5, v^2 + 5v - 1800\right\}. \tag{14}$$

In this we notice the last element of the set is a quadratic only in v, from which we may find the solutions using the normal formula and, when required in the question, we could back-substitute in any of the other equations to find corresponding values of t. The explicit variety for this system is therefore

$$\left\{\left[v = -45, t = -2\right], \left[v = 40, t = 2.25\right]\right\}.$$

The goal of the rest of this chapter is to implement an answer test in CAA which best assesses systems of equations and provides useful feedback to students. Given a question which results in a system of multivariate polynomials, we want to answer two questions:

1. Does the student's answer have the same variety as the teacher's? That is to say, has the student correctly described the situation?

2. If the student's answer is not correct, what useful information can we determine about their answer to improve their learning?

The answer to our first question is now, in principle, straightforward. Given a student's and a teacher's systems of equations, we need simply to compute the reduced Gröbner bases of the ideals which each generates. If the reduced Gröbner bases are the same, then so too are the ideals and hence their varieties. Since reduced Gröbner bases are a canonical form for systems of equations we can easily compare the sets of expressions using a CAS.

The answer to the second question requires a little more discussion. At the heart of Buchberger's Algorithm lies the Multivariate Division Algorithm, which has the same relationship to Buchberger's Algorithm as does Euclid's algorithm to polynomial division. An important and useful fact about Gröbner bases is this: an expression f is an element of an ideal I if an only if f can be reduced to zero, in the same way as with Gaussian elimination, by the elements of I's Gröbner basis using the Multivariate Division Algorithm.

This is the great appeal of Gröbner bases even when applied to systems of univariate polynomials or simple linear equations; by being able to glean information from a student's answer a system is better able to give them *meaningful feedback* to promote learning. Given a student's answer as a system of polynomials, these techniques can compare this answer to the teacher's, telling us when:

- The student's system is inconsistent and so its variety is the empty set.
- The student's system is underdetermined; its variety contains the teacher's.
- The student's system is overdetermined; at least one equation should not be there.
- Which equations are the cause of the above problems.

For pragmatic reasons we have some basic manipulations of a student's answer before we are able to use Gröbner basis techniques to assess their system of equations.

1. If appropriate, make all expressions lowercase, forcing effective case insensitivity to enable $X^2+1=0$ to be considered the same as $x^2+1=0$.
2. Evaluation of assignments, e.g. evaluate the system $\{d{=}90,\ d{=}v{\times}t\}$ to the equivalent $\{90{=}v{\times}t\}$.
3. Write all equations in the form *expression* = 0, then convert to a set of expressions.
4. Rationalize all expressions, and clear the denominator. This includes converting all floating point numbers into their rational number equivalent. E.g. convert 0.33 to 33/100. Note that the default option for STACK is to forbid the use of floating point numbers within expressions to prevent the student being penalized for using approximations such as 0.33 instead of 1/3.
5. Ensure the expressions are *polynomials*, e.g. free of trigonometrical and exponential operations.

At each stage, feedback could be given, depending on the particular circumstances and the needs of the teacher. In Figure 1 we have an implementation of the railway journey problem in STACK. Notice here, the system has established that this answer is equivalent to the system (14) with an extraneous equation $90=(v+6)(t-0.5)$ included. STACK then uses the Gröbner basis techniques described here to establish the properties, and where necessary generate feedback, in this case identifying the third equation as incorrect.

For each answer that a student gives, STACK works through a *Potential Response Tree*, a binary tree which allows a teacher to test for common mistakes associated with a question and

Figure 1. An implementation of the railway journey problem in STACK

In a railway journey of 90km an increase of 5 kilometers per hour in the speed decreases the time taken by 15 minutes.

Write a system of equations (one equation per line) to represent this situation using v as the speed of the train and t as the time.

```
90=v*t
90=(v+5)*(t-0.25)
90=(v+6)*(t-0.5)
```

Your last answer was interpreted as:

$$[90 = v \cdot t, 90 = (v+5) \cdot (t-0.25), 90 = (v+6) \cdot (t-0.5)]$$

Incorrect answer.
The entries in red below are those that are incorrect.

$$[90 = v \cdot t, 90 = (v+5) \cdot (t-0.25), 90 = (v+6) \cdot (t-0.5)]$$

Your mark for this attempt is 0. With penalties, and previous attempts, this gives 0 out of 1

tailor feedback in each case. We demonstrate this with Example 2, created by the authors.

Example 2

In central Paris, the Rue de la Paix and the Rue de Rivoli meet besides the Jardin des Tuileries at a right angle. At its other end the Rue de la Paix meets the Avenue de l'Opéra at the Palais Garnier. The Avenue meets the Rue de Rivoli at the Louvre.

Walking at 4kph it takes 36 minutes to complete the journey from the Louvre to the PalaisGarnierand back via the Jardin des Tuileries. Each of the roads is straight, and the area enclosed by them is 0.24km^2.

Using a for the length of the $2400m$ Avenue de l'Opéra, p for Rue de la Paix and r for Rue de Rivoli, and working in metres, write a system of equations which describes

1. The relationship between the lengths of the three roads.
2. The total distance around the roads.
3. The area enclosed by the roads.

This question requires a simple distance-rate-time calculation and then the application of theorems regarding triangles. Firstly we see that the distance around the roads is , and so the system of equations required is

$$\{a^2 = p^2 + r^2, a + p + r = 2400, \frac{pr}{2} = 240000\} \tag{15}$$

In the event that the students has not paid sufficient attention to the question requirements, and answered in kilometers, their answer will be the system

$$\{a^2 = p^2 + r^2, a + p + r = 2.4, \frac{pr}{2} = 0.24\} \tag{16}$$

When the student submits their answer, the first node on the potential response tree checks to see if their answer is equivalent to System 16. In the event that it is, the feedback to the student is "Your working should be in metres, not kilometres (otherwise your answer is correct)!", and the answer is subjected to no other tests. When

Figure 2. The potential response tree for example 2

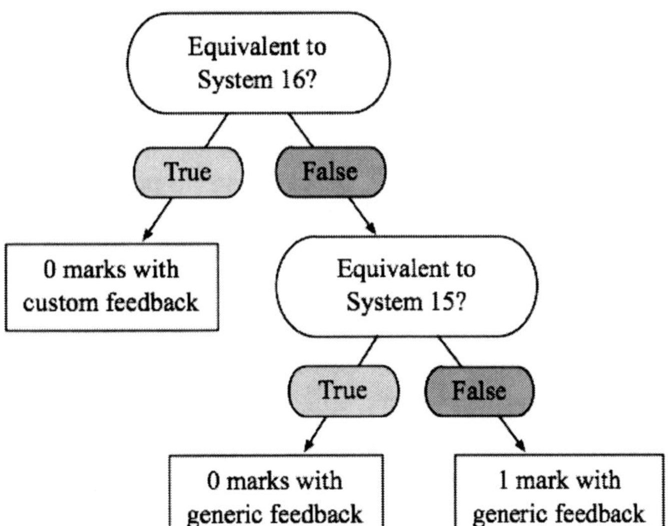

the answer is not equivalent to System 16, the second node of the potential response tree checks for equivalence with System 15, either marking the answer as correct or giving generic feedback of the kind in Figure 1. Figure 2 shows the potential response tree through which STACK works in the case of Example 2.

The main challenge presented by Gröbner bases is that Buchberger's Algorithm is not particularly efficient and computation may take several minutes with very complex systems on current hardware. This problem may be surmounted by applying more efficient algorithms, such as Faugère's F4 [1999] and F5 [2002] algorithms, which both offer speed increases over Buchberger's Algorithm. With computers becoming increasingly fast, issues relating to the speed of computation become less significant by the year, however. Systems such as (13) take a matter of milliseconds so the system as it stands is perfectly useable in most cases.

CONCLUSION

Systems of equations arise naturally as answers to the modelling step of word exercises. In this chapter we have explained how such systems of equations can be automatically assessed using Gröbner basis techniques. It would be perfectly straightforward to write contrived algebra problems for which Gröbner bases were obviously needed to assess whether the student's system was the "same" as the teacher's. The complexity of systems of equations arising in simple word exercises might appear to be more limited, typically consisting of only a small number of linear or quadratic terms. Even with such simple systems Gröbner bases offer a robust and effective method for assessment and feedback which is not provided by other methods, however. This is the natural algorithm for this task, from a mathematical and computational point of view, and hence we argue it is the right approach to use. These techniques scale up to more complex systems, and their simplification down to univariate or linear systems give them broad appeal as a tool for the teacher. We have also implemented these techniques as part of the STACK CAA system to assess answers in practice.

REFERENCES

Adams, W. W., & Loustaunau, P. (1994). *An introduction to Gröbner Bases*. American Mathematical Society.

Blum, W., & Niss, M. (1991). Applied mathematical problem solving, modelling, applications, and links to other subjects: State, trends and issues in mathematics instruction. *Educational Studies in Mathematics*, *22*(1), 37–68. doi:10.1007/BF00302716

Bradford, R., Davenport, J. H., & Sangwin, C. J. (2009). A comparison of equality in computer algebra and correctness in mathematical pedagogy. In *Proceedings of Calculemus*, (LNAI 5625 pp. 75-89).

Buchberger, B. (1965). *Ein Algorithmuszum Auffinden der Basis Elemente des Restklassenringsnacheinemnulldimensionalen Polynomideal*. PhDthesis, University of Innsbruck. (An algorithm for finding a basis for the residue class ring of a zero-dimensional polynomial ideal).

Buchberger, B. (1997). Introduction to Groebner bases. In Schwichtenberg, H. (Ed.), *Logic of computation, NATO ASI Series, Series F: Computer and Systems Sciences 157* (pp. 35–66). Berlin, Germany: Springer-Verlag.

Buchberger, B. (2006). An algorithm for finding the basis elements of the residue class ring of a zero dimensional polynomial ideal. *Journal of Symbolic Computation*, *41*(3-4), 475–511. doi:10.1016/j.jsc.2005.09.007

Clement, J., Lochhead, J., & Monk, G. S. (1981). Translation difficulties in learning mathematics. *The American Mathematical Monthly*, *88*(4), 286–290. doi:10.2307/2320560

Davenport, J. H., Siret, Y., & Tournier, E. (1993). *Computer algebra: Systems and algorithms for algebraic computation*. Academic Press Professional.

Euclid, . (1965). *The thirteen books of Euclid's elements, with introduction and commentary by Sir Thomas Heath*. Dover Publications.

Faugère, J. C. (1999). A new efficient algorithm for computing Gröbner bases. *Journal of Pure and Applied Algebra*, *139*(1-3), 61–88. doi:10.1016/S0022-4049(99)00005-5

Faugère, J. C. (2002).A new efficient algorithm for computing Gröbner bases without reduction to zero (F5). In *Proceedings of the 2002 International Symposium on Symbolic and algebraic computation* (p. 83). Association for Computing Machinery.

Hassmén, P., & Hunt, D. P. (1994). Human self-assessment in multiple choice. *Journal of Educational Measurement*, *31*(2), 149–160. doi:10.1111/j.1745-3984.1994.tb00440.x

Klai, S., Kolokolnikov, T., & Van Den Bergh, N. (2000). *Using Maple and the Web to grade mathematics tests. Advanced Learning Technology: Design and Development Issues*. Los Alamitos, CA: IEEE Computer Society.

Kluger, A. N., & DeNisi, A. (1996). Effects of feedback intervention on performance: A historical review, a meta-analysis,and a preliminary feedback intervention theory. *Psychological Bulletin*, *119*(2), 254–284. doi:10.1037/0033-2909.119.2.254

Mayer, R. E. (1981). Frequency norms and structural analysis of algebra story problems into families, categories, and templates. *Instructional Science*, *10*(2), 135–175. doi:10.1007/BF00132515

Mustoe, T., & Lawson, L. (2002). *Mathematics for the european engineer - A curriculum for the twenty-first century.Technical report*. The European Society for Engineering Education.

Pólya, G. (1981). *Mathematical discovery*. New York, NY: Wiley.

Recorde, R. (1557). *The whetstone of Witte*. London, UK: I. Kyngston.

Sangwin, C. J. (2011, November). Modelling the journey from elementary word problems to mathematical research. *Notices of the American Mathmatical Society*.

Sangwin, C. J., & Grove, M. J. (2006). STACK: Addressing the needs of the neglected learners. In *Proceedings of the First WebALT Conference and Exhibition January 5-6, Technical University of Eindhoven, Netherlands*, (pp. 81-95). Oy WebALT Inc, University of Helsinki.

Sangwin, C. J., & Ramsden, P. (2007). Linear syntax for communicating elementary mathematics. *Journal of Symbolic Computation, 42*(9), 902–934. doi:10.1016/j.jsc.2007.07.002

Shute, V. J. (2007). The future of assessment: Shaping teaching and learning . In Shute, V. J. (Ed.), *Tensions, trends, tools, and technologies: Time for an educational sea change* (pp. 139–187). Taylor and Francis Group.

Stedall, J. A. (2002). *A discourse concerning algebra: English algebra to 1685*. Oxford University Press.

Tuckey, C. O. (1904). *Examples in algebra*. London, UK: Bell & Sons.

KEY TERMS AND DEFINITIONS

Buchberger's Algorithm: Algorithm created by Bruno Buchberger for calculating the Gröbner basis of a system of multivariate polynomials.

Computer Aided Assessment (CAA): Software for the assessment of mathematics.

Computer Algebra System (CAS): Software for symbolic mathematics and the manipulation of mathematical expressions.

Gröbner Basis: A generating subset of an ideal. If two systems of equations have the same Gröbner basis, their varieties coincide.

Modelling: The process of describing a given situation in terms of mathematical equations and expressions.

System of Equations: A set of equations, each of which is held to be true.

Variety: The set of solutions of an equation or system of equations.

Word Exercise: A question in mathematical assessment presented in sentence form with a minimum of mathematics.

Chapter 14
Interactive Web-Based Tools for Learning Mathematics:
Best Practices

Barry Cherkas[1]
Hunter College of the City University of New York, USA

Rachael M. Welder
Hunter College of the City University of New York, USA

ABSTRACT

There is an abundance of Web-based resources designed for mathematics teachers and learners at every level. Some of these are static, while others are interactive or dynamic, giving mathematics learners opportunities to develop visualization skills, explore mathematical concepts, and obtain solutions to self-selected problems. Research into the efficacy of online mathematics demonstrations and interactive resources is lacking, but it is clear that not all online resources are equal from a pedagogical viewpoint. In this chapter, a number of popular and relevant websites for collegiate mathematics and collegiate preservice teacher education are examined. They are reviewed and investigated in terms of their interactivity, dynamic capabilities, pedagogical strengths and weaknesses, the practices they employ, and their potential to enhance mathematical learning both inside and outside of the collegiate classroom. Culled from these reviews is a working definition of "best practices": condensing difficult mathematical concepts into representations and models that clarify ideas with minimal words, thereby enabling a typical student to grasp, quickly and easily, the underlying mathematics.

DOI: 10.4018/978-1-60960-875-0.ch014

INTRODUCTION

The development of the Internet has provided mathematics teachers and educators at all levels with a wealth of information and a plethora of resources that were not previously available. Through this vast medium, myriad web-based materials that aim to enhance the teaching and learning of mathematics are continuously being developed. Some web-based resources are **static**, meaning that knowledge-seekers read passive content published on a website similar to material printed in a textbook. Other resources, however, are **interactive**, having the ability to provide the learner with a richer learning experience. Unfortunately though, many interactive websites do not actually teach students *how* to solve problems; instead, they deliver solutions not unlike an answer key, which can be useful for checking homework but not for developing knowledge or actively nurturing learning. On the other hand, some interactive websites are **dynamic** (Wikipedia, 2010), meaning that knowledge-seekers interact with web tools that generate fresh customized content based on user input. Interactivity is a major advance in delivering mathematics education with the power to reform the teaching and learning of mathematics.

The purpose of this chapter is to provide an overview of selected dynamic and potentially dynamic, interactive web-based mathematics resources to help readers identify effective practices for collegiate mathematics education. While there is a growing literature that studies classroom and assessment applications of technology [see e.g. Computer Algebra in Mathematics Education (2010)], we do not review or advocate any particular classroom or curriculum usage of the websites reviewed here. Instead, our goal is to expose college mathematics instructors to a variety of interactive and dynamic websites, for integration into the courses they teach, whether online or face-to-face. Furthermore, through our reviews, we aim to help college instructors develop a pedagogical view of the offerings and limitations of online tools, guiding them in their selection and evaluation of both existing websites and those yet to be developed. Since websites that aim to enhance learning in mathematics are continuing to evolve, it is important that educators are capable of identifying educationally sound web-based practices when selecting online resources for teaching and research purposes.

We have analyzed a number of highly ranked, interactive and dynamic web-based resources, relevant for collegiate mathematics education. In this chapter, we review a sample of select websites and discuss the effectiveness of the practices they employ, their pedagogical strengths and weaknesses, and their potential to enhance mathematics learning, in ways of which printed (and static) materials are not capable. We first address web-based resources that are appropriate for teaching and learning college level mathematics content. In this section, we discuss online resources based on the degree of user interaction and engagement required, starting with animations, followed by interactive tools, and ending with dynamic tools. The tools in this section cover mathematical material ranging from college algebra through calculus; so, in addition to addressing collegiate mathematics, many of the tools would also be appropriate for undergraduate courses designed for preservice secondary mathematics teachers. Afterwards, we address interactive and dynamic online resources relevant to the mathematical development of undergraduate preservice elementary and middle school teachers.

BACKGROUND

Types of Web-Based Resources

Many web-based resources are static, meaning that knowledge-seekers read passive content published on a website similar to material printed in a textbook. Some resources, however, are interactive, meaning that users interact with tools to explore a concept, without the need for custom user input. Still others are dynamic, meaning that knowledge-seekers interact with web tools that generate fresh customized content based on user input (Wikipedia, 2010). Utilizing animated demonstrations, interactive tools, and especially dynamic tools, both inside and outside of classrooms, is where the most likely benefits of the Internet lie and where the focus of future research might be most fruitful. The value of such resources resides in their ability to give learners the opportunity to develop visualization skills, explore mathematical concepts in innovative ways, and obtain solutions to self-selected problems. These options give users more control of their learning environment to meet their individual cognitive and developmental needs. Furthermore, interactive and dynamic web-based resources are more engaging and closer to the type of online activities students are involved in outside of school, like gaming and inhabiting virtual worlds (Brooks-Young, 2010). Often, animated and interactive tools can, in theory, be recast into dynamic tools using advanced technology. Admittedly, the underlying technologies of the individual demonstrations (such as animated GIF and applets) may not be adequate, but existing alternative technologies do permit the suggested dynamic improvements.

Selection Criteria

Given the enormous wealth of online resources for mathematics education, it is not possible in a single chapter to review more than a handful of the many worthy websites dedicated to learning mathematics. Therefore, our goals are to review a select sample of commendable websites that we deem best at serving the needs of college mathematics instructors and students and to cull from these reviews the characteristics of what we call "best practices" for interactive web-based mathematics tools. With that proviso, our selection criterion is based on several factors, which we discuss below.

One measure of the relevance of a website is the ranking it is given by major Western search engines such as Google, Yahoo!, and Bing. Rankings are largely correlated with the Internet traffic a website receives, as reported by Internet traffic measurement websites like Alexa (Alexa Internet, Inc., 2010), Compete (Compete, Inc., 2010), and Quantcast (Quantcast Corporation, 2010). To an extent, we take major search engine rankings and reported traffic levels into consideration when selecting resources for review. However, as we shall see below, website popularity, in and of itself, is not a guarantee of high quality or accurate mathematics. Therefore, we occasionally stray from popularity rankings to include unranked or low trafficked websites that offer what we believe to be worthwhile content for collegiate mathematics education.

Another consideration for selection was whether or not a website's design and user interface look and feel technologically current. Innovation is key to the initial design and implementation of interactive mathematics resources. However, we often see websites with very innovative mathematics tools that have not been upgraded to have current aesthetics or functionality. Online content that looks fresh and modern at one time will begin to look stale as newer technologies become commonplace. For contrast, we discuss one website, Demos with Positive Impact (Hill & Roberts, 2010a), whose appearance is dated by contemporary standards, but offers interactive demonstrations that have yet to be fully replicated by newer, more modern looking tools. This serves as a caution to web developers and publishers of online, digitized mathematics. Material needs frequent tending to have a continued look and feel of relevance in a world of constantly changing technology. Moreover, unlike printed material, older web pages may disappear without warning. For example, www.Arcytech.org was a highly successful and award winning educational website created by Jacobo Bulaevsky before he passed away in 2004. Although this website was working when we began writing this chapter, it has since become defunct.

In addition to a website being popular and current, another, and perhaps more significant, criterion for selection is that a website must offer (1) a wealth or preponderance of interactive tools that consistently deliver correct mathematics and (2) insight into the development of and reasoning behind the mathematical ideas discussed. Providing mathematically accurate information is not trivial; for contrast we review one very popular website below, WebMath.com (WebMath, 2010), which falls short of this criterion. To satisfy the latter specification of this criterion, we select tools that condense difficult mathematical concepts into representations and models that clarify ideas, with minimal words, thereby enabling a typical learner to quickly and easily grasp the underlying mathematics. This is our working definition of online mathematics resources employing "best practices."

It is important to note that all of the websites reviewed in this chapter offer at least part of their content to consumers for free. In general, Internet users seek web-based resources that provide free access to their materials. However, it clearly costs money for developers of online resources to create materials and maintain their websites. A few of the resources we discuss have been made possible by external funding sources. For example, Demos with Positive Impact, (Hill & Roberts, 2010a), was partially funded by NSF. Some are provided by companies that deliver free resources as part of their business of selling related products. Still others are created by nonprofit organizations, which fund their own in-house education websites, or educators, who often utilize technology resources provided by their institutions. On the other hand, some resources are solely funded by their developers, who are committed to the value of their work. It therefore becomes necessary for many free-access websites to obtain financial support through banner advertisements and subscriptions. Although advertisements are generally viewed negatively when resources are utilized in academic environments, this may just be a "necessary evil" if teachers and schools districts want to continue using such materials at no cost to themselves.

Who Visits Mathematics Websites?

Before reviewing mathematics-related websites, it is useful to have background information about the nature of the populations that visit these sites. As we previously mentioned, Quantcast (Quantcast Corporation, 2010) measures Internet traffic for all websites; they make this information publicly available. For many websites, Quantcast estimates several demographic characteristics of the sites' visitors. However, websites can directly interface with the Quantcast system to obtain more accurate demographic information. Quantcast uses the information it obtains to draw demographic inferences on the gender, age, ethnicity, education status, and income levels of each site's visitors.

We surveyed the demographic data published on quantcast.com for a number of websites committed to delivering mathematics education and have selected a sample of six websites: The Math Forum (Math Forum, 2010a), WebGraphing.com (Cherkas, 2010), Discovery Education's WebMath (WebMath, 2010), The Wolfram Demonstrations Project (2010a), The National Library of Virtual Manipulatives (Utah State University, 2010e), and Purplemath (Stapel, 2010). Five of these websites are discussed in this chapter while the sixth, Purplemath, which has no interactivity, is only included here since it is very highly ranked and has directly measured data. Our discussion will focus on ethnicity data, which has been reproduced for these websites in the six tables comprising Figure 1. As noted in Figure 1, four of the tables are Quantcast estimates while two are inferences based on data directly measured by Quantcast. In the tables, the term *index* "represents the delivery of a specific audience segment compared to the

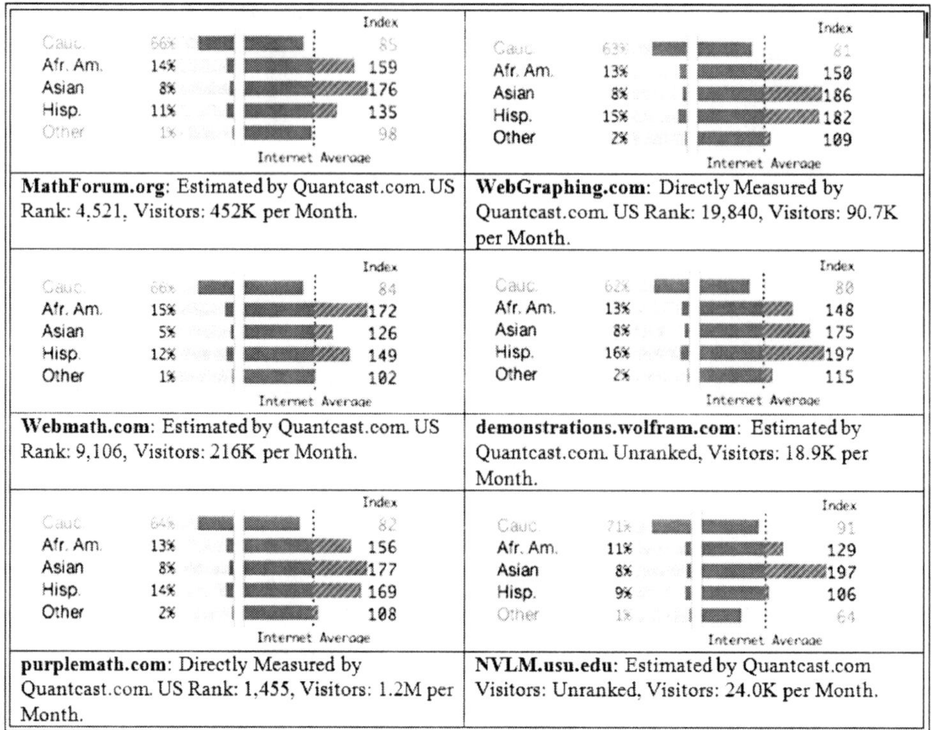

Figure 1. Inferential ethnicity data published on Quantcast.com (© 2010, Quantcast Corporation)

Internet average of 100" (Quantcast Corporation, 2010). "The index shows how an individual site's audience compares to the internet population as a whole. For example, an index of 100 indicated a site's audience is equivalent to the demographic make-up of the total Internet population." What is striking about the statistics seen in these tables is the consistent, disproportionately high use of these websites by ethnic minorities, especially the historically underserved populations of African American and Hispanic users. Perhaps less surprising is the disproportionately low use by Caucasians. Further, the disparity between the proportionately low percentage of Caucasian users and the high percentage of non-Caucasian ethnic minorities is stark. Admittedly, the accuracy of the demographics published by Quantcast cannot be confirmed (their inference model is proprietary); however, taken at face value, these ethnic differences deserve consideration. A noted black educator in the United States speculated on this data, that black students were searching the Internet for help after not getting what they needed in their schools.

When hypothesizing about the student visitors of mathematics websites, it seems plausible that many are independent learners. Such users, who may not be getting information about concepts presented in mathematics classrooms in a manner that they can use, are searching either for enrichment or alternative explanations and clarifications. The inferential data in Figure 1 suggest that there are a multitude of independent learners with the initiative to learn mathematics via the Internet. Based on the high volume of Internet traffic at mathematics-related websites, there is evidently a great deal of interest in learning via the Internet. Conceivably, the fact that many of these resources fill their pages with banner ads may discourage some teachers and schools from using or recommending these websites.

WEB-BASED TOOLS FOR COLLEGE MATHEMATICS CONTENT

There are countless websites that offer links to resources appropriate for college mathematics content. For the benefit of readers who are seeking resources beyond those reviewed here, we reference three websites that provide large collections of links to additional resources. Perhaps the most popular is The Math Forum at Drexel University, founded by Gene Klotz, which maintains an extensive collection of links to mathematics web resources at their Internet Mathematics Library (Math Forum, 2010a). They have a rather large staff of 25 people (Math Forum, 2010b) who maintain their enterprise. Another useful resource is Maths Online, housed at Universität Wien (Maths Online, 2010), designed by F. Embacher and P. Oberhuemer. This site is somewhat of a master list of links to other collections, although a check of a few links finds that there are some that are not current. This latter issue is probably not unique for any site that attempts to provide numerous links to other sites. Another extensive catalog of mathematics resources is housed at the University of Wisconsin Marathon County and managed by M. Maheswaran since 1994, see (Maheswaran, 2010). The listing is very crisp, making it easy to find what you want, and as of this writing it appears to be kept up-to-date (the date of last update is reported as two weeks before our date of retrieval).

Animations

We begin with a discussion of a few animations, which are not technically interactive, but are a valuable web resource because they cannot be replicated in a printed textbook. The website Demos with Positive Impact is the brainchild of David R. Hill and Lila F. Roberts who received NSF support to create web-based teaching tools (Hill & Roberts, 2010a). Their site has a number of demonstrations that are useful for class instruction as well as learner exploration, many contributed after the initial work of Hill and Roberts. Noteworthy are the animated visualizations for volumes of solids in calculus. There are separate demonstrations that elaborate on each of four methods for determining volumes of solids of revolution. Although the quality of the graphics dates back to 2002, the animations are classic in the way they visualize the generation of volume. Their washer method example (Hill & Roberts, 2010e), which consists of rotating a region in the first quadrant about the y-axis, is modeled by "$f(x)$=Making a bundt cake." This picture lends concreteness to the technique, which is a challenging visual concept to grasp. Besides the washer method, animations illustrate the methods behind volume calculations using the disk method (Hill & Roberts, 2010b), the shell method (Hill & Roberts, 2010c), and the method of sections (Hill & Roberts, 2010d). One improvement over the volume demonstrations shown on Demos with Positive Impact would be to have the ability for a user to enter a region for rotation and to have that region revolve about a user-selected axis or line in real time. The technology needed to do this does exist, as does the ability to show the computations for the integral that computes the desired volume. This would give the demonstration both interactive capability as well as user input ability, making it dynamic.

Another more encyclopedic website, Wolfram MathWorld, founded by Eric Weisstein in 1999 (Weisstein, 2010a), has over 100 animations among its 13,000 entries. The animated GIFs (Weisstein, 2010b) are rich in mathematics content, explaining in detail the mathematics behind the concept being demonstrated. For example, the "Ellipse" (Weisstein, 2010c) shows not only the animated generation of the ellipse based on the sum of the distances between the two foci, with a full explanation of the mathematics, but also includes supplementary material on the less-well-known trammel construction of an ellipse (Eves, 1965, p. 177). Weisstein's demonstrations are quite general, using variables instead of fixed values to

Figure 2. Volumes of revolution using cylindrical shells (© 2010, Wolfram Demonstrations Project. Used with permission.)

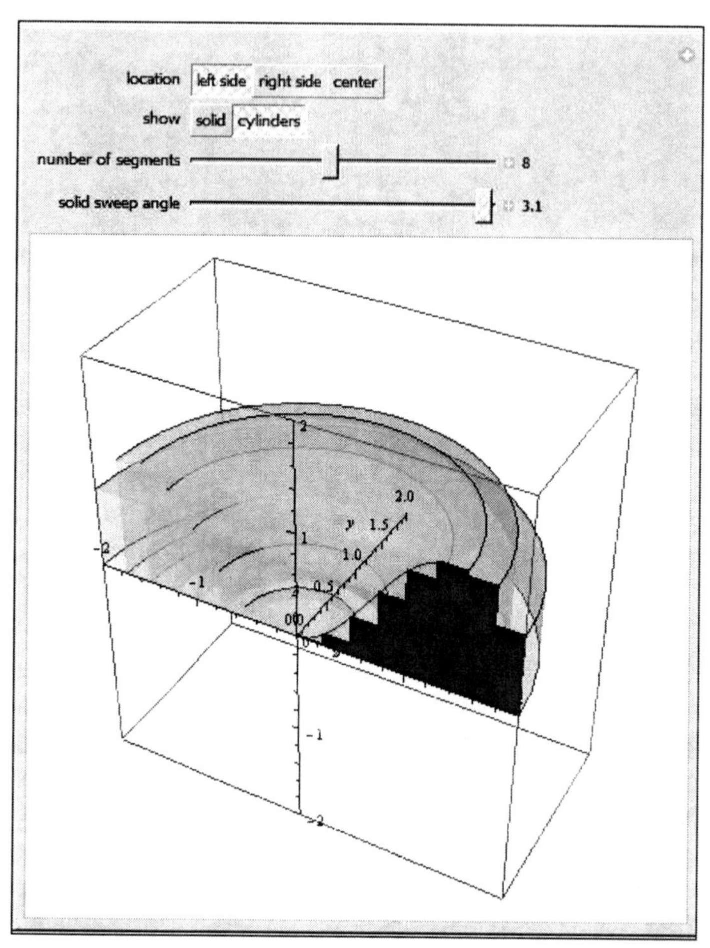

represent quantities under discussion. While the "Ellipse" demonstration could be made dynamic, the rich nature combining passive mathematics content with visually appealing animations makes this very satisfactory. Conceivably, a dynamic tool whereby users enter an actual equation of an ellipse centered at the origin—and explore how the equation changes if the ellipse is elongated by, say, pulling a point on either the semimajor or semiminor axes—would enable users to internalize the concepts being expressed through their tactile senses.

Interactive Tools

Moving up from animations to interactivity, there is the Wolfram Demonstrations Project. This is a large collection of interactive illustrations created by the community of *Mathematica* users, reviewed before publication by experts associated with Wolfram Research Inc. (http://www.demonstrations.wolfram.com). Anyone can preview a demonstration online, but to interact with it, a learner must download their free *Mathematica Player*. As of this writing, there are over 6,500 contributions, ranging in educational level from elementary mathematics to front-line research topics. One such demonstration, "Volumes of Revolution

Using Cylindrical Shells" (Wolfram Demonstrations Project, 2010c), treats the same problem as Hill and Roberts' "Solids of Revolution: The Method of Shells" (Hill & Roberts, 2010c), but with an interactive ability. That is, instead of a fixed animation, there are sliders that permit users to vary the number of cylinders and angular sweep, as well as toggle switches with additional controls (see Figure 2). Even more valuable, the user can rotate the 3D figure by dragging the cursor on the figure, giving a three-dimensional feeling for what is happening inside the solid when computing the volume of approximating shells. This demonstration could be made dynamic by adding the ability for the user to enter the initial function before revolving.

Students typically have great difficulty with word problems, and optimization problems in calculus are no exception. "The Wire Problem" is a standard optimization problem studied in first-semester calculus: maximize and minimize the total area of two geometric figures made from a fixed length of wire cut into two pieces. In the Wolfram Demonstrations Project of "The Wire Problem" (2010d), the problem begins by first having the user select a pair of geometric figures from a square, a triangle, and a circle (see Figure 3). The illustration enables learners to view what happens to the area function, which represents the sum of the areas of the two selected geometric figures, when the two perimeter lengths are continuously varied, using a slider, from zero to the length of the wire. This demonstration would be excellent to use in class to introduce the kind of thinking involved in solving optimization problems, posing questions such as: What is needed to determine the maximum?; Is it the same for the minimum? These questions could lead naturally to the need to formulate an equation for the area function, graph it, and use its derivative to find its minimum, additionally checking the interval endpoints for its maximum. This demonstration is already dynamic to the extent that the user can select from three geometric objects. Conceivably, additional geometric objects could be included like trapezoids, pentagons, and hexagons, giving learners more opportunities to explore these kinds of word problems.

In "Two Points Determine a Line" (Wolfram Demonstrations Project, 2010b), students are given the line $y = x$ with the points on the line at coordinates $(-2, 2)$ and $(2, 2)$ highlighted. Using the mouse, these points can be dragged to any locations on the grid, while the line connecting the point being dragged moves with the point. Students can watch the equation change continuously to represent the changing line being drawn (see Figure 4). By giving students complete control, this dynamic tool allows exploration and relates the analytical expression of a line to the visual features of the line. The coefficients can be rational or decimal and the grid can be limited to integers or remain open to any value. Interactive tools, such as this, are excellent for developing visualization skills. This interactive demonstration would be a great tool to use with preservice teachers at all levels, including elementary. This demonstration could be made dynamic by giving the user the option to enter a linear equation and have the application, or user, select a couple of appropriate coordinates to permit dragging for additional exploration.

Another large collection of interactive mathematics activities is on the website cut-the-knot.org, created by Alexander Bogomolny in 1996 (http://www.cut-the-knot.org/). Bogomolny has published over 1,000 interactive applets covering topics from elementary arithmetic through calculus. For calculus students and teachers, especially noteworthy is the applet "Function, Derivative, and Integral" (Bogomolny, 2010a) where students can drag the points along a given graph up and down and immediately see the effect on the function's derivative and integral (see Figure 5). In a recent calculus class of one of the authors, the students burst out with, "Wow!" when observing the screen display of interactive changes in

Figure 3. The wire problem. (© 2010, Wolfram Demonstrations Project. Used with permission.)

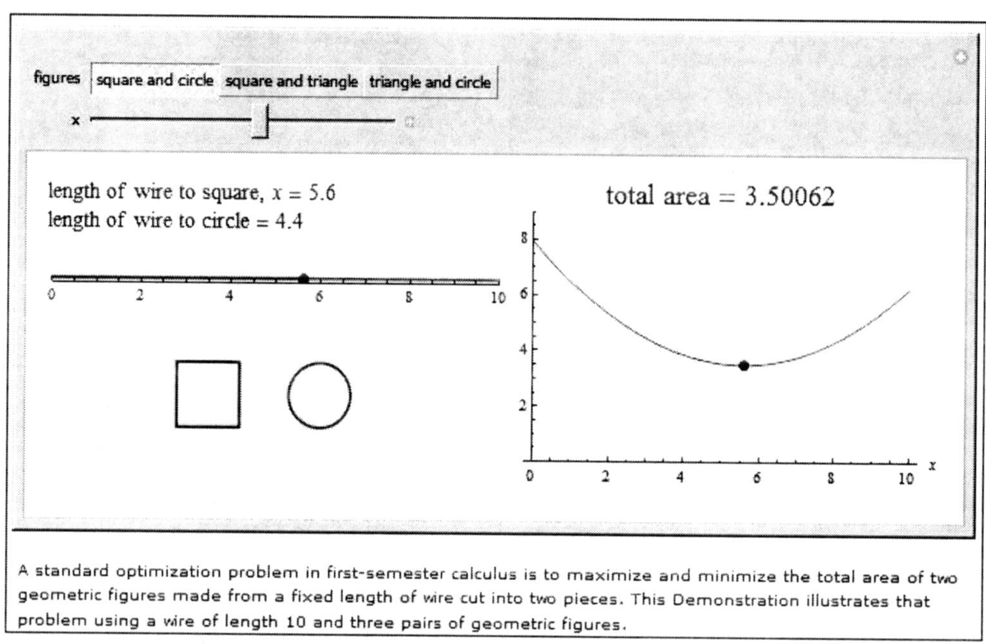

Figure 4. Two points determine a line (© 2010, Wolfram Demonstrations Project. Used with permission.)

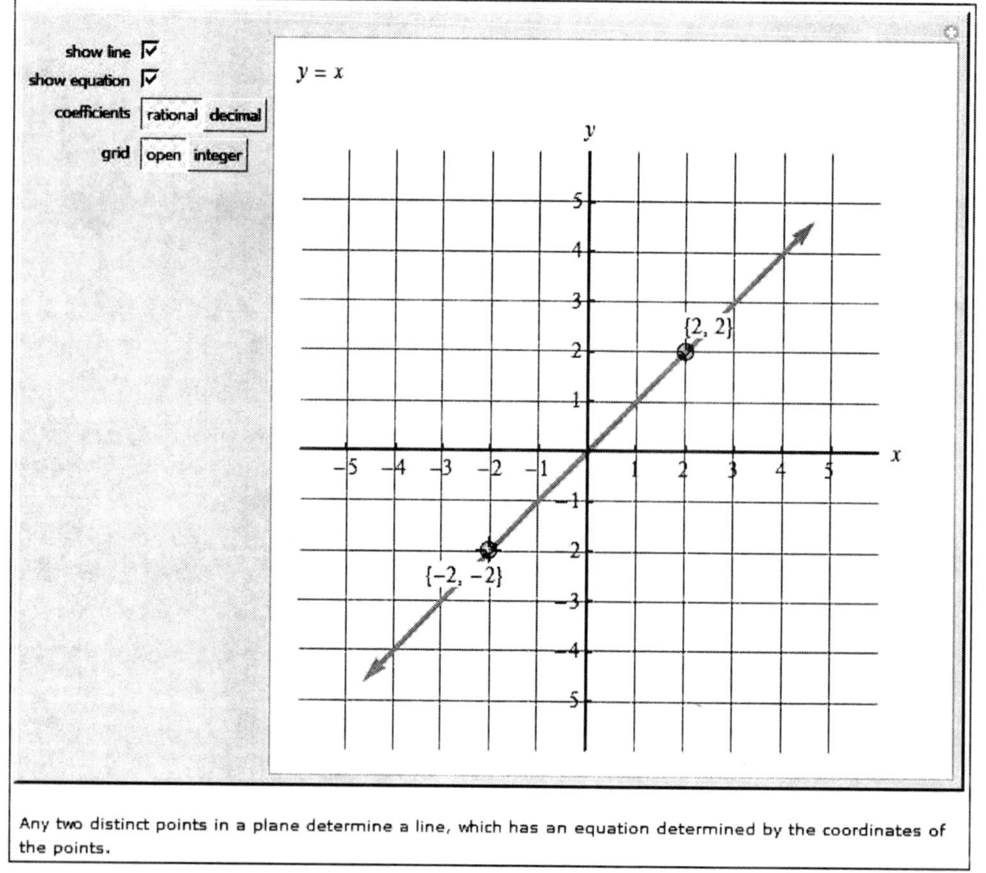

Figure 5. Function, derivative, and integral (© 2010, Alexander Bogomolny. Used with permission.)

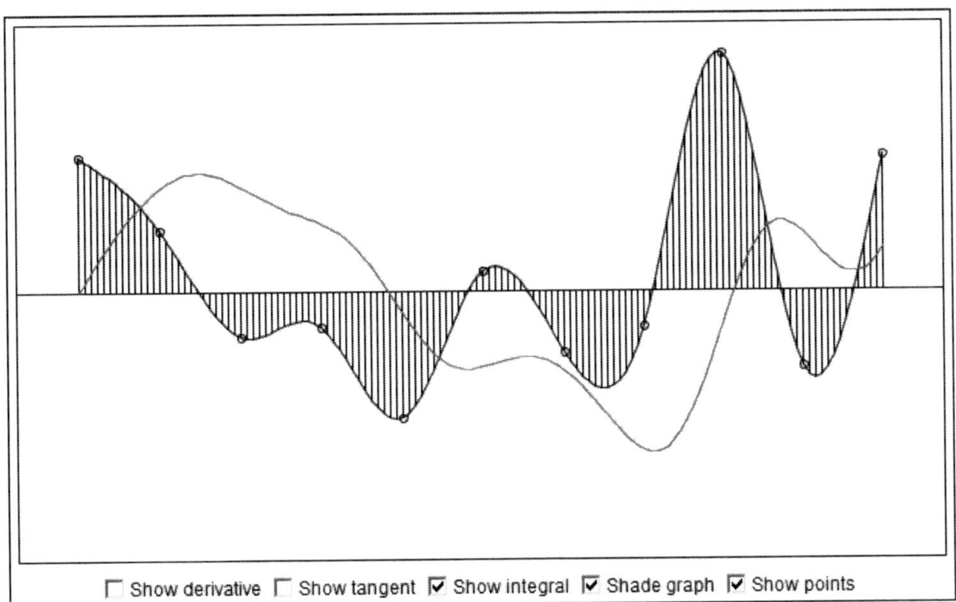

this demonstration. It would be useful to have a dynamic version of this interactive tool, whereby the user enters the function for consideration.

Also of interest is Bogomolny's applet "Riemann Sums–Function Integration" (Bogomolny, 2010c) where a slider for a given function enables rectangular approximations from $n = 1$ to $n = 100$ (see Figure 6). This demonstration simultaneously shows a given curve along with both the corresponding Riemann Sum and the Integral Value, visually demonstrating that these values get closer as n gets larger. What is especially clever about this is the ability to toggle between left, right, random, midpoint, lower, and upper rectangular sums and instantly observe the impact on the approximating sums. Once again, Bogomolny's demonstration could be improved by enabling instructors or learners to enter their own functions for interactive exploration.

Aside from these classroom activities, cut-the-knot.org has numerous exploratory examples on "Interactive Mathematics Activities" (Bogomolny, 2010b) to whet the appetite of the mathematically curious. This website offers a tremendous number of intriguing activities for those who delight in challenges ranging over topics like fallacies, puzzles, and visual illusions.

Moving on to three-dimensional interactive models (Weisstein, 2010d), MathWorld has over 400 applets based on LiveGraphics3D technology, a non-commercial Java applet created by Martin Kraus in 1997 (Kraus, 2010). These applets display and rotate three-dimensional graphics produced using *Mathematica* (http://www.wolfram.com/). Last updated in 2005, the LiveGraphics3D technology is not keeping up with current innovations in the underlying product *Mathematica*. However, the existing applets are useful as supplementary materials for multivariable calculus. The ability to manipulate a solid in three dimensions is excellent for developing the kind of visualization skills needed to understand calculus of two variables. Just for ellipses alone, MathWorld has applets for an ellipsoid, elliptic cone, elliptic cylinder, elliptic helicoid, elliptic hyperboloid, elliptic paraboloid, and elliptic torus, all with full mathematical details about their equations.

Figure 6. Riemann sums–function integration (© 2010, Alexander Bogomolny. Used with permission.)

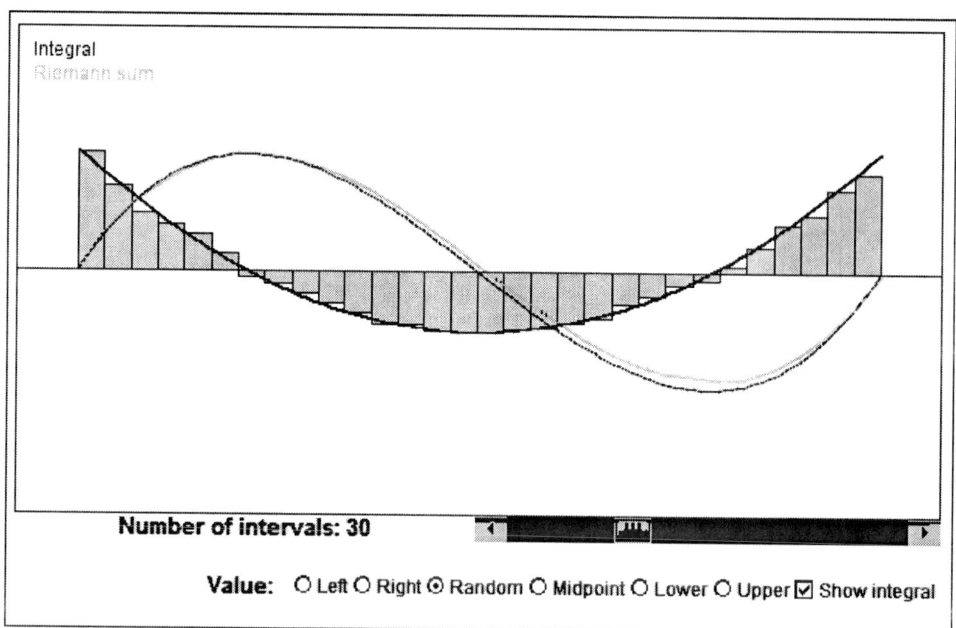

Dynamic Tools

Since 1999, George Beck's website Calc101.com (http://www.Calc101.com) has been giving step-by-step instructions for taking derivatives of user-entered functions (Beck, 2010a). This is especially useful for learning how to apply the chain rule, which buffaloes many calculus learners. Also notable for matrix algebra students are the solutions to self-selected problems, showing step-by-step computations for performing arithmetic with matrices or computing determinants, inverses, products, or transposes of matrices (Beck, 2010b). Beck's calculus tools are solid examples of dynamic web interactivity applied to non-geometric mathematics.

Graphing is an essential element of connecting visual to analytical mathematics, from algebra through calculus. Many teachers assign homework that requires students to use graphing calculators. With the emergence of websites that provide online graphing calculators, most of which are free, students and teachers often turn to these resources in lieu of having students purchase handheld models. By their very nature, these website are dynamic in the sense that users must enter a function to obtain a graph. Some permit the entry of random functions to assist users in how to work their online graphing calculators. The quality of the online graphs is generally superior to those on handheld graphing calculators, and in many ways, online graphing calculators are easier to use and often more convenient than traditional handheld models. The most popular online graphing calculator, Coolmath's "Online Graphing Calculator," (Lundin, 2010) appeals, by design, to pre-college students, but college students can also use it.

A slightly richer graphing experience is available at GCalc, where there are tools to zoom and trace (http://www.gcalc.net). In addition, GCalc enables students to quickly obtain several function graphs on the same set of axes. It offers several options, two of which are especially helpful for exploration: (1) "cross-hairs" that move with the mouse pointer and deliver coordinate values when hovering over a function graph, and (2) the ability to toggle between the graph appearing "continuous" or "discrete," enabling students to see the

Figure 7. Plot of ellipse, $x^2 + 2y^2 = 3$ *(© 2010, Wolfram Alpha LLC. Used with permission.)*

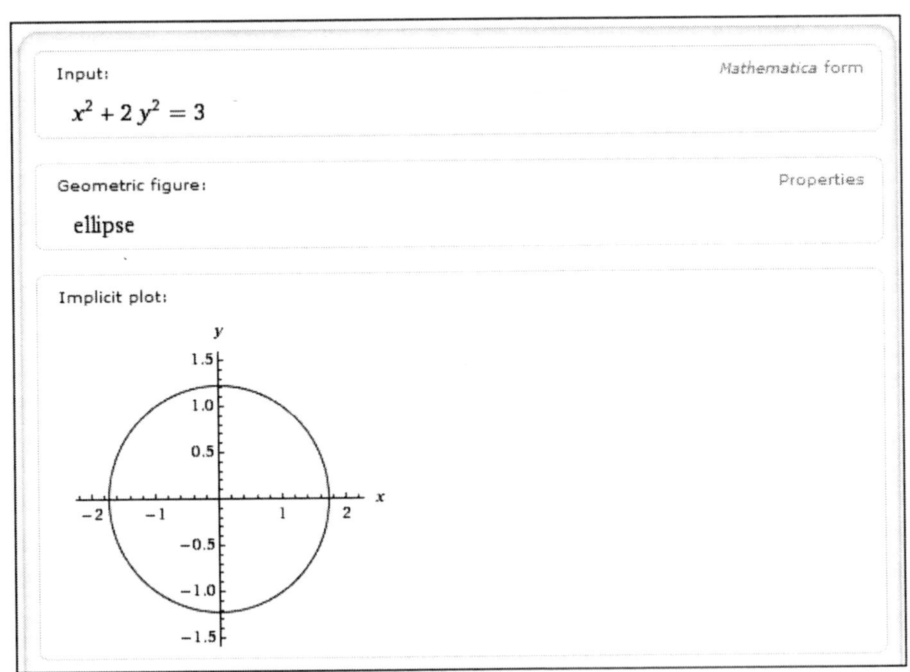

underlying points being plotted that connect the lines into a continuous graph. The tool's ease of use, together with the available options, makes this a useful graphing utility. The "Graphing Calculator" by Holt Online Learning has even more features, including point plotting, a table of values for the points plotted when graphing a function, and finding the intersection points among a set of equations (Holt, Rinehart, & Winston, 2010).

In 2009, Wolfram|Alpha (not to be confused with the Wolfram Demonstrations Project or Wolfram MathWorld cited above), self-described as a "computational knowledge engine," began operation (http://www.wolframalpha.com/). This site is a veritable goldmine for doing mathematics online. More specifically, Wolfram|Alpha delivers graphs with additional targeted information on the function or equation entered. For example, entering the equation $x^2 + 2y^2 = 3$ yields the information that the geometric figure is an ellipse and a learner can drill down (click a link) to get the foci, center, semi-axis lengths, area, perimeter, focal parameter, and eccentricity. Regrettably, when we entered the equation above, the resulting graph was circular in shape rather than the traditional elliptical shape. This would require astuteness on the part of a novice learner to read carefully the tick marks on the axes and dispel the cognitively-clashing perception that it is a circle (see Figure 7).

As for entering a function, such as $(x - 1)(x + 2)(x - 3)(x + 4)(x - 20)$, Wolfram|Alpha, unlike other graphing calculators except WebGraphing.com (Cherkas, 2010), determines function-dependent window dimensions that include essential mathematical features of the function. Typically, Wolfram|Alpha delivers two graphs, one local that includes all important points of interest and the other global that indicates the end behaviors of the function. In addition, this website provides step-by-step instructions for taking derivatives and computing indefinite integrals, including approximate values (no steps) for local maxima and minima. WebGraphing.com

Figure 8. Real and imaginary plot of $\sqrt{x^2-1}$ *(© 2010, Wolfram Alpha LLC. Used with permission.)*

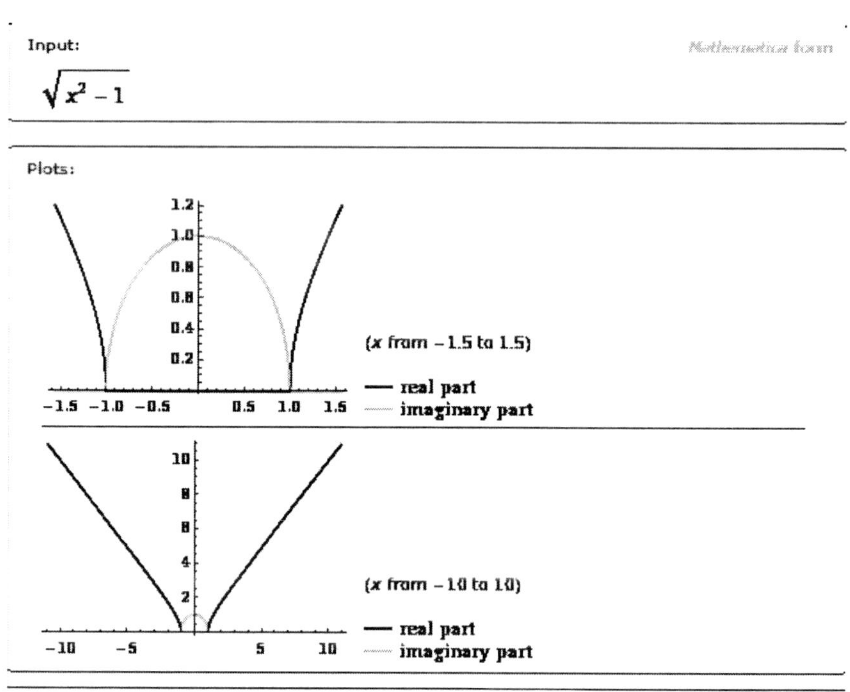

also delivers two graphs, both of which include all important points of interest, additionally showing asymptotes, discontinuities, and holes, in standard mathematical notation. There, the two graphs differ by color-coding; one graph shows increasing curve segments in one color and decreasing curve segments in another color, while the other graph shows concave up curve segments in one color and concave down curve segments in another color. Also included are complete calculus solutions with both symbolic and approximate values, as well as tutorial steps for determining these values.

Notably, unlike any other graphing calculator, Wolfram|Alpha plots imaginary parts of a function on the same axes as its real parts, using two separate colors to distinguish them. For example, the plot of $\sqrt{x^2-1}$, where the domain for real values is $|x| \geq 1$, shows the plot of the imaginary part on the interval $(-1, 1)$ (see Figure 8). This is an innovation worthy of imitation.

Solving equations and systems of equations are also important topics in mathematics courses from algebra to calculus. If one performs an Internet search of "quadratic equation solvers" (in quotation marks), Google reports "about 54,600" web pages. Since the topic of solving quadratic equations is studied in both middle and high schools, many websites that solve quadratic equations are designed with those students in mind. Yet students continue to work with these problems in undergraduate college algebra, so such websites are still beneficial for college students. Unfortunately, the vast majority of these sites do not actually teach students how to solve quadratics; instead, they deliver answers, often with inadequate or misleading explanations. For example, the solution to $x^2 = 2$ is typically offered as a decimal, $x = \pm 1.41421$, instead of the more suggestive answer using the radical symbol, $x = \pm\sqrt{2}$, which mathematics students learn to use when solving by hand. This is the case with interactive web tools at many highly ranked websites, including "Quadratic Equation Solver" (Solve My Math, 2010), "Solve a Quadratic Equation by Factoring" (WebMath, 2010), and "Quadratics" (QuickMath, 2010). Alternatively, both Wolfram|Alpha and WebGraphing.com deliver answers using radical notation and provide solution steps.

The popular website WebMath is a case in point. If a student enters $x^2 - 5x + 6 = 0$ into WebMath's tool "Solve a Quadratic Equation by Factoring," WebMath will factor the trinomial and provide the factored form, $(x - 3)(x - 2) = 0$. WebMath will then proceed to solve $x - 3 = 0$ and $x - 2 = 0$ for 3 and 2. However, there is no explanation provided for the steps needed to get the factors of the quadratic equation or the solutions to the linear equations. Further, if one enters the quadratic equation $x^2 - 1 = 0$, WebMath delivers mathematically misleading information. Instead of factoring $x^2 - 1$ into $(x - 1)(x + 1)$, it states: "First, we'll attempt to factor this quadratic equation as a trinomial. This polynomial has 2 terms. It must [sic] exactly three terms to be a trinomial. Since this quadratic equation cannot be factored as a trinomial we will not be able to solve it by factoring."

If the method of solution is not important, we suggest using Wolfram|Alpha.com for solving quadratic equations. There, if you enter $x^2 - 1 = 0$, the equation will first be rewritten as $x^2 = 1$, and then using the method of taking square roots, the correct solution will be given. In addition, Wolfram|Alpha delivers the graph of $y = x^2 - 1$, where the roots $x = -1$ or $x = 1$ are highlighted. Currently, the method of solution, taking square roots, is determined by Wolfram|Alpha and cannot be changed by the user.

WEB-BASED TOOLS FOR PRE-SERVICE ELEMENTARY AND MIDDLE SCHOOL MATHEMATICS TEACHER EDUCATION

When looking for online resources addressing elementary and middle school mathematics, one place to start is "Johnnie's Math Page," created by Johnnie Wilson (Wilson, 2010). This self-proclaimed, "Guide to the best interactive math tools and activities for kids and their teachers," offers a collection of approximately 700 links to online mathematics resources. The references on this website are categorized by content area (number, geometry, fractions, multiplication, measurement, statistics, and probability) and level (primary vs. intermediate). This website points to many large collections of interactive tools, including two of which will be discussed later in greater detail: the National Library of Virtual Manipulatives (Utah State University, 2010e) and "Interactivate" by Shodor (2010a).

Other notable collections of interactive mathematics tools, not discussed in this chapter, include: Electronic Examples (National Council of Teachers of Mathematics, 2010), Interactive Math Websites (Jefferson County Schools, 2010), Math Manipulatives (Deubel, 2010), Math Websites (Louisiana Department of Education, 2010), Mathematics Glossary (Alberta Education, 2007), and Primary Interactive Resources (Crickweb, 2010). In addition to base blocks, clocks, area models, and Venn Diagrams, described in this chapter, this abundance of resources includes virtual pattern blocks, tangrams, equation balances, function machines, geoboards, algebra tiles, and more.

Number Sense

The National Library of Virtual Manipulatives (NLVM), developed by mathematicians, math educators, and instructional design experts at Utah State University (Matti Math, 2010; Utah State University, 2010e) offers a rich variety of

Figure 9. Using 42 base block units to represent 42 (© 2010, Utah State University. Used with permission.)

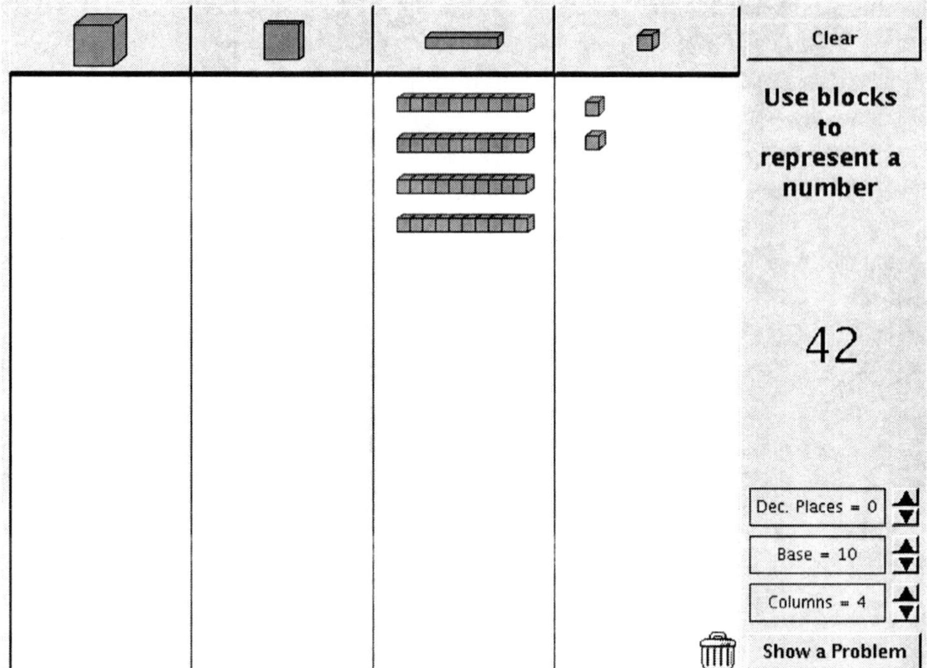

interactive tools and applets that can be used to help preservice teachers develop and extend their number sense. The manipulatives are organized by grade bands and content strands, in accordance with the National Council of Teachers of Mathematics (2000).

NLVM offers an interactive applet "Base Blocks" (Utah State University, 2010a), which allows learners to add or delete virtual base blocks and see how the numerical digits of the represented number change (see Figure 9 for an example; while the figure states "Download New Free Trial" all the tools mentioned here are offered online for free). Starting with a blank screen, students can add in (and later remove) any amount of units, tens (rods), hundreds (flats), or thousands (cubes) and see the numerical representation of the created amount. The screen is divided into columns, designated for each type of block, to reinforce the idea of place value. If more than ten blocks of any type are placed in a column, the student must use the mouse to group ten of the blocks together. When grouped by tens, blocks will automatically be replaced by one of the next larger blocks (for example, ten units grouped together are replaced by one ten block (rod)). The learner must then move this new block into its appropriate column to see the accurate numerical representation.

As the preservice teachers' understanding of place value advances, this interactive manipulative can be changed to include columns for up to three decimal places. Depending on the selected number of decimal places, the unit blocks automatically adjust from representing one whole unit to representing one-tenth, one-hundredth, or one-thousandth of a unit (see Figure 10). Furthermore, this interactive tool allows users to change the base of the number system with which they are working from base ten to base two, three, four, or five (see Figure 11 for an example in base five). This feature helps teachers deepen their knowledge of place value by working with non-base ten number systems.

Figure 10. Using 42 base block units to represent 0.42 when decimal places = 2 (© 2010, Utah State University. Used with permission.)

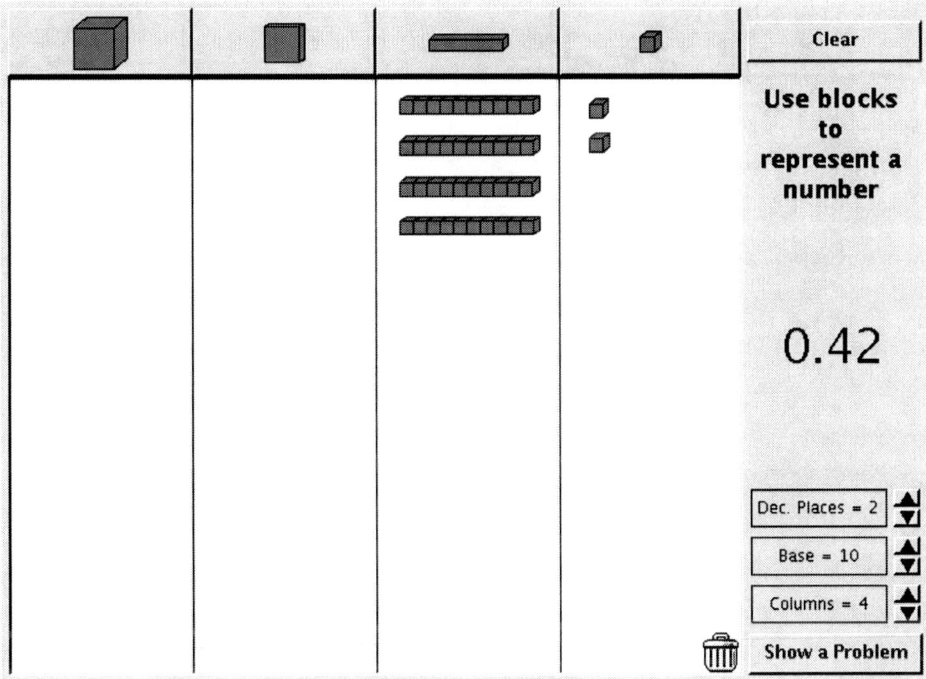

Shodor's website (http://www.shodor.org) provides an alternative way of looking at non-base ten numerals, through "Number Base Clocks" (Shodor, 2010b), part of their vast "Interactivate" collection of online activities for students grades 3-12 (Shodor, 2010a). This interactive tool provides four clocks to represent numerals with up to four digits. In the base ten setting, each clock face has ten ticks spaced equally apart around its circumference. The learners enter a value between zero and 624 and the clocks animate counting up to that value from right to left. Every time a clock completes a 360-degree cycle, the clock to its left moves one tick clockwise, emphasizing grouping and place value with continuous measurement. This tool is a great complement to usual explorations of place value, which tend to rely solely upon discrete models for grouping. We especially like the 'step' feature, which allows users to advance the clocks one step at a time.

The "Number Base Clocks" tool (Shodor, 2010b) can be set to show equivalents of base ten numerals in bases two through sixteen, which is another aspect that makes this tool unique; non-base ten materials tend to avoid bases greater than ten. When the tool is set to a non-ten base, five for example, the clocks are adjusted to only have five equally-spaced ticks. The users still enter a base ten numeral, but now the clocks will animate counting up the entered number of units in base five. Figure 12 shows base five clocks after moving seven units, representing how 7 in base ten is equal to 12 in base five. The equality between the expansions in the two bases is clearly displayed below the clocks with accompanying base notation. However, the notation uses the numeral "5" in the subscript for writing a base-five numeral, which can be misleading since the numeral "5" does not exist in a base five system. A suggestion would be to replace notation such as 12_{base5} with

Figure 11. Using 42 base block units to represent 132 base five (© 2010, Utah State University. Used with permission.)

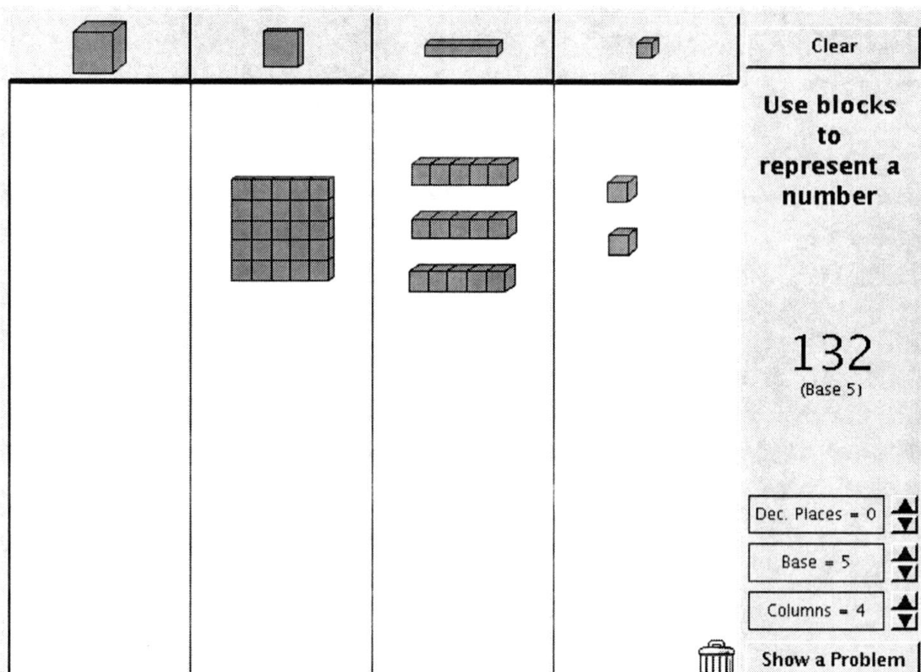

12_{five}. Writing "*five*" clarifies the base without using the numeral "5."

Either way, Shodor's "Number Base Clocks" tool (2010b) can be a great resource for preservice teachers to see consecutive numbers being illustrated, as they struggle with the idea that 10 follows 4 in writing out base five numerals for consecutive numbers. On the other hand, the way in which the clocks are labeled in bases other than ten could be misleading for teachers first learning how to write non-base ten numerals. Take the previous example in base five. The first clock on the right is comprised of five ticks labeled 0-4; but the five ticks on the clock to its immediate left are labeled 0, 5, 10, 15, and 20. These labels highlight the base ten equivalent of the base five numeral being represented, but do not help teachers to see how the number they entered should be written in base five. Instead of being able to write the represented base five numeral using the numerals the clock pointers end upon, the teacher must understand that the base five numeral is being represented by the number of ticks each pointer finishes away from the zero position. Knowing how challenging preservice elementary and middle school teachers find the concept of non-base ten number systems, this aspect of the "Number Base Clocks" tool may complicate their learning. An improvement would be to label all of the clocks in each base using the same numerals ranging from zero to one less than the selected base. This could be especially valuable when illustrating larger numbers (Figure 13 shows how 42 base ten is currently represented in base five).

Operations with Whole Numbers and Fractions

In addition to the aforementioned "Base Block" applet (Utah State University, 2010a), NLVM

Figure 12. Using animated clocks to illustrate 7 base ten as equivalent to 12 base five (© 2010, Shodor. Used with permission.)

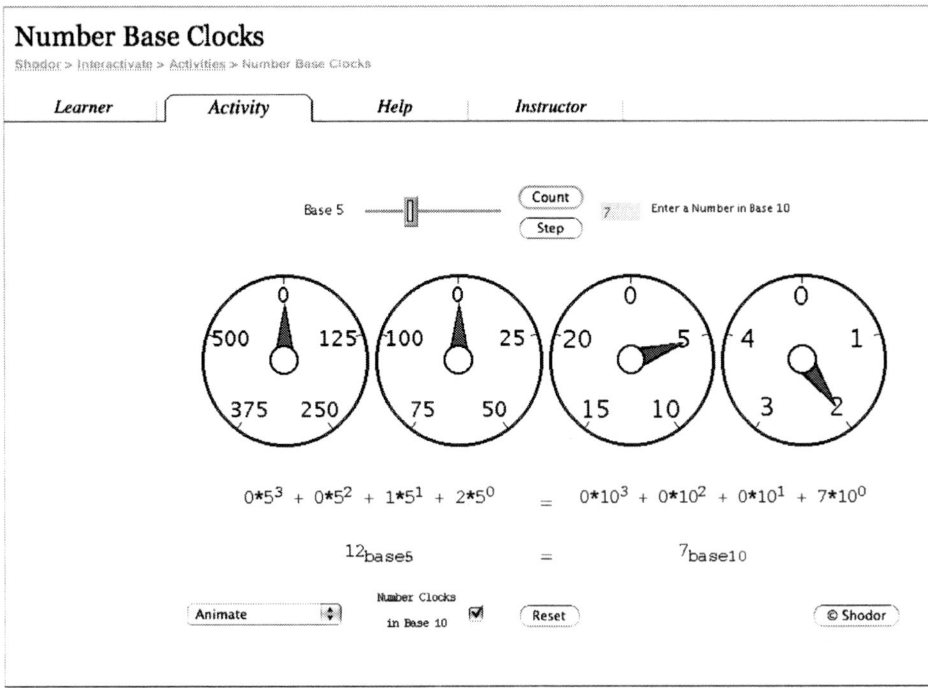

Figure 13. Using animated clocks to illustrate 42 base ten as equivalent to 132 base five (© 2010, Shodor. Used with permission.)

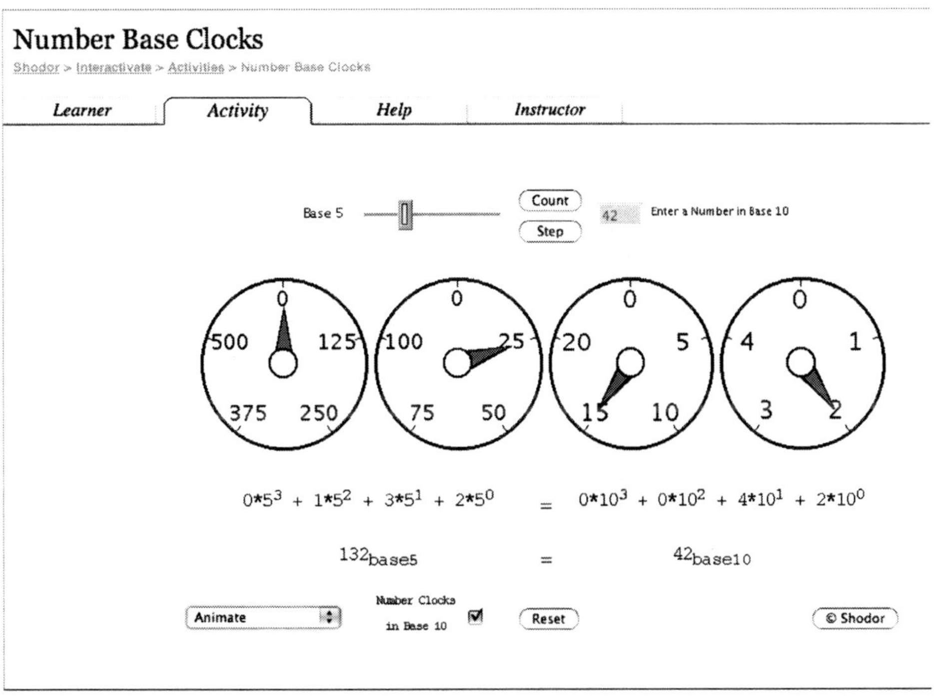

also provides applets for "Base Block Addition" (Utah State University, 2010b) and "Base Block Subtraction" (Utah State University, 2010c). These tools follow the same abacus format, emphasizing place value by keeping the blocks lined up in their respective columns for addition and subtraction. One feature, however, not available with the NLVM base blocks applets is the ability for the user to arrange base blocks freely on an open workspace. Such a feature could be beneficial when developing preservice teachers' conceptual understandings of whole number operations.

When constructing area models for multiplication of fractions, NLVM has an excellent applet "Multiplication of Fractions" (Utah State University, 2010d). The tool has two modes, "Proper Fractions" which can be used to model the multiplication of two fractions that are both less than one and "Improper Fractions" where fractions can be greater than one. Starting with "Proper Fractions," users are provided with a 1×1 rectangle for which each dimension can be divided into 2-8 equivalent sections (see Figure 14). They can subdivide the area of the rectangle and select desired dimensions. The two dimensions designated by the two factors are displayed using different colors (red and blue), and their product is clearly displayed in a third color (purple). The accompanying algorithm is also displayed using this color-coded system. Users can easily manipulate the sliders for each of the rectangle's dimensions to change factors and see how the resulting area model and product are changed.

The "Multiplication of Fractions" tool nicely emphasizes the meaning of the operation by providing the written expression "$\frac{1}{3}$ of $\frac{3}{5}$" above

Figure 14. Area model for multiplication of proper fractions (© 2010, Utah State University. Used with permission.)

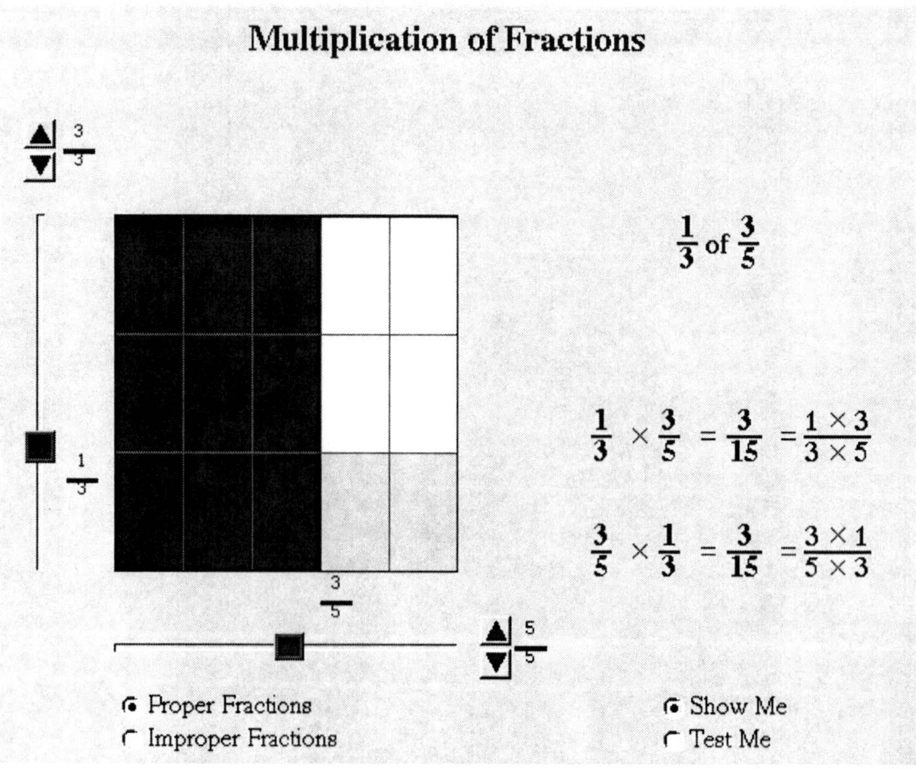

the procedural work for solving $\frac{1}{3} \times \frac{3}{5}$. Another useful aspect of this tool is that it always displays the product as an unsimplified quotient ($\frac{3}{15}$), which is vital for teachers to see when first building their conceptual knowledge of operations with fractions. Using an algorithm that produces a simplified fraction alone, such as $\frac{1}{\not{3}} \times \frac{\not{3}}{5} = \frac{1}{5}$, may build procedural knowledge but can also lead to misconceptions that similar "crossing out" procedures are valid for other operations (e.g. $\frac{1}{\not{3}} + \frac{\not{3}}{5} \neq \frac{1}{5}$). A criticism of this tool, however, is the order in which the elements of the equality statement in the procedural work are listed. The statement $\frac{1}{3} \times \frac{3}{5} = \frac{1 \times 3}{3 \times 5} = \frac{3}{15}$ highlights the steps of the standard algorithm more clearly than what is provided, $\frac{1}{3} \times \frac{3}{5} = \frac{3}{15} = \frac{1 \times 3}{3 \times 5}$.

As preservice teachers advance their understanding of multiplication of fractions, they can use the "Improper Fraction" mode of this tool to model the product of fractions ranging from 0-2 (see Figure 15). Here a 2×2 rectangle is given, for which each dimension can be divided into 2-16 equivalent sections.

Modeling multiplication of fractions greater than one is always a difficult concept for preservice elementary and middle school teachers. Having a dynamic tool such as this for them to interact with is extremely valuable in their development of this difficult concept. Both the "Proper Fractions" and "Improper Fractions" modes have a "Test Me" feature, which gives learners

Figure 15. Area model for multiplication of improper fractions (© 2010, Utah State University. Used with permission.)

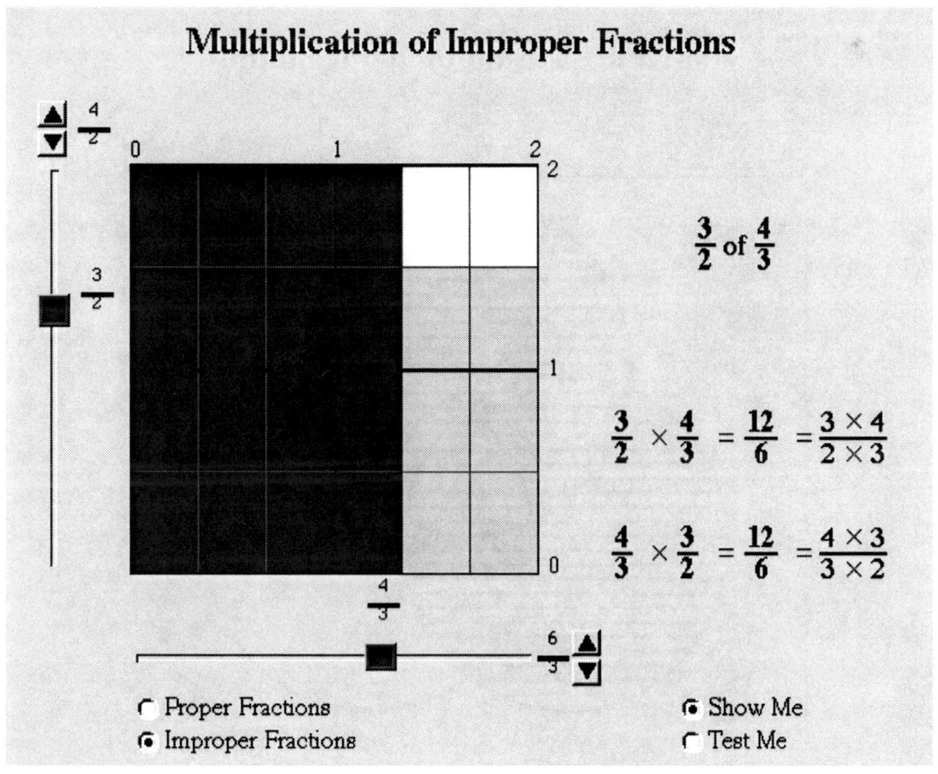

multiplication problems to model and solve and the ability to check their answers.

Venn Diagrams

Another notoriously difficult concept for elementary and middle school teachers is using Venn Diagrams. NLVM includes an interactive "Venn Diagrams" tool (Utah State University, 2010f) that provides a model of three intersecting circles that can be shaded using three different hatching designs (see Figure 16).

Users must hold down the shift key while clicking on a region to clear the shading of that portion without clearing all of the diagram's shading. Although this is described in the written instructions, which display to the right of the diagram, this feature is not intuitive and cannot be accessed through the graphical user interface of the tool. Having a "clear region" button that could switch the tool from shading to clearing the region clicked could enhance this tool's usability. The same goes for the feature that allows users to shade a set's complement. This can be performed by holding down the control key while clicking on the button for a particular set. Furthermore, the complement feature lacks the ability to shade the complement of a region that includes more than one particular set ($A \cup B$ for example).

Another enhancement to the NLVM "Venn Diagrams" tool (Utah State University, 2010f) would include having the shaded region be continually updated for the learners in set notation (similar to how the numerical representation is continually updated as base blocks are added or deleted in the NLVM's aforementioned "Base Blocks" tool). Teachers struggle with creating appropriate set notation for the set operations needed to describe portions shaded on a Venn Diagram. It would be helpful for teachers to be able to experience interactively how the notation for set operations changes as they click to shade and clear regions of a diagram.

Figure 16. Venn Diagram shaded to represent $A \cup B$ (© 2010, Utah State University. Used with permission.)

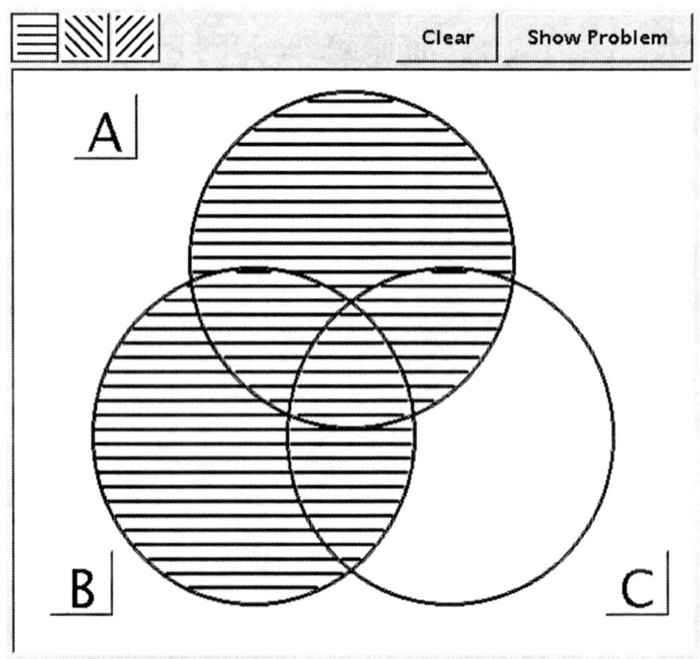

In addition to shading and writing set notation, there are other activities that are beneficial to use with preservice elementary and middle school teachers to build conceptual understanding of sets. "Interactivate" by Shodor (2010a) provides a "Venn Diagram Shape Sorter" (Shodor, 2010c) (see Figure 17). This courseware allows learners to create a Venn Diagram using up to two disjoint or intersecting circles, which are assigned rules using a drop-down menu of options. The users then sort 24 attribute blocks by dragging and dropping them onto the diagram. The shape must be dropped in the correct region or the tool will not allow the shape to be placed on the diagram. All 24 blocks must be sorted before the activity is complete, which helps teachers to realize that all shapes belong in the universe of the Venn Diagram regardless of the rules defining the sets. For increased mastery, it would be useful if the learners could create at least a third set in the Venn Diagram in this activity.

ReadWriteThink (http://www.readwritethink.org/), a nonprofit website maintained by the International Reading Association and the National Council of Teachers of English, with support from the Verizon Foundation, has an interactive tool that allows learners to generate their own Venn Diagrams (ReadThinkWrite, 2010) and sort sets of items they create (see Figure 18). Learners can choose to produce Venn Diagrams with either two or three intersecting circles and have the freedom to uniquely label each set. They can then create their own concepts, write descriptions for each, and drag and drop them into their Venn Diagrams.

Although there is no answer checking, this interactive tool allows the learners to be creative and develop their own meaningful sets of items. Such activities help preservice teachers think about how mathematics is integrated into the real world by bringing objects from everyday life into mathematics instruction.

Figure 17. Using a Venn Diagram to sort shapes by color and size (© 2010, Shodor. Used with permission.)

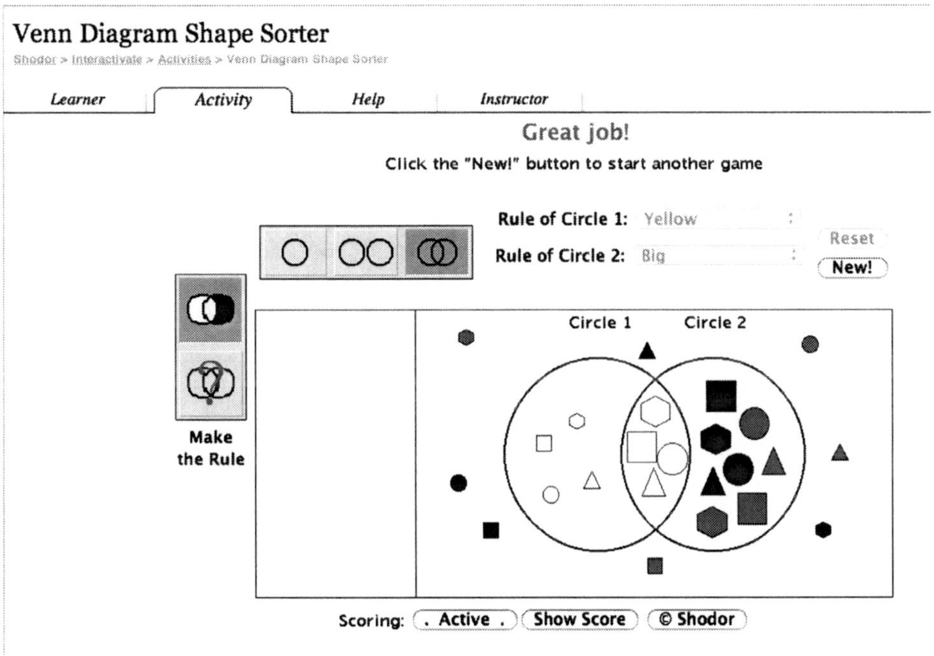

Figure 18. Creating a unique Venn Diagram and its concepts (© 2010, ReadThinkWrite. Used with permission.)

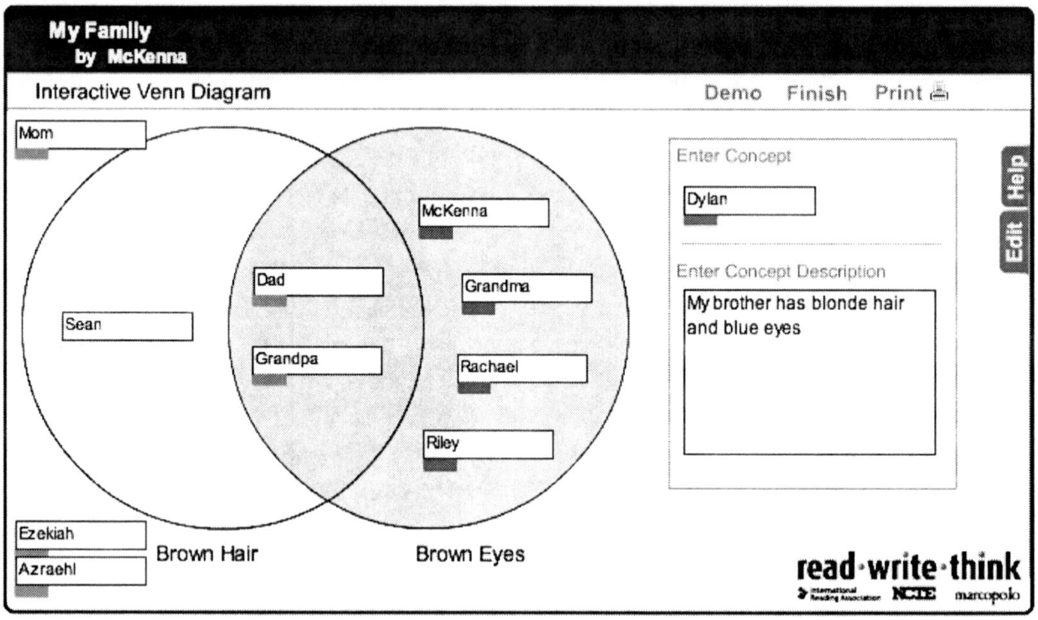

Geometry

GeoGebra (2010), developed by Markus Hohenwarter and an international team of programmers, offers an easy-to-use, interactive applet that can either be used directly in a web browser or downloaded for local use. Users are provided a blank two-dimensional plane (as either an axis or grid) on which they can place points and create lines and shapes. As the learners produce and manipulate objects by dragging points, updated information about the objects is displayed, including equations of lines, measurements of angles, and side lengths of created polygons. There is also an open field that allows users to input their own equations to be graphed. These dynamic features allow GeoGebra to be very versatile and useful for exploring a wide range of two-dimensional plane-geometry topics. Learners can move from investigating basic geometric principles, such as reflection, congruence, and similarity of polygons, to advanced ideas including tangent lines, ellipses, vectors, and hyperbolas.

Cinderella, developed at the Technical Universities of Munich and Berlin, is another example of interactive geometry software that learners can use to explore Euclidean Geometry by generating and controlling objects on a two-dimensional plane. The newest version of Cinderella is only available by purchase; however, an older version can be downloaded for free. Cinderella's website also offers a free gallery of "Math in Motion" interactive demonstrations (Cinderella, 2010) that cover a variety of advanced ideas. One example is a visual proof of the Pythagorean Theorem (Richter-Gebert & Kortenkamp, 2004). This tool allows the users to change the angles of a right triangle and see how the relationship among the squares created by the triangle's legs remains consistent (see Figure 19). This tool could be improved by providing the user updated information about the figures as they are manipulated, including angle measurements of the right triangle, areas of all resulting squares, and the sum of the areas of the two smaller squares.

Figure 19. Visual proof of Pythagoras' Theorem (© 2004, Jürgen Richter-Gebert & Ulrich Kortenkamp. Used with permission.)

The Wolfram Demonstrations Project also has many demonstrations addressing geometric topics (2010e). One such demonstration, "Interior Angles of a Triangle" (2010f), allows the user to alter the angles of a triangle and see how the sum of the three interior angles will always equal 180 degrees. Other demonstrations help learners interact with three-dimensional objects, which can be difficult to visualize. One example is "Cross Sections of Regular Polyhedra" (2010g), where users can fix three points on the edges of a polyhedron and see the cross section resulting from the intersection of the polyhedron and the plane created by the three points (see Figure 20). The user can rotate the polyhedron to see the polygonal cross section, shown in blue, from multiple angles. However, it would be more helpful to the learner if, as the points are manipulated on the polyhedron, the resulting polygonal cross section was also displayed two-dimensionally in addition to its three-dimensional representation. This could help users in visualizing and identifying the resulting cross-sectional polygon.

Moving on to the specialized topic of Non-Euclidean Geometry, we note that Carol Seaman and Stephen Szydlik have created a few interactive online tools (worksheets) to help learners explore lunes and triangles in spherical geometry (2002). This website accompanies an activity on the geometry of the surface of a Euclidean sphere, in the book, "Big Ideas in Mathematics for Future Middle Grades Teachers and Elementary Math Specialists: Big Ideas in Geometry" (Seaman & Szydlik, 2008). Users can manipulate points on a sphere and see angle measurements and areas of resulting lunes and spherical triangles. One interactive tool provides an updated sum of a spherical triangle's angles, highlighting the fact that the angles of triangles on spheres no longer add up to 180 degrees. Another tool helps learn-

Figure 20. Cross sections of regular polyhedra (© 2010, Wolfram Demonstrations Project. Used with permission.)

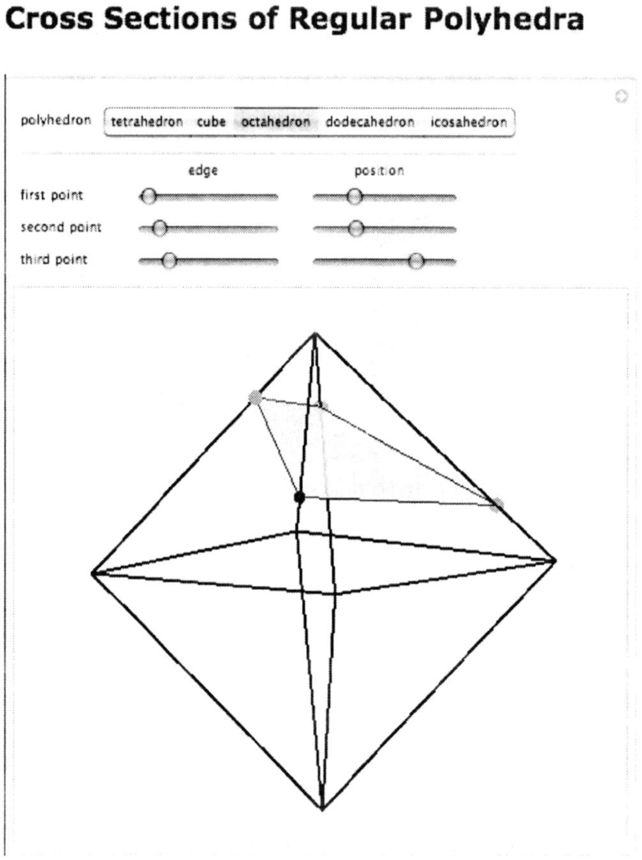

ers determine whether or not two spherical triangles can be similar without being congruent. One minor glitch of these last tools is that the user is able to drag the points off of the spheres, which could lead to confusion on part of the learner (see Figure 21).

The Importance of Implementing Online Tools with Preservice Teachers

Teachers are often resistant to integrating technology into their instruction. However, "barriers to using technology reported by teachers such as time, limited skill, fear of technology, and limited access to technology are partially addressed by easy-to-use [web-based learning tools] that are readily accessible in a wide variety of pedagogical formats," (Kay, Knaack, & Petrarca, 2009, p. 28). The interactive and dynamic online resources discussed throughout this chapter are all examples of web-based learning tools (WBLTs), defined by Kay, Knaack, and Petrarca (2009) as, "interactive web-based tools that support learning by enhancing, amplifying, and guiding the cognitive processes of learners," (pg. 28). When college instructors use interactive websites in both online and face-to-face college courses, preservice teachers gain experience with important pedagogical aspects of using technology in mathematics

Figure 21. Similar triangles on the sphere (with one point dragged off the sphere's surface) (© 2002, Carol Seaman & Stephen Szydlik. Used with permission.)

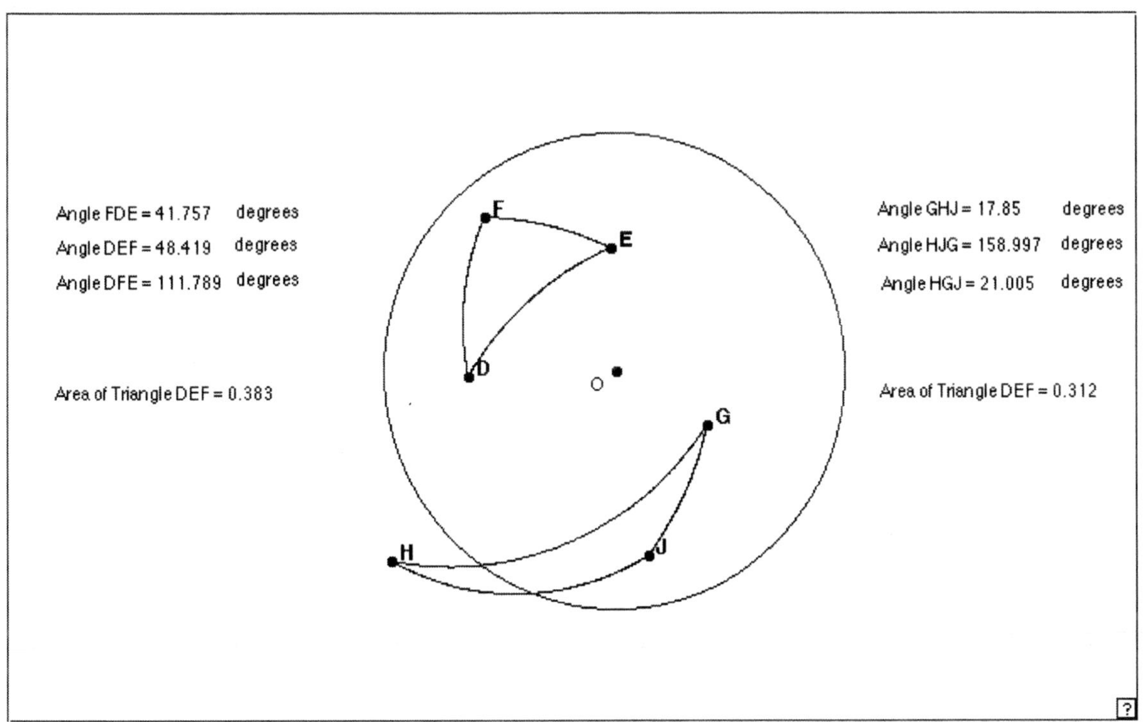

instruction, such as selecting materials that will be both engaging and easy-to-use.

The work of Means (2010) highlights the importance of effective classroom management on student learning gains with technology. Therefore, teachers need to be exposed to effective teaching practices that they can use to integrate technology into their own mathematics instruction. For example, it is important that preservice teachers have opportunities to observe efficient routines for transitioning students in and out of various software and technology usage. Kurz and Middleton (2006) showed that even short exposure with using technology can deepen preservice teachers' understandings of utilizing mathematics software and support their abilities to think about using technology with their future students. College instructors should refer to Kay (2006) who outlines ten key strategies for incorporating technology into preservice education based on his review of 68 refereed journal articles on introducing technology to preservice teachers.

FUTURE TRENDS AND RESEARCH DIRECTIONS

There is a clear trend in education as publishers are providing alternatives to their printed textbook offerings with electronic versions, i. e. ebooks. Until recently, ebooks presented digitized replicas of textbook pages (sometimes with supplemental CDs), which added little educational benefit beyond their portability. However, more recently ebooks have started incorporating digital media in new and innovative ways. For example, Pearson recently published the first calculus textbook to be offered as an ebook with built-in interactivity

(Briggs, Cochran, Gilette, & Schulz, 2010). This ebook combines static material from past versions of the printed text with 647 interactive demonstrations integrated into the written content. Cengage Learning is also working to produce an interactive ebook version of the most popular calculus book in the United States, Stewart's "Calculus" (Stewart, in press), for 2011 production. We expect this trend towards interactive ebooks to continue, spreading to all areas and levels of mathematics in the future. Much of mathematics is visual, and interactivity enhances the delivery of visualization. Even procedural mathematics can profit from interactivity, helping students to have yet another modality to grapple with difficult-to-grasp mathematical procedures in a game-like environment. As trends towards increased electronic and interactive learning materials continue, it will be essential for researchers to study the effects of these technological innovations on student learning.

With the forth-coming implementation of HTML5, it will be even easier for web-developers to integrate and Internet users to utilize interactive web-based resources. With HTML5, rich media elements (including interactive tools and video playback) will be native to the browser and no longer require the download and use of proprietary technologies like Flash and Mathematica Player (Keith, 2010). This innovation will eliminate the need for institutions to install and update a variety of plug-ins and external applications on the computers in their computer labs. Further, this has great importance for mobile devices (such as cell phones and tablet devices), which have limited computer capabilities but support browser implementations. These devices, which are currently unable to run third-party plugins, will now have the ability to display interactive web-based resources. This advancement may enable teachers to integrate more mobile technologies that students use on a regular basis outside of school into classroom settings, as suggested by Brooks-Young (2010).

Another trend in education is moving towards an increasing number of colleges and universities that are offering courses entirely online (Allen & Seaman, 2005). Yet, researchers have been questioning the quality of online experiences, especially of those designed for preservice teachers (Norton & Hathaway, 2008). Using and interacting with manipulatives is essential to developing preservice elementary and middle school teachers' mathematical knowledge for teaching, but students taking online courses will not have access to such physical manipulatives. We argue that when properly utilized in online mathematics courses, interactive virtual manipulatives and tools, as discussed in this chapter, have the potential to make online learning experiences for preservice teachers richer and more meaningful. Researchers need to explore how the integration of interactive web-based resources can facilitate learning when physical manipulatives are not available. In these as well as face-to-face teacher preparation classes, research is needed to explore any potential benefits or disadvantages afforded by the use of virtual manipulatives in addition to, or in lieu of, physical manipulatives.

Researchers could also view online mathematics resources from a multi-sensory learning perspective (Shams & Seitz, 2008). By design, web-based resources engage the visual senses; but those that are interactive also have the ability to engage the users' tactile senses. Furthermore, dynamic tools, which require user input, engage language and coding senses. Consequently, further research into the area of multi-sensory learning, using learning theories, could work to clarify how these different types of web-based resources can best be used to optimize learning for different learner styles.

Another area of research could extend from the work already put forth by Renkl (in press) and his colleagues (Atkinson, Derry, Renkl, & Wortham, 2008) on how students learn by reading worked-out mathematics examples. Many dynamic web-based mathematics tools, like calculator and solving tools, deliver worked-out solutions to problems selected by students. This area of research could be further developed in terms of learning mathematics through worked-out examples and solutions generated by online tools.

The magnitude of independent learning over the Internet suggests that the Internet is a vehicle for universal education in mathematics. Therefore, the audience for delivering mathematics over the Internet deserves greater attention. Specifically, in Figure 1 we identified a substantial audience of minority Internet users who appear to be independent learners. To the extent this includes traditionally underserved African-American and Hispanic minorities, this would appear to be ripe for further investigation.

In these and many additional areas, there is a great need for research into the efficacy of online mathematics demonstrations and interactive web-based resources. While there is an abundance of such materials available, there is a lack of research investigating whether or how they affect student learning. This research can and will take many paths as researchers and educators continue to explore emerging technologies and best practices for teaching mathematics online.

CONCLUSION

Web-based resources, especially those that are interactive, play an important role in mathematics e-learning. This chapter serves to apprise college mathematics instructors of a selection of educationally sound, web-based animations and interactive and dynamic tools, appropriate for undergraduate mathematics courses. We have reviewed these websites, highlighted their unique features, critiqued their deficiencies, raised questions about their pedagogical soundness, and identified best practices. Although we discuss representative websites for both collegiate mathematics and collegiate preservice teacher education, our selection is only a sample; we must note that many other worthy online mathematics resources go unmentioned.

Through our discussion, we have posited a hierarchy of online resources in terms of their degree of engagement for learning: static materials, animations, interactive tools, and dynamic tools. Although we consider all non-static types of web-based mathematics tools to be valuable aides in developing mathematical skills, we have clarified what is needed to create corresponding dynamic demonstrations for those that do not currently require user input. The Internet is fast becoming the universal teacher of mathematics and "best practices" for interactivity have a crucial role to play.

REFERENCES

Alberta Education. (2007). *Mathematics glossary*. Retrieved October 18, 2010, from http://www.learnalberta.ca/ content/ memg/ index.html

Alexa Internet, Inc. (2010). *Alexa: The Web information company*. Retrieved October 30, 2010, from http://www.alexa.com/

Allen, I., & Seaman, J. (2005). *Growing by degrees: Online education in the United States*. Retrieved September 28, 2006, from http://www.sloanc.org/ resources/ growing_by_degrees.pdf

Atkinson, R. K., Derry, S. J., Renkl, A., & Wortham, D. (2008). Learning from examples: Instructional principles from the worked examples research. *Review of Educational Research, 70*(2), 181–214.

Beck, G. (2010a). *Step-by-step derivatives*. Retrieved June 4, 2010, from http://calc101.com/ webMathematica/ derivatives.jsp

Beck, G. (2010b). *Step-by-step linear equations, matrices and determinants*. Retrieved June 4, 2010, from http://calc101.com/ webMathematica/ matrix-algebra.jsp

Bogomolny, A. (2010a). *Function, derivative, and integral*. Retrieved November 19, 2010, from http://www.cut-the-knot.org/ Curriculum/ Calculus/ CubicSpline.shtml

Bogomolny, A. (2010b). *Interactive mathematics activities*. Retrieved June 4, 2010, from http:// www.cut-the-knot.org/ Curriculum/ index.shtml

Bogomolny, A. (2010c). *Riemann sums–Function integration*. Retrieved November 19, 2010, from http://www.cut-the-knot.org/ Curriculum/ Calculus/ RiemannSums.shtml

Briggs, W. L., Cochran, L., Gilette, B., & Schulz, E. (2010). *Calculus: Early transcendentals*. Pearson/Addison-Wesley.

Brooks-Young, S. (2010). *Teaching with tools kids really use: Learning with web and mobile technologies*. Thousand Oaks, CA: Corwin.

Cherkas, B. (2010). *Online $\sqrt{Intelligent}$* graphing calculators. Retrieved June 4, 2010, from http:// www.webgraphing.com/ graphing_basic.jsp

Cinderella. (2010). *Cinderella: 2 examples*. Retrieved October 30, 2010, from http://cinderella.de/ files/ HTMLDemos/

Compete, Inc. (2010). *Website*. Retrieved October 30, 2010, from http://www.compete.com

Computer Algebra in Mathematics Education. (2010). *Website*. Retrieved November 4, 2010, from http://www.lkl.ac.uk/ research/ came/ index.html

Crickweb. (2010). *Crickweb.co.uk – Primary interactive resources*. Retrieved June 15, 2010, from http://www.crickweb.co.uk/

Deubel, P. (2010). *Math manipulatives, from computing technology for math excellence*. Retrieved June 15, 2010, from http://www.ct4me.net/ math_manipulatives.htm

Eves, H. (1965). *A survey of geometry* (revised ed.). Boston, MA: Allyn & Bacon.

GeoGebra. (2010). *GeoGebra*. Retrieved October 26, 2010, from http://www.geogebra.org/ cms/

Hill, D. R., & Roberts, L. F. (2010a). *Demos with positive impact*. Retrieved June 4, 2010, from http://mathdemos.gcsu.edu/ mathdemos/ index.html

Hill, D. R., & Roberts, L. F. (2010b). *The disk method for volumes of solids of revolution*. Retrieved June 4, 2010, from http://mathdemos.gcsu.edu/ mathdemos/ diskmethod/ diskmethod.html

Hill, D. R., & Roberts, L. F. (2010c). *Solids of revolution: The method of shells*. Retrieved June 4, 2010, from http://mathdemos.gcsu.edu/ mathdemos/ shellmethod/

Hill, D. R., & Roberts, L. F. (2010d). *Volumes by section*. Retrieved June 4, 2010, from http://mathdemos.gcsu.edu/ mathdemos/ sectionmethod/ sectionmethod.html/

Hill, D. R., & Roberts, L. F. (2010e). *The washer method for solids of revolution*. Retrieved June 4, 2010, from http://mathdemos.gcsu.edu/ mathdemos/ washermethod/

Holt, Rinehart, & Winston. (2010). *Holt online learning: Graphing calculator*. Retrieved June 4, 2010, from http://my.hrw.com/ math06_07/ nsmedia/ tools/ Graph_Calculator/graphCalc.html

Jefferson County Schools. (2010). *Interactive math websites*. Retrieved June 15, 2010, from http://jc-schools.net/ tutorials/ interact-math.htm

Kay, R. H. (2006). Evaluating strategies used to incorporate technology into preservice education: A review of the literature. *Journal of Research on Technology in Education*, *38*(4), 383–408.

Kay, R. H., Knaack, L., & Petrarca, D. (2009). Exploring teachers perceptions of Web-based learning tools. *Interdisciplinary Journal of E-Learning and Learning Objects*, *9*, 27–50.

Keith, J. (2010). *HTML5 for Web designers*. New York, NY: A Book Apart.

Kraus, M. (2010). *LiveGraphics3D homepage*. Retrieved on June 21, 2010, from http://wwwvis.informatik.uni-stuttgart.de/ ~kraus/ LiveGraphics3D/ index.html

Kurz, T. L., & Middleton, J. A. (2006). Using a functional approach to change preservice teachers' understanding of mathematics software. *Journal of Research on Technology in Education*, *39*(1), 45–65.

Louisiana Department of Education. (2010). *Math websites*. Retrieved June 15, 2010, from http://sda.doe.louisiana.gov/ ResourceFiles/ Math%20 websites.doc

Lundin, P. (2010). *Online graphing calculator*. Coolmath. Retrieved June 4, 2010, from http://www.coolmath.com/ graphit/

Maheswaran, M. (2010). *A catalog of mathematics resources on the WWW and the Internet*. Retrieved October 26, 2010, from http://mthwww.uwc.edu/ wwwmahes/ files/ math01.htm

Math Forum. (2010a). *Math Forum Internet mathematics library: Full table of contents*. Retrieved October 26, 2010, from http://mathforum.org/ library/ toc.html

Math Forum. (2010b). *Math Forum staff, 2008-2010*. Retrieved October 26, 2010, from http://mathforum.org/ staff.html

Maths Online. (2010). *Math links and online tools*. Retrieved October 26, 2010, from http://www.univie.ac.at/ future.media/ moe/ collections.html

Matti Math. (2010). *Store home, development*. Retrieved June 17, 2010, from http://www.mattimath.com/

Means, B. (2010). Technology and education change: Focus on student learning. *Journal of Research on Technology in Education*, *42*(3), 285–307.

National Council of Teachers of Mathematics. (2000). *Principles and standards for school mathematics*. Reston, VA: NCTM.

National Council of Teachers of Mathematics. (2010). *Electronic examples*. Retrieved June 7, 2010, from http://standards.nctm.org/ document/ eexamples

Norton, P., & Hathaway, D. (2008). Exploring two teacher education online learning designs: A classroom of one or many? *Journal of Research on Technology in Education*, *40*(4), 475–495.

Quantcast Corporation. (2010). *Glossary*. Retrieved December 6, 2010, from http://www.quantcast.com/ learning-center/ glossary

QuickMath. (2010). *Quadratics*. Retrieved June 4, 2010, from http://quickmath.com/ webMathematica3/ quickmath/ page.jsp?s1=equations&s2=quadratics&s3=basic

ReadWriteThink. (2010). *Interactive Venn diagram, 2 circles*. Retrieved June 7, 2010, from http://www.readwritethink.org/ classroom-resources/ student-interactives/ venn-diagram-circles-30006.html

Richter-Gebert, J., & Kortenkamp, U. (2004). *Cinderella.2 math in motion: Visual proof of Pythagoras' Theorem*. Retrieved October 30, 2010, from http://cinderella.de/ files/ HTMLDemos/ 1G01_Pythagoras.html

Seaman, C. E., & Szydlik, J. E. (2008). *Big ideas in mathematics fort future middle grades teachers and elementary math specialists: Big ideas in geometry*. Boston, MA: McGraw-Hill.

Seaman, C. E., & Szydlik, S. D. (2002). *Lunes and triangles in spherical geometry*. Retrieved October 28, 2010, from http://www.uwosh.edu/ faculty_staff/ szydliks/ elliptic/ elliptic.htm

Shams, L., & Seitz, A. R. (2008). Benefits of multisensory learning . *Trends in Cognitive Sciences*, *12*(11), 411–417. doi:10.1016/j.tics.2008.07.006

Shodor. (2010a). *Interactivate*. Retrieved June 7, 2010, from http://www.shodor.org/ interactivate/

Shodor. (2010b). *Number base clocks, from Interactivate*. Retrieved June 9, 2010, from http:// www.shodor.org/ interactivate/ activities/ NumberBaseClocks/

Shodor. (2010c). *Venn diagram shape sorter, from Interactivate*. Retrieved June 7, 2010, from http://www.shodor.org/interactivate/activities/ ShapeSorter/

Solve My Math. (2010). *Quadratic equation solver*. Retrieved June 4, 2010, from http://www. solvemymath.com/ online_math_calculator/ algebra_combinatorics/ equations/ quadratic_ equation.php

Stapel, E. (2010). *Purplemath*. Retrieved October 30, 2010, from http://www.purplemath.com/

Stewart, J. (in press). Single variable calculus e-book. *Cengage Learning*.

The Wolfram Demonstrations Project. (2010a). *Website*. Retrieved June 4, 2010, from http:// demonstrations. wolfram.com/index.html

The Wolfram Demonstrations Project. (2010b). *Two points determine a line*, (contributed by George Brown). Retrieved November 20, 2010, from http://demonstrations.wolfram.com/ TwoPointsDetermineALine/

The Wolfram Demonstrations Project. (2010c). *Volumes of revolution using cylindrical shells*, (contributed by Stephen Wilkerson). Retrieved November 20, 2010, from http://demonstrations. wolfram.com/ VolumesOfRevolution UsingCylindrical Shells/

The Wolfram Demonstrations Project. (2010d). *The wire problem*, (contributed by Marc Brodie). Retrieved November 20, 2010, from http:// demonstrations.wolfram.com/TheWireProblem/

The Wolfram Demonstrations Project. (2010e). *High school geometry*. Retrieved October 26, 2010, from http://demonstrations.wolfram.com/ education.html?edutag=High%20 School %20Geometry&start= 1&limit=20&sortmethod=recent

The Wolfram Demonstrations Project. (2010f). *Interior angles of a triangle*, (contributed by Jon McLoone). Retrieved October 26, 2010, from http://demonstrations.wolfram.com/ InteriorAnglesOfATriangle/

The Wolfram Demonstrations Project. (2010g). *Cross sections of regular polyhedra*, (contributed by Oleksandr Pavlyk and Maxim Rytin). Retrieved October 26, 2010, from http://demonstrations.wolfram.com/ CrossSectionsOf RegularPolyhedra/

Utah State University. (2010a). *Base blocks*. National Library of Virtual Manipulatives. Retrieved June 7, 2010, from http://nlvm.usu.edu/ en/ nav/ frames_asid_152_g_1_t_1.html?from=topic_t_1. html

Utah State University. (2010b). *Base blocks addition*. National Library of Virtual Manipulatives. Retrieved June 15, 2010, from http:// nlvm.usu.edu/en/nav/frames_asid_154_g_3_t_1. html?from=topic_t_1.html

Utah State University. (2010c). *Base blocks subtraction*. National Library of Virtual Manipulatives. Retrieved June 15, 2010, from http://nlvm. usu.edu/ en/ nav/ frames_asid_155_g_ 3_t_1. html?from=topic_ t_1.html

Utah State University. (2010d). *Fractions – Rectangle multiplication*. National Library of Virtual Manipulatives. Retrieved June 7, 2010, from http:// nlvm.usu.edu/en/nav/frames_asid_194_g_2_t_1. html ?from=topic_t_1.html

Utah State University. (2010e). *National Library of Virtual Manipulatives*. Retrieved June 7, 2010, from http://nlvm.usu.edu/

Utah State University. (2010f). *Venn diagrams*. National Library of Virtual Manipulatives. Retrieved June 7, 2010, from http://nlvm.usu.edu/en/ nav/ frames_ asid_153_g_ 2_t_1.html?open=instructions&from=topic_t_1.html

WebMath. (2010). *Solve a quadratic equation by factoring*. Retrieved June 4, 2010, from http://www.webmath.com/ quadtri.html.com

Weisstein, E. W. (2010a). *Wolfram MathWorld*. Retrieved June 19, 2010, from http://mathworld.wolfram.com/

Weisstein, E. W. (2010b). *Animated GIFs*. Retrieved June 19, 2010, from http://mathworld.wolfram.com/ topics/ AnimatedGIFs.html

Weisstein, E. W. (2010c). *Ellipse*. Retrieved June 19, 2010, from http://mathworld.wolfram.com/Ellipse.html

Weisstein, E. W. (2010d). *Interactive entries: LiveGraphics3D applets*. Retrieved June 21, 2010, from http://mathworld.wolfram.com/ Ellipse.html

Wikipedia. (2010). *Dynamic Web page*. Retrieved June 16, 2010, from http://en.wikipedia.org/ wiki/Dynamic_web_page

Wilson, J. (2010). *Johnie's math page*. Retrieved October 18, 2010, from http://jmathpage.com/

ADDITIONAL READING

Atkinson, R. K., & Renkl, A. (Eds.). (2007). Interactive learning environments: Contemporary issues and trends [Special Issue]. *Educational Psychology Review*, *19*, 235–399. doi:10.1007/s10648-007-9052-5

Aust, R., Newberry, B., O'Brien, J., & Thomas, J. (2005). Learning generation: Fostering innovation with tomorrow's teachers and technology. *Journal of Technology and Teacher Education*, *13*(2), 167–195.

Bullock, D. (2004). Moving from theory to practice: An examination of the factors that preservice teachers encounter as the attempt to gain experience teaching with technology during field placement experiences. *Journal of Technology and Teacher Education*, *12*(2), 211–237.

Chen, C., & Bradshaw, A. C. (2007). The effect of web-based question prompts on scaffolding knowledge integration and ill-structured problem solving. *Journal of Research on Technology in Education*, *39*(4), 359–375.

Doering, A., Hughes, J., & Huffinan, D. (2003). Preservice teachers: Are we thinking with technology? *Journal of Research on Technology in Education*, *35*(3), 342–361.

Engelbrecht, J., & Harding, A. (2005). Teaching undergraduate mathematics on the Internet, part I: Technologies and taxonomy. *Educational Studies in Mathematics*, *58*, 235–252. doi:10.1007/s10649-005-6456-3

Gadanidis, G., Gadanidis, J., & Schindler, K. (2003). Factors mediating the use of online applets in the lesson planning of pre-service mathematics teachers. *Journal of Computers in Mathematics and Science Teaching*, *22*(4), 323–344.

Hilbert, T. S., Renkl, A., Schworm, S., Kessler, S., & Reiss, K. (2008). Learning to teach with worked-out examples: A computer-based learning environment for teachers. *Journal of Computer Assisted Learning*, *24*, 316–332. doi:10.1111/j.1365-2729.2007.00266.x

Jacobs, K. L. (2005). Investigation of interactive online visual tools for the learning of mathematics. *International Journal of Mathematical Education in Science and Technology*, *36*(7), 761–768. doi:10.1080/00207390500271149

Johnson, S. (2005). *Everything bad is good for you: How today's popular culture is actually making us smarter*. New York, NY: Riverhead.

Kay, R. H., Knaack, L., & Muirhead, B. (2009). A formative analysis of instructional strategies for using learning objects. *Journal of Interactive Learning Research*, *20*(3).

Nguyen, D. M., & Kulm, G. (2005). Using web-based practice to enhance mathematics learning and achievement. *Journal of Interactive Online Learning*, *3*(3).

Renkl, A. (in press). Instruction based on examples . In Mayer, R. E., & Alexander, P. A. (Eds.), *Handbook of research on learning and instruction*. New York, NY: Routledge.

Renkl, A., & Atkinson, R. K. (2007). Interactive learning environments: Contemporary issues and trends. An introduction to the special issue. *Educational Psychology Review*, *19*, 235–238. doi:10.1007/s10648-007-9052-5

Russell, M., Bebell, D., O'Dwyer, L., & O'Connor, K. (2003). Examining teacher technology use: Implications for preservice and inservice teacher preparation. *Journal of Teacher Education*, *54*(4), 297–310. doi:10.1177/0022487103255985

Thompson, A. D. (2005). Scientifically based research: Establishing a research agenda for the technology in teacher education community. *Journal of Research on Technology in Education*, *37*(4), 331–337.

Wilson, L. (2009). Best practices for using games & simulations in the classroom. *Software and Information Industry Association* (*SIIA*). Downloaded on June 12, 2010, from http://www.siia.net/ index.php? searchword=math&ordering=newest&s earchphrase=all&limit=20&Itemid=317&option= com_search

KEY TERMS AND DEFINITIONS

Animations: Computer-generated graphics with motion

Dynamic Web-Based Resources: Websites that allow learners to interact with online tools that generate fresh customized content based on user input

Interactive Web-Based Resources: Websites that allow learners to interact with online tools to explore concepts, but do not require user input

Mathematical Demonstrations: Animations and interactive displays that visually exhibit a mathematical concept and/or allows exploration of the concept

Static Web-Based Resources: Websites that provide learners with passive content similar to material printed in a textbook

Web-Based Resources: Websites and web tools offered online, which require Internet access

ENDNOTES

1. Disclosure: One of the authors, Barry Cherkas, is the founder and owner of the website http://www.WebGraphing.com, which is referred to in this chapter.

Chapter 15
NAUK.si:
Using Learning Blocks to Prepare E-Content for Teaching Mathematics

M. Lokar
University of Ljubljana, Slovenia

P. Lukšič
University of Ljubljana, Slovenia

B. Horvat
University of Ljubljana, Slovenia

ABSTRACT

The lack of tools that are easy to use, but at the same time provide the functionality required for a quality education, and technical knowledge that is necessary for the implementation of electronic-based education, are currently the main two obstacles that hinder wider use of e-learning in schools as well as elsewhere. The NAUK group (http://www.nauk.si) is aiming to solve that problem by developing a new paradigm of learning blocks accompanied by tools for easy creation of content and its adaptation to the teachers' needs. When dealing with e-learning content it is our goal to allow teachers to be in control of the content, thereby putting them "back into the game."

DOI: 10.4018/978-1-60960-875-0.ch015

INTRODUCTION

The world we live in is currently undergoing substantial changes. Namely, we are witnessing the process of transition from the Industrial Age to the Information Age. In the last 100 years our lives have virtually been turned upside down. For example, a surgeon from the second half of the 19th century would be completely lost if he were to walk into a modern operating room. Not just because of all the new equipment; the change in the procedures performed is even greater.

What if a teacher travelled through time? Would he or she see any substantial changes in the educational process? The world is changing rapidly, but the educational system is not keeping pace. The currently prevailing educational model is still the same as the one established in the 19th century, developed to meet the needs of industrial economy. At the time, there were a certain number of children in the classroom, who were all taught in the same way, using the same approach and the same teaching materials (http://www.wearethepeoplemovie.com; Banathy, 1991; Education, n.d.).

The children sitting in the classrooms of today are different. They are the so called "net natives" (Prensky, 2001). Using information and communication technology is something completely natural for those pupils. Their approach to the process of gathering information and performing communication is different. Computers and communication devices are ubiquitous to them (Prensky, 2001; Lusoli & Miltgen, 2009; Evans, 2007). Furthermore, students are progressively becoming an increasingly heterogeneous group, mostly due to the lifelong learning initiative.

We live in a society where everything is individualized and personalized: computers are built to our exact specifications; we personalize our mobile phones with ringtones, wallpapers, skins, etc. Students, on the other hand, are repeatedly taught in the same way. If we take into account the fact that not all students are learning at the same pace, in the same environment, following the same learning path, and using the same methods, it soon becomes apparent that an individualized approach is absolutely essential. It has been widely confirmed by research that every individual assimilates information according to their own needs and interests. Learning styles vary as well. Some people are visual learners, some learn by auditory means, others kinesthetically (Dunn et al., 2002).

The current public education systems continue to assert that a "one-size-fits-all" full time classroom-based model can and will effectively serve all students (http://www.wearethepeoplemovie.com, Banathy, 1991). However, just as everything else, education needs to be customized.

There has been extensive research done regarding the appropriate role of technology in the educational process; therefore, we will not even attempt to cite the numerous sources. However, the findings can be neatly summarized in two sentences; both are quotations from the Teaching Matters booklet: A handbook for UTS academic staff from Institute for Interactive Media and Learning, University of Technology, Sydney (IML, 2009). The first one states that "New technologies should be used in the most appropriate way to provide a quality learning experience for students. ", whereas the second one determines that "The most effective kind of learning experience is determined not by the technology available, but by considering what is most appropriate for the students, the subject and the learning objectives and then selecting the most appropriate technology to use."

Therefore, it is apparent that the existing educational model is not appropriate anymore. Organizational issues shall not be discussed in this chapter, although they are numerous and need to be considered as well; two examples of such issues being: is the existing course model still sustainable, and is the formal division of students into different classes of equal size and age still appropriate? Instead, the chapter will focus on an issue that is crucial to the development of education, although it may not possess the immediate media visibility and is consequently not as highly politicized. The focus will be on the influence of the current changes in the society upon the teaching materials used in the educational process. The two main challenges regarding this part are:

- to establish the appropriate role of technology in the educational process and
- the requirement for the individualization and personalization of the educational process.

The role of the teacher in the 21st century needs to be redefined. The amount of "ex cathedra" lecturing is steadily diminishing. As stated in numerous papers and books (Kissing, 2008; Elliot 1993; Carlgren et al., 1994; Bryan, 2006; Keiny, 2002), the new role means that teachers at all stages of education should be oriented towards guiding the learner through the learning process. They are no longer "walking encyclopedias" or "talking textbooks" (Rodriguez & Kitchen, 2005) as this role has recently been successfully replaced by the internet. Instead, teachers are planners, strategists, researchers, pedagogical diagnosticians, work organizers, counselors, tutors, etc. Their main task is to guide a learner through pieces of information (teaching resources) towards knowledge, with the requirement to concretize the educational content and adapt it to the interests and abilities of a particular learner (Johnston-Wilder & Pimm, 2004).

In this chapter one of the key questions posed will be:

Are there any resources available that have been adapted to the redefined role of the teacher?

ORGANIZING AND USING TEACHING RESOURCES

The phase of organizing and choosing teaching resources is one of the fundamental steps in the learning process. At this step the teacher actually makes the decision how the learning process will be performed. It is at this step that factors, such as the class we are teaching, the pedagogical situation and other numerous issues that influence the learning and teaching process are taken into account.

It is very rare that the sum of these factors creates a situation in which the final decision is to take a certain textbook and use it from the first page to the last one. Combinations of different materials are usually prepared in this process of organizing the resources. Workbooks, tasks, pages on the Internet, etc., are chosen. There are countless choices to be made. The teacher then uses technology to "glue" resources together; from simple accessories like sticky tape and scissors to more sophisticated ones like the Copy and Paste functions of an operating system when resources are available electronically.

Only rarely do we encounter a learning situation where there exists an "ideal" resource, say a textbook that can be used without any change whatsoever. Why? Have you as a teacher ever considered how great it would be if you could have a slightly different textbook with a different sequence of examples, with a certain part omitted, some parts added from another source, etc.? The reason for such a wish is completely natural. Authors of resources (workbooks, for example) envisage a hypothetical (ideal) pedagogical situation with hypothetical students. But the actual teaching process always differs at least slightly from the hypothetical one that the author had in mind. Since good teachers should use resources in the most appropriate way, they are forced to combine and adapt various resources available.

What about e-resources, e.g. resources that use modern information communication technology (ICT)? As more and more teaching resources are available in this form, we should expect a teacher's task in managing the resources to be getting easier. Unfortunately, this is not usually the case. Several studies (Assche & Vuorikari, 2006; Lokar, 2006) have shown that teachers use few of the e-resources available. A somewhat surprising fact is that math teachers are especially slow to adopt such materials. Interviews with teachers (Lokar, 2006) exposed several reasons for this. The possibility of content modification is one of the properties math teachers demand but teaching materials most often lack. If teachers have the possibility of modifying the teaching material provided, they have a much more positive attitude towards using the particular material, as discovered by Hwang (2008). And the teachers' attitude towards the material used is perhaps the most important part of the usage of ICT in the teaching process. Math teachers, especially those teaching in upper primary and secondary schools, do not like using close form solutions or solutions where the complete didactical situation relies on a particular aspect of a certain tool; they want to be in control of the whole process (Lokar, 2006).

Thus it is not surprising that statements similar to the following one can often be encountered:

Using information and communications technology and electronic teaching materials in the teaching process has several advantages. The present generation of pupils is used to electronically delivered materials, so they expect to access information at school in the same way. As electronic teaching materials still have a scent of novelty, their use provides motivation. It also brings interactivity and through it immediate feedback. Moreover, using electronic teaching materials is cost efficient, as it allows infinite re-usage; suitable planning can also reduce photocopying. Time efficiency is another important aspect. It is possible to accomplish lots of routine tasks in a short time. The teacher prepares routine task exercises more easily on one hand and on the other hand, the pupil performs lots of experiments in learning through discovery. (Jakončič-Faganel & Lokar, 2006)

But are such statements really valid? Namely, the use of ICT in education and training has been a priority in most European countries during the last decade, but the progress has been uneven. As it was reported in the 2006 survey of several research studies (Balanskat et al., 2006), only a small percentage of schools have successfully introduced ICT into the curriculum, and demonstrate effective and appropriate ICT use to support and transform the teaching and learning. Most schools, however, were in the early phase of ICT adoption, characterized by uncoordinated provision and use, little enhancement of the learning process, some development of e-learning, but there has been no profound influence on learning and teaching.

The most interesting and relevant points for the teaching of mathematics in the summary of learning outcomes reported are:

- ICT has a positive impact on educational performance in primary schools, particularly in English as a foreign language, but less so in science and not at all in mathematics lessons.
- There is a positive association between the length of time of ICT use and the students' performance in PISA mathematics tests.
- Schools with higher levels of e-maturity demonstrate a more rapid increase in performance scores than those with lower levels.
- Schools with good ICT resources achieve better results than those that are poorly equipped.
- ICT investment impacts educational standards the most when the schools have an interest for making efficient use of it.

CONCERNS WHEN USING ICT IN THE TEACHING PROCESS

In the above mentioned report some contradictory facts are stated about the possibility of ICT usage having a positive impact on the teaching and learning of mathematics. Nevertheless, the opinion that technology has a positive influence on the teaching and learning of mathematics prevails, especially among the school policy makers. However, the question exists whether teachers share the same opinion about the advantages of incorporating ICT in the teaching process? A survey among Slovenian secondary school math teachers conducted in 2000, regarding computer algebra systems (CAS) and their usage in teaching, revealed that about 17% of the teachers are strongly opposed to using CAS in the classrooms. If we add merely a half of the 40% who did not respond, it can be deduced that more than a third of secondary school math teachers are opposed to the usage of CAS in math classrooms. Not to mention that just about 10% of the responses were in favor of using CAS in assessments. Unfortunately, the follow-up survey, planned for the current school year, has been postponed due to unexpected circumstances. However, from the present Slovenian activities regarding the incorporation of technology like CAS, CAGD (Computer Aided Geometric Design) and ICT into the teaching of mathematics, one can easily conclude that the teachers' opinions are largely the same as ten years ago.

Interviews with teachers revealed two main concerns to be:

- When using CAS and CAGD supported activities in the classroom, are the same goals attained as with conventional teaching methods?
- As the ultimate goal of all secondary education is still the success at the final external examination, why "waste" hours for introducing technology?

Besides these two concerns, several other negative comments were also expressed:

- Students merely look at pictures and icons – they do not read instructions anymore.
- Interactive tests can almost always be solved with a try-until-you-succeed approach or are much too restrictive, without providing sufficient feedback or allowing different ways of finishing the test.
- Electronic teaching materials (ETMs) frequently offer too much guidance without the possibility of turning this function off or fine tuning it according to the teachers' or learners' needs.
- Using ETMs means less verbal communication, which is a skill that most pupils lack.
- There is a shortage of suitable ETMs.
- The quality of some teaching materials is dubious.
- The ways of adapting the materials are too demanding.
- There is a lack of proper classification of the materials.

Further problems were identified; they were connected to the lack of use of ICT in pre-service and in-service teacher training, as efficient and proper use of ICT and ETMs requires a much higher level of didactical competence. In spite of all the research, there are still several concerns, expressed in (Lokar, 2000) and similarly in (Lokar, 2005), for example:

Even when someone is convinced that technology should by all means be used when teaching mathematics, he or she usually encounters several issues. How does one find proper answers to them, especially when he or she is in the position of trying to convince someone else about the benefits of such an approach?

Not all of the aforementioned concerns will be addressed here. Instead, the teachers' access to ETMs shall be the sole focus of this chapter. Namely, the possibility of modifying an ETM is one of the properties that teachers of mathematics demand. If teachers have at least the possibility to modify the teaching material prepared, they have a much better attitude towards its usage, which is

Figure 1. Two different models of preparing a resource

perhaps the most important part influencing the process of adopting ICT in the teaching process.

There is a conflict between the possibilities technology provides, the teachers' wishes and the e-materials available. Namely, all too often the materials are monolithic blocks (or at least their main parts are), constructed in the way that resembles an ordinary book or workbook. This demands that the teacher takes them as a whole, precisely in the order they were written in. Many projects focusing on the development of e-resources are complete portals where navigation through the resources must be followed in the exact way the author(s) had imagined. We encounter web portals with embedded flash animations, heavy and sophisticated usage of frames, applets without the source, which are impossible to adapt, etc.

Using an analogy to toys – a ship made of Lego® bricks has a far greater pedagogical potential as pre-constructed, unchangeable models. So the process should be changed from building resources in the form shown on the left side of Figure 1 to the resources prepared in the way as the model on the right side.

Following are some widely recognized problems associated with the existing e-learning content:

- It is often realized as a digitized book, multimedia-poor, with no real interactivity.
- It can only be used in one way (the content should be modified automatically – but following the same learning process).
- The instructions for the teacher are missing (how to present the material, what is the goal of the content at each step).
- The content is too strongly integrated into the presentation of the material – no changes are possible.
- Its structure is linear, although the process of learning is usually not.
- It has no contextual dependencies, which are useful when informing the student about his or her mistakes and the consequences resulting from these errors.
- It uses new teaching approaches insufficiently. Students will often use the content when a teacher is not present, therefore the concept of multiple interpretations of the same topic is very important, as well as motivation, progressive acquisition of knowledge, examinations, etc.

Too many resources are created from the point of view that the student is the final and independent user, where the author prescribes the way the resource is to be used. This is suitable (and even this can be debatable) for "self studying" (see Figure 2).

Figure 2. Usual author-student relation when dealing with resources

However, the basic proposition when these materials were being developed was that they were to be used in the learning process with a teacher present. Students are usually not exposed directly to the task as there is a teacher present in most cases, being the one who serves as an intermediary between the task and the student. Therefore, the teacher is actually in a worse situation than when using a classic textbook. These e-materials are often so technologically "closed" that there is no such tool as scissors, which are used when recombining classic, printed materials. Teachers often encounter problems if they want to use only a part of the content, not to mention the fact that it is not usually possible to adapt the materials at all.

As mentioned before, the pedagogical situation the author envisages does not always fit its purpose. This will be illustrated with a simple example. As part of a teaching resource we (the authors) want to illustrate the Thales' theorem. There are several possibilities; three of them are depicted in Figures 3-5.

Several examples of illustrating the Thales' theorem were prepared, also using other tools (Cabri Geometre and C.a.R.). When a group of teachers were asked which one was the most useful for their teaching and should thus be chosen for our resource, the responses were not uniform at all. As can be expected, teachers rated their usefulness regarding their typical pedagogical situations. As these were diverse, so were their opinions.

The questions that arise are evident. Who should decide on "the proper" part of the resource and how should this decision be implemented? Should that be the author or a teacher or even the end user (a student)? Should the part be fixed or should it allow personalization? The teacher is the one who comes into direct contact with the student. Should not therefore the teacher decide which materials are appropriate for the situation given? Why not use the possibilities offered by new technologies and at least give the teachers the chance to adapt the materials to their and their students' needs. Claims such as the following have often been postulated:

- Teachers do not want too many different interpretations of the same topic.
- Teachers are more or less passive, they want exactly the material specified, and then they will keep it and use exactly as is.
- Teachers do not possess the knowledge or the time to adapt and combine the materials in their own way.
- Only the author is the one who is aware of the proper sequence of different parts of the material.

Figure 3. Video instructions and a GeoGebra Applet with construction steps for illustrating the Thales' theorem

Thales' Theorem

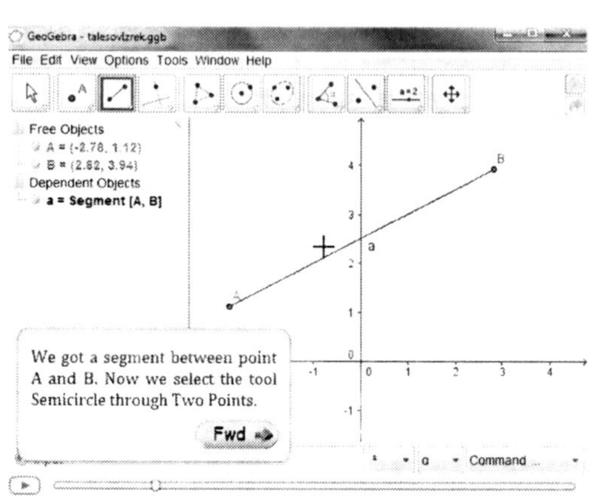

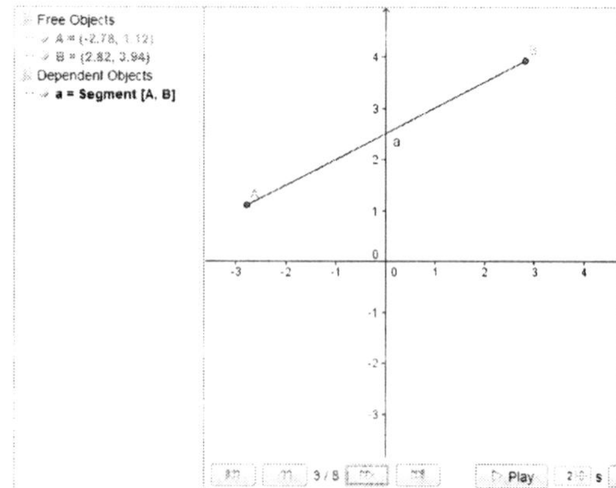

Figure 4. Video instructions for illustrating the Thales' theorem and a GeoGebra Applet for practicing

Thales' Theorem

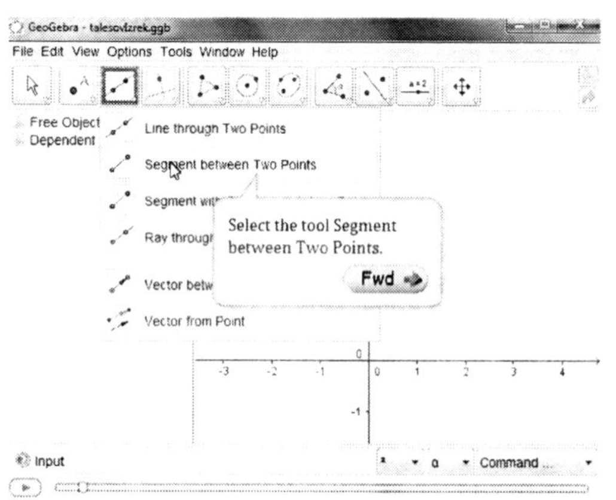

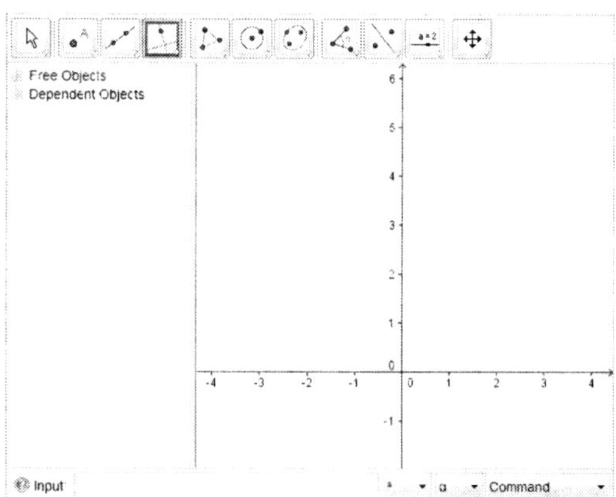

However, such claims simply cannot (and should not) apply to all the teachers.

When designing and evaluating a particular teaching resource the authors should envision the whole process of design, usage and modification of the resource. The entire life cycle of an e-learning material is well described in Assche and Vuorikari (2006) and is summarized in Figure 6.

The lower circle, where the process of reuse and adaptation is performed, is the part all too many resource authors neglect. Most of the teaching resources are meant for the teacher, who is present throughout the learning process and instructs the students how to use these resources. Therefore the authors of e-resources should recognize and acknowledge the role of the teacher.

Figure 5. A GeoGebra Applet with construction steps for illustrating the Thales' theorem and a GeoGebra Applet for practicing

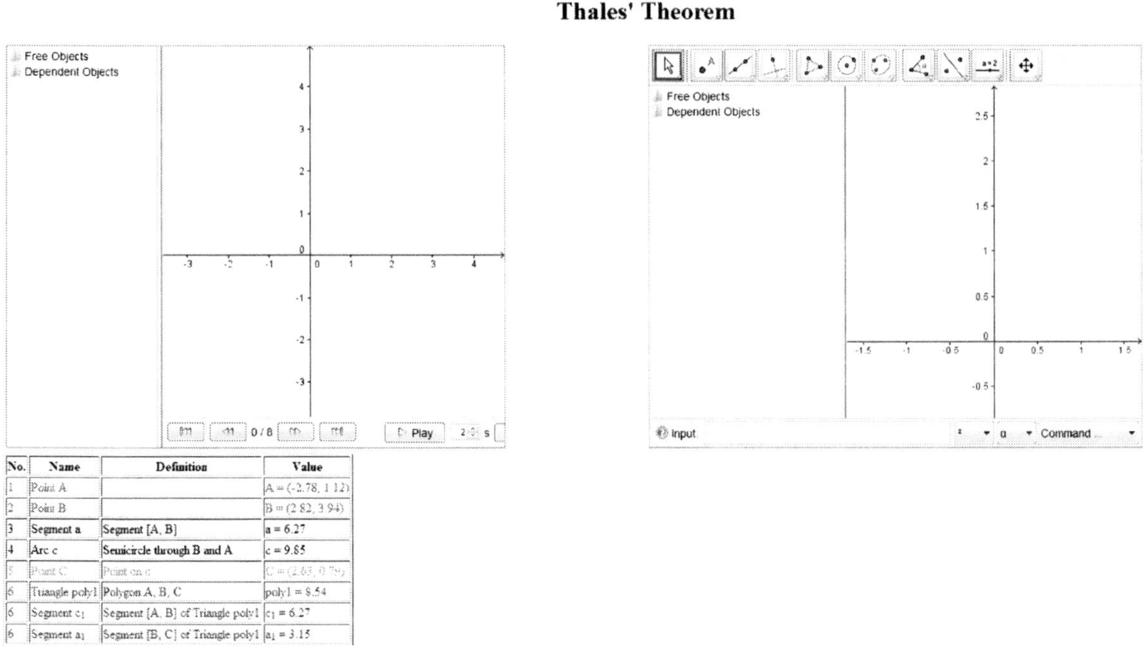

No.	Name	Definition	Value
1	Point A		A = (-2.78, 1.12)
2	Point B		B = (2.82, 3.94)
3	Segment a	Segment [A, B]	a = 6.27
4	Arc c	Semicircle through B and A	c = 9.85
5	Point C	Point on c	C = (2.63, 0.79)
6	Triangle poly1	Polygon A, B, C	poly1 = 8.54
6	Segment c_1	Segment [A, B] of Triangle poly1	c_1 = 6.27
6	Segment a_1	Segment [B, C] of Triangle poly1	a_1 = 3.15

Figure 6. The life cycle of an e-resource (Adapted from von Assche and Vuorikari, 2006)

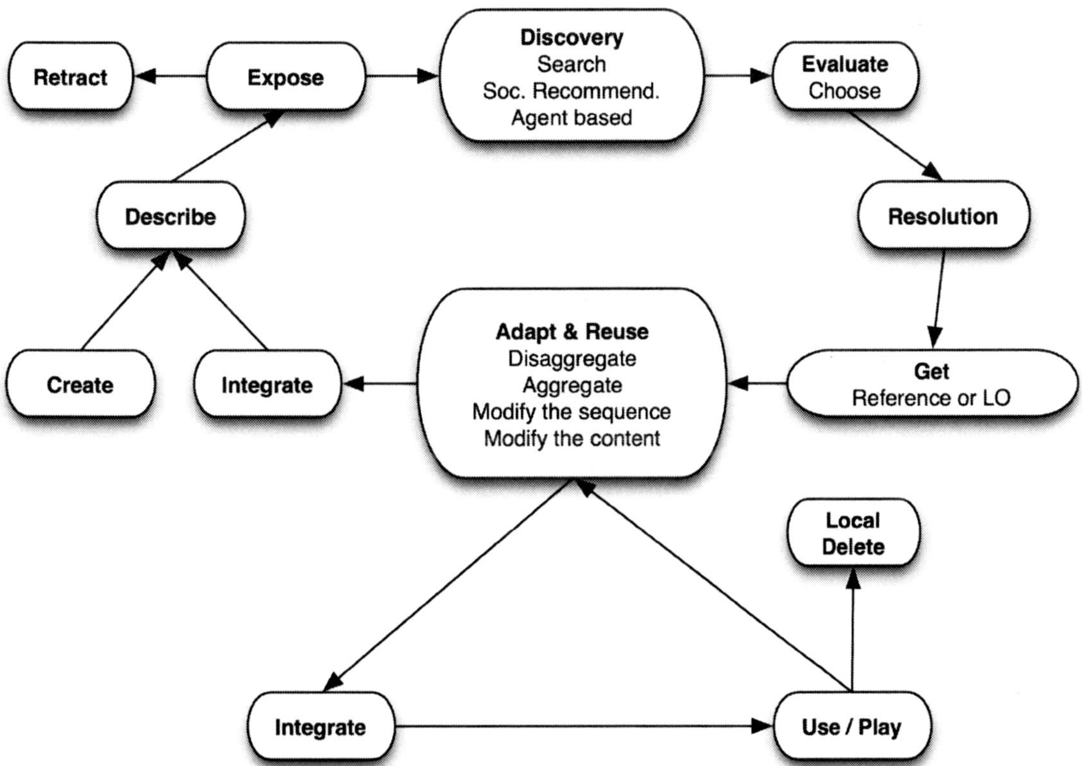

A DIFFERENT APPROACH TO MATH RESOURCE DESIGN

The discussion of theoretical aspects of mathematical e-resources design is quite lively. For example, there are disagreements about the appropriate ratio between procedural and conceptual knowledge obtained through mathematical activity when using ICT. In Berger (2009) a semiotic framework is used to illuminate the aspects of the design of mathematical resources, which may promote or hinder mathematical activity. Some core problems are emphasized in the paper, e.g. the problems arising in resource design when ICT is to be used in the teaching process. And, as it often happens, there are no final answers. The approach which is suitable in one pedagogical situation fails in another one. If resources were designed in a more flexible way, the epistemic value of the resources would be vastly improved. For example, instead of the author making a speculation about the precise ratio of both the procedural and the conceptual approach, the tasks could be designed in such a way that this ratio could easily be adapted to the needs of the user (Lokar, 2009).

As can be seen, a conflict exists between the possibilities offered by the technology, the teachers' wishes and the e-materials available. Several studies have shown that teachers need e-learning content that can easily be adapted and reused (Hwang, 2008). Therefore, the selection of proper technologies and tools for managing e-learning content and the establishment of a user-friendly and easy-to-use environment for creating and modifying the content are essential to ensure the support and popularization of e-learning.

The primary concerns of the authors of e-materials should therefore be:

- creation of basic building blocks,
- development of pre-combined models (that can be corrected or recombined), and
- provision of guidelines for the construction of new models.

What represents a basic building block depends on the particular learning situation. It can be a short explanation of a concept, a picture, an animation, a short video clip, a question, an exercise, an interactive game, etc. But there is more. The basic building blocks themselves should offer the possibility of being adapted, as well. The teacher should be able to reword a question, change the explanation slightly, add a link to another material on the topic in the feedback, and so on; in short, the teacher should be able to improve the building block itself.

The main ideas behind the new concept can be summarized into 5 points:

1. **The teacher must be in control.** Every teacher is unique and has a unique teaching style. Furthermore, the way a teacher teaches differs from class to class. Therefore, learning materials should not be limiting and prescriptive as to the way they can be used. The author should provide a learning path, but that path should be easily deconstructed, adapted and modified.
2. **Teaching resources should consist of small building blocks.** In this way everyone can construct their own learning path and have the possibility to combine their own resources with resources obtained elsewhere.
3. **Building blocks should be format and tool independent.** Building blocks should be easily obtained in different formats such as text files, HTML, XML format, SCORM, etc. This makes it easier for the users to embed the blocks into their own Internet pages, use them within their virtual classrooms, offer them on DVDs, etc.
4. **Teaching material should only be a sample combination.** A pre-constructed resource should only present one of several possible patterns. However, it does make sense that authors offer pre-constructed learning paths, as these paths show the possible use of basic building blocks.

5. **The power of metadata must be exploited.** All building blocks should have descriptions that enable a user to know about the content even before seeing it. Metadata also enables quality searching so a user can quickly obtain the resource he or she is looking for.

NAUK.SI: A PRACTICAL EXAMPLE

This part will show how concepts described above could be used in practice in preparing modern, high quality mathematical educational e-materials. Motivated by interviews with numerous teachers, who expressed their wish to be "in control" of the resources and following the analysis of the before mentioned research, an informal research group called NAUK was established. The word "nauk" means "education" or "lesson" in Slovenian, and is at the same time an acronym for NApredne Učne Kocke – Advanced Learning Blocks.

One of the aims of the group was to create an innovative web-based application for managing and serving e-learning content tailored to the needs of teachers. Teachers can choose between various animations, worksheets, question banks, dynamically generated questions and thus develop their own learning path. Each resource is supported by a brief explanation and a short preview. All resources can also be freely downloaded in various formats.

Another thing that has previously been neglected by other content creation tools is the process of knowledge extraction. Teachers do not only want some basic quiz type questions but often want to randomize questions, offer feedback for the most frequent errors, use structured questions that challenge the learner and therefore construct a nonlinear path through the process of examination and learning. Since each question is a knowledge object, all this is possible with the NAUK system (see Figure 7). Finally, the authors of the content have generally been people trained in ICT. Because teachers with little or no practice in the use of ICT should be able to use the software, it was designed to be very intuitive and user-friendly.

The NAUK group also found that it was not enough merely to offer content; it has to be inserted into an appropriate classification system and properly interlinked. A creation of large repositories of e-learning materials will start a new process; that is, a process of creation of e-learning

Figure 7. A three way relation when dealing with resources that includes the teacher

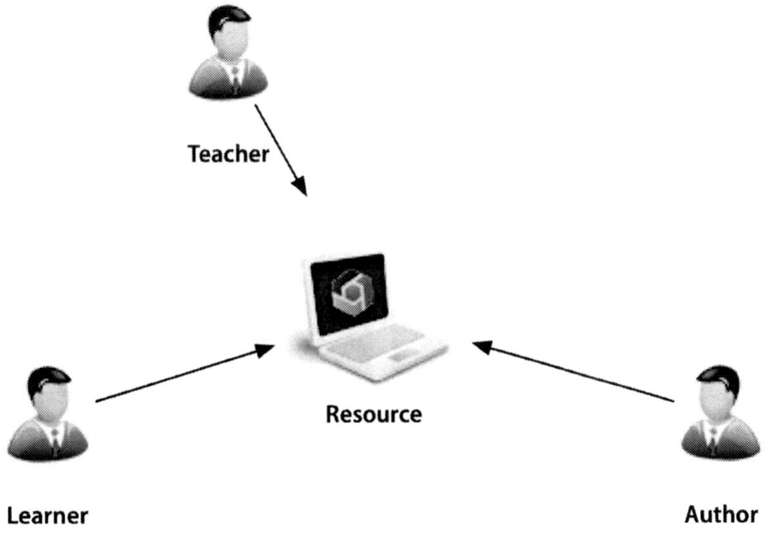

books that will someday become a supplement to at least a part of widely-used traditional teaching materials. Although traditional teaching materials can be used even decades after they were published (printed), this is not the case with e-learning materials. Since e-learning materials are built using different technologies and standards (Varlamis & Apostolakis, 2006), special care should be taken to develop the process that will enable the adaptation of e-textbooks to new technologies and standards in the not so distant future.

The NAUK group is currently involved in several projects in progress that are concerned with the creation of e-learning content for high-school mathematics, elementary- and high-school physics, elementary-school logic, all pre-faculty levels of computer science classes and faculty-level mathematics. Creating a repository of e-learning content – see Figure 8 – from four different fields of knowledge (at different levels), promises a greater range of users but also demands a greater responsibility from the group.

The basic idea of NAUK's approach can yet again be easily compared to the popular Lego® bricks; see Figure 9. The e-learning material should be built by creating: basic / simple building blocks, pre-designed e-learning material, which can later be customized, by using instructions for preparing customized e-learning material combining simpler building blocks.

Many repositories for learning content exist already, having been created in most cases as a result of EU projects, e.g. the InterGeo portal (http://i2geo.net) with resources on geometry, web-based environment for learning mathematics ActiveMath (http://www.activemath.org), Connexions repository (http://cnx.org/), online community for finding, authoring and sharing content Lemill (http://lemill.net/), portal for developing and delivering online and hybrid courses MERLOT (http://onlinecourses.merlot.org/), Slovenian Educational Network SIO (http://www.sio.si), Croatian national distance learning portal (https://lms.carnet.hr), etc. The portals mentioned above

Figure 8. The entry page of the NAUK repository

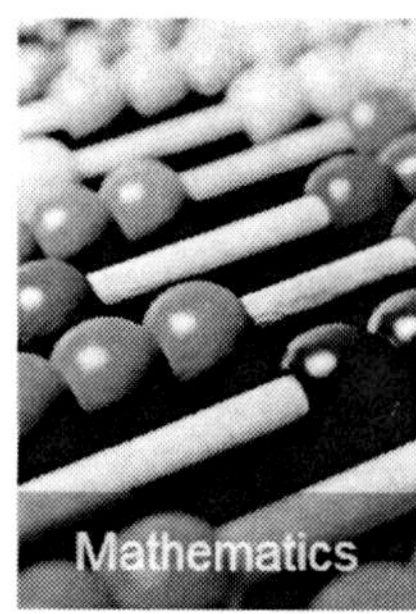

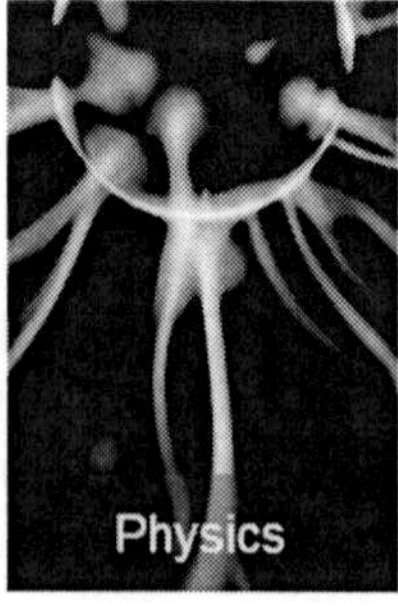

were used as a basis when trying to find a solution to the before mentioned problems; the solution later materializing as the NAUK portal (http://www.nauk.si). The main component of this application is a repository of materials, which, unlike the majority of the above mentioned systems, is not only intended to be an archive and repository of content, but offers the possibility of combining the existing materials into new learning units. Although some of the projects (ActiveMath, Connexions) also offer the possibility to create and combine content, this is either difficult to do or the interactive elements that the content prepared accordingly can include are very limited.

Sustainability and reusability of the NAUK created content are the two main advantages when compared to the existing monolithic presentations of e-learning content that can currently be seen all over the web. The main use case scenarios that were envisaged before creating the repository are:

- The teacher constructs the learning path, i.e. a complete learning course for teaching specific topics in the curriculum.
- The teacher using a virtual learning environment creates an assessment and imports it into the virtual learning environment.
- The teacher prepares homework with the same content as the teaching material he or she used while teaching, but with different data for every student.
- The teacher modifies and reuses previously prepared content.
- The teacher adds interactive elements or descriptions on transitions between the elements to previously prepared content.
- The teacher uses mathematical notation.
- The teacher comments and grades a previously prepared content.
- The teacher contributes his or her own content into the repository.
- The teacher creates new teaching materials or assessments.

Since the process of creation and modification of interactive elements should be as simple as possible and at the same time provide automatic computer based manipulation in the not so distant future, the NAUK group decided to use a similar

Figure 9. Analogy of the NAUK learning blocks paradigm with the LEGO® bricks

Figure 10. Example of the wiki-like syntax that is used in NAUK projects to describe e-learning content

markup syntax as that used by well-known wiki environments, e.g. by Wikipedia. Of course, NAUK's syntax contains additional tags, thereby enabling the addition of various multimedia elements and links between e-learning materials, adding responses to user input, etc. An example of the syntax is shown in Figure 10.

By using the NAUK services the teacher is able to take an existing content from the repository, adjust or supplement it, and publish it immediately in the repository. The other important functionality of the repository is the possibility of exporting the content in source code (text), HTML, SCORM or Common Cartridge standard. The teacher is able to use the e-learning content exported in SCORM in his/her own virtual learning environment. Thus, by using the NAUK export service the requirement for technical knowledge of the author (teacher) becomes obsolete.

Therefore, the teacher is no longer obliged to blindly follow the ideas of the original authors of the content, but is able to adapt the content to his or her needs. He or she can easily:

- take a few questions from the existing quizzes and make a new quiz,
- add or improve responses (feedback) depending on the accuracy of the answer to a question or an interactive part of the teaching material,
- take a previously constructed teaching material, remove or replace a certain section, change the order of chapters and slides, etc.,
- correct an animation or add his or her own example,
- assemble a context aware test from a database of questions, where the next question displayed depends on the accuracy of the answer to the previous question,
- add leaps in the learning pathway and thereby build a non-linear learning structure.

Figure 11. An assessment built automatically by the NAUK system following the scenario as shown in Figure 10. The learner is supposed to move the answers to correct locations to match sports with athletes.

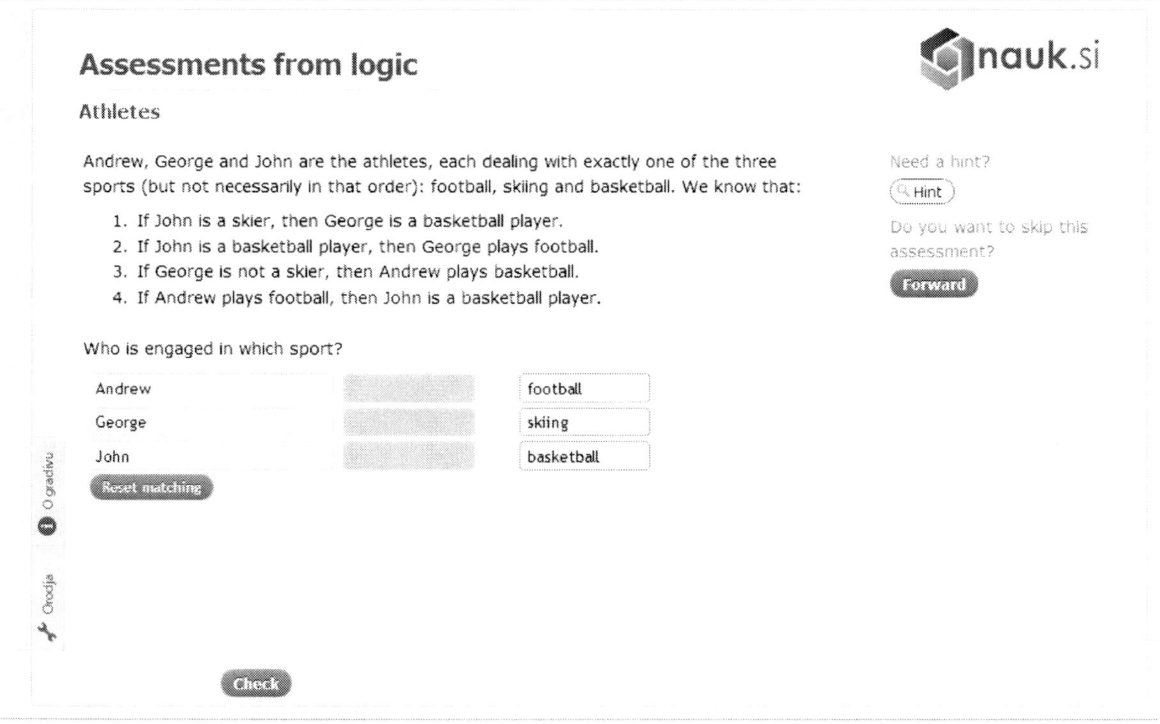

A feature that is absolutely necessary but often overlooked in the repositories of educational content is the implementation of efficient search engines. Most of the current repositories in Slovenia contain search by title, some of them also include search by content, but almost all of them lack the option to search by other metadata taxonomies: type of material, purpose, scope, popularity, level of difficulty, etc. This is the most pressing problem of the current Slovenian educational network - SIO (Čač et al., 2007), which is being filled with an increasing amount of material but numerous problems are encountered when searching for specific content due to the lack of proper classification. Teachers are therefore forced to review a great deal of content on the same subject to see that some consist only of a single PDF document, others are learning paths, others yet collections of links to other places on the Internet, etc. This is the reason why all e-learning content present in the NAUK repository must be metadata equipped, which enables the system to classify the materials using different taxonomies: curriculum, type of content, etc.

Teachers do not have to take care of the appearance (representation) of their teaching material, but only of the content, interactivity, multimedia add-ons and their place within the learning path of the e-learning material. An example of such an exercise can be seen in Figure 10 and the automatically generated presentation in Figure 11.

Authors can overlay the so-called "tools" above the multimedia content: video, image, data plot, measurements, etc. The currently available tools are: angle, distance, vector, vertical lines, horizontal lines, freehand drawing, stopwatch and polyline; see Figure 12. By using these tools the author can enable the learner to interact "naturally" while learning by solving puzzles, answering quizzes, measuring distances and angles be-

Figure 12. A truly interactive learning path constructed with the help of NAUK e-learning tools and concepts

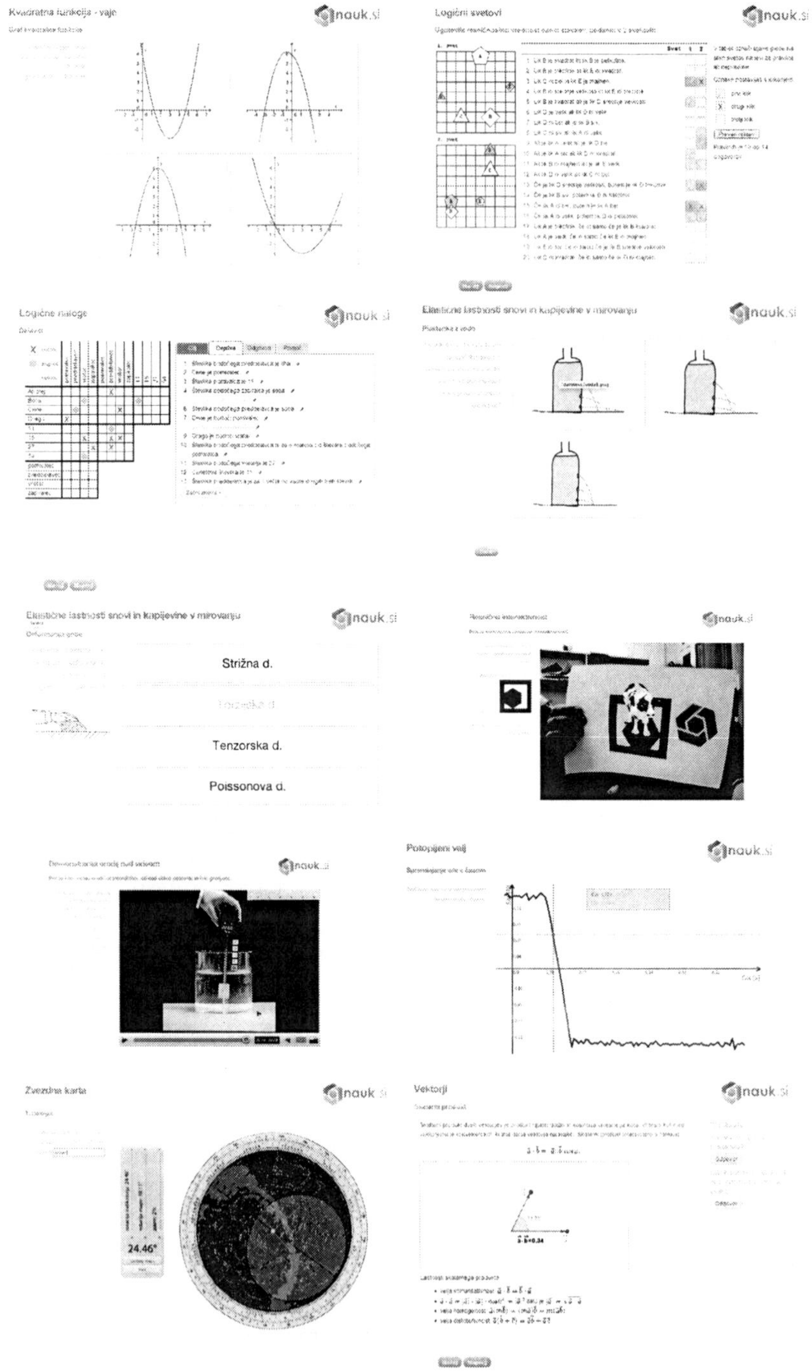

tween objects in images or videos, responding to questions by drawing an image or a vector, by creating a graph, etc. (Horvat & Lukšič, 2010)

One of the most important features of the present approach is that every interactive element triggers a transition to the next slide, which is selected automatically according to the current context of the learning process. The simplest example of this concept is probably the following one: a learner who makes a mistake and answers a question incorrectly is given a customized response and can be allowed (if this mistake is not too fundamental) to proceed to the next slide automatically, or is returned to another question, which has been slightly modified, e.g. made easier or changed in such a way that the learner will be forced to use the same learning process to solve the modified problem. Thus, the learning path is nonlinear.

FURTHER WORK

Informal interviews with many teachers as well as the first reactions of users have shown that the concepts and solutions similar to the one described above form a valuable approach that will provide higher quality teaching and learning. The NAUK group has decided to invest further efforts into upgrading the concepts presented currently. Therefore, the group has built a web based community, where it is possible to give opinions and comment on the existing materials as well as grade them. The group wants to make the process of content creation even more visually transparent when dealing with chapter editing and inclusion of other materials, using the ideas already seen on the Connexion in Flat World Knowledge portals (http://www.flatworldknowledge.com/). Still another goal is to enable content use on mobile devices, e-book readers, tablet PCs, etc.

Since word of good ICT solutions in the field of education spreads quickly (Centre for Educational Research and Innovation, 2009), all members involved in the NAUK projects hope for the success of the solutions and concepts presented, but are also aware that further development in this area relies heavily on the satisfaction of another group of end-users – the students.

CONCLUSION

The teachers have the right to be included in the e-learning process by preparing the content for their students. Therefore, teaching resources should be designed in a flexible way, supporting appropriate use of different ICT tools. Appropriate e-resource preparation should take into account the whole process of creation, design, usage and modification as only then we will get the e-resources teachers need and deserve.

REFERENCES

Balanskat, A., Blamire, R., & Kefalla, S. (2010). *A review of studies of ICT impact on schools in Europe*. ICT impact report. Retrieved June 15, 2010, from http://insight.eun.org/ shared/ data/ pdf/ impact_study.pdf

Banathy, B. H. (1991). *Systems design of education: A journey to create the future*. Englewood Cliffs, NJ: Educational Technology Publications.

Berger, M. (2009). *Designing tasks for CAS classrooms: Challenges and opportunities for teachers and researchers*. Paper presented at CAME6, Megatrend University, Belgrade, Serbia. Retrieved June 15, 2010, from http://www.lkl.ac.uk/ research/ came/ events/ CAME6/ index.html

Bryan, A. (2006). Web2, a new wave of innovation for teaching and learning? *EDUCASE Review, 41*(2), 32-44. Retrieved June 15, 2010, from http:// www.educause.edu/ ir/library/ pdf/ ERM0621.pdf

Čač, J., Čampelj, B., Flogie, A., Gajšek, R., Golob, M., & Harej, J. ... Turk, M. (2007). *Idejna zasnova programa projektov izdelave Slovenskega izobraževalnega omrežja*. Working report of the Program committee for the computerization of education, Ljubljana, Slovenia.

Carlgren, I., Handal, G., & Vaage, S. (1994). *Teachers' minds and actions: Research on teachers' thinking and practice*. Washington, DC: The Falmer Press.

Centre for Educational Research and Innovation. (2009). *Beyond textbooks: Digital learning resources as systemic innovation in the Nordic countries*. OECD Publishing. Retrieved June 15, 2010, from http://www.oecdbookshop.org/ oecd/ display.asp? CID=&LANG= EN&SF1= DI&ST1=5KSJ0TFD5DQ5

Dunn, R., Beaudry, J. S., & Klavas, A. (2002). Survey of research on learning styles. *California Journal of Science Education*, *2*(2), 75–98.

Education. (n.d.). In *Encyclopædia Britannica*. Retrieved July 1, 2010, from http://www.britannica.com/ EBchecked/ topic/ 179408/ education

Elliot, J. (1993). *Reconstructing teacher education*. London, UK: The Falmer Press.

Evans, J. (2007). *Tomorrow's students: Are we ready for the new 21st-century learners?* EDUCAUSE Podcast. Presented at the EDUCAUSE 2007 Annual Conference, Seattle, WA. Retrieved July 1, 2010, from http://www.educause.edu/ blog/ gbayne/ E07PodcastTomorrowsStudentsAre/ 167251

Horvat, B., & Lukšič, P. (2010). Learning science with advanced learning blocks. In S. Dolinšek, & T. Lyons (Eds.), *XIV. IOSTE Symposium, Socio-cultural and human values in science and technology education* (pp. 519-529). Ljubljana Institute for Innovation and Development of University of Ljubljana.

Hwang, D. (2008). *EDUNET: The core of Korea's knowledge bank.* Presented at the 2nd Strategic meeting EdReNe, Lizbona, Portugal. Retrieved June 15, 2010, from http://edrene.org/ seminars/ seminar2Lisbon.html

IML. (2009). *Teaching matters: A handbook for UTS academic staff.* Retrieved June 15, 2010, from http://www.iml.uts.edu.au/ learnteach/ resources/ tm/ teacherprep.html

Jakončič-Faganel, J., & Lokar, M. (2006). Quality of electronic materials for math teaching. In D. Quinney (Ed.), *Proceedings of the 3rd International Conference on the Teaching of Mathematics at the Undergraduate Level.* Istanbul, Turkey: John Wiley & Sons.

Johnston-Wilder, S., & Pimm, D. (Eds.). (2004). *Teaching secondary mathematics with ICT*. Open University Press.

Keiny, S. (2002). *Ecological thinking: A new approach to educational change*. Lanham, MD: University Press of America.

Kissing, M. (2008). *KeyShop – A new culture of learning*. Progress report of GRUNDTVIG Multilateral project. Retrieved June 15, 2010, from http://eacea.ec.europa.eu/ llp/ projects/ public_parts/ documents/ grundtvig/ gru_134022_ keyshop.pdf

Lokar, M. (2000). Some questions about technology and teaching. In B. Kutzler, V. Kokol-Voljč, M. Lokar, & J. Palčič (Eds.), *Exam questions and basic skills in technology-supported mathematics teaching: Proceedings of the 6th ACDCA Summer Academy* (pp. 129-132). Hagenberg, Austria.

Lokar, M. (2005). Nekaj vprašanj o tehnologiji in poučevanju. In Z. Labernik, & M. Varšek (Eds.), *Proceedings of 10th International Conference MIRK'05*, Piran, Slovenia.

Lokar, M. (2006). Electronic teaching and learning resources in math teaching in Slovenia. In D. Quinney (Ed.), *Proceedings of the 3rd International Conference on the Teaching of Mathematics at the Undergraduate Level*. Istanbul, Turkey: John Wiley & Sons.

Lokar, M. (2009). *Some issues on designing tasks for CAS classroom*. Paper presented at CAME6, Belgrade, Serbia, Retrieved June 15, 2010, from http://www.lkl.ac.uk/ research/ came/ events/ CAME6/ index.html

Lusoli, W., & Miltgen, C. (2009). *Young people and emerging digital services: An exploratory survey on motivations, perceptions and acceptance of risks*. Scientific and Technical Research Series, Luxembourg. Retrieved June 15, 2010, from http://ipts.jrc.ec.europa.eu/ publications/ pub.cfm?id=2119

Prensky, M. (2001). Digital natives, digital immigrants. *On the Horizon, 9*(5), 1-6. Retrieved June 15, 2010, from http://unesdoc.unesco.org/ images/ 0013/ 001390/ 139028e.pdf

Rodríguez, A. J., & Kitchen, R. S. (2005). *Preparing mathematics and science teachers for diverse classrooms: Promising strategies for transformative pedagogy*. Routledge.

van Assche, F., & Vuorikari, R. (2006). A framework for quality of learning resources . In Ehlers, U., & Pawlowski, J. M. (Eds.), *European handbook for quality and standardization in e-learning* (pp. 443–456). Springer. doi:10.1007/3-540-32788-6_29

Varlamis, I., & Apostolakis, I. (2006). The present and future of standards for e-learning technologies. *Interdisciplinary Journal of Knowledge and Learning Objects, 2*, 59-76. Retrieved June 15, 2010, from http://ijklo.org/ Volume2/v2p059-076 Varlamis.pdf

ADDITIONAL READING

Benkler, Y. (2006). *The Wealth of Networks*. Yale University Press.

Curriki (n.d.). An online community for creating and sharing open source curricula. http://www.curriki.org/.

Gerlič, I. (2003). *Stanje in trendi uporabe računalnika v slovenskih osnovnih in srednjih šolah*, Research report 2003 (in Slovene), Retrieved June 15, 2010, from http://www.ris.org/ 0000/ 00/ Publikacije/ Stanje_in _trendi_uporabe_racunalnika _v_slovenskih_osnovnih _in_srednjih_ solah_ _raziskovalno_porocilo/.

Heid, M. K., & Blume, G. W. (Eds.). (2008). *Research on technology and the teaching and learning of mathematics*, Volumes 1 & 2. Information Age Publishing.

Kadijevich, Dj. (2007). *Towards relating procedural and conceptual knowledge by CAS*. Paper presented at CAME5, University of Pècs, Hungary. Retrieved June 15, 2010, from http://www.lkl.ac.uk/ research/ came/ events/ CAME5/.

Kortenkamp, U. (in press). Interoperable Interactive Geometry for Europe. *The Electronic Journal of Mathematics and Technology.*

Libbrecht, P., Desmoulins, C., Kortenkamp, U., & Mercat, K. (in press). Crossing Cultural Boundaries with Interactive Geometry Resources . *The International Journal on Mathematics Education.*

Palfrey, J., & Gasser, U. (2008). *Born Digital: Understanding the First Generation of Digital Natives*. Basic Books.

Parker, K., & Chao, J. (2007). Wiki as a Teaching Tool. *Interdisciplinary Journal of Knowledge and Learning Objects*, 3, 57-72. Retrieved June 15, 2010, from http://ijklo.org/ Volume3/ IJKLOv3p057-072 Parker284.pdf.

Rosen, L. D. (2010). *Rewired, Understanding the iGeneration and the Way They Learn*. New York, NY: Palgrave MacMillan.

Semenov, A. (2005). *Information and communication technologies in schools: a handbook for teachers or how ICT Can Create New, Open Learning Environments*. France: UNESCO.

Sojka, P. (Ed.). *Proceedings of DML2008 Towards a Digital Mathematics Library*. Brno, Czech Republic: Masaryk University Press.

Sojka, P. (Ed.). *Proceedings of DML2009 Towards a Digital Mathematics Library*. Brno, Czech Republic: Masaryk University Press.

Sojka, P., & Plch, R. (2008). Technological Challenges of Teaching Mathematics in a Blended Learning Environment. *International Journal of Continuous Engineering Education and Life-Long Learning*, *18*(5/6), 657–665. doi:10.1504/IJCEELL.2008.022172

Wassermann, A. (2010). The challenge of a new hardware generation to mathematics education . In Bianco, T., & Ulm, V. (Eds.), *Mathematics Education with Technology, Experiences in Europe*. Augsburg: Universität Augsburg.

Zhao, J. (2008). Towards a User-centric Math Information Retrieval System. Bulletin of IEEE Technical Committee on Digital Libraries, 4(2). Retrieved July 15, 2010, from http://www.ieee-tcdl.org/ Bulletin/ v4n2/zhao/ zhao.html

Zhao, J., Kan, M., & Theng, Y. L. (2008). Math information retrieval: user requirements and prototype implementation. In R. Larsen (Ed.), *Proceedings of the 8th ACM/IEEE-CS joint conference on Digital libraries* (pp.187-196). Pittsburg, ACM.

Chapter 16
Software Tools Used in Math Refresher Courses at the University of Alcalá, Spain

J. G. Alcázar
University of Alcalá, Spain

M. Marvá
University of Alcalá, Spain

D. Orden
University of Alcalá, Spain

F. San Segundo
University of Alcalá, Spain

ABSTRACT

We describe our experience of using the following mathematical tools: an e-learning platform (Moodle), several components of the WIRIS software suite for mathematics education (the formula editor, WIRIS CAS, and WIRIS-Quizzes), the dynamical geometry package GeoGebra, the computational knowledge engine Wolfram Alpha, and the mathematics software system SAGE. Our aim in this chapter is two-fold: on the one hand, we report the use of these tools in Math refresher courses. On the other, we provide sufficient information about them for readers to decide on the usefulness of these tools in their own particular context (maybe different from that of a refresher course). More specifically, for each tool we give a general description, some comments on its use in Math refresher courses, and a list of (general) advantages and drawbacks.

DOI: 10.4018/978-1-60960-875-0.ch016

INTRODUCTION

E-learning (see for example Albano G. and Ferrari P.L., 2008; Descamps S.X., Bass H., Bolanos Evia G., Seiler R. and Seppala, M., 2006; Nichols M., 2003; Tavangarian D., Leypold M., Nölting K. and Röser M., 2004) essentially comprises learning/ teaching tools with computer support. Therefore, learning platforms, specialized software packages, scientific repositories, etc. can all be considered as e-learning tools.

These tools have obvious advantages: on the one hand, they can be used for (synchronous or asynchronous) online teaching, and they can improve classroom teaching; on the other hand, students usually find them interesting and attractive, which results in higher motivation to study. These advantages have encouraged many teachers to try them; however, when it comes to using a new tool (whether computer-supported or otherwise), teachers tend to be cautious: commonly, it is tested with a small number of students, so that everything can easily be kept under control; if the experience is successful, then the testing is extended to larger groups and to other contexts. Thus, it is useful to have some kind of test group, in order to evaluate the tool's capabilities and to identify its drawbacks.

The authors of this chapter, being no exception, have also started using e-learning tools with small groups of students. In the case of our university (University of Alcalá, Madrid, Spain), we found the perfect test group in the refresher courses, called, in our university, "zero courses". These are refresher courses in basic areas of science (essentially Mathematics, Physics and Chemistry), which were introduced at UAH (University of Alcalá) several years ago in order to provide a common foundation for all students about to start their degrees. In fact, this kind of course is offered in many other universities in Spain, and also in other countries (see for example http://pre.universia.es/que-estudiar/cursos-cero/index.htm, the web page of Waterloo University, Canada, http://de.uwaterloo.ca/preuniversity.html, or the web page of Dakota University, US, http://www.dsu.edu/disted/math-refresher.aspx, to give just a few examples). Zero courses in Mathematics typically cover such basic topics as:

- Algebra: inequalities, equations, and systems, matrices, determinants, polynomials.
- Calculus: sequences, functions, limits, derivatives, integrals.
- Discrete mathematics: combinatorics.
- Basic statistics.
- Geometry: trigonometry, affine plane geometry, conics.

At UAH, these courses are offered on many different degree courses, such as Engineering, Architecture, Biology, Environmental Sciences or Chemistry, but are not compulsory since not all the students need to refresh those topics. There are usually around 30 students on each of these courses, which generally last between twenty and thirty hours and are completed before the degree course begins (at the moment, the academic year at most Spanish universities begins in the third week of September, although this is likely to change in the future). The courses take place in a traditional classroom setting, although some online support is commonly provided. Furthermore, it has been decided that evaluation on these courses at the UAH should be merely informative, so that it has no impact on students' degree marks. As a consequence, the contents are more flexible than on a compulsory course, and the teacher can adapt the contents to the initial level of the students, which is evaluated in the first session.

In addition, for those students attending refresher courses this is usually their first academic experience (at UAH). Hence, and also because of the short duration of the course, it is clearly important to:

- Optimize time (no time to waste!),
- Present the topics covered in the course in an attractive way,
- Provide the students with materials that can help them to progress independently, even when the course is over.

The authors of this chapter have been teaching these courses for several years. Apart from other, more classical, tools (oral presentations, problem solving, etc.), the following virtual tools have been used (to different extents) in such teaching:

1. The e-learning platform Moodle.
2. The WIRIS formula editor and Computer Algebra System.
3. The WIRIS Quizzes package, combined with Moodle.
4. The dynamical geometry package Geogebra.
5. The computational knowledge engine Wolfram Alpha.
6. The mathematics software system SAGE.

Readers may be interested to learn that all of these tools, except for the third one, are free. As for their ease of use, they range from being usable from scratch (for example, tools 1, 2, 5) to being rather advanced (for instance, 6), while others (such as 3, 4) require some effort from the teacher, but not from the students. Due to these differences, some of them are more suited to the particular characteristics of the course than others, and the final decision of which to use lies with the teacher.

The aim of this chapter is to share with the readers our experience of using these tools; even though our emphasis is on their use in Math refresher courses, we also hope to give sufficient information for readers to decide on the usefulness of these tools in their own particular context. Thus, for each tool we provide:

- a brief description,
- a review of its main functionalities in the context of a refresher course,
- a list of advantages and drawbacks,

Furthermore, in the Conclusions section we also discuss the effectiveness of each tool in the context of Math refresher courses. Thus, after reading the chapter, hopefully the reader will have obtained both a general idea of what these tools can or cannot do, and also how relevant their use is in the case of a refresher course.

E-LEARNING PLATFORMS: MOODLE

Description of the Tool

E-learning platforms are virtual environments with three main capacities: (1) displaying downloadable information, as in a web page; (2) enabling interaction between participants (teacher and students); (3) helping to evaluate students. Such an environment is controlled by the teacher, who builds *courses* for different subjects within the general framework provided by the platform. There are many platforms of this kind; well-known examples include Blackboard Learning System (previously, WebCT), Moodle, Sakai, eCollege or TopClass, to cite just a few. A thorough comparison of different platforms can be found in the literature (see for example Graf S. and List B., 2005; Anguiano Gómez, C.E., González- Romero V.M. and Alvarez Gómez, M., 2005).

Moodle (see for example Dougiamas, M. and Taylor, P.C., 2002; Dougiamas, M. and Taylor, P.C., 2003; Rice W., 2006; Rice W., 2007) is a free learning platform which is becoming increasingly popular (according to http://moodle.org, there are currently 1,003,196 registered users, speaking over 78 languages in 212 countries) and which has a strong, well-organized community. The fact that it is a "free" tool not only means that it can be downloaded and used free of charge, but also that the code is open, so that anyone with some knowledge of programming languages can modify it and develop new Moodle functionalities. Hence, Moodle can be built in a collaborative way, and can be adapted to the particular needs of the user.

In the case of Moodle, the capabilities (1), (2), (3) above correspond to what Moodle calls *resources*, *activities* and *communications*, respectively. The *Resources* function includes the possibility of displaying text and hosting files that students can download (as in a web page), devising web-like screens for showing information more efficiently, and creating links to different websites. While the *resources* are not interactive, in the sense that only the teacher can create or modify them, *activities* are interactive and students are expected to participate. Activities are organized into *databases*, *surveys*, *quizzes*, *wikis*, *glossaries*, *assignments* and *lessons*. In our refresher courses we basically use *surveys*, *quizzes* and *wikis*, and we will speak a bit more about these in the subsections that follow. For the remaining activities we refer the reader to Cole J. and Foster H. (2007).

Using This Tool in Math Refresher Courses

The main functionalities that we use are quizzes, forums, chats, wikis and surveys. Let us briefly describe how we use each of these tools.

Quizzes

Moodle has a vast range of possibilities for creating quizzes and many different formats for the questions are available: true/false, multiple choice, short answer, numerical, essay, etc; the interested reader can explore this question further in Chapter 6 of Cole J. and Foster H. (2007). Since our refresher course students do not get any grades (the refresher course is not included in the degree), we are essentially interested in using quizzes for:

1. Obtaining information about the initial level of our students (to take this into account while teaching the course).
2. Obtaining information about the level achieved by our students at the end of the course (to evaluate the efficiency of the course).
3. Providing exercises that the students can complete independently.

In the first class of the course, our students are required to complete a quiz that evaluates their initial level. This test typically consists of twenty multiple-choice questions, which are corrected automatically by the system. Since Moodle provides statistics, we can rapidly identify the average level of each student and of the class as a whole; furthermore, we can also obtain the statistics corresponding to each question, and hence we can quickly detect the parts of the curriculum our students are less familiar with.

The same process is carried out at the end of the course. In this case the test is configured so that after sending the responses, the results are visible for the student. Hence, every student leaves the course with a "mark" (although it has no bearing on his/her degree grades). There are also other quizzes which are created for student self-evaluation. These quizzes are kept on the platform for the rest of the year so that the students can go back to them if they need to. In this sense, the quizzes can be configured so that right and wrong answers receive appropriate messages (see Figure 1), that typically contain information on "frequently-made mistakes". Furthermore, a quiz can be configured so that each new attempt contains the results of the preceding one; in this way, a quiz can be completed over several attempts.

The *quiz* activity can also be used to gather information about a topic, before addressing it in class. Assume, for instance, that we are going to address differentiation: obviously the initial test includes some questions on this matter, but maybe we want to have a clearer idea of what our

Figure 1. Feedback on a quiz question

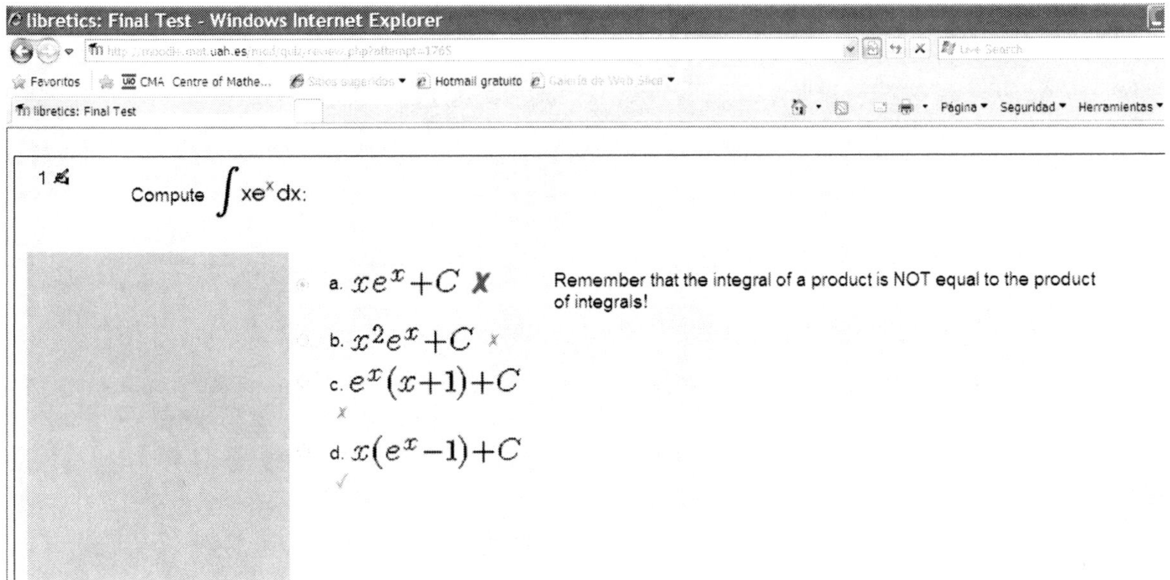

students already know. Thus, we assign them the task of completing the quiz at home. The system provides a statistical summary of the responses registered, and thus we can get an idea of our students' knowledge of the topic.

Forums and Chats

We use two types of forums: the News Forum, for announcements, and general forums, where students can start discussions and also participate in discussions created by others. In the News Forum only the teacher can post messages; moreover, any message posted is immediately e-mailed to the students. Hence, it is a good tool for general announcements, reminders, etc. In general forums, however, use is completely open to everybody (although the teacher obviously has control over the functioning of the forum).

In the case of general forums, we have observed that students do not usually participate spontaneously and a certain level of guidance and encouragement is commonly needed for this to happen, which has been also observed in Cole J. and Foster H. (2007), see page 80 there. In our experience, a strategy that generally works is to encourage (or "force") people to communicate in small groups; in such a situation, communication is generally easier. For this purpose, Moodle participants are first organized into groups by the teacher. Then the teacher assigns a task to each group (for example, the solution of a problem), and specifies that the steps of the solution must be carried out through the forum. Since not only wikis but also forums can be configured in Moodle in such a way that only the members of a same group can interact, we have an easy means of forcing communication in small groups.

Concerning chats, it is worth mentioning that the number of users that can interact through the Moodle chat is limited (often to just three or four simultaneous chats, see page 87 in Cole J. and Foster H., 2007). Hence, the purpose of this tool is basically to provide a space for the teacher and one or two students to meet in order to carry out "virtual mentoring".

Figure 2. Wikis

Matrices

Explain if each of the following statements is true, false, or true with some additional requirement.

(a) If A,B are matrices, then $(A+B)^2 = A^2 + 2AB + B^2$ False in general. It is true only if $A \cdot B = B \cdot A$

(b) If A,B are matrices, then $A \cdot B = 0 \Rightarrow A = 0$ or $B = 0$ False; take for example $A = \begin{pmatrix} 0 & 1 \\ 0 & 0 \end{pmatrix}$ and $B = \begin{pmatrix} 1 & 0 \\ 0 & 0 \end{pmatrix}$. It is true when either A or B are invertible. Why? I do not understand it.

(c) If A is symmetric, then A^2 is also symmetric. I think that it is true, but I do not know how to prove it. Use induction?

Wikis

Due to the short duration of the course, it is impossible to cover all the topics and solve all the exercises in the lectures. Thus, unsolved questions are placed on the virtual platform, and students are invited to solve them cooperatively by means of *wikis*. *Wikis* can be intuitively described as *online editable documents*; thus, if a wiki is placed in a Moodle course, all the participants on that course (teacher and students) can edit the document, which works as a "public blackboard" (see Figure 2). In our case, a typical wiki starts with a blank document containing a mathematical statement that must be proven, or a problem that must be solved. Different students make contributions (in a process which is supervised by the teacher) and after a certain time the solution takes shape. When the solution is finally reached, the teacher sends a message notifying students that the document needs no further editing. This process is controlled by the teacher, who can recover every previous version of the wiki, recognize the changes between two consecutive versions of the wiki, and organize the editing process in groups, if required.

Surveys

The *survey* activity (also *questionnaire*) serves the purpose of collecting data. In current versions of Moodle (at present, 1.9.8) this tool cannot be used to collect anonymous data (i.e. the answer of each participant is stored in association with the name of the participant). However, there are modules available for collecting anonymous data, based on phpESP, an open source questionnaire tool, which can be downloaded. We have installed one of these modules, and therefore on our courses we have the option of collecting both anonymous and non-anonymous data. We use the first option at the end of the course, for satisfaction surveys regarding our teaching. The second option can be used for other enquiries; a typical example would be: "Have you studied complex numbers at school?"

Advantages and Disadvantages of Using This Tool

The main advantages and drawbacks of using Moodle are summarized in Table 1.

In terms of the *advantages*, in general we can say that Moodle is a user-friendly, freely downloadable and open-source tool. This last aspect,

Table 1. Advantages and disadvantages of using Moodle

Advantages	Disadvantages
• Simple to use. • Free software, open source. • LaTeX language understood (forums, chats, quizzes). • Interaction with WIRIS or MathType. • Wikis integrated. • News Forum. • Strong community of users.	• Generally, you have to administer the platform yourself. • Limited quality in creating wikis and text. • Very limited quality in LaTeX expressions. • Limited potential in communication tools. • Basic operations such as loading files, inserting and modifying content, etc. are a bit slow. A more interactive screen could be desired.

i.e. the fact that the Moodle code is open to everybody and can be modified, has enabled us to devise our own Moodle resources (more specifically, a module for dividing the students into problem-solving groups, and another module for organizing mentoring). Also, Moodle understands LaTeX language, which can be introduced through the text editor. This saves time when writing in forums and chats, creating quizzes, etc. Furthermore, Moodle is able to interact with WIRIS (see the next section). On the one hand, this gives our students a tool for introducing mathematical symbols which does not require learning syntax; on the other, it gives them the option of using a CAS for computations (numerical and algebraic), again without the need to learn syntax.

Also, Moodle allows the use of wikis that can be configured so that the same wiki is only shared by members of a same group (i.e. all the other groups either cannot see, or can see but cannot edit, other groups' wikis). Last, but not least, Moodle has a strong, well-organized community of users. User forums are very active and it is easy to locate help if one runs into a problem. The program has a good help manual, and there are plenty of freely downloadable books, manuals, etc. (the webpage http://www.moodle.org is a good reference). Displaying courses in Moodle (or any e-learning platform) allows teachers to visualize students' activity. In this way, we get "hot" information for reflecting on the strengths or weaknesses of the kind of contents, activities, evaluation, etc. we are using on that course.

As regards the *disadvantages*: if you choose to use Moodle, you will probably also choose to host and administer your own Moodle server, and therefore you will have to tackle the kind of problems deriving from this situation; it is possible to hire external hosting and administration (information on this can be found on the Moodle webpage), but this has to be paid for. Also, in general, it can be said that the main merit of a virtual platform such as Moodle is the provision of a wide range of features in one package, such as communication tools, interaction tools, web-like tools, etc. In Moodle however, each of these when taken alone has a limited potential: therefore, if you are essentially interested in only one or two of these features, you should probably look for more specialized software. The same is the case with text edition, LaTeX processing (which is of quite low quality), communication tools, etc. Finally, although Moodle provides all the required features of a webpage, there are a number of simple processes which are basically concerned with the appearance of the Moodle site (creating and modifying content, loading and deleting files, etc.) that are reasonably fast to carry out when editing web-pages but that take rather more time with Moodle. It is not an exhausting amount of time, but one often wishes that these simple operations could be carried out more rapidly.

Figure 3. Using WIRIS CAS for computing primitives, 2-D and 3-D plotting, solving equation systems, etc. (2010, Maths for More. Used with permission)

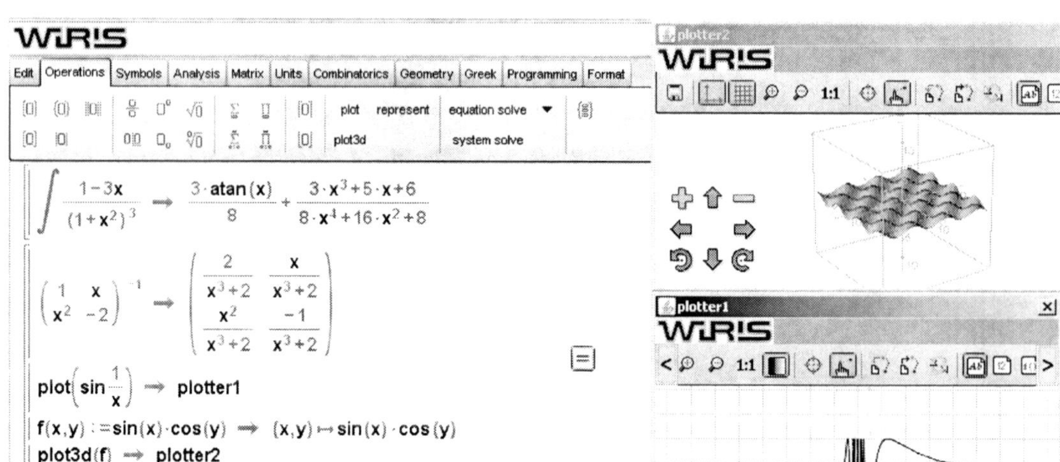

WIRIS

Description of the Tool

WIRIS (http://www.wiris.com/index.php) is the name of a mathematical software suite designed and developed for educational purposes. It was created by Maths for More (http://www.mathsfor-more.com/), a spin-off company of the Technical University of Catalonia, in Barcelona, Spain.

The WIRIS family consists of different interactive modules for writing and editing mathematical formulae, performing mathematical computations and handling dynamic geometry. This software is based on Java technology and is therefore independent of the browser and operating system. The cornerstone of this suite is the WIRIS Computer Algebraic System (hereafter, WIRIS CAS) and its ability to communicate with Moodle. In fact, WIRIS products can be integrated into Moodle via plug-in. We will focus on the following:

1. **WIRIS editor**: this is a free tool for creating mathematical formulae in HTML. The external appearance is similar to other equation editors found in text processing tools (e.g. Office Word, etc.). Users obtain access to a range of symbols, the Greek alphabet, operators, physical units, etc. so that mathematical expressions can be written easily. This editor supports MathML and OpenMath standards.
2. **WIRIS CAS**: this is an online platform for mathematical computations. The interface consists of a notepad where users can write text and formulas aided by different menus. Users can manipulate mathematical expressions and tackle a range of problems: solve limits, calculate derivatives, primitives and definite integrals, perform combinatorial analysis, solve different equation types, and handle matrices. It is also possible to plot 2D and 3D graphics (see Figure 3).

WIRIS CAS includes a dynamic geometry system. Three-dimensional facilities are especially noteworthy, since not many tools are currently available for dealing with these kinds of problems. Examples in the *2D Graphics* and *3D Graphics* entries of the WIRIS CAS help system give a fairly complete overview of what can be done.

Three-dimensional graphics can easily be rotated, zoomed, etc. The two-dimensional possibilities of WIRIS CAS as a Dynamic Geometry system should not be underestimated, although other packages (such as GeoGebra, which is discussed later) are more oriented to these tasks.

Furthermore, the programming menu includes an amazingly simple method for introducing programming structures.

3. **WIRIS Quizzes**: this is a plug-in which provides real communication between Moodle questionnaires and WIRIS CAS. By "real", we mean that answers may consist of mathematical expressions typed using the WIRIS editor, which can be interpreted and corrected by WIRIS CAS. This tool enables the creation of quiz questions with parameters which take random values from a range introduced by the quiz creator (the teacher). These parameters may correspond to numbers, algebraic expressions, graphics, etc. Thus, even if a student completes the same quiz several times, it is probable that he/she will always encounter different questions which are variations of a certain standard question. This provides the student with an impressive number of exercises.

Only the WIRIS editor is free, whereas the other WIRIS modules comprise proprietary software. In practice, many public educational portals give free online access to WIRIS CAS. The interested user can also try an English version of WIRIS CAS at the web address http://www.wiris.net/demo/wiris/en/index.html. WIRIS products are available in several languages, including English, Spanish, French, German, Portuguese, Catalan, Basque and Estonian.

WIRIS is becoming increasingly popular among secondary school pupils, and not only because of the free online access mentioned above: many textbook publishers at this level include interactive exercises and examples aided by WIRIS Player (see http://www.wiris.com/content/category/7/49/60/lang,es/). The main advantage of WIRIS tools is the interface: students do not need to learn a new language or syntax to start typing commands. Anyone familiar with mathematical notation and standard equation editors, such as those available in many office suites, should encounter no difficulties in operating WIRIS.

WIRIS CAS is capable of generating HTML documents, which allow one to create documents combining text and mathematical expressions (see http://www.wiris.com/demo/flash/materials-1.htm, http://www.wiris.com/demo/flash/materials-2.htm). Although WIRIS CAS is not designed for professional editing, it can generate materials in Web format. Furthermore, we can enrich these HTML documents by encapsulating applets generated with WIRIS CAS.

Using This Tool in Math Refresher Courses

We consider only the online versions of the equation editor and the CAS engine. WIRIS software is compatible with several e-learning platforms, such as Moodle. The WIRIS editor is similar to other available equation editors. Surprisingly, it is not possible to save formulae generated with the WIRIS editor in a file. It can be done only when used in combination with an e-learning platform; in this case the equation editor can be used for writing and inserting mathematical expressions in a text document. When used independently of an e-learning platform, at most we can drag and drop formulae onto a notepad in order to obtain the corresponding MathML code. WIRIS CAS improves on all these features, enabling users not only to write and save, but also to interact with (i.e. compute) mathematical expressions. WIRIS

Table 2. WIRIS quizzes equation

WIRIS CAS (symbolic computational power)	+	Moodle Quizzes (automatic evaluation and feedback)	=	WIRIS Quizzes

CAS syntax is very similar to standard mathematical notation and our students find it very simple and intuitive to use. Typically, students can use this software for checking their answers to the problems posed to them. WIRIS CAS sessions can be saved in different html formats. This feature seems slightly advanced to our average student, at least on their first encounter with this tool. On the other hand, this feature allows the incorporation of WIRIS CAS sessions into "ordinary" web pages containing, for instance, theoretical contents. Therefore, students can experiment with "live" examples illustrating contents presented therein. In both cases students quickly become skilled users: in fact, the relationship between WIRIS tools and Moodle is synergic and it is a good idea to use both tools together (see the paragraphs below).

WIRIS editor sessions are displayed simply by clicking on the icon with the square root of x. As mentioned in the Moodle section, we find wikis and forums useful on refresher courses. It seems obvious that the benefits of using these resources depend on their capacity to include mathematical expressions. Other cases in which this editor is needed are the following: sometimes students are asked (via Moodle) to choose topics to be emphasized during the course. In addition, Moodle provides an e-mail service and, again, we may need to write mathematics.

Another icon (consisting of a couple of square brackets) leads to a WIRIS CAS session (invoked from Moodle) and thus, we can incorporate a CAS session into the document we are editing, whether web pages, forums, wikis or e-mails (within Moodle). There is a huge difference between using WIRIS editor and WIRIS CAS for enclosing formulae in a document. In the first case, we are merely including an expression written in MathML. In the second case, we are including a complete WIRIS session, which will be displayed by double clicking the mathematical expression.

Last, but not least, let us briefly present WIRIS Quizzes. This is a plug-in for Moodle related to questionnaires. We offer our students two different kinds of questionnaires: a) for assessing their skills at the beginning and at the end of the course and b) for practicing techniques learned in secondary school. In what follows, we will show how WIRIS Quizzes provide substantial help with these tasks. The idea is best conveyed by the equation see the equation in Table 2.

Moodle provides a range of question types for building up questionnaires, and WIRIS editor and WIRIS CAS can be used with WIRIS Quizzes to devise the questions and answers. Namely, WIRIS Quizzes can be used to incorporate mathematics into multiple-choice questions, true-false questions, matching questions, essay questions and short-answer questions. In all these cases, the use of WIRIS Quizzes means that:

- Teachers can use formulas both in the statement of the question, in the options provided (e.g. for multiple-choice questions) and in the feedback provided after the question has been answered.
- The statement and the possible answers to the question are generated by an algorithm created with WIRIS CAS, including random elements. This is one of the main features of WIRIS CAS, which renders it extremely powerful (see below).

Table 3. Advantages and disadvantages of using WIRIS

Advantages	Disadvantages
• Regarded as a calculator, simple and intuitive to use. • Each help file (when found) contains a WIRIS CAS session providing "live" examples to interact with. • WIRIS CAS is available via public educational institutions. • Full integration of Moodle in the text editor. • WIRIS Quizzes engine substantially improves Moodle questionnaires with mathematical contents. • Currently, WIRIS tools are inexpensive for educational institutions. • Well established at secondary school level; many students are familiar with this tool. • Teaching resources compatible with interactive digital blackboards.	• Help system is chaotic. • There is no user's community. • The version of WIRIS products evaluated here depends on an Internet connection. • It seems rather slow, as it is Java based software. • WIRIS Quizzes in Moodle questionnaires is not as powerful as could be desired (see comments below).

In the case of the short-answer question type, students use WIRIS Editor to type the answer. Then, WIRIS CAS is used to check whether the answer is correct. Note that this includes the ability to recognize different, but correct, forms of expressing the same answer. For essay questions, WIRIS CAS is used to generate random statements, but the answers must be checked manually by the teacher.

Question generation can be enhanced by a program or algorithm. We can create statements which include random elements: not just numbers, but also functions, graphs, operations, etc, chosen from a suitable set previously defined by the teacher. Thus, from just one question, hundreds of different questions may be generated. Let us illustrate this idea. For instance, when editing a question concerning the derivative of the product of two elemental functions, we write #a and #b instead of providing concrete functions. From now on, #a and #b stand for variables ranging in a set defined by us. This set must be included in the WIRIS Program block provided. For instance, let us write the following code

```
a=random({sin(x), cos(x), tan(x),
ln(x), exp(x)})
b=random({sin(x), cos(x), tan(x),
ln(x), exp(x)})
```

By combining all the possible values of #a and #b, we obtain 10 different options. Thus, we have created 10 different questions. Moreover, every time the student enters the questionnaire, he/she will probably find a different question, because #a and #b are randomly chosen from the list {sin(x), cos(x), tan(x), ln(x), exp(x)}. Furthermore, if we add some code lines with the correct answer and the most frequent mistakes, for instance,

```
ok= da/dx ·b+ a·db/dx
false1= a·b+ a·db/dx
false1= da/dx ·b+ a·b
false1= da/dx ·db/dx
```

the system will correct students' answers and will provide them with very useful feedback. Generating questionnaires in this way, which contain questions with random statements, provides students with a large number of different exercises with which they can practice as much as they need.

Advantages and Disadvantages of Using This Tool

The main advantages and drawbacks of using the WIRIS family tools are summarized in the Table 3.

In our opinion, the WIRIS family tools are interesting and have a range of *advantages*. Writing mathematical expressions is imperative for us, and the WIRIS editor fulfills this need. The WIRIS editor is richer than other editors such as MathDox (http://www.mathdox.org/new-web/index.html) or DragMath (http://www.dragmath.bham.ac.uk/). Furthermore, WIRIS CAS is powerful enough to cover almost every computational need from elementary school up to first year university courses. For many purposes, no special syntax is required; where this is not the case, the equation editor is sufficient for introducing the intended computations (such as primitives, derivatives, etc.). Regarding accessibility, WIRIS CAS is freely available via many institutional educational sites and therefore it can be used directly on the Internet. Many students have used WIRIS in high school and several editors provide textbooks with WIRIS resources. In the help files system, commands are illustrated with examples, which are in themselves WIRIS CAS sessions. Thus, one can try the commands in the example, modify them and see the result, all within the help system. WIRIS editor and WIRIS CAS can be integrated into several e-learning platforms, such as Moodle. Consequently, platforms become fully functional for courses including mathematical contents, opening up a wide range of possibilities from a mathematical point of view. Finally, WIRIS Quizzes simplifies to an amazing extent the task of providing self-evaluation tests for students and self-correctable exams (richer than those based on yes/no or multi-choice questions).

Nevertheless, we encountered some *disadvantages*. It is easy to start working with WIRIS, but it is not a simple task to go beyond this point. WIRIS developers have focused on creating functions and functionalities, and they have not paid attention to document applications and to the organization of the help files system (see the online official resource http://www.wiris.com/wiris/manual/en/index.html). Often, it is difficult to find precise information and it is easy to feel lost. In fact, some useful commands and functions are undocumented. As a result, it is rather complicated (and frustrating) to become skilled and progress in deeper applications. In these cases, one feels the lack of a strong WIRIS user's community with which to share information. WIRIS Quizzes allows students to reply with mathematical expressions when answering short-answer type questions in Moodle (that is, the answer consists of a word, short sentence, formula, etc. provided by the student). Nevertheless, we cannot read these expressions. We only can compare whether this answer matches a set of possible responses previously stated by the programmers, and this seriously limits feedback. Of course, with open source software, users have the possibility of redressing these kinds of limitations on their own. Otherwise, users must wait for future releases.

GEOGEBRA

Description of the Tool

GeoGebra is, according to the help section of the official GeoGebra Web page, "dynamic mathematics software that joins geometry, algebra and calculus". In particular, GeoGebra includes a dynamic geometry system, a kind of tool that already has a firmly established position in the mathematical education toolbox: think of programs such as Cinderella (www.cinderella.de), Geometer's Sketchpad (www.dynamicgeometry.com) or Cabri (www.cabri.com), and for more background on the educational uses of these programs see King J. & Schattschneider D. (1997), or Recio T. (1998). However, GeoGebra is special in that it is not limited to this functionality: the dynamic geometry features of GeoGebra are wisely combined with some symbolic commands, a powerful and original spreadsheet view and an intuitive interface. Last, but by no means least, GeoGebra is free and open-source software. These elements, together with very complete support, training and documentation resources for the user community, render GeoGebra a very valuable tool for Geometry- or Calculus-oriented courses.

The name of the software refers to the key ingredient: objects in GeoGebra have a dual representation, combining geometric, visual representation with an algebraic description of the object. This approach, in terms of mathematical education, greatly enhances the interplay between Geometry and Algebra, providing high gains in terms of students' intuition and abstraction.

GeoGebra also includes some features for generating teaching material. GeoGebra constructions can be easily exported to web pages; more specifically, they can be exported to HTML files containing Java applets. And, with the latest versions of the software, the integration of GeoGebra applets into Moodle sites is extremely simple.

The GeoGebra team has invested much effort in promoting the existence of a large international community of users: GeoGebra has been translated into over thirty languages. And there is also a growing network of national or regional *GeoGebra Institutes*, designed to provide training and support for local communities of GeoGebra users. In our country, the use of GeoGebra in Spanish secondary schools is growing rapidly. There is also institutional support for this through the Spanish Instituto de Tecnologías de la Educación (Institute for Educational Technologies, www.ite.educacion.es), which organizes introductory GeoGebra courses for secondary school teachers. Furthermore, there are now four GeoGebra Institutes in Spain (see www.geogebra.org/cms/en/community for the world map of GeoGebra Institutes).

The place to start using GeoGebra is its official web page, www.geogebra.org. Thus, we refer readers to the excellent material available there: if you are completely new to GeoGebra, start with the *Introductory Materials* in the help section. In addition, the Geometry team of developers is very active; new, substantially improved versions are frequently released. The requirement for this software is Java, and there are Linux, Mac and Windows versions. The *Webstart* option in the download section is the best choice; its automatic update checker guarantees that you are using the latest version. You can also use a browser-based version, which can be very useful if you do not have administration privileges on the computer. Finally, there are off-line installers for users with a poor Internet connection.

Using This Tool in Math Refresher Courses

In math refresher courses, the main use of GeoGebra is illustrating basic notions and constructions in mathematics, especially plane geometry and calculus. Let us see first how it can be applied to illustrate geometry questions. On entering GeoGebra, following window is displayed (see Figure 4):

The central part of the window (the *Drawing Pad*, in GeoGebra terminology) presents the user with a representation of the coordinate plane, where the GeoGebra geometrical objects are to be drawn. The *Input Field* is below the Drawing Pad. The Drawing Pad is used to geometrically construct objects, using the geometric tools available in the Toolbar above; thus, you might, for example, draw a circle by using the appropriate icon. However, instead of using the Toolbar, you can type *"Circle[(1,3),2]"* (without the quotes) into the Input Field, press Enter, and the desired circle appears in the Drawing Pad. Furthermore, the equation of the circle appears in the *Algebra Window*, which is the column to the left of the Drawing Pad. This reinforces the correspondence between algebraic objects and geometry objects, an aspect which is not always sufficiently clear for first-year students.

Let us see an example of the use of Geogebra for teaching Calculus. We want to illustrate the idea that definite integrals are approximated by sums. Typing the command *"f(x)=x*(x-1)*(x+1)+2"* into the Input Field, followed by *"UpperSum[f, -1, 1, 15]"* gives the result in Figure 5.

Figure 4. Geogebra Window

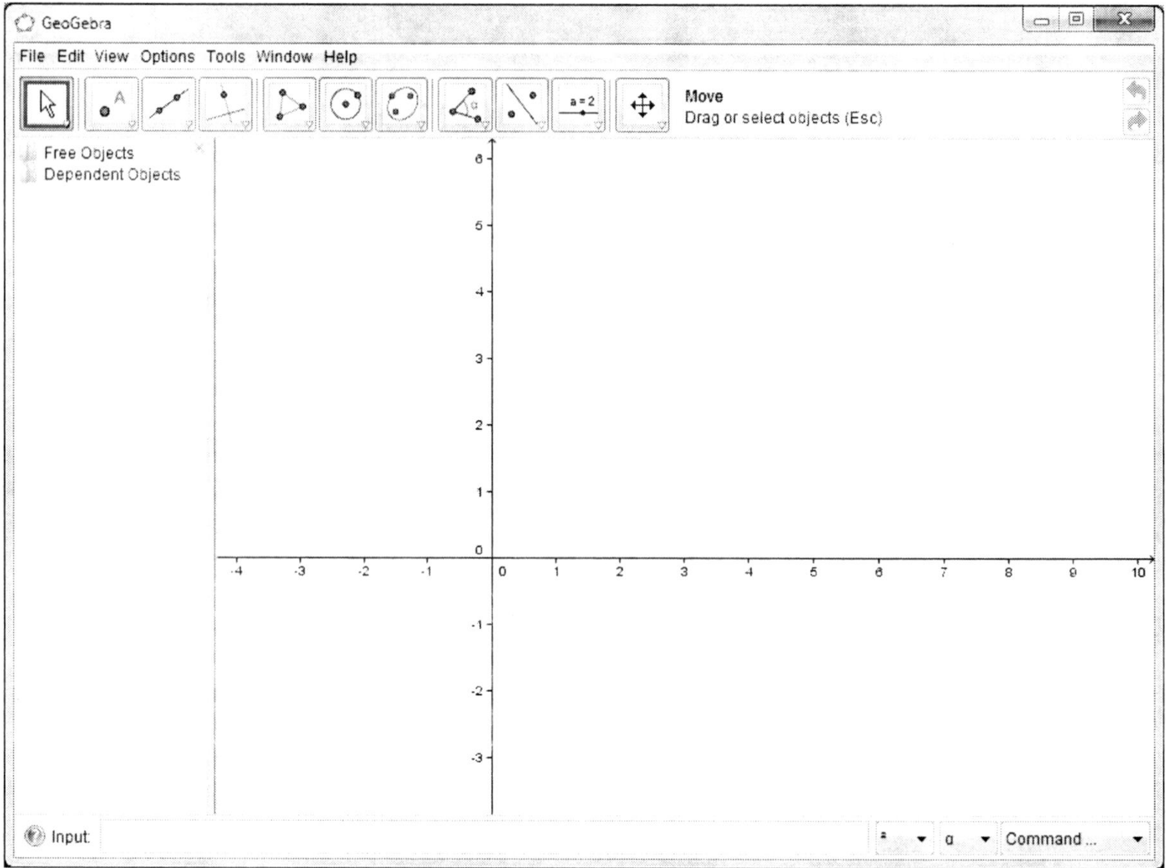

We can visualize the function together with the requested upper sum value, and compare this with the definite integral value. Next, we would like to show that as the number of points partitioning the interval increase, upper sums move closer and closer to the value of the definite integral. For this purpose, we use GeoGebra *sliders*. A slider produces a visual representation of the variable parameterizing the construction. In the Drawing Pad, this appears as a segment with a point on it. Dragging the point over the segment, the user changes the values of the variable, and simultaneously the GeoGebra construction changes to reflect this. Adding a slider to the construction in Figure 5, we control the number n of elements in the partition of the interval, simulating the convergence of the sums of the rectangle areas to the value of the definite integrals. Figure 6 shows the result of introducing such a slider, for $n=22$. Of course, this static figure does not capture the dynamism of the successive upper sums as the value of n is increased. This interactive -yet precise- representation is the main contribution made by dynamic mathematical software. We have observed that it helps the students to rapidly develop a deeper level of intuition.

In addition to definite integrals, we use Geogebra to illustrate:

- Elementary single-variable functions, as well as piecewise defined functions, and functions whose domain is restricted to a certain interval. Continuity. The functions

Figure 5. Explaining Definite Integrals with Geogebra

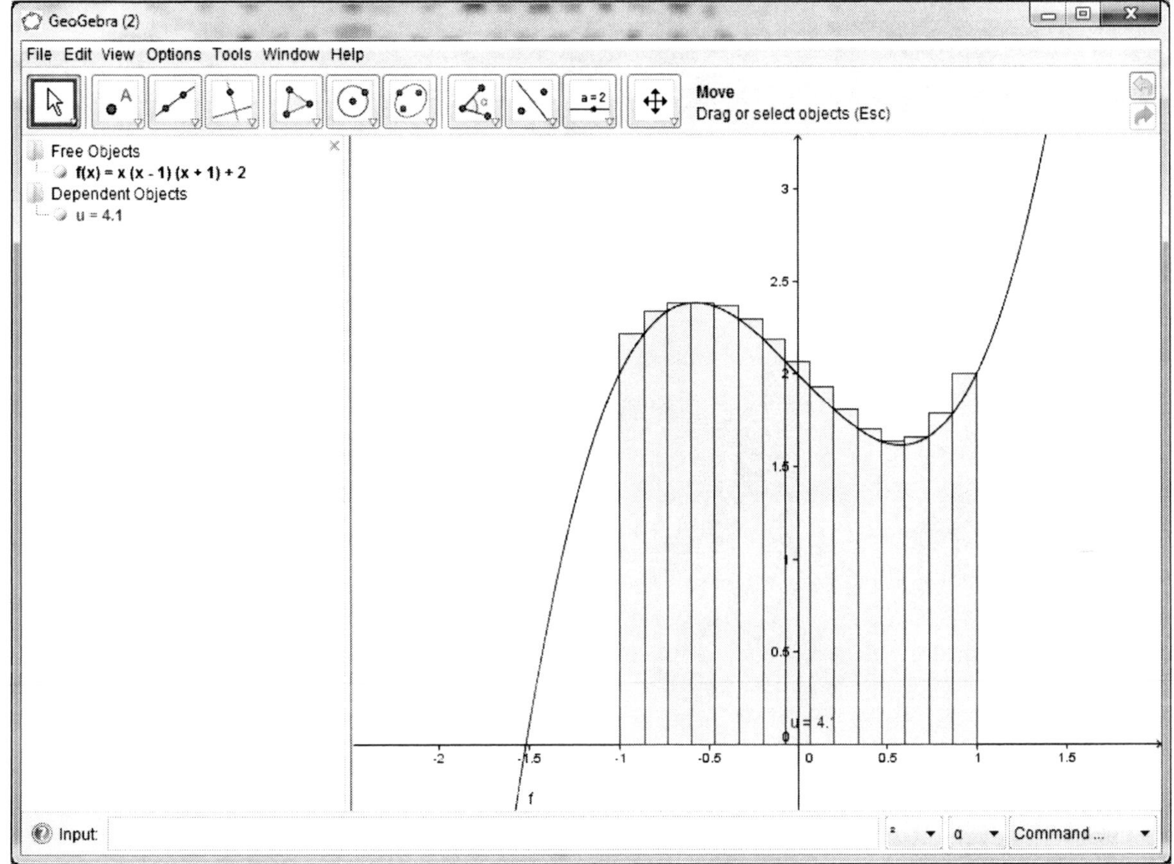

can depend on parameters, also represented with sliders.

- The derivative and primitive of a function. Differentiability.
- Extreme points, inflections, roots.
- Limits.
- Planar geometry.

GeoGebra version 3.2 has an additional new feature, called *Spreadsheet View,* which in our opinion could represent a very interesting educational resource. On the one hand, it can be used for illustrating the kind of notions that one usually associates with spreadsheets (statistics, regression analysis, etc.), while on the other, the objects stored in the spreadsheet cells are GeoGebra objects, and the operations that can be applied to them are GeoGebra commands. In addition, as with normal spreadsheets, the operations can be made to refer to cells using their relative position. Using simple cut and paste operations in the spreadsheet view, it is possible to perform many algorithmic operations, analogous to the loop structures of a programming language. For example, these are the steps to obtain the construction in Figure 7: (1) First, store the point (1.0) in the A1 cell of the spreadsheet. (2) Store in B1 a circle of center A1 (we can use the cell name to refer to its content) and radius equal to the semi-distance between A1 and the origin. (3) Store in C1 the midpoint between A1 and the origin. (4) Declare A2 to be equal to C1. (5) Copy and paste B1 and C1 to B2 and C2 respectively. We obtain a new circle and midpoint, using A2 as reference. (6) Finally, copy

Figure 6. Using sliders

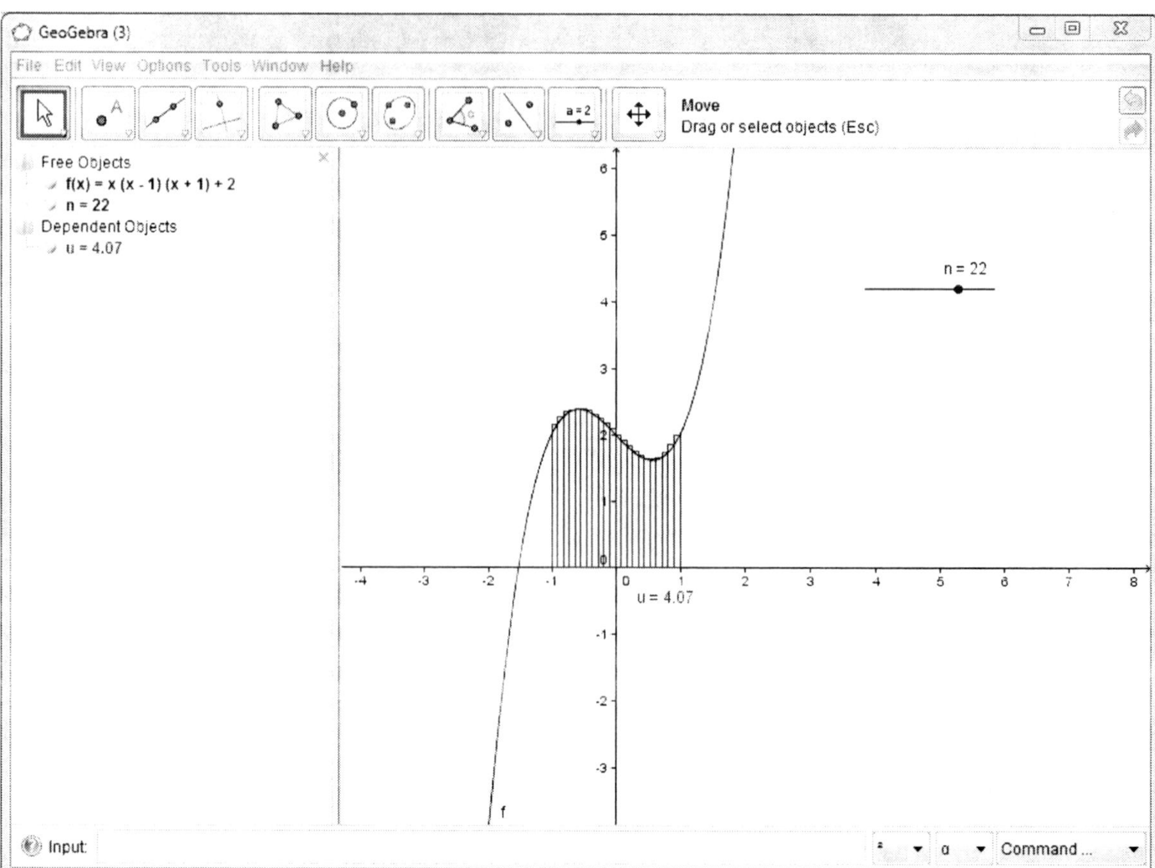

and paste the three cells in the second row into the third row, the fourth row and so on.

We use this approach to introduce students to algorithmic and iterative constructions, without needing to go into the details of a programming language. The successive iterations are visualized as cells of the spreadsheet.

Advantages and Disadvantages of Using GeoGebra

These are summarized in Table 4.

We have already mentioned in the preceding sections many of the advantages of GeoGebra. However, we also include here some remarks concerning those aspects of GeoGebra that need further improvement:

- The symbolic capacities of GeoGebra are very limited. GeoGebra takes symbolic input, but it stores numeric representations of the objects. This may change, however, if the above-mentioned project to communicate GeoGebra with other symbolic packages is successful, or if GeoGebra CAS, a version of GeoGebra with more symbolic power, is developed.
- GeoGebra does not cover three dimensional geometry and some important issues in plane geometry, such as implicitly defined curves.
- The use of Java poses some limitations on the performance and speed of GeoGebra. Such limitations are not important for standard use, but they often arise when the user

Figure 7. A construction with the spreadsheet

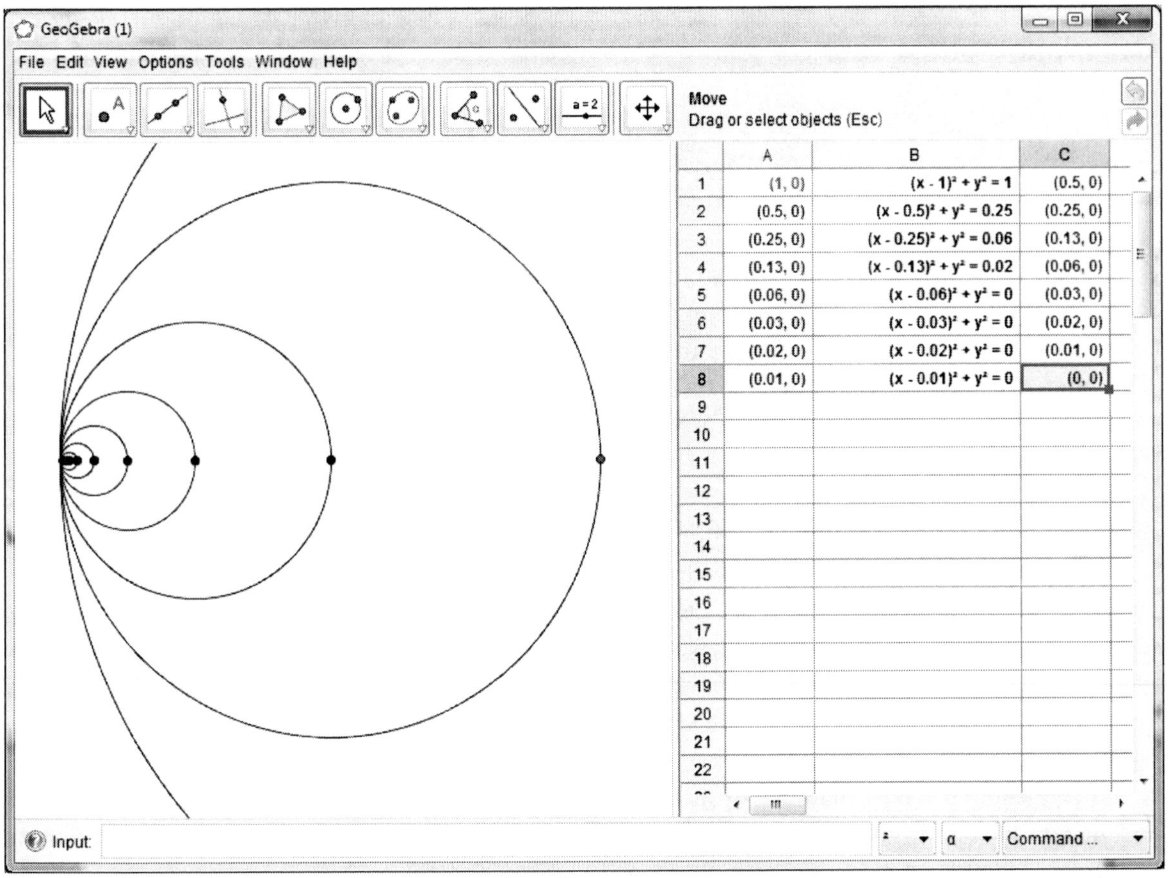

Table 4. Advantages and disadvantages of using GeoGebra

Advantages	Disadvantages
• Smooth learning curve for all users. • Very active community, providing all the required information, support and training. • GeoGebra software is free, multi-platform and open-source. • Very simple generation of web-based content (GeoGebra applets).	• No symbolic computations. • No support for 3D geometry or implicitly defined plane curves. • Limited computational power (Java based software.) • Limited integration with Moodle.

tries more complicated geometric constructions (e.g., to illustrate the notion of a fractal, etc).

- There is still room for improvement in the communication between GeoGebra and other programs, such as Wiris CAS. Although these can be used simultaneously, they are not really connected. Ideally, one would like to type, e.g., a function in a browser window, using Wiris Editor, or a similarly simple interface, and then have both GeoGebra and Wiris CAS receive and use the function definition. This goal does not seem remote, given the fact that all the software involved uses some variant of XML and JavaScript.

WOLFRAM ALPHA

Description of the Tool

Wolfram Alpha (http://www.wolframalpha.com) is an answer engine developed by Wolfram Research. Although it has a similar flavor to the omnipresent Google search engine, these two engine concepts differ in the output they provide to a given input. Thus, while Google returns a list of web pages or documents containing the answer, Wolfram Alpha computes a list of answers using available objective data and algorithms. The reader is encouraged to type, e.g., "square root" into both Google and Wolfram Alpha boxes and check the difference, in order to see for him or herself that, from the point of view of Mathematics, there is a notable difference between these two outputs, in favor of Wolfram Alpha. Wolfram Alpha is implemented entirely on Mathematica (http://www.wolfram.com/products/mathematica/index.html), proprietary computational software which implements a huge number of methods and models, including both basic and specialized mathematical tools. As a consequence, Wolfram Alpha presents an outstanding ability to answer mathematical queries.

Using This Tool in Math Refresher Courses

A comprehensive list of the uses of Wolfram Alpha on a refresher course would require much more space than is reasonable here. Instead, we list the topics which include functions that we have found to be appropriate in the context of a refresher course. An interested reader can either ask Wolfram Alpha or navigate through its Examples section (categories "Mathematics" and "Statistics & Data Analysis"), in order to find out what Wolfram Alpha is capable of doing with respect to a particular question.

- *Elementary Mathematics:* basic arithmetical operations, from addition and subtraction to powers and roots, including the possibility of working with fractions.
- *Numbers:* properties and operations relating integers, manipulation of complex numbers, and mathematical constants.
- *Plotting & Graphics:* 2D and 3D plots of functions, plots of the solution of bivariate equations or (single or multiple) inequalities.
- *Algebra:* equation solving, manipulation of polynomials and rational fractions, or matrices and linear algebra.
- *Calculus & Analysis:* sequences, their sums or products, limits, derivatives and integrals (both definite and indefinite).
- *Geometry:* plane figures and polygons, solids, plane geometry, and trigonometry.
- *Number theory:* primes and divisors.
- *Discrete mathematics:* combinatorics, graph theory, and recurrences.
- *Applied mathematics:* minimization, maximization (and, in general, optimization) of functions.
- *Logic & Set Theory:* Boolean functions and Venn diagrams.
- *Statistics & Data Analysis:* descriptive statistics (mean, median, etc.)

Advantages and Disadvantages of Using This Tool

Table 5 summarizes the main advantages and drawbacks of using Wolfram Alpha.

Examining the advantages in more detail, the main one is that Wolfram Alpha returns a very visual and complete answer, which includes quite a lot of information related to the query. As the reader may have discovered for him or herself, for the query "square root" one obtains plots, roots, derivative, integral, extrema and series representations. This makes it easier for the student to find the particular answer needed, and links

Table 5. Advantages and disadvantages of using Wolfram Alpha

Advantages	Disadvantages
• Very visual and complete answer. • User-friendly interface. • Query-related help. • Freely available, multi-platform.	• Lack of an editor to insert formulas. • Subtleties in the recognition of inserted text. • Absence of programming functionality. • Only online. • Only in English.

are provided to other properties which might be of interest. Along the same lines, the interface is extremely user-friendly; search engines are familiar to almost every student and therefore, so too is the interface of Wolfram Alpha. This encourages testing and experimenting, allowing the curious student to easily find out by him or herself what the tool can do, and how to do it. There is also a query-related help, as is usual with search engines, which guides the user in two ways once a query is performed. Firstly, if the query is not completely clear the engine offers different choices, with a "you might want..." type approach. Secondly, for some answers more details can be obtained if one is interested, e.g. the development of a derivative or an integral. See Figure 8 for an example.

Finally, it is interesting to note that Wolfram Alpha is freely available and multi-platform; the only requirements are an internet connection and a browser, hence there are no licenses to pay, nor demanding system requirements, since it can be used on all platforms, even smartphones. Such flexibility makes it easier for the students to integrate Wolfram Alpha into their daily learning process naturally.

As for the disadvantages, the main one might be the lack of an editor to insert formulas; although several syntaxes are understood for the same question, such as "integral of x^2 from 0 to 5" or "int (x^2, x=0..5)", users have to type the question via the keyboard, with no formula editor available. Although this might not seem dramatic, inserting matrices in the form $\{\{a_{11},...,a_{1n}\},...,\{a_{m1},..,a_{mn}\}\}$ is not as user-friendly as might be expected. Furthermore, there are subtleties in the recognition of inserted text; "1 + 2 + 3 + 4 + ... + n" will not be recognized, in contrast to "sum of x from 1 to n" or "sum(x, x=1..n)". Also, "distance between (2,3) and y=3-x" gives no answer, while "distance between point (2,3) and line y=3-x" does.

The user might also feel the lack of some kind of programming functionality; independently of whether the course includes notions of programming or not (ours do not), one might find it useful to use loops.

Finally, there are two limitations to Wolfram Alpha that should be pointed out. Firstly, there is currently no off-line version and, consequently, an internet connection is required in order to operate. Secondly, there are no other languages available to date other than English. It might be the case that some students are not sufficiently familiar with this language or, even if they are, it might well be the case that they are not so familiar with the mathematical terms in that language. Such a disadvantage is nevertheless mitigated by the number of online translators available.

SAGE

Description of the Tool

SAGE (http://www.sagemath.org) is a free, open-source, mathematics software system. On the one hand, it is aimed at integrating all the open-source mathematics software currently available. On the other, it is aimed at developing open-source packages to redress the shortcomings of other software.

Figure 8. Output for "derivate (x^2+x-1)/(x-1)" in Wolfram Alpha after clicking on the "Show steps" link

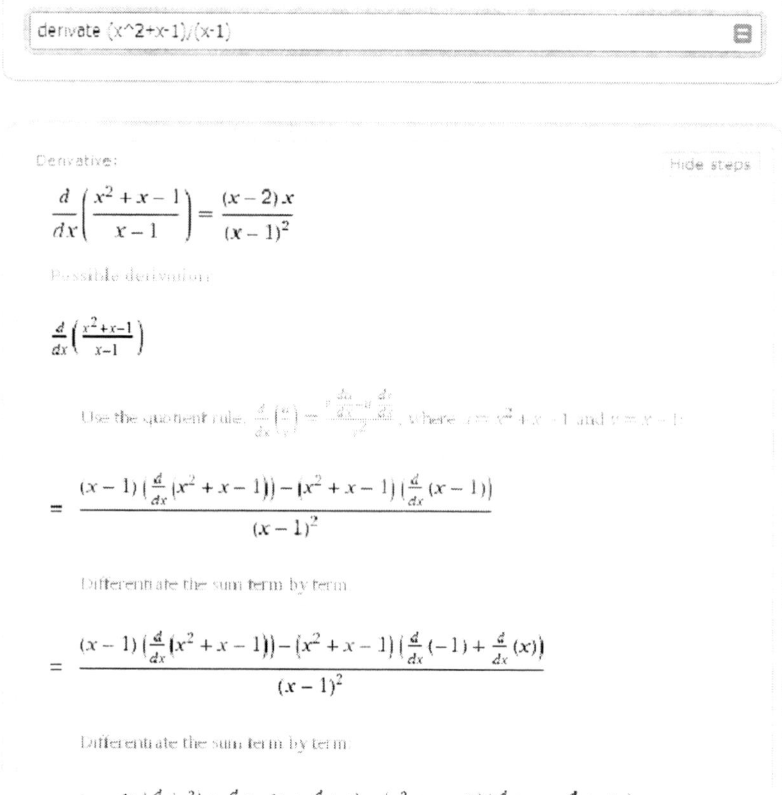

Hence, it is very complete, going much further than the basic needs of a refresher course and is suitable for research or professional purposes. The interested reader can find an online version on the web page.

Using This Tool in Math Refresher Courses

This is such a powerful tool that it makes no sense to list what it can do. Instead, the interested reader could consider it as a challenge to find a mathematical task which this software is not able to solve (not only those appropriate to a refresher course, but including even the most advanced tasks).

Although it might seem strange to consider the use of SAGE on refresher courses, our approach has been to offer it as a possibility for going beyond the basics, especially for the small, but usually present, proportion of students who already have a good understanding of the contents of the refresher course, and who tend to get bored if requested to solve problems they have already mastered. Since SAGE will be used on their forthcoming degree courses, these students can take the opportunity to begin to familiarize themselves with the system.

As for the teacher, it is easy to prepare teaching materials, since the possibility exists of exporting a worksheet in html format, and even publishing it in a SAGE repository.

Advantages and Disadvantages of Using This Tool

The main advantages and drawbacks of using Moodle are summarized in Table 6.

Table 6. Advantages and disadvantages of using SAGE

Advantages	Disadvantages
• Extremely powerful. • Might become standard for the entire degree course.	• Not for general use on refresher courses. • Unfriendly interface. • Special syntax. • Online version with frequent disruptions. • Off-line version Linux-native, not easy to install on Windows.

As regards the *advantages*, the main one is the above-mentioned power of the tool, which could well convert it into a companion tool for the entire university degree course, and even for future tasks such as research. On the other hand, there are general *disadvantages*, such as the unfriendly interface or the special syntax, in addition to the difficulties of installing it on Windows.

CONCLUSION

The authors have incorporated all the tools included in this chapter into their teaching activities; not only in math refresher courses but also on degree courses. We feel that students welcome new technologies and the associated strategies, and this belief is supported by student feedback.

With the exception of SAGE, which is a more advanced tool, the other tools described here are easy to use, suitable, useful and attractive for teaching purposes in math refresher courses. Some of them (Moodle, WIRIS and, at least in part, Geogebra) can interact with each other. Others (in part Geogebra, and Wolfram Alpha), cannot. Furthermore, Moodle, WIRIS editor, GeoGebra, Wolfram Alpha and SAGE are free, open-source software; thus, they require no investment from universities.

In terms of learning effectiveness and student satisfaction for each of the tools considered here, the main conclusions derived from our experience are the following:

- **Moodle** has been tested on a number of refresher courses, and the experience has always been successful. Learning how to use it implies a moderate effort on the part of both the teachers and the students, but these get used to it very quickly. In our experience, the tool is used extensively and the main deficiency, up to now, has been its scant utilization for carrying out virtual mentoring (students usually prefer a face-to-face encounter with the instructor, rather than a virtual meeting). The fact that the WIRIS editor cannot be used in chats (although LaTeX can) is, in this sense, a drawback that we plan to solve in the future.
- In our experience, the **WIRIS suite** is extremely useful on zero courses. Clearly, all of the benefits enumerated in our critical evaluation of the tool apply to zero courses, whereas many of the cited drawbacks will not be pertinent to refresher courses. Nowadays, students can access Internet at the University and at home. On these courses, WIRIS CAS provides our students with an easy-to-use tool for checking computations produced "by hand" and allows us to enrich web documents with WIRIS CAS sessions. Regarding its interaction with Moodle, we benefit from different WIRIS tools. The CAS engine enriches wikis, forums, e-mails and web pages. On the other hand, we set our students two different kinds of questionnaires: a) for grading their skills at the beginning and at the end

of the course and b) for exercising techniques learned in secondary school. For these purposes, WIRIS Quizzes are sufficient. Questionnaires are corrected by the system so that both students and teachers obtain rapid information about the *state of the art*. Moreover, simple programming allows us to automatically generate thousands of self-correctable training tests.

- Using **GeoGebra** to explore Geometry and Calculus, we have observed a constant increase in the motivation and interest of our students. The dynamic aspect of the constructions is a key ingredient of this reaction. Seeing applets running is beneficial for our students and helps them to quickly understand many notions through interacting with the constructions and exploring and trying out their ideas. The learning curve of the program is extremely smooth. However, many students will be tempted to devote more time to the possibilities of the software, which then becomes a distraction from the mathematics. Furthermore, learning to use GeoGebra independently takes some time, both for the teacher and the students. Although Geogebra is very user-friendly, one has to get used to it before being able to take full advantage of the program. Again, this takes time. Finally, the symbolic and algebraic features of GeoGebra are still very limited. Therefore, the software must be complemented with some other tool (e.g. Wiris). In the context of refresher courses, this implies that when using GeoGebra we are sometimes forced to leave the program, perform some computations using Wiris CAS -or some other software-, and then return with the results to GeoGebra. This can be tricky if the syntax is not coincident, and it takes time, which is a very limited resource for us.
- We have used **Wolfram Alpha** regularly on our refresher (and degree) courses, where its ease of use is always much appreciated by the students, who are usually amazed by the existence of a "mathematical search engine". Furthermore, the query-related help allows them to check their results easily, including the intermediate steps, which is very useful for derivatives and integrals (which many students have not practised sufficiently). On the negative side, the students usually feel the lack of a formula editor to provide easier interaction, as in the mathematical software they used in secondary education (e.g., WIRIS). However, they generally rate this tool as one of the most valuable resources on the course, and we find it interesting that both students and teachers consider it an everyday tool for quick queries.
- **SAGE** constitutes advanced mathematical software, and is far from being the main tool at a refresher course. We have used it to encourage outstanding students, who can thus familiarize themselves with a tool which will be used in their forthcoming courses.

REFERENCES

Albano, G., & Ferrari, P. L. (2008). Integrating technology and research in mathematics education: The case of e-learning . In Peñalvo, G. (Ed.), *Advances in e-learning: Experiences and methodologies* (pp. 132–148). doi:10.4018/978-1-59904-756-0.ch008

Anguiano Gómez, C. E. González- Romero, V. M., & Alvarez Gómez, M. (2005). Comparative study of e-learning platforms. In G. Richards (Ed.), *World Conference on E-Learning in Corporate, Government, Healthcare, and Higher Education 2005* (pp. 1877-1882).

Cole, J., & Foster, H. (2007). *Using Moodle-Teaching with the popular open source course management system*. O'Really Press. Retrieved from http://docs.moodle.org/ en/ Using_Moodle_book

Descamps, S. X., Bass, H., Bolanos Evia, G., Seiler, R., & Seppala, M. (2006). *E-learning mathematics*. Panel promoted by the Spanish Conference of Mathematics' Deans. International Conference of Mathematicians, Madrid, Spain, 2006.

Dougiamas, M., & Taylor, P. C. (2002). *Interpretive analysis of an internet-based course constructed using a new courseware tool called Moodle*. Higher Education Research and Development Society of Australasia (HERDSA) 2002 Conference, Perth, Western Australia.

Dougiamas, M., & Taylor, P. C. (2003). *Moodle: Using learning communities to create an open source course management system*. EDMEDIA 2003 Conference, Honolulu, Hawaii.

Graf, S., & List, B. (2005). *An evaluation of an open source e-learning platform stressing adaptation issues*. 5th IEEE International Conference on Advanced Learning Technologies, ICALT 2005, (pp. 163-165).

King, J., & Schattschneider, D. (1997). *Geometry turned on: Dynamic software in learning, teaching and research*. The Mathematical Association of America. Math Notes 41. ISBN 0-88385-099-0

Nichols, M. (2003). A theory for e-learning. *Journal of Educational Technology & Society*, *6*(2), 1–10.

Recio, T. (1998). *Cálculo simbólico y geométrico*. Madrid: Editorial Síntesis. (in Spanish)

Rice, W. (2006). *Moodle 1.9: E-learning course development*. PACKT Publishing.

Rice, W. (2007). *Moodle teaching techniques*. PACKT Publishing.

Tavangarian, D., Leypold, M., Nölting, K., & Röser, M. (2004). Is e-learning the solution for individual learning? *Journal of E-learning*, *2*(2).

Chapter 17
Formula Editors and Handwriting in Mathematical E-Learning

Morten Misfeldt
Aarhus University, Denmark

Anders Sanne
Norwegian University of Science and Technology (NTNU), Norway

ABSTRACT

Teaching and learning mathematics at university level is increasingly being supported by Learning Management Systems. In this chapter, we report from the e-learning initiative, DELTA, and in doing so we aim to describe how formulas, drawings, and other mathematical representations influence student communication. We describe a practice that combines handwriting and discussion forums facilitated by a Learning Management System (LMS). We have experienced lack of student activity in the discussion forums and introducing a new LMS (Moodle) with improved formula editor capabilities into the environment, does not seem to considerably improve the situation, whereas a scanner-based handwritten communication seems to successfully support the assignment communication between the students and the teacher.

DOI: 10.4018/978-1-60960-875-0.ch017

INTRODUCTION

Teaching and learning at university level increasingly takes advantage of online technology, such as Learning Management Systems (LMS), because they provide a number of advantages such as flexibility regarding time and place, easy distribution of information and support of collaboration among students (Engelbrecht and Harding, 2005, OECD, 2005).

As mathematics is a worldwide and comprehensive topic at undergraduate level (Carlson and Rasmussen, 2008) it is highly relevant to look into specific problems concerning teaching and learning mathematics online. This is the purpose of this chapter. The empirical basis of our discussion here is the distance learning program DELTA that has been running since 2005. Our focus is on the relation between technology for writing mathematics and the students' communication. We address the role of handwriting in mathematical e-learning, and how mathematical text is produced and distributed online through a LMS. We also explore the students' communication situation and how the technological environment supports or hinders this communication. More specifically, we address how teachers and students in DELTA cope with the many representations used in mathematical texts and describe the challenges this poses to e-learning of mathematics.

BACKGROUND

When teaching mathematics fully online, there are a number of aspects of mathematical communication that is worth considering. Firstly, the extent to which the employed interface (i.e. keyboard and mouse) and programs support or hinder mathematical communication. Some of the formulas, drawings and other types of representations are more difficult to create using a computer than it is to write them by hand. Secondly, technological challenges to mathematical notation could prompt students to describe mathematics in words rather than in the established mathematical notation or in other ways affect the types of representations used in mathematical work. Hence, we find it relevant to consider the implications of the multimodal (i.e. uses many types of representations) nature of mathematical text, and how this relates to learning and communication.

E-Learning and Mathematics

In 2005 OECD published a report surveying the use e-learning in tertiary education across the globe (OECD, 2005). The main results are that technology is increasingly available and used in tertiary education, but that the impact on classroom teaching and pedagogy is sparse. The only notable pedagogical impact is that the idea of a learning object has gained some momentum in supplementing classroom teaching. But the overall picture is unclear in the sense that a number of both positive, (for example flexible access to materials and resources and use of pedagogical techniques dependent on ICT) and negative (for example usability problems with digital tools and loss of face to face contact) effects of e-learning is laid out in the survey. The report points to lack of research evaluating the pedagogical value of e-learning.

A lot of literature, on the other hand, points to innovative or sensible practices and potentials of using e-learning (Jaques & Salmon, 2007, Hiltz & Goldman, 2005, MacDonald, 2008, Rattleff, 2008). The institutional culture seems to play some role; institutions with a long history of distributed teaching shows more potential for pedagogical development taking advantage of new technology (OECD, 2005).

The state of the art of communication technology is a persistent issue in e-learning of mathematics. This is reflected in a conference panel report (Descamps et al. 2006), which describes the current challenges of e-learning in mathematics. The report highlights that 'Tutor-student oral communication' is very important, and one of the reasons is that when writing down one's concerns the students must overcome a technological barriers that makes it a difficult task to write down a mathematical sign in a computer (Descamps et al., 2006).

There is no consensus about the importance of this technological barrier. In a report on Italian use of e-learning in mathematics, Osimo (2002) points out that writing mathematical formulae does not pose a serious threat to the possibility of creating online learning environments in mathematics. It should be noticed that the focus of this report is on the use of e-learning technology as a means to augment, rather than replace, campus teaching. This type of e-learning is sometimes denoted "blended learning" (Gynther, 2005, Macdonald, 2008). Contrary to Osimo's finding, a development project (Guzdial, 2002) involving a wiki-based collaboration tool to augment undergraduate university teaching observed resistance specifically to the technology that was introduced in the mathematics and science classes; a similar resistance was not observed in the teaching of other topics.

In relation to teaching mathematics fully online, Juan et al. (2008) points to the writing mathematical formalism online as one of seven observed problems, and suggest that students use as much plain (ASCII) text as possible when communicating mathematics.

A qualitative investigation has shown that professional mathematicians use computers as well as handwriting tools (e.g. pen and paper) to support their mathematical writing process. This investigation shows that pen and paper are used more in the early idea-generating phase of the work (Misfeldt, 2006). One of the reasons that these mathematicians sometimes prefer handwriting is that it better handles the many representations involved in mathematical work.

As we see previous research (Juan et al. 2008, Misfeldt 2006, Descamps et al. 2006) indicates that the use of handwriting, the nature of mathematical representations and how these are handled on a computer could be of relevance to the learning environment in a fully e-learning based initiative like DELTA. Yet, the exact impact of handwriting dependency on an e-learning initiative like DELTA is not clear.

The use of e-learning platforms often involves a pedagogical change as well as a change in transmitting media. Potentials regarding increased collaboration among students in e-learning are seen in many fields (Jaques & Salmon, 2007) including mathematics (Juan et al. 2008).

Mathematical Text

Mathematical text employs several forms of representations such as diagrams, algebraic formalism and natural language (Pimm, 1987, Ohallaran, 2005). The many types of representations are important to the learners development of mathematical concepts (Duval, 2006, Kress, Jewitt, Ogborn, & Tsatsarelis, 2001, Steinbring, 2006). Simultaneously, the many types of representations may pose a challenge to online mathematics communication (Mariotti, 2002). We consider mathematical text as multimodal (Kress & Van Leeuwen, 2001) in order to stress the simultaneous use of various modes of expressing meaning. In order to describe how this multimodality challenges online communication, we apply the concepts 'sign' and 'medium'.

In semiotics the central concept is the sign. Signs consist of a material signifier that signifies something, i.e. the signified, to someone, i.e. the interpreter. The material substance that is manipulated in order to produce signs is called the medium. Culturally developed systems of meaning using one or more media are called modalities (Kress & Van Leeuwen, 2001). To give an example, sound is a medium that can be manipulated to create signs such as utterances, and speech is a culturally developed system of meaning; a mode.

In the DELTA program, the typical cases of media are pen, paper and a computer. The mediation of mathematical signs in a computer is strongly dependent on the configuration of the programs one chooses to use. Therefore, we consider the computer with a specific configuration of programs to be a medium; i.e. we consider a computer with a word processor to be one medium and a computer with spreadsheet software to be another medium. Perhaps more relevant to this investigation, we consider a change in the LMS and functionalities of the discussion forum to be a change in the medium. In this connection we take a closer look at the affordance of media and modes, which constitutes both the constraints and possibilities that various media and modes pose for meaning making (Sellen & Harper, 2002).

In the following sections, we describe our research work with the DELTA program. Our research concern is to improve online teaching and learning in mathematics at undergraduate level. We describe the students' communication situation and how the technological environment supports or hinders the students' communication. More specifically, we address how the teachers and students in DELTA cope with the multimodal nature of mathematical text and the challenges this poses to e-learning.

THE USE OF MEDIA IN THE DELTA PROGRAM

DELTA[1] consists of eight online undergraduate mathematics courses at the Norwegian University of Science and Technology (NTNU). In terms of content, the subjects are identical to those taught on campus; i.e. the syllabuses and the exams are identical to the campus courses. In terms of format, the subjects have been adapted to distant learning. The typical DELTA-student is a teacher in upper secondary school who wants to qualify as a teacher in mathematics. Each course is worth 7.5 ECTS credits, and the eight DELTA courses are:

- Basic Calculus I
- Basic Calculus II
- Linear Algebra and Geometry
- Linear Algebra with Applications
- Number Theory
- Geometry
- Probability
- Statistical Methods

Information and Communication Technology (ICT) is used for communication, organization and facilitation of collaboration among students. The use of ICT is not a learning objective in itself. DELTA is based on the use of a Learning Management System. The LMS is the most important communication channel, and it is used to distribute texts and exercises and stream video lessons. The students are supposed to make active use of the discussion forums offered in the LMS. The specific concern in this chapter is the role of discussion forums and handwriting in learning and teaching mathematics online. The students have the possibility of participating in online discussions with teachers and fellow students, in a computer based (no handwriting) discussion forum, provided by the LMS, and the students scan their handwritten assignments and hand them in as PDF files via the LMS. The teachers use a pen and a tablet with their computers to work directly on the screen when they mark and comment on the students' assignments.

An Interventional Research Approach

The efforts described in this chapter simultaneously attempts to generate knowledge about the learning environment in online education in mathematics and to evaluate and improve various aspects of the educational initiative in DELTA. In this respect, we conduct design research (DBR Collective, 2003). A classical model for design research (Cobb 2001, p. 457) can be described by means of the design cycle. One important aspect of the cycle is the design intervention, together with a set of hopes, hypotheses or other forms of theoretically-based ideas about the workings of the intervention in a classroom situation, for instance. The other important aspect of the design cycle is the empirical investigation, where the combination of the designed intervention and the envisioned learning trajectory is put to the test.

The result of design research can be defined as 'the difference' between the theoretically based idea and the actual empirical investigation. We acknowledge that the result of the design research project is the developed design, the envisioned learning trajectory, the protocol of the empirical events recorded in the project, and the difference between the envisioned learning scenario and the empirical reality.

Our investigation is focused on obtaining a better understanding of how technology, culture, procedures, fellow students, and teachers affect the learning environment of the students who partake in DELTA.

More specifically, we have explored how teachers and students in DELTA cope with the multimodal nature of mathematical text first by interviewing students, and later by having all students in DELTA answer a questionnaire.

In order to gain qualitative insight into the students' communication situation we applied a relatively open approach. An interview study was conducted, mainly in search of relevant themes for a quantitative investigation. The interview guide was developed on the basis of the intuition and experience of the involved teacher and researcher and on the basis of a survey on literature. This open approach is inspired by Cobin and Strauss (2008). Three informants were interviewed over the phone. The interviews are transcribed and coded in an open way to facilitate the search for themes that related to the informants learning environment and that were of value to the informants.

The interviews showed that the students worked much on their own; they did this to be able to arrange their studies around all their other obligations. Nevertheless, the interview data pointed to a number of strong learning situations that the respondents had experienced when they were able to study together with another person, either a peer student or a mathematically skilled colleague. Furthermore, the interviews showed that the respondents was not supported by the discussion forums and occasionally had problems with respect to writing mathematical formalism in the discussion forum.

The Use of Discussion Forums

Based on the interview result, we developed a questionnaire, which the students have answered twice every year since 2006. In this continuous evaluation, we ask how the students use the discussion forum in relation to the courses. In every semester, only few of the students use the forum for asking questions often. However, the questions and answers that are posted are often read (several times every week) by many of the students. Weekly or occasionally a good part of the students have questions they would like to raise but choose not to post. Below, we present the total of the students' answers over a five year period.

Most of the students inform that they pose questions in the discussion forum 'rarely' or 'now and then' (Figure 1). Only a few of the students pose questions 'often', and in most of the semesters a small, but still noticeable, part of the students never pose questions in the discussion forum. This indicates that posing questions in the discussion forum is not a crucial aspect of participating in the DELTA program. Similarly, in most, but not all, semesters a smaller part of the students pose questions 'weekly' or 'several times a week'. This indicates that posing questions in the forum is something that most of the students do once in a while, while a few of the students do it on a more regular basis. Some of the students never pose questions; this indicates that active students do not necessarily pose questions on the forum.

Figure 1. (Q11) How often do you post questions to the discussion group?

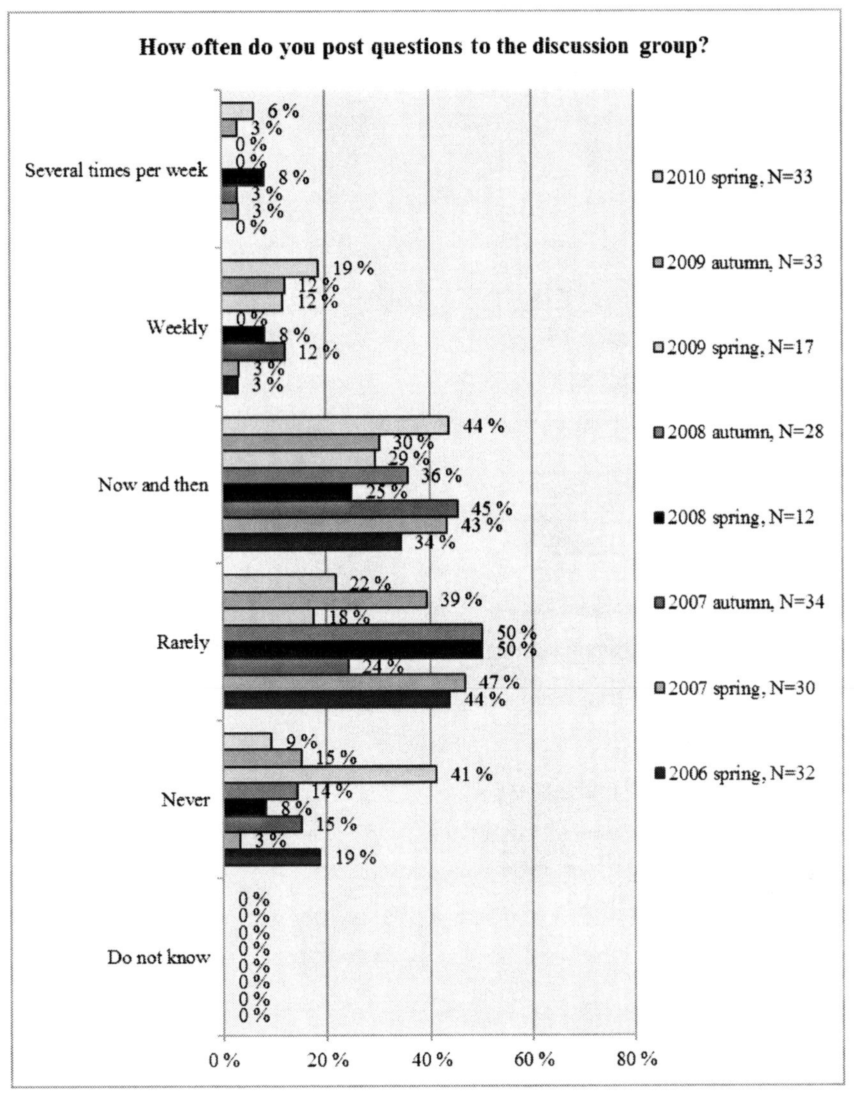

The number of students who answer questions posed by fellow students is close to the number of students that pose questions (Figure 2). We do not know whether those who never answer or pose questions are the same students or whether those who often answer and pose questions are the same. However, we can see that the group of students who never answers questions is bigger than the group of students who never asks questions in the online forum. This difference might be due to the fact that fewer students are actually able to answer the questions.

If we only look at the students' tendency to pose and answer questions in the discussion forum, the forum may appear unimportant to the students. Yet, when we ask how often questions and answers are read by the students we get an entirely different impression (Figure 3). Almost all of the students read the questions and answers on a weekly basis at least. From that perspective, the discussion forum becomes an important place to

Figure 2. (Q12) How often do you answer other students' questions?

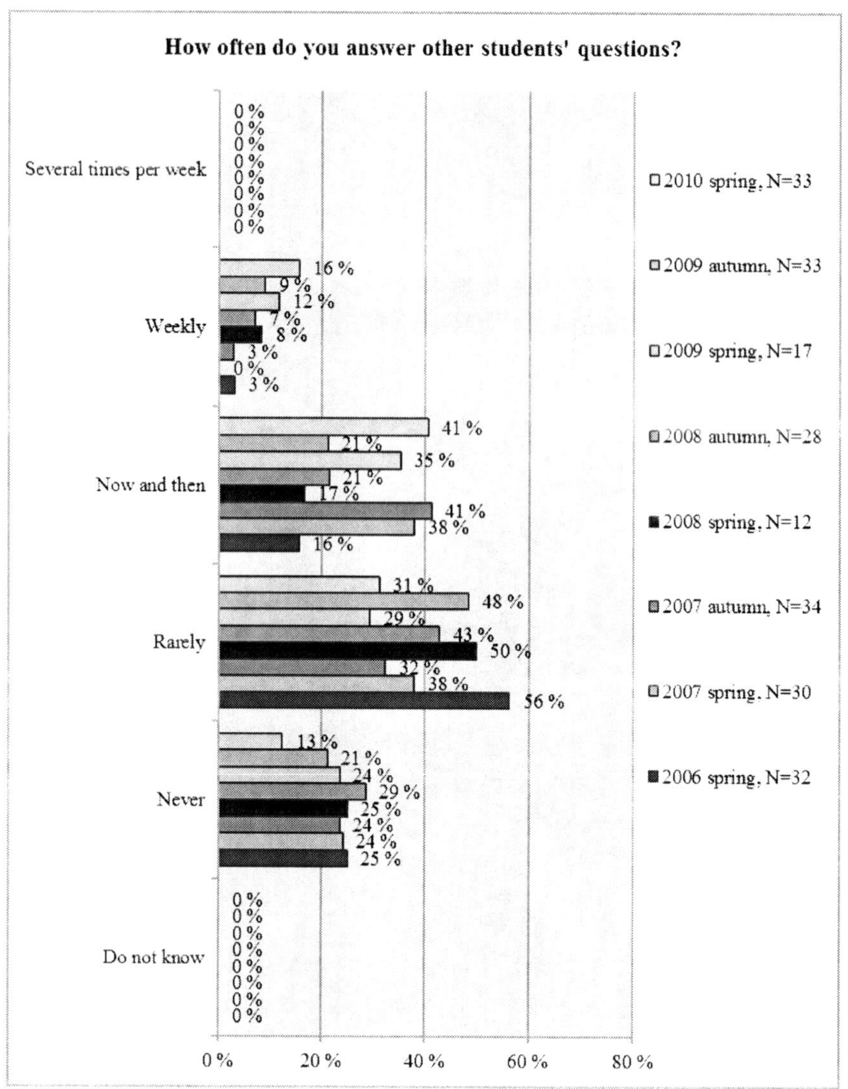

browse for knowledge and keep oneself updated on the challenges that the other students are facing.

More than half of the students have questions that they would like to have answered now and then (see Figure 4). These are questions the students could pose in the online forum, but they choose not to. Our questionnaire survey asks the students to give reasons for not posing questions. They give a number of reasons such as lack of time, problems with the mathematical interface to the discussion forum, and a feeling that the question is irrelevant because it relates to topics dealt with earlier in the course or at a different educational level.

The Students' Use of Media

In answering one of the questionnaire questions, the students explain how they typically communicate with peer students. The most typical way is face-to-face or via the LMS. From the students'

Figure 3. (Q13) How often do you read other's questions and answers?

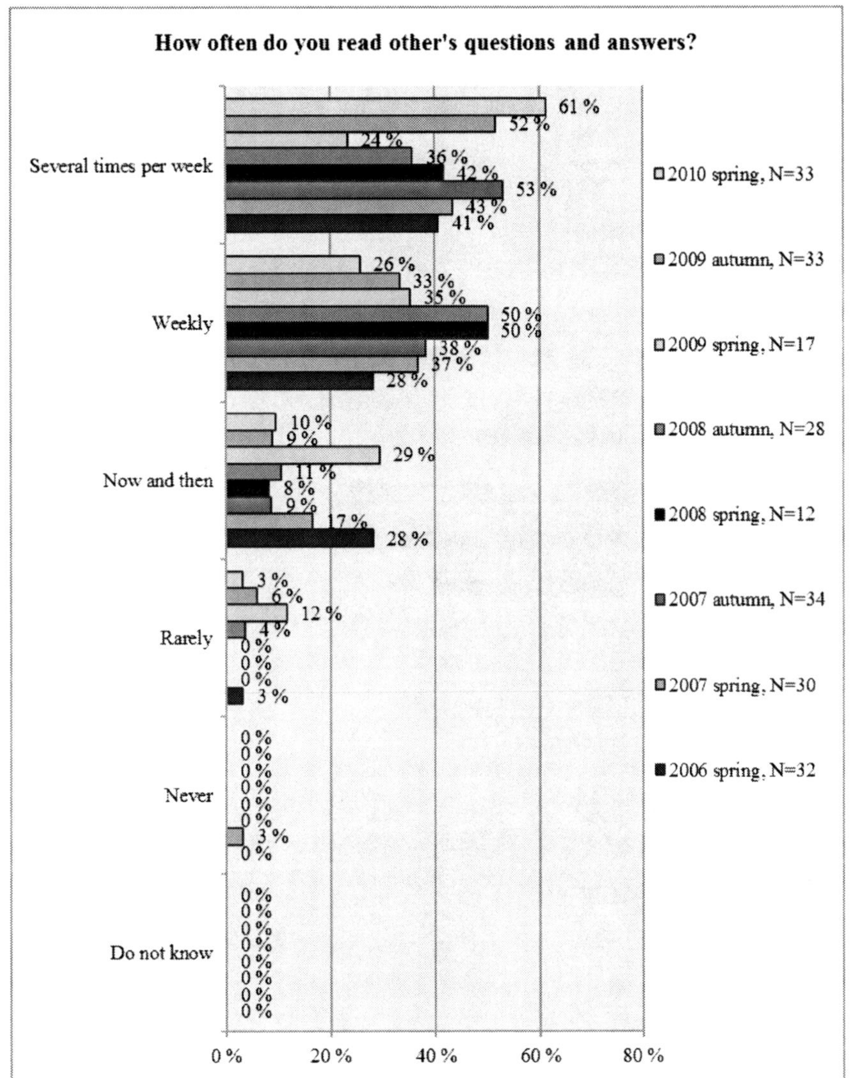

comments in the questionnaire it seems that the computer is mainly used to send and receive information. When they work with DELTA, paper is the dominant medium, followed by computer and scanner, as expressed by one student: "*I use pen and paper for calculating, computer to participate at Moodle and a scanner to scan my assignments*" (questionnaire response).

The students typically hand in handwritten exercises by scanning them and uploading them to the learning management system. The teachers mark the assignments by writing into the PDF file (for instance using Adobe Acrobat). The students' use of media in relation to DELTA is described in Table 1. The table comprises the answers from all the survey years.

From Table 1, we see that pen-and-paper and the computer are the only media that are typically used to work with mathematics.

The reason for choosing a handwriting approach is twofold. Firstly, the DELTA initiative uses the same exam as the campus-based programs

Figure 4. (Q14) How often do you have questions which you really would like answers to, but which you still don't pose?

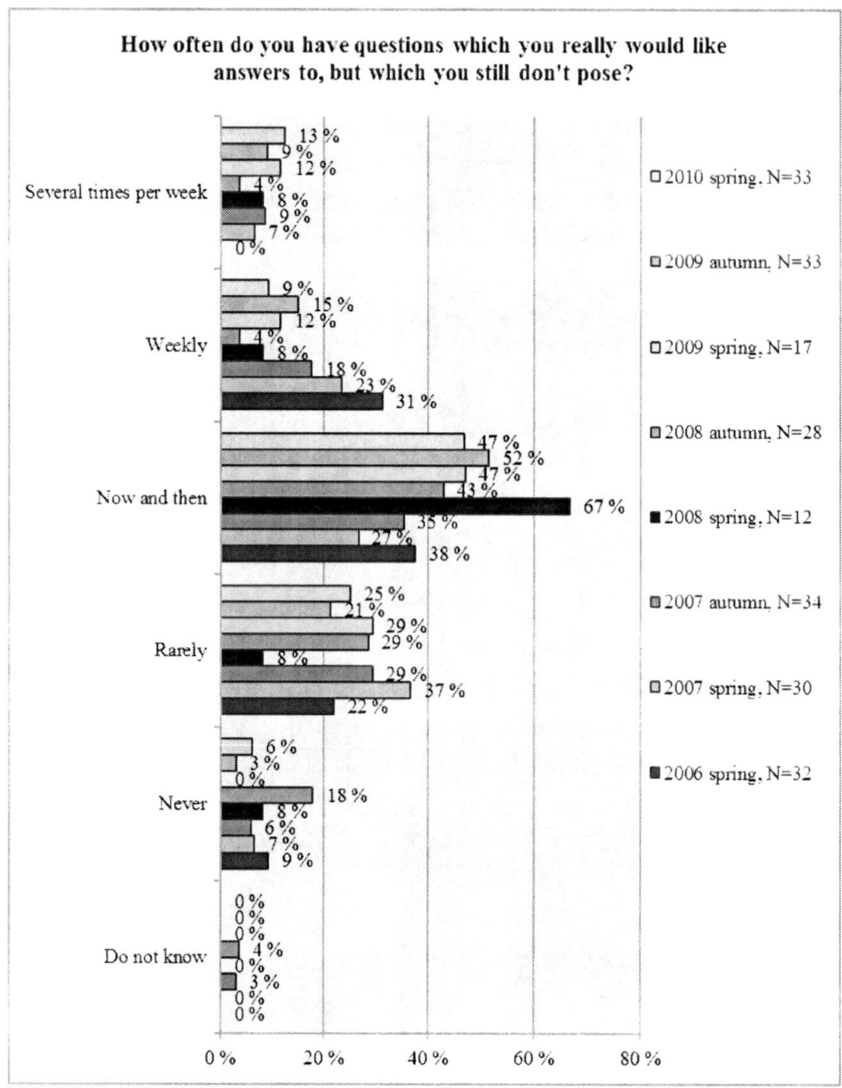

and this exam is a written test where the students typically hand in handwritten work. Hence, the technique of composing handwritten assignment work must also be trained in the DELTA program (see Figure 5).

The other reason for focusing on handwriting emerged from our work with DELTA. The combination of handwriting, scanning and using Adobe Acrobat proved very practical in supporting the students' ability to create multimodal texts. The assignment format proved much better at supporting mathematical formalism than the discussion forum, as the students typically used ASCII signs to communicate mathematics in the discussion forum.

Figure 6 shows how a student expresses a sequence of formulas in the discussion forum and what that sequence would look like in normal mathematical notation. It is obviously easier to interpret and work with the formula in standard notation, but in the discussion forum the students tend to only use the keyboard (ASCII) signs.

Table 1. Students' use of media in relation to their work in DELTA

How often do you use the following medium in your mathematics studies?							
Spring 2006 - Spring 2010							
N=191	Computer	Pen and paper	Blackboard	Phone	Scanner	Camera	Fax
Not answered	23.0%	25.7%	72.8%	66.5%	33.0%	73.3%	73.8%
Never	0.5%	0.0%	23.0%	16.8%	0.5%	23.6%	23.0%
Rarely	0.0%	0.0%	3.7%	3.7%	2.6%	0.5%	2.1%
Now and then	2.1%	1.0%	0.5%	6.3%	173%	2.6%	1.0%
Weekly	12.0%	9.9%	0.0%	4.7%	40.8%	0.0%	0.0%
Several times per week	62.3%	63.4%	0.0%	2.1%	5.8%	0.0%	0.0%

Figure 5. Excerpt from handwritten assignment with the student's question to the teacher and a comment from the teacher. The assignment routine in the DELTA program require the students to use a scanner and a PDF creator (such as adobe acrobat) and deliver their handwritten assignments as PDF-files through the LMS. The teacher works on the screen using a pen tablet for handwriting along with the note utilities in Adobe Acrobat, to mark and comment the assignment.

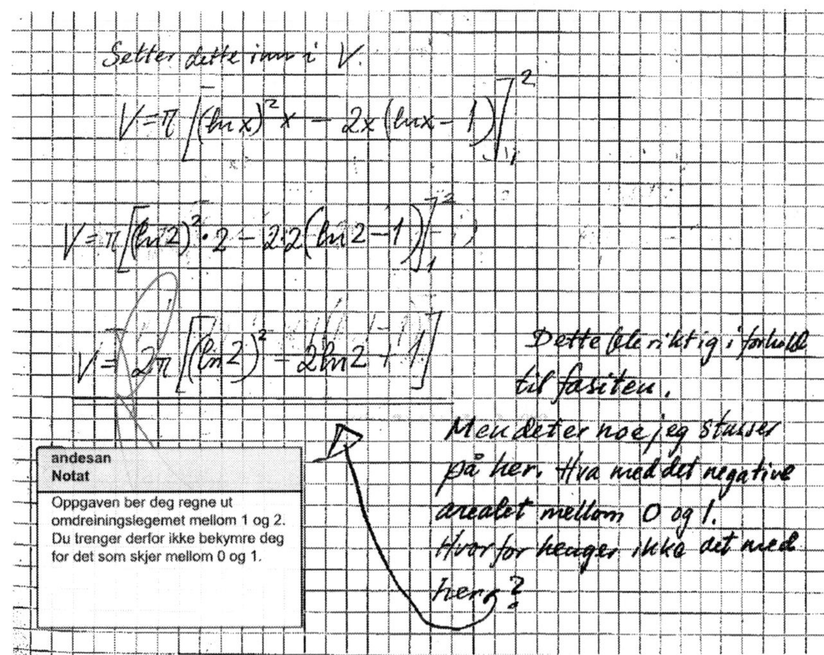

Change in the LMS

In order to improve the functionality of the learning management system regarding writing mathematics, we changed the LMS from *It's Learning* to *Moodle* after the first years of the DELTA program. The new system, Moodle (http://moodle.org), offered a much better embedded equation editor. We have used the algebra filter (http://docs.moodle.org/en/Algebra_filter) and the TeX notation filter

Figure 6. Example from the calculus discursion in our LMS. This is hard both to write and to read.

ASCII sample:

1+(x-1/(4x))^2= 1 + x^2-2x(1/(4x) +1/(4x)^2= 1 + x^2 -1/2+1/(4x))^2= x^2+1/2 +1/(4x))^2= (x+1/(4x^))^2 the square root of this then becomes x+1/(4x)

Student could have written this in standard mathematical notation as:

$$1+\left(x-\frac{1}{4x}\right)^2=1+x^2-2x\left(\frac{1}{4x}\right)+\frac{1}{(4x)^2}$$

$$=x^2+\frac{1}{2}+\frac{1}{(4x)^2}=\left(x+\frac{1}{4x}\right)^2 \text{ and}$$

$$\sqrt{\left(x+\frac{1}{4x}\right)^2}=\left(x+\frac{1}{4x}\right)$$

(http://docs.moodle.org/en/TeX_notation_filter), in Moodle (see figure 7 and 8). Furthermore we have embedded the mathematical software WIRIS (see www.wiris.com) into discussion forum posts.

With the algebra filter in Moodle, the students can write mathematics using syntax very similar to the ASCHII based "calculator code" showed in Figure 6. The algebra filter in Moodle automatically converts the student's input to small pictures via the TeX filter. The users are free to choose between the algebra filter and the TeX filter. We saw this as a big advantage of Moodle because the university teachers already know LaTeX from their everyday work. To help the students with the new way to edit equations, we provided an example sheet with a table (Table 2) showing how to type in the most common symbols and operators using both filters.

We were generally very satisfied with the system, but the functionalities regarding mathematical writing were not adopted by the students. Moreover, the tendency to write posts in the discussion forum and to answer other people's questions never increased. This is surprising and works against our hypothesis that one of the reasons most students only rarely wrote in the discussion forum was that the forum had insufficient functionalities regarding mathematical formalism. Yet, as the introduction of a new software environment that improved the students' possibilities for including mathematical formulas in their posts did not in any significant way change the students' tendency to write in the forum, there must be other reasons.

We see at least two reasons. We believe one explanation is that we have observed a general problem in which students' lacking will to write in online discussion forums is not related to mathematics as such, but rather to factors such as shy students and lack of process facilitation etc. This may very well be the case, as similar reasons have been found to explain the lack of written contributions in other online learning environments (Jaques & Salmon 2007, Salmon 2000). It appears obvious that this general problem of lack of willingness to write in online learning environments in part explains our observations.

Figure 7. The filter interaction in Moodle. The $$ starts the TeX filter, and the TeX code is automatically interpreted and shown as an image.

Fullscreen editor - Mozilla Firefox
http://moodle.math.ntnu.no/lib/editor/htmlarea/popups/fullscreen.php?id=23
Trebuchet
1 (8 pt)
Lang
This is an example of a posting with some mathematics. I can use the Moodle TeX filter to write an expression like this: $$\int_a^b f(x) dx = F(b)-F(a)$$
The LaTeX code written between the double $-signs shows up as well formatted mathematics.
Path:
Fullført
zotero

Figure 8. The TeX code is interpreted and shown as an image. When clicking the image you reopen the TeX code. The algebra filter works in a similar way.

An example posting
by Anders Sanne - Tuesday, 30 November 2010, 01:50 pm
This is an example of a posting with some mathematics. I can use the Moodle TeX filter to write an expression like this:
$\int_a^b f(x)dx = F(b) - F(a)$
The LaTeX code written between the double $-signs shows up as well formatted mathematics.
Edit | Delete | Reply

The other reason could be that problems of writing mathematics online concern more aspects than whether or not, a certain functionality exits, and can thus not simply be solved by introducing new functionalities. By looking at the students' free text comments in the questionnaire, we see that they sometimes state problems with writing formulas and drawing graphs as reasons for not posing questions in the discussion forum.

SOLUTIONS AND RECOMMENDATIONS

Handwriting in the DELTA Program

The students scan their handwritten assignments and hand them in via the LMS. Therefore, each student is required to use a scanner and upload handwritten multi page PDF files to the discus-

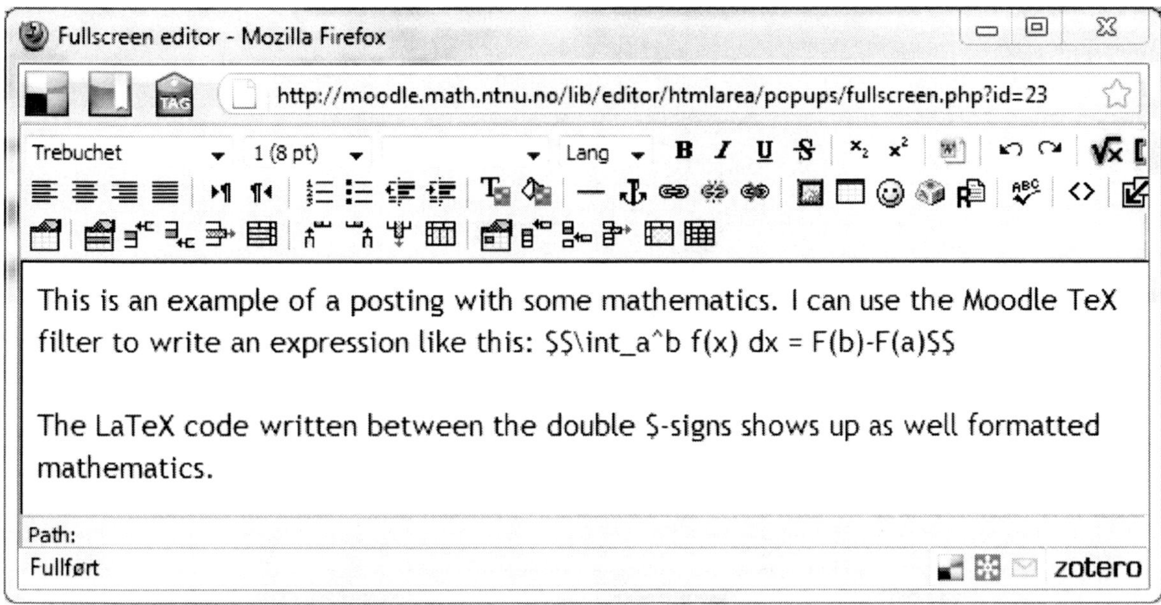

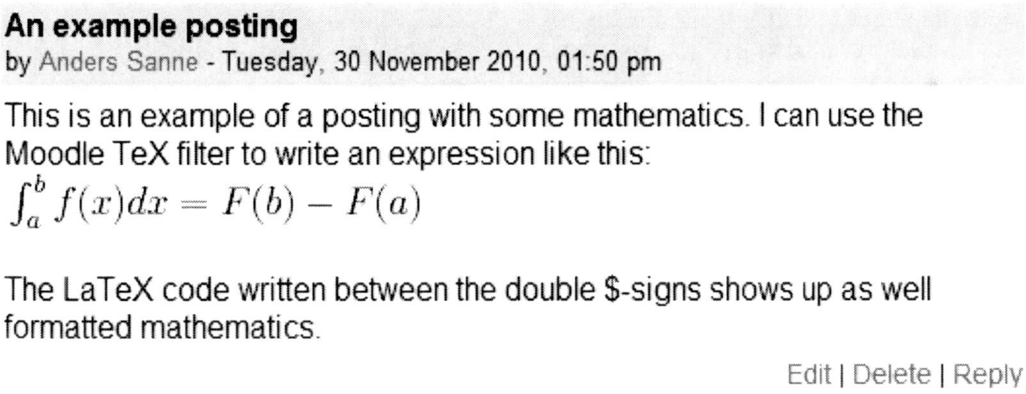

Table 2. Example sheet showing how to type in a the most common mathematical symbols and operators using the available algebra and TeX filters in Moodle. This sheet was provided to the students, when Moodle was introduced.

Algebra filter input	TeX filter input	Moodle output
@@x^2@@	$$x^{2}$$	
@@A=pi r^2@@	$$A=\pi r^{2}$$	
@@dy/dx=3x^2/y^3@@	$$\frac{dy}{dx}=\frac{3 x^{2}}{y^{3}}$$	
@@asin(x/y)@@	$$\mbox{sin}^{-1}\left(\frac{x}{y}\right)$$	
@@int(x/(x^2+4) dx)@@	$$\int \frac{x}{\left(x^{2}+4\right)} dx$$	
@@int(x/(x^2+4) dx,0,1)@@	$$\int_{0}^{1}\frac{x}{\left(x^{2}+4\right)} dx$$	
@@sqrt(x^2+y^2)@@	$$\sqrt{x^{2}+y^{2}}$$	
@@sqrt(x^2+y^2,3)@@	$$\sqrt[3]{x^{2}+y^{2}}$$	
@@x>=1@@	$$x\geq 1$$	
@@x<=pi@@	$$x\leq \pi$$	
@@x<>infty@@	$$x\not= \infty$$	
@@cos(x,2)+sin(x,2)=1@@	$$\cos^{2}\left(x\right)+\sin^{2}\left(x\right)=1$$	
@@cosh(x,2)-sinh(x,2)=1@@	$$\cosh^{2}\left(x\right)-\sinh^{2}\left(x\right)=1$$	
@@lim((x-2)/(x^2-4),x,2)=1/4@@	$$\lim_{x\to 2}\frac{\left(x-2\right)}{\left(x^{2}-4\right)} =\frac{1}{4}$$	
@@lim(x/(x^2+1),x,infty)=0@@	$$\lim_{x\to \infty} \frac{x}{\left(x^{2}+1\right)} = 0$$	

sion forum. The teachers use a pen and a tablet with their computers, and they work directly on the screen when they mark and comment on the exercises.

We have seen that pen & paper and scanner are frequently used by the students in the DELTA program. Furthermore, the combination of handwriting and scanner support the assignment routine that is used in the DELTA program. To some extent, this assignment routine resembles a classical campus-based format with frequent hand-in assignments and exercises that are marked by the teacher and returned to the students. One of the reasons for following such a classical scheme can be found in the assessment employed in the DELTA program. The DELTA students follow the same exams as the undergraduate mathematics students at NTNU, and these exams are paper and pencil-based, handwritten exams.

Apart from constituting a reasonable training platform for the written exam, the handwriting/scanner approach to the assignment work also allows the students in the DELTA program to express all the representations necessary to communicate mathematics in a reasonable way. In that sense, the handwriting/scanner approach to assignment work in mathematical e-learning environments supports the multimodal nature of mathematical text. Naturally, computers support the authoring of multimodal mathematical texts by including formulas, pictures, and tables just as the usability of the technology for creating mathematical formalism is continuously improved. Yet, our experience from the DELTA program suggests that the handwriting/scanner approach is a viable solution to the exchange of assignments between students and teachers.

Formula Editors in the Discussion Forum

The discussion forum obviously constitutes a resource for the students, as almost all the students read questions and answers on a weekly basis as a minimum. Yet, the participation and active posing of questions could be improved.

In that sense, it was interesting, and to some extent surprising, to observe that changing the learning management system to Moodle did not increase the activity in the online forum, just as the mathematical typesetting functionalities were not used.

A number of reasons may explain the low activity in the discussion forum. One reason may be that the pedagogy applied in the DELTA courses required relatively little online activity wherefore it may have been difficult for the students to self-organize meaningful collaboration without face-to-face interaction. Another reason might have been the lack of interface for writing mathematical text.

The first reason might be very important as the student training and general conditions in the DELTA program does not force the development of keyboard based instrumented techniques (Kieran & Drijvers, 2006) for mathematical communication, because the teacher-learner communication is mediated by handwriting. The inferred recommendation for supporting communication among students is to be cautious not to privilege one medium for the necessary teacher-student communication and use another one for voluntarily communication among students.

The attempt to address the latter problem by introducing Moodle as a learning management system with added functionalities did not prove successful. Moodle makes it possible to include mathematical formalism in forum posts, but it may not be particularly easy to use. Using formula editors tends to require some work and the formula editor comprised in Moodle does not differ significantly from others. Hence, it may be that the problem of writing mathematical formalism in the forum continues to be problematic, not because it is impossible to write, but *because it is not easy enough, and not entirely necessary to learn*. As a consequence, the students seem to choose to either not post their question or to post it using normal keyboard notation.

CONCLUSION

The main conclusions of the work presented in this chapter can be summarized in two observations. The first observation is that handwriting works fine in relation to e-learning of mathematics in the DELTA program. The second observation is that even though the discussion forum is used by the students in the DELTA program as a place to post questions on specific tasks and concepts, the forum is not as immediate a channel of communication between the students as we could wish. The improved formula editors are not adopted by the students who seem to prefer using ASCII signs when writing in the forum.

These observations allow us to conclude that handwriting continues to be a relevant way of communicating mathematics in e-learning programs; at least in the DELTA program where the pedagogical environment is effected by the close collaboration with the rest of the Norwegian University of Technology, which also entails shared (paper and pencil-based) exams. The process of communicating using handwriting that was adopted in the DELTA program may be beneficial for other programs as a supplement to other ways of communicating about assignments.

The question whether the improved formula editor (which was introduced into the user forum with the Moodle system) is adopted by the students, does not only concern the technology. Rather it seems that because the use of handwriting as main medium in the interaction between student and teacher is well-functioning it may leave the user forum and formula editor in the Learning Management System redundant. In that sense choosing one media for teacher – learner interaction and another to support discussion among learners can be an important part of the reason that the user forum is used less than we hoped for in DELTA.

REFERENCES

Carlson, M. P., & Rasumussen, C. (Eds.). (2008). *Making the connection: Research and teaching in undergraduate mathematics education*. Washington, DC: Mathematical Association of America.

Cobb, P. (2001). Supporting the improvement of learning and teaching in social and institutional context . In Carver, D., & Klahr, S. (Eds.), *Cognition and instruction: 25 years of progress* (pp. 455–478). Lawrence Erlbaum Associates.

Corbin, J. M., & Strauss, A. L. (2008). *Basics of qualitative research: Techniques and procedures for developing grounded theory*. Los Angeles, CA: Sage.

Descamps, S. X., Bass, H., Bolanos Evia, G., Seiler, R., & Seppala, M. (2006). E-learning mathematics. Panel promoted by the Spanish Conference of Mathematics Deans. In *Proc. of International Conference of Mathematicians*, Madrid, Spain, 2006. Retrieved October 27, 2010, from http://webalt.math.helsinki.fi/ content/ e16/ e301/e787/ eLearning Mathematics_ eng.pdf

Design-Based Research Collective. (2003). Design-based research: An emerging paradigm for educational inquiry. *Educational Researcher*, *32*(1), 5–8. doi:10.3102/0013189X032001005

Duval, R. (2006). A cognitive analysis of problems of comprehension in a learning of mathematics. *Educational Studies in Mathematics*, *61*(1), 103–131. doi:10.1007/s10649-006-0400-z

Engelbrecht, J., & Harding, A. (2005). Teaching undergraduate mathematics on the Internet. *Educational Studies in Mathematics*, *58*(2), 235–252. doi:10.1007/s10649-005-6456-3

Guzdial, M., Ludovice, P., Realff, M., Morley, T., & Carroll, K. (2002). *When collaboration doesn't work*. Presented at the Fifth International Conference of the Learning Sciences, Seattle.

Gynther, K. (2005). *Blended learning, IT og læring i et teoretisk og praktisk perspektiv*. København, Denmark: Unge Pædagoger.

Hiltz, S. R., & Goldman, R. (2005). *Learning together online*. Mahwah, NJ: Lawrence Erlbaum Associates.

Jaques, D., & Salmon, G. (2007). *Learning in groups: A handbook for face-to-face and online environments. Abingdon*. Oxon: Routledge.

Juan, A., Huertas, A., Steegmann, C., Coroles, C., & Serrat, C. (2008). Mathematical e-learning: State of the art and experiences at the Open University of Catalonia. *International Journal of Mathematical Education in Science and Technology*, *39*(4), 455–471. doi:10.1080/00207390701867497

Kieran, C., & Drijvers, P. (2006). The co-emergence of machine techniques, paper-and-pencil techniques, and theoretical reflection: A study of CAS use in Secondary School Algebra. *International Journal of Computers for Mathematical Learning*, *11*, 205–263. doi:10.1007/s10758-006-0006-7

Kress, G. R., Jewitt, C., Ogborn, J., & Tsatsarelis, C. (2001). *Multimodal teaching and learning: The rhetorics of the science classroom*. London, UK: Continuum.

Kress, G. R., & Van Leeuwen, T. (2001). *Multimodal discourse: The modes and media of contemporary communication*. London, UK: Arnold Publication.

Macdonald, J. (2008). *Blended learning and online tutoring: Planning learner support and activity design*. Hampshire, UK: Gower Pub Co.

Mariotti, M. A. (2002). The influence of technological advances on students' mathematics learning . In English, L. (Ed.), *Handbook of international research in mathematics education* (pp. 695–723). London, UK: Lawrence Erlbaum.

Misfeldt, M. (2006). *Mathematical writing.* Unpublished doctoral dissertation, The Danish University of Education, Denmark.

O'Halloran, K. (2005). *Mathematical discourse: Language, symbolism and visual images.* London, UK: Continuum.

OECD. (2005). *E-learning in tertiary education: Where do we stand?* Paris, France: Organisation for Economic Co-operation and Development.

Osimo, G. (2002). E-learning in mathematics undergraduate courses (an Italian experience). In I. Vakalis et al. (Eds.), *Proceedings of the 2nd International Conference on the Teaching of Mathematics.* John Wiley & Sons Inc.

Pimm, D. (1987). *Speaking mathematically: Communication in mathematics classrooms.* London, UK: Routledge and Kegan Paul Ltd.

Rattleff, P. (2008). Studerendes brug af videostreamet universitetsundervisning . In Birch Andreasen, L., Meyer, B., & Rattleff, P. (Eds.), *Digitale medier og didaktisk design.* Copenhagen, Denmark: Danmarks Pædagogiske Universitetsforlag.

Salmon, G. (2000). *E-moderating: The key to teaching and learning online.* London, UK: Kogan Page.

Sellen, A. J., & Harper, R. H. (2002). *The myth of the paperless office.* Cambridge, MA: MIT Press.

Steinbring, H. (2006). What makes a sign a mathematical sign? An epistemological perspective on mathematical interaction. *Educational Studies in Mathematics, 61*(1), 133–162. doi:10.1007/s10649-006-5892-z

ADDITIONAL READING

Alrø, H., & Skovsmose, O. (2002). *Dialogue and learning in mathematics education: intention, reflection, critique.* New York: Kluwer Academic Publishers.

Arnold, S., Shui, C., & Ellerton, N. (1996). Critical Issues in the Distance Teaching of Mathematics and Mathematics Education . In Bishop, A. J., Clements, M. A., Keitel, C., Kilpatrick, J., & Laborde, C. (Eds.), *International handbook of mathematics education* (*Vol. 2*, pp. 703–756). Dordrecht: Kluwer Academic Publishers.

Dominique, G., Ruthven, K., & Trouche, L. (2005). *The didactical challenge of symbolic calculators: turning a computational device into a mathematical instrument.* New York: Springer.

Jamieson, P. (2003). Designing More Effective On-campus Teaching and Learning Spaces: A Role for Academic Developers. *The International Journal for Academic Development, 8*(1/2), 119–133. doi:10.1080/1360144042000277991

McLuhan, M. (1964). *Understanding Media: the extensions of man.* New York: The New American Library Inc.

Sfard, A. (2008). *Thinking as communicating: human development, the growth of discourses, and mathematizing, Learning in doing.* New York: Cambridge University Press. doi:10.1017/CBO9780511499944

Steinbring, H. (2006). What Makes a Sign a Mathematical Sign? – An Epistemological Perspective on Mathematical Interaction. *Educational Studies in Mathematics, 61*(1), 133–162. doi:10.1007/s10649-006-5892-z

KEY TERMS AND DEFINITIONS

Algebra Filter: A formula editor that can be embedded in the Learning Management System Moodle. It is a simple version of the TeX filter.

Learning Management System: a Learning Management System (LMS) is a system to support teaching by facilitating communication between teacher and learner, constitute a shared archive of teaching materials, and facilitate the administrative aspects of an educational program. Examples of LMS are: Blackboard, Its learning, Fronter and Moodle.

Medium: The material substance that is manipulated in order to produce signs is called the medium. Examples are pen and paper, computer with a specific program, and sound.

Modality: Culturally developed systems of meaning using one or more media are called modalities. Oral speech is an example, algebra is another example.

Moodle: a free open source Learning Management System.

Sign: Signs consist of a material signifier that signifies something, i.e. the signified, to someone, i.e. the interpreter. Examples of signs are words, diagrams and formulas.

TeX filter: A formula editor that can be embedded in the Learning Management System Moodle. The filter allows the user to use TeX code to write mathematical formalism in all posts in Moodle.

ENDNOTES

1 In 2006 Norway Opening Universities (NOU) funded development of the DELTA program with 500,000 NOK. NOU is a national initiative for change and innovation in Norwegian higher education, and it supports Norwegian institutions of higher education by funding projects of developing ICT supported flexible learning and distance education courses through an annual application process.

Chapter 18
The Role of Technology in Mathematics Support:
A Pilot Study

Ciarán Mac an Bhaird
National University of Ireland Maynooth, Ireland

Ann O'Shea
National University of Ireland Maynooth, Ireland

ABSTRACT

In this chapter we will discuss the importance of using technology to enhance mathematics education and mathematics support. We present our initial steps in the use of technology in the National University of Ireland Maynooth as a pilot study. This essentially falls into two categories: the use of online courses to address mathematical issues faced by incoming at-risk students; and the development and use of additional resources such as pdfs (using touchscreen technology), podcasts and screencasts to complement existing services. We give a detailed description of the introduction, development, and implementation of these strategies including the advantages and disadvantages from both the teaching and learning perspectives. We also present the initial feedback concerning the use of these technologies with mathematics support services. This shows that students who made use of the help available reported that it had a significant impact on their learning experience. However, we will also discuss the major issue of getting students to actively engage with these extra supports. We also present the changes we are making to these services as a result of this pilot study and how they tie in with our long term strategy for a more complete mathematics support system for our students. We consider the implications for the future of mathematics education and mathematics support and give an overview of activities and resources already in existence.

DOI: 10.4018/978-1-60960-875-0.ch018

INTRODUCTION

The purpose of this chapter is to describe the first steps taken to implement the use of technology to supplement the mathematics support services in the National University of Ireland Maynooth (NUIM). We start by giving a brief overview of the development of mathematics support initiatives in the UK and Ireland in recent years; we discuss the use of technology and give a description of some research in this area. We then give an outline of mathematics at NUIM in order to provide context to our use of technology. Mathematics support services are a recent development at NUIM and technology was initially introduced as a pilot scheme to address certain issues that arose during reviews of the services. Using these supports as a case study, we look at the reasons why technology plays a role in providing students with a more complete and coherent support system. The student feedback and figures we present from the pilot study are mainly from the 2008-9 and 2009-10 academic years. The data reflects the pilot stage of implementation and mainly represents student usage and basic feedback on their experience. We focus on two areas: online mathematics courses; and supplementary electronic resources. In each section we look at the reasons behind these developments, the technologies involved, the development and implementation of the resources. We also discuss the feedback both from the teaching and the learning perspectives and we consider the issue of engagement with these resources. This is an area of major concern and something that should be seriously considered by anyone planning to develop additional electronic resources to support existing services. Finally we mention how we are using the data from the pilot study to provide a more coherent structure for the use and promotion of technology in mathematics support.

We see the use of technology as integral to the development of mathematics support but it should not be viewed as a replacement for one-to-one contact; rather it should be seen as a complement to this contact. This view is reinforced by the high levels of engagement of NUIM students with the drop-in sessions of the Mathematics Support Centre (MSC) and very low engagement with the online support courses. It is important to note that at present none of the mathematics support services in NUIM, whether electronic or face-to-face, are compulsory.

THE RECENT EXPANSION OF MATHEMATICS SUPPORT

There has been well documented growth in the area of mathematics support at third level in recent years in both Ireland (Gill et al., 2008) and the UK (Perkin & Croft, 2004). The reasons behind the establishment of mathematics support services are also well documented (Curriculum and Examinations Board, 1986; Lynch et al., 2003; Picker & Berry, 2001; Task Force on the Physical Sciences, 2002). These describe the situation at second level and some of the reasons for the increase in the numbers of students coming to study service mathematics at third level with high levels of mathematical deficiencies.

The mathematics support community offers a wide variety of services for students, particularly students who are deemed at-risk of failing. The effectiveness of these supports is widely researched (Mac an Bhaird et al., 2009). Croft (2008) has developed a website which contains reference to much of this research. This research allows for greater dissemination of services and the determination of best practice in mathematics support. This research can also be used to determine how best to deal with various student issues such as student anxieties, student engagement and student access to support services.

THE USE OF TECHNOLOGY IN MATHEMATICS EDUCATION

Over the last twenty years, technology has been used widely in mathematics education. Before we focus on its role in mathematics support, we will mention a selection of papers concerning the general situation.

The importance of e-learning is evident from the wide range and quality of reports in the area. For example the 2005 OECD (Organisation for Economic Co-operation and Development) report gives a measured overview of the use of technology at third level and the 2010 U.S. Department of Education report provides details on online learning at second level. Many of the other papers available discuss the role of technology in material delivery and support. Full descriptions of the extent to which technology, such as online teaching and learning is being used is well documented, for example see (Macdonald et al., 2001) and (Suanpang et al., 2003). Engelbrecht & Harding (2005) include a brief overview of papers which discuss the role of internet resources. Waldock (2008) presents evidence of a co-ordinated and integrated system which combines basic delivery of module material, module management, student support and tracking. Vidakovic et al. (2003) describe the development of a database for online formative assessment. Copley (2007) discusses the use of audio and video Podcasts to complement traditional lecturing. Brinkman et al. (2007) give a description of teaching discrete mathematics using a Virtual Learning Environment (VLE) with videos and a discussion board.

Many papers present evidence of the effectiveness of using technology in mathematics education. For example, Ruthven & Hennessy (2002) give a model for the successful use of computers and related resources at second level. Brinkman et al. (2007) give a detailed description of teaching mathematics in an online environment compared with traditional classroom methods and investigate the effect of online teaching on student attitudes and behavior. Karr et al. (2003) present data on a group of postgraduate Engineering Mathematics students who were exposed to one of the following: the traditional method of teaching; online teaching; a mixture of both. They found little difference in the final grades of the three groups. Becker and Dwyer (1998) consider the issue of learning type and found that more visually inclined learners tend to prefer the use of technology while more verbal learners preferred a face-to-face learning environment.

There are also a number of papers available on the implementation of technology in mathematics support services but there is very little analysis on the effectiveness of these supports. Hibberd et al. (2003) look at the challenges faced by establishing a suitable e-support system and give a detailed description of the aspects of mathematical study, particularly first-year support that can be substantially enhanced by the use of web-based learning environments. Samuels (2007) gives a very thorough overview of the reasons why new technologies should be embraced in mathematics support, a description of which technologies can be used, what this electronic support should be and some of the challenges facing the wider dissemination of such methods, for example teachers' or lecturers' perceptions towards these new teaching techniques. Lawson et al. (2008) give an overview of the electronic resources available at mathcentre (www.mathcentre.ac.uk), at mathtutor (www.mathtutor.ac.uk) and their mobile variants, as well as a description of the range of technological supports that can be used. They also give an overview of the extent to which these supports are being embraced.

The most pressing issues that hinder the development of electronic resources are financial and time constraints. However, the majority of the mathematical community freely share any electronic resources they develop. One example of this is the FETLAR project (http://www.fetlar.bham.ac.uk/) which aims to enable the open sharing of educational resources. There are also extensive online materials available from mathcentre, the Khan Academy (http://www.khanacademy.org/) and Just Math Tutoring (http://justmathtutoring.com/), to name but a few. The effectiveness of this support has not been widely analysed, for example there have been no significant studies carried out on the impact of the mathcentre website even though the number of hits is very high.

The resources are out there to be developed and accessed, for example Engelbrecht & Harding (2005) include an extensive list of website and online resources; students and teachers just need the opportunity and facility to access them. However, simply making the resources available is not sufficient. Khan (1997) emphasises that a meaningful learning environment should be created that fosters and supports learning. Reid and Petocz (2002) point out the importance of establishing a suitable structure to enhance the mathematics learning environment and ensure that students are aware of the existence of this structure and the support it can provide them. The issue is that we can provide all the links and resources we want but getting the students to actually engage is a problem. The material needs to be presented in a more interactive medium to help students engage.

The importance of technology in mathematics support is highlighted by a conference hosted by the Irish Mathematics Support Network in 2009. The conference covered a wide range of e-learning approaches being used internationally. A full description of this conference is available (Ní Fhloinn, 2010).

The majority of the studies presented here deal with the introduction of technology to complement or, in some cases, replace traditional methods of teaching. They deal with the difficulties that can arise both from the establishment of these supports and their suitability for different student types. It is clear from these studies that the implementation of technology use in education is a very complex issue, however they also highlight that technology has a vital role to play in the future of mathematics education.

THE USE OF TECHNOLOGY IN MATHEMATICS SUPPORT AT NUIM

NUIM has approximately 8000 students in total; there are 5800 undergraduates of which 950 study mathematics modules. The majority of these undergraduate students are studying service mathematics as part of their Humanities, Finance or Science degrees. The Department of Mathematics at NUIM has many recently established supports in place to help students if they experience difficulties. The department runs a very successful Mathematics Support Centre (MSC). The main service the MSC provides is a drop-in centre which commenced in 2007. The services of the MSC are revised each year and issues that need to be addressed are identified. Subsequently two online courses and three workshops (which use the touch screen technology Sympodium) were established. Research by Mac an Bhaird et al. (2009) shows that students at NUIM who avail of mathematics support services have a greater chance of succeeding in examinations than those who do not. However a small minority of at-risk students do not take advantage of the support available. There are also additional supports available for other students, for example a peer mentoring scheme has been initiated for penultimate year pure mathematics students and a drop-in service is also available for local secondary school students. Research is being carried out at NUIM into the reasons why some at-risk students do not avail of these supports and initial results can be found in Grehan et al. (2010).

NUIM uses Moodle (http://Moodle.org/) as a VLE and the majority of lecturers who teach service mathematics courses use this VLE for material dissemination. This is called supplemental web use as described in Barron (1998). The lecturers use a number of different techniques but very few of them post a full set of notes. This is done in order to encourage students to attend lectures and tutorials. This whole area of learning is discussed in more detail in Selden and Selden (1997).

The MSC decided to pilot the use of technology and electronic resources for a number of reasons. The main reason was that our centre can be extremely busy and sometimes students are not able to avail of all the help that they need. Employing online resources means that the students have access to suitable support material 24 hours a day and do not have to be on campus to access it. We also wish to cater for students with different learning styles and have found that technology has great potential in this area.

The MSC's plan for the use and development of electronic resources agrees with Hopper (2001, p.39), he states '*..the true potential of today's internet in higher education seems to be in support of traditional courses, far more than in the primary teaching role for complete courses..*'. It is also very important that the development of these resources should be seen to complement existing face-to-face and personal mathematics support, not simply as a more economical way of teaching. Samuels (2007) asserts that educational purpose and pedagogy should be the driving force behind the use of new technology.

We split the main description into two sections: online courses; and the development of Reusable Learning Objects (RLO's) to complement existing resources. In each section we look at the origins or reasons for the use of this approach, how the approach is developed and implemented and discuss the advantages and disadvantages of the approaches. Finally we discuss how we are using the initial feedback and experience to implement a more comprehensive and co-ordinated level of support using technology.

We also address the issue of getting students to engage with the resources. Brett (2004) considers the factors that determine students' engagement or lack of engagement with online materials. She found that the availability of home online access, familiarity with shared online environment, difficulties because of an already full timetable, mathematical fears, self-efficacy, and the students' level of mathematical knowledge impacted on their engagement with online resources. We feel that these factors are also reasons for students' lack of engagement with online resources at NUIM. As mentioned earlier, most students do engage with the drop-in service. Truluck (2007) discusses the negative effects of a lack of a personal contact between students and teachers involved in the learning process and claims that this can increase the risk of a sense of isolation among students. This highlights the importance of combining online resources with face-to-face supports.

METHODOLOGY

The supports discussed below were developed by the authors as part of a pilot study into the benefits of using technology in mathematics support. All RLO's were made available through Moodle and on the MSC website (http://supportcentre.maths.nuim.ie/). The supports were not restricted to specific class groups. As such, this made the collection of data difficult. It was decided to use anonymous online questionnaires which consisted mostly of Likert type questions and some open questions. Paper questionnaires were also distributed to class groups when possible. We are aware that there are serious issues associated with the use of online questionnaires and we realize that respondents do not form a representative sample of the users of the RLO's or the online courses. These methods of feedback and data collection were used due to time pressures and the pilot nature of the various projects.

Online Mathematics Courses

Origins

All students who register for a first year mathematics module in NUIM take a diagnostic test to determine their ability level in mathematics. The test covers basic topics in mathematics that students should be comfortable with from second level such as functions, algebraic manipulations and indices. Students who fail the diagnostic test are deemed at-risk. Originally students were assigned to an extra weekly tutorial. Basic mathematical concepts were reviewed during these tutorials. We found that attendance levels were low. One problem with trying to teach very basic material is that the students have seen it many times before and think that they know it well. Ten years ago, we decided to use CALMAT. This is a tutorial package which covers basic mathematical material and allows students to take diagnostic tests and review material with which they are not comfortable. The students were assigned to a weekly laboratory session and initially this approach was successful, but over time attendance at labs dropped. Two years ago, we reviewed our programme and decided to construct an online course for this material. We felt that this would allow students greater access to materials. There are a number of online courses and softwares available that offer to help remediate at-risk mathematics students, we chose to create our own courses through Moodle as this would allow us target the issues identified from the diagnostic test.

Implementation

The Mathematics Proficiency Course (MPC) was developed in 2008 and the Mathematics Foundation Course (MFC) in 2009. The MSC Director (the second author) designed and developed both courses and they are run through Moodle. The material covered includes basics on algebra, functions, equations, indices etc. and new topics are added each week. It is delivered using a combination of free online material available from mathcentre including text, iPod downloads, diagnostic tests and videos. A quiz is also created and added to the page so students can test if they have mastered the material. There is one workshop per week which is run by an experienced tutor. The workshop addresses many of the issues raised by Hopper (2001), such as the importance to students of being physically present in class and the benefits they receive in terms of a satisfying intimate and social learning experience if they just listen attentively in class.

Students who fail the diagnostic test (176 students in 2008-9, 144 students in 2009-10) are registered for the MPC so they can gain a better understanding of basic mathematical topics. The MFC was developed to cover some of the same material but at a slower pace. It is designed for students who are not studying a mathematics module but need mathematics for subjects such as Economics, Psychology, Sociology and Geography. Other students can also request to be added to these courses and all students who register with the MSC receive a weekly email outlining the details of the material to be covered on the online courses each week as well as a reminder of the follow-up workshops.

Outcomes

In 2008-9 262 students were enrolled for the MPC (note the MFC was not available); many of these were not registered for a mathematics module. The course consisted of 18 topics, it was viewed 6680 times and there were 960 quiz attempts. Feedback was gathered through an anonymous questionnaire on Moodle, and as expected the response was very low with 27 students completing the survey. Of these, 85% were registered for a Mathematics module and 15% were not. When asked how frequently they visited the proficiency course page, 41% said once a week, 22% said 2-3 times per week, 7.5% said daily, the remainder visited the module less than once a week. When asked which resources they used most often, 56% said quizzes, 33% said video files and 11% said summary texts. When asked which of the resources they found most useful, 37% said quizzes, 33% said video files, and 26% said summary texts.

In 2009-10, 225 students registered for the MPC course. The course was similar to the 2008-9 course except that an extra topic on statistics was added. The course had 3513 hits and attendance at the course dropped by 50% after six weeks. Only 10% of students completed the course. The MFC course was taken by 55 students. It had 871 hits and 5 students completed all topics. The feedback for both courses was very similar to that in 2008-9.

Students made many positive comments and the following are typical: 1) '*Helps to understand basic information needed to understand maths lectures and main exams*' 2) '*I found it very useful as it has been 16 years since I did the leaving cert, thanks.*' Students also commented on the fact that they had very busy schedules in college and the fact that the course was available 24 hours a day meant that they had an opportunity to work on the material and study at a pace that suits them.

Students' negative comments were principally with problems seeing the connection between the MPC material and the material covered in lectures etc, e.g. '*The topics covered were not always relevant but the topics taught were explained really well. For me more things dealing with differentiation and integration would have been useful*'. Comments like this raise a very significant issue with this type of remedial course, students rarely see that the topics are fundamental to their understanding of more advanced material in lectures. Trying to bridge this gap is a big challenge. Students also report that the courses can be impersonal and they miss direct one-to-one contact. To address this issue we have follow up workshops with an experienced tutor for each course and these workshops can often help students see the connection between the basics and their modules. This highlights the importance of having personal interaction for students to go hand-in-hand with the online courses. Unfortunately attendances at the workshops are also low, e.g. in 2009-10 49 students made 172 visits to the 20 MPC workshops and 26 students made 75 visits to the 20 MFC workshops. Students who attended regularly were very complementary and positive about their experiences but again the vast majority of at-risk students did not avail of the service.

Benefits

The main advantage that we see to these online courses is that they allow students 24 hour access to material. The students can work at their own pace and the video tutorials allow students to review topics as often as they need to. These web-based tools can be used to develop both alternative and complementary strategies to traditional face-to-face learning systems. These approaches permit delivery of instruction to students who are time- or place-constrained (Seufert, Lechner & Stanoevska, 2002). Other advantages are that they are not very time-consuming to develop, the topics and material are presented as RLO's and it is easy to maintain records of how students use the different materials. The MFC also allows us to support students from other departments.

Challenges

While we have found the courses to be very useful for students who use them, the low level of participation is of particular concern, especially as most of these students are at-risk. The courses are not compulsory so it is very difficult to ensure that students view and attempt the material. The main practical disadvantage of using online courses is that many students do not have access to an effective internet service outside NUIM. There is the added difficulty that many of the videos and clips will only play on certain browsers. Both these issues are beyond our control but they are very important to consider because they can be discouraging for students.

Conclusions

The online courses are seen as an important and integral way of addressing issues that students have, however we are concerned about the low numbers of students who are actually accessing these resources. We are investigating ways to make the courses more approachable and accessible to the at-risk students, as they are the students most likely to drop out and not avail of material and help. A related study (Grehan et al., 2010) has shown that these students often have a fear of mathematics and need positive intervention. Issuing these students with a mentor who shows them the importance of these supplementary courses may be beneficial. We are also considering plans to make the courses compulsory for students who fail the diagnostic test; it may become part of their continuous assessment grade. The authors could find no direct study which compares the rate of uptake of online materials between compulsory and non-compulsory courses but participation rates (Brett, 2004) in compulsory online modules are high.

The Development of RLO's to Complement Existing Services

Origins

At the end of the academic year 2007-8 the first author participated in three separate pilot projects in conjunction with the Quality Promotion Office (now the Centre for Teaching and Learning, CTL) at NUIM. The aim was to understand how to use and develop RLO's through the use of new teaching technologies. These technologies included Podcasting, Screencasting and the use of Sympodium software. The long-term goal was to determine the suitability of using these new mediums for the MSC. The pilot schemes began late in the academic year, so due to time constraints only a limited number of trials were feasible. Based on both the student reaction and feedback and the staff experiences, the MSC actively followed up on the use of these technologies and now sees them as an integral part of MSC services. We believe that the use of technologies such as Podcasts and Screencasts is central to providing suitable resources for students. A description of how to start projects in these areas is available (http://ctl.nuim.ie/e-learning).

This section will be divided into three subsections: Sympodium; Podcasts; and Screencasts. These technologies are used to produce various RLO's which complement existing mathematics material and courses in a variety of ways.

Sympodium

Sympodium (http://www2.smarttech.com/st/en-US/Products/Interactive+Pen+Displays/) is software which incorporates touch screen technology. The touchscreen unit is connected to a computer. This is then connected to an overhead projector and is used in classrooms. The user can either write on a blank document on the touchscreen, or on a pre-prepared document. The main advantage of this method of teaching is that you can record any written notes you have made during class and subsequently post them online. Students comment that they have time to listen and ask questions in class instead of rushing to write down the notes.

Implementation

The first author used Sympodium twice in all-class tutorials for First Year Science students during the pilot phase. He wrote on a blank document in class and posted this material online after the class for all the students to download. The feedback from the pilot scheme was very positive and a decision was made to use Sympodium in all future workshops run by the MSC.

Sympodium is used by the MSC to deliver its three weekly workshops. Two of these workshops supplement the online courses mentioned previously and act as follow up workshops for students who still have difficulties. These classes are student directed and students email the tutor with queries on topics that they would like covered. We have found that this reduces the embarrassment such students often suffer in asking questions in class. Students are also encouraged to listen in class and to ask questions rather than simply writing down the notes. The tutor uses Sympodium to

Table 1. Student responses to the Sympodium questionnaire

Statement	Strongly Agree	Agree	Neutral	Disagree	Strongly Disagree
The use of Sympodium made the class more interactive.	34.6%	52.0%	9.6%	1.9%	1.9%
The use of Sympodium enhanced the learning experience.	42.3%	40.4%	15.4%	1.9%	0.0%
The use of Sympodium in class was distracting.	0.0%	3.8%	7.7%	50.0%	38.5%
The use of Sympodium helped focus student attention.	32.7%	48.1%	15.4%	3.8%	0.0%
The use of Sympodium had no impact on class atmosphere.	0.0%	11.5%	15.4%	38.5%	34.6%
The use of Sympodium aided student learning of maths concepts.	32.7%	42.3%	23.1%	1.9%	0.0%
The use of Sympodium made it easier to take notes and make comments in class.	26.9%	42.3%	28.9%	1.9%	0.0%
The use of Sympodium made the class notes easier to view and follow.	42.3%	46.2%	7.7%	3.8%	0.0%

save the class notes in pdf form and then posts the class notes on the related Moodle course page each week. Relevant online links are also added to the material. A similar system is used for the third workshop which is the First Science Mathematics Workshop. In this class the tutor answers queries and issues that the students have which are related to the material that is covered in their mathematics lectures. Each week the tutor meets with the MSC Manager and the lecturers to discuss the topics emailed by students and then a general announcement is made to the class telling them which topics will be covered.

Outcomes

Detailed attitudinal feedback is not available for the use of Sympodium in the two weekly workshops which support the online courses but we do have some data from the pilot study and the First Science Mathematics Workshop. We also report on usage statistics for the resources created using Sympodium.

The notes from two initial workshops in the pilot scheme were posted onto the first year Integral Calculus Moodle site. 272 students had access to the notes and they were viewed 576 times. 52 students completed the anonymous questionnaire developed and distributed by the CTL in class. This consisted of 8 Likert type questions and Table 1 shows the students' responses to the statements given. They were asked to compare the class with Sympodium to a traditional class.

An online anonymous questionnaire was also issued to students about their experience during the First Science Mathematics Workshop and there was a very low response rate (11 in 2009-10 and 43 in 2008-9). However the feedback in general was very positive, particularly towards the use of Sympodium where questions along the lines of those asked in the pilot study were asked. In 2008-9 the 20 sets of notes from the workshop were posted onto the Moodle site for the related mathematics module. The material was available to 310 students and was accessed a total of 6641 times. In 2009-10 we decided to launch a site dedicated to this workshop to allow the possibility of adding additional materials to accompany the notes each week. 135 of the 342 First Science students registered for this site and they accessed the 20 sets of notes (not counting the additional videos and resources) a total of 1364 times. In 2009-10 55 students registered for the Mathematics Foundation Course and they viewed the 15 sets of workshop notes 106 times. 225 students registered for the Mathematics Proficiency Course and they viewed the 14 sets of workshop notes 351 times.

There has been a lot of positive feedback from students about the workshops in general. If we focus on the feedback on the use of the Sympodium unit the following comments were typical 1) '*The sympodium showed writing a little more clearly than what you would usually see in a lecture. It was nice to know that if you were taking down notes of your own, you could always ask to go back a page and clarify a point rather than rush down something that you know would be rubbed out*'. 2) '*the notes are on Moodle so you can take down extra notes to try help you remember why you're doing such things instead of rushing to get it all wrote down and only being able to half pay attention to how they are doing it*'

The small amount of negative feedback was principally about the Sympodium unit and followed the lines of '*It kept causing problems and many people who came when it wasn't working did not come back because you only got half a tutorial*'. This was no longer an issue in 2009-10.

Benefits

The most significant benefit (reported by students) was that all notes written in class can be recorded and posted online at a later time. Students reported that this allowed them to listen in class and ask questions without being under pressure to write down all the notes. They reported that this really assisted their understanding of the material. They have time to listen and to think about the material and ask questions. With these clear benefits for the students in mind, it was decided to use Sympodium in the workshops. It has been particularly beneficial as these workshops are put in place to be student-directed and to increase the amount of personal interaction and discussion between the students and the tutor. The fact that the notes are saved has facilitated this opportunity for students.

From a staff point of view it is relatively easy to use Sympodium. Staff also commented that it was very useful to have an accurate record of exactly what material had been covered in class. Friel et al. (2009) survey the benefits for staff and students of using such technology.

Challenges

The main disadvantages initially are the prohibitive costs (although there are group rates for third level) and the fact that setting up the unit can be very time consuming and problematic, and this is reflected by the comment above. However, Sympodium units have now been installed in most of the lecture theatres in the university so there are rarely any set-up problems.

Conclusions

On the whole we have been very impressed with using touchscreen technology and the benefits it brings to providing support. Students reported that they appreciated the fact that they could listen to explanations in the workshops without the pressure to write everything down. They then accessed the notes on Moodle later. However, again there is the issue of getting students to participate in these extra activities. Ebner and Nagler (2008) contains a good overview of a similar trial on the use of Sympodium. They report on both the student and staff feedback and their experience of using this technology.

Podcasts

The Podcasting software used included Audacity (http://audacity.sourceforge.net/) and iTunes (http://www.apple.com/itunes/). The wide variety of uses and applications for Podcasts are well documented. Evans (2008) gives a thorough analysis of the use of Podcasts and the feedback of students who use them. Chan & Lee (2005) discuss the use of Podcasts to help address the issue of student anxieties. The Podcasts we record are audio only.

During the pilot phase, one Podcast was recorded by the first author for his First Year Linear Algebra course. This class had a total of 218 students registered online. The Podcast was made at the end of term and contained a short description of details for exam preparation and other related advice. The Podcast was posted on the Moodle site for the course and 97.9% of the 218 registered students listened to it at least once, there were a total of 340 views of the resource (24 after the summer exam).

Forty eight students opted to comment on the use of the Podcast in the feedback section. Most of the feedback was positive and followed along the lines of these samples: 1) *It was helpful as it pointed out things that were important in the course. The information given was not rushed so there was time to take note and consider what was being said. It's easier to listen to because you can listen to it a few times if you don't catch everything the first time. You can also listen to it in your own time.* 2) *I found it helpful as you could listen to the material while on the go. However, I prefer examples to help understand the logic behind the Mathematics and this is not possible with a Podcast! I found the Podcast helpful as I could relisten to parts that I missed which is not possible in lectures. I think that using a Podcast might prove difficult to cover lecture material as it will be hard for the student to link the Podcast with lecture notes. All in all I think a Podcast is a good idea!*

Although very little could be established from the posting of one Podcast, the software was relatively easy to use and the Podcast was not time consuming to create. As many of the students pointed out the Podcasting has potential as a supplement to normal online facilities.

Implementation

A decision was made to use Podcasts to supplement existing online resources from the Engineering Mathematics First Aid Kit (http://www.mathcentre.ac.uk/staff/types/staff-resources/packs/). We are taking existing text resources and recording Podcasts to accompany them. This is part of another long term project to investigate the learning types (visual, auditory, kinesthetic) of incoming students, to make them aware of the most suitable medium for them to actively engage and interact with mathematics and provide suitable resources. This project is being funded by the National Digital Learning Repository (NDLR). This project is ongoing so as yet there is no feedback on the success. The Podcasts recorded to date and the associated texts are available at (http://supportcentre.maths.nuim.ie/resources/).

Benefits, Challenges and Conclusions

The clear benefit of Podcasts is that they are relatively easy to create and student friendly due to the huge number of students of that have iPods, (Chan & Lee, 2005). The main challenge is using them in a coherent fashion and getting the students to engage with the resources. The important factors to consider when recording are having a predetermined script with specific aims and goals, finding a quiet facility in which to make the recording, and keeping the recording short and to the point.

Screencasts

The Screencasting software used was Camtasia Studio. Pinder-Grover et al. (2008) give a description of how to use videos (Screencasts) in mathematics education and Peterson (2007) contains an overview of how Screencasts can be incorporated with online learning. In the pilot study, the first author picked a topic that students had difficulty with; he created a file which was approximately two pages in length. He then recorded a voiceover and was able to use a highlighter to specify which parts of the text he was taking about and essentially created a video (Screencast). He recorded two Screencasts on integration by substitution.

These were made available online for all first year students. Unfortunately, due to the editing difficulties, the Screencasts were only posted on the last week of term.

The Screencasts were available to 476 first year students and they were accessed 261 times. This low number was probably due to the fact that they were posted online during the last week of term. This also explains the rather low response in feedback from the students. 17 students filled out the online questionnaire developed by the CTL and answered all the questions. The feedback was as follows: Students were asked if the Screencasts had helped them to understand the material better, 77% agreed or strongly agreed and 18% were neutral. Students were asked if they preferred Mathematics in text format to Mathematics in Screencasts, 53% disagreed or strongly disagreed and 29% were neutral. Students were asked if they found the Screencast format difficult to follow, 82% disagreed or strongly disagreed. Students were asked if they found it easier to take notes during a Screencast than they did during traditional teaching sessions, 71% agreed or strongly agreed and 29% were neutral. Students were asked if they found it easier to follow the class material because of the Screencast, 88% agreed or strongly agreed. Students also commented on the benefits of the combination of the audio and visual aspects of the Screencast which helped with their understanding of the material.

Implementation

The MSC was so impressed with this facility that we applied for and received additional funding to record a further ten Screencasts. Due to the time consuming nature of creating Screencasts we decided on a long-term plan of development to complement current existing resources. Most research on the mathematical crisis in Ireland reports that students lack understanding of the context or applications of the mathematics that they encounter, for example Lynch et al. (2003). Indeed, context and application is an integral part of the current reform of second level mathematics in Ireland, Project Maths (www.ncca.ie/projectmaths).

We are using Screencasts to develop additional material for students to give context to material they are studying. Current topics include Algebra, Equations and Calculus. To date we have created 13 Screencasts. They are available on the MSC website and material related to these topics is also included. This project is funded by the NDLR (http://www.ndlr.ie/) and Meath County Council (http://www.meath.ie/Business/FurtherandHigherEducationOpportunities/). We created a special website for second level students in County Meath which contained the Screencasts and other relevant resources. Our aim was to introduce students to ways of thinking about mathematics that were different from what they encounter at school.

Recent funding has also been received from the NDLR to continue with the development of these resources, the new project will also involve the use of Screenr (http://screenr.com/) and Articulate (http://www.articulate.com/) to help develop the resources.

As the project has not yet been completed the number of hits on the site has been low. However, in addition both authors posted the relevant Screencasts onto the Moodle sites for their Calculus 1 and Linear Algebra 1 courses. Calculus 1 had 180 registered students and Linear Algebra 1 had 342 registered students. Eight Screencasts on Calculus were uploaded and these were viewed a total of 445 times. Five Screencasts on Linear Algebra were uploaded and these were viewed a total of 855 times. Students were not specifically asked about their opinion of the Screencasts, however in the end of semester evaluation form for the Linear Algebra course students were asked to comment on the extra resources posted on Moodle. The results were varied with many students accessing them but only if they had time, here is a typical positive response: *I looked at all the extra material because it was interesting to learn a little history of maths and how it was developed and the screen casts gave a good idea of the applications of linear algebra.* However, some of the students did not see the relevance of the Screencasts to their Mathematics modules: *No, I'm not that interested in the history behind the maths I'm doing, some people seemed to be though.*

An online survey was attached to the second level student website. Very few students responded but all responses were positive. The following comment '*I found the explanations of maths to be very interesting and find that this will give sense to the maths syllabus for kids*' suggests that we are going in the right direction.

Benefits, Challenges and Conclusions

Screencasting can act as a very important supplement to either lecture notes or tutorials. Students commented that the videos were very beneficial to them, they can access them at any time, they can pause and take notes and they can rewind to clarify a particular point. They also said that they found the commentary on the video very useful as it would explain how to get from one step to the next. The recording process was relatively straight forward; however the editing facility caused considerable difficulty. Ultimately, the effort was worth it and small videos were created that the students could access whenever they need. The Screencasts serve a different role to Podcasts, in that they have the added visual aspect. The main challenge is trying to present the Screencasts in a medium that will encourage students to avail of them.

DEVELOPMENTS

As a result of this pilot scheme to use technology to supplement mathematics support at NUIM we have identified three key areas that need to be addressed: 1) the provision of a cohesive electronic mathematics support service; 2) the establishment of full and proper evaluations of these services; 3) the development of initiatives to encourage student engagement with the electronic resources:

1. We conducted a thorough analysis of the main areas within mathematics that first year NUIM students have difficulties with. We then identified the areas where we felt there was a lack of suitable electronic support and have received funding to develop RLO's. We are currently working on *Limits* and *Sequences and Series*. When these resources are finished we aim to provide a comprehensive online mathematics support service which will be orientated towards specific subject areas within mathematics. To collect the various resources together into an effective and user friendly medium we are investigating the suitability of the software Articulate (www.articulate.com).
2. We will conduct a thorough analysis of the use and effectiveness of these resources including properly developed questionnaires which will be issued in class to ensure a balanced response from users and non-users of the supports.
3. At the start of the 2010-11 academic year we had a meeting to discuss the promotion of the online courses and resources to students. To this end, all first year lecturers and tutors regularly remind students of the topics covered online. We have also hired a student monitor who regularly checks student engagement with the material and contacts students who have failed the diagnostic test and who are not using the online course. A full description of the impact of this intervention will be completed at the end of the year.

CONCLUSION

We have outlined the use of technology in the MSC. Online resources are used to supplement existing support services. In our opinion the resources are useful because they allow students to work at material at their own pace. This is especially true with our online courses, Podcasts and Screencasts. Students can view videos or listen to Podcasts as often as they like. Unlike a normal lecture, they can pause or rewind if they do not understand.

It is also important that students have access to support when the MSC is closed. In fact, students can access online resources at any time and from any location. This is especially useful for mature students who often have family commitments which prevent them from spending long hours on campus. The use of online resources also allows us to provide support for students who are not registered for a mathematics module but who need to use mathematics.

However, as we have seen with all of the resources we have created; it is difficult to get the majority of students to engage. The online courses have low levels of engagement and the Screencasts and Podcasts are not used as often as we would like. We see the issue of engagement as a major obstacle in this area. Lecturers may spend a lot of time developing resources and this is wasted if students do not use them.

It is also essential when designing resources to investigate the resources that already exist. There seems to be no point in duplicating material. This is why projects such as FETLAR and the NDLR are invaluable. They allow people to share resources easily and efficiently.

We believe that the use of technology is essential to the continual development of mathematics support for students. In our experience of using both online courses and developing electronic resources, we have found that they are complement to existing mathematical resources and supports. They should not be seen as a replacement for face-to-face interaction, rather a supplement to existing workshops and drop-in services.

Although the data and feedback we collected was not comprehensive, it did indicate to us that it is in the best interests of both staff and students to embrace technology. Students have greater access to materials on a constant basis and staff will have a constant supply of RLO's that can be used to help with the student learning experience.

We are undertaking a number of initiatives to address the various issues raised from the pilot scheme and a full analysis will be available when it is completed.

REFERENCES

Barron, A. (1998). Designing web-based training. *British Journal of Educational Technology*, *29*(4), 355–370. doi:10.1111/1467-8535.00081

Becker, D., & Dwyer, M. (1998). The impact of student verbal/visual learning style preference on implementing groupware in the classroom. *Journal of Asynchronous Learning Networks*, *2*(2), 61–69.

Brett, C. (2004). Off-line factors contributing to online engagement. *Technology, Pedagogy and Education*, *13*(1), 83–95. doi:10.1080/14759390400200174

Brinkman, W. P., Rae, A., & Dwivedi, Y. K. (2007). Web-based implementation of the Keller Plan for self paced learning: A case study of teaching mathematics in an online video-based WebCT learning environment. *International Journal of Web-Based Learning and Teaching Technologies*, *2*(1), 39–69. doi:10.4018/jwltt.2007010103

Chan, A., & Lee, M. (2005). An MP3 a day keeps the worries away: Exploring the use of podcasting to address preconceptions and alleviate pre-class anxiety amongst undergraduate information technology students. In D. H. R. Spennemann & L. Burr (Eds.), *Good practice in practice: Proceedings of the student experience conference* (pp.58-70). Wagga Wagga, New South Wales.

Copley, J. (2007). Audio and video podcasts of lectures for campus-based students: Production and evaluation of student use. *Innovations in Education and Teaching International*, *44*(4), 387–399. doi:10.1080/14703290701602805

Croft, A. C. (2008). *Measuring the effectiveness of support centre resources*. Retrieved December 5, 2010, from http://www.mathcentre.ac.uk/ topics/ measuring-effectivess/ measuring-the-effectiveness-of-support-centres/

Curriculum and Examinations Board. (1986). *Mathematics education: Primary and junior cycle post-primary*. Curriculum and Examinations Board Discussion Paper, Dublin.

Ebner, M., & Nagler, W. (2008). Has the end of chalkboard come? A survey about the limits of interactive pen displays in higher education. In P. A. Bruck & M. Lindner (Eds.), *Proceedings of the 4th International Microlearning 2008 Conference* (pp. 79-91). Innsbruck University Press.

Engelbrecht, J., & Harding, A. (2005). Teaching undergraduate mathematics on the Internet. *Educational Studies in Mathematics*, *53*, 253–276. doi:10.1007/s10649-005-6457-2

Evans, C. (2008). The effectiveness of m-learning in the form of podcast revision lectures in higher education. *Computers & Education*, *50*(2), 491–498. doi:10.1016/j.compedu.2007.09.016

Friel, T., Britten, J., Compton, B., Peak, A., Schoch, K., & Van Tyle, W. K. (2009). Using pedagogical dialogue as a vehicle to encourage faculty technology use. *Computers & Education*, *53*(2), 300–307. doi:10.1016/j.compedu.2009.02.002

Gill, O., Johnson, P., & O'Donoghue, J. (2008). *An audit of mathematics support provision in Irish third level institutions*. CEMTL Report, University of Limerick.

Grehan, M., Mac an Bhaird, C., & O'Shea, A. (2010). Why do students not avail of mathematics support? A case study of first year students at the National University of Ireland Maynooth. In M. Joubert & P. Andrews (Eds.), *Proceedings of the British Congress of Mathematics Education 2010*, (pp. 254-258).

Hibberd, S., Litton, C., Chambers, C., & Rowlett, P. (2003). MELEES- e-support or mayhem? *MSOR Connections*, *3*(3), 29–34.

Hopper, K. B. (2001). Is the Internet a classroom? *TechTrends*, *45*(5), 35–43. doi:10.1007/BF03017086

Karr, C., Weck, B., Sunal, D., & Cook, T. (2003). Analysis of the effectiveness of online learning in a graduate engineering math course. *The Journal of Interactive Online Learning*, *1*(3), 1–8.

Khan, B. H. (Ed.). (1997). *Web-based instruction*. Englewood Cliffs, NJ: Educational Technology Publications, Inc.

Lawson, D. A., Carpenter, S. L., & Croft, A. C. (2008). Mathematics support: Real, virtual and mobile. *The International Journal for Technology in Mathematics Education*, *15*(2), 73–78.

Lynch, K., Lyons, M., Sheerin, E., Close, S., & Boland, P. (2003). *Inside classrooms: A study of teaching and learning*. Dublin, Ireland: Institute of Public Administration.

Mac an Bhaird, C., Morgan, T., & O'Shea, A. (2009). The impact of the mathematics support centre on the grades of first year students at the National University of Ireland Maynooth. *Teaching Mathematics and Its Applications*, *28*(3), 117–122. doi:10.1093/teamat/hrp014

Macdonald, C. J., Stodel, E. J., Farres, L. G., Breithaupt, K., & Gabriel, M. A. (2001). The demand-driven learning model: A framework for Web-based learning. *The Internet and Higher Education*, *4*, 9–30. doi:10.1016/S1096-7516(01)00045-8

Ní Fhloinn, E. (2010). The use of technology in mathematics support: An overview of the 4th Irish Workshop on Mathematics Learning and Support Centres. *MSOR Connections, 10*(2), 49-52.

OECD. (2005). *E-learning in tertiary education*. Paris, France: Organisation for Economic Co-operation and Development Policy Brief.

Perkin, G., & Croft, T. (2004). Mathematics support centres – The extent of current provision. *MSOR Connections*, *4*(2), 14–18.

Peterson, E. (2007). Incorporating screencasts in online teaching. *The International Review of Research in Open and Distance Learning, 8*(3). Retrieved December 5, 2010, from http://www.irrodl.org/ index.php/ irrodl/ issue/ view/ 28

Picker, S. H., & Berry, J. S. (2001). Investigating pupils' images of mathematics. *Proceedings of the 25th Conference of the International Group for the Psychology of Mathematics Education, vol. 4* (pp 49-56). Nottingham, UK: PME Proceedings.

Pinder-Grover, T., Mirecki Millunchick, J., & Bierwert, C. (2008). Work in progress - Using screencasts to enhance student learning in a large lecture material science and engineering course. *Proceedings of the 38th ASEE/IEEE Frontiers in Education Conference*. Retrieved December 5, 2010, from http://www.konferenslund.se/ pp/ SC_Pinder.pdf

Reid, A., & Petocz, P. (2002). Students' conceptions of statistics: A phenomenographic study. *Journal of Statistics Education, 10*(2). Retrieved December 5, 2010, from http://www.amstat.org/ publications/ jse/ v10n2/ reid.html

Ruthven, K., & Hennessy, S. (2002). A practitioner model of the use of computer-based tools and resources to support mathematics teaching and learning. *Educational Studies in Mathematics*, *49*, 47–88. doi:10.1023/A:1016052130572

Samuels, P. (2007). Mathematics support and new technologies. *MSOR Connections*, *7*(1), 10–13.

Selden, A., & Selden, J. (1997). Should mathematicians and mathematics educators be listening to cognitive psychologists? *MAA Research Sampler 2*. Retrieved December 5, 2010, from http://www.maa.org/ t_and_l/ sampler/ rs_2.html.

Seufert, S., Lechner, U., & Stanoevska, K. (2002). A reference model for online learning communities. *International Journal on E-Learning*, *1*(1), 43–54.

Suanpang, P., Petocz, P., & Kalceff, W. (2003, July). *E-student attitudes to learning business statistics online vs. traditional methods.* Paper presented at HERSA (Learning for unknown future), New Zealand.

Task Force on the Physical Sciences. (2002). *Report and recommendations of the task force on the physical sciences*. Retrieved December 5, 2010, from http://www.ul.ie/ ~childsp/ CinA/ Issue67/ TOC06_Report.htm

Truluck, J. (2007). Establishing a mentoring plan for improving retention in online graduate degree programs. *Online Journal of Distance Learning Administration*, *10*(1), 1–6.

U.S. Department of Education, Office of Planning, Evaluation, and Policy Development. (2010). *Evaluation of evidence-based practices in online learning: A meta-analysis and review of online learning studies.* Washington, D.C. Retrieved December 5, 2010 from http://www2.ed.gov/ rschstat/eval/tech/evidence-based-practices/ finalreport.pdf

Vidakovic, D., Bevis, J., & Alexander, M. (2003). Bloom's taxonomy in developing assessment items. *Journal of Online Mathematics and its Applications, 3*. Retrieved December 5, 2010, from http://mathdl.maa.org/ mathDL/ 4/ ?pa=content&sa =viewDocument &nodeId= 504

Waldock, J. (2008). Web-based student support and course management? *MSOR Connections*, *8*(2), 33–35.

About the Contributors

Angel A. Juan is an Associate Professor of Simulation and Data Analysis in the Computer Science Department at the Open University of Catalonia (UOC) as well as a Researcher at the Internet Interdisciplinary Institute (IN3). He also collaborates, as a Lecturer of Computer Programming and Applied Statistics, with the Department of Applied Mathematics I at the Technical University of Catalonia (UPC). He holds a Ph.D. in Applied Computational Mathematics (UNED), an M.S. in Information Systems & Technology (UOC), and an M.S. in Applied Mathematics (University of Valencia). His research interests include both service and industrial applications of computer simulation, probabilistic algorithms, educational data analysis, and mathematical e-learning. He has published several papers in international journals, books and proceedings regarding these fields. Also, he has been involved in several international research projects. He is an editorial board member of the Int. J. of Data Analysis Techniques and Strategies as well as of the Int. J. of Information Systems & Social Change, and a member of the INFORMS society. His e-mail is: ajuanp@uoc.edu

Antonia Huertas is an Associate Professor of Mathematics and Knowledge Representation in the Computer Sciences Department at the Open University of Catalonia (Barcelona, Spain). She holds a Ph.D. in Mathematics (University of Barcelona). Her research interests include knowledge representation and rationing and mathematical e-learning. Her e-mail is: mhuertass@uoc.edu

Sven Trenholm is currently a PhD research student at Loughborough University's Mathematics Education Center. Previously, for more than ten years, he taught as a fulltime mathematics instructor within the State University of New York. He holds an MSc in Curriculum Design and Instructional Technology (SUNY Albany) and a BSc and DipEd in Mathematics (McGill). His PhD research is focused on assessment approaches of tertiary mathematics e-learning instructors. His research interests also include disciplinary differences in approaches to e-learning, mathematics e-lecturing, efficacy of e-learning for courses in basic numeracy and psychological aspects of e-learning. Within these fields of interest, he has published journal papers and presented numerous times. His e-mail is: s.trenholm@lboro.ac.uk

Cristina Steegmann is currently a PhD research student at Open University of Catalonia (Barcelona, Spain). She has more than ten years of experience teaching mathematics online to Engineering students. Her PhD is focused on Mathematical e-learning in the context of the European area of higher education. As a result, she has participated in different research projects on those topics and is co-author of several papers and chapters published in international journals and books. Her e-mail is: csteegmann@uoc.edu

* * *

Buma Abramovitz (Abramovici) completed his undergraduate degree in Mathematics at the University of Bucharest (Romania) in 1974. He received his MSc in Mathematics degree from the Technion - Israel Institute of Technology in 1987 and his DSc degree from the same institution in 1992. In parallel he was involved in programs for gifted children. He has been an adjunct lecturer at Technion since 1992, and became a lecturer at Ort Braude College in 1993. His research interests include numerical solutions for Fredholm Integral Equations of the first kind and inverse problems and mathematic education. For many years Dr. Abramovitz has been participating in various projects about online learning and teaching in calculus.

Giovannina Albano is Assistant Professor of Geometry at the University of Salerno (Italy), since 1997, and for a long time she has been teacher in several mathematics courses at the Faculty of Engineering. Her research interests are in mathematics education and in educational models for e-learning environments, including knowledge domain representation, cooperative learning, computer-based mathematics learning and affective issues related to the use of e-learning platforms. She has contributed to the educational theoretical framework implemented in the e-learning platform IWT. She has been vice-project coordinator of the Italian Centre of Excellence "Methods and Systems for the learning and knowledge", and scientific leader of the research line "Virtual Scientific Experiments." She has been Italian representative at the Working Party for Learning Policies within IST Programme, V Framework Programme. She is involved in many national and European projects on e-learning & mathematics education.

Juan G. Alcázar is Assistant Professor in the Mathematics Department at the University of Alcalá (Madrid, Spain). He holds a Degree in Mathematics (Complutense University of Madrid, 1995) and a Ph.D. in Mathematics (University of Alcalá, 2007). He is an active researcher in the fields of constructive algebraic geometry, symbolic computation, and the applications of these in computer aided geometric design. He was a member of the InnovamatUAH group, until December 2009, and is a member of LibreTICs, of which he was the leader until September 2010.

Matthew Badger is a postgraduate student in the School of Mathematics at the University of Birmingham in the United Kingdom. He was awarded his undergraduate degree in mathematics by the University of Sheffield in 2006, before completing an MPhil in Group Theory at the University of Birmingham. Since 2008 he has been working towards a PhD under the supervision of Chris Sangwin, the title of which is "Problem solving in mathematics education and computer aided assessment." As part of his work he has made contributions to the computer aided assessment software STACK.

Miryam Berezina was born in Riga, Latvia. She received her MSc in Mathematics and Mathematics Education from Latvia's State University. Following her immigration to Israel, she studied at the Technion - Israel Institute of Technology and received her DSc from this institution. Dr. Berezina's research interests are differential geometry and mathematic education. She is a senior lecturer at Ort Braude College, Karmiel and an adjunct senior lecturer at the Technion. Together with Buma Abramovitz and Ludmila Shvartsman, she has written a textbook on the subject of Multivariable Calculus, which was published by Magnes Press of the Hebrew University of Jerusalem. For many years Dr. Berezina has participated in various projects about online learning and teaching in Calculus. She developed different assignments in Calculus for students' independent learning by means of Webassign.

Abraham Berman received his MSc in Mathematics from the Technion - Israel Institute of Technology in 1968 and his PhD in Applied Mathematics in 1970. He holds the Israel Pollak Academic Chair at the Technion where he is a Professor of Mathematics and the head of the Department of Education in Technology and Science. He holds visiting professorships and visiting research positions in many universities including the University of California, San Diego, the Institute for Advanced Studies in Princeton, the Centre de Recherche in Montreal and the University of Science and Technology of China. His research interests include spectral graph theory of nonnegative matrices, mathematic education, and giftedness.

Ciarán Mac an Bhaird received his PhD in Mathematics from the National University of Ireland Maynooth in 2007. He is a lecturer in the Department of Mathematics and Manager of the Mathematics Support Centre which he helped to establish in 2007. He researches and publishes in both mathematics and mathematics education and has postgraduate research students in both areas. He has received funding for a number of projects including the development of reusable learning objects in mathematics and he is a committee member of the Irish Mathematics Support Network. In 2010, he received the Sigma (The Centre for Excellence in Maths and Stats Support) Rising Star award in recognition of his contributions in this area.

Rolf Biehler is Professor for Didactics of Mathematics at the Institute of Mathematics in Paderborn since 2009 and is director of the Centre for Higher Mathematics Education Research. From 1999 to February 2009 he was Professor at the University of Kassel and one of the founders of the VEMA project. He studied mathematics and physics at the Universities of Marburg and Bonn and got his Ph.D. and his habilitation in didactics of mathematics from the University of Bielefeld. He co-edited the book 'Didactics of Mathematics as a Scientific Discipline' and he is currently co-editor of the Journal für Mathematik-Didaktik, the leading German journal for research in mathematics education. His specialities are the use of Information Technology in mathematics education, the didactics of probability and statistics, and research into teaching and learning mathematics in higher education.

Barry Cherkas holds a BS (1962) in Mathematics from Worcester Polytechnic Institute and both an MA (1965) and PhD (1968) from Georgetown University. Currently, he is a Professor of Mathematics at Hunter College of the City University of New York and the CUNY Graduate Center (Program in Urban Education). Over the years, he has written research and practitioner articles in mathematics and collegiate mathematics education. In 2003, he founded WebGraphing.com to deliver mathematical graphing over the Internet. He holds several US patents on function graphing systems and methods. He sees the Internet as having the potential to universalize learning, in general, and mathematics in particular, with dynamic interactivity as the key innovation to spark this advance in mathematics education. Besides attending legitimate theater often, his hobbies are largely fitness-related—sailing, mountain biking, and jogging—all while listening to new age music.

Ellen Clay is an Assistant Teaching Professor of Mathematics Education in the School of Education and Mathematician in Residence at the Math Forum at Drexel University. Her experience includes teaching mathematics at the university level, teaching middle school mathematics in the School District of Philadelphia, and working with pre-service, in-service, regular, and special education teachers from across the country through continuing professional development opportunities offered by the Math Forum. Ellen holds a doctorate of mathematics from The University of Louisiana. Her research interests include urban mathematics education and teachers' and students' development of instructional explanations around the fundamental mathematical concepts that underlie the entire secondary curriculum.

Hans Cuypers is an Associate Professor of Mathematics at Eindhoven University of Technology. He is leading the group in Discrete Mathematics. Besides his research in group theory and discrete and finite geometry, he is also interested in computer mathematics, focusing on interactive mathematical documents. Under his guidance, the software system MathDox, an open source system for presenting highly interactive mathematical documents and exercises, has been developed. Cuypers has been actively involved in various national and European projects concerned with e-learning of mathematics.

Blazenka Divjak is a Full Professor at the Faculty of Organization and Informatics, University of Zagreb, recently elected on the position of vice-rector for students and study programs at the University of Zagreb. She got her PhD in mathematics in 1998 and she teaches mathematics at undergraduate level, discrete mathematics and graph theory at graduate level, and R&D project cycles at doctoral level. She works actively on R&D projects and Bologna reform, quality assurance system, as well in implementation of e-learning. Professor Divjak published over 30 scientific papers in mathematics and related areas, more than 20 professional papers and participated at more than 50 international conferences.

Pascal Rolf Fischer got his degree (Staatsexamen) from Kassel University in the programme for future mathematics teachers. He specialized in e-learning and use of technology in mathematics education. Pascal R. Fischer has been working for VEMA since 2004 and he is responsible for the design of the Web-based material and for running and coordinating the bridging courses every year. His Ph.D. project is concerned with developing and evaluating the different blended learning course variants of VEMA. In this context, he is designing diagnostic tests and feedbacks for monitoring and evaluating students' learning processes and achievements when using the VEMA material. He is a member of the advisory board of the Service Centre for Teaching and of the Commission for Information Management at the University of Kassel. Since 2008 he is also working in the EU-project Math-Bridge and is here responsible for the pedagogical aspects.

Bas Giesbers obtained a Master degree in educational- and developmental psychology at Tilburg University, the Netherlands. He gained experience as an educational technologist and teacher in distance education and is currently working as project leader and researcher in e-learning at the department of Educational Research and Development of the Maastricht University School of Business and Economics. The projects he is involved in mainly concern remedial teaching, distance supervision (e.g. of internships), and teacher professionalization in the field of distance education. His research focuses on the support of collaborative (e-) learning by means of ICT in general and Web-videoconference in particular.

Reinhard Hochmuth is Professor of Analysis at the University of Kassel since 2005 and director of the Centre for Higher Mathematics Education Research. He received M.Sc. degrees in mathematics and psychology and a Ph.D. in mathematics in 1989 all from Freie Universität in Berlin. From 1996 to 1998 he was guest Professor in Columbia (South Carolina) and with the Laboratoiré d'Analyse Numerique at the Université Pierre et Marie Curie in Paris. After his habilitation in mathematics he worked as Associate Professor at the Technical University in Freiberg and as guest Professor at the Universities in Potsdam and Kassel. Since 2001 he is Research Fellow at the Zuse Institute in Berlin and since 2005 he is a member of the VEMA group in Kassel. His main research areas are teaching and learning mathematics in higher education and in analysis partial differential equations, wavelets, and nonlinear approximation.

Boris Horvat, PhD in Computer Science, does research in discrete mathematics, e-learning, & intelligent e-services. He has several years of experience in fields involving the Internet, multimedia, programming, and system integration.

Daniel Jarvis is an Associate Professor in the Schulich School of Education at Nipissing University in North Bay, Ontario. He teaches courses in the pre-service teacher education (mathematics), in-service teacher development, and graduate education programs. His research interests include technology, integrated curricula, teacher professional learning, and educational leadership. Dr. Jarvis has recently collaborated with colleagues in Canada and the UK on an international research project focusing on individual and departmental use of Computer Algebra Systems (CAS) in university mathematics instruction. He is currently also studying handheld/mobile technology use in secondary school mathematics instruction, as well as documenting (video) reform-oriented, problem-based mathematics teaching/learning practices in Grade 7/8 classrooms. Dan has taught online mathematics additional qualification courses for nearly a decade, and is intrigued by the interesting challenges and affordances associated with online learning, particularly in contexts involving experienced teachers of mathematics.

Wolter Kaper studied chemistry, and during his studies, became involved in the study of chemical education. His Ph.D. study was about finding new ways of making the entropy and energy concepts understandable to first year undergraduate chemistry majors. After his Ph.D. he has been teaching in a Master of Science Education program, as well as working as an educational advisor for the Department of Science at the University of Amsterdam. His primary interest is: how to make abstract concepts understood, particularly focussing on the role guided discovery and inductive reasoning methods can play to achieve so.

Birgit Loch is a Senior Lecturer in the Mathematics Discipline and Head of the Mathematics and Statistics Help Centre at Swinburne University of Technology in Melbourne, Australia. She holds a PhD in Applied Mathematics, with her current research interests focusing on online learning and effective technology use in mathematics education. These include but are not limited to tablet technology, mobile learning and Web 2.0 applications, and the engagement of academic staff in the use of technologies for learning and teaching, not just in mathematics, but across all disciplines. Before joining Swinburne in 2010, Birgit was the educational technology advisor at her previous university, where she also conducted a number of university-wide technology trials (for instance, lecture recording and Web conferencing software, and tablet technology), which all led to adoption.

Matija Lokar is employed at the Faculty of Mathematics and Physics, University of Ljubljana, as the Head of the Computer Centre and as a Senior Lecturer. He is actively researching and testing the new learning technologies. He collaborated on numerous national and international projects aimed at the use of ICT at various educational settings and is a member of CAME (Computer Algebra in Math Education) International Steering Committee. Currently he is also the head researcher in group NAUK – "Advanced Learning Blocks for Teachers." He wrote numerous scientific and research papers on the role and use of technology in all levels of education. He has almost 300 entries in COBISS Online bibliographic system.

Primož Lukšič, PhD in Computer Science, has collaborated on numerous national and EU funded projects aimed at promoting the use of ICT in science. He is also the author of many papers from the mentioned fields and is actively researching and testing new learning technologies.

Marcos Marvá is Assistant Professor in the Mathematics Department at the University of Alcalá (Madrid, Spain). He holds a Degree in Mathematics (University of Murcia, 1999). He is an active researcher in the field of dynamical systems (multi-time scale systems) and their applications in Ecology and Epidemics. He was a member of the InnovamatUAH innovation group, until December 2009, and is a member of LibreTICs, of which he has been the leader since October 2010.

Maria Meletiou-Mavrotheris is an Associate Professor at the European University Cyprus, and Director of the Research Laboratory in ICT-Enhanced Education. She has a Ph.D. in Mathematics Education (University of Texas, 2000), an M.Sc. in Statistics (University of Texas, 1994), an M.Sc. in Engineering (University of Texas, 1998), an M.A. in Open and Distance Learning (UK, Open University, 2008), a B. A. in Mathematics (University of Texas, 1993), and Teacher's Diploma in Elementary Education (Pedagogical Academy of Cyprus, 1990). Her research interests focus on the educational applications of advanced e-learning technologies in mathematics, statistics, science, and engineering. She has been involved, in the capacity of coordinator or research collaborator, in numerous locally or EU-funded projects exploring the utilization of open and distance education environments in formal education systems (at the elementary, secondary, or higher education level), as well as in adult education and vocational training.

Travis K. Miller is an Assistant Professor of Mathematics at Millersville University of Pennsylvania where he teaches a variety of mathematics courses, including those for future mathematics teachers, and supervises secondary mathematics student teachers. He earned his Doctorate in Curriculum and Instruction with a specialization in Mathematics Education from Purdue University. His recent research endeavors focus upon the use of asynchronous online discussions and personal response systems (clickers) in mathematics content courses for preservice elementary teachers. His work examines the effectiveness of implementations and elements of students' experiences in using the technology, including: students' approaches to using technology; students' perceptions of technology; and their development of conceptions of mathematics topics and the nature, teaching, and learning of mathematics. He and his wife, Emily, currently reside in Lancaster, PA.

Morten Misfeldt is Associate Professor at the department for Curriculum research at Aarhus University. Misfeldt works with the possibilities and challenges that Information and Communication Technology poses to expression of mathematics, learning environments at university level, and with design of learning games. Misfeldt teaches mathematics, mathematics education, and ICT and learning. Misfeldt is on the board of the Danish ICME organization.

Ann O'Shea holds a PhD in Mathematics from the University of Notre Dame, USA and has been a lecturer in the Mathematics Department at NUI Maynooth since 1992. She is the Director of the NUIM Mathematics Support Centre. She is course director of an MSc in Mathematics for Education which is aimed at out-of-field teachers. Her research interests lie in the area of mathematics education. In 2010, she received a national award for excellence in teaching from NAIRTL (The National Academy for the Integration of Research, Teaching and Learning).

Amílcar Oliveira is an Assistant Professor of Statistics in the Department of Sciences and Technology at the Universidade Aberta (UAb), Lisbon. He is a member of the Center of Statistics and Applications at the University of Lisbon. He holds a PhD in Mathematics -Statistical Modeling (UAb), and an M.S. in Statistics and Optimization (FCT-New University of Lisbon). His research interests include statistical modeling, joint regression analysis, statistical inference, simulation, statistical quality control, educational data analysis, and statistical e-learning. He has published several papers in international journals, books, and proceedings regarding these fields.

Teresa Oliveira is an Assistant Professor of Statistics in the Department of Sciences and Technology at the Universidade Aberta (UAb), Lisbon. She is a member of the Center of Statistics and Applications at the University of Lisbon. She holds a Ph.D. in Statistics and Operations Research – Experimental Statistics and Data Analysis (University of Lisbon), an M.S. in Statistics and Operations Research (Faculty of Sciences, University of Lisbon). Her research interests include experimental design, statistical modeling, joint regression analysis, statistical inference, simulation, statistical quality control, re-sampling techniques, educational data analysis, and statistical e-learning. She has published several papers in international journals, books, and proceedings regarding these fields. She is supervising several PhD and Master theses.

David Orden is Associate Professor in the Mathematics Department at the University of Alcalá (Madrid, Spain). He received his Ph.D. degree in Mathematics from the University of Cantabria in 2003. His research interests focus on discrete and computational geometry from geometric graphs, including triangulations, pseudotriangulations, rigidity, and crossings, to parallelization of geometric algorithms such as incremental randomized algorithms. His teaching activities have included 14 different courses in the last ten years, participating in 5 different projects and leading the group InnovamatUAH until December 2009. Since January 2010, he has been a member of the innovation group LibreTICs.

Diana Perdue is a creative, energetic advocate for the appropriate and effective use of technology in the classroom. Throughout her extensive career, she has consistently used inquiry-based, student-centered methodologies to help other teachers enhance their students' learning experience. During her tenure as Assistant Professor at West Texas A & M University and as Associate Professor at Virginia State University, she successfully incorporated the use of tools such as Blackboard, Voki, Moodle, Geometer's Sketchpad software, and graphing calculator technologies into her mathematics and mathematics education courses. As a Fulbright Scholar to Rwanda, Dr. Perdue served as the Director of E-learning at KIST (Kigali Institute for Science and Technology) and mathematics faculty member at KIE (Kigali Institute of Education). Her projects there explored the potential of using cell phone technology for educational purposes and meeting challenges facing teachers who wish to use technology in their classrooms.

Bart Rienties (PhD) is lecturer of higher education academic practices and initiatives at the Centre for Educational and Academic Development at the University of Surrey. As Economist and Educational Psychologist, he conducts multi-disciplinary research on work-based and collaborative learning environments and focuses on the role of social interaction in learning. His primary research interests are focussed on CSCL, the role of motivation in learning, the role of the teacher to design effective blended and online learning courses, and the role of social interaction in learning. Finally, he is chair of the international Educational Innovation in Economics and Business (EDINEB) Network.

Fernando San Segundo is Assistant Professor in the Mathematics Department at the University of Alcalá (Madrid, Spain). He received his Ph.D. degree in Mathematics from the University of Alcalá in 2010. His research interest is in symbolic computation and effective algebraic geometry of curves and surfaces.

Chris Sangwin is a Senior Lecturer in the School of Mathematics at the University of Birmingham in the United Kingdom. Since 2000 he has been seconded half time to the UK Higher Education Academy "Maths Stats and OR Network" to promote learning and teaching of university mathematics. In 2006 he was awarded a National Teaching Fellowship. His learning and teaching interests include (i) automatic assessment of mathematics using computer algebra, and (ii) problem solving using Moore method and similar student-centred approaches. Chris Sangwin is the author of a number of books, including "How Round is Your Circle," which is an attempt to promote the links between mathematics and engineering using physical models.

Anders Sanne is currently an Assistant Professor in Mathematics Education at the Norwegian University of Science and Technology (NTNU) in Trondheim, Norway. He has experience in teaching mathematics from upper secondary school, and from online in-service training courses for mathematics teachers. Earlier he worked in Clustra Systems Inc, a database software vendor which specialized in clustered, high-availability databases. He is board member of the Norwegian Association of Mathematics Teachers (LAMIS), member of the International GeoGebra Institute Advisory Board, and chair of the GeoGebra Institute of Norway. Sanne has been involved in international professional activities including organizing conferences and serving as program committee member.

Ludmila Shvartsman graduated from Voronezh State University (the former USSR) in 1982 and received her PhD in Physics and Mathematics in 1985 from the same university. She began teaching in 1988 as a teaching assistant in Yaroslavl Polytechnic Institute (Russia) and resigned from the Institute in 1993 at the rank of Associate Professor. After immigrating to Israel in 1993, she resumed her teaching career. Dr. Shvartsman is a senior lecturer at ORT Braude College and an adjunct Senior Lecturer at the Technion. Her research interests include differential equations and mathematical education at the undergraduate level. For many years she has been participating in various projects about online learning and teaching. In particular, since 2000 she developed different assignments in linear algebra and calculus for students' independent learning by means of Webassign.

Jason Silverman is an Assistant Professor of mathematics education in the School of Education at Drexel University, where he also serves at the Program Director for Mathematics Learning and Teaching. He has over 15 years of experience in mathematics education and has taught mathematics at the middle school, high school, and university levels. At Drexel, he teaches mathematics content and pedagogy courses for teachers at the undergraduate, Master's, and Doctoral level. Jason holds a BA in mathematics from Franklin and Marshall College as well as Master's degrees in both mathematics and mathematics education and a Doctorate in mathematics education from Vanderbilt University. His research focus involves supporting the development of mathematical knowledge for conceptual teaching, research in undergraduate mathematics education, discourse in mathematics classrooms, and technology in mathematics education. Jason has presented his research in numerous national and international conferences and been published in numerous peer reviewed books and journals.

Jorge Simosa is a student in Electrical Engineering and Computer Science at Massachusetts Institute of Technology (Cambridge, MA, USA). His academic curriculum ranges from electrical engineering topics such as circuit design to computer science topics such as software engineering. His research interests include communication networks, reliability & availability issues, and mathematical e-learning. He is a Junior Researcher at the Open University of Catalonia and the Public University of Navarre, within the HAROSA Community, completing research projects concerning structural reliability & availability and e-learning, including several publications in conference proceedings and international journals.

Dirk Tempelaar is Senior Lecturer at the department of Quantitative Economics of the Maastricht University School of Business & Economics, the Netherlands. His prime teaching is in quantitative methods: introductory courses mathematics and statistics for students in business, economics, and liberal arts. Following this responsibility, he has designed preparatory courses in mathematics and statistics directed at prospective students. These online remedial courses have taken place in all summers since 2003. Related to these initiatives, he has been actively involved in various national and European projects concerned with online, remedial learning of mathematics.

Evert van de Vrie is lecturer in Mathematics at the Open University in the Netherlands. His interests are in discrete mathematics and cryptology, parts of the computer science curriculum. He is involved in projects and activities supporting students starting in higher education with a lack in prior knowledge in mathematics. Within the Open University he is coordinating the preparation courses in Mathematics. In the Netherlands, he was involved in several cooperative projects of Dutch universities in this area. He participates in MathBridge, a European project realising online remedial courses in Mathematics. Homepage: http://www.open.ou.nl/evv

Henk van der Kooij is a member of the Freudental Institute for Science and Mathematics Education (FIsme), Utrecht University. His main interests are in mathematics education for senior high school, the bridge (or bridging the gap) between high school and higher education, assessment of mathematical skills and mathematics for the workplace. After being a teacher in Senior High School for 15 years, he changed to curriculum developmental work at FIsme. He also served as manager of national exams for the natural sciences and mathematics in the National Examination Board in the Netherlands.

Sybrand Schim van der Loeff is Associate Professor of Econometrics at the department of Quantitative Economics of the Maastricht University School of Business & Economics, the Netherlands. Dr. Schim van der Loeff did his graduate studies at The Erasmus University in Rotterdam, was a research fellow at the Center for Operations Research and Econometrics (CORE) Louvain, Belgium, and a visiting scholar at the Economics Department, Harvard University, Cambridge, Massachusetts, U.S.A. His research interest is in developing econometric methods for the estimation of dynamic panel data, and in effect studies in quasi-experimental settings.

Leendert van Gastel obtained a degree in mathematics at the University of Utrecht, and wrote a dissertation on algebraic geometry. He has worked at the CAN Expertise Centre for the introduction and support of the use of computer algebra. Since 2005, Leendert van Gastel is heading the Higher Education Group of the Science Faculty of the University of Amsterdam. The mission is to improve mathematics, science, and technology education at this faculty. Leendert van Gastel is currently project leader of the NKBW project (National Knowledge Bank on Basic Skills in Mathematics) funded by the Dutch SURF Foundation, a joint project with 18 Dutch higher education institutes. This project is focusing on the convergence between secondary and tertiary education in algebraic skills.

Thomas Wassong got his degree (Staatsexamen) from the Georg-August-University of Göttingen in mathematics, ethics, and computer science. He is one of the co-authors of a book about the Computer-Algebra-System MuPAD, written at his study times. After his studies 2008 he got a research assistant at the University of Kassel, and since 2009 he is research assistant at the University of Paderborn. Thomas Wassong is a member of the VEMA Group since 2008 and he is working within the EU-project Math-Bridge. In both projects he is mainly responsible for the technical aspects in the Kassel/Paderborn team. His research is focused on the professional development of teachers and pre-teachers, with an example being stochastic.

Rachael M. Welder is currently an Assistant Professor of Mathematics Education at Hunter College of the City University of New York. She earned a Ph.D. (2007) in mathematics, with specialization in mathematics education, from Montana State University. In addition, she holds an MS (2003) in mathematics from the University of North Dakota and a BS (2001) in mathematics and secondary mathematics teaching from the University of Mary. Her research interests focus on pre-service elementary teachers and their development of mathematical content knowledge for teaching. In addition to her love for mathematics, Dr. Welder has a huge affinity for animals. She is a dedicated animal rights advocate and proponent of living a vegan-lifestyle. She lives in Manhattan with her husband, Sean, and their two beloved cats and enjoys traveling back to the Midwest (weather permitting) to see her family.

Index

E

F

G

H

I

J

P

Q

R

S